Foundation Stage

Module A

Accounting Framework

ACCA Textbook

British Library Cataloguing-in-Publication Data

A catalogue record for this book is available from the British Library.

Published by AT Foulks Lynch Ltd
Number 4
The Griffin Centre
Staines Road
Feltham
Middlesex
TW14 0HS

ISBN 0 7483 3100 X

Acknowledgements

We are grateful to the Chartered Association of Certified Accountants, the Chartered Institute of Management Accountants and the Institute of Chartered Accountants in England and Wales for permission to reproduce past examination questions. The answers have been prepared by AT Foulks Lynch Ltd.

CONTENTS

		Page
Preface & format of the examination		iv
The syllabus		vi
The official ACCA teaching guide		ix

The role and principles of financial accounting and reporting

Applications of accounting conventions

Recording, handling and summarising accounting data

Chapter 1	Introduction to accounting	1
Chapter 2	The balance sheet	16
Chapter 3	The profit and loss account	34
Chapter 4	Preparing final accounts	48
Chapter 5	Ledger accounts and double-entry bookkeeping	70
Chapter 6	Ledger accounts and year-end adjustments	92
Chapter 7	The preparation of final accounts from a trial balance	115
Chapter 8	Accounting for fixed assets and depreciation	125
Chapter 9	Accounting for stocks	145
Chapter 10	Accounting for debtors and bad and doubtful debts	163
Chapter 11	Subsidiary records	185
Chapter 12	The journal	209
Chapter 13	Control accounts and computerised accounting systems	234
Chapter 14	Bank reconciliation statements	258

Preparing financial statements

Chapter 15	Incomplete records	265
Chapter 16	Accounting for clubs, societies and associations	303
Chapter 17	Partnership accounts	329
Chapter 18	Partnership accounts - partnership changes	351
Chapter 19	Accounting for limited companies	383
Chapter 20	Introduction to published company accounts	421
Chapter 21	Non-statutory aspects of published company accounts	444

Interpreting/using financial statements

Chapter 22	The cash flow statement	477
Chapter 23	Profit measurement and valuation	503
Chapter 24	Analysis and interpretation of final accounts	536
Glossary		571
Index		581

PREFACE

This Textbook is the ACCA's official text for paper 1, Accounting Framework, and is part of the ACCA's official series produced for students taking the ACCA examinations.

It has been produced specifically for paper 1 and covers the syllabus in great detail giving appropriate weighting to the various topics.

This Textbook is, however, very different from a reference book or a more traditional style textbook. It is targeted very closely on the examinations and is written in a way that will help you assimilate the information easily and give you plenty of practice at the various techniques involved.

Particular attention has been paid to producing an interactive text that will maintain your interest with a series of carefully designed features.

- **Activities**. The text involves you in the learning process with a series of activities designed to arrest your attention and make you concentrate and respond.

- **Definitions**. The text clearly defines key words or concepts. The purpose of including these definitions is **not** that you should learn them - rote learning is not required and is positively harmful. The definitions are included to focus your attention on the point being covered.

- **Conclusions**. Where helpful, the text includes conclusions that summarise important points as you read through the chapter rather than leaving the conclusion to the chapter end. The purpose of this is to summarise concisely the key material that has just been covered so that you can constantly monitor your understanding of the material as you read it.

- **Self test questions**. At the end of each chapter there is a series of self test questions. The purpose of these is to help you revise some of the key elements of the chapter. The answer to each is a paragraph reference, encouraging you to go back and re-read and revise that point.

- **End of chapter questions**. At the end of each chapter we include examination style questions. These will give you a very good idea of the sort of thing the examiner will ask and will test your understanding of what has been covered.

FORMAT OF THE EXAMINATION

The examination will have the following format:

	Number of marks
Multiple Choice Questions (MCQs) section: 30 MCQs	40
Essay section: 3 to 5 compulsory questions	60
(no question will carry more than 25 marks)	——
	100
	——

Time allowed: 3 hours

The overall balance in the paper will be in the region of 60% technical and 40% conceptual.

As the MCQ section will test mainly technical areas, the essay section will concentrate on conceptual issues and on the ability to communicate and present information.

A short supplement may be used in the essay section of the paper.

SYLLABUS

Foundation stage - Module A Paper 1: ACCOUNTING FRAMEWORK

Introduction

Paper 1 provides a broad introduction and overview of the financial accounting process. The syllabus covers all the essential aspects, without reaching the depth of complexity or variety of applications of later studies.

Chapter reference

(1)   **THE ROLE AND PRINCIPLES OF FINANCIAL ACCOUNTING AND REPORTING**   1-4, 13, 20, 21, 23

     (a)   Nature, principles and scope of accounting: role of financial accounting, management accounting, financial management and auditing.

     (b)   Nature, principles and scope of financial accounting

         (i)   the reasons for its current state of development
         (ii)   the influences on possible future developments.

     (c)   Nature, scope and purposes of financial and related records, accounts and statements.

     (d)   The users of financial accounts and statements, and their information requirements

         (i)   the adequacy of financial accounts and statements in meeting those needs
         (ii)   introduction to alternative methods to meet those needs.

     (e)   The structure of the regulatory system and its relationship to financial accounts and statements.

     (f)   The nature of the accounting profession and the role of the accountant.

     (g)   The nature and role of bodies which set accounting standards and guidelines.

     (h)   Ethics and independence of the accounting and auditing professions.

     (i)   The nature, role and significance of

         (i)   accounting theories and principles
         (ii)   accounting conventions (to include SSAP2)
         (iii)   accounting standards and guidelines (eg SSAPs, FRSs, IASs, SORPs)
         (iv)   Generally Accepted Accounting Practice (GAAP)
         (v)   legislative and quasi-legislative requirements.

     (j)   Applications of information technology in processing financial and related information.

(2)   **APPLICATIONS OF ACCOUNTING CONVENTIONS**   20, 21, 23

      (a)   The understanding, application and implications of accounting conventions.

      (b)   Principles of the conceptual framework debate.

      (c)   Standardisation versus accounting choice.

(3)   **RECORDING, HANDLING AND SUMMARISING ACCOUNTING DATA**   1-14, 21

      (a)   Double entry book-keeping and accounting systems

            (i)   form and content of accounting records (manual and computerised)
            (ii)   books of original entry, including journals
            (iii)   sales and purchase ledgers
            (iv)   cash book
            (v)   general ledger
            (vi)   trial balance
            (vii)   accruals, prepayments and adjustments.

      (b)   Methods of classifying expenditure between capital and revenue.

      (c)   Accounting treatment of

            (i)   fixed assets - tangible and intangible
                  -     depreciation - reasons for, and methods of providing for it (to include SSAP12)
                  -     research and development (to include SSAP13)
                  -     goodwill
            (ii)   current assets
                  -     stock (to include SSAP9 (except for long term contracts))
                  -     debtors, including bad debts
                  -     cash
            (iii)   liabilities
            (iv)   provisions and reserves
            (v)   post balance sheet events (to include SSAP17)
            (vi)   contingencies (to include SSAP18).

      (d)   Confirming and correcting mechanisms

            (i)   control accounts
            (ii)   bank reconciliations
            (iii)   suspense accounts and the correction of errors.

(4)   **PREPARING FINANCIAL STATEMENTS FOR**   15-21

      (a)   Sole traders: from simple incomplete records situations.

      (b)   Clubs or societies

            (i)   receipts and payments accounts
            (ii)   income and expenditure accounts.

(c)   Partnerships: changes in the constitution of a partnership; admission, change in profit sharing ratio and retirement including elementary treatment of goodwill.

(d)   Individual companies: profit and loss accounts and balance sheets for internal and external purposes in accordance with the Companies Act formats.

(5)   INTERPRETING/USING FINANCIAL STATEMENTS   22, 23, 24

(a)   Preparing cashflow statements in accordance with FRS1 and contrasting cash flow and funds flow concepts.

(b)   Preparing significant ratios for financial statements.

(c)   Appraising and communicating the position and prospects of a business based on given and prepared statements and ratios.

(d)   Appraising the validity of available information for user purposes.

THE OFFICIAL ACCA TEACHING GUIDE

Paper 1 - Accounting Framework

	Syllabus Reference	Chapter Reference
Session 1 *Introduction to Accounting*		

- identify the groups who make use of financial accounting primarily for decision making purposes   1a,b,c,d   1
- identify the groups who make use of financial accounting primarily for stewardship purposes
- describe the main financial statements available to users
- outline the purpose of each of the main financial statements
- explain the role of the accountancy profession within society
- indicate the role of the accountant in a variety of organisational contexts
- distinguish between management accounting, financial accounting, financial management and auditing
- identify non-financial statements (eg, the chairman's statement)
- identify the desirable qualities of accounting information
- explain the usefulness of each desirable quality for decision-making purposes
- explain the usefulness of each desirable quality for stewardship purposes
- briefly outline the main reasons for the present state of financial accounting
- briefly outline the main influences on possible future developments of financial accounting
- explain the difference between capital and revenue items

Session 2   *Balance Sheet and Profit and Loss Account*

- explain how the balance sheet equation and business entity convention underlie the balance sheet   1c   2, 3, 4
- define assets and liabilities
- explain how and why assets and liabilities are disclosed in the balance sheet
- draft a simple balance sheet in vertical format
- explain the matching convention and how it applies to revenues and expenses
- explain how and why revenues and expenses are disclosed in the trading and profit and loss account
- illustrate how the trading and profit and loss account and the balance sheet are inter-related
- draft a simple trading and profit and loss account in vertical format

Sessions 3/4   *Book-keeping Principles*

- identify the main data sources and records of an accounting system   3a   5, 6, 7
- explain the function of each data source and record
- outline the form of accounting records in a typical manual system
- outline the form of accounting records in a typical computerised system
- explain how double entry book-keeping relies upon the convention of duality and the balance sheet equation
- explain debit and credit
- distinguish between asset, liability, revenue and expense accounts
- explain the meaning of the balance on each type of account

	Syllabus reference	Chapter reference

- record cash transactions in a set of ledger accounts (note VAT is not examinable)
- record credit transactions in a set of ledger accounts (note VAT is not examinable)
- calculate and record the closing balance on these accounts
- identify the ledgers into which the double entry books are conventionally divided
- outline the advantages and disadvantages of dividing the ledger
- explain the nature and purpose of each ledger
- explain the meaning of the balance(s) in each ledger
- outline the nature and purposes of a trial balance
- extract the ledger balances into a trial balance
- list errors which would not be highlighted by a trial balance difference
- prepare a simple profit and loss account and balance sheet from the trial balance

Sessions 5/6   Day Books, Errors, Control, IT Implications

	Syllabus reference	Chapter reference
- identify the main books of original entry, including the transfer journal	1j	11, 12, 13
- state which transactions each book of original entry will deal with	3a,d	14

- state how the output of each book of original entry will be dealt with
- record transactions in the books of original entry and post them to the ledgers
- explain the nature and purposes of the journal
- illustrate the use of the journal, including the posting of journal entries into the ledger accounts
- identify the types of error which may occur
- indicate which of these errors could be detected by a trial balance
- illustrate the use of a suspense account and journal to correct errors
- draft a corrected profit and loss account and balance sheet
- explain the nature and purposes of a control account
- explain how control accounts relate to the double entry system
- construct a control account and the underlying individual accounts from books of original entry
- agree the control account balance with the sum of the balances on the underlying accounts
- explain the nature and purposes of a bank reconciliation statement
- explain why the bank statement and cash book balances may not agree
- make the cash book entries required to update the balance for outstanding items
- draft a bank reconciliation statement
- identify the relative advantages and disadvantages of manual and computerised accounting systems
- outline the major applications of information technology in processing financial and related information

Sessions 7/8   Fixed Assets and Depreciation, Liabilities

	Syllabus reference	Chapter reference
- define and give examples of fixed assets	3b,c	8, 21

- define and explain the purposes of depreciation in accordance with SSAP 12 'Accounting for Depreciation'
- outline and discuss the straight line, reducing balance, sum of the digits and revaluation methods of depreciation
- illustrate the application of each method
- explain the roles of consistency and subjectivity in accounting for depreciation

- explain the relationship between depreciation and asset replacement
- record the acquisition or revaluation of a fixed asset in ledger accounts
- record the charge for depreciation and the cumulative provision for depreciation in ledger accounts
- outline the accounting treatment of appreciating assets
- explain why it is necessary to depreciate appreciating assets, with reference to SSAP 12 'Accounting for Depreciation'
- explain and record the disposal of a depreciated fixed asset in ledger accounts
- account for changes in the estimated life and/or residual value of a fixed asset
- show and explain how the ledger account balances will be disclosed in the financial statements in accordance with SSAP 12 'Accounting for Depreciation'
- define and give examples of liabilities
- distinguish between current and long-term liabilities
- disclose liabilities on a balance sheet
- distinguish between liabilities and provisions

Sessions 9/10   *Current Assets and Liabilities*

- define stock and work in progress
- apply the prudence convention to justify the valuation at the lower of cost and net realisable value
- explain the FIFO (first in, first out), LIFO (last in, first out) and AVCO (average cost) methods of valuing stock
- calculate the stock and cost of sales figures under each method, given changes in prices
- indicate how stocks and work in progress will be disclosed in the financial statements in accordance with SSAP 9 'Stocks and Long-Term Contracts'
- outline the relative merits of continuous and period end stock records
- define a trade debtor
- explain the difference between a bad debt written off and a doubtful debt provision
- record bad and doubtful debts in ledger accounts
- disclose trade debtors in a balance sheet after bad debts and net of the doubtful debt provision
- show the corresponding charges or credits in the profit and loss account
- show bank and cash balances in a balance sheet
- describe the nature and purpose of an accrual
- record adjustments relating to accrued expenses and revenues in ledger accounts
- describe the nature and purpose of a prepayment
- record adjustments relating to prepaid expenses and deferred revenue in ledger accounts
- prepare a set of final accounts for a sole trader from a trial balance, after incorporating period end adjustments for depreciation, stock, prepayments, accruals, and bad and doubtful debts

The syllabus references for "Sessions 9/10" are 3b,c and chapter references 6, 7, 9, 10.

Session 11   *Accounting Conventions*

- explain the nature and purpose of accounting conventions
- outline and illustrate the application of the conventions of:
  - going concern
  - separate valuation

The syllabus reference for "Session 11" is 2a and chapter references 4, 20.

	Syllabus reference	Chapter reference

- accruals
- prudence
- consistency
- historic cost
- stable monetary unit
- money measurement
- materiality
- realisation
- objectivity
- business entity
- duality
- ♦ discuss the usefulness of these conventions

Session 12   **Accounting Policies, Conceptual Framework**

♦ explain the nature and purposes of SSAP 2 'Disclosure of Accounting Policies'	1i,2b,c	20, 21, 23

- ♦ outline the four accounting concepts identified in SSAP 2 'Disclosure of Accounting Policies'
- ♦ explain and give examples of accounting bases and accounting policies as defined in SSAP 2 'Disclosure of Accounting Policies'
- ♦ apply these fundamental accounting bases and policies to unfamiliar situations
- ♦ explain the nature and purposes of a conceptual framework
- ♦ discuss the purpose of each element of a conceptual framework
- ♦ outline potential benefits and drawbacks of an agreed conceptual framework
- ♦ outline the role of and general issues and ideas covered by the Statement of Principles (chapters 1-6). Note; a detailed knowledge of the content of these chapters is not examinable.

Session 13   **Goodwill, Research and Development**

♦ define goodwill	3c	21

- ♦ distinguish between purchased and non-purchased goodwill
- ♦ outline valuation methods for goodwill
- ♦ highlight how the valuation of goodwill differs from the conventional valuation of other fixed assets
- ♦ outline the alternative accounting treatments for goodwill
- ♦ define and explain research and development in accordance with SSAP 13 'Research and Development'
- ♦ classify expenditure as pure or applied research or as development
- ♦ disclose research and development expenditure in the financial statements in accordance with SSAP 13 'Research and Development'

Session 14   **Contingencies, Post-Balance Sheet Events**

♦ define a contingency in accordance with SSAP 18 'Accounting for Contingencies'	3c	21

- ♦ distinguish between the different categories of contingency
- ♦ account for each category of contingency in the financial statements in accordance with SSAP 18, 'Accounting for Contingencies'
- ♦ define a post balance sheet in accordance with SSAP 17 'Accounting for Post Balance Sheet Events'
- ♦ distinguish between the different categories of post balance sheet events

	Syllabus reference	Chapter reference

◆ account for each category of post balance sheet event in the financial statements in accordance with SSAP 17, 'Accounting for Post Balance Sheet Events'

Sessions 15/16   *Receipts and Payments/Income and Expenditure Accounts, Incomplete Records*

◆ describe the nature and purposes of a receipts and payments account   4a,b   15, 16
◆ identify the shortcomings of this type of report
◆ identify the type of accounting entity for which a receipts and payments account may be appropriate
◆ draft a receipts and payments account
◆ describe the nature and purpose of an income and expenditure account
◆ identify the type of accounting entity for which an income and expenditure account may be appropriate
◆ draft an income and expenditure account
◆ draft the corresponding balance sheet for a club or society
◆ distinguish between incomplete and limited accounting records
◆ calculate the net asset position and the profit for a sole trader business which has incomplete accounting records
◆ prepare final accounts for a sole trader from limited accounting records

Sessions 17/18   *Partnership Accounts*

◆ identify the existence of a partnership   4c   17, 18
◆ outline the advantages and disadvantages of operating as a partnership, relative to sole trading or as a company
◆ outline the conventional methods of dividing profit and maintaining equity between partners
◆ draft the appropriation account for a partnership
◆ distinguish between partners' capital and current accounts
◆ record the partners' shares of profits and losses and their drawings in the ledger accounts
◆ record introductions and withdrawals of capital in the ledger accounts
◆ draft the trading and profit and loss and appropriation account and the balance sheet for a partnership from a trial balance and period end adjustments
◆ explain why a revaluation is required after an admission, a change in the profit sharing ratio, or a retirement
◆ revalue the partnership after such a change, and calculate the goodwill
◆ make appropriate entries in the ledger accounts
◆ draft the partnership balance sheet after a change in the partnership
◆ draft the partnership balance sheet after a merger of two sole trader businesses

Sessions 19/20/21   *Accounting for Limited Companies*

◆ outline the advantages and disadvantages of operation as a limited company, rather than as a sole trader   4d   19-21
◆ distinguish between public and private limited companies
◆ identify the records which a limited company is required to keep by law
◆ indicate briefly the nature and purpose of share capital and reserves
◆ distinguish between capital and revenue reserves
◆ explain the nature and purpose of a dividend
◆ outline the nature of corporation tax
◆ explain the nature and purpose of a company's appropriation account

Syllabus
reference

Chapter
reference

- record tax and dividends paid and payable in the relevant ledger accounts
- draft a company trading and profit and loss and appropriation account for internal purposes
- distinguish between issued and authorised share capital, and between called up and paid up share capital
- distinguish between ordinary and preference shares
- record shares issued and held in the relevant ledger accounts
- illustrate the permitted uses of capital and revenue reserves
- record amounts transferred to and from reserves in the relevant ledger accounts
- draft a company balance sheet for internal purposes
- define a debenture
- outline the advantages and disadvantages of raising finance by issuing debentures rather than ordinary or preference shares
- define and illustrate gearing
- explain the importance of gearing
- define a bonus issue
- outline the advantages and disadvantages of this method if increasing a company's capital
- record a bonus share issue in ledger accounts
- define a rights issue
- outline the advantages and disadvantages of raising finance by this method
- record a rights issue in ledger accounts
- distinguish between the market value and the nominal value of a share
- explain why companies will be concerned with the market value of their shares
- determine the value of a share
- calculate the return on a shareholding
- outline the nature, scope and authority of accounting standards
- outline the Companies Acts' impact on financial accounting
- outline the role of the Stock Exchange in the regulation of financial reporting
- explain why the Companies Act 1985 and FRS 3 Reporting Financial Performance specify a layout for the external, published profit and loss account and balance sheet of a limited company
- outline the main provisions of the Companies Act 1985 and FRS 3 Reporting Financial Performance relating to the presentation of published accounts
- redraft an internal set of financial statements as an external set to comply with the law and FRS 3 Reporting Financial Performance

Session 22   *Cash Flow and Funds Flow*

- identify and illustrate circumstances where profit and liquidity are not directly related
- distinguish between the different definitions of funds
- prepare a simple funds flow statement from a list of transactions
- discuss the usefulness of a funds flow statement
- explain the distinction between cash flows and funds flows
- explain the need for a cash flow statement
- prepare a simple cash flow statement
- assess the usefulness of the information given by the cash flow statement
- outline the requirements of FRS 1 'Cash Flow Statements' (excluding group aspects)

5a   22

xiv

♦   prepare a cash flow statement in accordance with the requirements of FRS 1 'Cash Flow Statements' (for a single company)

♦   critically appraise the requirements of FRS 1 'Cash Flow Statements' (excluding group aspects)

Sessions 23/24   *The Theoretical and Operational Adequacy of Financial Reporting*

♦   outline other approaches to the conventional financial statements   1e,f,g,h   23

♦   suggest which users might find such approaches of particular value

♦   highlight the major shortcomings of historical cost accounting in times of changing price levels

♦   suggest how the shortcomings of historical cost accounting might be addressed

♦   describe the roles of the FRC, ASB, UITF and Review Panel

♦   explain the nature of SSAPs, FRSs, SORPs and IASs

♦   explain the relationship of accounting standards to the FRC, ASB, UITF and Review Panel

♦   discuss the relative merits of standardisation and choice of accounting treatment

♦   identify the elements of generally accepted accounting practice (GAAP)

♦   give examples of how GAAP is related to a conceptual framework

♦   outline the role of the financial accountant

♦   outline the ethical guidelines for accounting

♦   explain the role of the internal and external auditors in financial reporting

♦   explain why the external auditor should remain independent of the body being audited

Sessions 25/26   *Ratios, Interpretation, Usefulness*

♦   list the internal and external users of accounting information produced by a commercial undertaking   5b,c,d   24

♦   outline what information may be particularly relevant to each user group

♦   list the internal and external users of accounting information produced by a non-commercial undertaking

♦   outline what information may be particularly relevant to each user group

♦   discuss the shortcomings of interpretation

♦   explain why understandability is an important characteristic of financial statements

♦   identify the major techniques of interpretation
    - understanding the business' context
    - calculation of ratios
    - analysis of ratios
    - critical review

♦   describe the technique of ratio analysis and its potential shortcomings

♦   identify the ratios which primarily measure profitability

♦   calculate each ratio

♦   describe the meaning and purpose of each ratio

♦   indicate the limitations of each ratio

♦   identify the ratios which primarily measure liquidity and funds management

♦   calculate each ratio

♦   describe the meaning and purpose of each ratio

♦   indicate the limitations of each ratio

♦   identify the ratios which primarily help to appraise investment

♦   calculate each ratio

- describe the meaning and purpose of each ratio
- indicate the limitations of each ratio
- outline the nature, purpose and limitations of financial accounting
- appraise the validity of available information for user purposes
- express your own reasoned opinions on the usefulness of financial accounting

Session 27   *Review and Revision*
- Book-keeping and Financial Accounts

Session 28   *Review and Revision*
- Users, Concepts, Applications, Reports

1 INTRODUCTION TO ACCOUNTING

INTRODUCTION AND LEARNING OBJECTIVES

This chapter is intended to set the scene for the study of the accounting framework as preparation for the examination of that name.

Accounting is concerned with the use of financial and economic information to help people to make decisions. The people who use accounting information about a particular business fall into several groups: owners, managers and other employees, customers, suppliers, competitors and government. Accounting has two main areas: **financial accounting**, which is the subject of this book, and **management accounting**, which you will meet elsewhere in your studies. Accountants are not only concerned with these two areas, however.

At first glance, it might appear that all of the financial and economic information about a business will be encompassed in information about cash receipts and payments and their effect on the cash balance. Closer inspection shows that only a very limited impression of a business can be gained by looking just at cash. We therefore need other types of information as well as just the cash flows in order to make useful judgements about virtually any aspect of a business. In fact, two other principal sources of information have emerged over the history of accounting. The first of these is a statement which shows how much wealth the business possesses, what form that wealth takes and how the wealth of the business is committed to others. This is the **balance sheet**. The other source is a statement showing the extent to which the business has generated wealth, and the manner of doing so. This is the **profit and loss account**.

When you have studied this chapter you should be able to do the following:

*   Discuss the role of accounting and the various users of accounts

*   Identify the basic financial statements required in a set of accounts

*   Discuss desirable qualitative characteristics of financial statements.

---

1 THE ROLE OF ACCOUNTING

1.1 Introduction

When being introduced to a new subject it is often useful to begin with a definition of the subject. A definition can help identify the essential features of the subject and should, therefore, provide a logical starting point for further study. Over the years various broad definitions of accounting have appeared in the literature. One such definition, which is widely quoted and appears to enjoy widespread acceptance, was developed by the American Accounting Association (AAA). The AAA has defined accounting as:

> the process of identifying, measuring and communicating economic information to permit informed judgements and decisions by users of the information.

This particular definition of accounting emphasises the fact that accounting is concerned with providing economic information to users. Accounting is, therefore, a form of service. Users of accounting information require economic information because resources are scarce in relation to needs. In order to help make decisions concerning the most efficient allocation of scarce resources economic information is required.

It is important never to lose sight of the fact that accounting exists for a purpose – that of economic decision-making. Accounting is not an end in itself. It is unfortunate that some definitions of accounting appear to suggest that accounting is simply concerned with the preparation of financial statements. While this may describe what many who work in accounting do, it fails to emphasise the purpose of this activity.

1.2   The principal users of accounting information

In the business world there are various groups of users of accounting information. Each user group is concerned with particular types of economic decision. By identifying user groups and the kinds of decision they wish to make, it is possible to establish the type of accounting information that should be produced. The principal users of accounting information are outlined below.

(a)   Owners

Owners will usually invest in a business with a view to increasing their wealth. In order for prospective owners and existing owners to make decisions concerning whether to invest in, remain in, or disinvest from, a particular business they require information concerning the risks and rewards associated with that business. Where the owners leave the day-to-day running of the business to professional managers, information concerning the financial position and performance is required in order to assess whether the managers have acted honestly, efficiently and in the best interests of the owners.

(b)   Employees

Employees often have a substantial and long-standing relationship with a business. The principal concerns of employees are those of job security and remuneration. These matters, of course, are related to the survival and economic success of the business. Hence, information concerning the financial position and performance of the business should be of direct concern to employees.

(c)   Suppliers of goods and services

Suppliers of goods and services need to be satisfied that the business has the necessary cash resources to pay for the goods and services provided. Thus, suppliers are likely to have a particular concern with the liquidity of the business, that is, the availability of cash or near-cash assets to meet short-term obligations. However, some suppliers of goods and services may, like employees, have a substantial and long-standing relationship with a business and may be concerned with the ability of the business to honour and renew contracts over the long term. In such circumstances information concerning the general financial position and performance may be required in order to assess the long-term prospects of the business.

(d)   Lenders

Lenders provide finance for a business in addition to that provided by the owners. Lenders may provide finance on a short-term basis (say, less than 12 months) or for a longer term. For short-term lenders the principal concern will be the liquidity of the business. However, long-term lenders will be concerned with the long-term prospects of the business and will, therefore, require more general information concerning the financial position and performance of the business.

(e)   Customers

Customers may need information to satisfy themselves that the business is able to continue supplying goods or services at the required rate. This may arise where large contracts are involved and where detailed negotiations and binding commitments are being undertaken. Thus, a large retail business is likely to take a keen interest in the financial health of its suppliers in order to assess the security of existing contracts and the prospects for future contracts.

(f) Government

Government may have a number of reasons for requiring economic
business. Information relating to performance, such as profits, wih
taxation purposes. In addition, information relating to the resources of the bu.
profits of the business may help in deciding on the provision of financial supp.
particular business or industry. A government may wish to regulate the behaviou.
business. For example, it may have a policy to encourage widespread competition and to
prevent the growth of monopoly power. In such a situation information relating to output
and profits of a particular business may be useful to ensure that government policy is being
adhered to.

(g) Management

Management have responsibility for the day-to-day running of the business. Hence,
managers have to make many different types of economic decisions. These decisions relate
to such matters as product pricing, establishing output targets, evaluating investment
proposals, determining appropriate levels of stock and cash, determining financing
requirements. In order to make decisions on such matters it is clear that managers require a
considerable amount of detailed economic information. Indeed, the information needs of
managers are much greater than those of other user groups.

The user groups listed above may all be seen as having a potential stake in the continuing
survival and success of the business. However, for one particular user group this is unlikely
to be the case; indeed, the reverse may be true.

(h) Competitors

Competitors are likely to seek economic information concerning a rival business for two
reasons. First, the financial position and performance of the rival may be useful for
comparison purposes. By comparing their own performance with that of a rival some
evaluation of efficiency and effectiveness can be made. Second, the financial position of a
rival may provide clues concerning likely future strategies. For example, the build-up of
large amounts of stock by the rival may mark the beginning of an aggressive sales
campaign.

2 TYPES OF ACCOUNTING

2.1 Introduction

As stated above, managers require a considerable amount of detailed economic information in order
to plan and control the business. Moreover, they are in a position to ensure that they are provided
with the information they require. The other groups mentioned above often require less detailed
information. Generally speaking, they will be satisfied with a summary of the financial position and
performance of the business as a whole. They are also likely to be given only restricted access to
economic information relating to a business in order to safeguard the interests of the business.

This difference in the information needs of managers compared to other user groups has resulted in
accounting developing in two directions.

2.2 Management accounting

As the name suggests, management accounting is concerned with the provision of economic
information for management purposes. To help managers plan for the future, management
accounting information will incorporate forecasts concerning future activities and events. To help
managers control the business, management accounting information will also provide feedback on
current performance. By comparing current performance with earlier planned performance it is
possible for managers to see whether the business is on the right course and whether corrective
action is required.

It is important to note that the amount, the frequency and the format of the information presented to management will be determined by management themselves. Wide variations in management accounting practices can, therefore, occur between businesses.

2.3 Financial accounting

Financial accounting is concerned with providing economic information to 'outsiders' (that is, the other user groups identified above). The information provides a general overview of the financial position and performance of the business and is not as specific or detailed as the information produced for management. The information provided is essentially a review of past performance and current financial position. Forecast information is rarely disclosed for fear that it may help competitors or that the nature of the forecasts will be misunderstood by users. Financial accounting information relating to a particular business may be used as a basis for comparison with other businesses. To facilitate such comparisons it is useful if each business presents and prepares its financial accounting information in a similar way. The law and the accounting profession have intervened to ensure that the financial reports published by businesses are produced in a fairly uniform fashion.

The law is represented by the **Companies Acts 1985** and **1989.** They provide rules (covered in Chapters 19 and 20) about the information which companies need to disclose to the public and the manner in which it is disclosed. The accounting profession has complemented and extended the law with its own rules: Statements of Standard Accounting Practice (SSAPs) and Financial Reporting Standards (FRSs), usually together known as **accounting standards**. Chapter 21 describes the purpose of accounting standards and how they are set.

In practice, the division between management and financial accounting is not always as clear-cut as the above descriptions might suggest. For example, lenders negotiating future finance for a business may insist on receiving details of future plans and profit forecasts before agreeing to provide finance. Similarly, managers may benefit from receiving reports which provide a general overview of the financial position and performance of the business.

In this book the principal focus is on matters relating to financial accounting. This reflects the Foundation Stage, Accounting Framework, syllabus of the Chartered Association of Certified Accountants.

2.4 Other activities usually undertaken by accountants

There are several other activities undertaken by members of the accounting profession, as well as acting as financial and management accountants. The principal activities are:

(a) **Financial management**

Financial management is the task of making and implementing decisions about raising finance for the business and using that finance to make investments, usually in things like factories, machines and so on, which will help the business to generate more wealth. Not surprisingly, financial managers use accounting information to aid their decision making.

(b) **Auditing**

Auditors carry out independent reviews of financial statements and report their opinion of them. In virtually all cases the auditors are concerned with the extent to which financial statements are a fair representation of the reality which those statements seek to portray. To be able to form an opinion of the reliability of financial statements, it is essential that auditors have a good understanding of accounting. We shall take a slightly closer look at the role of auditors in Chapter 20.

(c) **Tax consultancy**

In the UK most of the work involved with giving advice to, and acting on behalf of, taxpayers in respect of their tax liabilities is done by accountants who have chosen to specialise in this type of work. This is in contrast to the situation which exists in most other parts of the world where such work is undertaken by qualified lawyers, who have chosen to specialise in taxation.

In many cases, a particular accountant is usually involved with more than one of these activities. For example, an accountant who works for a small business will probably be the financial accountant, the management accountant and the financial manager as well. On the other hand, large businesses break down each of these activities and have a different accountant looking after just one facet of each one. For example, a large business may have a financial manager who is just responsible for looking after decisions about raising new finance.

Auditors and tax consultants tend to work for firms of accountants. These firms offer their business and private clients a range of services.

2.5   The accounting profession in the United Kingdom

When people talk about the accounting profession they normally mean people who are members of one of the following professional bodies:

- The Chartered Association of Certified Accountants (ACCA)
- The Chartered Institute of Management Accountants (CIMA)
- The Chartered Institute of Public Finance and Accountancy (CIPFA)
- The Institute of Chartered Accountants in England and Wales (ICAEW)
- The Institute of Chartered Accountants in Ireland (ICAI)
- The Institute of Chartered Accountants of Scotland (ICAS)

Between them these bodies have almost 200,000 members. To become a member of any one of these professional bodies, it is necessary to undertake a period of professional training and experience and to pass a set of demanding examinations.

The accounting profession is greatly concerned with ethics. Each of the bodies has very strict rules about the required conduct, professionalism and competence of its members. Particularly important in this area are integrity, objectivity and independence. Each of the bodies has a disciplinary system which deals firmly with any member who is found to fall short of the high standards which it sets, including expelling the member from the organisation.

Though these bodies are independent of one another, they do co-operate to a considerable extent. Many accountants feel that the future of the UK profession lies with the bodies amalgamating into one large body. Other accountants feel that having a number of bodies enriches the profession.

3   ACCOUNTING SYSTEMS

3.1   The accounting information system

It has been seen that accounting is a process by which economic information relating to a business is gathered and then communicated to interested parties. In practice, each business will develop its accounting system in a way which the managers perceive best meets their own requirements and those of other users of accounting information. This means that accounting information systems can vary considerably in the level of sophistication and technology employed. Nevertheless, there are certain common elements underlying any accounting system which may be identified. These elements are as follows:

1   **Data collection** involves setting up appropriate procedures to ensure that relevant economic information is properly identified and captured.

2   **Data recording** involves ensuring that the data collected is classified in a logical and systematic fashion. This element is often referred to as 'bookkeeping'.

3   **Data evaluation** involves the analysis and interpretation of the data collected. Where options exist the costs and benefits associated with each option must be carefully assessed.

4   **Data reporting** involves shaping the information into reports which will satisfy the requirements of users at a reasonable cost. Data reporting can take the form of internal reporting (for management) or external reporting (for other user groups).

In this book all four of the above elements are considered. The book begins by examining the basic financial statements provided to users (that is, data reporting). This is done in order to provide an early appreciation of the final product supplied to users. The book then considers in some detail the data collection and recording procedures necessary to compile the financial statements. It is hoped these procedures will be easier to understand having gained an insight into the ultimate purpose of the procedures. Finally, the book considers the analysis and interpretation of financial reports (that is, data evaluation). This provides some understanding of the way in which financial reports are made in order to evaluate the financial health of a business.

3.2   Accounting for profit

It has been seen that, for a private commercial business, there are various groups with an interest in the accounting information produced by the business. In many cases, users require accounting information because they have a stake in the survival and prosperity of the business. However, it should be borne in mind that it is the owners who have ultimate control of the business. Owners invest in a business with the expectation that it will generate wealth (profit) for them. Hence, the generation of wealth is seen as a primary objective of private commercial business.

As a result of the central role of owners within the private sector the financial accounting reports prepared by businesses are primarily concerned with meeting owners' needs. Thus, emphasis is given to the amount of wealth (profit) generated during the year and the amount available to owners. As managers are employed by the owners to operate the business on their behalf it follows that management accounting reports will also be concerned with the wealth generated for the owners. This is not to suggest that other user groups will have no interest in the financial accounting reports produced. However, their needs may go beyond what is produced for the benefit of owners.

3.3   Accounting for not-for-profit organisations

Although the primary focus of this book is accounting as it relates to a private commercial business it is important to emphasise that there are many types of organisation which do not exist mainly for the pursuit of profit yet produce accounting information for decision-making purposes. Examples of such organisations include charities, trade unions, colleges, public utilities, clubs and associations, churches and nationalised industries. Accounting information may be used by those who have an important stake in the economic survival and prosperity of the organisation. Thus, the wealth generated by the organisation may still be relevant to some user needs. In addition, some users may require confirmation that the wealth of the organisation is being properly controlled and applied in a manner consistent with the objectives of the organisation.

3.4   Activity

For the following organisations state who you consider the major user groups to be and what their likely information needs are:

1   a trade union
2   a public sector college.

3.5   Activity solution

A **trade union** will have the following major user groups:

Members

Members of a trade union may wish to receive financial information concerning the performance and position of the union in order to make judgements concerning levels of subscriptions and the range and quality of benefits and services offered. Members may also wish to assess whether the funds are being applied efficiently and in a manner consistent with the objectives of the union.

Elected officials

Elected officials are accountable to the members for the way in which the union is run. They will, therefore, require information which will be of value in planning and controlling the activities of the union.

Employers

Employers may wish to receive financial information relating to a union where it is in conflict with members of the particular union. Employers may be interested to know the resources that the union has available to support an industrial dispute.

Government

Government may well wish to receive financial information relating to a trade union for a number of reasons. As an employer, it may wish to know the resources that the union has available to support an industrial dispute. In addition, information relating to the resources of the union may by of assistance in deciding on the level of financial support required for certain trade union reforms; for example, the introduction of more democratic election procedures. Information concerning the financial performance and position of the union may also be useful in helping to regulate the activities of the union.

Suppliers of goods and services/lenders/employees

These separate groups will have information needs which are the same as those for commercial businesses.

A public sector college

Students (or their elected representatives)

Students may seek financial information in order to assess whether the college is able to expand or maintain the range of facilities and services provided. They may also require confirmation that financial resources are being employed efficiently and in a manner consistent with college objectives.

Management

Managers of the college will need financial information in order to help plan and control the activities of the college. Some colleges are dependent on government funding whereas others rely on private funding. The information needs of college managers, however, are unlikely to differ substantially between sectors.

Government

Information about the financial resources of a college may be of value in determining the level of financial support for a particular college or group of colleges. Information concerning financial resources may also be useful in regulating the activities of a college, such as for setting student intake numbers.

Suppliers of goods and services/lenders/employees

These groups will have the same information needs as for commercial businesses.

3.6 **Is the reporting of cash flows sufficient?**

As stated earlier, the primary focus of accounting reports for a business is the wealth (profit) generated during a particular period. It may be thought that this is simply a matter of measuring the cash increase (or decrease) during the period. However, this is not usually the case. The following examples illustrate the inadequacy of reporting cash flows alone.

Example 1

Duncan, a student, decided to start a business selling T-shirts to fellow students in order to help finance his forthcoming summer holiday. On the first day of the summer term he paid £80 cash for T-shirts from a local wholesaler. He set up a stall in the Students' Union (for which there was no charge) and to his surprise and delight sold all his stock for £120 cash by the end of the day. What profit has he made?

Solution

The amount of wealth (profit) he generated can be calculated by deducting the cost of the T-shirts (£80) from the sales generated (£120). The profit generated is therefore £120 – £80 = £40.

This, of course, is also the difference between the cash received and the cash paid during the day. However, for most businesses it would be unusual to acquire stock for cash and sell it for cash within the same day.

Example 2

On the second day of the summer term Duncan spent all the cash available (£120) on the acquisition of more stock. However, sales during the second day were slower and by the end of the day he had only managed to sell half his stock for £90. Duncan was disappointed to find that, at the end of the second day, he was left with less cash than he began the day with. He concluded from this that he had operated at a loss and was having second thoughts about his business venture. Is his conclusion valid?

Solution

Although Duncan had less cash at the end of the day his overall wealth had actually increased. At the beginning of the day his wealth was represented by:

Cash	£120

However, at the end of the day his wealth was represented by:

Cash	£90	
Stock of T-shirts	£60	(that is, half of the stock acquired)
	£150	

Thus, Duncan increased his wealth by £30 (£150 – £120) during the second day even though his cash decreased.

This example illustrates the inadequacy of relying on cash alone to measure changes in wealth. Wealth can take many forms, including freehold land, machinery, motor vehicles and stock. Thus, to measure the changes in wealth of a business it is necessary to take account of all the different forms of wealth held.

It must be recognised, however, that cash is a particularly important form of wealth. Businesses must retain an uninterrupted capacity to pay their obligations as and when they fall due.

This means there must be sufficient cash for this purpose. Failure to maintain adequate cash balances can jeopardise the survival of the business.

4   THE BASIC FINANCIAL STATEMENTS

4.1   The statements required

In order for Duncan (see Examples 1 and 2) to assess the financial health of his business he requires answers to each of the following questions:

- How much wealth (profit) was generated during the period?
- What is the business wealth at the end of the period?
- What cash movements have occurred over the period?

In order to answer the first question a **profit and loss account** (also known as an **income statement**) can be drawn up for the period. This will show the wealth inflows as a result of sales and the wealth outflows as a result of expenses occurred to generate these sales. The difference between the wealth inflows and outflows will be the profit (loss) for the period.

The profit and loss account for the second day of Duncan's business would be as follows:

Profit and loss account for day 2

	£
Sales	90
less Cost of sales*	60
	30

*This represents the amount of stock consumed in that day (half of £120) rather than the total amount purchased (£120).

In order to answer the second question a **balance sheet** (also known as a **financial position statement**) can be drawn up. This will show the business wealth at a particular point in time. Thus, the balance sheet at the end of the second day will be as follows:

Balance sheet as at the end of day 2

	£	
Stock of unsold T-shirts	60	(half of £120)
Cash	90	
Duncan's business wealth	150	

In order to answer the final question a **cash flow statement** for the period is required. The cash flow statement would simply indicate the cash inflows and outflows occurring during the period and the effect of the net inflow (outflow) on the cash balance. The cash flow statement for the second day would be as follows:

Cash flow statement for day 2

	£
Cash inflows (from sales)	90
less	
Cash outflows (payments for stock)	120
Net cash flow	(30)
Opening balance	120
Closing balance	90

When taken together, these three financial statements provide a useful picture of the financial position and performance of the business. They may be prepared on the basis of historical data (as in this case) in order to establish past performance and position. Alternatively, they may be prepared on the basis of forecast data to gain some insight into likely future performance and position.

These statements are of fundamental importance and will be examined in more detail in subsequent chapters.

4.2 Activity

On the third day of the summer term Duncan decided to have a 'Grand Clearance Sale'. He reduced prices and generated £70 of sales (cash). At the end of the day he had stock remaining which originally cost £5.

Draw up the profit and loss account and cash flow statement for day 3 and the balance sheet at the end of day 3.

4.3   Activity solution

Profit and loss account for day 3	£
Sales	70
Less: Cost of sales*	55
Profit	£15

*This represents the amount of stock held at the commencement of trading (half of £120 = £60) less the amount of stock remaining at the end of the day (£5).

Cash flow statement for day 3	£
Cash inflows (from sales)	70
Less: outflows (payments for stock)	–
Net cash flow	£70

Since the opening cash balance was	£90
The closing balance must be	£160

Balance sheet as at the end of day 3	£
Stock of unsold T-shirts	5
Cash	160
Duncan's business wealth	£165

5   THE USEFULNESS OF ACCOUNTING INFORMATION

5.1   Introduction

The provision of accounting information involves the utilisation of scarce resources. Hence, managers should be convinced that the accounting information system represents a proper use of these resources and that the benefits of the system outweigh any costs. However, it is not easy to quantify the benefits to be derived from the system. Although various groups have an interest in receiving accounting information it is not always clear just how useful the information received is as a basis for making decisions.

Information can be defined as useful if it results in forming expectations about the outcome of future events and this, in turn, affects behaviour. Accounting reports which have no effect on behaviour do not represent information and their cost, therefore, cannot be justified. Generally speaking, it is difficult to assess the impact of accounting information on human behaviour. However, one situation arises where the impact of accounting information can be observed and measured. This is where the shares (that is, portions of ownership) of a company are traded on a Stock Exchange. There is a strong body of evidence to suggest that when a company announces its annual (and half-yearly) profits there is a significant change in the price of the shares and the number of shares traded. This suggests that a profit announcement leads to a change in expectations concerning the value of a company which in turn affects the share price as investors make decisions as to whether to buy or sell shares in a company. While this evidence provides some insight into the impact of accounting information there still remains the question as to whether the benefits outweigh the costs of producing the information. However, as both the law and the Stock Exchange require such information to be produced the point is, perhaps, only of academic interest.

5.2   Qualitative characteristics of financial statements

It has been argued that to be useful to users, accounting statements need to show the following four characteristics:

(a)   **Relevance**

Relevance is the potential for accounting information to have the ability to influence the decisions of users. This is the primary characteristic required of accounting information.

Unless it provides users with what they need to know, there is little point in producing the information. Accounting information needs to be relevant to the decisions which users need to make about the future; **predictive** relevance. It also needs to be able to help users to evaluate the effects of past decisions; **confirmatory** relevance.

(b)   **Reliability and objectivity**

Reliability is freedom from **material error or bias** and can be relied upon by users to represent faithfully that which it purports to represent. In being reliable, accounting information needs to reflect **economic substance** rather than strict legal form. For example, it is possible to acquire all of the aspects which are normally associated with owning a piece of manufacturing machinery (the right to use it, the need to repair it) in such a way that the strict legal position is that it is owned by someone else. In these circumstances it should be treated as an asset of the user, for accounting purposes. Accounting information needs to be objective, that is, **free from bias.** This means that the information should not be presented in such a way that it influences the decision-maker in a predetermined way. Reliable information will be **prudent** in nature. For example, the provision of accounting information frequently requires judgements to be made about partially completed transactions or events. In these circumstances those exercising the judgement should do so in a prudent and cautious manner, avoiding unjustified optimism. Accounting information also needs to be **complete,** as omissions can mislead.

(c)   **Comparability**

Comparability means that items or events which are essentially the same should be measured and presented in a consistent manner.

(d)   **Understandability**

Understandability is an important characteristic of accounting information. If accounting information is to be useful it must be understood by users. As different user groups are likely to have different levels of understanding of accounting, it is sometimes argued that they should receive different types of report. Thus, some companies produce a financial report for employees which is, in essence, a simplified version of the annual financial report sent to shareholders.

Whatever the level of understanding of users, accounting information should be expressed as clearly as possible.

6   CHAPTER SUMMARY

- Accounting is concerned with the provision of information of an economic/financial nature which will enable those who need to take decisions about an organisation to make better decisions. Financial accounting is concerned with reporting to people outside the business and it tends to report past events. Management accounting is concerned with the provision of information to managers and it tends to have a more forward-looking approach. The distinction between these two types of accounting is somewhat blurred, however.

- Members of the accounting profession are found doing work outside of the strict definition of accounting. Qualified accountants can be found working as financial managers, auditors and tax consultants.

- Throughout the history of accounting, three principal types of accounting statement have evolved and been accepted as being useful to users of accounting information. The profit and loss account or income statement shows how much wealth flowed into the business, and how much flowed out, as a result of its business activities during a particular period. It also shows the net effect on the wealth of the business. The balance sheet, or position statement, shows the form of the wealth of the business – how much is in the form of cash, how much is in the form of land and buildings and so on – and the extent that the wealth is committed to various people who have a stake in the business. The balance sheet depicts the financial position at a particular point in time. The third type of statement is the cash flow statement. This basically shows the cash received, the cash paid and the net effect on the cash of the business over a period.

- Ideally, accounting information should be relevant to the needs of those using it. It should be objective in the sense of being based on fact rather than opinion or bias. It should be produced relatively frequently and shortly after the conclusion of the events which it describes. It should be capable of being used to make comparisons between one business and another or between different time periods for the same business. Lastly it must be capable of being understood by those who use it.

7   SELF TEST QUESTIONS

(Note: the numbers in brackets show the paragraph number of this chapter where each answer can be found.)

7.1   Give a definition of accounting. (1.1)

7.2   State the principal groups of users of accounts. (1.2)

7.3   Give four examples of not-for-profit organisations. (3.3)

7.4   Name the three basic financial statements. (4.1)

7.5   State four desirable characteristics of accounting statements. (5.2)

8   EXAMINATION TYPE QUESTIONS

8.1   Relevance

(a)   Relevance is often regarded as the single most desirable characteristic of accounting information. Why?   **(8 marks)**

(b)   Distinguish between financial and management accounting.   **(7 marks)**

(Total: 15 marks)

8.2   Simon

Simon, a trainee accountant, wished to earn some extra income by selling a new type of food for those wishing to lose weight. The food, known as the 'Wigan Wonder Diet Food' can be purchased by agents from the manufacturers in minimum quantities of 100 packets at £3 per packet. Simon, who is an appointed agent, purchased 100 packets in week 1 and sold 80 packets to friends and relatives at £4.50 per packet. In week 2 Simon purchased a further 100 packets and sold 110 packets at £4.50 per packet. None of those who purchased the new diet food succeeded in losing weight in the first two weeks, and therefore, Simon met resistance when attempting to sell further quantities of the diet food in week 3. Simon decided to purchase no further diet food from the manufacturers and sold his remaining stock, to an uncle for dog food at £2 per packet.

(a)   Prepare a profit and loss account and cash flow statement for the business for each of the three weeks of trading.   **(12 marks)**

(b)   Prepare a balance sheet for the business at the end of each week of trading.   **(6 marks)**

8.3   User Groups

It has been suggested that, apart from owners/investors, there are six separate user groups of published accounting statements: the loan creditor group, the employee group, the analyst advisor group, the business contact group, the government and the public.

(a)   Taking any four of these six user groups, explain the information they are likely to want from published accounting statements.   **(12 marks)**

(b)   Are there any difficulties in satisfying the requirements of all four of your chosen groups, given the requirements of other users?   **(4 marks)**

9 **ANSWERS TO EXAMINATION TYPE QUESTIONS**

9.1 **Relevance**

(a)   If accounting information is said to be relevant this implies that it relates to the needs of those people and institutions who use it. Accounting has no justification for its existence other than its being useful. Clearly to be useful it must meet user needs, and it must be relevant. Thus relevance can be regarded as the single most desirable characteristic of accounting information.

It is possible for there to be a conflict between the desirable characteristics of accounting information. A good example of this is the potential conflict between relevance and objectivity. It may be that users of accounting information would find it useful to know the current selling price of (say) freehold premises owned by a business. Such information may help in deciding between retaining or selling the premises. However, the current value of the premises may be difficult to determine with substantial accuracy. There may be some disagreement between valuers on the appropriate figure to be placed on this resource. A more objective value which could be placed on the freehold premises would be its acquisition value, that is original cost. However, this information may be of little help in making decisions concerning whether to retain or sell the premises.

(b)   Management accounting is concerned with providing economic information to managers of organisations. The information is designed to help plan and control the activities of the organisation. To help managers plan, information concerning the likely future outcome of events and activities is provided. To help managers control the organisation, information concerning actual performance and position is provided. This information can then be compared with earlier planned performance to see whether the organisation is progressing according to plan.

Management accounting information can be provided in a format, frequency and volume to meet the needs of the managers. Wide variations in management accounting practices may therefore occur between businesses.

Financial accounting is concerned with providing economic information to 'outsiders', that is other users apart from management. Generally speaking, the information provided gives a general overview of financial position and performances. It is not normally specific or detailed in nature. Forecast information is rarely provided as this may affect the business's competitive position and may be misunderstood by less sophisticated users. As financial reports of different businesses are often compared it is helpful to users if each set of reports are produced in a uniform fashion.

The law and the accounting profession have introduced requirements to narrow areas of difference in the preparation of financial reports to outside users.

9.2 **Simon**

(a)   **Profit and loss account for week 1**

	£
Sales	360
Less: Cost of sales	240
Profit	£120

Profit and loss account for week 2

	£
Sales	495
Less: Cost of sales	330
Profit	£165

Profit and loss account for week 3

	£
Sales	20
Less: Cost of sales	30
Profit (loss)	£(10)

Cash flow statement for week 1

	£
Cash inflows (from sales)	360
Less: Cash outflows (payments for stock)	300
Net cash flow	60
Opening balance	0
Closing balance	£60

Cash flow statement for week 2

	£
Cash inflows (from sales)	495
Less: Cash outflows (payments for stock)	300
Net cash flow	195
Opening balance	60
Closing balance	£255

Cash flow statement for week 3

	£
Cash inflows (from sales)	20
Less: Cash outflows (payments from stock)	0
Net cash flow:	20
Opening balance	255
Closing balance	£275

(b) **Balance sheet as at end of week 1**

	£
Stock of unsold Diet Food	60
Cash	60
Simon's business wealth	£120

Balance sheet as at end of week 2

	£
Stock of unsold Diet Food	30
Cash	255
Simon's business wealth (120 + 165)	£285

Balance sheet as at end of week 3

	£
Stock of unsold Diet Food	0
Cash	275
Simon's business wealth (120 + 165 − 10)	£275

9.3   User Groups

(a)   **The loan creditor group** This group will normally be concerned with the long-term prospects of the business. Issues such as the level of likely future profit, the value of underlying assets and the level of gearing will be of importance in assessing the future. Where, however, loans are due for repayment in the short term, the liquidity of the business is likely to be of importance.

Employee group The principal concerns of employees are those of job security and remuneration. This means that information relating to likely future profits, likely future contracts and expansion or contraction programmes will be of interest to them. In addition to ascertaining the financial health of the business overall, employees may also wish to know the position and performance of the particular operating unit to which they are attached.

Government Government has a number of reasons for requiring accounting information from a business. Profits will be of interest for taxation purposes. In addition, profits may be of interest when deciding on whether to provide financial support for a particular business or industry. A government may also wish to regulate the behaviour of businesses and may use accounting statements to see whether regulations are being adhered to.

Public The public may require accounting statements for a variety of reasons. For example, information relating to profits of a large company may be of value when assessing employment prospects within the local community. The public may also require information of likely future prospects, the effect of the business on the local environment, the employment policies adopted, the contribution made to the local community and so on. There is an increasing expectation among sections of the public that businesses must be 'good citizens' within their adopted community.

(b)   In order to meet the needs of all user groups a great deal of information would have to be produced which would be both time consuming and costly. The accounting statements prepared for publication by companies are of a general purpose nature and are designed to meet the major requirements of all user groups apart from managers. However, information made publicly available must not hinder the competitiveness of the business.

2 THE BALANCE SHEET

INTRODUCTION AND LEARNING OBJECTIVES

In this chapter the balance sheet will be considered in some detail. The balance sheet is simply a statement of the assets of a business and the claims which can be made against those assets. The relationship between **assets** and **claims** is set out by the accounting equation. The terms assets and claims will be defined and discussed, to provide a full understanding of the nature of the balance sheet, and equally important, of its limitations. This discussion will include an introduction to some of the basic assumptions and conventions on which the balance sheet is based. These conventions will include business entity, duality, money measurement, cost, going concern and the stable monetary unit.

As the chapter develops, examples will be used to illustrate how the balance sheet is affected by a series of trading and non-trading activities. In the course of this the terms **revenue** and **expense** will be defined. These are the essential ingredients of profit.

Finally the chapter considers various categories of assets and claims, and illustrates alternative ways in which the balance sheet can be presented. Categories defined include fixed assets, current assets, capital (also referred to as equity), long- term liabilities and current liabilities.

Since the Foundation Stage syllabus for Accounting Framework relates mainly to private sector organisations which have a profit motive, all organisations will be referred to in this book as businesses except where they are clearly identified as otherwise, for example, clubs and societies. It should be noted, however, that the underlying principles of accounting apply to most types of organisation.

When you have studied this chapter you should be able to do the following:

- Discuss the nature of a balance sheet

- Define assets, liabilities and capital

- Explain the balance sheet equation

- Understand the accounting conventions that are commonly used in drawing up sets of accounts

- Explain the difference between fixed assets and current assets.

---

1 THE NATURE AND PURPOSE OF THE BALANCE SHEET

1.1 Assets and claims

A balance sheet is simply a statement which lists both the assets of a business and the claims against that business at some point of time. Assets are things of value to the business. Claims are financial obligations to people or groups of people.

1.2 Meaning of assets

More formally, **assets** may be defined as rights or other access to future economic benefits controlled by a particular business as a result of past transactions or events. Assets would therefore only appear in a balance sheet where:

- there remains a probable future benefit. For example a machine which was once useful but which is now defunct and has no second-hand value is not an asset and should not be shown in the balance sheet

- the business can control them. Thus the existence in the UK of a fairly effective road and rail transport service is useful (and valuable) to most UK businesses, but none of them would include the existence of this as an asset in their balance sheet because they cannot control it
- the benefit must have arisen from some transaction or event.

1.3 Meaning of claims

A **claim** is an obligation to transfer economic benefits as a result of past transactions or events. An amount of money borrowed by a business would be an example of a claim. Claims would only appear in a balance sheet where:

- they exist at the balance sheet date. Thus the transaction or event giving rise to a particular claim must have already occurred
- there is a probability that they will have to be met. Thus an amount which is owed by a business to someone who could not be traced would not normally be included in the balance sheet.

It may be the case that the business will have a claim against it only in the event of some future event occurring. For example a business may have a legal case for negligence proceeding against it, which may give rise to the need to pay damages. Such potential claims are known as **contingent liabilities**. Though knowledge of them may be an important piece of information about the business, such claims would not normally be included in the balance sheet.

Claims against businesses are of two main types:

- **external liabilities**, the obligations, often legally enforceable, to people outside the business
- **capital** (or **equity**), the amount of the claim which the owner has on the business.

1.4 The business entity convention

The reason for an owner having a claim against the business arises from the convention of **business entity**. This asserts that the business and the owner are separate *for accounting purposes*. This convention is necessary in order that the balance sheet of a business only reflects the assets of the business and does not include the owner's personal, non-business assets. The business entity convention is one of a number of conventions upon which accounting is based. Others will be introduced later in this chapter.

1.5 The balance sheet equation

The assets which appear in the balance sheet are only those of that particular business. They can only be acquired from finance supplied by claimants against the business. It must therefore be true to say that at any point in time for a particular business:

$$\textbf{Assets} = \textbf{Capital} + \textbf{Liabilities}$$

This is known as the **balance sheet equation**.

If the balance sheet equation must always hold true it must be the case that any alteration to the balance sheet value of any asset or claim must be compensated elsewhere. This could be through the increase or decrease in some other asset or through the increase or decrease in some claim. This is known as the **convention of duality** which holds that each transaction must have two effects such that the balance sheet is left in agreement after each transaction has been recorded. For instance, a business buying stock and paying by cheque causes an increase in stock which is precisely matched by a reduction in cash at bank.

An example may help to bring together some of the points which have arisen so far in the chapter.

Example

Ann Smith started a business. During the first week of trading the following transactions occurred.

1.   Ann opened a bank account for the business and paid in a cheque for £10,000 as her investment in the business.

2.   The business bought goods for resale (such goods are known as 'stock in trade' or 'inventory') for £3,000, paying by cheque.

3.   The business bought further stock in trade for £2,000 on credit (with the intention of paying for it at a later date).

4.   Stock which cost £1,500 was sold for £2,000. The buyer paid by cheque.

5.   Stock which cost £1,000 was sold for £1,500 on credit (the £1,500 will be paid by the customer at a later date).

6.   The business bought a delivery van for £3,000, paying by cheque.

Draw up the balance sheet after each of these transactions.

Solution

Each of these transactions will affect the balance sheet as follows:

Balance sheet after transaction 1

Assets	£	**Claims**	£
Cash at bank	10,000	Capital	10,000

The asset of cash increased by £10,000 and Ann (the owner of the business) acquired a claim of £10,000 against the business (capital). It should be clear from this transaction that the convention of business entity is essential if the balance sheet is to reflect the financial situation *of the business.*

Balance sheet after transaction 2

Assets	£	**Claims**	£
Cash at bank	7,000	Capital	10,000
(10,000 – 3,000)			
Stock in trade	3,000		
	10,000		10,000

Stock increased by £3,000 and cash decreased by £3,000. The claims were unaffected by this transaction.

Balance sheet after transaction 3

Assets	£	**Claims**	£
Cash at bank	7,000	Capital	10,000
Stock in trade	5,000	Trade creditors	2,000
(3,000 + 2,000)			
	12,000		12,000

Stock increased by £2,000, trade creditors (those who are owed money by the business for the supply of goods and services on credit) increased by £2,000. Neither cash nor capital were affected by this transaction.

Balance sheet after transaction 4

Assets		£	Claims		£
Cash at bank		9,000	Capital		10,500
(7,000 + 2,000)			(10,000 + 2,000 − 1,500)		
Stock in trade		3,500	Trade creditors		2,000
(£5,000 − £1,500)					
		12,500			12,500

The asset of stock decreased by £1,500 and that value left the business, to go to the customer. Since it is the owner of the business who gains from any increase in value, it is also the owner who suffers from any outflow of value. The effect of the reduction of stock is a reduction in the level of capital.

Of course this transaction is not all bad for Ann, since the stock leaving the business caused a £2,000 cheque to come into the business. This increased the cash by £2,000; it also increased capital by £2,000.

The net effect of this transaction on the capital is that it has increased by £500, because a profit of £500 was made as a result of selling stock which cost £1,500 for £2,000. This increase in capital was caused by a £500 net increase in assets (stock decreased by £1,500, cash increased by £2,000).

Balance sheet after transaction 5

Assets		£	Claims		£
Cash at bank		9,000	Capital		11,000
Stock in trade		2,500	(10,500 + 1,500 − 1,000)		
(£3,500 − £1,000)					
Trade debtors		1,500	Trade creditors		2,000
		13,000			13,000

As with transaction 4, the asset of stock decreased, in this case by £1,000, while the capital is reduced by £1,000. However, the transaction also results in an increase in the capital, amounting to £1,500 (the sale price) and an increase in an asset. The asset obtained in this case is an obligation from a customer to pay £1,500 at a future date. Those who owe money to the business for goods and services supplied on credit are known as trade debtors. The net effect of the transaction is to increase assets by £500 (an increase in trade debtors of £1,500 and a decrease in stock of £1,000) and capital by £500, the profit on the transaction (the result of selling for £1,500 stock which had cost £1,000).

Balance sheet after transaction 6

Assets		£	Claims		£
Cash at bank		6,000	Capital		11,000
(9,000 − 3,000)					
Stock in trade		2,500	Trade creditors		2,000
Trade debtors		1,500			
Delivery van		3,000			
		13,000			13,000

The van increased by £3,000 and cash decreased by £3,000. Neither stock nor the claims of the owner were affected by this transaction.

Note that each balance sheet 'balances'. This is to say that the sum of the assets equals the sum of the claims. This is what would be expected, given the conventions of business entity and duality. Note also that the heading to each of the above balance sheets specifies the particular point in time to which the balance sheet relates. In this sense the balance sheet can be viewed as a still photograph of the business. It depicts the situation at a particular instant. Shortly before or following that instant the picture may be different.

1.6   Activity

Following the pattern of the example above, draw up a series of balance sheets, one following each of the following transactions.

1   Peter starts a business by opening a business bank account and paying in a cheque for £5,000 from his own personal bank account.

2   The business bought stock in trade for £2,000, paying by cheque.

3   The business bought stock in trade for £1,000 on credit.

4   Stock in trade costing £1,600 was sold for £2,200, the buyer paying by cheque.

5   The creditor arising from transaction 3 was paid by cheque.

6   The business bought a machine for use in the business for £500, on credit.

7   The business borrowed £2,000, in the form of a cheque, from Peter's friend, Jones.

1.7   Activity solution

Peter's balance sheet after transaction 1

Assets	£	Claims	£
Cash at bank	5,000	Capital	5,000

Peter's balance sheet after transaction 2

Assets	£	Claims	£
Cash at bank	3,000	Capital	5,000
(5,000–£2,000)			
Stock in trade	2,000		
	£5,000		£5,000

Peter's balance sheet after transaction 3

Assets	£	Claims	£
Cash at bank	3,000	Capital	5,000
Stock in trade	3,000	Trade creditors	1,000
(2,000 + £1,000)			
	£6,000		£6,000

(Note that 'trade creditors' is the description usually applied to those who have advanced goods or services to a business on credit.)

Peter's balance sheet after transaction 4

Assets	£	Claims	£
Cash at bank	5,200	Capital	5,600
(3,000 + £2,200)		(£5,000 – £1,600 + £2,200)	
Stock in trade			
(£3,000 – £1,600)	1,400	Trade creditors	1,000
	£6,600		£6,600

Peter's balance sheet after transaction 5

Assets	£	Claims	£
Cash at bank	4,200	Capital	5,600
(£5,200 – £1,000)			
		Trade creditors	Nil
Stock in trade	1,400	£1,000 – £1,000	
	£5,600		£5,600

Peter's balance sheet after transaction 6

Assets	£	Claims	£
Cash at bank	4,200	Capital	5,600
Stock in trade	1,400	Trade creditors	500
Machine	500		
	£6,100		£6,100

Peter's balance sheet after transaction 7

Assets	£	Claims	£
Cash at bank	6,200	Capital	5,600
(4,200 + £2,000)			
Stock in trade	1,400	Trade creditors	500
Machine	500	Loan from Jones	2,000
	£8,100		£8,100

1.8   How often are balance sheets drawn up?

As will be seen in later chapters, a new balance sheet is not usually drawn up after each transaction as it has been in this example. This is principally because the complexity and quantity of transactions in the typical business would make it impractical to do so. In addition, users are unlikely to need balance sheets to be prepared so frequently. In principle, all transactions have the effect of altering the balance sheet in the way in which it was shown above. In practice, balance sheets are prepared periodically and will thus reflect the effect of a large number of transactions. This is illustrated below.

2   OTHER IMPORTANT CONVENTIONS AND PRINCIPLES

2.1   Introduction

Consideration has already been given to two accounting conventions. The business entity convention asserts that for accounting purposes the business and its owner are separate. The duality convention says that each transaction must have two effects. It might now be appropriate to consider some others, particularly since some of them have already been encountered, at least in terms of their practical effect.

2.2   Money measurement

The **convention of money measurement** asserts that accounting is only concerned with things that can be described in money terms and is not affected by those things which cannot. This means that a number of aspects of a business, which could be of great importance to users of accounts, will not be found on the balance sheet. These aspects include possession of such things as a skilled loyal workforce and a good reputation among customers.

2.3   Historic cost

The **historic cost convention** asserts that assets should be shown on the balance sheet at their original cost rather than at some assessment of current value. The basis of this convention is that actual cost tends to be a matter of demonstrable fact, current value tends to be a matter of opinion. Accounting tends to favour objectivity, sometimes at the expense of relevance.

2.4   Going concern/continuity

The **going concern** or **continuity** convention asserts that, unless there is evidence to the contrary, it is assumed that the business will continue more or less indefinitely. This convention has some bearing on the way in which long-term assets (fixed assets) are dealt with in the balance sheet (as will be seen later).

2.5   Stable monetary unit

The **stable monetary unit convention** assumes that the unit of currency in which the balance sheet is drawn up (the pound sterling in the UK) is not subject to alteration in value over time as a result, for example, of inflation. The implications of the invalidity of this assumption will be considered in Chapter 23.

2.6   Activity

1   What is a balance sheet?

2   Why must total claims always equal the total of the assets?

3   Why is it necessary to put a date in the heading of a balance sheet?

4   What is the 'balance sheet equation'?

5   Jim Brown has just paid £6,000 for a new car. Will this have an effect on the balance sheet of his business?

6   'Why is it that my capital is shown with the liabilities in the balance sheet of my business. Surely it is an asset?' This was said to you by Adrian Smith. Explain to him why he is wrong.

7   Which of the following would you expect to find on the balance sheet of a business? Explain your decisions.

    (a)   The fact that the business owes money.

    (b)   The fact that the owner has unusually good business skills.

    (c)   The fact that demand for the output of the business is expected to increase greatly in the future leading to a large increase in profits.

    (d)   The fact that the assets of the business are highly specialised and, in the main part, could only be used for the current purpose.

8   'The total of the assets in the balance sheet tells the owner how much his business is worth'. Is this true or false? Give reasons.

2.7   Activity solution

1   A balance sheet is a list of assets and claims of a business at some specific point in time.

2   The convention of duality ensures that the balance sheet, assuming no errors have occurred, will always show the same total for claims as it does for assets. Any alteration, irrespective of the reasons, in the balance sheet figure for any asset or claim must be accompanied by an alteration to another asset or claim such that the total for the assets equals the total for the claims.

3   Any balance sheet depicts the situation at some point in time. It is therefore important to tell the reader what this point in time is. This is particularly true since the assets and claims of a business can and do vary over time, sometimes dramatically so.

4   The balance sheet equation is:

$$\textbf{Assets = Capital + Liabilities}$$

5   If the car is for Jim's personal use and he pays for it using non-business funds there will be no effect on the balance sheet. If it is for Jim's personal use and it is bought using business funds, this is equivalent to a withdrawal of capital equal to the cost of the car. If the car is for business use and paid for from business funds it will be a business asset and it will appear as an asset on the balance sheet with the duality convention being satisfied by a decrease in cash or an increase in creditors. If the car is for business use, but is paid for from Jim's personal funds, it will appear as an asset on the business balance sheet with an equivalent injection appearing under capital.

6   This arises from the business entity convention. From the perspective of the business, Adrian is an outsider, so the balance sheet shows his investment in the business as a claim and not differently in principle from the liabilities. From Adrian's point of view his investment in the business is an asset.

7   (a)   This would appear in the balance sheet as creditors

    (b)   This would not appear in the balance sheet as such. Possibly its effect would manifest itself in the value of the assets, though this is not necessarily the case.

    (c)   This would not appear in the balance sheet.

    (d)   This would not appear in the balance sheet.

8   This statement is not true since the assets are not shown in the balance sheet at what they are worth, but at what they cost, subject to an allowance for depreciation of certain assets. The statement is also untrue due to the fact that the business may well have liabilities which will have the effect of reducing its value. The subject of depreciation will be taken up in later chapters.

3   CAPITAL (THE OWNER'S CLAIM)

3.1   Introduction

The nature of the transactions which have an effect on capital will now be examined in rather more detail. Probably the best way to approach this is through an example.

Example

Janet Strong has been in business for a little while and by 1 July 19X9 her business's balance sheet contained the following items:

Balance sheet at 1 July 19X9

Assets	£	Claims	£
Machinery	10,000	Capital	15,000
Motor van	3,000	Loan from bank	3,500
Trade debtors	2,000	Trade creditors	7,500
Stock in trade	6,000		
Cash at bank	5,000		
	26,000		26,000

During the next week the following transactions took place relating to the business:

1   Repaid £1,000 to the bank to reduce the loan

2   Bought some stock on credit for £4,000

3   Sold stock, which had cost £3,000, for £5,000 on credit

4   Received a cheque for £2,000 from a trade debtor

5   Paid £2,500 to trade creditors, paying by cheque

6   Paid a cheque for £250 for wages for the week to the only employee of the business

7   Paid a £500 cheque to the landlord of the business premises for rent and service charge for the week

8   Paid a cheque to Janet of £350 for her own use.

A revised balance sheet can be obtained by entering the effect of each of these transactions on the balance sheet, and then summarising the effect as at 8 July 19X9.

Janet's balance sheet after all of the transactions have been entered and summarised would appear as follows:

Balance sheet as at 8 July 19X9

Assets	£	Net £	Claims	£		Net £
Machinery	10,000	10,000	Capital	15,000		15,900
				−3,000	(3)	
				+5,000	(3)	
				−250	(6)	
Motor van	3,000	3,000		−500	(7)	
			−350		(8)	
Trade debtors	2,000	5,000				
	+5,000 (3)		Loan from bank	3,500		2,500
	−2,000 (4)			−1,000	(1)	
Stock in trade	6,000	7,000				
	+4,000 (2)					
	−3,000 (3)					
Cash at bank	5,000	2,400	Trade creditors	7,500		9,000
	−1,000 (1)			+4,000	(2)	
	+2,000 (4)			−2,500	(5)	
	−2,500 (5)					
	−250 (6)					
	−500 (7)					
	−350 (8)					
		£27,400				£27,400

The effect of each transaction can be identified by reference to the numbers in brackets. The figures in the 'net' columns are the resultant figures after all the transactions for the week have been recorded, in that they represent the position at 8 July 19X9. Strictly, the balance sheet at 8 July should contain only the figures in the 'net' column. The other figures are workings which keep track of the effect of individual transactions on the balance sheet.

Most of the above transactions are of the type which have already been met before but a few of them, notably those affecting the capital, require more explanation.

3.2   Transactions affecting capital

Transactions which affect the capital fall into three types:

(a)   **Injections of capital by the owner**

These occur when the owner wants to increase his investment in the business. There were no injections in this particular example.

(b)   **Those arising from trading activities**

Transactions (3), (6) and (7) are examples of such activities. They are distinguished from other transactions in that while the others simply involve swapping one asset for another, or paying off a creditor, or receiving money from a debtor, trading transactions involve actual increases and decreases in the wealth of the business. Transaction (6), for example, arose from employing someone for the week and paying him a wage. This was not the same as taking £250 out of the bank to replace it with another equally valuable asset. The £250 paid for wages has been lost to the business and as such it represents a reduction in the wealth of the business. This must be reflected somewhere in the balance sheet as well as in the cash at bank. If the business has lost wealth, it must be to the detriment of the owner; therefore it is to the capital that the reduction in wealth must be charged. It should be noted that this is not intended to suggest that employing people in general, or that Janet Strong employing someone during the first week in July in particular, is a waste of money. People are employed to help make the business successful, but whether that goal is achieved or not, they are still paid wages. It would normally be expected that the business would be compensated for the wages by higher sales or by savings in other types of cost.

Trading events which cause increases in capital, such as sales, are referred to as **revenues** and trading events which cause decreases in capital, such as stock used in making a sale, wages and rent, are known as **expenses**. Revenues less expenses equals profit (or loss).

(c) **Withdrawals of capital**

These occur where an owner, for a variety of reasons, takes part of their capital out of the business. The effect is to reduce assets and to reduce the owner's claims. However, it should be particularly noted that drawings of the owner, even if described as 'wages' or 'salary', are not an expense. The reward for the employee is wages or salary and for the owner it is profit. In spite of this it must be recognised that the amount of drawings *during a period* need not be related to the level of profit *during the same period*. For example, even in a period in which a loss is made, the owner may need to take out sufficient drawings to cover his personal living expenses. Over a longer time scale the relationship between profit and drawings is typically closer.

3.3 Summary of changes in capital

Janet Strong's capital changes during the week ended 8 July 19X9 could be summarised as follows:

		£
Opening capital		15,000
Add:	Injections	Nil
	Profit for the week	1,250
		16,250
Less: Drawings		350
Closing capital		15,900

The profit is arrived at by subtracting from the revenue (£5,000) the three expense items, namely stock sold (£3,000), wages (£250) and rent (£500).

You should note that the drawings are not a reduction in the profit for the week.

It will usually be the case that users of accounting information find it useful not only to know what profit has been made over a period, but how it arose. A user might, for example, be interested to know what level of sales gave rise to the profit figure and perhaps the relationship between the selling and buying prices of the stock sold. Not surprisingly this part of the capital area of the balance sheet is expanded and made available to users as the profit and loss account or income statement. This statement will be considered at greater length in the next chapter.

3.4 Activity

The following are transactions of a business for a period.

1 Stock in trade was bought on credit for £1,200.

2 The owner paid a trade creditor £1,500 for some stock in trade bought on credit recently. Since the owner did not have the business bank account cheque book with him, he drew a cheque on his personal account.

3 Stock in trade, which had cost £1,700, was sold on credit for £2,500.

4 The owner withdrew £500, by drawing a cheque on the business bank account, payable to himself.

5 Paid wages of £750 by cheque.

6 Paid bank interest of £100 by having the amount charged to the business bank account.

7 Received a £2,000 cheque from a trade debtor.

8 Paid a trade creditor £1,200 by a cheque drawn on the business bank account.

State the effect of each of the above on the balance sheet items. Where capital is affected, you should state whether the transaction is an injection of capital, a drawing, a revenue or an expense.

3.5   Activity solution

	Assets		Claims	
1	Stock in trade	+£1,200	Trade creditors	+£1,200
2			Trade creditors	−£1,500
			Capital (injection)	+£1,500
3	Stock in trade	−£1,700	Capital (expense)	−£1,700
	Trade in debtors	+£2,500	Capital (revenue)	+£2,500
4	Cash at bank	−£500	Capital (drawing)	−£500
5	Cash at bank	−£750	Capital (expense)	−£750
6	Cash at bank	−£100	Capital (expense)	−£100
7	Cash at bank	+£2,000		
	Trade debtors	−£2,000		
8	Cash at bank	−£1,200	Trade creditor	−£1,200

4   TYPES AND CLASSIFICATION OF ASSETS AND CLAIMS

4.1   Classification of assets

In balance sheets assets are usually classified as either fixed or current assets.

4.2   Fixed assets

These are the assets which are acquired by the business with the intention of retaining them in the business to help it to generate profit. Fixed assets are not acquired with the intention of reselling them at a profit though this may in fact happen. Fixed assets may be thought of as the 'tools' of the business. Sometimes these tools will be found to be unsuitable for the task which they were intended to perform, or the task may have altered, in which case they may not remain with the business for very long. Typically, however, fixed assets remain with the business for fairly long periods of time. Though plant and machinery, land and buildings are fairly typical fixed assets, not all fixed assets are **tangible.** Tangible assets are generally defined as assets having a physical embodiment, but may also include legal rights such as leases and securities. Some fixed assets are **intangible,** such as ownership of patents, copyrights, and licences.

A particularly important intangible asset is **goodwill.** This is the asset which arises from factors such as good reputation or a loyal workforce which might enable an existing business to expect to be able to generate higher profits than would be expected from a similar new business. Following the money measurement and historical cost conventions, goodwill built up in an existing business would not appear in its balance sheet. However, where a new owner buys an existing business, goodwill could well appear on the balance sheet of the new business. It would arise where the new owner paid more for the entire assets than the sum of their individual values, because it was judged that such things as the reputation of the established business had a value. The difference between the sum of the values of the individual assets and the price paid for them is the value of the goodwill. If this were not included in the balance sheet when *paid for* the balance sheet would not balance.

4.3   Current assets

These are assets which arise from day-to-day trading activities. They include assets which it is the business's express intention to turn into cash, as well as cash itself. Stock in trade, trade debtors, payments in advance and cash at bank are examples of typical current assets. Current assets do not typically remain in the business for as long as 12 months.

Note that what might be a fixed asset to one business could well be a current asset to another. Indeed even within the same business there could be two more or less identical assets, one of which could be current and the other fixed. For example, a motor car distributor could buy two identical cars on the same day. One might be put into the showroom for sale (a current asset − stock); the other might be intended for one of the staff to use, on a continual basis, to visit customers and others, as part of the job (a fixed asset − vehicles). The distinction between fixed and current assets is really one of intention rather than the nature of the asset.

4.4 Activity

Are the following assets of a retailing business fixed or current?

1. Delivery van
2. Cash at bank
3. Stock in trade
4. Trade debtors
5. Shop fittings
6. Cash registers
7. Cash in the cash registers
8. Insurance paid in advance

4.5 Activity solution

1. Fixed
2. Current
3. Current
4. Current
5. Fixed
6. Fixed
7. Current
8. Current – this is in effect a short term loan to the insurance company.

4.6 Classification of claims

Claims are usually classified under three main headings in the balance sheet. These are:

1. **Capital** (or owner's equity). This has been looked at in some detail already.
2. **Long-term liabilities.** These are liabilities which could not be demanded by their claimants in less than 12 months from the balance sheet date, for example a long-term loan.
3. **Current liabilities.** Liabilities for which payment could be demanded in less than 12 months. Typically the more major current liabilities are trade creditors and bank overdraft.

5 BALANCE SHEET FORMATS

5.1 Horizontal and vertical formats

If users are to understand a balance sheet and to find it fairly easy to use it is important that it is set out in some logical, orderly way. It is not really enough that it should be complete and arithmetically correct. An example of a logical, orderly layout is shown below:

Balance sheet as at 31 December 19X9

	£000	£000		£000
Fixed assets			**Capital**	
Land and buildings		80,000	Opening capital	102,000
Plant and machinery		28,000	*Plus:* Injections	10,000
Motor vehicles		25,000	Profit	17,000
		133,000		129,000

Current assets				Less: Drawings	6,000
Stock in trade	14,000				123,000
Trade debtors	10,000			**Long-term liabilities**	
Cash	3,000			Loans	25,000
		27,000			
				Current liabilities	
				Trade creditors	12,000
		160,000			160,000

This 'horizontal' layout clearly shows the assets and claims under the various headings. Note that assets are listed in increasing order of liquidity, that is, the least easily convertible into cash first and cash itself last. The claims go from the longest term to the shortest. The horizontal layout of two lists side by side highlights the equality of the total assets and total claims particularly clearly.

More popularly these days balance sheets are presented in a 'vertical' or 'narrative' form shown below:

Balance sheet as at 31 December 19X9

	£000	£000	£000
Fixed assets			
Land and buildings		80,000	
Plant and machinery		28,000	
Motor vehicles		25,000	
			133,000
Current assets			
Stock in trade	14,000		
Trade debtors	10,000		
Cash	3,000		
		27,000	
Less: **Current liabilities**			
Trade creditors		12,000	
Net current assets (working capital)			15,000
			148,000
Less: **Long-term liabilities**			
Loans			25,000
			123,000
Capital			
Opening capital			102,000
Plus: Injections			10,000
Profit			17,000
			129,000
Less: **Drawings**			6,000
Closing capital			123,000

Note that the vertical presentation does not change the basic figures nor the principles on which they are based, it simply rearranges the layout. What it does, however, is to give the information in a way which many people believe to be more logical and useful, for example, it shows a figure for current assets less current liabilities. This figure is known as **working capital** and it is regarded as a useful indicator of the financial health of the business. Chapter 24 will deal with this and other indicators in some detail.

How a business sets out its balance sheet is generally a matter of its own choice. Where the business is trading in the form of a limited company, however, the law in the UK prescribes the form. Accounting for limited companies will be dealt with in Chapters 19, 20 and 21.

The horizontal format will continue to be used for the next two chapters, mainly because it emphasises the convention of duality, and leads naturally into the system of double-entry bookkeeping.

5.2 Some additional points on balance sheets

When building up balance sheets by recording transactions it is a matter of judgement as to how many categories of assets and claims there are. For example, if a business owns two motor vehicles should these be shown under one heading in the balance sheet or should each one be shown separately? The answer must depend on whether users of the balance sheet would be helped by the additional information available if the vehicles are shown separately, or whether there would be a danger of giving an excess of information, and thus confusing readers. Judgements on the extent of aggregation of information must be made by those designing accounting systems and reports. At one extreme all the assets could be shown as one total figure labelled 'assets'. At the other, for example, each individual item of stock in trade could be separately shown in the balance sheet. The sensible approach lies somewhere between these two extremes.

In the examples and activities up to now, all transactions involving cash have gone through the bank. In fact most businesses maintain some sort of float of cash in the form of notes and coin, often referred to as 'petty cash' or 'cash in hand' (as opposed to cash at bank), and carry out some transactions in that form.

5.3 Using the balance sheet equation to determine the profit figure

It has been demonstrated that at any given moment:

$$\text{Assets} = \text{Capital} + \text{Liabilities}$$

It is worth mentioning at this point that under the UK legal system claims by creditors and other external bodies take priority over claims by the owner. Capital can therefore be seen as a residual claim on the assets of the business.

$$\text{Capital} = \text{Assets} - \text{Liabilities}$$

It has also been shown that:

$$\text{Opening capital} + \text{Injections} + \text{Profit (or} - \text{loss)} - \text{Drawings} = \text{Closing capital}$$

After adjusting for injections and withdrawals, the difference between opening and closing capital is profit (or loss) for the period.

Following on from these statements, it would be possible to deduce the profit for a period, without having knowledge of the various revenues and expenses. This is because if the assets and liabilities at the beginning and end of the period were known, the opening and closing capital figures could be deduced, so that knowledge of any capital injections or drawings during the period would enable the profit or loss to be calculated.

Example

Pat Cooper's business had the following total assets and liabilities at the beginning and at the end of January:

	1 January £	31 January £
Total assets	10,500	11,700
Total liabilities	4,300	5,600

During the month Pat made no injections of capital but withdrew £200. What was the profit (loss) for the month?

Solution

The profit figure could be deduced as follows:

Opening capital   10,500 – 4,300   = 6,200
Closing capital   11,700 – 5,600   = 6,100
Since Opening capital + Injections + Profit – Drawings = Closing capital
6,200 + 0 + Profit – 200   = 6,100
Profit = 6,100 – 6,200 + 200 =   £100

In Chapter 15, this approach will be used to derive the profit or loss figure for businesses with incomplete records.

6   CHAPTER SUMMARY

- This chapter explained the nature and purpose of the balance sheet. The balance sheet is a list of assets and claims for a business at a specified point in time. At any time the total assets must equal total claims. Accounting is based upon a number of basic rules or conventions. Those identified in this chapter included business entity, duality, money measurement, historic cost, going concern and stable monetary unit.

- The impact of a range of transactions on the balance sheet was illustrated. Some events recorded in accounting only cause the wealth of the business and of its owner(s) to change form. In other cases accounting events cause wealth to be increased or reduced. These events are known as revenues and expenses respectively. They will be considered in more depth in Chapter 3.

- Assets are classified as fixed assets or current assets. Claims are grouped as capital, long-term liabilities and current liabilities.

  - Balance sheets are usually set out in a logical and systematic way to ease their readers' understanding. The two-sided or horizontal format will be used for the next few chapters as it provides a logical introduction to the system of recording known as double-entry bookkeeping. In practice the vertical format is more commonly used and will be used elsewhere in this book.

7   SELF TEST QUESTIONS

7.1   Which of the following most accurately describes a balance sheet?

    (a)   a statement which shows how much profit a business has made and how it arose

    (b)   a statement which shows how much a business is worth

    (c)   a list of assets of and claims against a business

    (d)   a list of cash payments and receipts over a period. (1.1)

7.2   What does the going concern convention say?

    (a)   that unless there is evidence to the contrary, it is assumed that the business will continue more or less indefinitely

    (b)   that users of accounts will only be interested in the accounts as long as the business keeps going

    (c)   that it is impossible to prepare a balance sheet unless it is assumed that the business will continue more or less indefinitely

    (d)   that users are only concerned with the balance sheets of businesses which are expected to keep going. (2.4)

7.3   What is a revenue?

    (a)   some cash received

    (b)   a trading event which increases capital

    (c)   a trading event which reduces the owner's claim

    (d)   making a profit. (3.2 (b))

7.4　Why would a building be a fixed asset to a manufacturing business?

(a)　because it cannot be moved

(b)　because it would be held to help the business to generate revenue rather than being intended to be sold

(c)　because once the business owns the building it is difficult to sell it

(d)　because buildings never wear out. (4.2)

7.5　What can be deduced from knowledge of the opening and closing capital figures and the capital injections and withdrawals for a period?

(a)　how much the business is worth

(b)　how much cash has been spent during the period

(c)　how much the business owes to claimants

(d)　how much profit has been made during the period. (5.3)

8　EXAMINATION TYPE QUESTIONS

8.1　Transactions

The following transactions were entered into by a business during January:

1　Bought stock on credit for £4,000

2　Owner withdrew £100

3　Paid a trade creditor £1,200

4　Sold stock which had cost £1,800 for £2,500 on credit

5　Borrowed £2,000 as a long-term loan from Smith's Bank plc

6　Bought a piece of machinery (a fixed asset) for £1,500, paying by cheque

7　Received a cheque for £1,200 from a trade debtor

8　Paid rent in arrears for the month of £200, by cheque

9　Paid wages by cheque of £200

10　The owner took stock which had cost £50 for his own use.

State in the case of each of the above how the balance sheet would be affected. Follow the pattern shown below:

Transaction	Assets		Claims	
Transaction 1	Stock	+ £4,000	Trade creditors	+ £4,000

8.2　Mason

Richard Mason started a wholesale business on 1 March. The following is a summary of his transactions during his first month of trading:

- Richard transferred £10,000 from his own bank account to one opened in the name of 'Mason Enterprises'

- Richard's van, valued at £3,500, was transferred for use in the business

- Paid rent for the month of £1,000 on a warehouse, paying by cheque

- Bought stock on credit for £5,000

- Sold stock, which had cost £4,000, for £5,200 on credit

- Paid wages to an assistant, paying by cheque £350

- Paid general expenses, all by cheque, totalling £300

- Paid, by cheque drawn on the business account, the rent for the quarter to 31 May on Richard's flat, that is his personal dwelling, £650

- Received, by cheque, £4,300 from trade debtors

- Paid £3,200 to trade creditors by cheque.

(a)   Build up the balance sheet of Mason Enterprises.

(b)   Redraft the final balance sheet (that is, as at 31 March) in the standard vertical or narrative form (ignore depreciation).

9   ANSWERS TO EXAMINATION TYPE QUESTIONS

9.1   Transactions

Transaction	Assets		Claims	
Transaction 1	Stock	+£4,000	Trade creditors	+£4,000
Transaction 2	Cash at bank	−£100	Capital	−£100
Transaction3	Cash at bank	−£1,200	Trade creditors	−£1,200
Transaction 4	Stock	−£1,800	Capital	−£1,800
	Trade debtor	+£2,500	Capital	+£2,500
Transaction 5	Cash at bank	+£2,000	Bank loan	+£2,000
Transaction 6	Machinery	+£1,500		
	Cash at bank	−£1,500		
Transaction 7	Cash at bank	+£1,200		
	Trade debtor	−£1,200		
Transaction 8	Cash at bank	−£200	Capital	−£200
Transaction 9	Cash at bank	−£200	Capital	−£200
Transaction 10	Stock	−£50	Capital	−£50

9.2   Mason

(a)

Mason Enterprises
Balance sheet

Assets	£		£	Claims	£		£
Cash at bank	+10,000	(1)	8,800	Capital	+10,000	(1)	12,400
	−1,000	(3)			+3,500	(2)	
	−350	(6)			−1,000	(3)	
	−300	(7)			−4,000	(5)	
	−650	(8)			+5,200	(5)	
	+4,300	(9)			350	(6)	
	−3,200	(10)			−300	(7)	
					−650	(8)	
Van	+3,500	(2)	3,500	Trade creditors	+5,000	(4)	1,800
					−3,200	(10)	
Stock	+5,000	(4)	1,000				
	−4,000	(5)					
Trade debtors	+5,200	(5)	900				
	−4,300	(9)					
			£14,200				£14,200

(b)

Mason Enterprises
Balance sheet as at 31 March (in vertical form)

	£	£	£
Fixed assets			
Van			3,500
Current assets			
Stock	1,000		
Trade debtors	900		
Cash at bank	8,800		
		10,700	
Less: *Current liabilities*			
Trade creditors		1,800	
Net current assets (working capital)			8,900
			12,400
Capital			12,400

3 THE PROFIT AND LOSS ACCOUNT

INTRODUCTION AND LEARNING OBJECTIVES

This chapter will consider the profit and loss account (also known as the income statement). It will explain that the profit and loss account has a clear link with the balance sheet, and could be said to be in the nature of an appendix to the balance sheet, which summarises revenues and expenses.

We look in some detail at how the profit and loss account is constructed and at some of the accounting conventions and assumptions on which it is based.

In particular we focus on the derivation of revenues and expenses. The realisation convention, which deals with recognition of revenues, will be discussed. For example, should revenue be recognised as soon as a customer orders some goods, or when they are paid for, or at some other time? We make clear that in calculating profit the accruals convention will be used. This requires a distinction to be drawn between a revenue and a cash receipt, and an expense and a cash payment. In effect the accruals convention says that profit is the excess of revenues over expenses and not the excess of cash receipts over cash payments. For example, the purchase of stock for cash will result in a cash payment but not necessarily an expense. The expense will only arise when the stock has been used up.

The chapter will illustrate how a profit and loss account can be produced (together with a balance sheet) from basic data, including adjustments for prepaid and accrued expenses. The format of the profit and loss account will also be considered.

When you have studied this chapter you should be able to do the following:

- Explain the nature of the profit and loss account

- Discuss the application of the realisation convention and the accruals convention

- Calculate prepaid and accrued expenses.

---

1 THE NATURE AND PURPOSE OF THE PROFIT AND LOSS ACCOUNT

1.1 Introduction

It was seen in Chapter 2 that capital (the claim of the owner) of a business can be affected by three types of transaction, namely:

1 injections of new capital by the owner
2 withdrawals of capital by the owner
3 revenues and expenses from trading activities.

Revenues are events arising from trading which have the effect of increasing capital.
Expenses are the decreases in capital which arise from trading.

In practice, injections and withdrawals of capital are relatively rare events. In virtually all businesses, irrespective of their size, it is the trading transactions which dominate movements in the capital figure. Revenues and expenses occur almost constantly during working hours for most businesses, resulting in total in vast numbers over a period of a year, for instance. Given the number of trading transactions, it is necessary to have an appendix to the balance sheet which summarises the revenues and expenses and arrives at a net profit or loss. This statement is known as the **profit and loss account or income statement**.

Apart from the practical reason given above, there is a second and probably more important reason for producing this appendix to the balance sheet. The balance sheet at any given moment can only show the *total* net profit or loss. Most users of accounting information (including the owner) almost certainly want more than this. They probably want to know what the totals were for different types of sales; they also will want to know the total for each type of expense for the period. In other words, users will want to know how the particular level of profit has been earned (or perhaps how a loss was sustained), not just the amount of the profit or loss. Knowledge of the level of revenues and different expenses will help the user to make some assessment of past performance and to identify areas for future improvement. Thus knowledge of past performance will assist in planning for the future.

1.2   Accounts prepared annually

It is important to note that the profit and loss account relates to a particular period. This period could be of literally any length, up to a maximum of the entire life of the business. In fact virtually all businesses produce a profit and loss account on an annual basis, that is, every 12-month period. Many businesses, particularly larger ones, draw up a profit and loss account for shorter periods as well. A month (whether a calendar month, 4 weeks or 20 working days) is a popular period in larger businesses. The regular and frequent availability of information on revenues and expenses helps in the management of those businesses.

As well as preparing a profit and loss account on an annual basis virtually all businesses produce a balance sheet to coincide with the end of the period of the profit and loss accounts. So a particular business might choose to draw up a profit and loss account for the year to 31 December each year as well as a balance sheet at the close of business on 31 December. (Remember that the balance sheet shows the position at a point in time while the profit and loss account summarises trading for a period.) The annual profit and loss account and balance sheet are usually referred to as the **final** or **annual accounts**.

The pressure on UK businesses to produce final accounts comes from statute law in the case of businesses operating as limited companies and from the tax authorities for other businesses. In either case it is completely at the choice of the business as to which year end it chooses. One business can draw up its accounts to 31 December and another to 13 August.

1.3   Recording transactions

An example of recording transactions will now be considered. In working through this example, only entries relating to transactions involving injections and withdrawals of capital will be made in the capital section of the balance sheet, in the first instance at least. Transactions involving revenues and expenses will be shown in the profit and loss account. Only at the end of the period will the net profit or net loss be transferred to the capital area of the balance sheet. The other aspect of transactions affecting capital will be dealt with in the normal way. It should not be forgotten that the profit and loss account is simply an appendix to the balance sheet, so transactions recorded in the former will, in summary form, be recorded in the latter.

Example

Mary Carter has been in business for a few years. The balance sheet of the business at 31 December 19X8 was as follows:

Balance sheet at 31 December 19X8

Fixed assets	£	Capital	£
Freehold premises	25,000	At 31 December 19X8	34,000
Plant	12,000		
		Long-term liabilities	
		Loan from bank	20,000

Current assets			
Stock in trade	11,000		
Trade debtors	10,000	**Current liabilities**	
Cash at bank	5,000	Trade creditors	12,000
Cash in hand	3,000		
	£66,000		£66,000

During the year to 31 December 19X9 the following total transactions occurred:

1   Mary withdrew a total of £10,000 in cash

2   Stock in trade was bought, all on credit, for £34,000

3   Sales were made totalling £60,000 of stock in trade which had cost £37,000. Of the sales £51,000 were on credit and £9,000 for cash (that is, notes and coins)

4   A total of £16,000 was drawn from the bank in cash to augment the cash in hand

5   Electricity for the year paid by cheque totalled £2,000

6   Rates for the year paid by cheque totalled £1,000

7   Wages for the year all paid in cash totalled £10,000

8   Sundry expenses all paid in cash totalled £2,000

9   Trade creditors were paid a total of £36,000 all by cheque

10   Trade debtors paid a total of £54,000 all in cheques

11   The bank charged interest on the loan amounting to £3,000 for the year. This was deducted from the bank balance.

Show the effect of these summary transactions on Mary's balance sheet.

Solution

Balance sheet at 31 December 19X9

Fixed assets	£	£	Capital	£
Freehold premises		25,000	At 31 December 19X8	34,000
Plant		12,000	Add: Profit for the year	5,000
				39,000
			Less: Drawings	10,000 (1)
				29,000

Current assets				
Stock in trade	11,000	8,000		
	+34,000 (2)			
	−37,000 (3)			
			Long-term liabilities	
Trade debtors	10,000	7,000	Loan from bank	20,000
	+51,000 (3)			
	−54,000 (10)			
Cash at bank	5,000	1,000	**Current liabilities**	
	−16,000 (4)		Trade	10,000
	−2,000 (5)		creditors	12,000
	−1,000 (6)			+34,000 (2)
	−36,000 (9)			−36,000 (9)
	+54,000 (10)			
	−3,000 (11)			

Cash in hand	3,000		6,000
	−10,000	(1)	
	+9,000	(3)	
	+16,000	(4)	
	−10,000	(7)	
	−2,000	(8)	
	59,000		59,000

Profit and loss account for the year ended 31 December 19X9

Expenses	£		Revenues	£	
Cost of sales	+37,000	(3)	Sales	+60,000	(3)
Electricity	+2,000	(5)			
Rates	+1,000	(6)			
Wages	+10,000	(7)			
Sundry expenses	+2,000	(8)			
Bank interest	+3,000	(11)			
Total expenses	55,000				
Net profit	5,000				
	60,000			60,000	

The difference in using this approach, compared to that used in Chapter 2, is that instead of recording revenues as additions to capital on the balance sheet, they are listed in a separate profit and loss account. Similarly, expenses appear in the profit and loss account rather than as deductions from capital on the balance sheet. Since profit equals revenues less expenses it is necessary to add the profit calculated in the profit and loss account to the capital figure in the balance sheet. Losses need to be deducted.

1.4 Format of the profit and loss account

Since the profit and loss account is an appendix to the balance sheet the format in which it is kept is not particularly important at this stage. As set out above, revenues (increases in capital as a result of trading) and expenses (decreases in capital as a result of trading) are simply listed, and a profit or loss is calculated. It is then necessary to enter the amount of profit or loss on the balance sheet in order that the totals of both sides of the balance sheet are in agreement. In the example the revenues total £60,000, the expenses £55,000, giving a profit of £5,000, which is then added to the capital figure in the balance sheet.

The list of revenues and expenses is set out in the way shown above for a particular reason; it is essentially the same format as would be found in a profit and loss account in a system of ledger accounts. Ledger accounts will be dealt with in Chapter 5.

It should be noted that for *presentation* of the final accounts, the sections of the balance sheet would be individually subtotalled (for example, the fixed assets would be totalled). An appropriate format should also be used for the profit and loss account. Profit and loss formats will be discussed later in this chapter.

1.5 Activity

During the following year of Mary Carter's business (the year to 31 December 19X0) the following total transactions took place.

1   An additional piece of plant was acquired costing £3,000 which was paid for by cheque

2   Mary withdrew £5,000 in cash, drew a cheque to herself for £3,000 and she took stock in trade costing £2,000 for her own use

3   Sales of £63,000 were made of stock in trade which had cost £35,000. £12,000 of these were made for cash and the remainder on credit

4	Stock in trade was bought, all on credit, for £33,000
5	Trade creditors were paid £35,000, all by cheque
6	Trade debtors paid £48,000 by cheque
7	Electricity for the year, paid by cheque totalled £2,200
8	Rates for the year totalled £1,300. This was paid by Mary out of her own personal bank account because she had mislaid the business's cheque book at the time
9	Wages for the year totalled £9,200, all of which was paid in cash
10	A further £10,000 was borrowed from the bank and this was credited to the current account
11	Bank interest totalling £3,900 was charged to the current account
12	Sundry expenses for the year totalled £1,800, all paid in cash.

Draw up a balance sheet for Mary's business as at 31 December 19X0 to reflect these transactions and prepare the profit and loss account for the year ended 31 December 19X0.

1.6   Activity solution

Mary Carter
Balance sheet as at 31 December 19X0

	£	£		£	£
Fixed assets			**Capital**		
Freehold premises	+25,000	25,000	At 31/12/19X9		29,000
Plant	+12,000		Add: Profit for the year		9,600
	+3,000 (1)	15,000	Injection		1,300 (8)
					39,900
Current assets			Less: Drawings	−5,000 (2)	
Stock in trade	+8,000	4,000		−3,000 (2)	
				−2,000 (2)	
	−2,000 (2)				−10,000
	−35,000 (3)				29,900
	+33,000 (4)				
Trade debtors	+7,000	10,000			
	+51,000 (3)				
	−48,000 (6)				
			Long-term liabilities		
Cash at bank	+1,000	11,900	Bank loan	+20,000	
				+10,000	30,000
	−3,000 (1)				
	−3,000 (2)				
	−35,000 (5)				
	+48,000 (6)				
	−2,200 (7)		**Current liabilities**		
	+10,000 (10)		Trade creditors	+10,000	8,000
	−3,900 (11)			+33,000 (4)	
				−35,000 (5)	
Cash in hand	+6,000	2,000			
	−5,000 (2)				
	+12,000 (3)				
	−9,200 (9)				
	−1,800 (12)				
		£67,900			£67,900

Mary Carter
Profit and loss account for the year ended 31 December 19X0

	£			£	
Cost of stock sold	+35,000	(3)	Sales	+63,000	(3)
Electricity	+2,200	(7)			
Rates	+1,300	(8)			
Wages	+9,200	(9)			
Bank interest	+3,900	(11)			
Sundry expenses	+1,800	(12)			
Total expenses	53,400				
Net profit	9,600				
	£63,000			£63,000	

2   THE RECOGNITION OF REVENUES

2.1   The realisation convention

It is important that consideration be given to the question of the point at which revenue should be treated as having occurred. For example, should a sale be recorded in the accounts of the business:

- when the order is received from the customer
- when the goods pass to the customer
- when the customer pays for the goods?

There is no clear-cut, correct answer to this question. However, a convention, known as the **realisation convention,** tends to be followed here. The realisation convention asserts that the sale should normally be recognised when the goods physically pass to the customer and they are accepted. It is based upon the idea that at this point some objective measure of achievement (revenue) can be made, that there is acceptance by the customer of some kind of obligation to pay, and that there is a good chance that such payment will actually be made by the customer. It is important to recognise that the realisation convention may well mean that revenues may be recognised before cash is received. For example, when goods are sold on credit, revenue (sales) is normally recognised, with a corresponding increase in the current asset trade debtors. In such a case cash does not pass from the customer to the supplier at the same time as the goods pass in the opposite direction. Cash proceeds will arise at a later date. Indeed, a revenue may be recognised in one accounting period, with the associated cash not being received until a later period. For example, suppose that a business draws up its final accounts to 30 April each year. It makes a sale in April 19X8 which is paid for in May 19X8. This sale will be recognised in April and included in the total sales figure, for profit measurement purposes, during the year to 30 April 19X8. The balance sheet of the business as at 30 April 19X8 will therefore include (under current assets) a trade debtor in respect of the money due on this sale.

2.2   Deferred revenue

It is not unknown for goods to be paid for before they pass to the customer, but this is not, of itself, reason for the revenue to be recognised otherwise than at the time that the goods pass. At this stage, the transaction has not yet been completed, and revenue recognition would be premature. If goods are paid for by a customer in advance, the cash would increase, and a current liability, known as a deferred revenue, would be increased. When the goods pass to the customer the deferred revenue can be recognised as a revenue. Only when the goods have been supplied will profit have been earned.

2.3   Revenues relating to services

Where the subject of the sale is a service rather than a physical object, the position can be less straightforward. In general, revenues relating to services will be recognised on performance of that service. There are few problems with this where the service is quickly rendered and each service is individually identifiable, such as the services of a hairdresser or of a laundry. It can be more of a problem where the service is something like that provided by a landlord to a tenant or by an electricity board to its customers. Revenues such as rent receivable or interest receivable are typically recognised on a time basis for the period to which the particular agreement relates.

The recognition of revenues should not be seen as guaranteeing receipt of cash. The possibility of bad debts clearly exists, and this will be dealt with in Chapter 10. However, recognition in the way described above is a reasonable way of approaching most types of transaction. There are clearly other areas where revenue recognition can be particularly difficult (for example hire purchase transactions) but these are not within the syllabus. However it is important to realise that recognition of revenues is not always the clear-cut issue which it might be imagined to be.

3   MATCHING EXPENSES WITH REVENUES

3.1   The matching convention

Having established into which accounting period particular revenues fall, typically by following the realisation convention, it is necessary to ensure that the expenses relating to them are allocated to that same accounting period. Failure to match revenues with the expenses which arise in relation to them can cause very considerable distortions and therefore misleading information. The **matching convention** asserts that expenses should be matched to the revenues to which they relate such that both the revenue and the associated expenses incurred in earning the revenue are recognised in the same accounting period.

Where a manufactured product is made over two accounting periods it will be necessary to carry forward costs of production to the period in which the good is sold, so that these costs can be matched against revenues arising from the actual sale. Costs carried forward in this way must be shown as a current asset on the balance sheet, usually stock or work-in-progress, or finished goods.

Example

During the year ended 31 December 19X8 work was carried out on a contract for a particular product, with the resulting costs.

Stock used	£1,000
Wages (relating to this product)	£2,000

The product was sold in January 19X9 for £5,000.

Assuming that the business has a financial year which covers the period 1 January to 31 December, how would these items be treated in the 19X8 and 19X9 accounts?

Solution

No revenue would be recognised in the year ended 31 December 19X8. The £3,000 costs incurred as shown above would be reflected in the balance sheet as at 31 December 19X8, as a current asset (work-in-progress) £3,000. In 19X9 £5,000 revenue would be recognised, and the work-in-progress of £3,000 would become an expense, giving a profit on the transaction of £2,000. If the expenses had not been properly matched against revenues, but had been treated as an expense of 19X8, significant distortions in the profit calculation would have occurred. In 19X8 the transaction would have resulted in a decrease in profit of £3,000, while in 19X9 an increase in profit of £5,000 would have resulted.

3.2   Accruals accounting

Underpinning the realisation and matching conventions is the **accruals convention.** This asserts that a distinction needs to be drawn between a revenue and the cash receipt in respect of it; and between an expense and the cash payment which relates to it. In effect the accruals convention says that profit is the excess of revenues over expenses for a period, and not the excess of cash receipts over cash payments for the same period. Profit is concerned with increases in the net wealth of the business (and its owner) and wealth takes forms other than cash, as we explained in Chapter 1.

Example

Jim Moore's business draws up accounts each year to 31 December. Rent is paid for the business premises six months in advance on 1 April and 1 October each year. Recent rent payments and dates were as follows:

1 April 19X7	£4,000
1 October 19X7	£4,000
1 April 19X8	£5,000
1 October 19X8	£5,000

What amount would be charged for rent in the 19X8 profit and loss account?

Solution

The rent expense for the year ended 31 December 19X8 would be calculated as follows:

Period	£
1 January 19X8 to 31 March 19X8 (3/6 × £4,000)	2,000
1 April 19X8 to 30 September 19X8 (6/6 × £5,000)	5,000
1 October 19X8 to 31 December 19X8 (3/6 × £5,000)	2,500
Rent expense for the year ended 31 December 19X8	£9,500

The rent expense reflects the rate of rent applicable to the year 19X8, irrespective of the fact that £10,000 (£5,000 + £5,000) was actually spent on rent during that year.

This of course, leaves unanswered the question as to how to reflect in the balance sheet the fact that at the beginning and end of the accounting year 19X8, the business had paid rent from which future benefit was still to be derived.

At 1 January 19X8 Jim Moore's business still had the right to occupy its premises until 31 March 19X8. This represents an asset of £2,000 (3/6 × £4,000) and would be shown in the balance sheet as at 31 December 19X7 as such, under payment in advance (or prepayment) in the current assets.

Similarly the balance sheet as at 31 December 19X8 would include a payment in advance (prepayment) for rent of £2,500 (3/6 × £5,000), the rent from 1 January 19X9 to 31 March 19X9).

3.3 Expenses paid in arrears

In practice it is probably more common for expenses to be paid in arrears than in advance. Rent, rates and insurance premiums are relatively unusual in that they are typically paid in advance.

Example

Clare Andrews started a business on 1 April 19X8. During the first year she paid electricity bills for the business as follows:

Payment date	Amount (£)	Period of bill
14 July 19X8	314	1/4/19X8 to 30/6/19X8
12 October 19X8	207	1/7/19X8 to 30/9/19X8
14 January 19X9	348	1/10/19X8 to 31/12/19X8

Early in April 19X9 a bill of £388 for the quarter ended 31 March 19X9 was received from the Electricity Board.

What is the electricity expense for the year ended 31 March 19X9?

Solution

Though the cash payment for the year was only £869 (£314 + 207 + 348), the expense for the year includes the bill received after the financial year end and totals £1,257 (£869+388). The balance sheet at 31 March 19X9 reflects this by including the unpaid bill as a creditor, usually referred to as an accrued expense, (or an accrual) of £388. Note that the duality aspect of the accrued expense is upheld since an additional claim of £388 is entered in the balance sheet as a current liability with a corresponding reduction in capital. In fact the reduction in capital is achieved by including an additional expense of £388 in the profit and loss account.

When the last of the electricity bills is actually paid the appropriate entries in the balance sheet will be to reduce cash and to eliminate the £388 accrued expense from the current liabilities.

It is sometimes the case that the expense for a particular period is equal to the actual expenditure of cash. However, payment in advance, payment in arrears and the holding of stocks, both stock in trade and others such as stationery, are very common phenomena in practice and they will require adjustments of the type shown above. They are also very common in examination questions.

3.4   Activity

Soper's is a retail business whose final accounts are drawn up annually to 31 July. For each of the following, identify the expense for the year to 31 July 19X9 and any accruals or prepayments at that date.

1   Rent of £100 is paid monthly in advance at the beginning of each month.

2   Rates are paid half yearly in advance. Recent payments have been as follows:

	£
1 October 19X7	220
1 April 19X8	240
1 October 19X8	240
1 April 19X9	270
1 October 19X9	270

3   Bills for electricity, which are paid quarterly in arrears, have been paid as follows:

Payment date	Amount	Period of bill
20/7/19X8	410	1/4/19X8 to 30/6/19X8
14/10/19X8	360	1/7/19X8 to 30/9/19X8
23/1/19X9	442	1/10/19X8 to 31/12/19X8
12/4/19X9	478	1/1/19X9 to 31/3/19X9
14/7/19X9	432	1/4/19X9 to 30/6/19X9
15/10/19X9	366	1/7/19X9 to 30/9/19X9

3.5   Activity solution

	Expense for year	Prepayment or accrual
	£	£
1	1,200 (12 × £100)	None
2	500 (2/6 × 240) + 240 + (4/6 × 270)	90 prepayment
3	1,714 (2/3 × 360 + 442 + 478 + 432 + (1/3 × 366)	122 Accrual

3.6   Calculation of revenue for a period

Similar adjustments may arise with regard to cash receipts, in order to calculate revenue for a period. Revenues may be paid in advance, in which case they are carried forward as a liability in the period-end balance sheet, known as a **deferred revenue**. This deferred revenue will then become a revenue in the period to which it relates. Cash receipts associated with particular revenues may also be in arrears at the end of the period to which the revenue relates. Where this occurs they will be included as revenues in the profit and loss account and as a current asset in the period-end balance sheet. When cash is received this current asset will be eliminated.

Example

Jonathan Cater rents out part of his business premises from 1 January 19X5 at an annual rental of £1,000. His accounting year runs from 1 January to 31 December.

His cash receipts relating to rent are as follows:

	£
19X5	750
19X6	1,500
19X7	750

What amount will be shown in the 19X5, 19X6 and 19X7 accounts for these items?

Solution

In 19X5 the revenue (rent receivable) will be shown as £1,000, the amount of rent agreed for the period. This means that at the end of 19X5, £250 of the revenue has not been received. This will be shown as a current asset, debtors (rent receivable) £250.

In 19X6 £1,500 is received. This covers the £250 owing from 19X5, the £1,000 for 19X6, and £250 paid in advance for 19X7 (a deferred revenue). The revenue for the year is clearly £1,000. The £250 deferred revenue will be shown in the balance sheet as a current liability.

In 19X7 the deferred revenue will cease to be a liability, and will become a revenue. The £750 cash received means that, by the end of 19X7, the full £1,000 revenue has been received. The revenue for rent receivable will thus be shown as £1,000, and there will be no balances needed for rent receivable in the year end balance sheet.

The transactions for the three years can be recorded as follows, again conforming with the convention of duality.

19X5   At the time of cash receipt:
- increase cash
- increase the revenue (rent receivable)

    with £750

At the year end:
- increase a current asset, debtors (rent receivable)
- increase the revenue (rent receivable)

    with £250, the amount in arrears at the year end.

19X6   At the time of the cash receipt:
- increase cash
- increase the revenue (rent receivable)

    by £1,500, the amount received. The opening debtor needs to be set off against the revenue, as follows:
- reduce the revenue (rent receivable)
- reduce the opening debtors (rent receivable)

    by £250, the amount outstanding at the beginning of the year. In practice this adjustment will take place at the beginning of the period.

At the year end:
- reduce the revenue (rent receivable)
- increase a current liability (deferred revenue)

    by £250, the amount of cash received which relates to a revenue of 19X7.

19X7   At the beginning of the year:
- reduce the current liability (deferred revenue)
- increase the revenue (rent receivable)

    by £250, the amount relating to 19X7 which was received in 19X6.

At the time of the cash receipt:

-    increase cash
-    increase revenue (rent receivable)

by £750, the amount received.

3.7   Activity

Susan Boston rents premises from which she runs a retail business on the ground floor. The first floor is a self-contained flat which Susan sublets to a tenant.

The balance sheet at 31 December 19X6 showed, among other things, the following:

	£
Debtor for rent receivable	360
Prepaid rent payable	1,250

During the following three years the amounts received from the tenant and paid to the landlord were as follows:

	Receipts from tenant £	Payments to landlord £
Year to 31 December 19X7	1,560	3,750
Year to 31 December 19X8	1,440	3,750
Year to 31 December 19X9	1,680	5,000

Throughout the period covered by this question the annual rental due from the tenant was £1,440 and that due to the landlord was £5,000.

1   Show the rent receivable revenue and the rent payable expense which would appear in Susan's profit and loss account for each of the years ended 31 December 19X7, 19X8 and 19X9

2   Show the items which would appear in the balance sheets at the end of each of these three years.

3.8   Activity solution

Susan Boston

Year ended 31 December Rent receivable	Revenue £	Balance sheet item £
19X7	1,440	240 (debtor) (see note 2) (–360 + 1,560 – 1,440)
19X8	1,440	240 (debtor) (–240 + 1,440 – 1,440)
19X9	1,440	Nil (–240+1,680 – 1,440)
Rent payable		
19X7	5,000	Nil (see note 3) (+1,250 + 3,750 – 5,000)
19X9	5,000	1,250 (accrued expense) (0+3,750 – 5,000)
19X9	5,000	1,250 (accrued expense) (– 1,250 + 5,000 – 5,000)

1   Irrespective of the amount paid or received during the year the profit and loss account figures would be those specified by the leases or rental agreements, except in unusual circumstances.

2   The balance sheet item for 19X7 for rent receivable is deduced as follows:

	£
Amount due from tenant at 1/1/X7	360
Rent due for the year	1,440
	1,800

Less: Amount paid by the tenant during the year	1,560
Amount due from tenant at 31/12/X7	£240

The balance sheet item for the other years is deduced following similar logic.

3   The balance sheet item for 19X7 for rent payable is deduced as follows:

	£
Amount prepaid at 1/1/X7	1,250
Amount paid during the year	3,750
	5,000
Rent expense for the year	5,000
Amount outstanding at 31/12/X7	nil

The balance sheet item for the other years is deduced following similar logic.

An important example of the accruals convention, yet one which has yet to be considered, concerns the wearing out of fixed assets over their useful lives. Through factors like physical wear and tear and technological obsolescence, most types of fixed asset gradually lose their usefulness over time. Logically this should be recognised accounting period by accounting period, irrespective of the fact that the asset may neither have been bought nor sold during the period under review. The expression used for this expense is **depreciation**. The subject of depreciation is an important one, which will be considered in detail in Chapter 8.

3.9   Costs, expenses and expenditures

At this point it might be useful to distinguish between three terms with rather different meanings in accounting terms, namely costs, expenses and expenditure.

Costs represent financial sacrifices involved in acquiring assets, either by purchase, or by manufacturing them, or buying services. A cost will typically involve the payment of cash or the incurring of a liability. Costs become **expenses** as the assets involved are used up in the course of business. Thus when stock in trade is bought it represents a cost. As it is used in helping generate revenues it turns into an expense. With the exception of freehold land, which has an infinite life, typically all costs become expenses eventually. Sometimes the transformation is immediate as, for example, with sales staff salaries. Sometimes the transformation from cost to expense is slower and more gradual, for example with most types of fixed asset.

Expenditure is a rather less precise term. It tends to be used more or less synonymously with cost, meaning the acquisition of an asset. **Capital expenditure** is the term used to refer to the acquisition of fixed assets or that which adds to the value of fixed assets, such as improvements. **Revenue expenditure** is the term used to refer to the incurring of a cost related more to day-to-day trading, for example the payment of wages, electricity bills and the acquisition of stock.

4   CHAPTER SUMMARY

- The profit and loss account is in effect an appendix to the balance sheet in which revenues and expenses are compared and a net profit or loss deduced. Revenues are the increases in capital which can be attributable to trading activities. Expenses are the decreases in capital which can be attributable to trading activities.

- The realisation convention is important in identifying revenues. In essence the realisation convention asserts that the sale should normally be recognised when goods or services pass to the customer and are accepted by the customer. This is based on the idea that at this point some objective measure of achievement (the revenue) can be made, that there is acceptance of an obligation by the customer to pay, and that there is a reasonable chance that payment will be made.

- Expenses should be matched against appropriate revenues.

- The calculation of profit (or loss) follows the accruals convention. The accruals convention effectively says that profit is the difference between revenues and expenses and not cash receipts and payments. Profit is concerned with increases in the net wealth of the business and wealth takes forms other than cash.

5   SELF TEST QUESTIONS

5.1   For what period is a profit and loss account prepared?

(a)   one year

(b)   one month

(c)   six months

(d)   any length of time considered appropriate. (1.2)

5.2   When are sales normally recognised, according to the realisation convention?

(a)   when the customer pays

(b)   when the contract between the buyer and the seller becomes binding

(c)   when the goods are passed to the customer and are accepted

(d)   when the customer places the order. (2.1)

5.3   What is profit according to the accruals convention?

(a)   the amount of cash which is in the bank at the end of the accounting period

(b)   the difference between the total revenues and total expenses for the period

(c)   the difference between cash receipts and cash payments for the period

(d)   total sales less total costs for the period. (3.2)

5.4   What is accrued expense? (3.3)

5.5   What is the difference between capital expenditure and revenue expenditure? (3.9)

6   EXAMINATION TYPE QUESTIONS

6.1   Business rates

The following cash payments are made relating to rates for a business:

Payment date	Period covered	Amount
1/2/19X6	1/1/19X6–31/3/19X6	£150
1/5/19X6	1/4/19X6–30/9/19X6	£350
1/11/19X6	1/10/19X6–31/3/19X7	£350
1/4/19X7	1/4/19X7–30/9/19X7	£400
1/1/19X8	1/10/19X7–31/3/19X8	£400

Assuming a financial year ending on 31 December, identify the amounts which will be shown under the expense 'rates' for the years ended 31 December 19X6 and 19X7, together with the amounts and headings which will be included in the balance sheets as at 31 December 19X6 and 19X7.

(10 marks)

6.2   Business rents

A business rents a property to a tenant from 1 January 19X5, at an agreed rental of £5,000 per annum. The following cash receipts occur:

Receipt date	Amount
1/1/19X5	£1,250
1/4/19X5	£1,250
1/7/19X5	£1,250
1/10/19X5	£1,250
1/1/19X6	£1,250

1/4/19X6	£1,250
1/7/19X6	£1,250
1/10/19X6	£1,250
31/12/19X6	£1,250
1/4/19X7	£1,250
1/7/19X7	£1,250
1/1/19X8	£1,250

Assuming that the financial year is 1 January–31 December identify the amounts which will be included for the amounts in the accounts for the years ended 31 December 19X5, 19X6 and 19X7.

(8 marks)

7   ANSWERS TO EXAMINATION TYPE QUESTIONS

7.1   Business rates

	£
Expense	
19X6	
$(150 + 350 + \dfrac{350}{2})$	675
19X7	
$(350 + 400 + \dfrac{400}{2})$	775
Balance sheet entries as at 31 December	
19X6 Prepaid rates $(\dfrac{350}{2})$	175
19X7 Accrued rates $(\dfrac{400}{2})$	200

7.2   Business rents

19X5	
Revenue (rent receivable)	5,000
19X6	
Revenue (rent receivable)	5,000
Current liabilities (deferred revenue)	1,250
19X7	
Revenue (rent receivable)	5,000
Current asset (debtors: rent receivable)	1,250

4 PREPARING FINAL ACCOUNTS

INTRODUCTION AND LEARNING OBJECTIVES

This chapter will build on Chapter 3 and consider the profit and loss account in more detail. A detailed example will be used to illustrate how a profit and loss account and balance sheet interact. This example will include adjustments relating to prepayments, accruals and depreciation. It will also illustrate how the cost of sales figure can be calculated by estimating the cost of closing stock held, and how carriage and discounts are dealt with in the accounts.

We also discuss ways in which the profit and loss account can be set out so as to be most useful to users.

Finally we review a range of conventions which have implications for the final accounts.

When you have studied this chapter you should be able to do the following:

- Understand how a balance sheet and profit and loss account are drawn up incorporating complexities such as accruals, prepayments and depreciation

- Analyse the cost of sales figures charged to the profit and loss account

- Discuss a range of important accounting conventions.

---

1 PREPARING FINAL ACCOUNTS

1.1 Detailed example

The method for dealing with accrued and prepaid expenses at the end of the accounting period will now be considered by way of an example.

Example

The following is the balance sheet for Snowy White Traders as at 31 March 19X7:

Balance sheet as at 31 March 19X7

	£	£		£
Fixed assets			**Capital**	54,000
Buildings	40,000			
Machinery	12,000		**Long-term liability**	
Vehicles	8,000	60,000	Loan from George	20,000
Current assets			**Current liabilities**	
Stock in trade	5,000		Trade creditors	8,000
Trade debtors	8,000			
Cash at bank	6,000			
Cash in hand	3,000	22,000		
		82,000		82,000

During the year to 31 March 19X8, the following occurred:

1   Stock in trade was bought on credit for £87,000

2   Sales of £119,000 were made involving stock in trade which had cost £82,000. £84,000 of the sales were on credit and the remainder were settled immediately for cash

3	The trade debtors paid £86,000 by cheque
4	The trade creditors were paid £86,000 by cheque
5	Wages of £8,900 were paid in cash
6	The owner withdrew £17,800 in cash
7	Sundry expenses totalling £4,600 were paid in cash
8	Rates were paid by cheque amounting to £5,400

The following points are to be taken into account at 31 March 19X8:

9	Rates of £1,900 had been prepaid
10	Wages in arrears amounted to £200
11	There was a bill relating to cleaning amounting to £100 unpaid. Cleaning is included in 'Sundry expenses'
12	Interest of £2,000 is owed to George
13	Depreciation is to be charged for the year as follows:

On machinery	£1,200
On vehicles	£1,600

You are required to prepare

(a) the balance sheet at 31 March 19X8 and the profit and loss account to that date **incorporating transactions 1–8 only.**

(b) the balance sheet at 31 March 19X8 and the profit and loss account to that date **incorporating all the above transactions.**

Solution

(a) After incorporating transactions 1–8 the balance sheet and profit and loss account would appear as follows:

Balance sheet as at 31 March 19X8

	£	£		£	£
Fixed assets			**Capital**		
Buildings	40,000	40,000	At 1 April 19X7	54,000	
Machinery	12,000	12,000	Profit for the year		
Vehicles	8,000	8,000			
			Less: Drawings	−17,800 (6)	
				36,200	
Current assets					
Stock in trade	5,000	10,000			
	+87,000 (1)				
	−82,000 (2)		**Long-term liability**		
			Loan from George	20,000	
Trade debtors	8,000	6,000			
	+84,000 (2)				
	−86,000 (3)				
Cash at bank	6,000	600			
	+86,000 (3)				
	−86,000 (4)		**Current liabilities**		
	−5,400 (8)		Trade creditors 8,000	9,000	
			+87,000 (1)		
			−86,000 (4)		

Cash in hand	3,000		6,700	
	+35,000	(2)		
	−8,900	(5)		
	−17,800	(6)		
	−4,600	(7)		
			£83,300	£65,200

Profit and loss account for the year ended 31 March 19X8

	£		£		£		£
Cost of sales	+82,000	(2)	82,000	Sales	+119,000	(2)	119,000
Wages	+8,900	(5)	8,900				
Sundry expenses	+4,600	(7)	4,600				
Rates	+5,400	(8)	5,400				
Total expenses			£100,900				£119,000

At this stage:

Assets + Expenses = Capital − Drawings + Claims + Revenues
(83,300 + 100,900) = (54,000 − 17,800 + 29,000 + 119,000)
184,200 = 184,200

(b)   The adjustments for transactions 9–13 will be made as follows:

9   The rates payment during the year had included £1,900 which related to the following year. The expense is then reduced by £1,900, so that the total for the year is not the £5,400 paid but only £3,500. This £1,900 becomes a current asset because the business has paid for something from which it has yet to gain the benefit.

10   The wages arrears mean that the £8,900 paid for wages during the year did not represent the full extent of the expense because the business owed £200 for work done but not paid for. This £200 is thus added to the expense heading in the profit and loss account and included in the balance sheet as at 31 March 19X8 as a current liability, accrued expenses.

11   This was similar to 10 in that payments made during the year did not account for the entire expense incurred. Some cleaning had been done, but not yet paid for, requiring inclusion as an expense and as a current liability.

12   This is the same in principle as 10 and 11 and differs only in that there had been no expenditure during the year. Thus the whole expense is owed at the year end. It could be argued that the £2,000 should be added to the amount of the debt, but this would probably not be strictly correct since the interest is probably due for immediate payment (that is, it is a current liability) whereas the £20,000 is not. Outstanding loan interest is thus typically added to current liabilities.

13   Depreciation is in effect recognition of the fact that fixed assets tend to lose value as time passes. This loss of value is, by definition, an expense, hence it is shown as reducing the fixed assets in the balance sheet and as an expense in the profit and loss account.

Note that each of these 'adjustments' has two effects, such that after making allowance for the item the balance sheet is left in a state of equality. Thus the duality convention is maintained.

The last stage in the process is to calculate the profit or loss and transfer the result to the capital section of the balance sheet.

After having incorporated all of the adjustments for the year the balance sheet and profit and loss account would appear as follows:

Balance sheet as at 31 March 19X8

	£		£		£		£
Fixed assets				**Capital**			
Buildings	40,000		40,000	At 1 April 19X7			54,000
Machinery	12,000		10,800	Profit for the year			14,900
	−1,200	(13)					68,900
Vehicles	8,000		6,400				
	−1,600	(13)		Less: Drawings			−17,800 (6)
							51,100
Current assets							
Stock in trade	5,000		10,000				
	+87,000	(1)					
	−82,000	(2)		**Long-term liability**			
Prepayments	+1,900	(9)	1,900	Loan from George			20,000
Trade debtors	8,000		6,000				
	+84,000	(2)					
	−86,000	(3)					
Cash at bank	6,000		600				
	+86,000	(3)					
	−86,000	(4)		**Current liabilities**			
	−5,400	(8)		Trade creditors	8,000		9,000
					+87,000	(1)	
					−86,000	(4)	
Cash in hand	3,000		6,700				
	+35,000	(2)					
	−8,900	(5)		Accrued	+200	(10)	
2,300							
	−17,800	(6)		expenses	+100	(11)	
	−4,600	(7)			+2,000	(12)	
			£82,400				£82,400

Profit and loss account for the year ended 31 March 19X8

	£		£		£		£
Cost of sales	+82,000	(2)	82,000	Sales	+119,000	(2)	119,000
Wages	+8,900	(5)	9,100				
	+200	(10)					
Sundry	+4,600	(7)	4,700				
expenses	+100	(11)					
Rates	+5,400	(8)	3,500				
	−1,900	(9)					
Interest	+2,000	(12)	2,000				
Depreciation	+1,200	(13)	2,800				
	+1,600	(13)					
Total expenses			104,100				
Net profit			14,900				
			£119,000				£119,000

1.2   Activity

The balance sheet of Johnson's shop at 1 October 19X7 was as follows:

	£	£		£	£
Fixed assets			**Capital**		
Shop premises	45,000		At 1 October 19X7		51,000
Shop fittings	12,000				
Delivery van	4,000	61,000			
Current assets			**Current liabilities**		
Stock in trade	14,000		Trade creditors	12,000	
Cash in hand	2,000	16,000	Bank overdraft	14,000	26,000
		£77,000			£77,000

The following is a summary of the transactions which took place during the year to 30 September 19X8:

1   Sales were made, all for cash, of £145,000. The stock in trade sold cost £83,000

2   Stock in trade was bought, all on credit for £78,000

3   Cash of £113,000 was taken from the till (cash register) and paid into the bank

4   The trade creditors were paid £73,000 by cheque

5   Johnson borrowed £30,000 from Black which was paid into the bank. The loan is for 5 years

6   Wages of £17,000 were paid by cash

7   Rates of £2,900 were paid by cheque

8   Additional shop fittings costing £9,000 were bought and paid for by cheque

9   The bank charged overdraft interest of £2,000 direct to the account

10   Sundry expenses of £6,000 were paid in cash

11   Electricity bills of £1,600 were paid by cheque

12   The owners of the business withdrew £9,000 in cash.

At 30 September 19X8 you discover the following:

13   Interest £2,500 due to Black for the year was unpaid

14   Shop fittings are to be depreciated at 10% per annum on the total at the year end; the delivery van is to be depreciated by 20% per annum of the total at the year end

15   The rates payment during the year included £1,000 in respect of the period 1/10/19X8 to 31/3/19X9

16   The electricity bill for the quarter to 30/9/19X8 for £500 was unpaid.

Prepare a balance sheet as at 30 September 19X8 and a profit and loss account for the year to that date.

1.3   Activity solution

Johnson
Balance sheet as at 30 September 19X8

	£	£		£	£
Fixed assets			**Capital**		
Shop premises	+45,000	45,000	At 1 October 19X7	+51,000	51,000
			Add: Profit		27,600
					78,600
Shop fittings	+12,000	18,900			
	+9,000 (8)		*Less:* Drawings	–9,000 (12)	9,000
	–2,100 (14)				69,600

Shop premises	+45,000		45,000	At 1 October 19X7	+51,000		51,000
Delivery van	+4,000		3,200				
	−800	(14)		**Long-term liability**			
Current assets				Loan from Black	+30,000	(5)	30,000
Stock in trade	+14,000		9,000				
	−83,000	(1)					
	+78,000	(2)		**Current liabilities**			
Prepayment	+1,000	(15)	1,000	Trade creditors	+12,000		17,000
					+78,000	(2)	
					−73,000	(4)	
Bank	−14,000		40,500	Accrued expenses	+2,500	(13)	3,000
	+113,000	(3)			+500	(16)	
	−73,000	(4)					
	+30,000	(5)					
	−2,900	(7)					
	−9,000	(8)					
	−2,000	(9)					
	−1,600	(11)					
Cash in hand	+2,000		2,000				
	+145,000	(1)					
	−113,000	(3)					
	−17,000	(6)					
	−6,000	(10)					
	−9,000	(12)					
			£119,600				£119,600

Profit and loss account for the year ended 30 September 19X8

	£		£		£		£
Cost of stock sold	+83,000	(1)	83,000	Sales	+145,000	(1)	145,000
Rates	+2,900	(7)	1,900				
	−1,000	(15)					
Electricity	+1,600	(11)	2,100				
	+500	(16)					
Wages	+17,000	(6)	17,000				
Bank interest	+2,000	(9)	2,000				
Loan interest	+2,500	(13)	2,500				
Sundry interest	+6,000	(10)	6,000				
Depreciation	+2,100	(14)	2,900				
	+800	(14)					
Total expenses			117,400				
Net profit			27,600				
			£145,000				£145,000

Note that the bank balance has turned into a positive one by 30 September 19X8 and so should appear as a current asset. The closing balance sheet can be tidied up and shown as:

Balance sheet as at 30 September 19X8

	£	£		£	£
Fixed assets			**Capital**		
Shop premises	45,000		At 1/10/X7	51,000	
Shop fittings	18,900		*Add:* Profit	27,600	
Delivery van	3,200	67,100		78,600	
			Less: Drawings	9,000	69,600
Current assets					
Stock in trade	9,000		**Long-term liability**		
Prepayment	1,000		Loan from Black		30,000
Cash at bank	40,500				
Cash in hand	2,000	52,500	**Current liabilities**		
			Trade creditors	17,000	
			Accrued expenses	3,000	20,000
		£119,600			£119,600

2   STOCK IN TRADE AND THE COST OF SALES FIGURE

2.1   Determining the cost of sales

In the examples and activities so far, the cost of sales figure has been given as if the cost of each sale has been recorded as the sale was made. In some industries this approach is standard practice, particularly in larger businesses. However it is by no means the only way in which the cost of sales can be ascertained. Most smaller, less sophisticated businesses deduce the figure by taking the figure for stock purchases and adjusting it for the value of the stock at the beginning and at the end of the period concerned, typically obtained from a physical stock count.

The stock that the business starts a period with, plus that which it buys during the period, represents the maximum amount of stock which is available for sale during that period. If the cost of the amount which remains in hand at the end of the period can be ascertained, and deducted from the total of opening stock plus purchases, the result must be the cost of the stock which has left the business during that period. Provided that none of the stock has been returned to the supplier, or stolen or lost, or drawn for the personal use of the owner, that stock which has left the business must have been sold. Where returns and stock drawings occur the calculation becomes a little more complicated. Nevertheless, the necessary calculation can be summarised as follows.

	£
Opening stock	x
Add: Purchases	x
	x
Less: Returns to suppliers, stock lost, stock drawings (if any)	x
= Stock available for sale	x
Less: Closing stock	x
= Cost of sales (or cost of stock sold)	x

If the cost of sales figure is to be calculated in this way it requires that the stock is counted and valued at the end of each accounting period, or that reliable records of the physical stock are maintained from which the physical quantities can be deduced at any time.

Where this approach to deducing the cost of sales figure is used, the workings (in the style shown above) are usually included on the face of the profit and loss account. Deducing the cost of sales figure in this way is akin to deducing any expense item where there is some sort of prepayment or accrual.

In passing it is worth noting that the term 'cost of sales' is a misnomer, since it represents an expense, not a cost. Despite this the expression 'cost of sales' is widely used in practice.

Example

Barbara Casals runs a shop selling musical instruments. During the year to 31 January 19X9 purchases of stock totalled £68,000. The stock in hand was valued at £14,000 at 1 February 19X8 and at £17,000 at 31 January 19X9. During the year Barbara returned instruments costing £2,000 to the suppliers because they were found to be faulty on arrival at the shop. A violin which had cost £1,000 was stolen from the shop during the year and it had not been recovered.

The cost of sales figures for the year ended 31 January 19X9 would be calculated as follows:

	£	£
Opening stock (1/2/19X8)		14,000
Add: Purchases		68,000
		82,000
Less: Returns to suppliers	2,000	
Stock stolen	1,000	
		3,000
		79,000
Less: Closing stock (31/1/19X9)		17,000
Cost of sales		£62,000

Note that the other side of each of the items 'returns to suppliers' and 'stock stolen' must be recorded somewhere. Assuming that the returns are accepted by the supplier and that this reduced the amount owed by Barbara for purchases, the trade creditors' figure should be reduced by the £2,000. If the supplier is unwilling to accept the returned goods and cannot be forced to do so, the other aspect of this is an expense in the profit and loss account with the title 'cost of unsaleable stock' or similar.

The stock stolen gives rise to an expense item in the profit and loss account 'cost of stock stolen' or similar. Had any stock been drawn by the owner it would have been deducted from the owner's capital.

3 THE FORM AND CONTENT OF THE PROFIT AND LOSS ACCOUNT

3.1 Introduction

So far little consideration has been given to the layout of the profit and loss account but it will now be considered. For this purpose it is probably useful to distinguish between businesses which render a service as their activity and those which sell goods (merchant businesses). The accounts of manufacturers are outside the scope of the syllabus.

3.2 Service businesses

Where the business renders a service typically the profit and loss account simply deducts the expenses from the revenues, usually grouping the expenses in the most useful way.

For example, the profit and loss account of the Crystal Window Cleaning Company might be as follows:

Crystal Window Cleaning Company
Profit and loss account for the year ended 31 March 19X9

	£		£
Window cleaning costs*		Bills rendered to customers	x
Window cleaners' wages/			
depreciation of equipment/			
cleaning materials	x	Rent receivable	x
Administration costs*			
Rent/rates/insurance/			
heat and light/telephone,			
stationery	x		
Selling expenses*			
Salesperson's			
salaries/advertising	x		
Finance expenses*			
Interest/bad debts	x		
Total expenses	x		
Net profit	x		
	x		x

* These groupings are only suggestions as are the items included within each group. Each item would normally be shown separately and a subtotal given for each group.

As with the balance sheet, more common in practice is the vertical style shown below:

Crystal Window Cleaning Company
Profit and loss account for the year ended 31 March 19X9

	£	£
Bills rendered to customers		x
Rent receivable		x
		x
Less: Expenses:		
Window cleaning costs*		
Window cleaners' wages/depreciation		
of equipment/cleaning materials	x	
Administration costs*		
Rent/rates/insurance/heat and light/		
telephone/stationery	x	
Selling expenses*		
Salesperson's salaries/advertising	x	
Finance expenses*		
Interest/bad debts	x	
		x
Net profit		x

* with the relevant detail within these groups

3.3   Merchant businesses

Where the main activity of a business is to sell physical goods (for example, a retailer), it is usual to take the sales figure and the cost of sales into a separate statement (or at least a separate section) and to carry the net figure, known as **gross profit**, into the profit and loss account. The separate statement is known as the **trading account**. In presentation the trading account is shown before the profit and loss account.

The major reason for having a separate trading account is to deduce the gross profit as a separate figure. The usefulness of knowing the figure is something which will be considered in later chapters, particularly in Chapter 24.

In the horizontal or two-sided form, the trading and profit and loss account of a typical merchant business would look something as follows:

Southern Retailers
Trading and profit and loss account for the year ended 30 June 19X9

	£	£		£	£
Opening stock		x	Sales		x
Add: Purchases	x		*Less:* sales returns		x
Add: Carriage in	x				x
	x				
Less: Purchase returns	x				
	x				
	x				
Less: Closing stock	x				
Cost of sales	x				
Gross profit carried down	x				
	x				x
			Gross profit brought down		x
Administration expenses					
Rent/rates/insurance/heat					and
light/telephone/stationery	x				
Selling expenses			**Other revenues**		
Salesmen's salaries/commission/			Discount received	x	
transport/advertising/carriage out	x		Rent receivable	x	
			Interest	x	
				x	
Finance expenses					
Interest/bad debts/					
discounts allowed	x				
	x				
Net profit	x				
	x				x

Again the groupings are matters of judgement.

There are several incidental points which might usefully be mentioned here:

(a)   **Carriage in**

This is the cost of transporting goods to the premises of the business. This cost is usually borne by the supplier, but where it is borne by the buying business, it is treated as an additional element of the purchase cost and brought into the trading account, as shown above.

(b)   **Carriage out**

This is the cost of transporting stock which is the subject of sales to customers. As such it is a selling expense and appears in the profit and loss account.

(c)   **Returns**

These are either returns of purchases to suppliers or returns of sales by customers, sometimes referred to as returns out and returns in respectively. They are deducted from the purchases and sales figures respectively either on the face of the trading account or before those figures are entered in the trading account.

(d)   **Discounts**

There are basically two kinds of discount which might be available to businesses when they buy stock: trade discounts and cash discounts.

Purchasers might obtain a reduction in the price because they are in a particular line of business rather than private individuals. This is known as **a trade discount** and it can be related to the amount of trade which occurs between a particular supplier and customer. Trade discounts will arise typically in situations where one business is selling both to the general public, and to other businesses in the same or associated trades. Very often the same price lists are used, but a trade discount is given to the businesses in the same trade. Trade discounts are usually deducted from the price of the goods (or possibly, service) when the goods are bought. As such, trade discounts have the effect of reducing the purchase and sales figures. Since the pre-discount figures are typically never recorded, the sales and purchases figures are automatically shown net of this discount.

The other type of discount is one whereby credit customers are allowed to deduct a specified percentage of the amount owed for goods or services provided that they are paid for within a specified time after the purchase. These are known as **cash discounts** or **discounts for prompt payment**. The accounting treatment normally adopted reflects the fact that this discount is not really a reduction in the price, but an incentive to pay promptly. The sales and purchases are taken into the trading account at their full price (net of trade discount if relevant), any cash discounts allowed to credit customers are treated as an expense in the profit and loss account, and any cash discounts received from suppliers are treated as revenues in the profit and loss account. Thus cash discounts do not affect the gross profit. The entries for discount allowed and discount received in the trading and profit and loss account of Southern Retailers are cash discounts.

The trading and profit and loss account for merchant businesses can also be set out in the vertical or narrative form as follows:

Southern Retailers
Trading and profit and loss account for the year ended 30 June 19X9

	£	£	£
Sales			x
Less: Returns			x
			x
Less: Opening stock		x	
Purchases	x		
Add: Carriage in	x		
	x		
Less: Returns	x		
		x	
		x	
Less: Closing stock		x	
Cost of sales			x
Gross profit			x
Add: Other revenues			
Discounts received		x	
Rent receivable		x	
Interest		x	
			x
			x
Less: Administration expenses*		x	
Selling expenses*		x	
Finance expenses*		x	
			x
Net profit			x

* with the relevant detail within these groups.

3.4 Activity

During the year ended 31 October 19X8 Commercial Wholesalers, which buys all of its stock from the same suppliers, was involved in the following:

1   Bought stock which had a gross price of £630,000. Since Commercial Wholesalers is a trade buyer the supplier allowed a trade discount of 10%. The supplier also allowed customers to deduct 2% of the amount owed if customers paid within 30 days of receiving the goods. Commercial Wholesalers paid promptly for all of its purchases and claimed the full discount. There were no trade creditors outstanding at either the start or end of the year.

2   Commercial Wholesalers paid carriage totalling £25,000 to bring the purchases to its premises and spent £63,000 transporting stock sold to customers' premises.

3   Commercial Wholesalers made sales with a gross sales value of £980,000. It allowed a trade discount on exactly half of this value at 7.5%. In addition customers owing £620,000 successfully claimed a 2.5% cash discount (for prompt payment) during the year.

4   The value of the stock at 1 November 19X7 was £60,000 and at 31 October 19X8 it was £73,000.

Show, in vertical or narrative form, the trading account of Commercial Wholesalers for the year ended 31 October 19X8.

3.5 Activity solution

Commercial Wholesalers
Trading account for the year ended 31 October 19X8

	£	£	£
Sales(1)			943,250
Opening stock		60,000	
Add: Purchases(2)	567,000		
Add: Carriage in	25,000		
		592,000	
		652,000	
Less: Closing stock		73,000	
Cost of sales			579,000
Gross profit			£364,250

Notes

1   The sales figure is $\dfrac{980,000}{2} + \dfrac{(980,000 \times 92.5\%)}{2} = 490,000 + 453,250 = £943,250$

      This is because half of the £980,000 sales attracted a trade discount of 7.5%.

2   The purchases figure is £630,000 less 10% = £567,000. This is because all of the purchases attract a trade discount of 10%.

3   The discounts allowed and received for prompt payment (cash discounts) and the carriage out are all items which appear in the profit and loss account, not the trading account. Note also that since the price charged to a customer by a supplier is after deducting trade discount, the amount of the trade discount is not something usually recorded. Where trade discount is not mentioned in an exam question, you may assume either that it does not exist or that it has already been taken into account.

4   ACCOUNTING CONVENTIONS

4.1   Introduction

Accounting can be viewed as a language through which certain economic information about businesses and other organisations is stored, analysed and transmitted. As with any other language there are a number of accepted rules or conventions surrounding accounting. These rules have evolved over time, as they have with other languages, and tend to reflect the needs and convenience of users and compilers of accounting information. They also tend to reflect what is practical, rather than what is theoretically justifiable.

One reason for the practical emphasis of the accounting conventions is that there is no real agreement as to what is theoretically the correct way to do things. In fact it is probably the case that notions such as theoretical correctness simply do not apply to accounting any more than they apply to any other language. For example, there is no fundamental theory which asserts that each sentence should start with a capital letter and end with a full stop. However, it is a very practical rule since it enables a reader to know when one thought of the writer is coming to an end and the next one is beginning.

The rules of accounting are variously referred to as conventions, concepts, principles, postulates and assumptions. In this book they will be called conventions, reflecting the fact that they are simply an accepted, time-honoured way of doing things rather than rules based on fundamental truths or theories.

4.2   List of conventions

The more important conventions are identified below. Some of these have already been dealt with. These are as follows:

(a)   **Business entity**

For accounting purposes the business and its owner are separate. This is why owner's capital appears as an item in the balance sheet.

(b)   **Duality**

Each transaction must have two effects which are equal and opposite so that the balance sheet equation (Assets = Claims) always holds.

(c)   **Money measurement**

Accounting restricts itself to consideration of those aspects of a business which can be expressed in money terms.

(d)   **Historic cost**

Assets are shown in accounts at a value which is based on their monetary cost to the business.

(e)   **Going concern**

Unless the contrary is believed to be true, it is assumed that the business will continue indefinitely.

(f)   **Stable monetary unit**

The units in which accounting figures are expressed are assumed to remain of constant value. This means that inflation is ignored.

(g)   **Realisation**

Sales are normally recognised when the good being sold passes to the customer, or the service is rendered and is accepted by the customer.

(h)   **Matching**

Expenses should be matched to the revenue to which they relate such that both the revenue and its associated expenses are recognised in the same accounting period.

(i) **Accruals**

Profit (or loss) is the difference between revenues and expenses, properly matched, and not between cash receipts and payments.

4.3 Other general conventions

To these must be added some other, general, conventions:

(a) **Objectivity**

What appears in accounting statements should be objective. It should be based upon facts, not opinion. It should be free from bias and it should be capable of independent verification. This is important since users of accounting information would probably be disinclined to rely too much on it if it were to be substantially based on opinions of individuals. This point is given greater weight if the opinions involved are those of individuals with a vested interest. For example, how much reliance would a bank manager put on a set of final accounts for a business, submitted in support of an application for a loan to the business, where the accounts are based on the opinion of the owner of the business? This is one of the justifications for showing assets at cost, rather than some rather more subjective estimated current market value.

(b) **Prudence**

This is sometimes referred to as conservatism. Basically accounting errs on the side of caution. Where the outcome of a transaction is not known, a cautious or pessimistic view is taken of it. Profits should not be anticipated but only taken into account when they are realised. Possible losses should be anticipated. For example, where a sale has been made on credit and there is some doubt as to whether the debtor will pay the view tends to be taken that he will not. Trade debtors will thus be reduced and an expense included in the profit and loss account. This does not mean that no attempt will be made to recover the debt; the convention is purely concerned with the accounting treatment. Neither does it mean that it is automatically assumed that no debtor will pay until the money is actually received, merely that a cautious rather than an optimistic view is taken of uncertain outcomes.

(c) **Consistency**

Where different accounting treatments could be made of a particular type of transaction, then the one selected should be applied consistently. The consistency convention asserts that whatever attitude is taken in one period should be consistently applied. This is important since it enables more valid comparison of figures from one year to the next. Further examples of the need for consistency will emerge in later chapters.

(d) **Materiality**

Where the amounts involved are trivial it is not necessary to identify precisely the point at which costs become expenses. For example, in order to strictly follow the accruals convention it would be necessary to assess the physical quantities in hand and then to value every item of stock, not just stock in trade but also stocks of such things as stationery and unused food in the canteen, so that they could be treated as assets rather than as expenses in the final accounts. According to the materiality convention this should be ignored except where the value of these stocks is material. Thus the entire expense would be recognised in the accounting period in which the stock is acquired. What is meant by material is a matter of judgement for those preparing the final accounts. Also it will vary from business to business; what is a material amount to a small business may well be totally immaterial to a large multinational company.

Clearly there can be conflict between the conventions. For example, the cost convention says that assets should be shown at cost, but the prudence convention asserts that some stock in trade say, whose sale value has dropped below its cost, should be shown in the balance sheet at the lower value. In such a situation the prudence convention would be applied. Where the prudence convention and some other conventions conflict, the prudence convention will normally dominate. In practice such conflicts tend not to cause too many problems.

4.4   Activity

An acquaintance of yours, Harry Gee, has recently set up in business for the first time as a general dealer. The majority of his sales will be on credit to trade buyers but he will sell some goods to the public for cash. He is not sure at which point of the business cycle he can regard his cash and credit sales to have taken place. After seeking guidance on this matter from his friends, he is thoroughly confused by the conflicting advice he has received. Samples of the advice he has been given include:

'The sale takes place when:

1   you have bought goods which you know you should be able to sell easily

2   the customer places the order

3   you deliver the goods to the customer

4   you invoice the goods to the customer

5   the customer pays for the goods

6   the customer's cheque has been cleared by the bank.'

He now asks you to clarify the position for him.

(a)   Write notes for Gee, setting out, in as easily understood a manner as possible, the accounting conventions and principles which should generally be followed when recognising sales revenue.

(b)   Examine each of the statements 1 to 6 above and advise Gee (stating your reasons) whether the method advocated is appropriate to the particular circumstances of his business.

4.5   Activity solution

(a)   The accounting convention principally involved here is the **realisation convention** which asserts that sales should normally be recognised when the goods pass to the customer and they are accepted.
With certain types of sales the position may not be quite as straightforward as this, but in the case of H. Gee, the convention would seem to apply.

(b)   **Statement 1**
To treat the sale as having been made when the goods are bought would be in violation of the prudence (conservatism) convention even though they may be expected to sell easily. The prudence convention holds that profits and revenues should not be anticipated.

Statement 2

To recognise the sale when the order is placed is still generally considered to be too far away from the ultimate receipt of the cash for revenue to be recognised. At this stage the order has not been fulfilled, and goods have not been accepted by the customer. Revenue recognition at this point would generally be considered to be anticipating something which may not actually occur.

Statement 3

It is when the goods are delivered to the customer and they are accepted that the sale is recognised under the realisation convention.

Statement 4

Normally, invoicing the customer would take place more or less at the same time as delivery of the goods. Typically the mechanism in the accounting system that will trigger off delivery of the goods also leads immediately to the dispatch of the invoice. Where this is not the case, it is the physical transfer and acceptance of the goods which is the essential factor, according to the realisation convention.

Statement 5

With credit sales, provided that there is no reason to believe that the cash will not ultimately be received, waiting for the cash before the revenue is recognised is regarded as being excessively prudent. Businesses do not sell on credit except where they are reasonably confident that the customer will pay. Where sales are for cash, the goods pass and are accepted by the customer at the same time as the customer pays for the goods. Therefore, by coincidence, cash sales are recognised when the cash is paid, but in actuality they are recognised when the goods pass.

Statement 6

Once again this would be regarded in normal circumstances as being excessively prudent. Presumably the business would not accept payment by cheque unless there was a fair amount of confidence that the cheque would be honoured.

5 CHAPTER SUMMARY

- The profit and loss account is in effect an appendix to the balance sheet in which revenues and expenses are compared and a net profit or loss deduced. Typically the profit and loss account contains sufficient detail to enable useful conclusions to be drawn from its contents. Since cash payments and expenses are not always the same within a given time period, at the end of accounting periods prepaid and accrued expenses usually arise. Allowance must be made for these in the profit and loss account and in the balance sheet. Revenues are typically recognised for accounting purposes when the goods or the service passes to the customer and are accepted.

- The cost of sales figure is, in many businesses, deduced from knowledge of all the actual opening and closing stock and of the purchases for the period. In businesses which are involved in selling physical goods the derivation of the cost of sales figure and comparison of that figure with sales for the period to deduce the gross profit is carried out in the trading account, a subdivision of the profit and loss account.

- Accounting is based on the conventions of business entity, duality, money measurement, historic cost, going concern, stable monetary unit, realisation, matching, accruals, objectivity, prudence, consistency and materiality.

6 SELF TEST QUESTIONS

6.1   Cost of sales is:

    (a)   an asset

    (b)   a revenue

    (c)   an expense

    (d)   a liability. (2.1)

6.2   How is carriage inwards treated in the trading and profit and loss account?

    (a)   Added to the sales figure

    (b)   Treated as an expense in the profit and loss account

    (c)   Added to the purchases figure

    (d)   Deducted from the closing stock figure. (3.3)

6.3   How are discounts allowed for the prompt settlement of debts dealt with in the trading and profit and loss account?

    (a)   Treated as a revenue in the profit and loss account

    (b)   Treated as an expense in the profit and loss account

      (c)   Deducted from the sales figure

      (d)   Deducted from the purchases figure.

7   EXAMINATION TYPE QUESTIONS

7.1   Following Data

Prepare a profit and loss account for the year ended 31 December, and a balance sheet as at 31 December, based on the following data.

The following is the balance sheet of the business at the beginning of the year.

	£		£
Fixed assets		**Capital**	11,000
Buildings	10,000	**Loan**	5,000
Equipment	5,000	**Current liabilities**	
Current assets		Creditors	2,000
Stock of stationery	100	Accrued rates	100
Stock in trade	1,000		
Prepaid rent	100		
Debtors	900		
Cash	1,000		
	£18,100		£18,100

The following transactions took place during the year:

1   Stock was purchased on credit for £10,000

2   Stock was purchased for £2,000 cash

3   Cash sales amounted to £8,000

4   Credit sales amounted to £10,000

5   £200 of sales were returned

6   £300 of purchases were returned

7   £100 was paid for carriage on sales

8   £200 was paid for carriage on purchases

9   Wages of £3,000 were paid, all but £100 relating to the year

10   Rent of £500 was paid. The annual rent amounts to £500

11   Rates of £700 were paid. Of this £200 related to October to March, £250 to April to September and £250 to the following October to March

12   General expenses of £500 were paid

13   Stationery was purchased for £500 cash

14   Additional equipment was purchased on 1 January for £2,000, financed from an additional loan of this amount. The interest rate is 10% per annum

15   £1,000 of the loan was repaid on 30 June

16   Cash received from debtors amounted to £7,800, which was in satisfaction of debts of £8,000, the remainder being discount

17   Cash paid to creditors amounted to £6,750, which was in satisfaction of debts of £7,000, the remainder being discount

18   The owner withdrew £1,500 cash and £100 stock.

At the end of the year it was found that £50 of general expenses had not been paid for. It was also found that debts amounting to £100 were unlikely to be received. There was stock in hand of £3,000 and the value of stationery remaining was estimated at £150. The loan carried interest of 10% per annum. Depreciation to be taken at 10% on the book value of the equipment at the year end.

(24 marks)

7.2 Backwards and Forwards

'The historical cost convention looks backward but the going concern convention looks forwards.'

(a)   Explain clearly what is meant by:

    (i)   the historical cost convention

    (ii)   the going concern convention.

(b)   Does traditional financial accounting, using the historical cost convention, make the going concern convention unnecessary? Explain your answer fully.

(c)   Which do you think a shareholder is likely to find more useful – a report on the past or an estimate of the future? Why?

(15 marks)

7.3 Stock in Accounts

'The idea that stock should be included in accounts at the lower of historical costs and net realisable value follows the prudence convention but not the consistency convention.'

(a)   Explain clearly what is meant by:

    (i)   historical cost

    (ii)   net realisable value

    (iii)   prudence convention

    (iv)   consistency convention.

(b)   Do you agree with the quotation?

(c)   Explain, with reasons, whether you think this idea (that stocks should be included in accounts at the lower of historical cost and net realisable value) is a useful one. Refer to at least two classes of user of financial accounting reports in your answer.

(15 marks)

7.4 Accounting Situations

'If a business invests in shares, and the market value of the shares increases above cost, then until and unless the business sells them, no profit is made. If the business invests in stock for resale, and the market value of the stock falls below cost then the loss is recognised even though no sale has taken place.'

'If a business undertakes an intensive advertising campaign which will probably result in increased sales (and profit) in succeeding years it will nevertheless usually write off the cost of the campaign in the year in which it is incurred'.

Explain the reasoning behind the application of accounting principles in situations such as these and discuss the effect on the usefulness of accounting information in relation to users' needs.

Note: A share is a part of the ownership of a business.

(12 marks)

8   ANSWERS TO EXAMINATION TYPE QUESTIONS

8.1 Following Data

With a question involving rather more transactions it may well be easier to have separate columns for the pluses and minuses, since this makes subsequent addition easier.

Balance sheet as at 31 December

	+ £	− £	Net £		+ £	− £	Net £
Fixed assets				**Capital**			
Premises	10,000		10,000	Opening balance	11,000		11,000
Equipment	5,000	700 adj	6,300	Net profit	1,625		1,625
	2,000 (14)						12,625
				Less: Drawings		1,500 (18)	
						100 (18)	1,600
							11,025
Current assets							
Stationery#	100	450 adj	150				
	500 (13)						
Stock##	1,000	9,800 adj	3,000				
	10,000 (1)	300 (6)					
	2,000 (2)	100 (18)		Loans	5,000	1,000 (15)	6,000
	200 (8)				2,000 (14)		
Prepayments							
– rent	100	100 adj	100				
	100 adj						
– wages	100 adj		100				
– rates	125 adj		125				
Debtors	900	200 (5)	2,600				
	10,000 (4)	8,000 (16)		**Current liabilities**			
		100 adj		Creditors	2,000	300 (6)	4,700
					10,000 (1)	7,000 (17)	
Cash	1,000	2,000 (2)	50				
	8,000 (3)	100 (7)		**Accruals**			
	7,800 (16)	200 (8)		– rates	100	100 adj	–
		3,000 (9)		– general exps	50 adj		50
		500 (10)		– loan			
		700 (11)		interest	650 adj		650
		500 (12)					
		500 (13)					
		1,000 (15)					
		6,750 (17)					
		1,500 (18)					
			£22,425				£22,425

\# Or do adjustments to stationery as an expense.

\#\# Or do on profit and loss statement.

Profit and loss account for the year ended 31 December

Expenses	+ £	− £	Net £	Revenues	+ £	− £	Net £
Cost of sales	9,800 adj		9,800	Sales			
				− cash	8,000 (3)		8,000
				− credit	10,000 (4)		10,000
							18,000
Wages	3,000 (9)	100 adj	2,900	*less:* Returns	200 (5)		200
							17,800
Carriage	100 (7)		100				
Rent	500 (10)	100 adj	500	Discount			
	100 adj			received	250 (17)		250
Rates	700 (11)	125 adj	475				
			100 adj				
General	500 (12)		550				
expenses	50 adj						
Depreciation	700 adj		700				
Discount							
allowed	200 (16)		200				
Bad debts	100 adj		100				
Loan interest	650 adj		650				
Stationery	450 adj		450				
			16,425				
Net profit			1,625				
			£18,050				£18,050

8.2 Backwards and Forwards

(a) (i) The **historic cost convention** is that transactions are recorded in their accounts at the original price. An item then remains in the accounting records at that original figure until disposal. Assets, and therefore expenses, are recorded and evaluated at original cost, and profit is calculated as revenues less original cost of resources used.

(ii) The **going concern convention** is the assumption, in the absence of evidence to the contrary, that the business will continue to trade in the normal way into the foreseeable future. This enables the accountant to assume that stocks will eventually be sold, that fixed assets will continue to be used, and so on.

(b) Traditional financial accounting based on the historical cost convention does not make the going concern convention unnecessary. Traditional and current practice relies heavily on the going concern convention. Stocks are evaluated on the assumption that they will eventually be sold in the ordinary course of business. Fixed assets are depreciated over their estimated useful life to the business, and this requires the assumption that the business will continue to operate over the period of that useful life. Prepayments assume that the firm will operate and use the service acquired. Indeed the whole basis of the accruals convention is that the business is a continuing operation and the going concern convention is therefore crucial to current accounting practice even though that practice is based on the historical cost convention.

(c) The reason why shareholders need a report at all is because they wish to use the report to influence some future action or decision on their part. If this is not so then they have no use for the report, whatever its contents. However, the above does not strictly answer the question. The shareholders may well find a report on the past events extremely useful as a guide to predicting future outcomes and future trends. Equally, however, the shareholders may find management's estimate of future events to be directly useful. Perhaps the short answer to the question is: both!

8.3   Stock in accounts

(a)   (i)   Historic cost means the original cost of acquiring an item. This method of valuation forms the basis of the traditional approach to accounting.

(ii)   Net realisable value represents the estimated selling price of an item less any selling costs incurred. The selling price is based on the amount likely to be obtained, either in the ordinary course of business or in the event of any orderly liquidation.

(iii)   The prudence convention states that assumptions and estimates in financial statements should err on the side of caution. A pessimistic view is preferred to an optimistic view. A good example of the prudence convention in practice is the lower of cost or net realisable value rule in relation to stock valuation which is mentioned in the question.

(iv)   The consistency convention states that where different accounting treatments could be applied to a particular transaction, one should be selected and should be applied consistently over time. This is seen as important in facilitating comparability between years.

(b)   It can be argued that the lower of cost and net realisable value in relation to stock contravenes the consistency convention as it can lead to different bases for valuation being used in different periods. However, as this rule is designed to provide the most prudent figure for stock valuation, it can be argued that in adopting this rule we are being consistently prudent in our valuation approach.

(c)   The usefulness of the prudence convention will depend on the kind of decision which has to be made. The effect of using the lower of cost or net realisable value may be to understate the current value of the stocks. This may be useful if a pessimistic view is required by the user. For example, a lender or a shareholder may wish to adopt a pessimistic view in order to help assess the degree of risk associated with their respective investments in the business. However, a pessimistic view introduces bias into the accounts which may be to the advantage of some users but not others. A shareholder, for example, may decide to sell shares in a company at a lower price than he/she would have done if there had not been a pessimistic bias in the accounts. The lower price agreed, however, will be to the benefit of the investor who purchases the shares.

8.4   Accounting Situations

There are really three parts to this question and these will be dealt with one by one.

(a)   **Investment in shares**

This is concerned with the realisation and prudence conventions. The realisation convention asserts that revenues should not be recognised until the goods are passed to and are accepted by the buyer. The fact that a ready buyer (presumably a Stock Exchange market maker) may exist is not usually considered sufficient justification for this convention to be overruled. The prudent view would therefore tend to be taken and the gain on the shares would not be anticipated.

(b)   **Stock for resale**

Once again the prudence convention would tend to dominate, over what in this case would be the less conservative cost convention. Thus, the stock would be shown at its current value rather than at its historic cost, that is the potential loss would be anticipated.

(c)   **Advertising**

The matching convention would suggest that part, at least, of the cost of the advertising campaign is an expense of future years, rather than of the current year. However, unless there was great confidence that future benefits would occur as a result of the campaign, the prudence convention would tend to prevail. Thus, the cost of the campaign would normally be treated as an expense in the year of the campaign.

Cases a) and c) are both examples of ways in which the prudence convention can limit the usefulness of accounting statements. It would seem that showing the shares at their current market value and an element of the advertising cost as an asset would be more informative to users, yet it would not normally be done in this way.

5 LEDGER ACCOUNTS AND DOUBLE-ENTRY BOOKKEEPING

INTRODUCTION AND LEARNING OBJECTIVES

This chapter aims to provide an introduction to the system of ledger accounts, also known as double entry bookkeeping. The basis of the system will be explained, and related to the system of pluses and minuses used so far in the book. The detailed mechanics of the system will then be explained, and an example will be used to illustrate the process, including the trial balance and the completion of the final accounts. The handling of adjustments will be left to Chapter 6.

When you have studied this chapter you should be able to do the following:

- Understand the principles of double entry bookkeeping

- Draw up ledger accounts for specified transactions

- Extract a trial balance.

---

1 LEDGER ACCOUNTS – GENERAL BACKGROUND

1.1 Introduction

The aim of the chapters to date has been to provide a broad understanding of the basic principles of accounting, particularly of the balance sheet and the profit and loss account, and to enable readers to prepare final accounts from a set of transactions. It will no doubt have become apparent, however, while working through the activities, that the system adopted becomes more difficult to implement as the number of transactions increases. In practice a business with a large number of transactions would need to use a system which is able to cope rather more effectively with increased amounts of data. The system of pluses and minuses, made by hand on the face of a balance sheet and profit and loss account will not do. In practice a business is likely to use one, or a combination, of the following:

1   a manual system of ledger accounts – known as double-entry bookkeeping

2   a non-manual system (usually computerised).

Both of these are based on the principles developed already in this book, but with a capability to handle large volumes of data.

Students wishing to embark on a career in accountancy need to become familiar with these systems. This chapter deals specifically with the process of double-entry bookkeeping as a means of maintaining a record of transactions and preparing a set of final accounts.

1.2 Revision of the balance sheet equation

So far in the book the equation below has been used as the basis of a system for preparing final accounts:

$$\text{Assets} \quad = \quad \text{Capital} + \text{Liabilities}$$

At the end of a period of trading this equation can be been modified as follows:

Assets at the end of a period	=	**Capital at the beginning of the period**
		+ Injections of new capital during the period
		+ Net profit (– net loss) for the period
		– Drawings during the period
		+ External liabilities at the end of the period

Since Profit = Revenue – Expenses this can be modified as follows:

Assets	=	Opening capital
		+ Injections
		+ Revenue – Expenses
		– Drawings
		+ External liabilities

which can be rearranged as follows:

Assets	=	Opening capital
		+ Injections
+		+
Drawings		External liabilities
+		+
Expenses		Revenues

This equation must balance, unless mistakes have been made.

Clearly, if a list can be prepared which sets out the above components following a period of trading, it would be fairly straightforward to convert it into a set of final accounts. The procedure would be broadly the same as described in earlier chapters. Revenues and expenses would be summarised in a profit and loss account, from which the net profit or loss could be calculated. This figure would then be added to (or subtracted from) the capital, with drawings being deducted from the resulting figure.

2 LEDGER ACCOUNTS – DETAILED METHOD OF RECORDING

2.1 Ledgers and accounts

The book which is used to record transactions using the system of double-entry book-keeping is known as a **ledger**. This is why the system is referred to as **ledger accounts**.

The system of ledger accounts is based upon the equation shown above, and permits a system whereby assets, drawings and expenses may be effectively recorded on one side of the equation, while capital, liabilities and revenues may be recorded on the other side.

The basic record used in a system of ledger accounts is called an **account**. An account is a record of one or more items, relating to some person or thing, kept under an appropriate heading. The number of accounts kept will depend upon the amount of detail considered useful. The more accounts kept, the more detail is possible in preparing final accounts and other accounting reports of assistance to users. Of course this increase in usefulness must be balanced against the increased costs associated with it, and a sensible compromise decided on.

An account takes the following form:

Debit side			**Title**			**Credit side**	
Date	Detail	Folio	Amount	Date	Detail	Folio	Amount

Each transaction is recorded in accounts for the particular person or thing it affects. All transactions are entered in date order. An account is thus able to provide a history, which means that it can be useful in profit calculations. It is also able to provide a picture of the current position, so it can be useful for balance sheet purposes. In the final equation shown above, assets, drawings and expenses are shown on the left-hand side, while capital, liabilities and revenues are shown on the right-hand side. This means that if all assets, drawings and expenses are put on the left-hand side of the relevant accounts, and all capital, liabilities and revenues on the right-hand side, the total of the left-hand sides of all accounts will equal the total of the right-hand sides of all accounts. In accounting the words debit and credit are used to denote the side of an account on which an entry is made.

They should not be seen as necessarily implying that something is good or bad. The word debit simply means to make an entry on the left-hand side, and credit means to make an entry on the right-hand side. This means that assets, drawings and expenses are debited, while capital, liabilities and revenues are credited.

Consider the situation where a proprietor starts a business with £10,000, deposited in a business bank account on 1 January. This involves an increase in an asset and an increase in capital. The two accounts will therefore appear as follows:

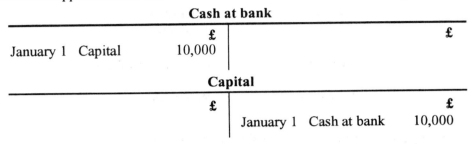

Cash at bank

	£		£
January 1 Capital	10,000		

Capital

	£		£
		January 1 Cash at bank	10,000

Note that the date is recorded, along with the detail and amount. The detail column in each ledger account provides a cross-reference facility, and shows the title of the account in which the corresponding double entry is being made. In the format of an account shown earlier there was an additional column included, namely the folio column. This provides an additional cross-reference facility, and usually includes the code or number given to the account entered in the detail column. It is rarely used in textbooks or examinations, and will not be used in this chapter.

Suppose now that on 2 January equipment is bought on credit, for £3,000. The entries in the ledger accounts will be as follows:

Equipment

	£		£
January 2 Creditors	3,000		

Creditors

	£		£
		January 2 Equipment	3,000

At this stage it can be seen that the total of the debits (£13,000) equals the total of the credits, so the convention of duality is satisfied. It should, however, also be noted that so far every transaction has involved a debit entry and a credit entry. This is why this form of recording is known as **double-entry bookkeeping.**

Certain transactions, such as the purchase of equipment for cash, result in an increase in one asset and a corresponding decrease in another asset. An increase in equipment means that an equipment account must be debited. The question remains as to what should be done with the decrease in cash. Clearly it is possible to show the decrease in cash as a deduction on the debit side of the account, and this would be in line with the system of pluses and minuses used earlier. However, having different signs on the same side of an account is likely to lead to errors. In practice therefore, the method which is normally adopted is to *show decreases on the opposite side to increases*. Thus a decrease in an asset or an expense is shown on the credit side of an account, while a decrease in capital, a liability or a revenue is shown on the debit side. Whenever an account needs to be totalled all that has to be done is to add up each of the two sides and calculate the difference.

Suppose, following on from the accounts used so far, that on 3 January further equipment costing £1,000 is purchased by cheque. The entries for this transaction would be recorded as follows:

Equipment

		£		£
January 2	Creditors	3,000		
January 3	Cash at bank	1,000		

Cash at bank

		£			£
January 1	Capital	10,000	January 3	Equipment	1,000

The above method of recording decreases in items means that for every debit there is still a corresponding credit. Duality therefore becomes double-entry bookkeeping.

2.2 Balancing an account

In order to ascertain how much cash was on hand on 4 January the two sides are totalled. The difference is £9,000. Since the debit side (increases) is greater than the credit side (decreases), the £9,000 clearly represents cash in hand. The problem is how to show this as a balance in hand and preserve the double entry.

The method used is known as **balancing off** an account. First the difference between sides is calculated as before. This amount is then added to the smaller side, so that the two sides balance. The two sides can then be double underlined, indicating that they are not to be included in any further additions. To preserve double entry the balance is then carried down onto the larger side. The balancing off of the cash account will thus appear as follows:

Cash at bank

		£				£
January 1	Capital	10,000	January	3	Equipment	1,000
				4	Balance c/d	9,000
		£10,000				£10,000
January 4	Balance b/d	9,000				

where b/d means brought down to the next section of the account and c/d means carried down from the last section of the account; b/f and c/f, meaning brought forward and carried forward, are often used as an alternative, particularly at the start and end respectively of pages in the ledger.

2.3 Further transactions

Continuing the transactions from above, assume that on 5 January, with the bank manager's approval, a cheque for £10,000 is paid for stock. If double entry is completed and the cash amount is balanced off the accounts will appear as follows:

Stock

		£		£
January 5	Cash at bank	10,000		

Cash at bank

			£				£
January	4	Balance b/d	9,000	January	5	Stock	10,000
	5	Balance c/d	1,000				
			£10,000				£10,000
				January	5	Balance b/d	1,000

The balance brought down on the cash at bank account is a credit balance. From what has been said before it is clear that such a balance must represent a liability or a revenue. This seems a little strange in that cash is normally an asset. In this case the answer is quite simple. The liability arose when a cheque was paid out for an amount which was more than was currently held in the bank account. The business is now in overdraft, and owes the bank £1,000.

From this it can be seen that some accounts can change from assets into liabilities using the normal rules of double entry. No special treatment is required. This is most likely to be true of cash at bank and personal accounts, where a debtor may become a creditor and vice-versa.

Following on from earlier sections of this chapter, it should be clear that expenses are initially treated in the same way as assets, while revenues are initially treated in the same way as liabilities.

Suppose now that the business paid rent of £500 by cheque on 6 January, and that cash sales to the value of £2,500 (received in the form of a cheque) were made on 7 January. The accounts, after balancing off the cash at bank account, would appear as follows:

Cash at bank

		£				£
January 7	Sales	2,500	January	5	Balance b/d	1,000
				6	Rent	500
				7	Balance c/d	1,000
		£2,500				£2,500
January 7	Balance b/d	1,000				

Rent

		£		£
January 6	Cash at bank	500		

Sales

	£			£
		January	7 Cash at bank	2,500

The rules for double entry recording can now be summarised as follows:

Type of account	Increase	Decrease
Asset	debit	credit
Liability	credit	debit
Capital	credit	debit
Expense	debit	credit
Revenue	credit	debit
Drawings	debit	credit

2.4   Activity

Complete the following:

Transaction 1 has been completed as an illustration.

Transaction	Effect	Ledger entry
1 January 1 – Started a trading business by putting £15,000 into a business bank account	increase cash at bank £15,000 increase capital £15,000	debit cash at bank £15,000 credit capital £15,000
2 January 4 – Bought equipment for £3,000 paid by cheque		

3 January 5 – Bought furniture
from D. Perks for £800 on credit

4 January 7 – Purchased stocks
for resale for £2,000 paid by cheque

5 January 10 – Paid D. Perks by cheque

6 January 18 – Bought equipment
from A. Harvey for £2,000 on credit

7 January 25 – Purchased further stock
on credit from J. Golding, for £1,500

8 January 28 – Borrowed £5,000 from
Island Building Society

9 January 31 – Paid an additional
£2,000 into the business bank account

10 January 31 – Cash sales £250.

2.5 Activity solution

Transaction	Effect	Ledger entry
1 January – Started a trading business by putting £15,000 into a business bank account	increase cash at bank £15,000 increase capital £15,000	debit cash at bank £15,000 credit capital £15,000
2 4 January – Bought equipment for £3,000, paid by cheque	increase equipment £3,000 reduce cash at bank £3,000	debit equipment £3,000 credit cash at bank £3,000
3 5 January – Bought furniture from D. Perks for £800 on credit	increase furniture £800 increase creditors (D. Perks) £800	debit furniture £800 credit D. Perks £800
4 7 January – Purchased stock for resale for £2,000, paid by cheque	increase stock £2,000 decrease cash at bank £2,000	debit stock £2,000 credit cash at bank £2,000
5 10 January – Paid D. Perks by cheque	reduce D. Perks £800 reduce cash at bank £800	debit D. Perks £800 credit cash at bank £800
6 18 January – Bought equipment from A. Harvey for £2,000 on credit	increase equipment £2,000 increase creditor (A. Harvey) £2,000	debit equipment £2,000 credit A. Harvey £2,000
7 25 January – Purchased further stock on credit from J. Golding, for £1,500	increase stock £1,500 increase creditor (J. Golding) £1,500	debit stock £1,500 credit J. Golding £1,500
8 28 January – Borrowed £5,000 from Island Building Society	increase cash at bank £5,000 increase loan £5,000	debit cash at bank £5,000 credit loan £5,000
9 31 January – Paid an additional £2,000 into the business bank account	increase cash at bank £2,000 increase capital £2,000	debit cash at bank £2,000 credit capital £2,000
10 31 January – Cash sales £250	increase cash increase sales	debit cash £250 credit sales £250

2.6 Distinction between bank and cash

In practice, a distinction is usually drawn between transactions carried out through the bank (recorded in a 'cash at bank' account) and transactions carried out using money (recorded in a 'cash in hand' account). This distinction is often not drawn in examination questions, which assume a single account for cash being maintained. This latter approach will be used in the remainder of this chapter. It is important, however, to note that examination questions should be read carefully to establish whether separate accounts are needed for cash at bank and cash in hand, or whether a cash account will suffice. Certain topics, such as incomplete records (dealt with in Chapter 15), will almost certainly require a distinction to be drawn between the two.

2.7   A worked example of the recording process

In order to reinforce the above points consider the following transactions for a business for the month of January:

1	January 1	– Peter Anniss puts in £50,000 cash to start a new business of his own, calling it 'Pete's Products'
2	January 1	– Borrows £15,000 from the Natsouth Bank
3	January 3	– Buys a small workshop for £30,000 cash
4	January 6	– Buys equipment for £10,000 cash
5	January 8	– Buys stock for resale for £8,000 on credit
6	January 10	– Buys further stock for £5,000 cash
7	January 12	– Stock which cost £1,500 is sold for £2,500 cash
8	January 15	– Stock which cost £2,000 is sold for £2,700 on credit
9	January 18	– Cash of £6,500 is paid to a creditor
10	January 20	– Peter pays a creditor £500 from his personal funds
11	January 20	– Cash of £1,200 received from a debtor
12	January 22	– Peter withdraws £500 cash from the business for his private use
13	January 24	– Goods which cost £1,600 are sold for £1,800 cash
14	January 25	– Stock to the value of £1,000 is bought on credit
15	January 26	– Wages of £300 are paid
16	January 28	– Miscellaneous expenses of £50 are paid in cash.

Transaction 1 would result in an increase in cash (an asset) and an increase in capital. The entries in the ledger accounts would be:

debit cash	£50,000
credit capital	£50,000

Transaction 2 results in an increase in cash and an increase in a liability. The entries in the ledger accounts would thus be:

debit cash	£15,000
credit loan (Natsouth Bank)	£15,000

Transaction 3 results in an increase in one asset (premises) and a decrease in another (cash). The entries in the ledger accounts would thus be:

debit premises	£30,000
credit cash	£30,000

Transaction 4 results in an increase in equipment (an asset) and a decrease in cash (an asset). The double entry is thus:

debit equipment	£10,000
credit cash	£10,000

Transaction 5 results in an increase in stock (an asset) and an increase in creditors (a liability). The double entry is thus:

debit stock	£8,000
credit creditors	£8,000

Transaction 6 results in an increase in stock and a decrease in cash. The double entry is thus:

debit stock	£5,000
credit cash	£5,000

Transaction 7 results in an increase in cash and an increase in revenues, together with a reduction in stock and an increase in expenses. The double entry is thus:

debit cash	£2,500
credit sales	£2,500
debit cost of sales	£1,500
credit stock	£1,500

Transaction 8 results in an increase in debtors and an increase in revenues, together with a reduction in stock and an increase in expenses. The double entry is thus:

debit debtors	£2,700
credit sales	£2,700
debit cost of sales	£2,000
credit stock	£2,000

Transaction 9 results in a reduction in cash and a reduction in creditors. The double entry is thus:

debit creditors	£6,500
credit cash	£6,500

Transaction 10 results in an increase in capital (an injection) and a reduction in creditors. The double entry is thus:

debit creditors	£500
credit capital	£500

Transaction 11 results in an increase in cash and a decrease in debtors. The double entry is thus:

debit cash	£1,200
credit debtors	£1,200

Transaction 12 results in a reduction in capital (drawings) and a reduction in cash. The double entry is thus:

debit drawings	£500
credit cash	£500

It should be noted that drawings are usually recorded in a drawings account during the accounting period, and the total subsequently transferred to the capital account at the end of the period.

Transaction 13 results in an increase in cash and an increase in revenues, together with a decrease in stock and an increase in an expense (cost of sales). The double entry is thus:

debit cash	£1,800
credit sales	£1,800
debit cost of sales	£1,600
credit stock	£1,600

Transaction 14 results in an increase in stock and an increase in creditors. The double entry is thus:

debit stock	£1,000
credit creditors	£1,000

Transaction 15 results in an increase in an expense (wages) and a decrease in cash. The double entry is thus:

debit wages	£300
credit cash	£300

Transaction 16 results in an increase in an expense (miscellaneous expenses) and a decrease in cash. The double entry is thus:

debit miscellaneous expenses	£50
credit cash	£50

After balancing off the accounts with entries on both sides the completed set of accounts for the business (Pete's Products) would appear as follows:

Capital

	£		£
January 31 Balance c/d	50,500	January 1 Cash	50,000
		20 Creditors	500
	£50,500		£50,500
		Balance b/d	50,500

Cash

	£		£
January 1 Capital	50,000	January 3 Premises	30,000
1 Loan		6 Equipment	10,000
(Natsouth Bank)	15,000	10 Stock	5,000
12 Sales	2,500	18 Creditors	6,500
20 Debtors	1,200	22 Drawings	500
24 Sales	1,800	26 Wages	300
		28 Misc expenses	50
		31 Balance c/d	18,150
	£70,500		£70,500
February 1 Balance b/d	18,150		

Loan (Natsouth Bank)

	£		£
		January 1 Cash	£15,000

Premises

	£		£
January 3 Cash	£30,000		

Equipment

	£		£
January 6 Cash	£10,000		

Stock

	£		£
January 8 Creditors	8,000	January 12 Cost of sales	1,500
10 Cash	5,000	15 Cost of sales	2,000
25 Creditors	1,000	24 Cost of sales	1,600
		31 Balance c/d	8,900
	£14,000		£14,000
February 1 Balance b/d	8,900		

Stock

			£				£
January	8	Creditors	8,000	January	12	Cost of sales	1,500
	10	Cash	5,000		15	Cost of sales	2,000
	25	Creditors	1,000		24	Cost of sales	1,600
					31	Balance c/d	8,900
			£14,000				£14,000
February 1		Balance b/d	8,900				

Creditors

			£				£
January	18	Cash	6,500	January	8	Stock	8,000
	20	Capital	500		25	Stock	1,000
	31	Balance c/d	2,000				
			£9,000				£9,000
				February 1		Balance b/d	2,000

Debtors

			£				£
January	15	Sales	2,700	January	20	Cash	1,200
					31	Balance c/d	1,500
			£2,700				£2,700
February 1		Balance b/d	1,500				

Cost of sales

			£			£
January 12		Stock	1,500	January 31	Balance c/d	5,100
	15	Stock	2,000			
	24	Stock	1,600			
			£5,100			
						5,100
Balance b/d			5,100			

Sales

		£				£
January 31	Balance c/d	7,000	January	12	Cash	2,500
				15	Debtors	2,700
				24	Cash	1,800
		£7,000				£7,000
			Balance b/d			7,000

Drawings

		£		£
January 22	Cash	500		

Wages

		£		£
January 26	Cash	300		

Miscellaneous expenses

		£		£
January 28	Cash	50		

2.8   The trial balance

At this point every transaction has been recorded in ledger accounts, using a system of double entry. It should thus now be possible to extract a list of balances which gives the identity referred to earlier, namely:

Assets		Capital
+		+
Drawings	=	Liabilities
+		+
Expenses		Revenues

A list can thus be prepared, known as a trial balance, which sets out the debit and credit balances, as follows:

Pete's Products
Trial balance as at 31 January

	Debit	Credit
Assets	£	£
Cash	18,150	
Debtors	1,500	
Premises	30,000	
Stock	8,900	
Equipment	10,000	
Drawings	500	
Expenses		
Cost of sales	5,100	
Miscellaneous expenses	50	
Wages	300	
Capital		50,500
Liabilities		
Loan (Natsouth Bank)		15,000
Creditors		2,000
Revenues		
Sales		7,000
	£74,500	£74,500

It can be seen from the above that:

1   The totals of the debit balances and the credit balances are equal. This must always be true unless an error is made, since for every debit there is an equivalent credit.

2   All debit balances represent assets, drawings or expenses while all credit balances represent capital, liabilities or revenues.

A list of balances such as that shown above is referred to as a trial balance. Note that the balances are all calculated on the same day, so such a list should be headed 'Trial balance as at ... (date)'.

If the totals of the trial balance agree there is some reason to suppose that the double entry has been correctly made, hence the use of the word trial. Certainly if it does not agree some rechecking of the entries is required. There are however certain types of error which will not be disclosed by a trial balance, because the totals will still agree even if an error has been made. For example, suppose that on January 6 the purchase of equipment was misread as £1,000 and the double entry was made accordingly. The trial balance would still balance, even though the accounts would be incorrect. Alternatively, if the miscellaneous expenses had been wrongly debited to wages the trial balance would still agree, while the accounts would be incorrect.

Obviously there are serious limitations on the effectiveness of the trial balance as a check on the correctness of the accounts, but it is still normally used as part of the system of checks. Other checks (such as control accounts) are also used to confirm the accuracy of the accounts. These will be dealt with in later chapters.

2.9   Activity

1   What 'difference' would be caused in a trial balance by the following errors?

(a)   £20 paid for repairs to premises was debited to premises

(b)   discount received of £123 was credited as £231

(c)   rent paid was credited to the rent account as well as to cash.

2   A trial balance does not agree. State the possible nature of the error in each of the following cases?

(a)   the difference is £25 and there is a transaction of this amount

(b)   the difference is £180 and there is a transaction of £200

(c)   the difference is £9 and there is a transaction of £45

(d)   the difference is £8 and there is a transaction of £4

(e)   the difference is £8.55 and there is a transaction of £9.50.

2.10   Activity solution

1   (a)   The trial balance would still agree, although the premises would be overstated while the expenses would be understated.

(b)   The credit side would exceed the debit side by £108.

(c)   The credit side would exceed the debit side by *twice* the amount of rent paid.

2   (a)   Single entry.

(b)   One figure recorded as £20 instead of £200.

(c)   Transposition of numbers, £54 not £45.

(d)   Two entries on the same side.

(e)   One side posted as 95p instead of £9.50.

3   LEDGER ACCOUNTS – THE PREPARATION OF FINAL ACCOUNTS

3.1   The trading and profit and loss account

In a system of ledger accounts the profit and loss account is a formal part of the ledger accounting system. At the end of an accounting period revenues and expenses of that period are transferred to the profit and loss account. The net profit or loss is subsequently transferred to the capital account, as are drawings. The balance sheet is nothing more than a list of balances in the ledger accounts at the end of a period which must, by definition, be assets, liabilities or part of the owner's claim.

While in the above paragraph the profit and loss account has been referred to as if it were a single account, it is more typical to find it split into two accounts, corresponding with the trading and profit and loss accounts referred to in Chapters 3 and 4.

Example

By way of illustration of the above, the accounts of Pete's Products for January are shown below, incorporating trading and profit and loss accounts.

Capital

		£				£
January	31	Drawings	500	January	1 Cash	50,000
	31	Balance c/d	51,550		11 Creditors	500
					31 Profit and loss	1,550
			£52,050			£52,050
				February	1 Balance b/d	51,550

Cash

			£				£
January	1	Capital	50,000	January	3 Premises	30,000
	1	Loan	15,000		6 Equipment	10,000
		(Natsouth Bank)			10 Stock	5,000
	12	Sales	2,500		18 Creditors	6,500
	20	Debtors	1,200		22 Drawings	500
	24	Sales	1,800		26 Wages	300
					28 Misc expenses	50
					31 Balance c/d	18,150
			£70,500			£70,500
February	1	Balance b/d	18,150			

Loan (Natsouth Bank)

			£				£
January	31	Balance c/d	15,000	January	1 Cash	15,000
			£15,000			£15,000
				February	1 Balance b/d	15,000

Premises

			£				£
January	3	Cash	30,000	January	31 Balance c/d	30,000
			£30,000			£30,000
February	1	Balance b/d	30,000			

Stock

			£				£
January	8	Creditors	8,000	January	12	Cost of sales	1,500
	10	Cash	5,000		15	Cost of sales	2,000
	25	Creditors	1,000		24	Cost of sales	1,600
					31	Balance c/d	8,900
			£14,000				£14,000
February	1	Balance b/d	8,900				

Equipment

			£				£
January	6	Cash	10,000	January	31	Balance c/d	10,000
			£10,000				£10,000
February	1	Balance b/d	10,000				

Creditors

			£				£
January	18	Cash	6,500	January	8	Stock	8,000
	20	Capital	500		25	Stock	1,000
	31	Balance c/d	2,000				
			£9,000				£9,000
				February	1	Balance b/d	2,000

Debtors

			£				£
January	15	Sales	2,700	January	20	Cash	1,200
					31	Balance c/d	1,500
			£2,700				£2,700
February	1	Balance b/d	1,500				

Cost of sales

			£				£
January	12	Stock	1,500	January	31	Trading	5,100
	15	Stock	2,000				
	24	Stock	1,600				
			£5,100				£5,100

Sales

			£				£
January	31	Trading	7,000	January	12	Cash	2,500
					15	Debtors	2,700
					24	Cash	1,800
			£7,000				£7,000

Drawings

			£				£
January	22	Cash	500	January	31	Capital	500
			£500				£500

Wages

			£				£
January	26	Cash	300	January	31	Profit and loss	300
			£300				£300

Miscellaneous expenses

			£				£
January	28	Cash	50	January	31	Profit and loss	50
			£50				£50

Trading

			£				£
January	31	Cost of sales	5,100	January	31	Sales	7,000
	31	Gross profit	1,900				
			£7,000				£7,000

Profit and loss

			£				£
January	31	Wages	300	January	31	Gross profit	1,900
	31	Miscellaneous expenses	50				
	31	Net profit – to capital	1,550				
			£1,900				£1,900

3.2   The balance sheet

The trading and profit and loss accounts as shown above are ledger accounts and part of the double-entry system. A variety of alternative formats exists for presenting this information in the final accounts, but the principles remain. The balance sheet, which is given below, is simply a list of debit and credit balances, representing assets and liabilities and the owner's claim. Alternative formats are also acceptable, indeed, narrative formats are more widely found in practice, and will be used increasingly in this and subsequent chapters.

Balance sheet as at 31 January

Fixed assets	£	£	Capital	£
Premises		30,000	Opening balance	50,000
Equipment		10,000	Injections	500
		40,000		50,500
			Net profit	1,550
				52,050
Current assets			Less: Drawings	500
Stock	8,900			51,550
Debtors	1,500			
Cash	18,150			
		28,550	**Loan**	15,000
			Current liabilities	
			Creditors	2,000
		£68,550		£68,550

4 CHAPTER SUMMARY

- This chapter has set out the essential features of the manual system of recording known as double-entry bookkeeping. Entries for each item for which records are maintained are made in an appropriate ledger account, with debit entries being made on the left-hand side of the account, and credit entries being made on the right-hand side. Debit entries represent increases in assets, expenses and drawings, and decreases in capital, liabilities and revenues. Credit entries represent decreases in assets, expenses and drawings, and increases in capital, liabilities and revenues. Each transaction requires both a debit entry and a credit entry in the ledger accounts, hence the name *double-entry* bookkeeping.

- On completion of the entries for a period a trial balance may be extracted, which is a list of account balances at the end of a period, before any adjustments are made. Agreement of the trial balance is necessary before the accounts can be made to balance, since non-agreement means that an error in recording or adding up has been made.

- At the end of the period all revenue and expense accounts can be transferred to the trading and profit and loss accounts and a profit or loss can be calculated. This amount will need to be recorded in the capital account. Any remaining balances must reflect assets or claims. These can then be grouped appropriately to form the balance sheet.

- From your understanding of accruals accounting it should be apparent to you that in reality the ledger accounting process is not likely to be quite as easy as implied above, since the illustrations used to date ignore adjustments. These are the subject of the next chapter.

5 SELF TEST QUESTIONS

5.1   A business makes a sale on credit. Which is the correct double entry?

    (a)   debit sales, credit trade debtors   X

    (b)   debit cash, credit sales

    (c)   debit trade debtors, credit sales

    (d)   debit trade debtors, credit cash. (2.7)

5.2 At the end of a period of trading the trial balance of a business was in agreement. Does this imply:

(a) that the business has made a profit for the period?

(b) that the accounting entries for the period have all been correctly made? ∝

(c) that there had been a debit entry for every credit entry?

(d) that a set of final accounts should now be produced for the period? (2.8)

6 EXAMINATION TYPE QUESTIONS

6.1 Transactions

Complete the following:

				Effect	Ledger entry
(a)	January	1 –	Started business with £10,000 in a bank account	↑ bank 10,000	debit cash + credit (capital)
(b)	January	2 –	Bought stock on credit from F. Edwards and Co to the value of £5,000		
(c)	January	5 –	Cash sales £150		
(d)	January	10 –	Purchased equipment for £750 paid by cheque		
(e)	January	12 –	Paid wages of £150 by cheque		
(f)	January	15 –	Paid rent of £300 by cheque		
(g)	January	20 –	Paid electricity bill of £200 by cheque		
(h)	January	22 –	Sold goods to P. Nock for £200 on credit		
(i)	January	28 –	Cash sales £75		
(j)	January	31 –	Paid F. Edwards and Co's bill by cheque		

(10 marks)

6.2 Ledger Accounts

(a) Record the following in ledger accounts:

April 1 – A. Slacker invests £3,000 in a business

3 – Purchases £1,300 of stock for cash

4 – Purchases equipment for £400 cash

5 – Purchases £1,500 of stock on credit

9 – Pays rent of £250

10 – Pays fuel and electricity bills amounting to £120

11 – Pays general expenses of £100

19 – Sells goods for £2,000 cash. The cost of these sales was £1,200

20 – Sells goods for £1,900 on credit. The cost of these sales was £1,200

21 – Withdraws £500 in cash

28 – Pays £1,000 to creditors

29 – Receives £1,250 from debtors

30 – £25 is drawn from the bank and held as a petty cash float

(b) Prepare a trial balance as at 30 April.

(c) Prepare a trading and profit and loss account for the month and a balance sheet as at 30 April. Assume that the expenses paid all relate to the month of April and that there are no accruals.

(20 marks)

6.3 Characteristics

It has been suggested that published accounting statements should attempt to be relevant, understandable, reliable, complete, objective, timely and comparable.

(a)   Explain briefly in your own words the meaning of these terms, as they apply to accounting.

(b)   Are there any difficulties in applying all of them at the same time?

(12 marks)

7   ANSWERS TO EXAMINATION TYPE QUESTIONS

7.1   Transactions

Transaction	Effect	Ledger entry
1 1 January – Started business with £10,000 in a bank account	increase cash in bank £10,000 increase capital £10,000	debit cash at bank £10,000 credit capital £10,000
2 2 January – Bought stock on credit from F. Edwards and Co to the value of £5,000	increase stock £5,000 increase creditor (F. Edwards and Co) £5,000	debit stock £5,000 credit F. Edwards £5,000
3 5 January – Cash sales £150	increase cash in hand £150 increase sales £150	debit cash in hand £150 credit sales £150
4 10 January – Purchased equipment for £750 paid by cheque	increase equipment £750 decrease cash at bank £750	debit equipment £750 credit cash at bank £750
5 12 January – Paid wages of £150 by cheque	increase wages £150 decrease cash at bank £150	debit wages £150 credit cash at bank £150
6 15 January – Paid rent of £300 by cheque	increase rent £300 decrease cash at bank £300	debit rent £300 credit cash at bank £300
7 20 January – Paid electricity bill of £200 by cheque	increase electricity £200 decrease cash at bank £200	debit electricity £200 credit cash at bank £200
8 22 January – Sold goods to P. Nock for £200 on credit	increase debtors (P. Nock) £200 increase sales £200	debit P. Nock £200 credit sales £200
9 28 January – Cash sales £75	increase cash in hand £75 increase sales £75	debit cash in hand £75 credit sales £75
10 31 January – Paid F. Edwards and Co's bill by cheque	reduce creditors £5,000 (F. Edwards and Co) reduce cash at bank £5,000	debit F. Edwards and Co £5,000 credit cash at bank £5,000

Note: In many examination questions it is not necessary to separate cash in hand and cash at bank, but simply to have a single cash account.

7.2   Ledger Accounts

(a)

Capital

		£			£
April 30	Drawing	500	April 1	Bank	3,000
April 30	Balance c/d	3,530	April 30	Net profit	1,030
		£4,030			£4,030
			May 1	Balance b/d	3,530

Stock

		£			£
April 3	Bank	1,300	April 19	Cost of sales	1,200
April 5	Creditors	1,500	April 20	Cost of sales	1,200
			April 30	Balance c/d	400
		£2,800			£2,800
May 1	Balance b/d	400			

Equipment

		£			£
April 4	Bank	400	April 30	Balance c/d	400
		£400			£400
May 1	Balance b/d	400			

Rent

		£			£
April 9	Bank	250	April 30	Profit and loss	250

Creditors

		£			£
April 28	Bank	1,000	April 5	Stock	1,500
April 30	Balance c/d	500			
		£1,500			£1,500
			May 1	Balance b/d	500

Fuel and electricity

		£			£
April 10	Bank	120	April 30	Profit and loss	120

General expenses

		£			£
April 11	Bank	100	April 30	Profit and loss	100

Cost of sales

		£			£
April 19	Stock	1,200	April 30	Trading	2,400
April 20	Stock	1,200			
		£2,400			£2,400

Sales

		£				£
April 30	Trading	3,900	April	19	Bank	2,000
			April	20	Debtors	1,900
		£3,900				£3,900

Debtors

		£				£
April 20	Sales	1,900	April	29	Bank	1,250
			April	30	Balance c/d	650
		£1,900				£1,900
May 1	Balance b/d	650				

Drawings

		£			£
April 21	Bank	500	April 30	Capital	500

Bank

		£				£
April	1	Capital	3,000	April	3	Stock	1,300

			£				£
April	1	Capital	3,000	April	3	Stock	1,300
April	19	Sales	2,000	April	4	Equipment	400
April	29	Debtors	1,250	April	9	Rent	250
				April	10	Fuel and electricity	120
				April	11	General expenses	100
				April	21	Drawings	500
				April	28	Creditors	1,000
				April	30	Bank	25
				April	30	Balance c/d	2,555
			£6,250				£6,250
May 1		Balance b/d	2,555				

Petty cash

		£			£
April 30	Cash	25	April 30	Balance c/d	25
		£25			£25
May 1	Balance b/d	25			

(b) and(c)

Trading account

		£			£
April 30	Cost of sales	2,400	April 30	Sales	3,900
April 30	Profit and loss (Gross profit)	1,500			
		£3,900			£3,900

Profit and loss account

		£			£
April 30	Rent	250	April 30	Trading	1,500
April 30	Fuel and electricity	120		(Gross profit)	
April 30	General expenses	100			
April 30	Capital (Net profit)	1,030			
		£1,500			£1,500

Trial balance as at 30 April

	Debit	Credit
	£	£
Capital		3,000
Equipment	400	
Stock	400	
Creditors		500
Rent	250	
Fuel and electricity	120	
General expenses	100	
Sales		3,900
Cost of sales	2,400	
Drawings	500	
Debtors	650	
Bank	2,555	
Petty cash	25	
	£7,400	£7,400

Balance sheet as at 30 April

Fixed assets	£	£	**Capital**	£
Equipment		400	Opening balance	3,000
			Net profit	1,030
				4,030
Current assets				
Stock	400		Less: Drawings	500
Debtors	650			3,530
Bank	2,555			
Petty cash	25		Current liabilities	
		3,630	Creditors	500
		£4,030		£4,030

7.3 Characteristics

(a)   **Relevant** This is often considered to be the primary quality required of accounting information. To be relevant, accounting information must have the potential to influence the decisions of users. It reflects the basic point that accounts are prepared to meet the needs of users and must therefore be appropriate for this purpose.

Understandable If accounting statements are to be useful they must be understood by users. As different types of users have different levels of understanding of accounting it is sometimes argued that they should receive different types of accounting reports. Whatever the level of understanding of the user the accounting statements should be set out as clea. . as possible.

Reliable This means that accounting statements should be capable of independent verification. It is important for users to have confidence in the statements.

Complete This means that accounting statements should provide a total picture of financial position and performance. It is not acceptable to provide a selective view of the entity's position. This may result in users obtaining a distorted perspective on the entity even though the information provided may be both relevant and reliable.

Objective This means that the information must be free from bias. It is important that information is not slanted in such a way that it favours one group of users at the expense of another. This quality should help engender confidence in the accounting statements prepared.

Timeliness Timeliness has two aspects. The first is concerned with the time lag between the end of the accounting period and the production of the accounting statements. If the time lag is too long the accounting statements will lose their relevance for decision-making purposes. The second aspect is concerned with the frequency of accounting statements. The more frequent the production of accounting statements the greater the costs involved but the more up-to-date the information provided.

Comparable This means that items or events which are essentially the same should be measured and presented in the same manner. This helps users when evaluating data over time or between different entities.

(b)   There is tension between certain of these qualities and certain trade-offs may have to be made. For example, timely information may require that some degree of completeness is sacrificed, relevance may require the sacrifice of some reliability, understandability may require the sacrifice of some degree of completedness.

6 LEDGER ACCOUNTS AND YEAR-END ADJUSTMENTS

INTRODUCTION AND LEARNING OBJECTIVES

Chapter 5 provided an introduction to the ledger accounting process. This chapter shows you how adjustments can be handled within the ledger accounting framework.

In dealing with the accruals convention it is necessary to separately identify assets, expenses, liabilities and revenues. Certain accounts may need to be examined carefully to establish the categories into which their entries fit. Nevertheless, it should be clear from the discussion so far that the question as to whether an account represents an expense, revenue, asset or liability needs to be determined only at the end of a period, when preparing a set of final accounts.

Recordings in the accounts will generally reflect:

- any opening balances on an account, brought down from a previous period
- any cash paid or received during the period
- any credit transactions carried out during the period
- any adjustments made at the end of the period, which require the carrying down of balances reflecting assets or liabilities
- any transfer to the trading or profit and loss accounts, reflecting the amount of any revenue or expense for the accounting period.

In the examples used in Chapter 5 the assumption was made that expenses relate to the period in which they were paid, and that there were no prepayments or accruals. Similar assumptions were made regarding revenues. In fact, as was made clear in Chapters 3 and 4, a variety of adjustments will be needed, since the matching convention requires expenses to be matched against revenues. The adjustments needed will generally relate to:

- prepayments of expenses
- accrued expenses
- prepayment of revenues (deferred revenues)
- revenues due but not received
- depreciation
- stock
- bad and doubtful debts.

The adjustments for the first six of these are dealt with in this chapter. The adjustments for depreciation and stock are dealt with in outline only at this stage, and will be dealt with in more detail in Chapters 8 and 9. The adjustments for bad and doubtful debts are left entirely to Chapter 10.

When you have studied this chapter you should be able to do the following:

- Deal with all the adjustments listed above in ledger accounts
- Prepare a set of final accounts from these ledger accounts.

1   PREPAYMENT OF EXPENSES

1.1   Introduction

Amounts prepaid by a business at the end of a period represent assets, and must therefore appear as debit balances brought down on the appropriate account. The expense for the period, which must be transferred to the profit and loss account, will thus be calculated by deducting the amount prepaid from the total of the account to date.

1.2   Example

By way of illustration assume that rent of £1,250 is paid by a business in a financial year. The financial year of the business concerned is from 1 January to 31 December 19X7. Assume also that the £1,250 paid for rent relates to a period of 15 months ending on 31 March 19X8. The payment of the rent will require a double entry in the ledger accounts, namely:

debit rent	£1,250
credit cash	£1,250

However, examination of the information at the year end should indicate that this amount covers a period of 15 months, and the accounting period relates to the period January–December 19X7. Only £1,000 of the rent is an expense of the 19X7 accounting period. The remaining £250 will become an expense in 19X8. However, at 31 December 19X7 it represents an asset, a prepayment, and is thus carried down as a debit balance. The rent account for the financial year 1 January–31 December 19X7 would appear as follows:

Rent

19X7		£	19X7			£
Dates paid	Cash	1,250	December 31	Profit and loss	1,000
			31	Balance c/d	250
		£1,250			£1,250
19X8					
January 1	Balance b/d	250			

The profit and loss account would have a corresponding debit for rent amounting to £1,000 and the prepayment would be shown on the balance sheet as a current asset.

Using ledger accounts, any balance brought down from a previous period will be dealt with automatically at the end of the period. For example, assume, following on from the previous example, that in 19X8 a further £750 of rent is paid, covering the remainder of the year. The rent account would thus appear as follows in 19X8.

Rent

19X8		£	19X8		£
January 1	Balance b/d	250	December 31 Profit and loss	1,000
Dates paid	Cash	750		
		£1,000		£1,000

A corresponding debit for rent of £1,000 would appear in the 19X8 profit and loss account.

If the amount paid in 19X8 had been £1,000, covering the year ending 31 March 19X9, the rent account would appear as follows:

Rent

19X8			£	19X8			£
January 1	Balance b/d		250	December	31	Profit and loss	1,000
Dates paid	Cash		1,000		31	Balance c/d	250
			£1,250				£1,250
19X9							
January 1	Balance b/d		250				

The balance brought down represents a prepayment as at 31 December 19X8, and so would appear on the balance sheet as at that date, as a current asset.

2   ACCRUED EXPENSES

2.1   Introduction

Amounts owing by a business at the end of a period represent liabilities, and must therefore appear as credit balances brought down on the appropriate account. The expense for the period, which is transferred to the profit and loss account, will be calculated by *adding* the amount owed at the end of a period to the total of the account to date.

2.2   Example

By way of illustration, assume rent of £750 is paid on 1 January 19X7, covering the period 1 January to 30 September 19X7. Assume also that the financial year of the business is 1 January to 31 December 19X7. The rent account for 19X7 would appear as follows:

Rent

19X7			£	19X7			£
January	1	Cash	750	December	31	Profit and loss	1,000
December	31	Balance c/d	250				
			£1,000				£1,000
				19X8			
				January	1	Balance b/d	250

A corresponding debit of £1,000 for rent would be made in the profit and loss account. The £250 closing balance would be shown in the balance sheet as at 31 December 19X7 as a current liability, accrued expenses.

If in 19X8 cash payments of £1,250 were made, covering the period 1 October 19X7 to 31 December 19X8, the rent account for the year would appear as follows:

Rent

19X8			£	19X8			£
Dates paid	Cash		1,250	January	1	Balance b/d	250
				December	31	Profit and loss	1,000
			£1,250				£1,250

It is possible for an account to be shown as an asset at the beginning of the year, yet become a liability at the end of the year, and vice versa. For example, suppose that cash payments of £1,500 had been made in 19X8 covering the period 1 October 19X7–31 March 19X9. The rent account for 19X8 would then appear as follows:

Rent

19X8		£	19X8			£
Dates paid	Cash	1,500	January	1	Balance b/d	250
			December	31	Profit and loss	1,000
			December	31	Balance c/d	250
		£1,500				£1,500
19X9						
January 1 Balance b/d		250				

The £250 closing balance would be shown in the balance sheet as at 31 December 19X8 under current assets, as a prepayment.

3   PREPAYMENT OF REVENUES (DEFERRED REVENUES)

3.1   Introduction

Deferred revenues at the end of a period represent liabilities, and must therefore appear as a credit balance brought down. The revenue due for a period, which will be transferred to the profit and loss account, will be arrived at by *deducting* the amount of deferred revenue at the end of the period from the total of the account to date.

3.2   Example

By way of illustration assume that rent is received in the financial year 1 January to 31 December 19X7, amounting to £1,250, covering the period 1 January 19X7 to 31 March 19X8. The rent receivable account for 19X7 would appear as follows:

Rent receivable

19X7		£	19X7			£
December 31	Profit and loss	1,000	Dates received	Cash		1,250
31	Balance c/d	250				
		£1,250				£1,250
			19X8			
			January	1	Balance b/d	250

A corresponding credit entry of £1,000 for rent receivable would be made in the profit and loss account, and the £250 closing balance would be shown in the balance sheet as at 31 December 19X7 under current liabilities, deferred revenue.

The deferred revenue will automatically be dealt with in the next period. For example, assume that in 19X8 rent is received amounting to £750, covering the period 1 April to 31 December. The rent receivable account for 19X8 would be as follows:

Rent receivable

19X8		£	19X8			£
December 31	Profit and loss	1,000	January	1	Balance b/d	250
			Dates received	Cash		750
		£1,000				£1,000

4   REVENUES DUE BUT NOT RECEIVED

4.1   Introduction

Revenues relating to a period, but not received by the end of that period, represent assets, and must therefore appear as debit balances. The revenue due for the period, which will be transferred to the profit and loss account, will be arrived at by *adding* the amount outstanding at the end of the period to the total of the account to date.

4.2   Example

For example assume that rent is received in the financial year 1 January to 31 December 19X7, amounting to £750, covering the period 1 January to 30 September. The 'rent receivable' account for 19X7 would appear as follows:

Rent receivable

19X7			£	19X7			£
December	31	Profit and loss	1,000	Dates received		Cash	750
				December	1	Balance c/d	250
			£1,000				£1,000
19X8							
January	1	Balance b/d	250				

The £250 closing balance would be shown on the balance sheet as at 31 December 19X7 as a current asset, debtors, rent receivable.

Accounts related to revenues may move from having opening debit balances (representing assets) to closing credit balances (representing liabilities) and vice versa. For example, following on from the above figures, assume that in 19X8 rent of £1,500 is received, covering the period 1 October 19X7 to 31 March 19X9. The rent receivable account for 19X8 would appear as follows:

Rent receivable

19X8			£	19X8			£
January	1	Balance b/d	250	Dates received		Cash	1,500
December	31	Profit and loss	1,000				
	31	Balance c/d	250				
			£1,500				£1,500
				19X9			
				January	1	Balance b/d	250

The £250 closing balance would be shown on the balance sheet as at 31 December 19X8 as a current liability, deferred revenue.

4.3   Activity

J. Gray prepared his final accounts on 31 December 19X7. The following balances appeared, among others, in his ledger, after the final accounts had been prepared:

	Debit £	Credit £
Rent payable		800
Rates	500	
Loan		50,000
Interest on loan		1,250

1   What information can you derive from each of these balances?

2   Open the accounts named above and enter the balances.

3   During the next year the following transactions took place affecting the above accounts:•
         1 April paid rent of £2,400, relating to the year ending 31 August

•   1 May paid rates of £2,400, relating to the year following 31 March

•   30 September paid one year's interest on loan at 10%

•   30 September made a repayment of £10,000 on the loan account

Make the necessary entries to record these transactions. Balance off the accounts, incorporating any adjustments necessary, showing transfers to the trading and profit and loss accounts and

4.4   Activity solution

1   £800 accrual for rent at 31 December 19X7.
        £500 prepayment for rates at 31 December 19X7.
        A loan of £50,000 is outstanding at 31 December 19X7.
        £1,250 accrual for loan interest at 31 December 19X7.

2/3

Rent payable

19X8			£	19X8			£
April	1	Cash	2,400	January	1	Balance b/d	800
December	31	Balance c/d	800	December	31	Profit and loss	2,400
			£3,200				£3,200
				19X9			
				January	1	Balance b/d	800

Rates

19X8			£	19X8			£
January	1	Balance b/d	500	December	31	Profit and loss	2,300
May	1	Cash	2,400	December	31	Balance c/d	600
			£2,900				£2,900
19X9							
January	1	Balance b/d	600				

Loan

19X8			£	19X8			£
September	30	Cash	10,000	January	1	Balance b/d	50,000
December	31	Balance c/d	40,000				
			£50,000				£50,000
				19X9			
				January	1	Balance b/d	40,000

Loan interest

19X8			£	19X8			£
September	30	Cash	5,000	January	1	Balance b/d	1,250
December	31	Balance c/d	1,000	December	31	Profit and loss	4,750
			£6,000				£6,000
				19X9			
				January	1	Balance b/d	1,000

4.5   Activity

From the information given below you are required to show the rent payable account and the interest payable account in the ledger of a business, for the year ending 30 June 19X8, showing clearly any prepayments of accruals at that date, and the transfer to profit and loss account for the year.

The balances on the account at 1 July 19X7 were:

	£
Rent prepaid	2,000
Interest accrued	500

Payments made during the year ended 30 June 19X8 were as follows:

19X7

21 August	Rent – covering the 3 months ending 30 November:	£3,000
31 August	Interest – covering the 3 months ending 31 August:	£1,500
10 November	Rent – covering the 3 months ending 28 February:	£3,000
30 November	Interest – covering the 3 months ending 30 November:	£1,500

19X8

3 March	Rent – covering the 3 months ending 31 May:	£3,000
31 March	Interest – covering the 3 months ending 28 February:	£1,500
31 May	Interest – covering the 3 months ending 31 May:	£1,500

4.6   Activity solution

Rent

19X7			£	19X7		£
July	1	Balance b/d	2,000			
August	21	Cash	3,000			
November	10	Cash	3,000			
19X8				19X8		
March	3	Cash	3,000	June 30 Profit and loss		12,000
June	30	Balance c/d	1,000			
			£12,000			£12,000
				July	1 Balance b/d	1,000

Interest payable

19X7			£	19X7			£
August	31	Cash	1,500	July	1	Balance b/d	500
November	30	Cash	1,500				
19X8				**19X8**			
March	31	Cash	1,500	June	30	Profit and loss	6,000
May	31	Cash	1,500				
June	30	Balance c/d	500				
			£6,500				£6,500
				July	1	Balance b/d	500

5   LEDGER ACCOUNTS RELATING TO STOCK

5.1   The cost of sales

When the accounts of Pete's Products (see Chapter 5) were prepared, all purchases of stock were debited to the stock account. When stock was sold two sets of double entry were carried out:

1   Debit cash or debtors with the amount of sales; credit sales (a revenue)

2   Debit cost of sales (an expense) with the *cost price* of the stock issued; credit stock with the same amount.

The use of ledger accounts does not pose any particular problems in this area, and the above entries are appropriate whenever the cost of sales is *known at the time of the sale*. It is not unusual however, to find the stock account expanded to enable the number and cost of the various stock purchases to be included. An example is given below.

Stock

Date	Detail	Quantity	Price	£	Date	Detail	Quantity	Price	£

As has been made clear in earlier chapters, before entry 2 above can be made, the cost of the sale just made must be known. In practice this may not happen. For example, consider a small retail shop. Every time a can of beans is sold, do you see the shopkeeper running off with it to debit a cost of sales account? Inevitably the answer is 'No'. Such retailers are likely simply to enter the sale on the till or cash register, and collect the cash. At the end of an appropriate period, perhaps every day (but perhaps longer), the total of the amounts entered in the till or cash register (the total sales) can be credited to sales, and the total cash collected can be debited to cash. Given that most retailing organisations have a large product range it is clear that detailed entries relating to stock issues and cost of sales are unlikely to be found in too many cases. Interestingly many larger retailing organisations are now using computer-based coding systems which do permit the cost of sales to be known immediately, and which provide a means of keeping a detailed track of stock items.

5.2   Determining the cost of sales

Where the entries are confined to sales and cash or debtors, it is clearly still necessary for a calculation of cost of sales to be made before a profit figure can be calculated for an accounting period. The necessary steps for this were set out in Chapter 3. Essentially the total stock available at the beginning of a period is added to the figure for purchases of stock during the period. This will give the cost of the total amount of stock available for sale. If no stock is left at the end of the period this figure will represent the cost of sales for the period. If, however, there is stock in hand at the end of the period, and there usually will be, the cost of sales will be arrived at by deducting the figure for closing stock from the total available for sale.

The usual method of recording for this type of business will be to debit the opening stock and purchases to two accounts, 'Stock' and 'Purchases', though sometimes these are combined in one stock account. At the end of the period the balances on these accounts can be transferred to a cost of sales account. The closing stock can be counted and valued, using an appropriate valuation base. The stock account can then be debited with the amount of closing stock, while the cost of sales account will be credited. The cost of sales account can then be transferred to the trading account, where it will be set against sales and a gross profit figure will be calculated.

5.3   Example

By way of illustration assume that a business has opening stock valued at £1,000. Purchases during the year were as follows:

January	credit	£1,000
March	credit	£2,000
September	cash	£3,000

Closing stock is valued at £1,500. The accounts would appear as follows:

Stock

			£			£
January	1	Balance b/d	1,000	December 31 Cost of sales		1,000
			£1,000			£1,000
December	31	Cost of sales	1,500			

Purchases

			£			£
January	31	Creditors	1,000	December 31 Cost of sales		6,000
March	31	Creditors	2,000			
September	30	Cash	3,000			
			£6,000			£6,000

Cost of sales

		£			£
December 31	Stock (opening)	1,000	December 31	Stock (closing)	1,500
	Purchases	6,000	31	Trading account	5,500
		£7,000			£7,000

The cost of sales account is frequently bypassed, with the adjustment shown above being made in the trading account. If this were done, and sales for the period were £10,000, the trading account would appear as follows:

Trading account

		£			£
December 31	Stock (opening)	1,000	December 31	Sales	10,000
31	Purchases	6,000	31	Stock (closing)	1,500
31	Profit and loss (Gross profit)	4,500			
		£11,500			£11,500

The gross profit is credited to the profit and loss account.

5.4   Alternative approach

An alternative, and perhaps more logical approach, is to have only one account for stock and purchases. This would be debited with the opening stock for the period (as the balance brought down) and with purchases of stock made during the accounting period. At the end of the period, when the figure for the closing stock has been ascertained, the closing stock amount will be credited to the account (as a balance carried down), with the corresponding double entry being the balance brought down into the new accounting period.

Continuing to use the same illustrative figures the account would appear as follows:

Stock (and purchases)

			£				£
January	1	Balance b/d	1,000				
	31	Creditors	1,000				
March	31	Creditors	2,000	December	31	Trading (cost of sales)	5,500
September	30	Cash	3,000		31	Balance c/d	1,500
			£7,000				£7,000
January	1	Balance b/d	1,500				

The cost of sales figure (£5,500) is the 'balancing figure' on the account. The corresponding debit is, of course, to the trading account.

5.5   Purchase returns and carriage in

In reality the figure for purchases may need to be adjusted to deal with purchases returns and carriage in. Carriage paid on purchases can be debited to a carriage in account during the accounting period, with a subsequent transfer to the trading account at the end of a year. Purchases returns can be credited to a separate purchases returns account (along with a debit to creditors), with the purchases returns account being transferred to the trading account at the period end. Sales returns can also be recorded in a separate sales returns account during the accounting period, and be transferred to the trading account at the period end.

By way of illustration, consider the following figures relating to a business for the year ended 31 December 19X7.

		£
1 January	Stock in hand	1,000
1 February	Credit purchases	2,000
1 March	Cash sales	4,000
1 April	Cash purchases	5,000
1 May	Credit sales	5,000
1 June	Purchase returns	500
1 August	Cash sales	3,000
15 August	Sales returns	300
1 October	Cash purchases	2,000
	Carriage on purchases (cash)	300

On 31 December the closing stock is valued at £3,000.

These transactions would be recorded in the appropriate accounts, including the trading account (which is part of the ledger accounts system) for the period, as shown below. The accounts for cash, debtors and creditors have not been balanced off since the above transactions represent only part of the entries for these accounts.

Stock

			£				£
January	1	Balance b/d	1,000	December	31	Trading	1,000
			£1,000				£1,000
December	31	Trading	3,000				

Purchases

			£				£
February	1	Creditors	2,000	December	31	Trading	9,000
April	1	Cash	5,000				
October	1	Cash	2,000				
			£9,000				£9,000

Sales

			£				£
December	31	Trading	12,000	March	1	Cash	4,000
				May	1	Debtors	5,000
				August	1	Cash	3,000
			£12,000				£12,000

Purchase returns

			£				£
December	31	Trading	500	June	1	Creditors	500
			£500				£500

Carriage in

			£				£
October	1	Cash	300	December	31	Trading	300
			£300				£300

Cash (extracts only)

			£				£
March	1	Sales	4,000	April	1	Purchases	5,000
August	1	Sales	3,000	October	1	Purchases	2,000
				October	1	Carriage in	300

Creditors (extracts only)

			£				£
June	1	Purchase returns	500	February	1	Purchases	2,000

Debtors (extracts only)

			£				£
May	1	Sales	5,000	August	15	Sales returns	300

Sales returns

		£			£
August 15	Debtors	300	December 31	Trading	300
		£300			£300

Trading

			£				£
December	31	Stock	1,000	December	31	Sales	12,000
December	31	Purchases	9,000	December	31	Purchase	500
December	31	Sales returns	300			returns	
December	31	Carriage in	300	December	31	Stock	3,000
December	31	Profit and loss	4,900				
			£15,500				£15,500

5.6 Presentation in final accounts

The trading account shown above is as it would appear in the *ledger accounts*. When the *final accounts* are being prepared for presentation to users, rather different formats are typically employed. The more usual presentations are as follows:

Normal horizontal format

Trading account for the year ended 31 December 19X7

	£	£			£
Opening stock		1,000	Sales		12,000
Purchases	9,000		*Less:* returns		300
Less: Returns	500				11,700
	8,500				
Carriage in	300				
		8,800			
		9,800			
Less: Closing stock		3,000			
Cost of sales		6,800			
Gross profit		4,900			
		£11,700			£11,700

Narrative or vertical format

Trading account for the year ended 31 December 19X7

	£	£	£
Sales			12,000
Less: Returns			300
			11,700
Opening stock		1,000	
Purchases	9,000		
Less: Returns	500		
	8,500		
Carriage in	300		
		8,800	
		9,800	
Less: Closing stock		3,000	
Cost of sales			6,800
Gross profit			£4,900

Again there is the alternative of having just one account for stock and purchases. The account can be used to collect all of the factors which affect the cost of sales: opening stock, purchases, purchase returns, carriage in and closing stock. These entries would be made in the account as the accounting period progresses. In this case the relevant account would be as follows:

Stock (and purchases)

		£			£
January 1	Balance b/d	1,000	June 1	Creditors	500
February 1	Creditors	2,000			
April 1	Cash	5,000	December 31	Trading (cost of sales)	6,800
October 1	Cash	2,000			
	Cash	300		Balance c/d	3,000
		£10,300			£10,300
January 1	Balance b/d	3,000			

This approach has the advantage that just one figure is shown for cost of sales in the trading account. For the typical user of the accounts this might make the trading account easier to read.

6   DEPRECIATION

6.1   Why depreciation is required

It has already been shown that over time, or with use, the benefits of fixed assets are used up, with the result that, for accounting purposes, part of the cost of an asset becomes an expense, known as **depreciation**, in each accounting period. The basis of deciding on an appropriate amount to include for depreciation will be discussed in detail in Chapter 8, as will the detailed accounting entries. However, it is useful to identify at this stage the broad implications in terms of the ledger accounts and final accounts of a business.

Effectively, the depreciation of a fixed asset will result in a reduction in the balance sheet values of the fixed asset, and an increase in an expense. This expense will be charged to the profit and loss account for the appropriate period. Following the logic of ledger accounts, this means that the following double entry is required;

> Debit profit and loss with depreciation (an expense)
>
> Credit the appropriate fixed asset account.

This means that an amount is included as an expense. It also means that the fixed asset account will show a reduced closing balance at the end of the period, which will be reflected in the balance sheet.

6.2   Example

By way of illustration, assume that a business has equipment which cost £5,000 on 1 January 19X7, which is expected to last 5 years. It therefore decides to depreciate the asset by £1,000 each year. In the first year of use the relevant accounts would appear as follows:

Equipment

19X7		£	**19X7**		£
January 1	Cash	5,000	December 31	Profit and loss	1,000
			December 31	Balance c/d	4,000
		£5,000			£5,000
19X8			**19X8**		
January 1	Balance b/d	4,000			

Profit and loss (extracts)

19X7		£	19X7		£
December 31	Depreciation	1,000			

The profit and loss account will be closed in the normal way. In future years the same double entry with regard to a depreciation will be made, with the result that the value of the equipment will constitute a lower figure in the balance sheet each year. At the end of five years it will be reduced to a value of zero.

7   CHAPTER SUMMARY

- This chapter has shown how adjustments are dealt with in the ledger accounting process.

- At the end of the accounting period any adjustments for prepayments, accruals and so on need to be made, with appropriate balances being transferred to the next accounting period in the form of a balance carried down. Revenues and expenses are then transferred to the trading and profit and loss account. Remaining balances can be summarised into a balance sheet at the year end.

- The adjustments for depreciation and stock were introduced.

- You should now be in a position to record a set of transactions in ledger accounts, make any adjustments to these accounts which arise at the year end, and prepare a set of final accounts.

8   SELF TEST QUESTIONS

8.1   At the end of an accounting period there is a £50 accrued expense for electricity. How would this normally be dealt with in the accounts at the year end?

    (a)   included in trade creditors

    (b)   carried down as a debit balance in the electricity account

    (c)   credited to cash at bank account

    (d)   carried down as a credit balance on the electricity account. (2.1)

8.2   A business has opening stock of £10,000, spends £95,000 (net of trade discount) on purchases of stock, returns stock which had cost it £950 (net of trade discount), is given £2,000 cash discount on its stock purchases, and has closing stock of £12,000. What is the cost of sales for the year?

    (a)   £97,000

    (b)   £92,050

    (c)   £95,200

    (d)   £90,050 (5.5)

9   EXAMINATION TYPE QUESTIONS

9.1   Wholesale Business

The ledger accounts of PAF and Co, which is a wholesale business which rents two premises, both of which have sub-tenants, included the following account balances:

	At 31 December 19X8	At 31 December 19X9
	£	£
Rent payable		
– prepayments	500	300
– accruals	200	400
Rent receivable		
– payments in advance	600	—
– amounts outstanding	200	300
Creditors	10,000	8,000
Debtors	12,000	10,000

During the year to 31 December 19X9 the following transactions occurred:

- Rent paid by cheque £5,000

- Rent received by cheque £3,000

- Creditors paid by cheque £60,000, in satisfaction of debts of £61,000, the difference being discount

- Cheques received from debtors £100,000, in satisfaction of debts of £102,000, the difference being discount.

Record the above in the appropriate accounts for the year 19X9, including sales and purchases (the balances of which are to be derived) and balance off the accounts, showing the amount of any transfer to the trading and profit and loss account where appropriate.

(20 marks)

9.2   Nazgul

The following were the balances on the ledger accounts of A. Nazgul on 30 November 19X7, eleven months into the financial year.

	Debit £	Credit £
Capital		30,000
Sales		150,000
Stock (1 January)	20,000	
Wages and salaries	19,000	
Purchases	100,000	
Debtors		
– A. Orc	3,000	
– B. Gnome	4,000	
– C. Goblin	12,000	
Creditors		
– S. Sauron		7,000
– G. Gandalf		13,000
Heating and lighting	1,000	
Rent and rates	1,300	
General expenses	3,000	
Drawings	11,000	
Cash	25,700	
	£200,000	£200,000

Open ledger accounts, bring down the above balances, and record the following transactions for December.

December	3	Sales on credit to A. Orc £6,000
	6	Cash sales £1,000
	10	Purchases on credit from S. Sauron £10,000
	12	Pays S. Sauron £7,000
	12	Pays G. Gandalf £6,000
	15	Pays rates of £1,000 which relate to the half year ending on 31 March 19X8
	16	Receives £3,000 from A. Orc
	16	Receives £12,000 from C. Goblin
	20	Cash sales £4,000
	27	Pays wages £2,000
	30	Sales on credit to B. Gnome £5,000
	30	Drawings were made of £1,000.

Then prepare a trading and profit and loss account for the year to the end of December, incorporating the following notes. Carry forward balances where appropriate.

The following additional information is available as at 31 December:

- Closing stock was valued at £15,000
- Wages of £1,000 were outstanding
- General expenses of £500 were owing.

(30 marks)

9.3   Table

Complete the following table on the assumption that there were no opening balances involved:

	Relating to the period		At the end of the period	
	Paid/received	Due for period	Prepayments	Accruals/deferred revenues
	£	£	£	£
Rent payable	10,000		1,000	
Rates and insurance	5,000			1,000
General expenses		6,000	1,000	
Loan interest payable	3,000	2,500		
Rent receivable		1,500		1,500

Then record the above in ledger accounts.

(12 marks)

10   ANSWERS TO EXAMINATION TYPE QUESTIONS

10.1   Wholesale Business

Rent payable

		£			£
19X9			**19X9**		
January 1	Balance b/d	500	January 1	Balance b/d	200
Various	Bank	5,000	December 31	Profit and loss	5,400
December 31	Balance c/d	400	December 31	Balance c/d	300
		£5,900			£5,900
19X0			**19X0**		
January 1	Balance b/d	300	January 1	Balance b/d	400

Rent receivable

		£			£
19X9			**19X9**		
January 1	Balance b/d	200	January 1	Balance b/d	600
December 31	Profit and loss	3,700	Various	Bank	3,000
			December 31	Balance c/d	300
		£3,900			£3,900
19X0			**19X0**		
January 1	Balance b/d	300			

Creditors

19X9		£	19X9		£
Various	Bank and discount	61,000	January 1	Balance b/d	10,000
December 31	Balance c/d	8,000	Various	Purchases	59,000
		£69,000			£69,000
19X0			19X0		
			January 1	Balance b/d	8,000

Debtors

19X9		£	19X9		£
January 1	Balance b/d	12,000	Various	Bank and discount	102,000
Various	Sales	100,000	December 31	Balance c/d	10,000
		£112,000			£112,000
19X0			19X0		
January 1	Balance b/d	10,000			

Sales

19X9		£	19X9		£
December 31	Trading	£100,000	Various	Debtors	£100,000

Purchases

19X9		£	19X9		£
Various	Creditors	£59,000	December 31	Trading	£59,000

Discount allowed

19X9		£	19X9		£
Various	Debtors	£2,000	December 31	Profit and loss	£2,000

Discount received

19X9		£	19X9		£
December 31	Profit and loss	£1,000	Various	Creditors	£1,000

Bank (extracts)

19X9		£	19X9		£
Various	Rent receivable	3,000	Various	Rent payable	5,000
Various	Debtors	100,000	Various	Creditors	60,000

10.2 Nazgul

Capital

19X7		£	19X7		£
December 31	Drawings	12,000	November 30	Balance b/d	30,000
December 31	Balance c/d	40,700	December 31	Net profit	22,700
		£52,700			£52,700
			19X8		
			January 1	Balance b/d	40,700

Sales

19X7		£	19X7		£
December 31	Trading	166,000	November 30	Balance b/d	150,000
			December 3	A. Orc	6,000
			December 6	Cash	1,000
			December 20	Cash	4,000
			December 30	B. Gnome	5,000
		£166,000			£166,000

Stock

19X7		£	19X7		£
January 1	Balance b/d	20,000	December 31	Trading	20,000
		£20,000			£20,000
19X8					
January 1	Balance (trading)	15,000			

Wages/salaries

19X7		£	19X7		£
November 30	Balance b/d	19,000	December 31	Profit and loss	22,000
December 27	Cash	2,000			
31	Balance c/d	1,000			
		£22,000			£22,000
			19X8		
			January 1	Balance b/d	1,000

Purchases

19X7		£	19X7		£
November 30	Balance b/d	100,000	December 31	Trading	110,000
December 10	S. Sauron	10,000			
		£110,000			£110,000

A. Orc (Debtor)

19X7		£	19X7		£
November 30	Balance b/d	3,000	December 16	Cash	3,000
December 3	Sales	6,000	December 31	Balance c/d	6,000
		£9,000			£9,000
19X8					
January 1	Balance b/d	6,000			

B. Gnome (Debtor)

19X7		£	19X7		£
November 30	Balance b/d	4,000	December 31	Balance c/d	9,000
December 30	Sales	5,000			
		£9,000			£9,000
19X8					
January 1	Balance b/d	9,000			

C. Goblin (debtor)

19X7		£	19X7		£
November 30	Balance b/d	12,000	December 16	Cash	12,000
		£12,000			£12,000

Drawings

19X7		£	19X7		£
November 30	Balance b/d	11,000	December 31	Capital	12,000
December 30	Cash	1,000			
		£12,000			£12,000

Cash

19X7		£	19X7		£
November 30	Balance b/d	25,700	December 12	S. Sauron	7,000
December 6	Sales	1,000	December 12	G. Gandalf	6,000
December 16	A. Orc	3,000	December 15	Rates	1,000
December 16	C. Goblin	12,000	December 27	Wages	2,000
December 20	Sales	4,000	December 30	Drawings	1,000
			December 31	Balance c/d	28,700
		£45,700			£45,700
19X8					
January 1	Balance b/d	28,700			

S. Sauron (creditor)

19X7		£	19X7		£
December 12	Cash	7,000	November 30	Balance b/d	7,000
December 31	Balance c/d	10,000	December 10	Purchases	10,000
		£17,000			£17,000
			19X8		
			January 1	Balance b/d	10,000

G. Gandalf (creditor)

19X7		£	19X7		£
December 12	Cash	6,000	November 30	Balance b/d	13,000
December 31	Balance c/d	7,000			
		£13,000			£13,000
			19X8		
			January 1	Balance b/d	7,000

Heating and lighting

19X7		£	19X7		£
November 30	Balance b/d	1,000	December 31	Profit and loss	1,000
		£1,000			£1,000

Rent and rates

19X7		£	19X7		£
November 30	Balance b/d	1,300	December 31	Balance c/d	500
December 15	Cash	1,000	December 31	Profit and loss	1,800
		£2,300			£2,300
19X8					
January 1	Balance b/d	500			

General expenses

19X7		£	19X7		£
November 30	Balance b/d	3,000	December 31	Profit and loss	3,500
December 31	Balance c/d	500			
		£3,500			£3,500
			19X8		
			January 1	Balance b/d	500

Trading account
for the year ended 31 December 19X7

	£		£
Opening stock	20,000	Sales	166,000
Purchases	110,000		
	130,000		
Less: Closing stock	15,000		
Cost of sales	115,000		
Gross profit	51,000		
	£166,000		£166,000

Profit and loss account
for the year ended 31 December 19X7

	£		£
Heating and lighting	1,000	Gross profit	51,000
Rent and rates	1,800		
General expenses	3,500		
Wages and salaries	22,000		
	28,300		
Net profit	22,700		
	£51,000		£51,000

Balance sheet as at 31 December 19X7

Current assets	£	£	**Capital**	£	£
Stock		15,000	Opening balance		30,000
Prepayments		500	Net profit		22,700
					52,700
Debtors – A. Orc	6,000				
– B. Gnome	9,000		Less: Drawings		12,000
		15,000			40,700
Cash		28,700	**Current liabilities**		
			Creditors – S. Sauron	10,000	
			– G. Gandalf	7,000	
					17,000
			Accruals		1,500
		£59,200			£59,200

In practice the trading and profit and loss accounts are more typically presented in a combined vertical format, and the balance sheet is also typically presented in a vertical format. The final accounts for this question are given below in this alternative format.

Trading and profit and loss account
for the year ended 31 December 19X7

	£	£
Sales		166,000
Less:		
Opening stock	20,000	
Purchasers	110,000	
	130,000	
Closing stock	15,000	
Cost of sales		115,000
Gross profit		51,000
Less: other expenses		
Heating and lighting	1,000	
Rent and rates	1,800	
General expenses	3,500	
Wages and salaries	22,000	
	28,300	
Net profit		£22,700

Balance sheet as at 31 December 19X7

Current assets	£	£
Stock	15,000	
Prepayments	500	
Debtors	15,000	
Cash	28,700	
		59,200
Less:		
Creditors due within a year		
Creditors	17,000	
Accruals	1,500	
		18,500
		£40,700
Capital		
Opening balance		30,000
Net profit		22,700
		52,700
Less: Drawings		12,000
		£40,700

10.3 Table

Rent payable, due for period = £9,000

Rates and insurance, due for period = £6,000

General expenses, paid in period = £7,000

Loan interest payable, prepayment at end of period = £500

Rent receivable, received during period = £3,000

Rent payable

	£			£
During period cash	10,000	End of period	Profit and loss	9,000
		End of period	Balance c/d	1,000
	£10,000			£10,000
Beginning of next period Balance b/d	1,000			

Rates and insurance

	£			£
During period cash	5,000	End of period	Profit and loss	6,000
End of period Balance c/d	1,000			
	£6,000			£6,000
		Beginning of next period	Balance b/d	1,000

General expenses

	£			£
During period cash	7,000	End of period	Profit and loss	6,000
		End of period	Balance c/d	1,000
	£7,000			£7,000
Beginning of next period Balance b/d	1,000			

Loan interest payable

	£			£
During period cash	3,000	End of period	Profit and loss	2,500
		End of period	Balance c/d	500
	£3,000			£3,000
Beginning of next period Balance b/d	500			

Rents receivable

	£			£
Profit and Loss	1,500	During period Cash	3,000
End of period Balance c/d	1,500		
	£3,000		£3,000
		Beginning of next period Balance b/d	1,500

7 THE PREPARATION OF FINAL ACCOUNTS FROM A TRIAL BALANCE

INTRODUCTION AND LEARNING OBJECTIVES

This short chapter focuses on one part of the process covered in the previous two chapters, namely the preparation of a set of final accounts from a trial balance, after incorporating a series of adjustments. This part of the process builds on the basic double-entry system. It provides an opportunity for examiners to test students' understanding without requiring them to prepare lots of detailed ledger accounts. As a result, questions of this type appear regularly in examinations. Such questions should test students' ability to convert the basic data contained in the accounts into a set of final accounts, after incorporating a series of year-end adjustments.

This general approach is likely to continue throughout the professional examinations. The types of business may become more complex (for instance, partnerships and companies), as do the adjustments, but the underlying principles remain the same.

When you have studied this chapter you should be able to do the following:

- Deal with exam questions that call for the preparation of a set of accounts from a provided trial balance and adjustments required.

---

1 FINAL ACCOUNTS FROM A TRIAL BALANCE

1.1 Introduction

The preparation of a complete set of accounts can be quite a time-consuming task. This means that in examinations, many of which are limited to three hours, questions on ledger accounts generally deal with only a relatively small part of the overall process. One of the more common approaches used by examiners to test understanding of the recording process, particularly with regard to the impact of transactions on the final accounts, is to give a trial balance for a business, taken out on the last day of the year, together with a detailed list of adjustments which need to be taken into account, and ask the student to prepare a set of final accounts from this information. Such an approach has the advantage (from an examiner's point of view) of eliminating the need for a student to complete a set of detailed ledger accounts, which should be fairly straightforward, if rather repetitive, but does require the student to display understanding of year-end adjustments and final accounts.

It was shown in Chapter 5 that the trial balance usually represents a summary of the ledger accounts at the end of an accounting period, before any end-of-period adjustments are made. It is the result of the double entry made throughout the period. If a complete set of accounts were being kept all that would be necessary would be the transfer of the revenues and expenses of the period to the trading and profit and loss accounts, subject to any end of period adjustments, and the transferring of the net profit and drawings to the capital account. This would in turn enable all balance sheet items to be identified.

Where an examiner simply asks for the final accounts there is no need to show the closing of the individual accounts to the trading and profit and loss accounts. If adjustments are difficult or confusing it may be advisable to show *selected* accounts, or equivalent workings. Similarly, accounts for assets and liabilities need not be shown, since their inclusion in the balance sheet will be taken to indicate understanding in this area.

1.2   Suggested procedure

The suggested procedure for dealing with this kind of question is as follows:

Step 1   Set out a pro-forma trading account, profit and loss account and balance sheet (that is, draft final accounts without any figures). You should by now have a clear idea as to the kind of layout you wish to use, and its likely content, in terms of items. This is particularly true of the trading account and the balance sheet. It is suggested that the narrative (vertical) presentations are used, since they are now more common in practice. You should, however, always read the question carefully, since an examiner may ask for a particular approach to be used. A certain amount of flexibility may need to be retained for profit and loss account items. You are advised to allow plenty of room to make any adjustments that are necessary. (As you become more proficient in this area you may not need to set out pro-formas, but will be able to insert figures in the appropriate position.)

Step 2   Go down the trial balance, and put all the assets and liabilities into their appropriate position on the balance sheet, and all the revenues and expenses into their appropriate position in the trading and profit and loss accounts. No double entry is needed since, as was pointed out above, the trial balance figures are the result of the double entry.

Step 3   Make the necessary end-of-period adjustments. Since no double entry will have been made for these there will be a double effect on the final accounts. Most adjustments will affect both the balance sheet and the trading and profit and loss accounts.

Step 4   Total the figures on the trading and profit and loss accounts, calculate the gross and net profits, transfer the profit figure to the capital section of the balance sheet, and total the balance sheet.

Example

As an example, consider the following trial balance, which was extracted from the accounts of a business as at 31 December 19X7.

	£	£
Sales		150,000
Sales returns	3,000	
Purchases	70,000	
Carriage in	1,000	
Stock – 1 January	10,000	
Wages	20,000	
Administration expenses	25,000	
Insurance	1,000	
Selling and distribution expenses	10,000	
Purchases returns		500
Drawings	10,000	
Capital		50,000
Premises	20,000	
Equipment	20,000	
Debtors	15,000	
Creditors		10,000
Cash	5,500	
	£210,500	£210,500

At the year end (31 December) the following information is available:

1   £1,000 of the wages relate to the next accounting period
2   £2,000 is owed for administration expenses relating to 19X7
3   Equipment is to be depreciated by £4,000
4   Closing stock is estimated to have cost £8,000.

You are required to prepare the balance sheet at 31 December 19X7 and the trading and profit and loss account to that date.

Solution

If the first two steps identified above are carried out the results will be as shown below:

Trading and profit and loss account for the year ended 31 December 19X7

	£	£	£
Sales			150,000
Less: Returns			3,000
			147,000
Opening stock		10,000	
Purchases	70,000		
Less: Returns	500		
	69,500		
Carriage in	1,000		
		70,500	
		80,500	
Less: Closing stock			
Cost of sales			———
Gross profit			
Add other revenues			———
Less: **Other expenses**			
Wages	20,000		
Administration expenses	25,000		
Insurance	1,000		
Selling and distribution	10,000		
Net profit		£	

Balance sheet as at 31 December 19X7

	£	£	£
Fixed assets			
Premises			20,000
Equipment		20,000	
Current assets			
Stock			
Prepayments			
Debtors	15,000		
Cash	5,500		
Less: **Current liabilities**			
Creditors	10,000		
Accruals	———		
Net current assets		£	

Capital
Opening balance   50,000
Net profit
Less: Drawings   10,000

                                                                      £

Stage 3 requires a consideration of the adjustments.

Adjustment 1 arises because £1,000 of the wages paid relate to the following year. If a wages account were to be drawn up it would appear as follows:

Wages

19X7		£	19X7			£
Various dates Cash		20,000	December 31	Profit and loss		19,000
			December 31	Balance c/d		1,000
		£20,000				£20,000
19X8						
January 1 Balance b/d		1,000				

In other words, of the £20,000 paid, £19,000 represents an expense of the year, while £1,000 represents a current asset, a prepayment at the end of the year. In an examination it should not be necessary to complete accounts for all items requiring adjustment, as long as the correct adjustments are made to the final accounts. In the case of adjustment 1 all that is needed is to reduce the figure for the expense – wages – by £1,000, and to increase prepayments in the balance sheet by the same amount.

Adjustment 2 relates to an accrued expense, namely the fact that £2,000 is owed for administration expenses. This represents an additional expense which is due (and therefore must be added to the administration expenses in the profit and loss account) but which is unpaid at the year end. It must therefore also appear as an accrual in the balance sheet.

Adjustment 3, the depreciation of equipment by £4,000, results in an additional expense in the profit and loss account, and a reduction in the equipment. The reduction may thus be made on the balance sheet.

Adjustment 4 relates to the cost of sales and the closing stock. Since the closing stock is valued at £8,000 the figures for cost of sales in the trading account (that is, opening stock + purchases – purchases returns + carriage in) must be reduced by the amount of the closing stock, while the stock figure in the balance sheet must reflect the amount of the stock in hand at the year end.

After these adjustments, and the totalling and transfers set out in step 4, the final accounts should appear as follows:

Trading and profit and loss account for the year ended 31 December 19X7

	£	£	£
Sales			150,000
Less: Returns			3,000
			147,000
Opening stock		10,000	
Purchases	70,000		
Less: Returns	500		
	69,500		
Carriage in	1,000		

		70,500	
		80,500	
Less: Closing stock		8,000	
Cost of sales			72,500
Gross profit			74,500
Less: **Other expenses**			
Wages	20,000	19,000	
	−1,000		
Administration expenses	25,000	27,000	
	+2,000		
Insurance	1,000	1,000	
Selling and distribution	10,000	10,000	
Depreciation		4,000	
			61,000
Net profit			£13,500

Balance sheet as at 31 December 19X7

Fixed assets	£	£	£
Premises			20,000
Equipment		20,000	
		−4,000	16,000
			36,000
Current assets			
Stock	8,000		
Prepayments	1,000		
Debtors	15,000		
Cash	5,500		
		29,500	
Less: **Current liabilities**			
Creditors	10,000		
Accruals	2,000		
		12,000	
Net current assets			17,500
			£53,500
Capital			
Opening balance			50,000
Net profit			13,500
			63,500
Less: Drawings			10,000
			£53,500

It may be argued that showing the workings on the face of the final accounts makes the end result less neat than it might be. Against this, the above approach has the advantage that an examiner can clearly see the workings which have gone into the final accounts. On balance the showing of workings in this way is favoured, even at the cost of a slight loss in neatness.

2   CHAPTER SUMMARY

- In many examinations time does not permit the examiner to ask for full sets of ledger accounts. In many cases examiners ask for a set of final accounts to be prepared from a trial balance, thus eliminating the early part of the process described in Chapters 5 and 6. It is important to adopt a sound technique in dealing with such questions, since time is always a problem in examinations. It should be noted that in practice, questions requiring the preparation of final accounts from a trial balance are likely to include some (or all) of the adjustments described in Chapters 8–10, as well as those discussed in this chapter.

3   EXAMAMINATION TYPE QUESTIONS

3.1   Business Accounts I

The following trial balance was extracted from the accounts of a business as at 31 December 19X7.

	£	£
Sales		300,000
Sales returns	5,000	
Carriage in	2,000	
Wages	50,000	
Premises	120,000	
Equipment	40,000	
Creditors		25,000
Rent and rates	5,000	
Heating and lighting	4,000	
Discount allowed	2,500	
Discount received		1,500
Purchases	160,000	
Purchases returns		5,000
Carriage out	2,000	
Stock – 1 January	15,000	
Debtors	30,000	
Rent receivable		3,000
Administration expenses	8,000	
Insurance	1,500	
Cash	9,500	
Capital		140,000
Drawings	20,000	
	£474,500	£474,500

At the year end the following additional information is available:

1   £500 of administration expenses remain unpaid

2   £300 of insurance relates to the following year

3   Bad debts of £500 are to be written off

4   £500 of rent is still owing to the business

5   £200 of wages are outstanding, relating to overtime worked in December

6   Closing stock is valued at £20,000

7   Equipment is to be depreciated by £8,000.

Prepare a trading and profit and loss account for the year ended 31 December 19X7, and a balance sheet as at 31 December 19X7.

3.2   Business Accounts II

The following trial balance was extracted from the accounts of a business as at 31 December 19X5.

	£	£
Advertising	14,000	
Bad debts	600	
Bank charges	200	
Capital		50,000
Discount allowed	500	
Discount received		600
Furniture and fittings	5,000	
Administration expenses	12,000	
Rates and insurance	3,000	
Heating and lighting	2,000	
Plant and machinery	15,000	
Purchases	80,000	
Purchases returns		1,000
Sales		200,000
Sales returns	2,000	
Distribution expenses	8,000	
Wages	40,000	
Repairs to plant	1,000	
Debtors	25,000	
Creditors		15,000
Drawings	20,000	
Stock	10,000	
Cash	28,300	
	£266,600	£266,600

At the year end the following additional information is available:

1 Closing stock is valued at £12,000

2 Depreciation of £3,000 on plant and machinery, and of £1,000 on furniture and fittings, is to be provided for

3 Rates and insurance prepaid amounts to £500

4 Accrued administration expenses amount to £500.

Draw up a trading and profit and loss account for the year ended 31 December 19X5, and a balance sheet as at that date.

4   ANSWERS TO EXAMINATION TYPE QUESTIONS

4.1   Business accounts I

Trading and profit and loss account for the year ended 31 December 19X7

	£	£	£
Sales			300,000
Less: returns			5,000
			295,000
Less:			
Opening stock		15,000	
Purchases	160,000		
Less: returns	5,000		
		155,000	
Carriage in		2,000	

		172,000	
Closing stock		20,000	
Cost of sales			152,000
Gross profit			143,000
Add: **Other revenues**			
Rent receivable	3,000		
	500	3,500	
Discount received		1,500	
			5,000
			148,000
Less: **Other expenses**			
Wages	50,000		
	200	50,200	
Rent and rates		5,000	
Heating and lighting		4,000	
Discount allowed		2,500	
Carriage out		2,000	
Administration expenses	8,000		
	500	8,500	
Insurance	1,500		
	−300	1,200	
Bad debts		500	
Depreciation		8,000	
			81,900
Net profit			**£66,100**

Balance sheet as at 31 December 19X7

	£	£	£
Fixed assets			
Premises			120,000
Equipment		40,000	
		−8,000	32,000
			152,000
Current assets			
Stock		20,000	
Prepayments		300	
Debtors	30,000		
	−500	29,500	
Rent owing		500	
Cash		9,500	
		59,800	
Current liabilities			
Creditors	25,000		
Accruals	500		
	200		
		25,700	
Net current assets			34,100
			£186,100

Capital

Opening balance	140,000
Net profit	66,100
	206,100
Less: Drawings	20,000
	£186,100

4.2   Business Accounts II

Trading and profit and loss account for the year ended 31 December 19X5

	£	£	£
Sales			200,000
Less: Returns			2,000
			198,000
Opening stock		10,000	
Plus: Purchases	80,000		
Less: Returns	1,000		
		79,000	
		89,000	
Less: Closing stock		12,000	
Cost of sales			77,000
Gross profit			121,000
Add: **Other revenues**			
Discount received			600
			121,600
Less: **Other expenses**			
Advertising		14,000	
Rates and insurance		2,500	
Wages		40,000	
Depreciation		4,000	
Bad debts		600	
Bank charges		200	
Heating and lighting		2,000	
Distribution		8,000	
Repairs		1,000	
Administration		12,500	
Discount allowed		500	
		85,300	
Net profit		£36,300	

Balance sheet as at 31 December 19X5

	£	£	£
Fixed assets			
Plant and machinery			12,000
Furniture and fittings			4,000
			16,000
Current assets			
Stock		12,000	
Prepayments		500	
Debtors		25,000	
Cash		28,300	
		65,800	
Less: **Liabilities due within 12 months**			
Creditors	15,000		
Accruals	500		
		15,500	
Net current assets			50,300
			66,300
Capital			
Opening balance			50,000
Net profit			36,300
			86,300
Less: Drawings			20,000
			£66,300

8 ACCOUNTING FOR FIXED ASSETS AND DEPRECIATION

INTRODUCTION AND LEARNING OBJECTIVES

This chapter is concerned with accounting for fixed assets, and the associated depreciation charges. It has been made clear that the benefit of an asset is used up over time, and that the benefit used up will result in an expense and a reduction in the figure recorded in the accounts for that asset. This chapter explains the nature of depreciation and identifies the more common ways in which depreciation is calculated. The chapter also shows how depreciation and fixed asset movements, including asset disposals, are recorded in the ledger accounts.

When you have studied this chapter you should be able to do the following:

- Understand the nature of depreciation

- Calculate depreciation charges under the straight-line method and the reducing-balance method

- Account for revaluations and disposals of fixed assets

- Recognise that it is SSAP 12 that lays down standard accounting practice in this area.

---

1 DEPRECIATION OF FIXED ASSETS – BASIS

1.1 Introduction

In Chapter 2 it was seen that for an asset to be defined as such certain criteria must be met. One of these criteria is that an asset must be capable of providing future benefits. In the case of fixed assets it is common for the benefits to extend over several periods. However, the life of a fixed asset is limited (with the exception of freehold land) and, eventually, the asset will be used up in the process of generating revenue. This using up of the asset is referred to as **depreciation**. More formally, depreciation has been defined as:

Definition   The measure of the wearing out, consumption or other reduction in the useful economic life of a fixed asset whether arising from use, effluxion of time or obsolescence through technological or market changes *(Statement of Standard Accounting Practice 12)*.

Normally, a portion of the value of the fixed asset will be used up in each accounting period of its life in order to generate revenue. It has been seen that to calculate profit for a period it is necessary to match expenses with the revenues they help earn. In determining the expenses for a period it is important, therefore, to ensure that an amount is included to represent the amount of fixed assets consumed during that period (that is, depreciation).

In essence, depreciation involves allocating the cost of the asset (less any residual value) over its useful life. In order to calculate the depreciation charge for an accounting period, the following factors must be determined.

1.2 Cost

The cost of an asset will include all amounts necessary to acquire the asset, to bring the asset to its required location and to make it ready for use. In order to acquire certain assets such as freehold property, legal costs may have to be incurred. Such costs can be regarded as forming part of the total cost of the asset as they are necessary to obtain the asset. Similarly, costs incurred in bringing the asset to its required location should be regarded as an integral part of the total cost of the asset.

Costs of installing the asset and setting it up for use should also be properly included as part of total cost.

The cost of subsequent improvements and alterations to a fixed asset increase its cost in the accounts. By contrast, the costs of repairs and overhauls of assets do not increase the assets' book value. Usually the costs of repairs and overhauls are treated as expenses of the accounting period in which the work is done.

1.3   Useful life

An asset may be viewed as having a physical life and an economic life. Most fixed assets will suffer physical deterioration through usage and the passage of time. Although care and maintenance may succeed in extending the physical life of an asset, typically it will, eventually, reach a condition where the benefits have been exhausted. However, a business may not wish to keep an asset until the end of its physical life. There may be a point when it becomes uneconomic to continue to use the asset even though there is still some physical life left. The economic life of the asset will be determined by such factors as technological progress and changes in demand. For purposes of calculating depreciation it is the economic life rather than the physical life of the fixed asset which is important. However, determining the economic life of an asset may be difficult as the factors influencing economic life are often unpredictable and outside the control of the business.

1.4   Residual value

At the end of the useful life of an asset the business will dispose of it and any amounts received will represent its residual value. This, again, may be difficult to estimate in practice. The cost of the asset less the residual value will represent the total amount to be depreciated.

1.5   Activity

Arundel Enterprises purchased a new motor car for a sales representative. The invoice received contained the following information:

	£	£
New Vauxhall Cavalier		10,400
Road Fund Licence	100	
Petrol	10	
Delivery charge	45	
Number plates	60	
Burglar alarm system	150	
		365
		10,765
Part exchange allowance		6,200
Amount due		£4,565

It is estimated that the new car will have a useful life of three years and will have a residual value of £6,350.

Calculate the total amount to be depreciated in respect of the new car.

1.6   Activity solution

	£
New Vauxhall Cavalier	10,400
Add:	
Delivery charge	45
Number plates	60
Burglar alarm system	150

Total cost	10,655
Less: Estimated residual value	6,350
Total amount to be depreciated	£4,305

2 DEPRECIATION METHODS

2.1 Introduction

It has been seen that cost less residual value determines the total amount to be depreciated and the useful life provides the time period over which the fixed asset should be depreciated. The final requirement is a depreciation method which will allocate, in a systematic way, the total amount to be depreciated between each accounting period of the asset's useful life.

There are various methods of depreciation available. However, most businesses appear to adopt one of the two methods described below.

2.2 Straight-line method

This method is widely used and is simple to calculate. It is based on the principle that each accounting period of the asset's life should bear an equal amount of depreciation. As a result the depreciation expense relating to the asset will be a constant charge in the profit and loss account. The formula for calculating the charge is:

$$Dsl = \frac{C - R}{N}$$

where:

Dsl	=	Annual straight-line depreciation charge
C	=	Cost of the asset
R	=	Residual value of the asset
N	=	Useful life of the asset (years)

By way of illustration, assume that a business purchases a new machine for £3,000 on 1 April 19X3. It is estimated that the machine will have a residual value of £800 and an expected useful life of four years. The business has an accounting year ending on 31 March.

Calculation of the annual depreciation charge using the straight-line method is as follows:

$$Dsl = \frac{C - R}{N}$$

$$Dsl = \frac{£3,000 - £800}{4}$$

$$= £550$$

A figure of £550 would therefore be charged as the appropriate depreciation expense in each of the four profit and loss accounts covering the useful life of the asset. In each annual balance sheet the machine would be shown at its original cost less any amounts depreciated to date. At the end of the second year, for example, extracts from the financial statements will be as follows:

Profit and loss account for the year ended 31 March 19X5 (Extract)

Depreciation of machinery	£550

Balance sheet as at 31 March 19X5 (Extract)

	£	£
Machine at cost	3,000	
Less: Accumulated depreciation*	1,100	
		1,900

* This represents the total depreciation during the first two years.

The cost of the machine less the accumulated depreciation to date (£1,900) is referred to as the **written-down value (WDV)** or **net book value (NBV)**. It is important to appreciate that this figure does not attempt to represent the current market value of the machine (except at the time of disposal). Rather it is the unexpired portion of the original cost. Depreciation is a process of allocation not valuation.

The straight-line method derives its name from the fact that both the annual depreciation charge and accumulated depreciation charge, when graphed against time, result in a straight line.

It can be argued that the pattern of depreciation charges relating to an asset should attempt to match the pattern of benefits derived from that asset. Thus, where the benefits from an asset are likely to be constant over its life the straight-line method of depreciation would be appropriate as it results in a constant depreciation charge. In practice it may be difficult to assess the pattern of benefits relating to an asset. In such cases the straight-line method may often be chosen simply because it is easy to understand and calculate.

2.3 Reducing-balance method

This method provides a high annual depreciation charge in the early years of an asset's life but the charge diminishes as the asset ages. To achieve this pattern of depreciation a fixed annual depreciation percentage is applied to the written-down value of the asset. Thus, depreciation is calculated as a percentage of the reducing balance.

To illustrate this, assume that a business purchases a motor van for £10,000 on 1 January 19X5. It is estimated that the van has a useful life of four years and a residual value of £256. The annual depreciation rate is calculated at 60% of the written-down value. The business has its accounting year end on 31 December.

Using the reducing-balance method, the annual depreciation charge for each of the four years will be as follows:

31 December		£
	Cost	10,000
19X5	Depreciation charge (60% cost)	6,000
	Written-down value	4,000
19X6	Depreciation charge (60% WDV)	2,400
	Written-down value	1,600
19X7	Depreciation charge (60% WDV)	960
	Written-down value	640
19X8	Depreciation charge (60% WDV)	384
	Residual value	£256

It can be seen that this method can result in substantial differences from one year to the next in the annual depreciation charge relating to an asset. To illustrate the effects of the depreciation charges on the financial statement relevant extracts for the year ended 31 December 19X7 are shown below:

Profit and loss account for the year ended 31 December 19X7 (Extract)

Depreciation of motor van £960

Balance sheet as at 31 December 19X7 (Extract)

	£	£
Motor van at cost	10,000	
Less: Accumulated depreciation*	9,360	
		640

*This represents the total amount depreciated in the first three years.

In the above example the fixed depreciation percentage was given. To derive this percentage the following formula can be used:

$$Dp = (1 - \sqrt[N]{R/C}) \times 100\%$$

where:
$$Dp = \text{Fixed depreciation percentage}$$
$$N = \text{Useful life of the asset (years)}$$
$$R = \text{Residual value of the asset}$$
$$C = \text{Cost of the asset}$$

However, in the Foundation-level Accounting Framework examination the depreciation percentage is usually given and does not, therefore, have to be calculated.

For certain assets the benefits derived may be high in the early years, but may decline as the asset ages. For such assets the reducing-balance method of depreciation would be appropriate insofar as it matches the pattern of benefits. However, this method is sometimes supported for another reason as discussed below.

The total expense associated with an asset is made up of two elements: a depreciation expense and a maintenance expense. For certain assets the maintenance charges rise as the asset ages. Thus, in order that total expenses remain constant it is necessary for the depreciation charge to adopt the opposite pattern, that is, to be high in the early years and to decline as the asset ages. This argument seems valid only if there is some justification for maintaining total asset expenses at a constant level (that is, the level of benefits remains constant).

2.4 Activity

A business purchases a microcomputer for £4,400 on 1 January. It has an estimated useful life of four years and a residual value of £275. The business has its accounting year end on 31 December.

1　　Calculate the annual depreciation charge using the straight-line method

2　　Calculate the annual depreciation charges using the reducing-balance method

3　　Show the relevant balance sheet extracts for Year 3 under each depreciation method.

Note: Work to the nearest £.

2.5 Activity solution

1　　Straight-line method

$$Dsl = \frac{C - R}{N}$$

$$= \frac{(4,400 - 275)}{4}$$

$$= £1,031$$

2　　Reducing-balance method

$$Dp = (1 - \sqrt[4]{R/C}) \times 100\%$$

$$= 50\%$$

	£
Cost	4,400
Year 1 Depreciation charge – (50% of cost)	2,200
Written-down value	2,200
Year 2 Depreciation charge – (50% of WDV)	1,100
Written-down value	1,100
Year 3 Depreciation charge – (50% of WDV)	550
Written-down value	550
Year 4 Depreciation charge – (50% of WDV)	275
Residual value	£275

3   **Balance sheet extracts**

	£	£
Straight-line method		
Microcomputer at cost	4,400	
Less: Accumulated depreciation	3,094	
		1,306
Reducing-balance method		
Microcomputer at cost	4,400	
Less: Accumulated depreciation	3,850	
		550

2.6   Total depreciation charged

It must be emphasised at this point that, whichever method of depreciation is selected, the total depreciation to be charged will be the same. It is simply the allocation of the total depreciation charge between accounting periods which is affected by the choice of method.

3   OTHER ISSUES

3.1   Depreciation and subjectivity

Depreciation provides a good example of the fact that accounting is not a precise science. Some accounting measurements require the exercise of judgement which may vary between individuals. In the case of depreciation, judgment is normally required concerning:

- the estimated useful life of the asset
- the estimated residual value
- the appropriate method of depreciation.

Different judgements concerning the above would result in different calculations of the annual depreciation charge and, therefore, different calculations of net profit between years.

3.2   Depreciation and asset replacement

It is sometimes believed that the purpose of depreciation is to provide for the replacement of the asset at the end of its useful life. This is *not* the conventional view of depreciation. As stated earlier, depreciation is simply an attempt to allocate, in a systematic manner, the cost of the asset (less any residual value) over its useful life. The view that depreciation is linked to asset replacement assumes that the business intends to replace the asset, which is not always the case. Where it is the intention to replace the asset the process of depreciation does not normally involve setting aside each year a sum equivalent to the annual depreciation charge for replacement purposes. Even if this were done, the cash accumulated at the end of the asset's life might be insufficient to replace it because of inflation and technological change.

3.3   Appreciation of fixed assets

Not all fixed assets depreciate. Freehold land is an example of an asset which has generally appreciated in value over the years. Given this situation many consider it appropriate to revalue such an asset in the books. This, of course, would represent a departure from both the (historic) cost convention, which states that assets should be recorded at cost, and the convention of prudence, which states that gains should not be recognised until they are realised. Nevertheless, it has become increasingly common for businesses periodically to revalue freehold land and property where there is a significant difference between the current value and original cost.

Any gain arising on revaluation represents a capital gain which does not occur in the normal course of trading. Therefore, it should not pass through the profit and loss account. Instead, it is transferred to the owner's capital account. The appropriate accounting entries are:

- Debit   Asset account
- Credit   Capital account

      with the amount of the gain on revaluation

Where the revaluation of an asset takes place this should be done by a suitably qualified, independent person. This would help retain some degree of objectivity.

It is not unknown for assets which are expected to depreciate over their useful lives to appreciate in value over the short term. Such assets might be revalued and the new value put into the balance sheet as described above. However, the asset should still be depreciated with the periodic depreciation expense being based on the valuation rather than on cost.

An example of an asset which depreciates in the long term though it may appreciate in the short term is a lease of land and buildings. During a period of rapidly rising property prices, such as that experienced in the UK in the late 1980s, a lease lasting 20 years say, could easily increase in market value despite the fact that its life is shortening. For example, a lease to occupy premises for 20 years from 1987 to 2007 which cost £100,000 in 1987 could quite conceivably have increased in value to £120,000 by 1989, despite the fact that two years of its life had elapsed.

There is as much justification in revaluing a depreciating asset whose value has increased in the short term as there is in revaluing a non-depreciating asset like freehold land. The benefits of revaluating a depreciating asset are that the asset is shown at a more relevant value in the balance sheet, but also that the depreciation expense for periods after the revaluation more reasonably reflects the economic benefit of using the asset. In such cases, though clearly the cost convention is violated, revaluation does lead to a more prudent depreciation expense for periods after the revaluation.

4   ACCOUNTING FOR DEPRECIATION

4.1   Accounting entries necessary

In order to illustrate the accounting entries necessary to record depreciation consider the following example:

Example

A business acquired two fixed assets for cash on 1 June 19X2. These were:

1   a 20-year lease on a freehold shop costing £40,000
2   a motor car costing £7,000 which has an estimated useful life of six years and a residual value of £326.

The lease is depreciated at the rate of 5% per annum on cost (using the straight-line method). The motor van is depreciated at the rate of 40% per annum on the reducing balance. The business has an accounting period end on 31 May.

Show the ledger account entries for these assets for 19X3, 19X4 and 19X5.

Solution

Accounting entries concerning the purchase of assets have already been considered in a previous chapter. Where an asset is purchased for cash the appropriate entries are:

- Debit   Asset account
- Credit   Cash with the cost of the asset

A separate account will be opened for each class of asset.

Before considering the accounting entries for depreciation it is necessary to calculate the annual depreciation charge. The depreciation charge for each of the first three years will be as follows:

Year ended 31 May	Lease £	Motor van £
19X3	2,000	2,800
19X4	2,000	1,680
19X5	2,000	1,008

Once the depreciation charge for a particular year has been calculated the relevant account entries are:

- Debit   Profit and loss account
- Credit   Provision for depreciation account

  with the amount of the annual depreciation charge

The debit entry is in recognition of the fact that depreciation is an expense and, therefore, must be charged to the profit and loss account. As the profit and loss account is an integral part of the double-entry system, and as depreciation represents a year-end adjustment, it is acceptable to debit the depreciation expense directly to the profit and loss account.

The credit entry to the provision for depreciation account completes the double entry. Though there is no reason of principle why the depreciation charged in the profit and loss account should not be credited to the relevant fixed asset account, this is not usually done in practice. The normal treatment is to open a separate accumulated depreciation account for each type of fixed asset, that is an accumulated depreciation account for each fixed asset account, unless there are some fixed assets which are not depreciated. The objective of maintaining accumulated depreciation accounts separate from the fixed asset accounts is to enable both the total cost and accumulated depreciation figures for each type of fixed asset to be identified. It is normal practice to show fixed assets on the face of the balance sheet as:

	£
Cost	x
Less: Accumulated depreciation	x
Net book value (or written-down value)	x

The accumulated depreciation accounts are usually referred to as **provisions**. A provision is usually defined as an amount set aside out of profits to provide for any known expense, the amount of which cannot be accurately determined.

The balance on the provision for depreciation account is carried forward and accumulated until such time as the asset is disposed of. What happens to it then will be discussed later in this chapter.

The relevant accounting entries and balance sheet extracts relating to the above example for each of the first three years are as follows:

Lease

19X2		£	19X2	£
June 1	Cash	40,000		

Motor van

19X2		£	19X2	£
June 1	Cash	7,000		

Provision for depreciation – lease

19X3		£	19X3		£
May 31	Balance c/d	2,000	May 31	Profit and loss	2,000
		£2,000			£2,000
			June 1	Balance b/d	2,000
19X4			**19X4**		
May 31	Balance c/d	4,000	May 31	Profit and loss	2,000
		£4,000			£4,000
			June 1	Balance b/d	4,000
19X5			**19X5**		
May 31	Balance c/d	6,000	May 31	Profit and loss	2,000
		£6,000			£6,000
			June 1	Balance b/d	6,000

Provision for depreciation – motor van

19X3		£	19X3		£
May 31	Balance c/d	2,800	May 31	Profit and loss	2,800
		£2,800			£2,800
			June 1	Balance b/d	2,800
19X4			**19X4**		
May 31	Balance c/d	4,480	May 31	Profit and loss	1,680
		£4,480			£4,480
			June 1	Balance b/d	4,480
19X5			**19X5**		
May 31	Balance c/d	5,488	May 31	Profit and loss	1,008
		£5,488			£5,488
			June 1	Balance b/d	5,488

Profit and loss account for the year ended 31 May (Extracts)

			£	£
19X3	Depreciation:	lease	2,000	
		motor van	2,800	
				4,800
19X4	Depreciation:	lease	2,000	
		motor van	1,680	
				3,680
19X5	Depreciation:	lease	2,000	
		motor van	1,008	
				3,008

Balance sheet as at 31 May (Extracts)

	£	£
19X3 Lease at cost	40,000	
Less: Accumulated depreciation	2,000	
		38,000
Motor van at cost	7,000	
Less: Accumulated depreciation	2,800	
		4,200

19X4 Lease at cost	40,000	
Less: Accumulated depreciation	4,000	
		36,000
Motor van at cost	7,000	
Less: Accumulated depreciation	4,480	
		2,520
19X5 Lease at cost	40,000	
Less: Accumulated depreciation	6,000	
		34,000
Motor van at cost	7,000	
Less: Accumulated depreciation	5,488	
		1,512

4.2   Activity

For the above example show the relevant accounting entries and balance sheet extracts for the years ending 31 May 19X6 and 19X7

4.3   Activity solution

Provision for depreciation – lease

19X6		£	**19X5**		£
May 31	Balance c/d	8,000	June 1	Balance b/d	6,000
			19X6		
			May 31	Profit and loss	2,000
		£8,000			£8,000
			June 1	Balance b/d	8,000
19X7			**19X7**		
May 31	Balance c/d	10,000	May 31	Profit and loss	2,000
		£10,000			£10,000
			June 1	Balance b/d	10,000

Provision for depreciation – motor van

19X6		£	**19X5**		£
May 31	Balance c/d	6,093	June 1	Balance b/d	5,488
			19X6		
			May 31	Profit and loss	605
		£6,093			£6,093
			June 1	Balance b/d	6,093
19X7			**19X7**		
May 31	Balance c/d	6,456	May 31	Profit and loss	363
		£6,456			£6,456
			June 1	Balance b/d	6,456

Profit and loss account for the year ended 31 May (extracts)

			£	£
19X6	Depreciation	– lease	2,000	
		– motor van	605	
				2,605
19X7	Depreciation	– lease	2,000	
		– motor van	363	
				2,363

Balance sheet as at 31 May (extracts)

		£	£
19X6	Lease at cost	40,000	
	Less: Accumulated depreciation	8,000	
			32,000
	Motor van at cost	7,000	
	Less: Accumulated depreciation	6,093	
			907
19X7	Lease at cost	40,000	
	Less: Accumulated depreciation	10,000	
			30,000
	Motor van at cost	7,000	
	Less: Accumulated depreciation	6,456	
			544

4.4 Using a depreciation expense account

When accounting for depreciation it is sometimes the practice to debit the annual depreciation charge to a depreciation expense account rather than directly to the profit and loss account. The appropriate accounting entries would therefore be:

- Debit   Depreciation expense account
- Credit   Provision for depreciation account

               with the annual depreciation charge.

The balance on the depreciation expense account is transferred to the profit and loss account when the final accounts are prepared. Hence, the accounting entries will be:

- Debit   Profit and loss account
- Credit   Depreciation expense account

               with the amount of the annual depreciation charge.

This approach adds a further stage to the process of accounting for depreciation. In an examination, where there is severe time pressure, this approach is not recommended. However, the depreciation expense account can be useful as it will be debited with annual depreciation charges relating to each type of asset, with the total depreciation charge being debited to the profit and loss account.

5 DISPOSAL OF FIXED ASSETS

5.1 Introduction

It was stated above that when calculating the amount to be depreciated, estimates must be made concerning the useful life of the asset and the residual value. These estimates may prove to be inaccurate and, thus, when the asset is disposed of, some adjustment will be necessary. If it proves that the total depreciation charge had been underestimated an additional charge to cover under-depreciation must be made in the profit and loss account for the year in which the asset is disposed. Similarly, if it proves that the total depreciation charge had been overestimated, the profit and loss account in the year of the asset disposal should be credited with the excess depreciation relating to the asset.

The following example can be used to illustrate the way in which under- or over-depreciation can be calculated.

Example

A business purchased cleaning equipment on 1 January 19X3 for £3,000 cash. The business depreciated the equipment at the rate of 20% per annum using the straight-line method. The equipment is sold on 1 January 19X5 for £1,750. The business has its accounting year end on 31 December.

What adjustment is required on disposal of the asset?

Solution

The adjustment necessary, as a result of disposal of the asset, can be calculated as follows:

	£
Cost of equipment	3,000
Less: Accumulated depreciation	
(2 years @ £600 pa)	1,200
Written-down value	1,800
Sales proceeds	1,750
Under-depreciation	£50

It can be seen that the sale proceeds are £50 less than the written-down value and, therefore, an additional charge to the profit and loss account is required. This charge is referred to as either under-depreciation or loss on sale. Where the selling price is in excess of the written-down value the profit and loss account is credited with over-depreciation or profit on sale.

5.2   Accounting for asset disposal

The disposal of a fixed asset must be recorded in the accounts. The first step is to open a fixed asset disposal account. A separate disposal account will typically be opened for each class of asset. Once this has been done the original cost of the asset must be transferred to the disposal account. The relevant accounting entries are:

- Debit   Asset disposal account
- Credit   Asset account with the cost of the asset

These entries eliminate the asset disposed of from the asset account. The second step is to transfer the accumulated depreciation relating to the asset to the asset disposal account. The accounting entries are:

- Debit   Provision for depreciation account
- Credit   Asset disposal account

  with the amount of accumulated depreciation

  relating to the asset being disposed of.

These entries eliminate the relevant accumulated depreciation from the provision for depreciation account.

The third step is to transfer the sale proceeds to the asset disposal account. The accounting entries are:

- Debit   Cash/Bank/Debtor account
- Credit   Asset disposal account

    with the sale proceeds.

Once the above entries have been completed the balancing figure on the asset disposal account will represent under- or over-depreciation arising on disposal. This balance will be transferred to the profit and loss account at the end of the accounting period.

Example

These accounting entries can be illustrated using the information contained in the previous example:

Cleaning equipment

19X3		£	19X5		£
January 1	Cash	3,000	January 1	Disposal	3,000
		£3,000			£3,000

Provision for depreciation – cleaning equipment

19X3		£	19X3		£
December 31	Balance c/d	600	December 31	Profit and loss	600
		£600			£600
19X4			19X4		
December 31	Balance c/d	1,200	January 1	Balance b/d	600
			December 31	Profit and loss	600
		£1,200			£1,200
19X5			19X5		
January 1	Disposal	£1,200	January 1	Balance b/d	£1,200

Disposal – cleaning equipment

19X5		£	19X5			£
January 1	Cleaning equipment	3,000	January	1	Provision for depreciation	1,200
				1	Cash – sale proceeds	1,750
			December 31		Profit and loss under-depreciation	50
		£3,000				£3,000

5.3   Disposals during an accounting year

In practice, fixed assets can be purchased and sold at any time during the accounting year. It is important, therefore, to be clear about how to deal with purchases and sales occurring part way through a year. Typically, one of two approaches is used to deal with this:

1   To calculate a depreciation charge for assets purchased or disposed of during the year based on the fraction of the year for which the asset is held.

2   To provide a full year's depreciation in the year of purchase and none in the year of disposal irrespective of the period for which the asset is held.

In an examination it is necessary to read the question carefully to see which of the two approaches is required. Where no indication of the required approach is given it is advisable to use the first method cited.

5.4   Activity

At the beginning of the financial year commencing on 1 April 19X5, a company had a balance on plant account of £372,000 and on provision for depreciation of plant account of £205,400.

The company's policy is to provide depreciation using the reducing-balance method applied to the fixed assets held at the end of the financial year at the rate of 20% per annum.

On 1 September 19X5 the company sold for £13,700 some plant which it had acquired on 31 October 19X1 at a cost of £36,000. Additionally, installation costs totalled £4,000. During 19X3 major repairs costing £6,300 had been carried out on this plant and, in order to increase the capacity of the plant, a new motor had been fitted in December 19X3 at a cost of £4,400. A further overhaul costing £2,700 had been carried out during 19X4.

The company acquired new replacement plant on 30 November 19X5 at a cost of £96,000, inclusive of installation charges of £7,000.

Calculate

(a)   the balance of plant at cost at 31 March 19X6

(b)   the provision for depreciation of plant at 31 March 19X6

(c)   the profit or loss on disposal of the plant.

5.5   Activity solution

		£	£
(a)	Plant at cost 1 April 19X5		372,000
	Less: Disposals during the year – plant	36,000	
	– Installation costs	4,000	
	– New motor	4,400	
			44,400
			327,600
	Add: Acquisitions during the year		96,000
	Plant at cost 31 March 19X6		£423,600

Note that the cost of repairs and overhauls did not form part of the cost of the plant disposed of.

		£	£
(b)	Provision for depreciation at 1 April 19X5		205,400
	Less: Depreciation relating to asset sold		
	– year to 31 March 19X2 (20% × £40,000)	8,000	
	– year to 31 March 19X3		
	(20% × (£40,000–£8,000))	6,400	
	– year to 31 March 19X4		
	(20% × (40,000–£14,400+£4,400))	6,000	
	– year to 31 March 19X5		
	(20% × (£44,400–£20,400))	4,800	
			25,200
			180,200
	Add: Depreciation for the year		
	(20% × (423,600–£180,200))		48,680
	Provision for depreciation at 31 March 19X6		228,880

(c)	Cost of plant disposed of	44,400
	Less: Accumulated depreciation	25,200
	Written-down value	19,200
	Proceeds on sale	13,700
	Loss on disposal	£5,500

6 SSAP 12 – ACCOUNTING FOR DEPRECIATION

6.1 Detail of SSAP 12

SSAP 12 (see the first page of this chapter) deals with accounting for depreciation. In general the standard follows the approach set out in this chapter. Some of the detail contained in SSAP 12 will be discussed later in chapter 21 of this text.

7 CHAPTER SUMMARY

- This chapter has introduced you to the concept of depreciation. You should be aware that depreciation is a process of allocation of cost, rather than a process of valuation.

- Alternative approaches are possible, giving different figures for the depreciation expense. The two most common methods are straight-line depreciation and reducing-balance depreciation. Their use will depend on the type of asset and its pattern of use. Each method can be calculated using mathematical formulas, but their use depends ultimately on the accountant's judgement. Clearly accounting is not a precise science.

- The chapter also covered the treatment of fixed assets and depreciation in the ledger accounts, including methods for dealing with the disposal of fixed assets.

8 SELF TEST QUESTIONS

8.1 The purpose of depreciation is:
   (a) to set aside an amount out of profits to provide for asset replacement
   (b) to ensure that expenses for a period contain some measure of the amount of an asset consumed in generating revenue for that period
   (c) to ensure that fixed assets are shown at their current market value on the balance sheet
   (d) to arrive at a conservative calculation of profits for the period. (1.1)

8.2 Define the residual value of a fixed asset. (1.4)

8.3 State a formula for calculating the annual depreciation charge using the straight-line method. (2.2)

8.4 What is the correct accounting entry to reflect the upwards revaluation of a fixed asset?
   (3.3)

8.5 What entries are made in a fixed asset disposal ledger account? (5.2)

8.6 Does SSAP 12 require the use of the straight-line method? (6.1)

9 EXAMINATION TYPE QUESTIONS

9.1 Following Terms

(a) Explain the following terms as used by accountants:
   (i) asset
   (ii) fixed asset

        (iii)   current asset

        (iv)   depreciation.

(b)   Do you regard each of the following as an asset of a business for accounting purposes? Explain your answers.

        (i)   a screwdriver bought some years ago

        (ii)   a machine hired by the business

        (iii)   the good reputation of the business with its customers.

(c)   The fixed assets in the balance sheet of a company have been summarised as follows:

			£m
Land at valuation			3
Buildings at cost			1
Plant and equipment	– cost	2.0	–
	– depreciation	1.5	0.5
			£4.5

Explain the meaning of this £4.5m figure to one of the company's shareholders, and comment on its relevance from a shareholder's point of view. **(15 marks)**

(ACCA, June 1992)

9.2   Firm Estimates

A firm buys a fixed asset for £10,000. The firm estimates that the asset will be used for 5 years, and will have a scrap value of about £100, less removal expenses. After exactly $2\frac{1}{2}$ years, however, the asset is suddenly sold for £5,000. The firm always provides a full year's depreciation in the year of purchase and no depreciation in the year of disposal.

(a)   Write up the relevant accounts (including disposal account but not profit and loss account) for each of years 1, 2 and 3:

        (i)   Using the straight-line depreciation method (assume 20% pa);

        (ii)   Using the reducing-balance depreciation method (assume 40% pa).

(b)   (i)   What is the purpose of depreciation? In what circumstances would each of the two methods you have used be preferable?

        (ii)   What is the meaning of the net figure for the fixed asset in the balance sheet at the end of year 2?

(c)   If the asset was bought at the beginning of year 1, but was not used at all until year 2 (and it is confidently anticipated to last until year 6), state under each method the appropriate depreciation charge in year 1, and briefly justify your answer. **(20 marks)**

9.3   Providing depreciation

(a)   To what extent, and in what way, if at all, does providing depreciation ensure that a business can afford to replace its fixed assets?

(b)   If profits are good and liabilities are bad, why are they on the same side of the balance sheet? **(8 marks)**

(ACCA, June 1991)

9.4   Accounting Terms

(a)   Explain clearly the following accounting terms in a manner which an intelligent non-accountant could understand in the context of a profit-oriented organisation:

(i)   expense

(ii)   matching

(iii)   prudence

(iv)   objectivity.

(b)   Your client has received the following invoice, and has come to you for advice.

'From: Marketing Services plc

Due for our services for the three months 1 October to 31 December 19X2.

	£
Agreed monthly fee for general advice three months at £1,000 per month	3,000
Supply of new colour photocopier on 1.10.X2, with five year guarantee, for use by your marketing department	10,000
Deposit paid by us on your behalf for television advertising time in February 19X3	5,000
Full cost of advertising campaign in newspaper, from 1 November to 30 November 19X2	50,000

Payable in total by 31.1.X3.'

Required

Write a letter to your client suggesting, for each of the four items on the invoice, how each item is likely to affect the expenses figure for the accounting year ended 31 December 19X2. You should explain your suggestions, and justify them by reference to accounting conventions.

(15 marks)

(ACCA, December 1992)

10   ANSWERS TO EXAMINATION TYPE QUESTIONS

10.1   Following Terms

(a)   An **asset** is a probable future benefit obtained or controlled by a particular business as a result of some past transactions or events affecting the business.

A **fixed asset** is an asset which is acquired by a business with the intention of retaining it, with a view to generating profit.

A **current asset** is an asset which arises from day-to-day trading activities, which is expected to change its state in the short term.

Depreciation is a measure of the wearing out, consumption or other reduction in the useful economic life of an asset, whether arising from use, time or obsolescence. It is an allocation of the differences between cost and residual value of the asset, spread over its useful life.

(b)   (i)   Strictly yes. In practice materiality will have caused the cost to have been treated as an expense on acquisition.

        (ii)   No, such a machine cannot normally be an asset as it has not been acquired, nor can it be completely controlled by the business.

        (iii)   No, since it has not been acquired, nor is it easily measurable in money terms.

(c)   The £4.5m consists of land at valuation, buildings at cost, and depreciated plant. When the land was valued and the time the buildings were purchased are relevant facts. If the valuation is recent, but the buildings were purchased several years ago, adding these two figures together is like adding apples and oranges. The figure for plant net of depreciation reflects a process of allocation rather than valuation. It is doubtful whether this amalgamation of figures adds much to the owner's understanding.

10.2   Firm Estimates

(a)   (i)

Fixed asset account

		£			£
Year 1	Bank (creditor)	10,000	Year 3	Disposal	10,000

Provision for depreciation – fixed assets account

		£			£
Year 1	Balance c/d	1,980	Year 1	Profit and loss	1,980
Year 2	Balance c/d	3,960	Year 2	Balance b/d	1,980
				Profit and loss	1,980
		£3,960			£3,960
Year 3	Disposal a/c	£3,960	Year 3	Balance b/d	£3,960

Disposal of fixed asset account

		£			£
Year 3	Fixed asset at cost	10,000	Year 3	Prov. for depreciation	3,960
				Bank (debtor)	5,000
				'Loss' on sale – profit and loss	1,040
		£10,000			£10,000

(ii)

Fixed asset account

		£			£
Year 1	Bank (creditor)	10,000	Year 3	Disposal	10,000

Provision for depreciation – fixed asset account

		£			£
Year 1	Balance c/d	4,000	Year 1	Profit and loss	4,000
Year 2	Balance c/d	6,400	Year 2	Balance b/d	4,000
				Profit and loss	2,400
		£6,400			£6,400
Year 3	Disposal a/c	£6,400	Year 3	Balance b/d	£6,400

Disposal of fixed asset account

		£			£
Year 3	Fixed asset at cost	10,000	Year 3	Provision for depreciation	6,400
	Profit on sale- Profit and loss	1,400		Bank (debtor)	5,000
		£11,400			£11,400

(b)   (i)   To calculate profit for a period it is necessary to match expenses with the revenues they help earn. In determining the expenses for a period it is important to ensure that an amount is included to represent the amount of fixed assets consumed in the process of generating revenue. This amount is referred to as **depreciation.**

It can be argued that the pattern of depreciation charges relating to an asset should attempt to match the pattern of benefits derived from that asset. Thus, where the benefits of an asset are likely to be constant over its life the **straight-line method** of depreciation is appropriate. Where the benefits of an asset are high in the early years and decline in later years the **reducing-balance method** is appropriate.

The reducing-balance method is sometimes proposed where maintenance expenses relating to an asset increase over its useful life. In order to ensure total expenses (depreciation charge plus maintenance charges) remain constant it is necessary for the depreciation charge to decrease as maintenance charges increase.

(ii)   The net figure on the balance sheet at the end of year 2 is referred to as the **written-down value** (WDV) or **net book value** (NBV) of the asset. It represents the cost of the asset less the amounts depreciated to date. It is important to appreciate that depreciation is a process of allocation rather than valuation. That is, the written-down value reflects the unexpired cost rather than the current market value of the assets.

(c)   As depreciation is an attempt to match expenses with the revenues they help earn there should be no depreciation charge in year 1. The asset will generate no revenues in year 1.

10.3   Providing Depreciation

(a)   There is no direct connection between depreciation and providing funds for replacement. Depreciation is the allocation of cost over an asset's useful life. As such there will be an expense charged in the profit and loss account which will not require a cash outflow. Other things being equal this will result in a cash inflow. Whether other things *will* be equal is far from obvious. In practice funds raised from operating activities tend to be spent in a variety of ways. Even if an amount equal to the depreciation charged were to be set aside as a cash reserve, it is unlikely that the amount provided would enable the asset to be replaced, given inflation. Of course, in many instances, technological change means that the asset would be replaced by something fundamentally different from the original.

(b)   Both profits and liabilities represent claims on the assets of the business. Liabilities represent claims of external parties, while profits increase the claim of the owners.

10.4   Accounting Terms

(a)   The definitions of the four accounting terms are given in the Glossary.

(b)   Your letter should include the following points:

The £3,000 for general advice should be matched to the revenues which it helped to generate between 1 October and 31 December 19X2 (matching convention). This probably means that it should be treated as an expense in the accounting year ended 31 December 19X2. If the advice did not help to generate any revenues, the £3,000 should be written off immediately in 19X2 (prudence convention).

The photocopier will be used over more than one accounting period, therefore the depreciation (cost less residual value) must be matched against the revenues of the relevant periods. Thus the total depreciation must be apportioned to the accounting periods concerned (matching convention). This may be done on an equal basis (straight-line depreciation) or on some other basis. An estimate will need to be made of the economic life of the copier and of its residual value. These need to be estimated on a prudent basis (prudence convention).

The advertising which is to take place in 19X3 would normally be matched against the revenues which it helped to generate (matching convention). This would probably be the 19X3 revenues, therefore the £5,000 would be treated as an expense of 19X3. It could be argued that the £5,000 expenditure may not generate any revenues and therefore should be written off against the 19X2 revenues (prudence convention). This latter treatment would normally be seen as an excessively prudent approach, however.

Following the same logic as was used in respect of the £5,000 (above), the £50,000 would be written off against the revenues of 19X2 (matching convention). It could be argued that the £50,000 might help to generate revenues in 19X3, so some part of it should be matched to those revenues. This would normally be regarded as a breach of the prudence convention, however.

9 ACCOUNTING FOR STOCKS

INTRODUCTION AND LEARNING OBJECTIVES

This chapter aims to provide you with an understanding of the problems of valuing stock, and its effect on the calculation of the expense – cost of sales, and its consequent impact on profit. Various methods of recording stock and cost of sales will be discussed and illustrated.

The problems associated with the valuation of stocks of manufactured goods will be introduced. SSAP 9 will be outlined, and the 'lower of cost or net realisable value' rule discussed.

When you have studied this chapter you should be able to do the following:

- Explain the problems of stock valuation

- Demonstrate the major methods of recording and valuing stock

- Explain the importance of stock valuation in the measurement of profit and financial position.

1 THE VALUATION OF STOCKS (INVENTORY)

1.1 Introduction

The valuation of stock in a systematic and logical fashion is of vital importance when preparing the final accounts of a business. It has been seen in Chapters 3 and 4 that stock values are used in determining cost of sales, an important expense item, and therefore have an influence on the calculation of profit. In addition, stock held at the end of the year will appear in the balance sheet. In certain industries stock represents a substantial proportion of total assets held and can, therefore, influence the assessment of financial position.

The valuation of stock is not a straightforward process. Various methods of stock valuation exist and each method can result in different calculations of profit and financial position. However, before dealing with the different methods of stock valuation it is necessary to understand the ways in which stocks are recorded in the accounts of a business. This is because the type of recording procedure can influence the way in which particular valuation methods are employed.

There are two ways in which stocks may be recorded by a business, the periodic method and the continuous (perpetual) method. Both of these methods are considered below.

1.2 Periodic method

With this method all purchases of goods for stock are recorded in a purchases account. The appropriate accounting entries are:

- Debit   Purchases
- Credit   Trade creditors/cash

with cost of goods purchased.

Any returns of purchases would be recorded in a separate purchase returns account. The accounting entries are:

- Debit   Trade creditors/cash
- Credit   Purchase returns

with cost of goods returned.

While purchases less returns provide an indication of the net amount purchased during a year, it does not indicate the cost of the goods sold. To derive this figure an adjustment is necessary in respect of opening and closing stocks. The cost of sales figure is calculated as follows:

	£	£
Opening stock		x
Add: Purchases	x	
Less: Returns	x	
	x	
	x	
Less: Closing stock		x
Cost of sales		x

The closing stock figure is derived by physically counting and valuing stock held at the end of the period. The closing stock for the period is carried forward and becomes the opening stock for the next period. Hence it is only necessary to undertake a physical count and a valuation of closing stock as opening stock would have been counted and valued in the preceding period.

This method of recording stock is simple to operate and can be employed satisfactorily by a business which holds small quantities of stock. However, where a business holds large quantities of stock it is likely that managers will wish to monitor stock movements more closely. The periodic method does not provide an indication of stock balances held during the year. To derive such information for stock replacement decisions a physical count is necessary, which may be time-consuming and expensive.

It is important to recognise that under the periodic method a figure for closing stock is required in order to calculate cost of sales, and hence profit for the period. Where managers require monthly profit reports it would therefore be necessary to undertake a stock count and valuation at the end of each month.

1.3 Continuous (perpetual) method

Under this method, as the name implies, a continuous record of inflows and outflows of stock during a period is kept. A separate stock account is opened for each line of stock and by comparing inflows with outflows it is possible to calculate the balance of stock in hand at any point in time. A typical format for a stock account is shown below:

	Stock								
	Debit Goods received			Credit Goods issued			Balance		
Date	Quantity	Cost/unit £	Total cost £	Quantity	Cost/unit £	Total cost £	Quantity	Cost/unit £	Total cost £

When this method is employed a purchases account is not kept. Instead, *purchases of stock* are recorded in the appropriate stock account. The accounting entries are:

- Debit   Stock
- Credit   Trade creditors/cash

                 with cost of goods purchased.

When *goods are sold* the following entries are made:

- Debit Cost of sales
- Credit Stock

with the cost of the goods sold.

The balance on the cost of goods sold account at the end of the year is transferred to the trading account. It is important to note that the above double entry will be carried out in addition to the recording of the sale in the sales account and the customer's account/cash.

Where there are *purchase returns* the following entries are made:

- Debit Trade creditors/cash
- Credit Stock

with the cost of the goods returned.

Adoption of the continuous recording method does not dispense with the need for stock counts. A physical count will be necessary from time to time, perhaps annually, in order to maintain a check on the accuracy of the stock records.

2 STOCK VALUATION METHODS

2.1 Introduction

Stock valuation presents a problem where the cost of stock purchases changes during a period. In order to illustrate the problem consider the following example.

A builders merchant purchases sand for resale. During the month of June the following transactions took place:

June 1	Opening balance	10 tonnes @ £20
4	Purchases	8 tonnes @ £22
15	Purchases	6 tonnes @ £24
23	Purchases	4 tonnes @ £26
		28

During the month 20 tonnes of sand were sold, 9 tonnes on 6 June and 11 tonnes on 18 June.

At the end of the month the builders merchant has 8 tonnes (28 − 20) of sand remaining in stock. However, it would probably not be possible to identify when this was originally purchased. During the month the cost of the sand rose and therefore the cost of the remaining stock of sand cannot be determined with indisputable precision. In order to derive a figure for the cost of the remaining stock certain assumptions must be made. There are three main approaches to determining the cost of stock, each of which employs different assumptions. These three approaches are:

1   First in – first out (FIFO)
2   Last in – first out (LIFO)
3   Weighted average cost (AVCO)

2.2 First in – first out (FIFO)

This method derives the cost of stock as if the first item held in stock will be the first to be issued. This means the oldest stocks are assumed to be used first. It should be emphasised that this assumption concerning the flow of goods through the business need not correspond to the physical flow. It is simply a convenient way of deriving the cost. To illustrate how the FIFO method works, see below. In working through this example the continuous recording method is employed:

Date	Goods received			Goods issued			Balance		
	Quantity (tonnes)	Cost per tonne	Total cost	Quantity (tonnes)	Cost/unit tonne	Total cost	Quantity (tonnes)	Cost/unit tonne	Total cost
		£	£		£	£		£	£
June 1							10	20	200
4	8	22	176				10	20	200
							8	22	176
6				9	20	180	1	20	20
							8	22	176
15	6	24	144				1	20	20
							8	22	176
							6	24	144
18				1	20	20			
				8	22	176			
				2	24	48	4	24	96
23	4	26	104				4	24	96
							4	26	104

The stock account begins with the opening balance on 1 June of 10 tonnes @ £20 each. A further 8 tonnes costing £22 each are added on 4 June. On 6 June the first issue is taken from the opening balance of 10 tonnes leaving only 1 tonne @ £20 remaining. This procedure of pricing goods issued as if they come from the earlier stocks acquired is continued throughout.

At the end of the month the stock in hand is costed as if it consists of the most recent purchases (4 @ £24 plus 4 @ £26 = £200). The goods issued are costed as if they consist of the earlier purchases. This means that during a period of rising prices, the FIFO method will show the higher-priced (that is, the more recent) stocks remaining in stock at the period end and appearing on the balance sheet, and the lower-priced (that is, the less recent) stocks included in cost of sales during the period. This has led to the criticism that during a period of inflation the FIFO method tends to understate cost of sales and, hence, overstate profit. Stock appearing on the balance sheet, however, will tend to be shown at a realistic figure.

2.3   Last in – first out (LIFO)

With this method goods issued are costed as if the most recent stock purchased is the first used. It therefore applies the opposite assumption to the FIFO method. The previous example will again be used to show how the LIFO method operates. The continuous recording method is again employed.

Date	Goods received			Goods Issued			Balance		
	Quantity (tonnes)	Cost per tonne	Total cost	Quantity (tonnes)	Cost/unit tonne	Total cost	Quantity (tonnes)	Cost/unit tonne	Total cost
		£	£		£	£		£	£
June 1							10	20	200
4	8	22	176				8	22	176
							10	20	200
6				8	22	176			
				1	20	20	9	20	180
15	6	24	144				6	24	144
							9	20	180
				6	24	144			
				5	20	100	4	20	80
23	4	26	104				4	26	104
							4	20	80

The stock account again begins with the opening balance on 1 June of 10 tonnes @ £20 each and a further 8 tonnes costing £22 each are added on 4 June. On 6 June 9 tonnes of stock are issued. The first 8 of these are taken from the most recent purchases (that is, 8 tonnes @ £22 each) and the remaining tonne is taken from the earlier purchases (that is, 10 tonnes @ £20 each). This procedure of costing goods issued from the most recent purchases first is continued throughout.

At the end of the month the stock in hand consists of 4 tonnes @ £20 plus 4 @ £26 = £184. The goods issued, which will be transferred to the cost of sales account will be priced as if they consist of the more recent purchases. Thus during a period of rising prices the LIFO method will show the lower-priced (that is, the less recent) stocks remaining in stock at the period end and appearing on the balance sheet, and the higher-priced (that is, the more recent) stocks included in cost of sales during the period. The LIFO method has been supported as appropriate for inflationary conditions as it results in a realistic figure for cost of sales and, hence, profit. However, it has the disadvantage that stock values appearing on the balance sheet tend to be understated.

The LIFO method is not acceptable in the UK for tax purposes and this has reduced its practical importance.

2.4 Weighted average cost (AVCO)

With this method new stock enters into a common pool and loses its separate identity. The cost of new stock purchased is added to the cost of existing stock held and a weighted average cost is derived (the average cost being weighted according to quantity). All subsequent issues of stock are then recorded at that weighted average cost until further purchases of stock occur and a new weighted average figure is computed.

The same information that was used earlier will be used again to illustrate this method. The continuous recording method will again be employed.

Date	Goods received			Goods issued			Balance		
	Quantity (tonnes)	Cost per tonne	Total cost	Quantity (tonnes)	Cost/unit tonne	Total cost	Quantity (tonnes)	Cost/unit tonne	Total cost
		£	£		£	£		£	£
June									
1							10	20	200
4	8	22	176				8	22	176
							18	20.89	376
6				9	20.89	188	9	20.89	188
15	6	24	144				6	24	144
							15	22.13	332
18				11	22.13	243	4	22.13	89
23	4	26	104				4	46	104
							8	24.12	193

During a period of rising prices the AVCO method will produce a cost of sales figure and a closing stock figure which falls between the two extremes of FIFO and LIFO. However, this method is sometimes criticised on the grounds that the price at which stock is issued is somewhat artificial, in that stock may not have been purchased at that figure.

In our example the cost of stocks rose during the period. This resulted in each method producing a different cost of sales figure and a different closing stock value for the balance sheet:

	Cost of sales (total goods issued) £	Closing stock £
FIFO	424	200
LIFO	440	184
AVCO	431	193

However, the different valuation methods only result in different profit figures between years. Over the whole life of the business the total profits will be unaffected by the choice of stock valuation method.

It is important to recognise that the different figures produced by each method occurred as a result of changing prices. Where prices are constant each method will produce the same cost of goods sold and closing stock values.

2.5 Activity

Auto Supplies carries one item of stock which has the following details:

Balance at 1 November	20 units @ £40
Purchased 5 November	16 units @ £50
Purchased 9 November	20 units @ £60
Purchased 23 November	24 units @ £64

During November 42 units were sold. The business sold 18 units on 7 November and 24 units on 14 November. The business employs the continuous method of stock recording.

Calculate the cost of sales for November and the value of closing stock based on each of the three valuation methods discussed above.

2.6 Activity solution

FIFO

Date	Goods received			Goods issued			Balance		
	Quantity	Cost/ unit	Total cost	Quantity	Cost/ unit	Total cost	Quantity	Cost/ unit	Total cost
Nov		£	£		£	£		£	£
1							20	40	800
5	16	50	800				20	40	800
							16	50	800
7				18	40	720	2	40	80
							16	50	800
9	20	60	1,200				2	40	80
							16	50	800
							20	60	1,200
14				2	40	80			
				16	50	800			
				6	60	360	14	60	840
23	24	64	1,536				14	60	840
							24	64	1,536

Cost of sales (goods issued) £1,960   Closing stock £2,376

LIFO

Date	Goods received			Goods issued			Balance		
	Quantity	Cost/ unit	Total cost	Quantity	Cost/ unit	Total cost	Quantity	Cost/ unit	Total cost
Nov		£	£		£	£		£	£
1							20	40	800
5	16	50	800				16	50	800
							20	40	800
7				16	50	800			
				2	40	80			
							18	40	720
9	20	60	1,200				20	60	1,200
							18	40	720
14				20	60	1,200			
				4	40	160	14	40	560
23	24	64	1,536				24	64	1,536
							14	40	560

Cost of sales (goods issued) £2,240   Closing stock £2,096

AVCO

Date	Goods received			Goods issued			Balance		
	Quantity	Cost/ unit	Total cost	Quantity	Cost/ unit	Total cost	Quantity	Cost/ unit	Total cost
Nov		£	£		£	£		£	£
1							20	40	800
5	16	50	800				16	50	800
							36	44.44	1,600
7				18	44.44	800	18	44.44	800
9	20	60	1,200				20	60	1,200
							38	52.63	2,000
14				24	52.63	1,263	14	52.63	737
23	24	64	1,536				24	64	1,536
							38	59.82	2,273

Cost of sales (goods issued) £2,063   Closing stock £2,273

3 STOCK VALUATION METHODS RECONSIDERED

3.1 Introduction

When illustrating the operation of each stock valuation method above the continuous method of stock recording was employed. This continuous method permits a close matching of purchases and issues of stock. It is also possible, however, to operate each valuation method using the periodic method of stock recording. With the periodic method, issues of stock are not separately identified and recorded. It is therefore necessary to make some assumption about the point at which issues of stock occur. For purposes of calculation it is assumed that all issues occur on the last day of the accounting period.

To illustrate how each valuation method operates under the periodic method of stock recording the same basic information used in the examples in the previous section will continue to be used.

3.2   First in – first out (FIFO)

Cost of sales

As the first stocks purchased are costed as if they are the first to be sold the cost of sales figures will include the first 20 tonnes purchased.

Date June	Quantity (tonnes)	Cost per tonne £	Total cost £
1	10	20	200
4	8	22	176
15	2	24	48
			£424

Closing stocks

The stock remaining will represent the most recent acquisitions.

Date June	Quantity (tonnes)	Cost per tonne £	Total cost £
15	4	24	96
23	4	26	104
			£200

3.3   Last in – first out (LIFO)

Cost of sales

As the most recent stocks purchased are costed as if they are the first to be sold the cost of sales figure will include the last 20 tonnes purchased.

Date June	Quantity (tonnes)	Cost per tonne £	Total cost £
23	4	26	104
15	6	24	144
4	8	22	176
1	2	20	40
			£464

Closing stock

The stock remaining will represent the earliest acquisition.

Date June	Quantity (tonnes)	Cost per tonne £	Total cost £
1	8	£20	£160

3.4   Weighted average cost (AVCO)

The weighted average cost of all stocks purchased will be calculated at the end of the period.

Date June	Quantity (tonnes)	Cost per tonne £	Total cost £
1	10	20	200
4	8	22	176
15	6	24	144
23	4	26	104
	28		£624

$$\text{Average cost} \qquad \frac{£624}{28} \qquad = \qquad £22.28$$

Cost of sales

All stocks will be issued at the weighted average cost shown above. Hence, cost of goods sold will be:

20 tonnes @ £22.28 =   £446

Closing stock

Stock remaining at the end of the period will be valued at the weighted average cost shown above. Hence, closing stock will be:

8 @ £22.28 =   £178

3.5   Comparison of the systems

A comparison of stock valuation methods under each recording system reveals the following:

Cost of sales	Continuous £	Periodic £
FIFO	424	424
LIFO	440	464
AVCO	431	446

Closing stock	Continuous £	Periodic £
FIFO	200	200
LIFO	184	160
AVCO	193	178

As can be seen the FIFO method is unaffected by the stock recording procedures employed. However, the LIFO method produces a higher closing stock and lower cost of goods sold figure under the continuous method than the periodic method. This is due to the fact that, during a period of rising prices, stock issues (that is, cost of sales) under the continuous method will be at progressively higher amounts, whereas under the periodic method stock issues will be at the most recent prices. The AVCO method produces a higher closing stock figure and lower cost of sales under the continuous recording method than under the periodic recording method. This is because during a period of rising prices, stock issues under the continuous method are based on earlier, and therefore lower-priced, items. However, under the periodic method stock issues are weighted to include the most recently purchased, and therefore higher-priced items.

3.6   Activity

Refer to the information in the activity in paragraph 2.5. Calculate the cost of sales figure and closing stock value under the FIFO, LIFO and AVCO methods of stock valuation using the periodic system of stock recording.

3.7   Activity solution

FIFO

Cost of goods sold

Date	Quantity	Cost/unit £	Total £
Nov 1	20	40	800
Nov 5	16	50	800
Nov 9	6	60	360
	42		£1,960

Closing stock

Date	Quantity	Cost/unit £	Total £
Nov 9	14	60	840
Nov 23	24	64	1,536
	38		£2,376

LIFO

Cost of goods sold

Date	Quantity	Cost/unit £	Total £
Nov 23	24	64	1,536
Nov 9	18	60	1,080
	42		£2,616

Closing stock

Date	Quantity	Cost/unit £	Total £
Nov 9	2	60	120
Nov 5	16	50	800
Nov 1	20	40	800
	38		£1,720

AVCO

Date	Quantity	Cost/unit £	Total £
Nov 1	20	40	800
Nov 5	16	50	800
Nov 9	20	60	1,200
Nov 23	24	64	1,536
	80		£4,336

Weighted average cost – £4,336/80 = £54.20
Cost of goods sold
42 units £54.20 = £2,276
Closing stock
38 units £54.20 = £2,060

4   STOCKS OF MANUFACTURED GOODS

4.1   Different types of stocks held

When a business is engaged in the manufacture of goods it can hold three types of stocks: raw materials, work-in-progress (part finished goods) and finished goods. In the case of work-in-progress and finished goods it is necessary to be clear as to what may properly be included in the total cost, whichever method of stock valuation is employed. The cost of such stock will include all costs incurred in bringing the product to its current location and condition. This will include the cost of purchases of raw materials (including associated costs such as carriage and duties) and **conversion costs**. Conversion costs are any costs involved in converting raw materials to the final product. This will include labour, expenses directly related to the product and an appropriate share of production overheads.

By way of illustration, consider the following example.

Example

A business has the following details relating to production and sales for a year:

Sales 900 units at £600
1,000 units are produced with the following costs being incurred:
Opening stock 200 units at £100 each
Purchases 1,050 units at £100 each
Closing stock 250 units at £100 each

Production wages	£150,000
Production overheads	£100,000
Other overheads*	£100,000

*These relate to general administration, selling and distribution.

Given that production exceeds sales, the question inevitably arises about what should be the value attached to the closing stock. Should it incorporate a share of the wages and overheads, for instance?

Clearly cost of production should include an appropriate share of production wages and production overheads. Costs associated with other overheads are expenses of the business which cannot be deemed to be costs of production. The following profit calculation would seem appropriate:

	£	£
Sales (900 units)		540,000
Cost of production (1,000 units)		
Materials		
Opening stock	20,000	
Purchases	105,000	
	125,000	
Less: Closing stock	25,000	
Cost of materials used	100,000	
Wages	150,000	
Production overheads	100,000	
Cost of production (1,000)	350,000	
Less: Closing stock		
100 units at £350	35,000	
Cost of sales		315,000
Gross profit		225,000
General overheads		100,000
Net profit		£125,000

The costs of production are deemed to have been spread over the units produced. Any unsold units are then valued at a figure which reflects a share of these costs. This means that when the stock is eventually sold, the overheads associated with its manufacture will be properly matched with the revenues earned.

5 LOWER OF COST OR NET REALISABLE VALUE RULE

5.1 Application of the prudence convention

Determining the cost of stock does not solve the problem of valuation. The convention of prudence demands that a cautious view be taken of stock values appearing on the balance sheet. Thus, where it is estimated that the net realisable value (NRV) (selling price less associated selling costs) is below the cost of stock then the net realisable value is taken as the appropriate balance sheet figure. In most cases, particularly during a period of rising prices, net realisable value will be above the cost of stock. When this occurs the lower cost figure should be used in the balance sheet. It would not be appropriate to use net realisable value in this case as the convention of prudence demands that profits should not be recognised until they are realised. Where possible the comparison of cost with net realisable value should be made for each separate item of stock. However, if this is impractical groups or categories of stock can be compared.

By way of illustration consider the following example.

Example

A dealer in second-hand cars has 5 vehicles in stock at the end of the financial year. These are:

Car	Cost	Net realisable value
	£	£
Ford	2,300	3,100
Renault	5,500	5,300
Jaguar	3,800	4,500
Datsun	4,000	4,600
Vauxhall	1,800	1,900
	£17,400	£19,400

The value of the stock at 'the lower of cost and net realisable value' is:

Car	£
Ford	2,300
Renault	5,300
Jaguar	3,800
Datsun	4,000
Vauxhall	1,800
	£17,200

Note that the appropriate stock figure is not £17,400.

5.2 Activity

A business has an item of stock which had cost it £1,000. It is now obsolete and cannot be used for production purposes without modification costing £300, after which it could be used as a substitute for another product which would cost £800 to purchase.

What value should be included in the balance sheet for this item?

5.3 Activity solution

Cost = £1,000

Net realisable value = £800 – £300 = £500

∴ Lower cost and net realisable value = £500

5.4   Activity

A business has included in its accounts an item of stock which had cost it £10,000. The business has no further use for this stock. It can be scrapped for £5,000 or sold for the following:

	£
Sale proceeds	8,000
Less: Trade discount	800
	7,200
Less: Cash discount	200
	7,000
Less: Costs of disposal	500
	£6,500

What figure should be included in the accounts for this item?

5.5   Activity solution

Since it is more beneficial to sell the stock rather than scrap it it is the sale figures which are relevant. The net realisable value is £6,700, that is the final figure shown plus the cash discount. The discount would appear in the profit and loss account.

6   SSAP 9 – STOCKS AND LONG-TERM CONTRACTS

6.1   Key points of SSAP 9

SSAP 9 deals with the problems of valuation of stock and work-in-progress. Essentially it formalises much of what has been said so far in the chapter. The standard aims to develop greater uniformity in the valuation methods used and in the information disclosed in financial statements. We shall consider SSAP 9 in rather more detail in chapter 21.

6.2   Stock adjustments

One type of examination question involving stocks requires a recalculation of the final stock figure of a business. Adjustments to the stock figure provided may have to be made to correct errors or to ensure stocks are valued in accordance with recognised accounting principles. When tackling this type of question it is important, where necessary, to apply the 'lower of cost or net realisable value' rule discussed above. It may also be important to ensure that all stocks owned by the business are included wherever they may be located. Thus, goods sold to customers on a sale or return basis, for example, will be included as part of the stocks owned by a business unless the customer has signified acceptance of the goods.

7   CHAPTER SUMMARY

- This chapter has identified the importance of stock valuation in the calculation of profit and the establishment of financial position. The periodic and continuous methods were discussed, as were the systems of FIFO, LIFO and AVCO. The problems of valuing stocks of manufactured goods were briefly discussed as was the 'lower of cost or net realisable value' rule.

8   SELF TEST QUESTIONS

8.1   During a period of rising prices which method of stock valuation will give the highest profit figure for the period?

(a)   FIFO

(b)   LIFO

(c)   AVCO (2.4)

8.2   During a period of rising prices which method of stock valuation will give the highest closing stock figure?

    (a)   FIFO

    (b)   LIFO

    (c)   AVCO (2.4)

8.3   A second-hand car dealer has three cars in stock at the year end, as follows:

	Cost £	Realisable value £
A	10,000	8,000
B	10,000	12,000
C	10,000	11,000

What figure should appear for stock in the balance sheet? (5.1)

8.4   Explain what is meant by the statement 'Stock is valued at cost'.

What are the main difficulties associated with this statement? (4.1, 5.1)

9   EXAMINATION TYPE QUESTIONS

9.1   Businessperson

A businessperson started trading with a capital in cash of £6,000 which was placed in the business bank account at the outset.

The transactions, none of which were on credit, were as follows (in date sequence) for the first accounting period. All takings were banked immediately and all suppliers were paid by cheque. He traded in only one line of merchandise.

Purchases		Sales	
Quantity	Price per unit	Quantity	Price per unit
No	£	No	£
1,200	1.00		
1,000	1.05		
		800	1.70
600	1.10		
		600	1.90
900	1.20		
		1,100	2.00
800	1.25		
		1,300	2.00
700	1.30		
		400	2.05

In addition expenses of £1,740 were incurred, of which £570 were still owed at the end of the period.

Prepare separately using both the FIFO (first in – first out) and the LIFO (last in – first out) methods of stock valuation:

    (a)   a statement of cost of sales for the period

    (b)   a balance sheet at the end of the period.

Note: Workings are an integral part of the answer and must be shown.   **(22 marks)**

9.2 Managing Director

If you were the Managing Director of a business, which method of stock valuation (FIFO, LIFO, AVCO) would you use if you wished to:

(a) report the lowest profit figure

(b) report the highest profit figure

(c) show inventory at a figure which would be closest to its current cost

(d) best match cost of sales with revenue? **(10 marks)**

9.3 Idea

'The idea that stock should be included in accounts at the lower of historical cost and net realisable value follows the prudence convention but not the consistency convention.'

(a) Explain clearly what is meant by:

    (i) historic cost

    (ii) net realisable value

    (iii) prudence convention

    (iv) consistency convention.

(b) Do you agree with the quotation? Why or why not?

(c) Explain, giving reasons, whether you think this idea (that stocks should be included in accounts of the lower of historical cost and net realisable value) is a generally useful one. Refer to at least two classes of user of financial accounting reports in your answer.

(10 marks)

10 ANSWERS TO EXAMINATION TYPE QUESTIONS

10.1 Businessperson

(a)

Cost of sales (FIFO)

Quantity	Cost per unit £	Total cost £
800	1.00	800
400	1.00	400
200	1.05	210
600		
800	1.05	840
300	1.10	330
1100		
300	1.10	330
900	1.20	1,080
100	1.25	125
1300		
400	1.25	500
		£4,615

Cost of sales (LIFO)

Quantity	Cost per unit	Total cost
800	1.05	840
600	1.10	660
900	1.20	1,080
200	1.05	210
1100		
800	1.25	1,000
500	1.00	500
1300		
400	1.30	520
		£4,810

(b)

Balance sheet at end of period (FIFO)

	£	£
Stock (see workings)		1,285
Bank (see workings)		7,050
		£8,335
Opening capital	6,000	
Net profit (see workings)	1,765	7,765
Creditors		570
		£8,335

Balance sheet at end of period (LIFO)

	£	£
Stock (see workings)		1,090
Bank (see workings)		7,050
		£8,140
Opening capital	6,000	
Net profit (see workings)	1,570	7,570
Creditors		570
		£8,140

Workings

Purchases and sales calculations

Purchases			Sales		
Quantity	Cost per unit £	Total cost £	Quantity	Price per unit £	Total price £
1200	1.00	1,200	800	1.70	1,360
1000	1.05	1,050	600	1.90	1,140
600	1.10	660	1100	2.00	2,200
900	1.20	1,080	1300	2.00	2,600
800	1.25	1,000	400	2.05	820
700	1,30	910			
		£5,900			£8,120

Closing stock calculation

Closing stock = Purchases – Cost of sales

FIFO closing stock = £5,900 – £4,615 = £1,285

LIFO closing stock = £5,900 – £4,810 = £1,090

Profit calculation

	FIFO £	LIFO £
Sales	8,120	8,120
Less: Cost of sales	4,615	4,810
Gross profit	3,505	3,310
Less: Expenses	1,740	1,740
Net profit	£1,765	£1,570

Closing bank balance calculation

	£	£
Opening balance		6,000
Add: Cash from sales		8,120
		14,120
Less: Cash for purchases	5,900	
Expenses (£1,740 – £570)	1,170	7,070
Closing balance		£7,050

10.2   Managing Director

(a)   On the assumption that stock prices are rising, LIFO. If they are constant it will make no difference. If they are falling, FIFO.

(b)   On the assumption that stock prices are rising, FIFO. If they are constant it will make no difference. If they are falling, LIFO.

(c)   Under normal circumstances FIFO will result in stock being included in the balance sheet at values which reflect the latest prices borne. Given that these values reflect the latest prices paid by the business for goods actually bought, there may still be a considerable difference between the value included in the balance sheet and the current value.

(d)   Matching is best achieved by setting the expenses used up against revenues. LIFO comes closest to doing this. Nevertheless it should be recognised that ultimately the best matching is revenues and current cost. Current cost represents an opportunity cost, but does not quite fit the normal definition of historic cost, and is not used for measuring profit. Whether it should be used remains a relevant question, which will be briefly addressed later in this book. It is permitted by the Companies Act 1985, subject to a revaluation reserve being introduced.

10.3   Idea

(a)   (i)   Historic cost is the original price paid for an item.

(ii)   Net realisable value is the amount which it is expected can be obtained for an asset, less any trade discounts and any other costs associated with completion of the item or subsequent disposal.

(iii)   Prudence is a convention which states that when there is doubt about a figure the accountant should err on the cautious side.

(iv)   Consistency is a convention which states that various accounting policies, assumptions and methods should be followed consistently.

(b)   On the face of it the quotation is true. However, prudence is the more important convention.

(c)   The advantage is one of prudence. Both creditors and shareholders are likely to prefer a situation in which they can rely on the fact that all anticipated losses are recognised in the accounts.

10 ACCOUNTING FOR DEBTORS AND BAD AND DOUBTFUL DEBTS

INTRODUCTION AND LEARNING OBJECTIVES

Where a business sells goods and services on credit, it must accept that there is a risk that some customers will not pay the amount due. Well-managed businesses take care not to sell on credit where there is a high probability of default. They also establish systems and routines to try to ensure that all trade debts are collected within a reasonable time. Despite this, even the best managed businesses accept that, almost inevitably, some trade debts will turn 'bad'. Thus, at any point in time, the total debtors outstanding may include debtors who will fail to pay.

In this chapter we consider the problems of bad or doubtful debts. We begin by considering the problem of bad debts and go on to explain how they are dealt with in the accounts. We then consider the problem of doubtful debts and the reasons why this form of debt should be treated differently in the accounts. We shall see that bad and doubtful debts raise important issues concerning the recognition of revenue and the portrayal of financial position. We shall also see that this is another area where subjective judgement must be exercised in order to derive the profit or loss for the period and the financial position at the end of the period.

When you have studied this chapter you should be able to do the following:

*   Distinguish between bad and doubtful debts

*   Account for bad debts in the ledger accounts

*   Account for doubtful debts in the ledger accounts

*   Account for bad debts who subsequently pay what is due.

---

1   BAD DEBTS

1.1   Introduction

When preparing a balance sheet it is important to ensure that proper account is taken of the problem of non-payment. Failure to take this into account could mean that the assets of debtors would be overstated and the balance sheet would therefore contravene the prudence convention and present a misleading picture. Thus, to ensure that the debtors figure on the balance sheet represents a realistic estimate of *recoverable* debts some adjustment to the total debtors figure may be necessary. Once it has become reasonably certain that a particular debtor will not pay all or part of a debt, the amount concerned should be written off (treated as an expense). Note that there is no question of cancelling the original sale when a debt is recognised as being bad.

It is important to be clear about the distinction between a bad debt and a sales return. Typically, sales are realised in accordance with the realisation convention, that is, when the goods or services pass to the customer and are accepted. If it is subsequently conceded by the seller that the goods or services were faulty, the seller will cancel the sale by accepting a sales return. As a result the customer's trade debtor account (assuming a credit sale) will be credited. The corresponding debit entry will be made either directly into the sales account or in a sales returns account. The overall effect of a sales return is to cancel the debt in the customer's account and to cancel the sale, so that the sales figure (net of any returns) in the trading account for the period reflects sales *accepted* by the customer.

By contrast, when a bad debt is recognised, the fact that the goods or services had originally been passed to, and been accepted by, the customer is not affected. The occurrence of a bad debt means that what had been believed to be, and had been treated as, an asset, is now known not to be an asset, but a trade debt. Thus, an expense needs to be recognised. When a bad debt is recognised it is charged as an expense in the profit and loss account. The corresponding credit entry is made in the account of the debtor concerned.

It should be said here that one of the reasons for a bad debt arising is as a result of a dispute. The buyer may believe that the sale should be cancelled as he believes that the goods or services were lacking in some respect. The seller may disagree and refuse to accept a sales return.

The overall effect on net profit is identical, irrespective of whether an item is treated as a sales return or as a bad debt. However, the gross profit will be different according to the treatment. Since the gross profit figure is regarded as a useful measure of sales effectiveness, it is important that sales returns and bad debts are clearly distinguished and correctly treated.

1.2   Bad debts and the matching convention

Following the matching convention, expenses should be charged in the same accounting period, as far as possible, as that in which the revenues to which they relate are recognised. Thus it is necessary to charge bad debts to the accounting period in which the sale which gave rise to the debt concerned was recognised. This can pose problems where, as will typically be the case in practice, trade debts are outstanding at the end of an accounting period. It is quite likely that some of these debts, unpaid at the end of the period in which the sale was made, will prove to go bad in the subsequent accounting period. To comply with the matching convention, and to ensure that period-end trade debtors are not overstated, it is necessary to make a judgement about the extent of the bad debt potential of the trade debts at the end of the accounting period and to treat that amount as an expense. The period-end trade debtors can thus be reduced by this amount, ensuring, as far as possible, that they are not overstated. More detail on how this is done in practice is given below.

1.3   Accounting for bad debts

Where there is evidence to suggest that a debt is irrecoverable the amount outstanding cannot be regarded as an asset, as it is incapable of providing future benefits. In such circumstances it is necessary to write off the debt, resulting in a reduction in the appropriate trade debtors account. If the bad debt relates to a sale made during the same accounting period, it will be regarded as an expense of that period and be charged to the profit and loss account. If the bad debt relates to a sale made in an earlier period the treatment set out in the next section (Doubtful debts) must be followed.

The remainder of this section assumes that the bad debts identified relate to sales made in the current accounting period.

When a bad debt has been identified the amount must be transferred from the individual debtor's account to a bad debts account. The accounting entries are:

Debit   Bad debts
Credit   The individual debtor's account
           with the amount of the bad debt

This will eliminate the asset in the books and record the relevant amount as an expense.

At the end of the accounting period it will be necessary to write off the bad debts by transferring the balance on the bad debts account to the profit and loss account. The accounting entries will be:

Debit   Profit and loss
Credit   Bad debts
           with the total bad debts for the period

In order to illustrate these accounting entries consider the following example.

Example

The Mayflower Secretarial Agency found that during the accounting year ended 31 December 19X6 two clients failed to pay the amounts due. Mr A. Black owed £120 and Ms J. Green owed £85, both of which amounts arose from credit sales made during the year ended 31 December 19X6. It was believed that both amounts were irrecoverable. In order to write off the debts the accounting entries would be as follows:

Mr A. Black

19X6			£	19X6			£
September	10	Fees	120	December	31	Bad debts	120
			£120				£120

Ms J. Green

19X6			£	19X6			£
November	15	Fees	85	December	31	Bad debts	85
			£85				£85

Bad debts

19X6			£	19X6			£
December	31	Mr A. Black	120	December	31	Profit and loss	205
		Ms J. Green	85				
			£205				£205

Profit and loss account for the year ended 31 December 19X6 (extract)

	£
Bad debts written off	205

1.4 Bad debts subsequently recovered

Occasionally an amount due may be treated as a bad debt and written off in the relevant accounting period, and the amount due may eventually be received in a later period. When this occurs the amount is recognised as a revenue in the period in which it is received. The accounting entries will be:

Debit	Cash/Bank account
Credit	Bad debts recovered account
	with the amount recovered

At the end of the accounting period the balance on the bad debts recovered account will be transferred to the profit and loss account. Hence, the accounting entries will be:

Debit	Bad debts recovered account
Credit	Profit and loss account
	with the total amount recovered during the period

An alternative approach to dealing with bad debts recovered is to credit the amount to the bad debt account. The amounts recovered would therefore be offset against the bad debts for that period. However, this is a less informative approach than the method outlined above.

2   DOUBTFUL DEBTS

2.1   The application of prudence

As has already been pointed out, the trade debtors at the end of an accounting period may be overstated. It is thus necessary at the end of each accounting period to estimate the extent of potential bad debts in the existing trade debts, taking a prudent view of the matter. Any bad debts written off represent debts which the business is reasonably certain cannot be recovered. However, there may also be debts outstanding at the year end which are uncertain of recovery but which cannot be categorised as bad debts at the year end. Following the convention of conservatism, these doubtful debts must also be taken into account by the business.

There are two approaches to estimating the amount of the doubtful debts associated with the debtors at the end of a period. The first approach involves an examination of the individual debtors' accounts in the sales ledger and deriving a total of those considered doubtful. The second approach relies on past experience to identify a likely proportion of total debtors which may prove irrecoverable. With this approach an overall percentage may be applied to the debtors figure to derive the amount of doubtful debts. Alternatively, a different percentage may be applied to each age category of debtors. In the table below the debts are categorised according to age and the doubtful debt percentage rises as the period outstanding increases. The longer the period outstanding the greater the risk that a debt will prove to be bad.

Age categories of debtors			
Period	**Amount outstanding**	**Doubtful debts provision**	**Amount of outstanding**
	£	%	£
1–30 days	60,000	1	600
31–60 days	20,000	2	400
61–90 days	12,000	4	480
91–120 days	6,000	8	480
>120 days	3,000	10	300
			£2,260

2.2   Accounting for doubtful debts

Once the amount of the period-end doubtful debt figure is deduced, the accounting entry is:

Debit   Profit and loss account

Credit   Provision for doubtful debts account (often also known as bad debt provision) with that figure

A provision is usually defined as an amount set aside out of profit to provide for any known expense, the amount of which cannot be accurately determined.

The doubtful debt provision at the end of an accounting period serves two purposes:

- It is deducted from the trade debtors figure in the balance sheet so that the net figure is a prudent estimate of the realisable value of those debts. It should be recognised that the provision for doubtful debts represents a total provision. As such it need not, and typically cannot, be identified with individual debtors

- It provides a credit balance against which bad debts arising from the period-end debts will be written off.

2.3 Recognition of bad debts

The treatment shown so far deals with:

1 The writing off of bad debts in the period in which the associated sale was recognised

2 The setting up of a provision against which can be set any bad debts which arise in future periods on sales associated with the current or previous periods.

This still leaves unanswered the question as to how bad debts which arise in future accounting periods should be treated. The answer is that when a debt associated with a sale recognised in a past accounting period is recognised as being irrecoverable the entries are:

Debit	Provision for doubtful debts account
Credit	The individual debtor's account
	with the amount of the bad debt

Any amount remaining on the provision account at the end of the subsequent accounting period is either explicitly credited to the profit and loss account of that period, or netted against the bad and doubtful debt expense of the period. Such an amount represents an over-provision for doubtful debts.

Any shortfall in the amount of the provision means that bad debts arising in the current period from previous period sales could not be fully covered by the provision and would need to be written off to the current period profit and loss account as an expense.

2.4 Summary of accounting entries

The entries relating to bad and doubtful debts can be summarised as follows:

Bad debts arising in the period in which the associated revenue was recognised

Debit	Bad debts account
Credit	Individual debtor account

At the period end the balance on the bad debts account will be transferred to the profit and loss account thus

Debit	Profit and loss account
Credit	Bad debts account

Doubtful debts in the period end debtors

Debit	Profit and loss account
Credit	Provision for doubtful debts

Bad debts arising in a period subsequent to that in which the associated revenue was recognised

Debit	Provision for doubtful debts account
Credit	Individual debtor account

Any balance remaining on the provision for doubtful debts account will be transferred to the profit and loss account of a subsequent accounting period. If bad debts written off to the provision account exceed the amount of the provision, the balance will be written off to the profit and loss account as an expense. If bad debts written off to the provision account are less than the amount of the provision the balance will be written off to the profit and loss account as a revenue.

Bad debts recovered

Debit	Cash/bank account
Credit	Bad debts account (if recovered in the period in which they were written off)
	or
	Bad debts recovered account (if recovered in a subsequent period)

The balance on the bad debts recovered account will be transferred to the profit and loss account at the end of the period.

The balance sheet at the period end will show debtors (after bad debts have been written off), less the amount of the provision for doubtful debts, which should result in a prudent figure appearing.

Example

Video Supplies maintains just one total trade debtors account to which are debited all credit sales. The business keeps a copy of each credit sales invoice on a file until payment has been received. In this way a check can be kept on the makeup of the balance on the trade debtors account. Video Supplies started trading on 1 January 19X3.

The following relates to Video Supplies during its first five years of trading:

Year ended	Total credit sales	Total cash received from debtors	Bad debts written off arising from credit sales in:	
			current year	previous year
	£	£	£	£
19X3	42,100	38,300	200	–
19X4	48,800	47,900	250	150
19X5	50,500	49,700	200	100
19X6	44,300	44,400	200	200
19X7	47,700	47,200	100	200

Video Supplies created a provision for doubtful debts of 5% of the trade debtors balance carried down at each year end. £100 of the 19X7 cash receipts related to a debt previously written off.

Write up the relevant ledger accounts for the period.

Solution

The relevant accounts would appear as follows:

Total trade debtors

		£			£
19X3	Credit sales	42,100	19X3	Cash	38,300
				Bad debts	200
				Balance carried down	3,600
		£42,100			£42,100
19X4	Balance brought down	3,600	19X4	Cash	47,900
	Credit sales	48,800		Bad debts	250
				Provision for doubtful debts	150
				Balance carried down	4,100
		£52,400			£52,400
19X5	Balance brought down	4,100	19X5	Cash	49,700
	Credit sales	50,500		Bad debts	200
				Provision for doubtful debts	100
				Balance carried down	4,600
		£54,600			£54,600

Total trade debtors (continued)

		£			£
19X6	Balance brought down	4,600	19X6 Cash		44,400
	Credit sales	44,300	Bad debts		200
			Provision for doubtful debts		200
			Balance carried down		4,100
		£48,900			£48,900
19X7	Balance brought down	4,100	19X7 Cash (47,200 – 100)		47,100
	Credit sales	47,700	Bad debts		100
			Provision for doubtful debts		200
			Balance carried down		4,400
		£51,800			£51,800
19X8	Balance brought down	4,400			

Note that the amounts transferred to the provision for doubtful debts are the bad debts which arose in a year subsequent to that of the associated sale.

Provision for doubtful debts

		£			£
19X4	Trade debtors	150	19X3	Profit and loss	
	Profit and loss	30		(5% × £3,600)	180
		£180			£180
19X5	Trade debtors	100	19X4	Profit and loss	
	Profit and loss	105		(5% × £4,100)	205
		£205			£205
19X6	Trade debtors	200	19X5	Profit and loss	
	Profit and loss	30		(5% × £4,600)	230
		£230			£230
19X7	Trade debtors	200	19X6	Profit and loss	
	Profit and loss	5		(5% × £4,100)	205
		£205			£205
			19X7	Profit and loss	
				(5% × £4,400)	220

Note that a provision is set up at the end of each period. Bad debts which relate to revenues associated with that period, but which arise in subsequent periods, are written off against the provision, and any balance (under- or over-provision) is transferred to the profit and loss account of the next period.

Bad debts recovered

		£			£
19X7	Profit and loss	100	19X7	Cash	100

Bad debts

		£			£
19X3	Trade debtors	200	19X3	Profit and loss	200
19X4	Trade debtors	250	19X4	Profit and loss	250
19X5	Trade debtors	200	19X5	Profit and loss	200
19X6	Trade debtors	200	19X6	Profit and loss	200
19X7	Trade debtors	100	19X7	Profit and loss	100

The profit and loss account for 19X7 would thus include the following items:

	Dr £	Cr £
Bad debts written off	100	
Bad debts recovered		100
Provision for doubtful debts	220	
Provision for doubtful debts written back		5

These may be netted to a debit of £215, which might be shown as an expense 'bad and doubtful debts'. The balance sheet at 31 December 19X7 would include the following (under Current assets):

	£	£
Trade debtors	4,400	
Less: Provision for doubtful debts	220	
		4,180

In practice, just the net figure of £4,180 would probably be shown.

3 BAD AND DOUBTFUL DEBTS – AN ALTERNATIVE PRACTICAL APPROACH

3.1 Using a single bad debts account

We have just considered the logical approach to dealing with bad and doubtful debts and it is important that you are clear as to how it works. However, an alternative approach can be used which is simpler to operate but which gives the *same* total charge to the profit and loss account for bad and doubtful debts. It does not provide as much information as the method set out above. In practice this may not be important. On the other hand the alternative approach does not require that the treatment of a bad debt written off should vary depending on whether or not the debt is associated with a revenue of the current accounting period. This can simplify matters in practice, since it avoids the need to keep debtor records separate for each accounting period.

With this alternative approach, a bad debts account is opened and all bad debts, irrespective of when the associated revenue was recognised, are written off to it. There is also a provision for the doubtful debts account on which the provision is carried.

When a debt is recognised as being bad the double entry is:

Debit	Bad debts account
Credit	Individual debtors' accounts
	with any debts written off

The bad debts account is transferred to the profit and loss account at the end of the accounting period.

At the end of the first period a provision for doubtful debts is set up, with the following double entry:

Debit	Profit and loss account
Credit	Provision for doubtful debts account
	with the amount of the provision needed

The total charge to the profit and loss account for the first period is thus the sum of the bad debts written off and the amount transferred to the provision.

In subsequent periods bad debts continue to be written off to the bad debts account, not to the provision account as described earlier. This means that the provision will be unchanged through the second period. The amount of provision needed at the end of this period can be established, and the necessary adjustment made to the balance on the provision account.

If the provision needs to be *increased* the double entry will be:

Debit	Profit and loss account
Credit	Provision for doubtful debts account
	with the amount of the increase in the provision needed

If the provision needs to be *decreased* the double entry will be:

Debit	Provision for doubtful debts account
Credit	Profit and loss account
	with the amount of the decrease in the provision

The total charge to the profit and loss account in any period is thus the sum of the bad debts actually written off in the period, plus any increase in the provision for doubtful debts or minus any decrease in the provision. This will give the same total charge for bad and doubtful debts as the more detailed method described earlier. In practice, the distinction between the bad debts account and the provision account is an artificial one. In examination questions and solutions, however, this method is typically required.

Example

The bad debts account for Video Supplies for 19X3 and 19X4 would be as follows:

Bad debts

		£			£
19X3	Trade debtors	200	19X3	Profit and loss	200
		£200			£200
19X4	Trade debtors (250 + 150)	400	19X4	Profit and loss	400
		£400			£400

Note that bad debts are written off to the bad debts account as they arise. As was mentioned above, this represents a distinct advantage over the method described earlier since there is no need to identify the period in which the associated revenue was recognised in respect of each bad debt written off.

The provision for doubtful debts account would appear as follows:

Provision for doubtful debts

		£			£
19X3	Balance carried down	180	19X3	Profit and loss (5% × £3,600)	180
		£180			£180
19X4	Balance carried down	205	19X4	Balance brought down	180
				Profit and loss ((5% × £4,100) − £180)	25
		£205			£205
			19X5	Balance brought down	205

Looking back at the earlier example it can be seen that the various profit and loss account items relating to bad and doubtful debts were:

Year	Bad debts written off	Doubtful debts provision	Doubtful debts provision written back		Net
	£	£	£		£
19X3	200	180	–	380	(= 200+180)
19X4	250	205	30	425	(= 400+25)

Thus it can be seen that the alternative approach gives the same net profit and loss account charge as does the route which follows the more logical, but more protracted steps.

3.2   Activity

Show the bad debts account and the provision for doubtful debts account of Video Supplies for the years 19X5, 19X6 and 19X7 and demonstrate how the alternative, more direct approach gives the same net expense as did the approach used in the earlier example.

3.3   Activity solution

Bad debts

		£			£
19X5	Trade debtors	300	**19X5**	Profit and loss	300
	(200 + 100)	£300			£300
19X6	Trade debtors	400	**19X6**	Profit and loss	400
	(200 + 200)	£400			£400
19X7	Trade debtors	300	**19X7**	Cash	100
	(100 + 200)			Profit and loss	200
		£300			£300

Provision for doubtful debts

		£			£
19X5	Balance carried down (5% × £4,600)	230	**19X5**	Balance brought down	205
				Profit and loss (balancing figure)	25
		£230			£230
19X6	Balance carried down (5% × £4,100)	205	**19X6**	Balance brought down	230
	Profit and loss (balancing figure)	25			
		£230			£230
19X7	Balance carried down (5% x £4,400)	220	**19X7**	Balance brought down	205
				Profit and loss (balancing figure)	15
		£220			£220
			19X8	Balance brought down	220

Figures arrived at using more logical approach

Year	Bad debts written off	Bad debts written back	Doubtful provision	Doubtful provision written back	Net (= same as above)
	£	£	£	£	£
19X5	200	–	230	105	325 = 300 + 25
19X6	200	–	205	30	375 = 400 – 25
19X7	100	100	220	5	215 = 200 + 15

3.4 Activity

AZ Engineering Co has the following information relating to its business:

Year ended 31 December	Total debtors £	Bad debts £
19X2	38,400	1,700
19X3	46,200	1,920
19X4	42,600	1,850
19X5	45,000	1,960

The business commenced on 1 January 19X2. The total debtors figure is prior to bad debts being transferred to a bad debts account. A provision of 5% on total debtors (after bad debts have been written off) is to be created in the first year of trading and maintained for each following year.

Show the relevant ledger accounts, profit and loss extracts and balance sheet extracts for each of the four years identified above, assuming that the more direct method is used to deal with bad and doubtful debts.

3.5 Activity solution

Bad debts

		£			£
19X2	Trade debtors	1,700	19X2	Profit and loss	1,700
		£1,700			£1,700
19X3	Trade debtors	1,920	19X3	Profit and loss	1,920
		£1,920			£1,920
19X4	Trade debtors	1,850	19X4	Profit and loss	1,850
		£1,850			£1,850
19X5	Trade debtors	1,960	19X5	Profit and loss	1,960
		£1,960			£1,960

Provision for doubtful debts

		£			£
19X2	Balance carried down (5% × (38,400 − 1,700))	1,835	**19X2**	Profit and loss	1,835
		£1,835			£1,835
19X3	Balance carried down (5% × (46,200 − 1,920))	2,214	**19X3**	Balance brought down Profit and loss	1,835 379
		£2,214			£2,214
19X4	Profit and loss Balance carried down (5% × (42,600 − 1,850))	176 2,038	**19X4**	Balance brought down	2,214
		£2,214			£2,214
19X5	Balance carried down (5% x (45,000 − 1,960))	2,152	**19X5**	Balance brought down Profit and loss	2,038 114
		£2,152			£2,152
			19X6	Balance brought down	2,152

Profit and loss account for the year ended 31 March (extracts)

		£
19X2	Bad debts written off	1,700
	Provision for doubtful debts	1,835
19X3	Bad debts written off	1,920
	Increase in provision for doubtful debts	379
19X4	Bad debts written off	1,850
	Decrease in provision for doubtful debts	(176)
19X5	Bad debts written off	1,960
	Increase in provision for doubtful debts	114

Balance sheet at 31 March (extracts)

		£	£
19X2	Debtors	36,700	
	Less: Provision for doubtful debts	1,835	
			34,865
19X3	Debtors	44,280	
	Less: Provision for doubtful debts	2,214	
			42,066
19X4	Debtors	40,750	
	Less: Provision for doubtful debts	2,038	
			38,712
19X5	Debtors	43,040	
	Less: Provision for doubtful debts	2,152	
			40,888

3.6 Final points

Accounting for doubtful debts is, in some ways, similar to accounting for depreciation. In both cases a provision is created by crediting a provision account and debiting the profit and loss account. In both cases the balance on the provision account is deducted from the relevant asset in the balance sheet. However, it is usual for the depreciation provision to *accumulate* from one year to the next, since at the end of an asset's life its cost less depreciation provision should be equal to the estimated disposal value. With a doubtful debts provision the amount of the provision will typically relate to the amount of debtors, and there is not the same cumulative effect.

Bad and doubtful debts represent a further area of accounting where there is an element of subjectivity. The exercise of judgement is required in determining which debts should be considered bad and the amount which should be considered doubtful. Different judgements may result in different calculations of expense (and hence profit) and different values being placed on debtors in the balance sheet in a particular year.

In an examination, problems concerning bad and doubtful debts often appear as part of a larger problem concerning the preparation of financial statements. Thus it is common for adjustments for bad and doubtful debts to form part of a series of adjustments necessary to prepare the final accounts.

4 CHAPTER SUMMARY

- This chapter has introduced you to the problems of revenue recognition which are related to bad and doubtful debts. To comply with the matching convention, and to ensure that the trade debtors appearing on the balance sheet are not overstated, it is necessary to make a judgement concerning the amount of bad debts arising and to treat these as an expense of the business. The amount of bad debts written off will also be deducted from the total of trade debtors which appears on the balance sheet at the end of the period.

- A bad debt is one where there is reasonable certainty that the amount owing cannot be recovered. However, at the year end there may also be debts which, although they cannot be classified as being bad, nevertheless are uncertain of recovery. Following the convention of conservatism, these doubtful debts should also be taken into account when preparing the profit and loss account and balance sheet. We have seen that a provision should be created for doubtful debts in the profit and loss account and the provision at the year end should be deducted from the total of trade debtors in order to derive a prudent figure for the amount owing from credit sales.

- The treatment of bad and doubtful debts once again serves to emphasise the point that accounting is not a precise science. Although objectivity is viewed as being a desirable quality of accounting information some degree of subjectivity is inevitable. Judgement is required when deciding upon the amount of bad debts and the amount of doubtful debts to be accounted for during a period. These judgements cannot be avoided if we are to make a reasonable assessment of the financial performance and position of a business.

5 SELF TEST QUESTIONS

5.1   Outline the double entry required to account for bad debts. (1.3, 1.4)

5.2   Distinguish between bad and doubtful debts. Why is it necessary to account for these types of debt in the profit and loss account and balance sheet? (2.1)

5.3   The balance carried forward to the new accounting period as the provision for doubtful debts should be:

    (a)   the amount of the bad debt written off in the previous accounting period

    (b)   an estimate of the amount of bad debts which will occur in the following accounting period

    (c)   an estimate of the amount included in the trade debtors carried forward to the next accounting period which will prove to become bad debts

    (d)   5% of the trade debts carried forward. (2.2)

5.4   Outline the double entry required to account for bad debts recovered. (2.4)

6   EXAMINATION TYPE QUESTIONS

6.1   Balances

(a)   You are given the following balances at 1 January 19X1: Debtors £10,000; Bank overdraft £5,000; Provision for doubtful debts £400. You ascertain the following information:

	£
Sales for the year 19X1 (all on credit)	100,000
Sales returns for the year 19X1	1,000
Receipts from customers during 19X1	90,000
Bad debts written off during 19X1	500
Discounts allowed during 19X1	400

At the end of 19X1 the provision for doubtful debts is required to be 5% of debtors, after making a specific provision for a debt of £200 from a customer who has gone bankrupt.

	£
Sales for the year 19X2 (90% on credit)	100,000
Sales returns for the year 19X2 (90% relating to credit customers)	2,000
Receipts from credit customers during 19X2	95,000
Debtor balances settled by contra against creditor balances during 19X2	3,000
Bad debts written off during 19X2 (including 50% of the debt due from the customer who had gone bankrupt, the other 50% having been received in cash during 19X2)	1,500
Discounts allowed during 19X2	500

At the end of 19X2 the provision for doubtful debts is still required to be 5% of debtors.

Write up the debtors and provision for doubtful debts accounts for 19X1 and 19X2, bringing down the balances at the end of each year and showing in those accounts the double entry for each item.

(b)   The normal accounting approach with credit sales, as illustrated in part a) above, is to recognise revenue on the sale when it is made, and then to allow for the possibility of some bad debts. Outline, with reference to appropriate accounting conventions, the justification for this approach.   **(18 marks)**

(ACCA, June 1988)

6.2   Rimmer

L. Rimmer prepared his final accounts at 31/12/19X4 and carried down a provision of £127 on his provision for doubtful debts account.

During 19X5 the following debts were written off. J. Barnes, £26; W. Morris, £32; P. Watson, £19; and M. Williams & Co, £25. The first two debts were written off on June 30 and the last two on September 30.

On 31 December 19X5 Rimmer decided to write off as bad a debt of £20 owing from T. Payne, who had died. The remaining debtors then amounted to £3,500 and Rimmer decided to adjust the provision for doubtful debts to 4% of this total.

Throughout 19X6 the following debts were written off as bad: T. Allen, £18; N. Collins, £41; S. Matthews, £37; and A. Thomas, £62.

At 31 December 19X6 outstanding debtors totalled £3,250 and Rimmer decided to maintain the provision for doubtful debts at 4%.

Show the following:

(a)   Bad debts accounts for 19X5 and 19X6

(b)   Provision for doubtful debts account for 19X5 and 19X6

(c)   Profit and loss extracts for 19X5 and 19X6 in respect of bad and doubtful debts

(d)   Extracts from the balance sheets for 19X5 and 19X6 in respect of debtors.   **(14 marks)**

6.3   Fletcher

The following trial balance was extracted from the books of H. Fletcher, a trader, as at 31 December 19X7.

	£	£
Capital account		205,000
Purchases	465,000	
Sales		609,000
Repairs to buildings	8,480	
Motor car	9,600	
Car expenses	3,180	
Freehold land and buildings	100,000	
Balance at bank	5,300	
Fixtures and fittings	14,600	
Wages and salaries	86,060	
Discounts allowed	10,610	
Discounts received		8,140
Drawings	24,000	
Rates and insurances	2,480	
Bad debts	3,590	
Provision for bad debts, 1 January 19X7		1,400
Trade debtors	52,130	
Trade creditors		40,350
General expenses	15,860	
Stock in trade, 1 January 19X7	63,000	
	£863,890	£863,890

The following matters should be taken into account:

1   Stock in trade, 31 December 19X7, £88,000.

2   Wages and salaries outstanding at 31 December 19X7, £3,180.

3   Rates and insurances paid in advance at 31 December 19X7, £450.

4   The provision for bad debts is to be reduced to £1,000.

5   During 19X7, Fletcher withdrew goods, valued at £2,000, for his own use. No entry has been made in the books for the withdrawal of these goods.

6   The item 'Repairs to buildings, £8,480' includes £6,500 for alterations and improvements to the buildings.

7   One third of the car expenses represents the cost of Fletcher's motoring for private, as distinct from business, purposes.

8   The motor car and fixtures are to be depreciated at 10% per annum.

Prepare a trading and profit and loss account for the year 19X7 and a balance sheet as on 31 December 19X7.   **(20 marks)**

6.4   Yeats

The following final balance was extracted from the books of J. Yeats, a trader, at 31 December 19X9:

	£	£
Carriage inwards	6,310	
Capital account at 1 January 19X9		500,000
Motor vans	200,000	
Stock at 1 January 19X9	164,000	
Balance at bank	116,860	
Purchases	1,593,690	
Sales		2,224,000
Trade debtors	290,000	
Trade creditors		157,600
Rent and rates	56,080	
Salaries	350,400	
General expenses	44,720	
Motor expenses	25,600	
Discounts allowed	40,400	
Discounts received		37,600
Insurance	17,600	
Bad debts	30,400	
Provision for doubtful debts 1 January 19X9		8,000
Provision for depreciation on vans		60,000
Drawings	50,000	
Disposal		6,000
Returns inwards	7,140	
	£2,993,200	£2,993,200

The following matters should be taken into account:

(a)   After examination of the debtors accounts, it was decided to:

    (i)   write off a bad debt of £12,000;

    (ii)   make a specific provision in the accounts for the following doubtful debts,

       •   £5,000 from Wordsworth

       •   £3,000 from Coleridge

    (iii)   make a general provision of 5% on the other debtors.

(b)   Goods unsold at 31 December 19X9 had cost £201,600 but Yeats expected to sell them at £232,470.

(c)   Salaries accrued at 31 December 19X9 amounted to £32,000.

(d)   The rent for the premises is £40,000 a year, payable quarterly in arrears, but the instalment due on 31 December 19X9 was not paid until 15 January in the next year.

(e)   Insurance paid in advance at 31 December 19X9 amounted to £2,000.

(f)   Depreciation is to be provided for on the motor truck at the rate of 20% per annum straight line on cost.

(g)   General expenses include £3,060 relating to the telephone account which is made up of:

    •   Rent – three months in advance from 30 November 19X9 at £420.

    •   Calls – three months ended 30 November 19X9 at £2,640.

(h)   It has been agreed with the Inland Revenue (Taxation Office) that 12.5% of the rent and rates relate to private use.

Prepare a trading and profit and loss account for the year to 31 December 19X9, and a balance sheet as at 31 December 19X9.   **(20 marks)**

6.5 Prepare and Submit

The balance on the provision for doubtful debts account on 1 January 19X1 was £1,000, equal to 5% of debtors at that date.

In the 12 months to 31 December 19X1 sales are £90,000, cash receipts from sales are £80,000 and bad debts (charged to the provision account) are £600. The doubtful debts provision balance at close of business on 31 December 19X1 is required to be 5% of debtors.

In the 12 months to 31 December 19X2 sales are £100,000, cash receipts from sales are £110,000 and bad debts (charged directly to expenses) are £400. The doubtful debts provision balance at close of business on 31 December 19X2 is required to be 5% of debtors. (The change in treatment of bad debts in the second year does not imply that any adjustment or correction should be made in relation to the first year).

Required

Prepare the provision for doubtful debts account for the period 1 January 19X1 to 1 January 19X3, clearly bringing down the balance at the end of each year, and indicating the double entry for each item in the account. Submit necessary workings in a convenient form. **(12 marks)**

(ACCA, December 1993)

7 ANSWERS TO EXAMINATION TYPE QUESTIONS

7.1 Balances

(a)

Debtors account

19X1		£	19X1		£
Jan 1	Balance b/d	10,000	Dec 31	Returns	1,000
				Cash received	90,000
Dec 31	Sales	100,000		Bad debts	500
				Discount allowed	400
				Balance c/d	18,100
		£110,000			£110,000
19X2			19X2		
Jan 1	Balance b/d	18,100	Dec 31	Returns	1,800
Dec 31	Sales	90,000		Cash received	95,000
				Contra item	3,000
				Bad debts	1,500
				Discount allowed	500
				Balance c/d	6,300
		£108,100			£108,100
19X3					
Jan 1	Balance b/d	6,300			

Provision for doubtful debts account

19X1		£	19X1		£
Dec 31	Balance c/d	1,095	Jan 1	Balance b/d	400
	(£200 + 5% £17,900)		Dec 31	Profit and loss account	695
		£1,095			£1,095
19X2			19X2		
Dec 31	Profit and loss account	780	Jan 1	Balance b/d	1,095
	Balance c/d 5% £6,300	315			
		£1,095			£1,095
			19X3		
			Jan 1	Balance b/d	315

Note: The above solution is consistent with the approach used in this book, that is, the provision for doubtful debts accounts is shown separately from the bad debts account. Thus, changes in the provision for doubtful debts will be adjusted in that account and any bad debts arising will be written off to the bad debts account. An alternative approach is to write off bad debts arising from credit sales in the previous year to the provision for doubtful debts account. Bad debts arising in the current year would still be written off to a separate bad debts account. However, there is insufficient information in the question about bad debts to adopt this approach.

(b)   The **realisation convention** states that, normally, a sale is recognised at the point where the goods are passed to, and accepted by, the customer and not when the cash is ultimately received. When the goods have been accepted by the customer at an agreed price the value of the sale can be objectively determined and there is, normally, reasonable certainty that the cash will ultimately be received.

Where cash is not eventually received for a credit sale, the amount of the debt should be written off. The bad debt is regarded as a business expense and the **matching convention** states that expenses must be matched with the revenues they help earn when determining profit for the period.

Where there is a possibility that a debt will eventually prove to be bad the **prudence convention** states that all losses – whether actual or anticipated – should be taken into account. Failure to take account of possible losses could lead to an overstatement of profit for the period end and overstatement of assets at the end of the period. It is also important to take account of possible losses arising in a particular period because of the **matching convention.** It would be incorrect to record sales in one period and associated bad debts in a subsequent period.

7.2   Rimmer

Provision for doubtful debts

		£			£
19X5			**19X4**		
Dec 31	Bal b/d	140	31 Dec	Bal b/d	127
			19X5		
			31 Dec	Profit and loss	13
		140			140
19X6			**19X6**		
Dec 31	Profit and loss	10	Jan 1	Bal b/d	140
	Bal c/d	130			
		£140			£140
			19X7		
			Jan 1	Bal b/d	130

Bad debts

			£			£
19X5				**19X5**		
Jun 30	Debtors (JB)		26	Dec 31	Profit and loss	122
	Debtors (WM)		32			
Sep 30	Debtors (PW)		19			
	Debtors (MW)		25			
Dec 31	Debtors (TP)		20			
			£122			£122
19X6				**19X6**		
Dec 31	Debtors	(TA)	18	Dec 31	Profit and loss	158
		(NC)	41			
		(SM)	37			
		(AT)	62			
			£158			£158

Profit and loss extracts

19X5	Bad and doubtful debts	135
19X6	Bad and doubtful debts	148

Balance sheet extracts

19X5	Debtors	3,500	
	Less Provision	140	
			3,360
19X6	Debtors	3,250	
	Less Provision	130	
			3,120

7.3 **Fletcher**

Trading and profit and loss account
for the year ended 31 December 19X7

	£	£
Sales		609,000
Less: Cost of sales		438,000
Gross profit		171,000
Add: Discounts received		8,140
Reduction in provision for Bad debts		400
		179,540
Wages and salaries	89,240	
Discounts allowed	10,610	
General expenses	15,860	
Car expenses	2,120	
Repairs to buildings	1,980	
Rates and insurance	2,030	
Bad debts	3,590	
Depreciation – fixtures and fittings	1,460	
– motor vehicles	640	
		127,530
Net profit		£52,010

Balance sheet as at 31 December 19X7

	£	£	£
Fixed assets			
Land and buildings		106,500	
Furniture and fittings	14,600		
Less: Accumulated depreciation	1,460	13,140	
Motor car	9,600		
Less: accumulated depreciation	960	8,640	128,280
Current assets			
Stock		88,000	
Debtors	52,130		
Less: Provision for bad debts	1,000	51,130	
Rates and insurances prepaid		450	
Bank		5,300	
		144,880	
Less: **Current liabilities**			
Creditors	40,350		
Accrued wages and salaries	3,180	43,530	101,350
			£229,630
Opening Capital			205,000
Add: **Net profit**			52,010
			257,010
Less: **Drawings**			27,380
			£229,630

7.4 Yeats

*Trading and profit and loss account
for the year ended 31 December 19X9*

	£	£
Sales		2,224,000
Less: Returns inwards		7,140
		2,216,860
Less: Cost of sales	1,556,090	
Carriage inwards	6,310	1,562,400
Gross profit		654,460
Discounts received		37,600
Profit on disposal		6,000
		698,060
Less:		
Salaries	382,400	
Rent and rates	57,820	
General expenses	45,320	
Motor expenses	25,600	
Discount allowed	40,400	
Insurance	15,600	
Bad and doubtful debts	55,900	
Depreciation – motor vans	40,000	663,040
Net profit		£35,020

Balance sheet as at 31 December 19X9

	£	£	£
Fixed assets			
Motor vans at cost		200,000	
Less: Accumulated depreciation		100,000	100,000
Current assets			
Stock		201,600	
Debtors	278,000		
Less: Provision for bad debts	21,500	256,500	
Prepayments		2,280	
Bank		116,860	577,240
			677,240
Current liabilities			
Creditors		157,600	
Accrued expenses		42,880	200,480
			£476,760
Capital at 1 January 19X9			500,000
Add: Net profit			35,020
			535,020
Less: Drawings			58,260
			£476,760

7.5   Prepare and Submit

Provision for doubtful debts account

		£			£
31.12.X1	Debtors	600	1.1.X1	Balance b/d	1,000
	Balance c/d	1,470	31.12.X1	Profit and loss	1,070
	(5% × £29,400)				
		2,070			2,070
31.12.X2	Profit and loss	520	1.1.X2	Balance b/d	1,470
	Balance c/d	950			
	(5% × £19,000)				
		1,470			1,470
			1.1.X3	Balance b/d	950

Workings

Debtors account

		£			£
1.1.X1	Balance b/d	20,000	31.12.X1	Cash	80,000
	(100/5 × £1,000)			Bad debts	600
31.12.X1	Sales	90,000		Balance c/d	29,400
		110,000			110,000
1.1.X2	Balance b/d	29,400	31.12.X2	Cash	110,000
31.12.X2	Sales	100,000		Profit and loss	400
				Balance c/d	19,000
		129,400			129,400
1.1.X3	Balance b/d	19,000			

11 SUBSIDIARY RECORDS

INTRODUCTION AND LEARNING OBJECTIVES

This chapter examines the accounting records required for a business in some detail. We have already considered in an earlier chapter the principles of double entry and the need for separate accounts for each type of transaction. In this chapter, we build on these points by considering the practical problems of maintaining accounts and the need for a system of subsidiary records. We will examine the most common forms of subsidiary records and show how these are related to the double entry accounts.

We will also consider the need for the double entry accounts to be organised in a logical and systematic manner. The book in which the accounts are kept is referred to as the **ledger**. However, in a business of any size, a single ledger is impractical. We will see how the various accounts of a business may be allocated to different divisions or categories in order to produce a number of ledgers. The nature and purpose of each of the ledgers which are typically maintained will be examined

When you have studied this chapter you should be able to do the following:

- Explain why subsidiary books are used in operating business accounts

- Explain the split of the ledger into cash book, sales ledger, purchase ledger, etc.

- Prepare journals for posting to ledger accounts

- Write up the cash book and petty cash book.

1 PRACTICAL ISSUES RELATING TO DATA COLLECTION AND RECORDING

1.1 Introduction

Chapter 5 set out the basis of a system of ledger accounts which is both logical and complete in itself. However, in practice it is normally not possible to record transactions directly into the ledger accounts, other than for the smallest of businesses. It is necessary to devise a system of recording items prior to their entry in the ledger (usually referred to as subsidiary records or a system of original or prime entry). The principal reasons for this are as follows:

(a) The *sheer volume of transactions* may mean that several people need to be involved in the recording process. This will make it necessary to devise a system which breaks down the process into parts, each of which can be made the responsibility of one person. There are several reasons for this, the most important of which is the fact that it is virtually impossible for more than one person at a time to work on a particular book. Another factor which makes division of the bookkeeping task a practical option is the benefit derived from individuals specialising in part of the work, so that they become more familiar and proficient with their task. A third factor is that responsibility for a particular set of tasks can be given to one individual, so that person can be held accountable should errors occur in that part of the work.

(b) Any system of recording needs to give consideration to issues relating to **internal check** and **internal control**. Errors and fraud become very much easier as systems become devolved, unless automatic checking processes are built in. Internal check relates to the particular checks which are built into the day-to-day transactions, which operate as part of the routine system, thus ensuring that the work of one person is verified by the work of another. Internal control is the entire system of controls operated by a business to ensure effective performance. Clearly, in designing systems of recording, appropriate weight must be given to ensuring that adequate checks are built in, to reduce the possibility of error or fraud, and that information needed for effective control can be provided easily and conveniently.

(c)   Closely related to issues of internal check and internal control is the *need for appropriate documentation of transactions*. It is important in devising appropriate systems of recording to recognise that, as the number of transactions grow, there is a greater need to ensure that the system of recording is linked with documentary evidence, thus providing the information necessary to check and prove the accuracy of the accounts. The word **audit** is used to describe the process of assessing the truth and fairness of a set of accounts. The ability to audit a set of accounts is important, and requires a clear set of documentary evidence leading from the original transaction to its inclusion in a set of final accounts. The evidence is frequently described as the **audit trail**. A second aspect of the documentation of transactions is that a variety of documents (for instance, sales invoices, credit notes, orders and receipts) will need to be prepared in the normal course of business. A system of recording and documentation should be devised which enables the necessary documents to be prepared and coordinated with the recording process.

In practice the range of systems that can be devised to deal with these problems is vast. These range from completely manual systems, through to fully computerised systems. Most examination questions in this area are based upon the assumption that a fully manual system is in operation, and the form and content of a typical manual system are described in detail in later sections of this chapter. In practice this emphasis is misplaced, since most systems are now entirely or largely computerised. Therefore a review of computerised systems is also given below. With these reservations in mind, it is nonetheless possible to outline the likely components of a system of subsidiary record keeping, and to relate these to the three sets of reasons given above.

1.2   The volume of transactions

The problem of the volume of transactions is normally solved by such things as the following:

(a)   The ledger may be subdivided into various component parts, with responsibility for a particular division being given to one individual

(b)   Responsibility for the initial recording of certain transactions can be given to particular individuals. Responsibilities will typically be subdivided to cover such things as sales, sales returns, purchases, purchases returns, cash receipts, and cash payments, and appropriate subsidiary records will be maintained. These subsidiary records then become the basis for the recording in the ledger accounts

(c)   A system of original entry can be devised which enables ledger entries to be made at a convenient time, using totals where appropriate.

Considerations of internal check will typically lead to a subdivision of responsibilities such that one person may carry out part of the recording in the ledger accounts, with a second person completing it. Any errors or fraud would thus be more likely to be found. Most systems also use totals in accounts, where possible. This makes the balancing off of accounts a much less onerous task, and is likely to enable information of use in maintaining control to be more easily extracted from the accounts.

With regard to the question of documentation and an audit trail, it is usual to find that the system devised permits a clear link to be established between the document supporting a transaction and the final accounts.

1.3   Subsidiary books

A typical manual system of accounting would involve the following:

- A set of ledger accounts which are suitably subdivided

- A system whereby every transaction is recorded in a subsidiary book prior to entry in the ledger accounts. Typical subsidiary books are as follows:

Credit transactions

Sales book

Sales returns book

Purchases book

Purchases returns book

Cash transactions

Cash book or cash journals

Other transactions

Journal

These are dealt with in more detail below.

1.4   The division of the ledger

The book in which accounts are kept is generally referred to as the ledger, hence the term ledger accounts. While the number of transactions relating to a business is small all the accounts may be kept in one single ledger. However, after a business has reached a certain size, the number of transactions which require recording will become so large that the operation of one ledger will become both cumbersome and difficult to implement. Clearly as a business expands the volume of transactions will require the employment of more than one person to maintain the accounts, and some kind of division of the ledger is needed if both are to be able to work at the same time. The division is likely to be based upon the particular jobs each person has been given. The actual split depends very much on the type of business. There are no hard and fast rules, but the following split is fairly typical, and should be assumed to be that used in examination questions, unless there is clear evidence to the contrary.

- **The cash book**

    This normally includes the accounts relating to cash and bank.

- **The sales ledger**

    This ledger contains the personal accounts of the individual trade debtors. It is also commonly referred to as the debtors ledger.

- **The purchases ledger**

    This ledger contains the personal accounts of the individual trade creditors. It is also referred to as the creditors or bought ledger.

- **The nominal ledger**

    This ledger normally contains the accounts relating to revenues and expenses, which are to be transferred to the trading and profit and loss accounts at the year end.

- **The general ledger**

    This contains the accounts remaining.

In some cases accounts of a confidential nature, such as capital or drawings or salaries of senior staff, may be kept in a separate **private ledger**. Frequently the items shown above as being in the nominal ledger, general ledger and private ledger are combined in a single general ledger. The sales and purchases ledger may be further subdivided as the number of trade debtor and trade creditor accounts increase.

1.5   Activity

Using the ledger divisions suggested above identify the ledger in which the following accounts would be found:

1	Sales	2	Purchases
3	J. Bloggs (a trade debtor)	4	P. Anniss (a trade creditor)
5	Discount received	6	Cash
7	Premises	8	Wages
9	Drawings	10	Loans

1.6   Activity solution

1   Sales – nominal ledger

2   Purchases – nominal ledger

3   J. Bloggs – (a debtor) – sales ledger

4   P. Anniss (a creditor) – purchases ledger

5   Discount received – nominal ledger

6   Cash – cash book

7   Premises – general ledger

8   Wages – nominal ledger

9   Drawings – general ledger

10   Loans – general ledger

1.7   Activity

Identify the accounts which will require entries, and the ledgers in which these accounts will be kept, for the following transactions:

1   Purchases of stock costing £100, on credit from A. Nock

2   Sales of goods for £500 on credit to P. Harvey

3   Sale of goods for cash £300

4   Cash paid to A. Nock £505

5   Cash paid for new equipment £600

6   Cash drawings £1,000

7   Wages paid of £150

8   Purchases of stock costing £400 from M. Druse

1.8   Activity solution

1   Debit purchases – in nominal ledger
Credit A. Nock – in purchases ledger

2   Debit P. Harvey – sales ledger
Credit sales – in nominal ledger

3   Debit cash – in cash book
Credit sales – in nominal ledger

4   Debit A. Nock – in purchases ledger
Credit cash – in cash book

5   Debit equipment – in general ledger
        Credit cash – in cash book

6   Debit drawings – in general ledger
        Credit cash – in cash book

7   Debit wages – in nominal ledger
        Credit cash – in cash book

8   Debit purchases – in nominal ledger
        Credit M. Druse – in purchases ledger

1.9   Advantages of splitting the ledger

The advantage of a split such as that suggested above is that it enables work to be carried out by more than one person at the same time. The likelihood of two people wanting to use the same ledger at the same time is thus considerably reduced. However, consideration of the second activity above should make it clear that this possibility is not completely eliminated, particularly with regard to the cash book, the nominal ledger and the general ledger, and further refinements are necessary to avoid such an occurrence.

2   SUBSIDIARY BOOKS IN DETAIL

2.1   Introduction

The division of the ledger will have no effect on the number of entries made in the accounts, since detailed recording of all entries will still occur. However, the use of subsidiary books as a system for recording transactions *prior to entry in the accounts* provides a way of reducing the amount of detail which needs to be included in the accounts. The system also enables a much clearer division of duties to be devised which eliminates the problems of overlapping use of ledgers identified in the preceding section. It also provides a way of linking the accounts with the documentary evidence needed to audit the accounts. It should be emphasised at the start that these subsidiary records are designed to support, but do not form part of, the double-entry accounting system.

2.2   Subsidiary books – credit transactions

Typically four books are opened to cover credit transactions:

- **The sales book**

  This records all sales on credit.

- **The purchases book**

  This records all credit purchases.

- **The sales returns book** (or **returns in book**)

  This records all returns of credit sales.

- **The purchases returns book** (or **returns out book**)

  This records returns of credit purchases.

These books are known as day books, books of original (or prime) entry, or subsidiary books. They are *not* part of the double-entry system, being subsidiary to, or preliminary to, that system.

The basic idea of these books is that when sales or purchases are made *on credit*, the detail is entered in the sales or purchases book, which is merely a list of sales or purchases, showing date, customer or supplier, invoice number and amount. This ensures that a record exists, from which the appropriate entries can be made in the ledger accounts, which also provides reference to supporting documents detailing the transaction. The actual entering of the transactions into the accounts (known as posting) can take place *at some later and more convenient time*, using *totals* if this is considered appropriate. Indeed it is important to note that the two parts of the double entry *need not take place at the same time, or be made by the same people*. Clearly they have to be completed before the accounts can be balanced off and a trial balance extracted, but considerably more flexibility exists with a system of subsidiary records than a system of double entry without subsidiary records. It should be noted that if the double entry does not need to be made by the same person it becomes much easier to make one person responsible for the accounts in a particular ledger. For example, a person can be given responsibility for the sales ledger, and can make single entries to the debit of the individual accounts in that ledger, while someone else can be given responsibility for the nominal ledger. This person would simply have to credit the sales account in the nominal ledger with the total of the sales book for the period concerned. Provided that a sound system is devised there is no reason for any particular person to have his work held up because of lack of access to necessary information.

Example

The form of the sales book is generally along the lines given below:

Date	Detail	Invoice number	Folio	Amount
19X7				**£**
January 1	A. Driver	J001	S070	10.50
1	W. Barrow	J002	S005	99.99
1	B. Fry	J003	S075	2.13
1	Z. Zorn	J004	S214	7.30
1	Y. Young	J005	S212	20.08
		Total to sales account		**£140.00**

The basic system for sales is essentially as follows: the seller sends an invoice to the customer, with a copy being retained, which then acts as the **prime document** or **voucher**. (By prime document or voucher is meant the documentary evidence which initiates the recording of the transaction.) The relevant information is then recorded in the sales book as illustrated. At the end of each day (or whatever period is considered reasonable) the total is posted to the credit of the sales account in the nominal ledger, and individual debits are made in the personal accounts of the debtors in the sales ledger. It should be noted that there is no saving in the number of postings to the sales ledger, but that postings may be made at a convenient time.

2.3 Explanation of the form of the sales book

In the illustration used above, hypothetical invoice numbers and folio references are used. The invoice number gives a reference back to the voucher, which is filed away to provide detailed back up to the accounts when needed. The voucher itself should provide more details about the transaction, including customer order numbers and correspondence. Such an approach ensures that there is a clear audit trail. The folio column is simply a cross reference facility to the customer account number in the sales ledger.

The ledger accounts relating to the sales book given in the example are as follows:

Sales ledger
A. Driver

			£	
January 1	Sales	SB1	10.50	

W. Barrow

			£	
January 1	Sales	SB1	99.99	

B. Fry

			£	
January 1	Sales	SB1	2.13	

Z. Zorn

			£	
January 1	Sales	SB1	7.30	

Y.Young

			£	
January 1	Sales	SB1	20.08	

Nominal ledger
Sales

				£
	January 1	Debtors	SB1	140.00

2.4 Form of the other books

The purchases book follows the same principles as the sales book, except that the total is debited to the purchases account in the nominal ledger, and the detailed figures are credited to individual personal accounts in the purchases ledger.

The books dealing with returns of sales or purchases also follow the same principles, with totals being posted to the appropriate returns account and detailed postings being made to individual accounts in the sales and purchases ledgers.

The vouchers for sales returns are generally copies of credit notes sent to the customer, files of which can be kept to substantiate the sales return figure. Credit purchases will result in an invoice from the supplier, which can be recorded in the purchases book and then kept in suitably ordered files. There is no one correct method of filing invoices, as long as the object of the provision of an audit trail is achieved. A method commonly used is one where invoices are filed in creditor order, alongside orders, thus enabling a check to be made on such things as the quantities ordered, contract prices, while ensuring a safeguard against duplicate payments. Returns of purchases will typically require a goods returned note or a credit note received from the supplier as a voucher. These can be entered into the purchases returns book and be subsequently filed alongside invoices and orders for checking and reference purposes.

Subsidiary books may be prepared in the form of **analysis books** if required. For example, a business selling four different types of product would probably require a breakdown of the sales figure by product. This could be achieved by the use of an analysis sales book with headings such as that shown below.

Date	Detail (customer)	Invoice	Folio	Total	1	2	3	4

The first five columns follow the kind of format described above. The last four columns represent an analysis of total sales under product headings. The totals of the last four columns should equal the overall total cost column. The postings to the accounts would be four postings to a sales account for each type of product, being the total of each of the last four analysis columns, and detailed postings to the debtors ledger, these being posted from the overall total column, in detail, in the usual way.

It is also frequently convenient to have a form of purchases book which will record all inward invoices, whether they relate to purchases of stock or other costs. If this is so the principles are similar to the analysis sales book described above. A total column will be provided and as many analysis columns as are considered necessary. An example is given below.

Date	Detail	Invoice	Folio	Total	Purchases	Rates	Fuel	Ledger

The total column provides a cross check on the analysis columns. The totals of the analysis columns will be posted to the debit of the appropriate account. Detailed postings will be made to individual creditors accounts. If an analysis purchases book is used the purchases ledger typically contains all the creditors accounts, and not merely those relating to purchases. Note also the ledger column in the example shown above. This is for miscellaneous items which cannot conveniently be put into one of the analysis columns. The ledger column thus needs posting in detail. The double- entry postings from an analysis purchases book therefore consists of debits to the appropriate accounts of the totals of the analysis columns, plus detailed debits posted from the ledger column, matched by detailed postings from the total column to the credit side of the personal accounts in the purchases ledger.

2.5   Activity

You are to enter up the purchases book and the purchases returns book from the following details, then to post the items to the appropriate accounts in the purchases ledger and the nominal ledger. Postings to the nominal ledger are to be made monthly.

January	1	Credit purchases from H. Howard £50
January	3	Credit purchases from T. Dance £100
January	7	Credit purchases from A. Fiddler £75
		Credit purchases from B. Nice £35
		Credit purchases from R. Webb £55
		Credit purchases from F. Weck £25
January	9	Goods returned to A. Fiddler £15
		Goods returned to H. Howard £10
January	15	Credit purchases from H. Howard £125
January	20	Credit purchases from A. Fiddler £25
		Credit purchases from R. Webb £50
		Credit purchases from B. Green £100
January	25	Goods returned to R. Webb £5
		Goods returned to B. Green £5
January	31	Credit purchases from C. Blue £50

2.6   Activity solution

Purchases book				
Date	**Detail**	**Invoice**	**Folio**	**Amount**
				£
Jan 1	H. Howard		PL25	50
3	T. Dance		PL10	100
7	A. Fiddler		PL15	75
7	B. Nice		PL40	35
7	R. Webb		PL90	55
7	F. Weck		PL92	25
15	H. Howard		PL25	125
20	A. Fiddler		PL15	25
20	R. Webb		PL90	50
20	B. Green		PL20	100
31	C. Blue		PL05	50
	Total to purchases account		G1	£690

Purchases returns book				
Date	**Detail**	**Invoice**	**Folio**	**Amount**
				£
Jan 9	A. Fiddler		PL15	15
9	H. Howard		PL25	10
25	R. Webb		PL90	5
25	B. Green		PL20	5
	Total to purchases returns account		G2	£35

Nominal ledger
Purchases account G1

			£			£
January 31	Creditors	PB1	690			

Purchases returns G2

	£				£
		Jan 31	Creditors	PRB1	35

Purchases (Creditors) Ledger
C. Blue (5)

	£				£
		Jan 31	Purchases	PB1	50

A. Fiddler (15)

			£						£
January 9	Purchase returns	PRB1	15	Jan	7	Purchases	PB1	75
January 31	Balance	c/d	85		20	Purchases	PB1	25
			£100						£100
				Feb 1		Balance	b/d	85

B. Green (20)

			£				£
January 25	Purchases returns PRB1		5	Jan 20	Purchases		£100
January 31	Balance c/d		95				
			£100				£100
				Feb 1	Balance b/d		95

H. Howard (25)

			£					£
January 9	Purchases returns	PRB1	10	Jan 1	Purchases	PB1	50
			£175					£175
				Feb 1	Balance b/d		165

B. Nice (40)

			£				£
				Jan 7	Purchases	PB1	35

R. Webb (90)

				£					£
Jan	25	Purchases returns	PRB1	5	Jan	7	Purchases	PB1	55
	31	Balance c/d		100		20	Purchases	PB1	50
				£105					£105
					Feb	1	Balance b/d		100

F. Weck (92)

			£				£
				Jan 7	Purchases	PB1	25

T. Dance (10)

			£				£
				Jan 3	Purchases	PB1	100

2.7 The principles of subsidiary books

It is important to note that the *principles* underlying the books described in this section may be used, even if no book is formally kept. For example, invoices may be kept in a box and posted monthly. Detailed postings to the purchases ledger may be made from each invoice, and the total of the box of invoices (probably add listed to provide a check) may be posted to the purchases account.

3 SUBSIDIARY BOOKS – CASH TRANSACTIONS

3.1 Introduction

Various ways of maintaining records relating to cash are possible. At the simplest level a cash account may be maintained in a ledger devoted solely to cash transactions. Even in a case such as this it may well be worthwhile combining the two elements of cash (cash in hand and cash at bank) into a **two-column cash book** as shown in the following example.

Example

The cash and bank accounts for a business are as shown below:

Cash in hand

			£					£
January	1	Balance b/d	90	January	10	Postage		10
	31	Sales	400		31	Bank		460
					31	Balance c/d		20
			£490					£490
February	1	Balance b/d	20					

Cash at bank

			£					£
January	1	Balance b/d	1,000	January	25	Wages		100
	31	Cash	460		27	V. Horn		
						(a creditor)		800
					31	Balance c/d		560
			£1,460					£1,460
February	1	Balance b/d	560					

These two accounts could be combined into a two-column cash book as follows:

Cash book

			Folio	Cash	Bank				Folio	Cash	Bank
				£	£					£	£
January	1	Balance	b/d	90	1,000	January	10	Postages		10	
	31	Sales		400			25	Wages			100
	31	Contra			460		27	V.Horn			
								(a creditor)			800
							31	Contra		460	
							31	Balance	c/d	20	560
				£490	1,460					£490	1,460
February	1	Balance	b/d	20	560						

The bank column contains details of payments made by cheque and of cheques received and payments into bank. The word 'contra' indicates that the second part of the double entry is on the other side of the cash book. This particular transaction was paying £460 previously held as notes or coins into the bank.

3.2 Double entry of cash transactions

It needs to be recognised that the entry of a transaction in the cash book represents only part of the double-entry process. The equivalent double entry must be made before the accounts can be completed. Using the figures from the two-column cash book shown above further postings would be required to the debit of postages (£10), wages (£100), V. Horn (£800), and to the credit of sales (£400). In effect the cash book acts as *both* a ledger account and a book of prime entry. Receipts of cash are debited to the cash book immediately, with some kind of reference being given to the receipt number given, or the cheque number, thus preserving the audit trail. At a later and more convenient time the credit entry can be made by the appropriate person in the appropriate ledger. Payments of cash, which should only be made when approved by a responsible official will be recorded on the credit side of the cash book, and at a later and more convenient time the corresponding debit postings can be made. While there are no hard and fast rules about the actual methods used, there should nevertheless be an easy reference from the cash book credit side to the voucher supporting the payment. The cash book is obviously an **account**. To the extent that it contains details for posting to other ledger accounts it can also be said to be a book of **prime entry**.

3.3 Three-column cash books

To encourage customers to pay their accounts within a reasonable time cash discounts can be offered. Discounts can be both allowed or received. The ledger entries for a discount allowed are to debit discount allowed and credit the personal account of the debtor concerned. The ledger entries for discount received are to credit the discount received account and to debit the personal account of the creditor concerned. Where discounts are given, cash paid or received will be net of discount, and the postings from a two-column cash book will reflect this. In effect this will result in the entries in the personal accounts of debtors and creditors being rather time-consuming, since two entries will need to be made in these accounts, at different times. In practice this problem can be overcome by the use of a three-column cash book, with a third column being added to the cash book to keep track of discounts at the time that cash is paid or received. This column is not part of the ledger accounting system, but a memorandum column, enabling the two components of cash and discount to be identified at the same time.

Example

The following items relating to cash and discount occur in a business:

March	1	Opening balances – cash in hand £100, cash at bank £1,000
	2	Receives cash of £90 from D. Not in settlement of a debt of £100
	3	Receives a cheque for £190 from J. Broom in settlement of a debt of £200
	6	Pays a cheque of £50 to B. Brush in settlement of a debt of £55
	7	Pays a cheque of £95 to J. Cater in settlement of a debt of £100

These transactions would appear in a three-column cash book as follows:

Cash book

		Discount	Cash	Bank				Discount	Cash	Bank
		£	£	£				£	£	£
March 1	Balance b/d		100	1,000	March 6	B. Brush		5		50
2	D. Not	10	90		7	J. Cater		5		95
3	J. Broom	10		190	7	Balance c/d			190	1,045
		20	190	1,190				10	190	1,190
March 7	Balance b/d		190	1,045						

All the relevant postings can be completed from this information. The cash received has already been entered in the cash book on the debit side. The total discount allowed (to debtors) over the period is the total of the discount column on the debit side. This figure can thus be posted to the debit of the discount allowed account in the nominal ledger. The amount of debts cleared by debtors will be the sum of the cash received and the discount allowed. This can be ascertained by simply adding the cash and discount columns in the three-column cash book. The total for each debtor can then be credited to the appropriate debtor account, or alternatively the two figures for cash and discount can be posted at the same time. Similar logic can be used to that used for the credit side of the cash book. The cash paid out has already been recorded in the cash book. The total of the discount column can be credited to the discount received account in the nominal ledger. The total of the cash and discount columns can then be debited to the appropriate individual debtor accounts, thus completing the double entry.

3.4 Activity

Write up a three-column cash book from the following details, balance off at the end of the month, and show the relevant discount allowed account as it would appear in the general/nominal ledger.

April	1	Opening balance – cash £100, bank £600
	2	Bought goods for £250 paying by cheque
	3	Further cash of £50 is paid into the business by the owner
	7	Paid J. Golding £100 owing to him, by means of a cheque for £95, £5 discount being received
	10	Cash sales £100
	13	H. Phipps paid us his account of £50 by cheque for £45, the difference being discount
	17	Paid W. Lawrence £60 owing to him by means of a cheque for £55
	20	Received cash in settlement of the following accounts, on which we agree to allow 10% discount
		S. Hughes – £50, A. Howard – £60, G. Manne – £80
	22	Paid £150 cash into the bank
	26	Paid the following accounts by cheque, a discount of 5% being allowed. T. Morphew £20, K. Williams £40, J. Barry £60
	30	Paid wages of £25 in cash

3.5 Activity solution

Cash book

Date	Details	fo	Disc	Cash	Bank	Date	Details	fo	Disc	Cash	Bank
			£	£	£				£	£	£
April 1	Balance b/d			100	600	April 2	Purchases				250
3	Capital			50		7	J Golding		5		95
10	Sales				100	17	W. Lawrence		5		55
13	H. Phipps		5		45	22	Contra			150	
20	S. Hughes		5	45		26	T. Morphew		1		19
20	A. Havard		6	54		26	K. Williams		2		38
20	G. Manne		8	72		26	C. Barry		3		57
22	Contra				150	30	Wages			25	
						30	Balance c/d			246	281
	To discount						To discount				
	allowed	NL	£24	£421	£795		received	NL	£16	£421	£795
May 1	Balance	b/d		246	281						

Nominal ledger

Discounts allowed account

			£		£
April 30	Cash Book	CBI	24		

3.6 Cash journals

A very large proportion of the transactions carried out by a business will result in the receipt or payment of cash, so a cash book may well be heavily used. Since every item in a cash book requires an additional posting to complete the double entry, the recording of cash transactions may still be quite tedious. Cash journals represent a possible way of reducing the amount of detailed posting needed, and also separate the responsibility for the recording of cash receipts and cash payments.

Lists of money received are kept in a **cash receipts journal**, and lists of money paid are kept in a **cash payments journal**. The totals of these lists are posted periodically to a cash account, which is clearly then much simpler. Indeed the cash account may then be kept in the general ledger, being essentially a summary account. Detailed postings will be from the cash journals.

The form of a cash receipts journal is normally similar to the following:

Cash receipts journal						
Date	Detail	Receipt number	Folio	Discount	Cash	Bank

In effect this kind of journal is nothing more than the debit side of a three-column cash book. The totals of the cash and bank columns will need to be posted to the debit side of the cash and bank accounts. Thereafter postings will be the same as for the debit side of the three-column cash book.

The cash payments journal will usually take a similar form, with a cheque number or similar reference being substituted for the receipt number. The totals of the cash and bank columns will need to be posted to the credit side of the cash and bank accounts. Thereafter postings will be the same as for the credit side of the three-column cash book.

Clearly the use of cash journals of the type described above will not save any detailed posting, as compared with a three-column cash book. The major advantage of such journals is the separation of the recording of receipts and payments. In order to save posting it is necessary to use **analysis cash journals**. The columns actually used will depend upon the particular needs of the business, but the format of such journals is likely to be along the lines shown below:

Cash receipts journal										
Date	Detail	Receipt No.	TOTAL	Sales		Interest	Rent	Sales ledger	Discount	Sales ledger
				Product A	Product A					

Cash payments journal										
Date	Detail	Cheque No.	TOTAL	Purchases	Wages	Rent and rates	Petty cash	Misc exps	Purchases ledger	Discount	Purchases ledger folio

3.7 Posting the cash journals

The postings for the cash receipts journal set out above would be as follows:

1   Post the total of the total column to the debit of the cash account

2   Post the total of the discount column to the debit of the discount allowed account

3   Post the totals of all the other columns (except the sales ledger column) to the credit of the appropriate revenue account

4   Post the individual amounts in the sales ledger column, together with the associated discount, to the credit of the personal accounts in the sales ledger.

The postings for the cash payments journal set out above would follow similar principles, as follows:

1   Post the total of the total column to the credit of the cash account

2   Post the total of the discount column to the credit of the discount received account

3   Post the totals of all the other columns (except the purchases ledger column) to the debit of the appropriate expense account

4   Post the individual amounts in the purchases ledger column, together with the associated discount, to the debit of the personal accounts in the purchases ledger.

If necessary a further column, usually known as a ledger column, can be kept in either cash journal for all those items which cannot be analysed to one of the other columns. Any entries in the ledger columns would need to be posted in detail. Where such an additional column is used the folio column would show all the references for the detailed postings, not simply those to the sales or purchases ledger.

It can be seen that the use of analysis cash journals can provide a considerable saving in posting time when compared with the cash book or simple cash journals.

The cash journals need not be set out exactly as above. There are innumerable options. What matters is that the basic principles are followed. These can be summarised as a listing, substantiated by vouchers, which can be used to post both entries in the accounts, where possible substituting totals for detailed entries.

3.8 Petty cash book

A widely recognised principle of good accounting systems is that payments should be made by cheque as much as possible. This reduces the likelihood of fraud or theft because there is a much clearer audit trail with cheques than with cash.

There will, however, almost invariably be a few small transactions where cash payments are necessary. The normal solution is to make all the major payments by cheques, which are recorded in the cash payments journal, and to keep a small amount of cash (hence the name **petty cash**) on the premises, from which small payments can be made if necessary. Obviously some method of recording and control of petty cash payments is necessary. This usually takes the form of a **petty cash book**, a typical layout of which is given below. (Note that if a petty cash system is used the cash payments journal will only record cheque payments.)

Petty cash book										
Receipts	Folio	Date	Detail	Voucher No	TOTAL	Stationery	Postage	Travelling	Sundries	Ledger

The number of analysis columns varies with the needs of the business.

The operation of the petty cash book is normally as follows:

- There will usually be an agreed maximum amount which can be held. This amount is known as an **imprest** or **float**. When this amount is drawn on the bank an entry will be made in the cash payments journal to reflect it. The cheque is then handed to the petty cashier, who cashes it and holds the cash on the premises. The petty cash book, which is a ledger account, is then debited with the amount received, while the cash account is credited.

- When payments are made details are recorded on vouchers, consecutively numbered. If possible these should be accompanied by receipts obtained. They should also be authorised by a responsible official. These payments are then recorded on the credit side of the petty cash book in both the total column and the appropriate analysis column.

- At the end of whatever period is considered appropriate (every month, say), the total amount spent is ascertained. This amount is then reimbursed from the bank account, so that at the end of each month the cash in hand is the amount of the imprest or float. Thus at any moment the sum of the remaining cash float and the total of the vouchers should equal the imprest.

- At the end of each period, the total of each analysis column is posted to the appropriate account in the nominal ledger, thus completing the double entry. The petty cash book, as with the cash book, can therefore be seen to be both a book of prime entry and a ledger account.

The double entry is as follows:

1   Giving a cheque to the person in charge of petty cash – debit petty cash, credit cash at bank

2   Spending of the petty cash – debit totals of the individual analysis columns to the appropriate accounts, credit petty cash

3   Subsequent reimbursement – debit petty cash, credit cash at bank.

As with other analysis books, the use of an analysed petty cash book minimises posting, and means that posting only needs to be done once in a given period.

Note that there is ample documentary evidence to support petty cash payments in the form of vouchers giving details of the transaction and, where possible, receipts from suppliers. Control can be fully exercised in that the value of the cash in hand plus the value of the vouchers issued should always equal the amount of the total float.

In practice it may be necessary for an organisation to permit a number of individuals or departments to hold petty cash floats. Each individual or department will then keep its own petty cash book.

3.9   Activity

The Oakhill Printing Co. Ltd operates its petty cash account on the imprest system. It is maintained at a figure of £80 on the first day of each month.

At 30 April 19X7 the petty cash box held £19.37 in cash. During May 19X7, the following petty cash transaction arose:

Date 19X7			Amount £
May	1	Cash received to restore imprest	to be derived
	1	Bus fares	0.41
	2	Stationery	2.35
	4	Bus fares	0.30
	7	Postage stamps	1.70
	7	Trade journal	0.95
	8	Bus fares	0.64
	11	Correcting fluid	1.29
	12	Typewriter ribbons	5.42
	14	Parcel postage	3.45
	15	Paper clips	0.42

15	Newspapers	2.00
16	Photocopier repair	16.80
19	Postage stamps	1.50
20	Drawing pins	0.38
21	Train fare	5.40
22	Photocopier paper	5.63
23	Display decorations	3.07
23	Correcting fluid	1.14
25	Wrapping paper	0.78
26	String	0.61
27	Sellotape	0.75
27	Biro pens	0.46
28	Typewriter repair	13.66
30	Bus fares	2.09
June 1	Cash received to restore imprest	to be derived

Open and post the company's petty cash account for the period 1 May to 1 June 19X7 inclusive and balance the account at 30 May 19X7.

In order to facilitate the subsequent double-entry postings, all items of expense appearing in the 'payments' column should then be analysed individually into suitably labelled expense columns.

3.10 Activity solution

Receipts	fo	Date	Detail	Voucher no	Total	Travel	Stationery	Postage	Office sundries	Repairs
					£	£	£	£	£	£
19.37		May 1	Balance b/d							
60.63		1	Cash							
			Bus fares	1	0.41	0.41				
		2	Stationery	2	2.35		2.35			
		4	Bus fares	3	0.30	0.30				
		7	Postage	4	1.70			1.70		
			Trade journal	5	0.95				0.95	
		8	Bus fare	6	0.64	0.64				
		11	Correction fluid	7	1.29		1.29			
		12	Typing ribbon	8	5.42		5.42			
		14	Parcel post	9	3.45			3.45		
		15	Paper clips	10	0.42		0.42			
			Newspaper	11	2.00				2.00	
		16	Copier repair	12	16.80					16.80
		19	Postage	13	1.50			1.50		
		20	Drawing pins	14	0.38		0.38			
		21	Train fare	15	5.40	5.40				
		22	Copier paper	16	5.63		5.63			
		23	Display	17	3.07				3.07	
			Corr fluid	18	1.14		1.14			
		25	Wrap paper	19	0.78		0.78			
		27	St ring	20	0.61		0.61			
			Sellotape	21	0.75		0.75			
			Biro pens	22	0.46		0.46			
		28	Typwv. repair	23	13.66					13.66
		30	Bus fares	24	2.09	2.09				
					71.20	£8.84	£19.23	£6.65	£6.02	£30.46
		31	Balance c/d		8.80					
£80.00					£80.00					
£8.80		Jun 1	Balance b/d							
£71.20		1	Cash							

Note to solution

Other layouts and different expense columns could have been equally correct.

On 1 June £71.20 will be received, making the balance £80, the agreed float.

4 SUBSIDIARY BOOKS – OTHER TRANSACTIONS

4.1 Use of the journal

A subsidiary book is one in which a record of transactions is made prior to entry in the ledger. The main reasons for subsidiary books have already been identified:

- The reduction in the amount of detail included in ledger accounts

- Assisting in the scheduling of work in particular to avoid the situation arising where more than one person requires a particular ledger at the same time

- The linking of documentary evidence with the ledgers, and the provision of an audit trail. This third reason is extremely important, and many people consider that *all* transactions should be recorded in a book of original entry prior to posting to the ledger.

So far in this chapter credit transactions relating to sales, purchases and returns have been covered, together with cash transactions. There are still a number of transactions which do not pass through any of the above books. Any such items are therefore recorded in another book of original entry, known as the **journal**.

The form of the journal is as follows:

	folio	Dr	Cr
		£	£
Date Name of account/s to be debited Name of account/s to be credited Narrative description of the transaction			

It should be noted that the journal is not part of the ledger (that is, the double-entry system). It still has to be posted in the same way as any other book of original entry. Unlike the other books there are no savings of the time because of the posting of totals, since all items have to be posted in detail. The main advantage of the journal is to complete the system of original entry, thus ensuring that every transaction goes through a book of original entry. The format shown above can provide much more detailed information about a transaction than can an entry in the ledger, and can conveniently be linked with documentary evidence.

4.2 Advantages of the journal

This in turn leads to the following advantages of the journal:
- The risk of omission of one or both entries is reduced, particularly where more than one ledger is kept and one is in use at the required time. Some form of distinctive ticking off of items posted must be devised

- Because more information as to the nature of a transaction can be given in the journal than in the ledger, complicated entries can be more easily understood

- Frauds, irregularities or errors become easier to find because full reasons are given for a particular transaction

- It ensures better continuity if staff changes, because it provides an explanation of more unusual past transactions.

5 CHAPTER SUMMARY

- This chapter has shown why it is necessary to have a system of subsidiary records in which details of transactions are recorded, prior to their inclusion in the ledger accounts. It has also identified the typical range of subsidiary books kept when a manual system is used, and a possible format for each. These include:

  - **Sales book** – for recording credit sales

  - **Purchases book** – for recording credit purchases

- **Sales returns book** – for recording sales returns
- **Purchases returns book** – for recording purchases returns
- **Cash book** – or cash journals – for recording cash and bank transactions
- **Petty cash book** – for recording expenditure in the form of cash; used when most transactions relating to expenditure are paid by cheque and recorded in a cash payments journal
- **Journal** – recording any transactions not included elsewhere.

- The subsidiary records provide considerable advantages in terms of organisation of the accounting system, in that they permit jobs to be broken down into parts, with particular individuals being given responsibility for the posting to the ledgers of particular transactions, or parts of transactions. Greater specialisation can occur, internal control can be improved, documentary evidence can be conveniently linked to the records to provide an audit trail, and a certain amount of unnecessary detail can be eliminated.

- Typically the ledger accounts are subdivided into convenient groups of accounts, designed to fit with the system of subsidiary records. The divisions identified are:
  - **Nominal ledger** – dealing with items to be included in the profit and loss account
  - **Cash book** – dealing with the cash and bank account
  - **Sales ledger** – dealing with debtors
  - **Purchases ledger** – dealing with creditors
  - **General ledger** – dealing with remaining items.

6   SELF TEST QUESTIONS

6.1   Identify the typical divisions of the ledger. (1.4)

6.2   Why does a business require subsidiary records as well as double-entry records? (2.2)

6.3   Which of the following books of prime entry is part of the 'double entry'?

   (a)   Sales (day) book
   (b)   Cash book
   (c)   Journal
   (d)   Purchases returns book. (3.2)

6.4   How should the period total of the discount column on the credit side of a three-column cash book be posted?

   (a)   Debit discounts allowed account
   (b)   Credit discounts received account
   (c)   Credit discounts received account, debit purchase ledger control account
   (d)   Debit discounts allowed account, credit sales ledger control account. (3.3)

6.5   Which of the following statements relating to petty cash is true?

   (a)   The imprest is the amount of petty cash left at the end of the month
   (b)   The imprest is equal to the sum of the balance, plus the total petty cash payments so far that month
   (c)   The imprest is the total of the payments for the month
   (d)   The imprest is the minimum amount to which the petty cash balance is allowed to fall before more cash is drawn from the bank. (3.8)

7 EXAMINATION TYPE QUESTIONS

7.1 Sales Items

Record the following in the sales book and sales return book, using analysis columns if appropriate. Then post to the sales ledger and the nominal ledger. Totals are to be posted to the nominal ledger monthly.

February	1	Sold quantity of product A to A. Crook for £100
		Sold quantity of product A to B. Best for £50
		Sold quantity of product B to B. Best for £50
February	4	Sold quantity of product C to G. Worth for £120
		Sold quantity of product B to N. Ord for £65
February	5	Product B returned by N. Ord to the value of £10
		Product A returned by B. Best to the value of £5
February	12	Sold quantity of product A to A. Crook for £80
		Sold quantity of product B to B. Best for £60
		Sold quantity of product C to A. Crook for £100
		Sold quantity of product C to G. Worth for £80
February	15	Product B returned by B. Best to the value of £10
		Product A returned by A. Crook to the value of £5
February	21	Sold quantity of product C to A. Crook for £110
		Sold quantity of product C to B. Best for £50
		Sold quantity of product A to N. Ord for £30
February	27	Product A returned by N. Ord to the value of £5

(20 marks)

7.2 Cash Payments Journal

Write up the cash payments journal and indicate the postings you would make to the ledger accounts, for the following payments by cheque:

January	1	Payments to creditors	
		– A £95 in satisfaction of a debt of	£100
		– B £90 in satisfaction of a debt of	£100
		– C £180 in satisfaction of a debt of	£200
	5	Paid wages	£100
	7	Paid rent	£20
	9	Paid miscellaneous expenses	£10
	11	Paid wages	£100
	13	Paid for fuel	£20
	17	Purchased fixed asset for cash	£200
	19	Paid wages	£100
	21	Paid rent	£20
	23	Payments to creditors	
		– D £95 in satisfaction of a debt of	£100
		– E £90 in satisfaction of a debt of	£100
	27	Paid for fuel	£30
	30	Paid electricity bill	£20

(18 marks)

7.3 Cash Book Entries

The following information is to be recorded:

1	Opening balances are cash £50 and bank overdraft	£100
2	Cash sales	£500

3	Credit purchases from P	£400
4	Wages paid in cash	£100
5	Bankings	£200
6	Credit sales to Q	£300
7	Paid P £250 less 10% discount, by cheque	
8	Received cash from Q, £200 less 5% discount	
9	Send goods to R on approval (that is, on sale or return), cost £60 selling price	£135
10	Wages paid by cheque	£100
11	R returns one third of the goods he was sent on approval, accepts one-third and delays a decision on the remaining third	
12	Bank charges notified of £30	
13	Receive balance due from Q, less discount of 4%, in cash.	

Open all necessary accounts, including a three-column cash book or otherwise, and record this information. Include any closing entries you consider necessary in relation to the transactions with R. Close off the accounts and prepare partial trial balance. Entries may be cross-referenced by the number of the transaction rather than by narrative.

(18 marks)

(ACCA, June 1991)

8 ANSWERS TO EXAMINATION TYPE QUESTIONS

8.1 Sales Items

Sales book

Date February	Detail	Invoice	Folio	Total £	A £	B £	C £
1	A. Crook			100	100		
1	B. Best		postings	100	50	50	
4	G. Worth			120			120
4	N. Ord		in	65		65	
12	A. Crook			180	80		100
12	B. Best		detail	60		60	
12	C. Worth			80			80
21	A. Crook			110			110
21	B. Best			50			50
21	N. Ord			30	30		
				£895	£260	£175	£460

To Sales A/B/C accounts in total

Sales returns book

Date February	Detail	Credit note	Folio	Total £	A £	B £	C £
5	N. Ord		Postings	10		10	
5	B. Best			5	5		
15	B. Best		in	10		10	
15	A. Crook			5	5		
27	N. Ord		detail	5	5		
				£35	£15	£20	£–

To: Sales returns A/B/C accounts in total

A. Crook

			£				£
Feb 21	Sale – Prod A	SB1	100	Feb 15	Return – Prod A	SRB1	5
12	Sale – Prod A	SB1	80				
	Sale – Prod C	SB1	100	28	Balance	c/d	385
21	Sale – Prod C	SB1	110				
			£390				£390
Mar 1	Balance	b/d	385				

B. Best

			£				£
Feb 1	Sale – Prod A	SB1	50	Feb 5	Return – Prod A	SRB1	5
	Sale – Prod B	SB1	50	15	Return – Prod B	SRB1	10
12	Sale – Prod B	SB1	60				
21	Sale – Prod C	SB1	50	28	Balance	c/d	195
			£210				£210
Mar 1Balance		b/d	195				

N. Ord

			£				£
Feb 4	Sale – Prod B	SB1	65	Feb 5	Return – Prod	SRB1	10
21	Sale – Prod A	SB1	30	27	Return – Prod A	SRB1	5
			28	Balance	c/d	80	
			£95				£95
Mar 1	Balance	b/d	80				

G. Worth

			£				£
Feb 4	Sale – Prod C	SB1	120	Feb 28	Balance	c/d	200
12	Sale – Prod C	SB1	80				
			200				200
Mar 1Balance		b/d	200				

Sales account (product A)

			£
February 28	Debtors	SB1	260

Sales account (product B)

			£
February 28	Debtor	SB1	175

Sales account (product C)

				£
	February 28	Debtors	SB1	460

Sales returns account (product A)

			£	
February 28	Debtors	SRB1	15	

Sales returns account (product B)

			£	
February 28	Debtors	SRB1	20	

8.2　Cash Payments Journal

Cash payments journal

Date	Detail no	ch.	fo	Total £	Wages £	Rent rates £	Fuel and electricity £	Sundries £	Other £	PL £	Disc £
Jan 1	A	1		95						95	5
	B	2		90						90	10
	C	3		180						180	20
5	Wages	4		100	100						
7	Rent	5		20		20					
9	Misc expenses	6		10				10			
11	Wages	7		100	100						
13	Fuel	8		20			20				
17	Fixed asset	9		200					200		
19	Wages	10		100	100						
21	Rent	11		20		20					
23	D	12		95						95	5
23	E	13		90						90	10
27	Fuel	14		30			30				
30	Fuel	15		20			20				
				£1,170	£300	£40	£70	£10	£200	£550	£50
				To cash	To wages	To rent /rates	To Fuel and electricity	To sundries	Post in detail		

The total of the discount column will be posted to the discount received account. The individual figures in the discount column will be debited to individual creditor accounts in the purchases ledger.

8.3　Cash Book Entries

Cash book

	Discount allowed £	Cash received £	Bank £		Discount received £	Cash paid £	Bank £
(1)		50		(1)			100
(2)		500		(4)		100	
(5)			200	(5)		200	
(8)	10	190		(7)	25		225
(13)	4	96		(10)			100
				(12)			30
Balance c/d			255	Balance c/d		536	
	14	836	455		25	836	455
Balance b/d		536		Balance b/d			255

Purchases

	£	
(3)	400	

Wages

	£		£
(4)	100		
(10)	100	Balance c/d	200
	200		200
Balance b/d	200		

Cost of sales

	£	
(11)	20	

Stock on sale or return

	£	
(11)	20	

Bank charges

	£	
(12)	30	

Sales

	£		£
(11)	45	(2)	500
(11)	45	(6)	300
Balance c/d	845	(9)	135
	935		935
		Balance b/d	845

P's account

	£		£
(7)	250	(3)	400
Balance c/d	150		
	400		400
		Balance b/d	150

Q's account

	£		£
(6)	300	(8)	200
		(13)	100
	300		300

R's account

	£		£
(9)	135	(11)	45
		(11)	45
		Balance c/d	45
	135		135
Balance b/d	45		

	Dr	Cr
	£	£
Cash and bank	536	255
Discounts allowed and received	14	25
Purchases	400	
Sales		845
Wages	200	
Stock on sale or return	20	
Cost of sales		20
Bank charges	30	
P		150
R	45	
Cash and bank opening difference	50	
	1,295	1,295

12 THE JOURNAL

INTRODUCTION AND LEARNING OBJECTIVES

Chapter 11 included a brief introduction to the journal and its uses. In this chapter we will consider the journal in more detail. We will see how various transactions relating to a business will be recorded using this book. Specifically, we will see how a set of books for a business can be opened, how we record the purchase of fixed assets and how we make year-end adjustments using the journal. The correction of errors and the clearing of a suspense account will also be dealt with in the journal and will be considered in this chapter.

At the end of the chapter there is a worked example, which is designed to reinforce your understanding of subsidiary books and the use of the journal. This is an integral part of the text and should be studied carefully.

When you have studied this chapter you should be able to do the following:

- Explain common uses of the journal

- Correct errors through the journal

- Make year-end adjustments through the journal.

1 THE JOURNAL – USES

1.1 Introduction

In Chapter 11 we saw that any transactions which do not pass through one of the other books of original entry will pass through the journal. You will recall that the form of the journal is as follows:

	folio	Dr	Cr
		£	£
Date Name of account/s to be debited Name of account/s to be credited Narrative description of the transaction			

We saw also in Chapter 11 that there are no definitive rules about the format of subsidiary records. As the journal is a kind of 'clearing up' book of original entry, it is therefore impossible to say with certainty that the journal should be used for a particular type of transaction. Nevertheless, the following are typically the main uses to which the journal is put.

- Entries needed to open a new set of books
- Purchases and sales of fixed assets on credit. This may not be true if an analysis purchases book is used, because a column may be allocated for that type of asset
- Correction of errors
- Other transfers.

Each of these uses is considered below.

1.2   Opening entries

In practice, opening entries are usually complicated, because capital is frequently represented by several types of asset minus several types of liabilities. If these were simply entered directly into the ledger accounts it would probably prove extremely difficult at a later date to tell what the opening assets and liabilities were. Cross- referencing is also difficult using ledger accounts only.

Example

C. Gover opened his accounts with the following assets and liabilities:

Land and Buildings £50,000; Fixtures and Fittings £5,000; Stock £25,000; Cash £2,500; Debtors – D. Harvey £2,500, P. Gover £5,000; M. Newman £5,000; Creditors – M. Bolwell £5,000, G. Paul £1,000.

This sort of situation may well arise when a business has been carried on for some time without proper accounts being kept.

Clearly the total of the entries in the debit column of the journal must be equal to the total of the entries in the credit column. If this were not the case the ledgers would not balance once the postings had been made. Here it is necessary to calculate the capital figure, being assets less liabilities (£89,000). The journal entry to record this transaction would be as follows:

		folio	Dr	Cr
			£	£
January 1	Land and buildings	GL1	50,000	
	Fixtures and fittings	GL2	5,000	
	Stock	NL1	25,000	
	Cash	CB1	2,500	
	D. Harvey	SL70	2,500	
	P. Gover	SL60	5,000	
	M. Newman	SL100	5,000	
	M. Bolwell	PL20		5,000
	G. Paul	PL45		1,000
	Capital	GL3		89,000
	Being opening balances on			
	commencement of business		£95,000	£95,000

1.3   Purchase and sales of fixed assets

When fixed assets are bought on credit no accounting problems should be encountered. The necessary double entry is a debit to the fixed assets account and a credit to the suppliers account. The main purpose of recording it in the journal is to provide, in the narrative, the necessary reference to documentary evidence.

Example

On 1 August a motor van is purchased on credit from Castle Road Garage for £2,500. The journal entry for this would appear as follows:

		folio	Dr	Cr
			£	£
August 1	Motor van	GL9	2,500	
	Castle Road Garage	GL11		2,500
	Being the purchase of motor van			
	G413 GDB invoice A209 refers			
	(or similar)			

Creditors relating to fixed assets will normally be recorded in the general ledger. However, where an analysis purchases book is used, and the purchase of fixed assets is recorded in that book, creditors relating to fixed assets will probably be kept in the purchases ledger.

1.4 Correction of errors

Errors which require correction through the journal fall into two categories:

- Errors which do not affect the agreement of the trial balance
- Errors which do affect the agreement of the trial balance.

Each of these is explained below.

1.5 Errors which do not affect the agreement of the trial balance

These errors are often found in practice.

- Errors of omission – where an entry has been completely omitted from the books
- Errors of commission – where a wrong account has been debited or credited
- Errors of principle – where an account of completely the wrong type has been debited or credited (An error of commission would be something like the crediting of the wrong creditors personal account due to a similarity of names, whereas an error of principle involves an incorrect entry in an account which is of a *fundamentally* different nature to the correct account).
- Compensating errors – where an error or errors on one side of the accounts is matched by equal and opposite errors on the other side of different accounts
- Errors relating to a complete reversal of entries, where the debit entry is made on the credit side, and the credit entry is made on the debit side
- Errors in the subsidiary book – an error which will be effectively posted to both sides of the accounts for an incorrect amount.

Where errors of these types occur all that is necessary is for adjusting entries to be made, eliminating the incorrect entry. Some reference back to the place of the error should be made in the narrative.

Example

Wages paid to D. Anthony amounting to £100 had been omitted from the books. In this case all that is required is the insertion of the entries into the journal and subsequent posting to the accounts. The correction of this omission would thus appear in the journal as follows:

		folio	Dr	Cr
			£	£
January 15	Wages	NL3	100	
	Cash	CB		100
	Being payment of wages to D. Anthony on 31 December – previously omitted. Refer to wages sheet ...			

Note that the main objective of the journal is satisfied, in that it provides a cross- reference for documentary evidence, thus preserving a clear audit trail. Note, however, that posting to the ledgers is still needed, but that this can take place at a later and more convenient time.

1.6   Activity

Indicate whether the following errors are errors of commission or of principle. Journalise the necessary corrections.

1   Sales of £150 to John Smith were debited to the account of Joan Smith

2   £500 wages paid for improvements to the factory had been debited to the wages account.

1.7   Activity solution

1   An error of commission.

2   An error of principle.

Date	Detail	Folio	Dr £	Cr £
January 1	John Smith	SL	150	
	Joan Smith	SL		150
	Being correction of invoice 0100 entered in wrong personal account – originally recorded in sales book on 23 December			
January 1	Buildings	GL	500	
	Wages	NL		500
	Being wages paid which relate to improvements, see time sheets for December Nos. 19/20			

1.8   Activity

Identify the nature of the following errors and journalise the necessary corrections:

1   The sales book was overcast by £100 (that is, the total was £100 too high). By complete coincidence a new vehicle purchased for £4,800 had been incorrectly debited as £4,900.

2   A payment of £25 to A. Messenger had been entered as a debit in the cash book and as a credit in his personal account.

3   Purchases amounting to £54 from M. Anne had been recorded in the purchases book as £45.

1.9   Activity solution

1   Compensating error.

2   Complete reversal of entries.

3   Error in the subsidiary book.

Date	Detail	Folio	Dr £	Cr £
(1) January 2	Sales	NL	100	
	Vehicles	GL		100
	Being correction of overcasting of sales day book 30 November and wrong debit to vehicles – journal 30 June refers			
(2) January 2	A. Messenger*	PL	50	
	Cash	CB		50
	Being correction of payment of cash incorrectly recorded as a receipt on 3 December			
(3) January 2	Purchases	NL	9	
	M. Anne	PL		9
	Being correction due in error of original entry – purchase invoice J0101 refers – also purchases book 15 December			

* Note: need to double amount of original entry. This is needed to cancel out the original entry and replace it with correct entry.

1.10 Errors which affect the agreement of the trial balance

All of the errors introduced so far have been errors which do not affect the agreement of the trial balance. By recording the corrections in the journal and subsequently posting them to the correct accounts all the necessary cross-references can be given. Not all errors are of this type. Some will prevent the trial balance from agreeing. This result is usually attributable to such things as incorrect additions and the making of incorrect entries on one or both sides of the accounts.

Where a trial balance does not agree it is advisable to check that all ledger account balances have been correctly included in the trial balance. Corrections of any errors in listing should result in a revised trial balance, but will not change the accounts. If the trial balance still does not agree the next stage in the correction process is to make it agree by making a single entry into an account known as a **suspense account**. This will enable the business to produce draft accounts for the business if required. However, the error (or errors) which lead to the creation of the suspense account must be discovered before the final accounts are prepared. Even a relatively small amount on the suspense cannot be dismissed as being immaterial as it may hide much larger compensating errors on each side of the accounts.

The suspense account becomes effectively part of the double-entry system and so, when the error is eventually found, the balance on the suspense account must be cleared by using the process of double entry. The correction of errors is also supported by an entry in the journal. The original errors are thus corrected in the books through the double-entry system with the posting from the journal acting as the correction.

Example

Suppose that in the trial balance of a business there is an excess of debits over credits of £64. It is thus necessary to open a suspense account and enter £64 on the credit side, thus making the trial balance agree.

At a later date the following two errors were found.

- In posting the total of the sales book at the end of August the total of £21,100 was read as £21,000

- A sale of £95 to J. Dix had been correctly recorded in the sales book, but had been posted to his account as £59.

The first error means that sales have been under-recorded by £100, and the second that a debtor (J. Dix) has been under-recorded by £36. The net effect of these two transactions will be to have £64 too little on the credit side. The amount was put in the suspense account.

When these errors were originally made they represented (in effect) single-sided entries, thus preventing the trial balance from agreeing. The opening of the suspense account provided the double entry to match these errors. Since the accounts are now in balance any corrections made must involve a double entry. Obviously the object of the corrections is to put right the original errors and to eliminate the suspense account. If a balance remains on the suspense account, further errors remain to be found.

The £64 credited to suspense account to make the trial balance agree consists of a credit of £100 due to the error on sales, and a debit of £36 due to the error on the account of J. Dix.

In order to correct the accounts and to eliminate the suspense account the following adjustments are necessary.

		folio	Dr	Cr
			£	£
March 31	Suspense	GL	100	
	Sales	NL		100
	Being correction of misposting of salesbook SB15 on 31/8/19X8			
March 31	J. Dix	SL	36	
	Suspense	GL		36
	Being correction of misposting from SB27 on 6/9/19X8, £95 being read as £59			

It should be remembered that *only* those items which affect the agreement of the trial balance will be corrected using the suspense account.

1.11   The effect on profit of clearing the suspense account

Sometimes you are required to deal with errors by showing their effect on the profit (or loss) of the business as well as on the suspense account balance. It is usually necessary to prepare a statement to show the effect on profit. There is no set format for such a statement although the following format is often used.

Statement showing the effect on net profit (loss) for the period

	£	£
Net profit for the year		x
Error 1	(x)	
Error 2	(x)	
Error 3		x
Error 4	(x)	
Error 5		x
	(x)	x
Deduct errors resulting in a decrease in profit		(x)
Revised profit (loss) for the period		x

The activity below requires this type of statement as well as adjustments to the suspense account.

1.12 Activity

The draft final accounts of RST Ltd for the year ended 30 April 19X9 showed a net profit for the year after tax of £78,263.

During the subsequent audit, the following errors and omissions were discovered. At the draft stage a suspense account had been opened to record the net difference.

1		Trade debtors were shown as £55,210. However,
	(a)	bad debts of £610 had not been written off,
	(b)	the existing provision for doubtful debtors, £1,300, should have been adjusted to 2% of debtors.
	(c)	a provision of 2% for discounts on debtors should have been raised.
2		Rates of £491 which had been prepaid at 30 April 19X8 had not been brought down on the rates account as an opening balance.
3		A vehicle held as a fixed asset, which had originally cost £8,100 and for which £5,280 had been provided as depreciation, had been sold for £1,350. The proceeds had been correctly debited to bank but had been credited to sales. No transfers had been made to the disposals account.
4		Credit purchases of £1,762 had been correctly debited to the purchases account but had been credited to the supplier's account as £1,672.
5		A piece of equipment costing £9,800 and acquired on 1 May 19X4 for use in the business had been debited to the purchases account. (The company depreciates equipment at 20% per annum on cost.)
6		Items valued at £2,171 had been completely omitted from the closing stock figure.
7		At 30 April 19X9 an accrual of £543 for electricity charges and an insurance prepayment of £162 had been omitted.
8		The credit side of the wages account had been under-added by £100 before the balance on the account had been determined.

Using relevant information from that given above:

1   Prepare a statement correcting the draft net profit after tax

2   Post and balance the suspense account. (*Note:* the opening balance of this account has not been given and must be derived.)

1.13 Activity solution

1   Statement correcting draft net profit after tax

			Effect on draft profit	
			Increase	**Decrease**
			£	**£**
(a)	(i)	Bad debts		610
	(ii)	Doubtful debts provision adjustment (£1,300 – [(55,210 – 610) × 2%])	208	
	(iii)	Discount provision adjustment [(£54,600 – (1,300 – 208)] × 2% (see note)		1,070
(b)		Rates		491
(c)		Sales cancelled		1,350
		Loss on disposal of vehicle (£1,350 – (8,100 – 5,280))		1,470
(d)		No effect on profit		
(e)		Purchase cancelled	9,800	

		£	£
	Depreciation (£9,800 × 20%)		1,960
(f)	Omitted stock	2,171	
(g)	Accrued electricity		543
	Prepaid insurance	162	
(h)	Wages undercast	100	
	Total corrections	12,441	£7,494
		7,494	
	Net increase in profit	4,947	
	Draft profit	78,263	
	Revised profit after tax	£83,210	

2

Suspense account

	£		£
(d) Creditors (1,762 – 1,672)	90	(b) Rates	491
(h) Wages	100		
Opening balance (balancing figure)	301		
	£491		£491

Note: It would be illogical to provide for discounts allowed on debts which had already been provided for as bad.

2   OTHER TRANSFERS

2.1   Using the journal to record year-end adjustments

The journal can be, and frequently is, used to record any other transfers which are considered necessary. Typically year-end adjustments will be first recorded in the journal.

For example, consider this year-end adjustment – depreciation for the year is to be £2,000. This will involve a debit to the profit and loss account in the nominal ledger and a credit to the appropriate depreciation provision account in the general ledger. However, an adjustment of this nature has two problems associated with it.

- How are the people in charge of the two ledgers going to be notified of the required entries?
- What will the documentary evidence be for the transaction?

The answer to the first of these questions is that the entries must first be recorded in the journal, for subsequent posting to the two ledgers. As regards documentary evidence, some kind of authorisation is necessary from management. In practice there will usually be a routine whereby one person or department is responsible for such authorisations. These can be sent in memorandum form to the person in charge of the journal, who can then enter them in the journal. They can subsequently be posted to the ledgers as and when convenient. As before there exists a clear audit trail back from the ledger, though the journal, back to the person authorising the transaction. The cross-reference in the folio columns in the ledger should refer back to the journal page number. In the journal the folios will show clearly where the ledger accounts can be found, while the narrative will provide the necessary reference back to the authorisation or voucher.

In some organisations the journal takes the form of consecutively numbered journal papers. The form is much the same, but there is much more room for the narrative, as only one transaction is recorded on each paper. The authorisations received can be attached to the papers.

Adjustments for bad debts and the bad debts provision follow much the same procedure. This will usually involve authorisations from the credit control department to the journal clerk, recording in the journal, and subsequent posting to the sales ledger to credit debtors accounts, to the nominal ledger to debit bad debts and to the general ledger to credit the bad debts provision.

For prepayments and accruals, it is usual to find that the department necessary for paying bills prepares lists of prepayments and accruals at the year end. These can then be recorded in the journal and subsequently posted.

Example

At the end of its financial year (31 March 19X4) a business has a prepayment relating to rates of £100, and an accrual relating to heating and lighting of £50. These would be journalised as follows:

		folio	Dr	Cr
			£	£
March 31	Rates (19X4/5)	NL	100	
	Rates (19X3/4)	NL		100
	Prepayments of rates as lists prepared by credit control department–31 March			
March 31	Gas (19X3/4)	NL	50	
	Gas (19X4/5)	NL		50
	Accrual as lists prepared by credit control department 31 March			

3 SUBSIDIARY RECORDS – A WORKED EXAMPLE

3.1 Introduction

To help reinforce the chapters on subsidiary records and the journal, let us work through the following exercise.

N. Bumpo has been in business for some time, though without keeping double- entry records. On 1 January 19X3 he had the following assets and liabilities.

> Premises £100,000; Equipment £20,000; Vehicles £10,000; Stock £10,000
>
> Debtors – O. Edwards £2,000, M. Richards £1,000; Bank £5,000; Cash £500
>
> Creditors – R. Duke £1,000, R. Mant £500.

These should be recorded in the journal and then posted to the relevant accounts.

The daily transactions for January are given below. These should be recorded in the appropriate subsidiary book and posted to the accounts. A trial balance is to be extracted on 31 January. N. Bumpo decides that the ledger will consist of a general ledger, a nominal ledger, a purchase ledger, a sales ledger and a cash book. He also decides to keep a journal, sales and purchases books, as well as two returns books. Invoices are to be recorded in the subsidiary books on the day that they are received or issued, but postings from the subsidiary books only need to be made at the end of the month.

The transactions for the month are:

January	1	Bought goods on credit from C. Man £800, A. Con £600 and D. Done £1,000
	2	Paid insurance of £1,000 by cheque, which related to the year
	3	Sold goods on credit to R. Cumming £1,000, M. Scott £1,500 and M. Revill £500
	7	Cash sales of £300. Paid miscellaneous expenses of £200 in cash
	8	Received cheques from O. Edwards £1,800 and M. Richards £900 in settlement of their debts of £2,000 and £1,000
	10	M. Revill returned £100 worth of goods
	12	Bought goods on credit from C. Man £400, R. Hard £1,000 and R. Weck £1,150
	13	Returned goods to R. Weck £150

14	Paid the following amounts by cheque: Motor expenses £250, R. Duke £1,000, R. Mant £500. Stamps and stationery were bought for £150 cash.		
17	Sales were made on credit to R. Cumming £900, N. Itch £700 and A. Crook £1,000		
18	Goods were returned by R. Cumming and N. Itch to the value of £100 each		
20	Paid C. Man a cheque for £760 in settlement of a debt of £800		
	Paid A. Con a cheque for £600 in settlement of a debt of that amount		
	Paid D. Done a cheque for £950 in settlement of a debt of £1,000		
22	Received cheques from the following in respect of the sales made of them on 3 January and the returns of 10 January		
	R. Cumming £900, M. Scott £1,350, M. Revill £360		
23	Purchased a new piece of furniture on credit for £1,000 from Pty Ltd		
24	Stamps and stationery were purchased for £100 cash		
26	Sales were made on credit to R. Cumming £1,000, N. Itch £1,150 and H. Nelson £800		
28	Goods were returned by R. Cumming to the value of £100 and by N. Itch to the value of £150		
	Paid C. Man a cheque for £380 in settlement of a debt of £400		
	Paid R. Hard a cheque for £1,000 in settlement of a debt of £1,000		
	Paid R. Weck a cheque for £950 in settlement of a debt of £1,000		
30	Received cheques from the following in respect of the sales (less returns) of 17 and 18 January		
	R. Cumming £720, N. Itch £540.		
	Cash was received from A. Crook of £1,000.		

3.2 The subsidiary records

The opening entries would be recorded in the journal, together with the transaction of 23 January, the purchase of fixed asset on credit. The remaining items would be recorded in the four day books or the cash book. The subsidiary records should appear as follows.

The journal				
		folio	Dr	Cr
			£	£
January 1	Premises	GL1	100,000	
	Equipment	GL2	20,000	
	Vehicles	GL3	10,000	
	Stock	NL1	10,000	
	Debtors – O. Edwards	SL1	2,000	
	M. Richards	SL2	1,000	
	Bank	CB1	5,000	
	Cash	CB1	500	
	Creditors – R. Duke	PL1		1,000
	R. Mant	PL2		500
	Capital	GL4		147,000
	Being opening balances – see N. Bumpo's memorandum		£148,500	£148,500
January 23	Furniture	GL5	1,000	
	Pty Ltd	GL6		1,000
	Being purchase of new bureau – invoice no. P101 refers			

Sales book

				Detail	Invoice	Folio	Amount
							£
January	3		R. Cumming	J001	SL3	1,000
			M. Scott	J002	SL4	1,500
			M. Revill	J003	SL5	500
	17		R. Cumming	J004	SL3	900
			N. Itch	J005	SL6	700
			A. Crook	J006	SL7	1,000
	26		R. Cumming	J007	SL3	1,100
			N. Itch	J008	SL6	1,150
			H. Nelson	J009	SL8	800
			To sales account		NL2	£8,650

Sales returns book

Date			Detail	Invoice	Folio	Amount
						£
January	10		M. Revill	JC001	SL5	100
	18		R. Cumming	JC002	SL3	100
			N. Itch	JC003	SL6	100
	28		R. Cumming	JC004	SL3	100
			N. Itch	JC005	SL6	150
			To sales returns account		NL3	£550

Purchases book

Date			Detail	Invoice	Folio	Amount
						£
January	1		C. Man	M001	PL3	800
			A. Con	C999	PL4	600
			D. Done	D003	PL5	1,000
	12		C. Man	M008	PL3	400
			R. Hard	H007	PL6	1,000
			R. Weck	W986	PL7	1,150
			To purchases account		NL4	£4,950

Purchases returns book

Date			Detail	Invoice	Folio	Amount
						£
January	13		R. Week	W986	PL7	150
			To Purchases returns account		NL5	£150

					Cash book					
Date	**Detail**	**Folio**	**Disc**	**Cash**	**Bank**	**Date**	**Detail**	**Folio**	**Disc**	**Cash**	**Bank**
			£	£	£				£	£	£
Jan 21	Balance	J1		500	5,000	Jan 21	Insurances				1,000
7	Sales	NL2		300		7	Misc expenses	NL7		200	
8	O. Edwards	SL1	200		1,800	14	Motor expenses	NL8			250
	M. Richards	SL2	100		900		R. Duke	SL1			1,000
22	R. Cumming	SL3	100		900		R. Mant	PL2			500
	M. Scott	SL4	150		1,350		Stationery	NL9		150	
	M. Revill	SL5	40		360	20	C. Man	PL3	40		760
30	R. Cumming	SL3	80		720		A. Con	PL4			600
	N. Itch	SL6	60		540		D. Done	PL5	50		950
	A. Crook	SL7		1,000		24	Stationery	NL9		100	
						28	C. Man	PL3	20		380
							R. Hard	PL6			1,000
							S. Weck	PL7	50		950
						31	Balance	c/d		1,350	4,180
	To discount						To discount				
	allowed	NL10	730	1,800	11,570		received	NL11	160	1,800	11,570
Feb 1	Balance			1,350	4,180						

3.3   Recording in the ledger accounts

At this stage every transaction has been recorded in the subsidiary books. These now need to be posted to the appropriate accounts. The subdivision of the ledgers, and the individual accounts contained in each, are shown below. Note that the cash book is both a subsidiary book and the accounts for cash and bank.

General ledger

Premises						GL1
			£			£
January	1	Balance	J1	100,000		

Equipment						GL2
			£			£
January	1	Balance	J1	20,000		

Vehicles						GL3
			£			£
January	1	Balance	J1	10,000		

Capital						GL4
		£				£
			January	1	Balance	J1	147,000

Furniture						GL5
		£				£
January 23Pty Ltd		J1	1,000			

				Pty Ltd			GL6
			£				£
				January 23	Furniture	J1	1,000

Nominal ledger
Stock NL1

			£				£
January 1	Balance	J1	10,000				

Sales NL2

			£				£
				January 7	Cash	CB1	300
				31	Debtors	SB1	8,650

Sales returns NL3

			£		£
January 31	Debtors	SRB1	550		

Purchases NL4

			£		£
January 31	Creditors	PB1	4,950		

Purchases returns NL5

		£				£
			January 31	Creditors	PRB1	150

Insurance NL6

			£		£
January 2	Cash	CB1	1,000		

Miscellaneous expenses NL7

			£		£
January 7	Cash	CB1	200		

Motor expenses NL8

			£		£
January 14	Cash	CB1	250		

Stationery NL9

			£		£
January 14	Cash	CB1	150		
24	Cash	CB1	100		

Discount allowed   **NL10**

			£					£
January 31	Debtors	CB1	730					

Discount received   **NL11**

			£					£
				January 31	Creditors	CB1		160

Sales ledger
O. Edwards   **SL1**

			£					£
January 1	Balance	J1	2,000	January	8	Cash & disc	CB1	2,000
			2,000					2,000

M. Richards   **SL2**

			£					£
January 1	Balance	J1	1,000	January	8	Cash & disc	CB1	1,000
			1,000					1,000

R. Cumming   **SL3**

			£					£
January	3	Sales	SB1	1,000	January	18	Sales returns	SRB1	100
	17	Sales	SB1	900		22	Cash & disc	CB1	1,000
	26	Sales	SB1	1,100		28	Sales & disc	SRB1	100
					30	Cash & disc	CB1	800
					31	Balance	c/d	1,000
			3,000					3,000
February 1	Balance	b/d	1,000					

M. Scott   **SL4**

			£					£
January	3	Sales	SB1	1,500	January	22	Cash & disc	CB1	1,500
			1,500					1,500

M. Revill   **SL5**

			£					£
January	2	Sales	SB1	500	January	10	Sales returns	SRB1	100
					22	Cash & disc	CB1	400
			500					500

N. Itch   SL6

			£					£
January 17	Sales	SB1	700	January	15	Sales returns	SRB1	100
26	Sales	SB1	1,150		28	Sales returns	SRB1	150
					30	Cash & disc	CB1	600
					31	Balance	c/d	1,000
			1,850					1,850
February 1	Balance	b/d	1,000					

A. Crook   SL7

			£					£
January 17	Sales	SB1	1,000	January	30	Cash & disc	CB1	1,000
			1,000					1,000

H. Nelson   SL8

			£		£
January 26	Sales	SB1	800		

Purchases ledger
R. Duke   PL1

			£					£
January 14	Cash	CB1	1,000	January	1	Balance	J1	1,000
			1,000					1,000

R. Mant   PL2

			£					£
January 14	Cash	CB1	500	January	1	Balance	J1	500
			500					500

C. Man   PL3

			£					£
January 20	Cash & disc	CB1	800	January	1	Purchases	PB1	800
28	Cash & disc	CB1	400		12	Purchases	PB1	400
			1,200					1,200

A. Con   PL4

			£					£
January 20	Cash	CB1	600	January	1	Purchases	PB1	600
			600					600

	D. Done								**PL5**

			£						£
January 20	Cash & Discount	CB1	1,000	January	1	Purchases	PB1	1,000
			1,000					1,000

	R. Hard								**PL6**

			£						£
January 28	Cash	CB1	1,000	January	12	Purchases	PB1	1,000
			1,000					1,000

	R. Weck								**PL7**

			£						£
January 13	Purchases returns	PRB1	150	January	12	Purchases	PB1	1,150
28	Cash & disc	CB1	1,000					
			1,150					1,150

In practice both the purchases ledger and the sales ledger would be in alphabetical order.

3.4 Preparation of the trial balance

It is now possible to draw up a trial balance as follows:

Trial balance as at 31 January

		Dr £	Cr £
Cash book balances –	Bank	4,180	
	Cash	1,350	
General ledger balances:			
	Premises	100,000	
	Equipment	20,000	
	Vehicles	10,000	
	Capital		147,000
	Furniture	1,000	
	Pty Ltd		1,000
Nominal ledger balances:			
	Stock	10,000	
	Sales		8,950
	Sales returns	550	
	Purchases	4,950	
	Purchases returns		150
	Insurance	1,000	
	Miscellaneous	200	
	Motor expenses	250	
	Stationery	250	
	Discount allowed	730	
	Discount received		160

Sales ledger balances:

O. Edwards		
M. Richards		
R. Cumming	1,000	
M. Scott		
M. Revill		
N. Itch	1,000	
A. Crook		
H. Nelson	800	

Purchases ledger balances:

R. Duke		
R. Mant		
C. Man		
A. Con		
D. Done		
R. Hard		
R. Weck		
	£157,260	£157,260

3.5 Preparation of the final accounts

Since the two sides of the trial balance agree it is possible to proceed to the preparation of final accounts. Assume that Bumpo wants final accounts prepared for January, and that the following adjustments are found to be necessary.

1   Insurance prepaid amounts to £920

2   Salaries and wages accrued were £750

3   Depreciation was to be included for January, amounting to £200 for equipment and £200 for vehicles

4   Stock at the end of January is valued at £10,500.

These adjustments can then be made in the journal, and subsequently posted to the accounts. For example, the journal entry for the adjustment relating to insurance would thus appear as follows:

			£	£
January 31	Insurance (February)	NL6	920	
	Insurance (January)	NL6		920
	Being insurance prepaid – see memo from × 30 January			

After posting this, the insurance account will appear as follows:

				Insurance				**NL6**
			£					£
January	2	Cash	CB1	1,000	January	31	Balance c/d J2	920
						31	Profit and loss	80
				£1,000				£1,000
February	1	Balance b/d	J2	920				

Sometimes the adjustment takes the form of a transfer to profit and loss of the amount due, the prepayments and accruals being taken care of automatically. Sometimes both adjustment and profit and loss amount are recorded in the journal and subsequently posted. There seems little need for both. Either will give the desired result.

Similar entries need to be made for the remaining adjustments, and trading and profit and loss accounts completed. In the ledger accounts the normal two–sided format for these accounts will be used. When presented, however, the trading and profit and loss account is likely to be in a narrative format such as shown below.

Trading and profit and loss account for January

	£	£	£
Sales		8,950	
Less: returns			550
			8,400
Opening stock		10,000	
Purchases	4,950		
Less: Returns	150		
		4,800	
		14,800	
Less: Closing stock		10,500	
Therefore cost of goods sold			4,300
Gross profit			4,100
Other revenues			
Discount received			160
			4,260
Other expenses			
Insurance		80	
Miscellaneous expenses		200	
Motor expenses		250	
Stationery		250	
Discount allowed		730	
Salaries and wages		750	
Depreciation – equipment		200	
vehicles		200	
Net profit			2,660
			£1,600

The balance sheet as at 31 January would appear as follows:

Balance sheet as at 31 January

	£	£	£
Fixed assets			
Premises			100,000
Equipment – cost		20,000	
– depreciation provision		200	
			19,800
Vehicles – cost		10,000	
– depreciation provision		200	
			9,800
Furniture – cost			1,000
			130,600

Current assets

Stock	10,500	
Prepayments	920	
Debtors	2,800	
Bank	4,180	
Cash	1,350	
	19,750	

Current liabilities

Creditors	1,000	
Accruals	750	
	1,750	

Net current assets		18,000
		148,600

Capital

Opening capital		147,000
Net profit		1,600
		148,600

4 CHAPTER SUMMARY

- This chapter has shown you how the journal can be used to record various types of transactions. The journal is not part of the double-entry system and has to be posted in the same way as any other book of original entry. The main advantage of the journal is to support the system of original entry by ensuring that every transaction goes through a book of original entry. The format of the journal shown above can provide much more detailed information about a transaction than can an entry in the ledger. Moreover, journal entries can be easily linked with documentary evidence.

- Examination questions requiring students to journalise certain transactions are fairly common. The majority of such questions relate to the types of issues referred to above. However, in certain instances journal entries are required as a means of showing the impact of a set of transactions on the ledger accounts, without actually showing the accounts themselves. In such cases the appropriate ledger entries should simply be shown in the journal, together with an appropriate narrative.

- A worked example involving the use of the journal and other subsidiary records preceded this summary. It should be emphasised that other forms of subsidiary records could be used, so the example should be seen as one of a variety of approaches. It should nevertheless provide a useful illustration of the interaction of the various parts, and the way in which they feed into the final accounts.

5 SELF TEST QUESTIONS

5.1 Identify the types of entries which are typically shown in the journal. (1.1)

5.2 Identify and explain each of the types of error which may occur and which do not affect the agreement of the trial balance. (1.5)

5.3 What is a suspense account? (1.10)

6   EXAMINATION TYPE QUESTIONS

6.1   Cosy Corners

The books of account of Cosy Corners are handwritten with great care by a small team of bookkeepers under the eagle eye of the office manager. This redoubtable person has however recently taken extended leave, with unfortunate results, since the month-end trial balance will not balance; the credits exceed debits by £318.

You are asked to help and after inspection of the ledgers discover the following errors:

1   A balance of £48 on a debtors account had been omitted from the schedule of debtors, the total of which was entered as debtors in the trial balance

2   A small piece of machinery purchased for £800 had been written off to repairs

3   The receipts side of the cash book had been undercast by £300

4   A total of one page of the sales day book had been carried forward as £3,092 whereas the correct amount was £3,902

5   A credit note for £120 received from a supplier had been posted to the wrong side of his account

6   An electricity bill for the sum of £78, not yet accounted for, was discovered in a filing basket

7   Mr Smith paid £540 to clear his account. His personal account has been credited but the cheque has not yet passed through the cash book.

(a)   Write up the suspense account to clear the difference

(b)   State the effect of each error on the accounts.

(12 marks)

6.2   Bookkeeper

The bookkeeper of a firm posted to the credit of a suspense account a difference of £150 in a trial balance of the accounts at 31 December 19X1.

The auditor finds the following errors:

1   A receipt of £75 from A. Green had been credited to the account of C. Batt

2   A purchase of goods from D. Mann had been debited to his account. The amount was £75

3   £50 charged to manufacturing wages related to the cost of installing new plant

4   The purchases day book had been undercast by £100

5   A purchase of goods from C. Shearer had been correctly entered in the purchases day book as £160, but had been entered in his account as £60.

Prepare the suspense account and the journal entries necessary to correct the accounts.

(12 marks)

6.3   Investigation

On preparing a trial balance you discover that credits exceed debits by £126, an amount which you enter into a suspense account. Subsequent investigation reveals the following errors:

1   The sales day book for January had been overcast by £100

2   The purchase of goods from J. Smith had been entered correctly in the purchases day book as £100 but posted to his account as £110

3   The sale of goods to P. Jones amounting to £110 had been recorded in the sales book as £100

4   Discount received from S. Brown of £10 had been credited to her account

5   £50 cash paid for advertising has been debited to the personal account of the advertising company

6   £100 received from the sale of an asset had been credited to sales. The asset was shown in the books at £300 cost, while cumulative depreciation amounted to £250

7   A credit purchase of goods (£200) from R. Archer had been credited to P. Gunn

8   The purchase day book was undercast by £50 on February 28

9   A credit sale of goods to J. Smith of £200 had been credited to his account

10   Machinery purchased for £1000 had been debited to purchases

11   £50 charged for repairs to the owner's house had been paid and included in sundry expenses

12   Bank charges of £10 had been entered in the cash book but the double entry had not been completed

13   A sale of goods to P. Binns had been correctly recorded in the sales book as £95 but posted to his account as £59

14   The total of the sales returns book for August, amounting to £100, had been credited to the purchases returns account

15   The total of the discount allowed column (£220) in the cash book had not been posted to the discount allowed account

16   A total in the purchases day book was carried forward as £635 instead of £365

17   A page in the sales book – total £650 – was omitted from the amount posted to sales account.

(a)   Prepare journal entries necessary to correct the above errors

(b)   Prepare the suspense account.

Note: the opening balance of the suspense account will have to be derived accordingly.

(20 marks)

6.4   Appropriate Treatment

The bookkeeper of the company which employs you as its accountant has consulted you about some transactions for which she does not know the appropriate accounting treatment. The company's accounting year ended on 31 March 19X6 and draft accounts have already been prepared.

The transactions are:

1   An account for goods bought on credit from Dominion Supplies Ltd for £127.54. This transaction, which is to be settled in contra against that company's account in the debtors ledger, has not yet been recorded at all

2   The company has sold a vehicle, which originally cost £7,800 and on which £4,500 depreciation had been provided, for £2,700. The bookkeeper has debited bank account and credited vehicles account with the sale proceeds but this has not affected any other entries

3   The company has traded in another vehicle which originally cost £8,300 and on which £6,900 depreciation had been provided, at an agreed valuation of £1,800. The only ledger entry made by the bookkeeper so far has been a debit to vehicles account and a credit to the supplier's account of the difference of £8,700 between the cost of the new vehicle and the trade-in value of the old vehicle

4   The company had acquired additional warehouse space from 1 October 19X5 at an annual rental of £3,000, payable quarterly in advance. The actual payments have been made on the due dates (1 October 19X5 and 3 January 19X6), but in preparing the draft accounts for the year ended 31 March 19X6 the bookkeeper mistakenly thought that these payments were made in arrears and had raised an accrual

5   The company has sub-let part of the premises referred to in (4) above at a quarterly rental of £240, payable in advance from 1 January 19X6. The tenant paid the rental for the March 19X6 quarter on 3 January 19X6 and for the June 19X6 quarter on 21 March 19X6. The bookkeeper has debited both the amounts to bank account and has credited them to premises account.

Open the company's journal and make the appropriate entries for the above transactions.

Note: The narrative is an integral part of each journal entry and must be shown.

(18 marks)

7   ANSWERS TO EXAMINATION TYPE QUESTIONS

7.1   Cosy Corners

(a)

Suspense

	£		£
Balance b/d	318	Debtors	48
		Cash	300
Sales	810	Creditors	240
		Cash	540
	£1,128		£1,128

(b)   **Effects**

(1)   debtor increased by £48
       suspense reduced by £48

(2)   increase machinery
       reduce repairs

(3)   increase cash
       reduce suspense

(4)   increase suspense
       increase sales

(5)   reduce supplies by £240 (twice the amount of the errors)
       reduce suspense by £240

(6)   increase expense
       increase liabilities

(7)   increase cash
       reduce suspense

7.2   Bookkeeper

Suspense

	£		£
D. Mann	150	Balance b/d	150
C. Shearer	100	Purchases	100
	250		250

(a)	Dr C. Batt	75	
	Cr A. Green		75
	Being correction of misposting		
(b)	Dr Suspense	150	
	Cr D. Mann		150
	Being correction of misposting		
(c)	Dr Plant	50	
	Cr Wages		50
	Being capitalisation of wages		
	relating to plant installation		
(d)	Dr Purchases	100	
	Cr Suspense		100
(e)	Dr Suspense	100	
	Cr C. Shearer		100
	Being correction of misposting		

Note: Journal entries should provide some kind of cross-reference to the original error

7.3   Investigation

(a)   Journal entries (excluding narrative)

(1)	Dr Sales	100	
	Cr Suspense		100
(2)	Dr J. Smith	10	
	Cr Suspense		10
(3)	Dr P. Jones	10	
	Cr Sales		10
(4)	Dr S. Brown	20	
	Cr Suspense		20
(5)	Dr Advertising	50	
	Cr Advertising Co		50
(6)	Dr Sales	100	
	Dr Disposal (cost)	300	
	Dr depn prov	250	
	Cr asset (cost)		300
	Cr Disposal (dp)		250
	Cr Disposal (proceeds)		100
(7)	Dr P. Gunn	200	
	Cr R. Archer		200
(8)	Dr Purchases	50	
	Cr Suspense		50
(9)	Dr J. Smith	400	
	Cr Suspense		400
(10)	Dr Machinery	1,000	
	Cr Purchases		1,000
(11)	Dr Drawings	50	
	Cr Sundry exps		50
(12)	Dr Bank charges	10	
	Cr Suspense		10
(13)	Dr P. Binns	36	
	Cr Suspense		36
(14)	Dr Purchases returns	100	
	Dr Sales returns	100	
	Cr Suspense		200

(15)	Dr Discount allowed	220	
	Cr Suspense		220
(16)	Dr Suspense	270	
	Cr Purchases		270
(17)	Dr Suspense	650	
	Cr Sales		650

(b)

Suspense account

		£				£
Balance b/d		126	(1)	Sales		100
(16)	Purchases	270	(2)	X		10
(17	Sales	650	(4)	A		20
			(8)	Purchases		50
			(9)	X		400
			(12)	Bank charges		10
			(13)	W		36
			(14)	Purchases returns		100
			(14)	Sales returns		100
			(15)	Discounts allowed		220
		£1,046				£1,046

7.4   Appropriate Treatment

Journal

		Dr £	Cr £
(1)	Purchases	127.54	
	Dominion Supplies Ltd. (creditor)	127.54	
	To Dominion Supplies Ltd. (creditor)		127.54
	Dominion Supplies Ltd. (debtor)		127.54
	Purchase of goods on credit from Dominion Supplies Ltd. and settlement of debtors account in contra		
(2)	Vehicles	2,700.00	
	To Disposals		2,700.00
	Transfer of proceeds received from sale of vehicle to Disposals		
	Disposals	3,300.00	
	Depreciation provision	4,500.00	
	To Vehicles		7,800.00
	Transfer to Disposals of written-down value on sale of vehicle		
	Profit and loss	600.00	
	To Disposals		600.00
	Transfer of loss on sale of vehicle		
(3)	Vehicles	1,800.00	
	To Disposals		1,800.00
	Transfer of trade-in value on disposal of vehicle		
	Disposals	1,400.00	
	Depreciation provision	6,900.00	
	To Vehicles		8,300.00

	Transfer to Disposals of written-down value on trade-in of vehicle		
	Disposals	400.00	
	To Profit and loss		400.00
	Transfer of profit on trade-in of vehicle		
(4)	Accruals	750.00	
	To Profit and loss		750.00
	Transfer to correct error in cancellation of one quarter's rent wrongly accrued		
(5)	Premises	480.00	
	To Profit and loss – rent receivable		240.00
	Deferred revenue – rent		240.00
	Transfer of amounts wrongly credited to Premises account		

13 CONTROL ACCOUNTS AND COMPUTERISED ACCOUNTING SYSTEMS

INTRODUCTION AND LEARNING OBJECTIVES

As the volume of transactions for a business increases, so does the potential for error. A great deal of time can be spent in searching for and eliminating errors. One method used to narrow down the area of search in identifying errors is the use of **control accounts**. These accounts provide a useful check on the accuracy of an individual ledger. In this chapter we examine their rationale and operation. The relationship between control accounts and other forms of accounting records is also explained.

In practice, many businesses now use computerised accounting systems. This chapter provides you with an introduction to the principles of computerised systems; the advantages of a computerised system over a manual system are considered in some detail as well as problems of control and security arising from computerised systems.

When you have studied this chapter you should be able to do the following:

- Explain the advantages of operating control accounts

- Prepare control accounts from given accounting transactions

- Discuss the impact of computerisation on accounting systems.

---

1 RATIONALE FOR CONTROL ACCOUNTS

1.1 Introduction

The reasons for the subdivision of the ledger were identified earlier in Chapter 11. However, it is clear that errors made will still require careful checking of *all* ledgers and their contents, unless a method can be devised of providing a check on the accuracy of an individual ledger. If an individual ledger can be checked or balanced separately, this is of considerable help in identifying the location of any errors which arise. Control accounts provide such a self-checking or self-balancing system. They are most widely used for the the sales and purchases ledgers. They also offer a means of agreeing the total trade debtors and total trade creditors figures which appear on the trial balance. If these totals can be agreed using control accounts, the search for any errors affecting the trial balance can be confined to other ledgers. This is likely to be extremely helpful in practice as the sales and purchases ledgers of a business often contain a large number of transactions

1.2 Purpose of a control account

The basic idea of a control account is that it *summarises* all of the transactions which have been recorded in the sales and purchases ledgers. As we shall see, the source of entries for the control accounts is the books of original entry which we discussed in Chapter 11. Using the information gleaned from these sources, we should be able to derive a total trade debtors and total trade creditors outstanding at the end of an accounting period. If the control account balance for either the sales or purchases ledger at the end of a period agrees with the total of the balances of the individual accounts in that ledger, there is an *implication* that the entries have been correctly made. As has already been seen, this is not necessarily true, since a variety of errors can be made which will not prevent the agreement of the trial balance. Nevertheless, control accounts do provide a further check on the accounts, since if the control account balance does not agree with the total of the balances of the individual accounts an error must have been made, either in the postings to the accounts, or in the control account. Because control accounts are essentially summaries of the transactions contained within a particular ledger they are sometimes referred to as **total accounts**.

1.3 An illustration

By way of illustration, consider the entries made in the sales ledger. This ledger contains the personal account of debtors. These accounts will be debited with the amount of any sales, and credited with the amounts of any returns, cash received, discount allowed and bad debts. With a large number of debtors accounts the scope for error is considerable, and control accounts are particularly useful in such cases. Indeed, control accounts are probably most widely used for the sales and purchases ledgers, where they are effectively total debtors accounts and total creditors accounts. They may also be found for groups of homogeneous accounts such as wages, where a large number of individual accounts are involved.

A **sales ledger control account** would typically appear as follows:

Sales ledger control

			£					£
January	1	Balance b/d	x	January	31	Sales returns		x
	31	Sales	x		31	Discount allowed		x
					31	Cash		x
					31	Bad debts		x
					31	Purchases ledger control		x
					31	Balance c/d		x
			£x					£x
February	1	Balance b/d	x					

Most of the items included are self-explanatory. Perhaps the only one which is not is the entry relating to the purchases ledger control account. This entry arises where there are balances on both creditor accounts and debtor accounts for the same individual or business. A person or business may be both customer and supplier, and it is sometimes necessary to set off one balance against the other. In such cases entries will be needed in the personal accounts in both the sales ledger and the purchases ledger, together with corresponding entries in the two control accounts. These are sometimes referred to as contra entries. Sometimes a sales ledger may contain accounts with credit balances, where, for instance a customer who has paid his account in full is given a credit note for goods returned at a later date. In such cases it is common (and this appears in examination questions) to keep the debit and credit balances separate, and to carry them forward on the appropriate side.

Example

Kingsbridge Components started business on 1 January. During the first week of trading the following transactions relating to debtors occurred.

January	1	Sold goods to M. Harvey for £100 on credit
		Sold goods to J. Cater for £200 on credit
	3	Sold goods to I. Ibbetson for £250 on credit
	4	Sold goods to J. Williams for £250 on credit
	5	Goods which had cost £20 were returned by M. Harvey
		Goods which had cost £20 were returned by J. Williams
	6	Received cash from J. Cater amounting to £180, with £20 being allowed as discount
		Received cash from I. Ibbetson amounting to £230, with £20 being allowed as discount
	7	Sold goods to J. Wigg for £200 on credit
		Sold goods to R. Young for £100 on credit
		Wrote off the debt of M. Harvey as bad

The subsidiary books for these transactions, assuming that a sales book, sales returns book, cash receipts journal, and a journal are kept, would appear as follows:

Sales book

				£
January	1	M. Harvey		100
	1	J. Cater		200
	3	I. Ibbetson		250
	4	J. Williams		250
	7	J. Wigg		200
	7	R. Young		100
				£1,100

Sales returns book

				£
January	5	M. Harvey		20
	5	J. Williams		20
				£40

Cash receipts journal

			Cash	Sales ledger	Discount
			£	£	£
January	6	J. Cater	180	180	20
	6	I. Ibbetson	230	230	20
			£410	£410	£40

The journal

			Debit	Credit
January	7		£	£
		Bad debts	80	
		M. Harvey		80
		Being debt written off as bad		

When posted to the ledger accounts the folio reference in the subsidiary books will be the reference number of the appropriate account.

The ledger accounts relating to these transactions would appear as follows when posted from the subsidiary records.

Sales ledger

M. Harvey

				£						£
January	1	Sales	SB1	100		January	5	Sales returns	SRB1	20
							7	Bad debts	J1	80
				£100						£100

J. Cater

			£					£
January	1	Sales	SB1	200	January	6	Cash & discount	CRJ1	200
				£200					£200

I. Ibbetson

			£					£
January	3	Sales	SB1	250	January	6	Cash & discount	CRJ1	250
				£250					£250

J. Williams

			£					£
January	4	Sales	SB1	250	January	5	Sales returns SRB1	20
						7	Balance	c/d	230
				£250					£250
January	7	Balance	b/d	230					

J. Wigg

			£		£
January	7	Sales	SB1	200	

R. Young

			£		£
January	7	Sales	SB1	100	

Nominal ledger

Discount allowed

			£		£
January	7	Debtors	CRJ1	40	

Sales

	£					£
		January	7	Debtors	SB1	1,100

Bad debts

			£		£
January	7	M Harvey	J1	80	

Sales returns

			£		£
January	7	Debtors	SRB1	40	

General ledger

Cash

			£			£
January 7	Debtors	CRJ1	410			

The sales ledger control account would appear as follows:

Sales ledger control

			£					£
January 7	Sales	SB1	1,100	January	7	Sales returns	SRB1	40
					7	Cash	CRJ1	410
					7	Discount	CRJ1	40
						Bad debts	J1	80
					7	Balance	c/d	530
			£1,100					£1,100
January 7	Balance b/d		530					

If the entries in the individual debtor accounts in the sales ledger, and those in the control account, have been correctly made, the balance on the control account should equal the sum of the balances on the individual debtor accounts. In this case the balance of £530 equals the sum of the balances on the accounts of J. Williams (£230), J. Wigg (£220) and R. Young (£100). Any errors in posting, other than compensating errors, would mean that this equality would not occur. Where there are differences between the control account balance and the sum of the individual account balances the ledger entries relating to these transactions clearly need to be checked.

1.4 The purchases ledger control account

A purchases ledger control account would typically appear as follows:

Purchases ledger control

			£				£
January	31	Purchase returns	x	January	1	Balance b/d	x
	31	Discount received	x		31	Purchases	x
	31	Cash	x				
	31	Sales ledger control	x				
	31	Balance c/d	x				
			£x				£x
				February	1	Balance b/d	x

Example

Balances and transactions affecting a company's control accounts for the month of May 19X2 are listed below:

	£	
Balances at 1 May 19X2:		
Sales ledger	9,123	(debit)
	211	(credit)
Purchases ledger	4,490	(credit)
	88	(debit)

Transactions during May 19X2:

Purchases on credit	18,135
Allowances from suppliers	629
Receipts from customers by cheque	27,370
Sales on credit	36,755
Discounts received	1,105
Payments to creditors by cheque	15,413
Contra settlements	3,046
Allowances to customers	1,720
Bills of exchange receivable	6,506
Customers' cheques dishonoured	489
Cash receipts from credit customers	4,201
Refunds to customers for overpayment of accounts	53
Discounts allowed	732

Balances at 31 May 19X2:

Sales ledger	136	(credit)
Purchases ledger	67	(debit)

Post the sales ledger and purchases ledger control accounts for the month of May 19X2 and derive the respective debit and credit closing balances on 31 May 19X2.

Solution

Sales ledger control

			£				£
May	1	Balance b/d	9,123	May	1	Balance b/d	211
	31	Sales	36,755		31	Cheques	27,370
	31	Dishonoured cheques	489		31	Purchases ledger control	3,046
	31	Cash refunds	53		31	Allowances	1,720
	31	Balance c/d	136		31	Bills of exchange receivable	6,506
					31	Cash	4,201
					31	Discount allowed	732
					31	Balance c/d	2,770
			£46,556				£46,556
June	1	Balance b/d	2,770	June	1	Balance b/d	136

Purchases ledger control

			£				£
May	1	Balance b/d	88	May	1	Balance b/d	4,490
	31	Allowances	629		31	Purchases	18,135
	31	Discount received	1,105		31	Balance c/d	67
	31	Cheques	15,413				
	31	Sales ledger control	3,046				
	31	Balance c/d	2,411				
			£22,692				£22,692
June	1	Balance b/d	67	June	1	Balance b/d	2,411

Several slightly more unusual transactions were introduced in this example. Allowances to debtors may be regarded as sums allowed to customers for some particular reason, such as damage to the goods sold. An appropriate account would need to be opened to reflect this, and a specific individual debtor account would be credited. Since a control account is nothing more than a summary of the individual accounts in a ledger the figure for such allowances must also be reflected in the sales ledger control account. Similar logic applies to cash refunds. Cheques which have been dishonoured will result in a debit to the individual debtor account (thus re-establishing the debt in the accounts) and a credit to cash. Again, the total relating to such entries in the debtors accounts must be included in the control account. Bills of exchange are negotiable instruments which are effectively a promise to pay at a future date. Bills of exchange receivable would thus be seen as eliminating any debt, by substituting a current asset (bills receivable). Allowances from suppliers follow the same principles as allowances to customers, but with the entries reversed.

1.5   Entering totals in control accounts

When entering amounts in a control account it is usual to use totals wherever possible. In other words, the entry for sales in the sales ledger control account should come from the total/s of the sales book. Sales returns should represent a posting of the total/s of the sales returns book, and so on. The use of totals has several advantages.

- It provides a check on the accuracy of the postings from the subsidiary records, and the addition in those subsidiary records

- It results in the control account having a limited number of entries, which makes it possible to extract total balances extremely quickly, a factor which may be important to management

- The control account can be easily and quickly kept by someone other than the person making the detailed postings, a factor which improves internal control and makes fraud more difficult, since collusion would be necessary for the fraud to be successful.

Control accounts clearly duplicate the entries in individual accounts, albeit in total. Both sets of entries cannot be part of the double entry, so a choice must be made about whether the control accounts or the individual accounts are part of the double entry, and which are memoranda (that is, subsidiary records supporting the ledger accounts). Typically, the control accounts relating to debtors and creditors are treated as a formal part of the double entry, with the detailed debtor and creditor accounts being seen as supporting memoranda accounts. Whichever view is taken, the end product remains the same. Ledgers which have control accounts are sometimes called **self-balancing ledgers**.

In examination questions it is common to be given the situation in which the control account balances and the totals of the individual accounts do not agree, and to be required to get them to agree. In such a question it is important to recognise that some errors will affect the control account, while other errors will affect the total of the individual accounts. The best approach is thus to have two separate adjustment processes going on at the same time, one for the control account and one for the total of the individual ledgers. Correction of these two separate figures should lead to a reconciliation.

Where examination questions on suspense accounts and correction of errors are linked with control accounts it is necessary to specify whether the control account or the individual accounts are to be taken as part of the double entry, since it is errors affecting the trial balance which lead to the opening of a suspense account.

1.6   Activity

The trial balance of Happy Bookkeeper Ltd, as produced by its bookkeeper, includes the following items:

Sales ledger control account	£110,172
Purchases ledger control account	£78,266
Suspense account (debit balance)	£2,315

You have been given the following information:

1   The sales ledger debit balances total £111,111 and the credit balances total £1,234

2   The purchases ledger credit balances total £77,777 and the debit balances total £1,111

3   The sales ledger includes a debit balance of £700 for business X, and the purchases ledger includes a credit balance of £800 relating to the same business X. Only the net amount will eventually be paid

4   Included in the credit balance on the sales ledger is a balance of £600 in the name of H. Smith. This arose because a sales invoice for £600 had earlier been posted in error from the sales day book to the debit of the account of M. Smith in the purchase ledger

5   An allowance of £300 against some damaged goods had been omitted from the appropriate account in the sales ledger. This allowance had been included in the control account

6   An invoice for £456 had been entered in the purchases day book as £654

7   A cash receipt from a credit customer for £345 had been entered in the cash book as £245

8   The purchase day book has been overcast by £1,000

9   The bank balance of £1,200 had been included in the trial balance, in error, as an overdraft

10   The bookkeeper had been instructed to write off £500 from customer Y's account as a bad debt, and to reduce the provision for doubtful debts by £700. By mistake, however, he had written off £700 from customer Y's account and increased the provision for doubtful debts by £500

11   The debit balance on the insurance account in the nominal ledger of £3,456 had been included in the trial balance as £3,546.

Record corrections in the control and suspense accounts. Attempt to reconcile the sales ledger control account with the sales ledger balances, and the purchases ledger control account with the purchases ledger balances. What further action do you recommend?

Note: In this question it should be assumed that the control accounts are part of the double entry and are thus reflected in the trial balance.

1.7   Activity solution

There are essentially four types of error in this question.

1   Errors in picking up figures in ledger accounts and putting them in the trial balance.

2   Errors affecting only the control accounts. These may also affect the suspense account since this answer assumes that the sales and purchases ledger control accounts are part of the double entry and that the individual personal accounts of trade debtors and trade creditors are memorandum in nature.

3   Errors affecting only the individual accounts in the sales and purchases ledgers.

4   Errors affecting both control accounts and the individual accounts.

The first type of error should normally be picked up before a suspense account is opened. If it is not, as in this case, the corrections will need to be reflected in the suspense account.

Suspense account

	£		£
Balance b/d	2,315	(ix) TB extraction error correction *	2,400
(xi) TB extraction error correction *	90	Balance c/d	5
	£2,405		£2,405
Balance b/d	5		

* There is no 'double entry' in respect of these since they correct errors which are not part of the double entry.

Errors relating to the control accounts can be corrected through the control accounts as follows:

Sales ledger control account

	£		£
Balance b/d	110,172	(iii) Contra re business X (PL control account)	700
(x) Debt incorrectly written off	200	(vii) Cash book error correction	100
		Balance c/d	109,572
	£110,372		£110,372
Balance b/d	109,572		

Purchase ledger control account

	£		£
(iii) Contra re business x (SL Control account)	700	Balance b/d	78,266
(vi) Correction of day book error	198		
(viii) Daybook overcast	1,000		
Balance c/d	76,368		
	£78,266		£78,266
		Balance b/d	76,368

Errors relating to the individual accounts in the sales and purchases ledger can then be corrected, with the following effect:

Sales ledger accounts balances

	£
Balances per sales ledger accounts	111,111(Dr)
Less: Credit balances	1,234(Cr)
	109,877 (Dr)

Corrections required to sales ledger accounts

		Dr	Cr	
(iii)	Contra re business X		700	
(iv)	H. Smith	600		
(v)	Damaged goods allowance		300	
(vii)	Cash book error correction		100	
(x)	Debt incorrectly written of	200		
		£800	£1,100	300 (Cr)
	Revised total of sales ledger account balances			£109,577 (Dr)

Purchase ledger accounts balances

	£
Balances per purchases ledger account	77,777 (Cr)
Less: Credit balances	1,111 (Dr)
	76,666 (Cr)

Corrections required to purchase ledger accounts

		Dr	Cr	
(iii)	Contra re business X	700		
(iv)	M. Smith		600	
(vi)	Correction of day book error	198		
		£898	£600	298 (Dr)
	Revised total of purchase ledger account balances			£76,368 (Cr)

The revised totals of the individual accounts in the sales and purchases ledgers can then be compared with the revised control account balances.

The purchase ledger account balances total now agrees with the control account balance. The sales ledger accounts balances total does not agree with the control account by £5. There were no ledger accounting errors which affected the trial balance difference. However the two trial balance errors ((ix) and (xi)) leave the trial balance difference at £5. Further checking of both the sales ledger and of the nominal/general ledger may be required in order to correct the accounts.

However, if only one error remains it is possible that the control account, rather than the ledgers, is incorrect.

As well as corrections to the accounts already dealt with in this answer, the following entries will need to be made in the nominal/general ledger to correct the errors already discovered:

		£
(vi)	Credit Purchases account	198
(vii)	Debit Cash book	100
(viii)	Credit Purchases account	1,000
(x)	Credit Bad debts written off account	200
	Debit customer/account	200
	Debit Provision for doubtful debts account	1,200
	Credit Provision for doubtful debts expense account	1,200

The trial balance will also need to be corrected for items (ix) and (xi).

2 COMPUTERISED ACCOUNTING SYSTEMS

2.1 Introduction

The principles and components of a manual accounting system such as that described in earlier chapters have not changed significantly for many years. A manual system of subsidiary records and ledgers is perfectly capable of providing a complete and efficient system for recording the transactions of a business. It is undoubtedly adequate for many small businesses. Nevertheless as a business grows in size and complexity a number of problems and weaknesses of manual systems become apparent. The more important of these are as follows.

- Considerable duplication of effort exists. Figures entered in a subsidiary book subsequently need posting and other documents relating to the business (for instance the preparation of invoices and cheques) are likely to reflect the same basic information

- The level of analysis permitted is fixed by the format of the subsidiary books, unless further detailed analysis is carried out as a supplementary exercise. Since the format of the subsidiary books is not typically changed very often, a manual system can be rather inflexible

- As the volume of transactions increases so the pressure on a manual system, and the difficulty of exercising adequate control over that system, increase significantly

- A manual system does not typically enable a rapid response to be made to requests for more information or summary information (although devices such as control accounts do go some way towards dealing with this problem)

- Any accounting system is related to a variety of other systems in a business, such as sales invoicing, personnel and wages, stock control and purchasing. However, the typical manual system is fairly self-contained, with its own procedures for ensuring that information provided by the other system is properly included in the accounting records. This is likely to prove wasteful of resources, and reinforces the concerns about duplication identified earlier.

Computerised accounting systems can overcome many of these problems, although they bring with them a need for other considerations of control and security to be taken into account.

2.2   The development of computerised accounting systems

Computerised accounting systems have developed rapidly over the last few years, principally because of significant changes in technology and its associated cost. Until relatively recently computerised accounting systems were found only in large organisations, generally operated by the use of what were referred to as **batch processing techniques**. Batches of documents, broadly corresponding to those found in the subsidiary books, were typically punched onto paper tape and fed into the computer for analysis and printing. Accounts were sometimes maintained on a computer file, and sometimes were posted manually from summary computer analyses. The accounting department was typically simply one of the user groups of the data-processing department. Output and methods thus followed the principles of a manual system fairly closely. The major advantage of computerisation was the ability to handle large volumes of data in an effective way.

In more recent years changes in technology have resulted in the production of a range of relatively cheap, compact, high-powered computers capable of being operated by non-specialists. Coupled with this has been the development of large amounts of business software (programs written to deal with specific business problems). This has meant that the computerised accounting function could be decentralised and the accounting department could take control over all aspects of it. It has also meant that small businesses can now operate computerised accounting systems cheaply and effectively.

2.3   Activity

What is the point in studying the manual system of accounting given that, nowadays, most businesses have computer-based accounting systems?

2.4   Activity solution

Manual systems are still being operated by some organisations and therefore it is necessary to be familiar with manual records for this purpose. In addition, computerised systems employ the same principles as a manual system. If you are familiar with a manual system, you will find it easier to understand computerised systems.

2.5   Management information systems (MIS)

Perhaps the greatest step forward which can be associated with the advances in technology in this area is the development of **management information systems (MIS)**. An MIS can be defined as a system which is designed to collect, analyse and distribute throughout the organisation information relevant to the management of the entire organisation. This will typically include information needed for both internal and external users, and information of both an accounting and a non-accounting nature. Typically an MIS will have a number of component parts (or sub-systems), of which the accounting system is one (but frequently the largest and most formalised). Other parts might include information systems targeted towards marketing, personnel, production scheduling and long-range planning/corporate strategy.

In principle, there is no need for an MIS to be computer-based. In practice, however, the growth of MIS is very closely linked to advances in computer technology, since computers typically provide the most economical and efficient means of storing data and analysing it to provide necessary and appropriate documentation and information for an organisation. Particularly important in this context is the concept of the **database**. This refers to the storage of data in an appropriate way (one which can be accessed and analysed easily), supported by software which effectively 'manages' the data through such things as the selection, updating, analysing, sorting and printing of appropriate information. Some of this will relate to relatively routine parts of the activities of the organisation, such as sales invoicing, payment of wages and payment of cheques to suppliers. If print routines relating to such activities are carried out on special preprinted stationery such as invoices, wage slips and cheques to suppliers, most documents needed by the organisation can be prepared as part of the overall MIS. Other software may relate more to forecasting and modelling, and may be rather less routine and more subjective. The use of spreadsheets and other financial modelling packages provide examples. These can be particularly useful for building forecasts relating to such things as sales, profits and cash. As such they are a useful addition to the decision-making process.

2.6   Requirements of a management information system

The typical requirements of an MIS are:

- A large mainframe or minicomputer supported by microcomputer processors or workstations, and a variety of different input and storage devices such as code readers, mark-sensing devices, disks, magnetic tapes, printers and microfiche copiers

- Good operating system software and controls to manage and manipulate the system effectively

- A well-designed database, including information from both within the organisation and outside it. Typically, the accounting part of this information will be internally generated

- A communication system which ensures that data is collected and fed into the data base, while reports and other information are distributed to appropriate parts of the organisation.

Most large organisations are likely to operate with a mainframe computer and an MIS. Small or medium organisations, even if unable to support a sophisticated MIS, are still likely to take advantage of the opportunities provided by computerised accounting systems. The typical system of a small or medium-sized business will use one or more workstations linked to a controlling processor, which in turn controls various other devices, like printers, screens and disk drives. The complexity of the hardware will depend upon user needs. Software, the programs actually operating the computerised system, may be purchased 'off-the-shelf' or 'tailored'. 'Off-the-shelf' packages provide the facility to run a range of accounting routines, but with no facility to adapt the routines to suit the particular needs of the business. 'Tailored' packages provide a more specific solution to the needs of a particular business.

2.7   Accounting software packages

The more straightforward accounting packages typically operate by the use of a menu-driven screen. This means that the user has a choice (the menu) of a range of accounting tasks which can be carried out (for example, raising invoices or posting purchases ledger payments). The user can then determine which part of the accounting system is to be used, and access it through the memory. The routines used within a package typically lead the user through the transactions, and provide instructions to ensure that data is entered correctly.

The various routines in a package usually cover a particular aspect of the data collection and recording process. It is thus common to find that there are separate elements of a package dealing with the same kind of divisions that were used in the manual system described above. However, the use of a computerised system has considerable advantages over a manual system in terms of integration. In a properly designed and integrated package, all the various sections of the package can draw on information fed into the computer, so that the necessary double entry and updating takes place automatically. This facility clearly saves time and unnecessary duplication of effort because an entry need only be made once for its effect to be dealt with elsewhere automatically. For example, if the preparation of sales invoices is linked with the sales ledger and the nominal ledger, the issuing and printing of sales invoices will automatically lead to the customer's account being debited in the sales ledger, and the sales account being credited in the nominal ledger.

2.8   Activity

Obtain information about two 'off-the-shelf' accounting software packages which are available to a small business. Compare and contrast the tasks which they can perform.

2.9   Main elements of a computerised system

The essence of a computerised accounting system is that a record (known as a **file**) is maintained for each item to be found in a set of accounts. In certain cases, such as debtors and creditors, these files will need to be broken down into a more detailed set of records, relating to the personal accounts of individual debtors and creditors. Similar principles are likely to apply to stock and wages. The computer files are updated regularly to reflect the current transactions.

In order to operate effectively, a computerised system must be based upon a sound system of coding. A coding system is nothing more than the designation of an appropriate reference number for each type of record or transaction. The codes designated must be sufficiently sophisticated to enable detailed records to be kept where needed, and for total figures to be extracted automatically, for inclusion in regular reports used for control purposes, or in final accounts. Properly coded information can then be fed into the computer in a variety of ways (for instance keyboard, tape, mark sensing, scanning) so that the records can be updated, analysed, and printed out as required. The method used to update records is one of pluses and minuses, so computerised accounting systems are perfectly consistent with the approach used in Chapter 3.

In practice, many software packages use similar terminology to those used in a manual system. For example, many of the screen displays and printed output use the terms debit and credit, and accounts are often shown in the traditional format. Data files are often given names which indicate the part of a manual system which they replace; for instance, the data file containing records relating to debtors is often referred to as the sales ledger. However, the programs actually process the information entered in the computer by manipulating the data files using pluses and minuses. Typically there are no ledgers or day books as such, but a number of data files which are regularly updated, from which the appropriate information and documentation can be obtained.

The typical printed output from a computerised accounting system will include the following:

- The standard accounting reports (trading and profit and loss account and balance sheet) together with such supporting information as is deemed appropriate (for example, some kind of cash book, stock records). Where information contained in a data file is directly accessible on an on-line basis the need for printed output is reduced or eliminated
- Whatever documents are needed to carry on the business of the organisation. Typically these include the sales invoices and credit notes, customer statements, cheques to creditors and suppliers, pay slips and associated end-of-year tax documents
- Other reports generated for some special purpose an age profile of debts, stock reports. The information contained in the data files can also be transferred to a spreadsheet or modelling package, where it can be manipulated or modelled, and printed out as necessary.

2.10   Computerised systems and error reduction

Computerised systems clearly provide the opportunity to produce more accurate reports, analyses and other information than would be expected from a manual system. The fact that a single entry can be made into the system, which will then be 'managed' by an appropriate software package, so that postings, analyses and final accounts can all emerge routinely from the system, should eliminate a number of errors, including the following:

- errors of posting from a subsidiary book to a ledger account
- errors relating to arithmetic, notably totals and balances
- reversal of entries
- postings to the wrong account (though see below).

The balancing of control accounts is also unlikely to be a problem, since the software will typically amend individual records for debtors and creditors *and* provide a control total automatically, from the data into the data files.

2.11   Potential problems of computerised systems

In spite of these advantages, as has already been mentioned, computerised accounting systems bring with them further problems of control and security. Those areas of most relevance include the following.

- The need to ensure that all inputs are carefully coded and verified before entry into the system. A computer system will not prevent errors of omission. Nor will it prevent an incorrect posting if an input is incorrectly coded

- While the general principles relating to internal control procedures are still valid, they will need to be modified in a computerised accounting system. As far as possible the work of one person should still act as some kind of check on that of another. The separation of duties discussed earlier in the chapter remains a feature of this. Documentation to provide the necessary audit trail and supporting evidence is still needed. However, the same amount of documentation as in a manual system may not be required in a computer system. Similarly the use of a computer package may mean that the separation of duties is not as easy as with a manual system

- A computerised system will require additional security checks to ensure that only authorised users can obtain access to the data files. This typically takes the form of some kind of password being given to authorised users, which needs to be input into the computer before access to the data file can be obtained. Other security procedures will need to be devised to ensure the protection of the hardware, software and the data files in the event of such things as fire, theft, breakdown and sabotage. Such procedures include a controlled environment with restricted access, back-up copies of programs and data files, and agreements giving access to equivalent hardware in the event of a breakdown

- Given that inputs are 'managed' by the software, it is necessary to ensure that the software itself remains uncorrupted. Again access to the software must be restricted to authorised users. Computer audit software, in particular audit interrogation software, allows management to ensure that the software is still doing what it is supposed to be doing.

In the final analysis it is important to recognise that a computerised system follows the same broad principles as a manual system. Computerised systems are likely to be used where:

- there is a large number of transactions

- where advantages exist with regard to the printing of documents and analyses necessary to the continued efficient running of the business

- where savings can be achieved by a system of automatic postings, which become possible with a properly integrated system.

3   CHAPTER SUMMARY

- This chapter has explained the nature of control accounts and their place in terms of the control process. We have seen that control accounts help narrow down the area of search for errors in the accounts by providing a self-balancing or self-checking system for the sales and purchases ledgers. Control accounts contain a summary of the transactions which have been recorded in the sales and purchases ledgers, using the books of original entry for their source data. Control accounts may form part of the double-entry system or may simply be used as memoranda records.

- The chapter has also provided a broad outline of the principles underlying a computerised accounting system. We have also considered the benefits of a computerised system and the circumstances in which computerised systems are likely to be used. In practice, a computerised system includes substantially more than a system of accounts. It will deal with the preparation of a large number of documents and related analyses that are essential to the efficient operation of the business.

4   SELF TEST QUESTIONS

4.1   What are the purposes of maintaining control accounts for debtors and creditors?   (1.2, 1.5)

4.2   Which of the following statements is true of the sales and purchases ledger control accounts?

(a)   The control account is always considered part of the double entry

(b)   The individual ledger accounts are always considered part of the double entry

(c)   Both the control account and the individual ledger accounts are considered part of the double entry

(d)   Either, but not both the control account and the ledger accounts, may be considered as part of the double entry. (1.5)

4.3   What are the main weaknesses of a manual accounting system? (2.1)

4.4   Identify the problems of control and security which need to be considered when employing a computerised accounting system. (2.11)

5   EXAMINATION TYPE QUESTIONS

5.1   Figures

From the following figures prepare the control accounts for debtors and creditors as they would appear in the ledger as at 31 December 19X1

30 June 19X1

	£
Sales ledger balances	8,349
Purchases ledger balances	5,280

1 July to 31 December 19X1

Cash received from debtors	27,375
Cash paid to creditors	17,222
Discount allowed	635
Discount received	772
Bad debts written off	44
Sales on credit	25,835
Purchases on credit	15,408
Returns inwards	128
Returns outwards	166

During the period a debit balance of £15 on the purchases ledger was transferred to the sales ledger.

(8 marks)

5.2   Monthly Postings

The subsidiary records of your business consist of the following:

(i)   sales book

(ii)   sales returns book

(iii)   purchases book

(iv)   purchases returns book

(v)   journal

(vi)   three-column cash book

Postings are made monthly, using totals where possible. A sales ledger control account and a purchases ledger control account are also kept, again using totals where possible.

At the end of each month the individual personal account balances in the sales ledger are add listed, and compared with the sales ledger control account balance. The same is done for the purchases ledger. The sales ledger list for November reveals an add list total of £8,004 compared with a control account balance of £8,250. For the same month the creditors add list totals £5,480, and the control account balance is £5,200.

Subsequent investigation reveals the following:

(a)   A purchase of goods from A. Brown, correctly recorded in the purchases book, had been debited to his account. The amount was £50

(b)   £100 cash paid for purchases from B. Goode had been debited to his account. No entry had been made in the control account

(c)   The sales book was overcast by £100

(d)   The purchase of goods from C. Valley had been correctly recorded in the purchases book, as £150, but had been credited to his account as £510

(e)   Discount received from D. Green, of £10, had been credited to his account

(f)   The total of the sales returns book, amounting to £100, had been credited to the purchases returns account, and debited to the creditors control account. The correct detailed postings had been made to the debtors accounts.

(g)   The add list for debtors was found to be £100 too little

(h)   Sales amounting to £39, to E. Williams, had been correctly recorded in the sales book, but posted as £93

(i)   A payment to N. White, a creditor, of £50, had been debited to M.White

(j)   A credit note had been included with a batch of invoices in entering the sales book. This related to goods returned by F. Dagg, amounting to £25.

Complete the statements below, where necessary, showing the appropriate adjustments to the control accounts balances or the add list total of the personal accounts, to ensure that agreement is reached.

Debtors

	Control Account	Add list of personal accounts
	£	£
	8,250	8,004
(a)		
(b)		
(c)		
(d)		
(e)		
(f)		
(g)		
(h)		
(i)		
(j)		
	———	———
equals		
	———	———

Creditors

Control account	Add list of personal accounts
£	£
5,200	5,480

(a)

(b)

(c)

(d)

(e)

(f)

(g)

(h)

(i)

(j)

_____   _____

                              equals

_____   _____

Show all adjustments as + or −.   **(12 marks)**

5.3   Many systems

(a)   Why are many accounting systems designed with a purchase ledger (creditors   l e d g e r) control account, as well as with a purchase ledger (creditors ledger)?

(b)   The following errors have been discovered:

   (i)   An invoice for £654 has been entered in the purchase day book as £456

   (ii)   A prompt payment discount of £100 from a creditor had been completely omitted from the accounting records

   (iii)   Purchases of £250 had been entered on the wrong side of a supplier's account in the purchase ledger

   (iv)   No entry had been made to record an agreement to contra an amount owed to F. Xavier of £600 against an amount owed by X of £400

   (v)   A credit note for £60 had been entered as if it was an invoice.

           State the numerical effect on the purchase ledger control account balance of correcting each of these items (treating each item separately).

(c)   Information technology and computerised systems are rapidly increasing in importance in data recording. Do you consider that this trend will eventually remove the need for control accounts to be incorporated in the design of accounting systems? Explain your answer briefly.   **(15 marks)**

(ACCA, December 1988)

5.4   Excel Stores

The bookkeeper of Excel Stores Ltd prepared a schedule of balances of individual suppliers' accounts from the creditors ledger at 30 June 19X4 and arrived at a total of £86,538.28.

He passed the schedule over to the accountant who compared this total with the closing balance on the creditors ledger control account reproduced below:

Creditors ledger control

19X4			£	19X4			£
June	30	Purchases returns	560.18	June	1	Balance b/d	89,271.13
	30	Bank	96,312.70		30	Purchases	100,483.49
	30	Balance c/d	84,688.31		30	Discount received	2,656.82
					30	Debtors ledger control (contras)	3,049.75
			£192,561.19				£195,261.19
				July		Balance b/d	84,688.31

During his investigation into the discrepancy between the two figures, the accountant discovered a number of errors in the control account and the individual ledger accounts and schedule. You should assume that the total of each item posted to the control account is correct except to the extent that they are dealt with in the list below:

1   One supplier had been paid £10.22 out of petty cash. This had been correctly posted to his personal account but has been omitted from the control account.

2   The credit side of one supplier's personal account had been under-added by £30.00.

3   A credit balance on a supplier's account had been transposed from £548.14 to £584.41 when extracted on to the schedule.

4   The balance on one supplier's account of £674.32 had been completely omitted from the schedule.

5   Discounts received of £12.56 and £8.13 had been posted to the wrong side of two individual creditors' accounts.

6   Goods costing £39.60 had been returned to the supplier but this transaction had been completely omitted from the returns day book.

(a)   Prepare a statement starting with the original closing balance on the creditors ledger control account then identifying and correcting the errors in that account and concluding with an amended closing balance, and

(b)   Prepare a statement starting with the original total of the schedule of individual creditors, then identify and correct errors in that schedule and conclude with an amended total.   **(15 marks)**

5.5   Trading Business

The sales ledger control account of a trading business for the month of November 19X3 was prepared by the accountant, as shown below:

Sales ledger control

	£		£
Opening debit balance b/d	27,684.07	Opening credit balance b/d	210.74
Credit sales	31,220.86	Allowances to customers	1,984.18
Purchase ledger contras	763.70	Cash received	1,030.62
		Cheques received	28,456.07
Discounts allowed	1,414.28	Cash received (on an account previously	
		written off as a bad debt)	161.20
Closing credit balance c/d	171.08	Closing debit balance	
		c/d (balancing figure)	30,416.18
	£61,253.99		£61,258.99
Opening debit balance b/d	30,416.18	Opening credit balance b/d	171.08

The bookkeeper balanced the individual customers' accounts and prepared a debtors' schedule of the closing balances which totalled £25,586.83 (net of credit balances).

Unfortunately both the accountant and the bookkeeper had been careless, and in addition to the errors which the accountant had made in the control account above, it was subsequently discovered that:

1   In an individual debtor's account, a debt previously written off but now recovered (£161.20) had been correctly credited and redebited but the corresponding debit had not been posted in the control account

2   Discounts allowed had been correctly posted to individual debtors' accounts but had been under-added by £100 in the memorandum column in the combined bank and cash book

3   Allowances to customers shown in the control account included sums totalling £341.27 which had not been posted to individual debtors' accounts

4   A cheque for £2,567.10 received from a customer had been posted to his account as £2,576.10

5   The credit side of one debtor's account had been over-added by £10 prior to the derivation of the closing balance

6   A closing credit balance of £63.27 on one debtor's account had been included in the debtors schedule among the debit balances

7   The purchase ledger contras, representing the settlement by contra transfer of amounts owed to credit suppliers, had not been posted to individual debtors' accounts at all

8   The balance on one debtor's account, £571.02, had been completely omitted from the debtors' schedule.

Identify and effect the adjustments to the sales ledger control account and debtors schedule, as appropriate, so that the net balances agree at 30 November 19X3.   **(15 marks)**

5.6   New Clerk

A new clerk takes over responsibility for some of the sales records on 1 January 19X2. The summary figures he receives from his predecessor are as follows: (at 1 January 19X2)

	£
Sales ledger control account	10,000
Sales ledgers – total of debit balances	10,483
Sales ledgers – total of credit balances	497

At 31 December 19X2, after his first year of responsibility, the clerk arrives at the following summary figures:

	£
Sales ledger control account	16,600
Sales ledgers – total of debit balances	15,547
Sales ledgers – total of credit balances	551

On investigation, you find the following facts, all of which relate to between 1 January 19X2 and 31 December 19X2.

(i)   The June sales total had been added as £9,876 when it should have been correctly added as £8,967.

(ii)   A sales invoice which should have been charged to A's ledger account with an amount of £642 had actually been charged to B's ledger account with an amount of £426.

(iii)   A credit note for customer D of £123 had been incorrectly treated as a sales invoice in her ledger account. (Customer D's account had a large debit balance at 31 December 19X2).

(iv)   Contra entries of £800, correctly entered in the separate ledger accounts, had been omitted from the control accounts.

(v)   Cash discounts given of £74 have been completely ignored by the clerk.

Required

(i)   Calculate, with necessary workings, the adjusted figures at 31 December 19X2 for sales ledger control account, total of sales ledger debit balances and total of sales ledger credit balances.

(ii)   Produce a clear statement of the net amount of the remaining errors which the clerk appears to have made during the year 19X2 which have not yet been discovered.   **(15 marks)**

(ACCA, December 1993)

6   ANSWERS TO EXAMINATION TYPE QUESTIONS

6.1   Figures

Sales ledger control

19X1		£	19X1		£
June 30	Bal b/d	8,349		Cash	27,375
	Sales	25,835		Discount allowed	635
	PL control	15		Bad debts	44
				Returns	128
			Dec 31	Bal c/d	6,017
		£34,199			£34,199
Bal b/d		6,017			

Purchases ledger control

	£			£
Cash	17,222	Balance b/d		5,280
Discount received	772	Purchases		15,408
Returns	166	SL control		15
Balance c/d	2,543			
	£20,703			£20,703
		Bal b/d		2,543

6.2   Monthly Postings

Debtors

	Control account	Add list of personal accounts
	£	£
	8,250	8,004
a)		
b)		
c)	−100	
d)		
e)		
f)	−100	
g)		+100
h)		−54
i)		
j)	−50	−50
	£8,000	£8,000

equals

Creditors

	Control account £		Add list of personal accounts £
	5,200		5,480
(a)			+100
(b)	−100		
(c)			
(d)			−360
(e)			−20
(f)	+100		
(g)			
(h)			
(i)			
(j)			
	£5,200	equals	£5,200

6.3   Many Systems

(a)   Detailed creditor accounts are necessary to enable control to be kept of each individual creditor. The purpose of also keeping a purchases ledger control account is:

    (i)   To act as a check on the accuracy of the detailed postings in the purchases ledger. This check may be carried out by a different person from the one preparing the purchases ledger, which should also make fraud more difficult.

    (ii)   To provide a summary account which permits the balance relating to creditors in total to be derived quickly and easily, together with associated transactions.

(b)

	Increase £	Decrease £
(i)	198	
(ii)		100
(iii)	No Effect	
(iv)		400
(v)		120

(c)   No, though the approach changes somewhat. In a computerised accounting system it should be possible both to derive detailed records and a total record (effectively the control account), from the same single input of data. This requires a satisfactory system of coding, but, properly programmed, there should be no arithmetic problems or mispostings. The total figure will still be used to assist management in planning and decision making. Perhaps more importantly, a computerised system brings with it the need to ensure adequate control with regard to the system as a whole.

Particular areas of note include:

- the need for a system of checking, coding and verification of data before entry into the computer system

- the need for clearly documented evidence of what is contained in the computer system

- internal control mechanisms need to be reconsidered in the light of a different system being introduced

- security procedures need to be implemented to prevent loss, unauthorised use of or access to the computer files, and manipulation of the files.

6.4   Excel Stores

(a)

Control account

		£
Original closing balance as at 30 June 19X4		84,688.31
(1)	deduct payment made and omitted	(10.22)
(2)	no effect	
(3)	no effect	
(4)	no effect	
(5)	no effect	
(6)	deduct purchases return omitted	(39.60)

Other errors

	£
Discount received should be debited to the control account	(2,656.82)
	(2,656.82)
Debtors ledger control contras should be debited to the control account	(3,049.75)
	(3,049.75)
The credit side has been incorrectly totalled – increase by	200.00
The closing balance is incorrect – it should be increased by	11,000.00
plus the transposition error on the debit side total	2,700.00
Revised closing balance	£87,125.35

(b)

Schedule of creditors

		£	£
Original total as at 30 June 19X4			86,538.28
Item No.			
Add:			
(1)	no effect		
(2)		30.00	
(4)		674.32	
			704.32
			87,242.60
Less:			
(3)	(584.41 – 548.14)	36.27	
(5)	(12.56 + 8.13)	20.69	
		20.69	
(6)		39.60	
			(117.25)
Amended total as at 30 June 19X4			£87,125.35

6.5   Trading Business

Sales ledger control

	£
Balance as at 30 November 19X3	30,416.18
	(171.08)
	30,245.10

Errors in control account

Purchase ledger contras on wrong side	(763.70)
	(763.70)
Discount allowed on wrong side	(1,414.28)
	(1,414.28)
Incorrect balance c/d due to errors in control account total (credit side)	(1,005.00)

Errors in transactions listed

Bad debts recovered needs corresponding debit in debtors	161.20
(2) Reduce by extra discount	(100.00)
	£24,945.34

Schedule of debtors	£
Balance as at 30 November 19X3	25,586.83
(1) No effect	
(2) No effect	
(3) Reduce by allowances	(341.27)
(4) Increase by amount of overposting of cash	9.00
(5) Increase by amount of overaddition on credit side	10.00
(6) Reduce by 2 × amount	(63.27)
	(63.27)
(7) Reduce by amount of contras	(763.70)
(8) Increase by amount omitted	571.02
	£24,945.34

6.6   New Clerk

(i)

Sales ledger control account

		£		£
31.12.X2	Balance b/d	16,600	Correction to June sales (9,876 – 8,967)	909
			Omitted contra	800
			Omitted cash discounts	74
			31.12.X2 Revised balance c/d	14,817
		£16,600		£16,600

1.1.X3	Balance b/d	14,817	

List of sales ledger balances

	£
Total (net of credit balances)	14,996
Add: Net increase in balances relating to error in posting invoice (642 – 426)	216
Less: Error in posting credit note (2 × 123)	(246)
Less: Omitted cash discounts	(74)
Revised total	£14,892

(ii)　Remaining error　(14,892 – 14,817)　　　　　　　　　　　　　£75
　　　　(excess of ledger balances over control account balance)
　　　　Error at 1 January 19X2
　　　　10,000 – (10,483 – 497)　　　　　　　　　　　　　　　　£14
　　　　(excess of control account balance over ledger balances)
　　　　Thus the errors made during 19X2 total £89 (that is £75 + 14).

14 BANK RECONCILIATION STATEMENTS

INTRODUCTION AND LEARNING OBJECTIVES

Most businesses maintain a current account with one of the high street banks. Typically the business will pay all, or most, of its receipts of money into this account. Most bills which the business incurs will be paid by a cheque drawn on the bank. Some businesses will receive money from customers by direct bank transfers. Many businesses make some payments by direct bank transfers. Periodically the bank will send a statement to its customers, showing all of the transactions which have passed through the customer's account and the resultant balance at the end of the period to which the statement relates. On receipt of a bank statement one of the business's staff will normally try to confirm that the balance shown by the statement equals the balance on the cash at bank account. This should be the case since both the bank statement and the cash at bank account should contain exactly the same information.

In practice the two balances rarely agree at a given time. Usually when a business receives a cheque the appropriate entry is made on the debit side of the cash at bank account. Then the cheque will be paid into the bank and it will subsequently be included in the bank statement. The lag between the time of the entry in the books of the business and of its inclusion in the statement means that the cash at bank account and the bank statement will not always include all of the same items at the same time. There are other perfectly valid reasons for the two balances not agreeing. The objective of the **bank reconciliation statement** is to show that the disagreement between the two balances is for perfectly proper and explainable reasons.

When you have studied this chapter you should be able to do the following:

- Understand the reasons why a cash book and a bank statement are unlikely to show the same balance for an account

- Prepare a bank reconciliation statement to identify the differences.

---

1 BANK RECONCILIATION STATEMENTS

1.1 Introduction

Banks send statements to their customers setting out in detail the transactions relating to the account of the customer which have occurred over a specific period. This statement provides the customer with an effective means of checking the accuracy of the entries in the accounts relating to cash at bank. Similarly, the cash at bank account should provide a means of checking the bank statement. Any differences which cannot be explained by the procedure given below will presumably relate to errors in either the cash account or the bank statement.

1.2 Reasons for differences between the cash book balance and the bank statement balance

Theoretically it might be expected that a bank statement and cash at bank account would fairly readily agree. In practice this is not the case, for a variety of reasons, the principal ones being as follows:

- Certain items recorded in the accounts as having been received may not actually have been paid into the bank, or they may have been paid into a different bank and not yet have been transferred to the customer's bank (or branch). Such amounts will thus not be shown on the bank statement

- Money banked shortly before the issue of the bank statement may not appear on the statement

- Cheques paid out to suppliers, which have been recorded in the cash at bank account, may not have been paid in by the supplier, and will thus not appear on the bank statement. These are generally referred to as unpresented cheques.

- Certain payments on the bank statement may not appear in the cash at bank account. Such things as bank charges (charges made by the bank to its customers for the service it renders them) will typically be omitted from the cash at bank account, since they will not be known until the bank statement arrives. Amounts collected by suppliers by direct transfer from one customer to another, or which are paid by standing order, ie a standing instruction from the customer to the bank to make a particular repeated payment, are also sometimes omitted from the accounts.

- Certain receipts on the bank statement, relating to such things as collections from customers using direct debit, giro transfers etc, may also be omitted from the accounts.

- Cheques which have been dishonoured, or returned for some reason, may appear on the bank statement without the necessary corrections appearing in the accounts.

1.3 Drawing up a reconciliation statement

Clearly, therefore, the job of reconciling the cash at bank account with the bank statement can be quite complex. It is frequently necessary to prepare a bank reconciliation statement, which sets out the balances on the cash at bank account and the bank statement, and reconciles the two. Several examination questions have been set requiring such statements.

The best approach in practice is undoubtedly to go through the bank statement and to identify any items which have been omitted from the cash at bank account. These items can then be recorded in the accounts, and a revised cash at bank balance can be derived. The cash at bank account and the bank statement can then be reconciled as follows:

1   Balance as shown in cash at bank account
2   Add unpresented cheques
3   Deduct payments into bank not shown on the bank statement
4   This should equal the balance shown on the bank statement.

If this is not the case rather more extensive checking will be needed to ascertain where the error has occurred. Since errors may occur on the bank statement it is sometimes necessary to revise the balance as shown on the statement, or to include a further step in the reconciliation process.

Example

The cash book of a business shows a favourable bank balance of £3,856 at 30 June 19X7. After comparing the entries in the cash book with the entries on the related bank statement you find that:

1   Cheques amounting to £218 entered in the cash book have not yet been presented for payment to the bank
2   An amount of £50 entered on the debit side of the cash book has not been banked
3   An amount of £95 has been credited by the bank to the account in error
4   The bank has debited and then credited the bank statement with an amount of £48, being A. Jones' cheque which it forwarded on 1 July 19X7 marked 'insufficient funds – return to drawer'
5   Interest of £10 has been charged by the bank, but not yet entered in the cash book
6   A cheque from a customer incorrectly entered in the cash book as £88 had been correctly entered by the bank as £188.

    (a)   Show the additional entries to be made in the cash book and bring down the corrected balance.

    (b)   Prepare a bank reconciliation statement.

    (c)   Explain the reasons for preparing a bank reconciliation statement.

Solution

The additional entries which need to be made in the cash book are as follows:

	£	
Bank balance shown in cash book	3,856	(in hand)
Add amounts paid in which are on the statement but not in the cash book	–	
Deduct amounts paid out which are on the bank statement but not in the cash book, interest (item 5)	10	
	3,846	
Adjust for others errors identified in the cash book		
item 4, credit cash, debit A. Jones	– 48	
item 6, debit cash £100, credit customer £100	+100	
Revised cash book balance	£3,898	(in hand)

Bank reconciliation statement as at 30 June 19X7		
Balance as cash book	3,898	(in hand)
Add unpresented cheques (item 1)	218	
	4,116	
Deduct payments into bank not shown on bank statement (item 2)	50	
Balance at bank	£4,066	(in hand)

In this case the balance shown on the bank statement will be £4,161, because £95 has been credited in error (item 3). As pointed out above, this £95 could have been included as the final stage in the reconciliation process, thus completing the reconciliation between the bank balance shown in the cash book and the (incorrect) balance shown on the bank statement.

1.4   Approach to examination questions

In many examination questions examiners appear to want a bank reconciliation statement prepared which reconciles the existing cash at bank account with the bank statement. Under such circumstances the process becomes slightly more involved than shown above, with the following revised process being necessary:

1   Balance shown in cash at bank account

2   Add amounts paid in which are on the bank statement but not in the account

3   Deduct amounts paid out which are on the bank statement but not in the account

4   This should give the revised correct balance on the account

5   Add unpresented cheques

6   Deduct payments into bank not shown on the bank statement

7   This should equal the balance shown on the bank statement.

When reconciling a cash at bank account with a bank statement it is important to recognise that the bank statement is effectively a copy of the account which the bank has for the customer. Hence a business which has a sum of money in a bank account will show this as a debit balance in its accounts (since it represents an asset), while the bank will show it as a credit balance (since it represents a liability). Similarly payments made by a business will be credits in its accounts, but debits in the bank's own account (and hence a debit on the bank statement). In reconciling the two balances it must be clearly recognised that transactions will appear on the opposite side of the accounts.

2 CHAPTER SUMMARY

- This chapter has identified the need to reconcile the balance as shown in the bank account with that shown in the business' accounts. There are various reasons why the balance on the cash at bank account and the bank statement may not agree. These include:

  Timing differences. Items paid into the bank and cheques drawn on the bank may be included in the cash at bank account in the books of the business, but they may not yet have appeared on the bank statement.

  Omissions. Items charged to or paid to the customer's account and shown on the bank statement may have been overlooked in writing up the cash at bank account. For example, bank charges.

  Errors made by either the bank or the business. For example an error in adding up the figures in the cash at bank account in the books of the business when balancing the account.

- It is therefore useful to draw up a statement reconciling the two balances to prove that any difference between them is purely caused by timing differences. Any errors or omissions should be identified during the reconciliation process and can be corrected by the business or by the bank, depending on who made the error or omission.

3 SELF TEST QUESTIONS

3.1 Which one of the following, which explain the difference between the cash book balance and the bank statement balance, is a genuine bank reconciliation statement item, as opposed to an error or omission which requires an entry in the cash book?

   (a) An unpresented cheque

   (b) Overdraft interest

   (c) A standing order

   (d) A credit transfer. (1.3)

3.2 Is a debit balance in the cash book an asset or a liability? (1.4)

4 EXAMINATION TYPE QUESTION

4.1 Fuller

The bank account of Fuller Ltd, prepared by the company's bookkeeper, was as shown below for the month of October 19X6.

Bank account

19X6 October		£	19X6 October		Cheque no	£
1	Balance b/d	91.40	2	Petty cash	062313	36.15
3	McIntosh and Co	260.11	3	Freda's Fashions	062314	141.17
3	Malcolm Brothers	112.83	6	Basford Ltd	062315	38.04
3	Cash sales	407.54	8	Hansler Agencies	062316	59.32
14	Rodney Photographic	361.02	9	Duncan's Storage	062317	106.75
17	Puccini's Cold Store Ltd	72.54	9	Aubrey plc	062318	18.10
20	Eastern Divisional Gas Board – rebate (August direct credit)	63.40	10	Secretarial Services Ltd	062319	28.42
22	Grainer's Garage	93.62	14	Trevor's Auto Repairs	062320	11.75
29	Cash sales	235.39	15	Wages cash	062321	115.52
31	Balance c/d	221.52	16	Towers Hotel	062322	44.09
			17	Bank charges (September)	–	12.36

20	Broxcliffe Borough Council	SO	504.22
21	Eastern Area Electricity Board	DD	196.83
24	Eastern Divisional Gas Board	DD	108.64
28	Petty cash	062323	41.20
30	Wages cash	062324	119.07
31	Salaries transfers	–	337.74

£1,919.37   £1,919.37

November		
1	Balance b/d	221.52

In early November, the company's bank sent a statement of account which is reproduced below.

Statement of account with Lowland Bank plc

Account: Fuller Ltd Current Account No 10501191

Date of issue: 1 November 19X6

19X6 October	Description	Debit £	Credit £	Balance £
1	BCE		175.02	90.45
2	CR		175.02	265.47
2	062310	111.34		154.13
3	062312	9.18		144.95
3	062309	15.41		129.54
3	CR		780.48	910.02
7	062313	36.15		873.87
10	ADJ		12.90	886.77
15	062315	38.04		848.73
16	062314	141.17		707.56
17	CR		443.56	1,151.12
20	SO	504.22		646.90
21	062317	106.75		540.15
21	DD	196.83		343.32
21	062320	11.75		331.57
22	141981	212.81		118.76
22	ADJ	10.00		108.76
22	062319	28.42		80.34
22	062320	11.75		68.59
22	CR		93.62	162.21
24	ADJ		212.81	375.02
27	INT (loan account)	26.35		348.67
27	062321	115.52		233.15
28	062322	44.09		189.06
28	DD	108.64		80.42
30	CGS	9.14		71.28
31	ADJ		11.75	83.03

Abbreviations: BCE = Balance; CR = Credit; ADJ = Adjustment; SO = Standing order; DD = Direct debit; INT = Interest;

CGS = Charges. Balances are credit unless marked OD

Prepare the company's bank reconciliation statement as at 31 October 19X6.   **(15 marks)**

5   ANSWER TO EXAMINATION TYPE QUESTION

5.1   Fuller

Bank reconciliation at 31 October 19X6

	£	£
Balance shown in cash at bank account 31 October 19X6		221.52 cr
Add: amounts paid out which are on the bank statement but not in the account		
— interest	26.35	
— charges	9.14	35.49
Which should give the revised correct balance on the account		257.01 cr
Add: unpresented cheques		
— 062316	59.32	
— 062318	18.10	
— 062323	41.20	
— 062324	119.07	
— salary transfer	337.74	575.43
		318.42
Deduct payments into bank not shown on the bank statement		
— cash sales		235.39
Which should equal the balance shown on the bank statement		£83.03

Notes

1   Amounts paid in, which are on the bank statement but not on the account. In this question several of the items in the bank account have clearly been paid in together. This needs to be recognised in reconciling the two sets of figures (£260.11 + £112.83 + £407.54 = £780.48). Once this has been recognised, three figures can be identified which are on the credit side of the bank statement which do not appear on the debit side of the bank account, namely £12.90, £212.81, and £11.75. The first of these presumably relates to an earlier period, and will be dealt with in more detail later. The other two would appear to be corrections of errors made in the bank, since they cancel out earlier incorrect transactions on the other side.

2   Amounts paid out, which are on the bank statement but not in the account. The only two items (apart from the items referred to in 1 above which were cancelled out) were interest and bank charges.

3   Unpresented cheques can be identified by comparing the payments in the bank account with the debit side of the bank statement. This comparison would also identify the fact that bank charges for September were included in the October bank account. Such charges would have been included on the September bank statement.

4   Payments into the bank which have not yet been recorded on the bank statement can be identified by comparing the debit side of the bank account with the credit side of the bank statement. Two such payments can be identified: £63.40 relating to a direct credit in August, and £235.39 relating to cash sales. The first of these was presumably credited to the bank statement in August, so is already included in the statement balance. The sales figure needs to be adjusted.

5   While examination questions seldom require a reconciliation of the opening balances it is nonetheless interesting to consider the reasons why the opening balances do not reconcile. A reconciliation can be drawn up as follows:

		£	£
Balance as bank account			91.40
Less: Bank charges relating to September			12.36
			79.04
Plus: cheques drawn in previous periods, not yet presented (it is assumed that earlier cheque numbers than those in the bank account will have been drawn in an earlier period)			
— 62309		15.41	
— 62310		111.34	
— 62312		9.18	135.93
			214.97
Plus: Direct credit to bank in August			63.40
			278.37
Less: Credits appearing on the October statement entered in the September bank account		175.02	
12.90		187.92	
Bank balance			90.45

This last procedure can be fairly time consuming, and is seldom necessary in examinations. It is given here to provide an indication of the kind of assumptions that may need to be made, and the kind of problems which may be encountered.

15 INCOMPLETE RECORDS

INTRODUCTION AND LEARNING OBJECTIVES

This chapter is concerned with the preparation of the profit and loss account and balance sheet in circumstances where there is not a full set of double-entry ledger accounts maintained by the business.

Small businesses do not necessarily need to maintain a full set of double-entry books in order to meet their accounting information needs. Usually small business managers, who are often the owners, can obtain the information they need to manage the business from other sources. For example, the stock in trade levels of a small business can often be ascertained by physical observation, just as effectively as can be done through the use of constantly updated accounting records. Thus the expense of maintaining a full, up-to-date set of accounts is not justified by the benefits which it is likely to give the managers. Despite this, it is still necessary to produce annual accounts. This might be because managers might find it useful to have a summary of trading and the position of the business from time to time. Even more important in practice is the need to produce accounts which can be used by the Inland Revenue to establish the income tax liability of the the owners of the business.

Provided that the managers of the business retain sufficient information (bank statements, invoices and so on), it is possible for someone with some accounting training to use these to produce annual accounts. The accounts would be prepared by establishing totals rather than by writing up the accounts in the progressive, piecemeal way which would have occurred had a full set of books been maintained throughout the year. The final accounts should contain exactly the same figures as would have been obtained had a full set of books been maintained.

When you have studied this chapter you should be able to do the following:

*   Understand why small businesses might not need to keep a full set of double entry accounts

*   Prepare accounts from such incomplete records

*   Calculate the value of lost assets in situations of incomplete records.

---

1   THE BACKGROUND TO INCOMPLETE RECORDS

1.1   Small businesses

So far only businesses which maintain a full set of double-entry accounts have been considered. In practice not all businesses go to these lengths. A full set of ledger accounts is only likely to be found in a business which is large enough to employ at least a part-time bookkeeper, or sophisticated enough to have adopted some kind of computerised accounting system, and to be employing someone to operate such a system.

Apart from the cost factor, many small businesses do not find it necessary to keep a full set of double-entry accounting records, for two main reasons:

1   The annual accounts (profit and loss account and balance sheet) can be prepared at the year end, without there being a full set of ledger accounts maintained, provided that the management of the business (usually the owner in the case of small businesses) keeps some minimal records.

2   A full set of double-entry records would not provide the business with any information which would be particularly useful on a day-to-day basis.

This chapter is principally concerned with the task identified in 1, but before going on to look more closely at this, it is worth considering the second reason in more detail. Generally, detailed double-entry accounts serve a much wider purpose than simply providing a basis for the preparation of the annual accounts. Provided that the ledger accounts are kept up to date they can be used by management in the running of the business. For example, a system which includes individual debtors' balances in the sales ledger, and a control account will tell the business how much is owed by credit customers in total, how much each customer owes and how long the debt has been outstanding, all of which is vital information in the management of trade debtors. Though the small business could also benefit from this approach, it is likely that the same benefits can be achieved much more simply. For example, a file of unpaid sales invoices could be maintained, invoices being switched to a 'paid' file when the cash is received from the customer. This would tell the small business all that it needs to know about trade debtors, without going to the trouble of keeping a full and up-to-date set of double-entry records. Similar points arise with most other uses to which larger businesses put their double-entry accounts, such as the management of stock-in-trade or the management of trade creditors.

Cash is probably the only area which it is difficult to manage without some up-to-date records, since cash is generally dealt with partly through a bank account, and cannot always be physically checked at will. However, in the case of cash at bank, a small business could easily ask its bank to provide up-to-date statements at short, regular intervals (say, weekly) and use these as a substitute for an up-to-date cash at bank account in the business's own books. On the other hand it would be a simple matter to maintain a cash book showing receipts and payments and periodic balances without going all the way to producing a full set of ledger accounts.

1.2   Legal requirements to keep accounts

There is no legal requirement in the UK for all businesses to keep detailed double-entry records. There is not even a *direct* requirement that all businesses produce an annual profit and loss account and balance sheet, though there is a requirement that businesses which are limited companies do so. However, where businesses do not produce annual accounts, the Inland Revenue can make life difficult for their owners. Since it is on the basis of accounting profit that the owners are assessed for income tax, if no annual accounts are produced, the Inland Revenue make estimates, usually overestimates, of the profit. The only way in which the owners of the business can show that the estimate is excessive is to produce (or have produced) annual accounts. This is not a criticism of the activities of the Inland Revenue; they need some mechanism to encourage production of annual accounts by small businesses, given that Parliament has continually ruled that business owners should be taxed on the basis of the profit earned.

It is probably true to say that for most small businesses the only reason for producing annual accounts is to provide the basis for agreeing the tax liability with the Inland Revenue. Even small limited companies probably only produce annual accounts for tax purposes and to comply with company law.

1.3   Businesses which keep no accounting records

Imagine that an accountant in practice is confronted by a client who owns a van from which greengroceries are sold. The client has no bank account. Stock is bought from a local wholesale market, with the account being settled in cash at the end of each month. The greengroceries are sold to householders on a door-to-door basis. Most customers pay immediately but some are allowed to settle at the end of each week. No records are kept. The client wants to know how much profit has been made during the past year.

Obviously it is not possible to arrive at a full set of accounts, but an accountant could probably get enough information to arrive at a profit or loss figure. In doing this it is important to remember that the balance on the owner's capital account at the end of each year is deduced as follows:

	1	**Balance at the start of the year**
plus	2	**Capital introduced**
plus	3	**Profit for the year** (or *less* loss for the year)
less	4	**Drawings**
equals	5	**Balance at the end of the year**

A moment's reflection should make it clear that if 1, 2, 4 and 5 are known, it would be a relatively simple matter to derive 3. In practice it is likely that:

1 could be found from the previous year's balance sheet;

2 could probably be remembered by the client (and may well be zero in any case);

4 could also probably be remembered, or at least estimated, particularly if the client was in the habit of drawing a fixed amount each week;

5 the capital balance at the year end, could be deduced by listing the client's assets and liabilities as at that date. In a small unsophisticated business this would be quite feasible provided that it is done at, or very shortly, after, the year end so that the items were still clear in the mind of the client.

1.4 Example

Suppose that the circumstances described above have actually occurred and that the accountant discovers the following:

1   The client started the business on 1 June 19X7 by introducing £1,000 into the business which was immediately invested in a second-hand van costing £900, and £100 worth of stock.

2   No further capital was introduced into the business during the year, but the client withdrew £100 each week except for the week immediately after Christmas and the week of the Easter holiday, when nothing was withdrawn.

3   At the end of the year (31 May 19X8), the client still had the van (which he believed would last two more years and then be worth nothing), £95 was owed (subsequently received) by various customers for greengrocery sales on credit, £265 was owed to various wholesalers for stock bought on credit, the stock left had cost him about £55 and there was a cash float of £370.

In deducing the profit the following approach would need to be taken:

There was no opening capital, but there was an injection of capital of £1,000. Drawings may be calculated as £5,000, being £100 per week for 50 weeks.

Since capital = assets – liabilities, the closing capital balance may be ascertained as follows:

Assets	**£**	
Van	600	(assuming straight-line depreciation)
Stock	55	
Debtors	95	
Cash	370	
	1,120	
Liabilities		
Creditors	265	
Capital	**£855**	

(This statement is often referred to as a **statement of affairs**)

The profit for the year may thus be calculated as follows:

	£
Opening capital	Nil
Capital introduced	1,000
	1,000
Plus: Net profit	x
Less: Drawings	5,000
Closing capital	£855

The net profit must therefore have been £4,855.

In practice it is unlikely that the Inland Revenue would accept a profit figure deduced in this way more than occasionally, where for example records had been accidentally destroyed. Inspectors of taxes usually insist on seeing a set of accounts which show, among other things, the gross profit, partly because they can then assess the credibility of the accounts by reference to the gross profit/sales ratio.

The approach which has just been explored does serve as a reminder of an important fact, that is, that net profit is the net increase in capital (and therefore in net assets) after accounting for any injections of new capital and drawings by the owner.

It is also worth noting that the owner may fail to keep business transactions separate from personal ones. For example, bills relating to personal and domestic expenses may be paid from business funds, and business expenses may be paid from personal funds. Transactions of this nature should be seen as drawings or injections of capital respectively.

1.5   Activity

Bill Brewer is a self-employed carpenter whose annual accounts are prepared by you from copy invoices and notes which Bill keeps. Immediately following the financial year end of 31 December 19X7, Bill sorted through the various bits of paper which he had accumulated during the year and made two piles, one of invoices and notes to hand to you, the other of useless papers and circulars. Unfortunately, as a result of a misunderstanding between Bill and his wife, the pile of useful papers was used to light the fire and the other one was retained. This left Bill with no records of any transactions for the year. Since most of his transactions were in cash, copy bank statements would be virtually useless as a basis for preparing a full set of accounts.

Bill is able to tell you the following:

1   He systematically took £100 each week from the business's cash balance

2   He paid the following personal expenses from the business bank account;

(a)   for Council Tax £540

(b)   domestic electricity £420

(c)   holiday costs £1,270.

3   He bought new tools costing £300 during the year and he threw away some old tools which had cost him £200 in 19X4 (three years earlier)

4   He had not introduced any new capital into the business

5   At 31 December 19X7:

(a)   he had work-in-progress valued at £290

(b)   he had £360 in the business petty cash box

(c)   he owed £140 to the local timber merchant

(d)   he had a stock of useable timber which cost £150

(e) he was owed £770 by customers who had yet to pay (but who Bill was very confident would pay) for work done by him during 19X7

(f) he still had the same van as last financial year.

Bill's business bank statement showed that at 31 December 19X7 he had a balance (in hand) of £1,260. Bill's balance sheet at 31 December 19X6 was, in summary, as follows:

Fixed assets	Cost	Depreciation	Net
	£	£	£
Motor van	3,000	1,200	1,800
Tools	1,200	500	700
	£4,200	£1,700	£2,500
Current assets			
Stock and work-in-progress	640		
Trade debtors	350		
Cash at bank	490		
Cash in hand	180	1,660	
Current liabilities			
Trade creditors		440	1,220
			£3,720
Capital account			£3,720

Bill depreciated both his van and his tools at 20% per annum straight line. None of his tools were more than three years old. A full year's depreciation is taken on assets held at the year end.

Deduce Bill's profit for the year to 31 December 19X7.

1.6 Activity solution

Bill Brewer

1 The opening capital balance is £3,720.

2 The capital introduced is zero.

3 The drawings were:

	£
Weekly cash (52 × £100)	5,200
Council tax	540
Electricity	420
Holiday	1,270
	£7,430

4 The closing capital balance is calculated as follows:

Fixed assets	Cost	Depreciation	Net
	£	£	£
Fixed assets			
Van	3,000	1,800	1,200
Tools	1,300	640	660
	4,300	2,440	1,860

Current assets

Stock and work-in-progress	440	
Trade debtors	770	
Cash at bank	1,260	
Cash in hand	360	2,830

Current liabilities

Trade creditors	140	2,690
Closing capital (at 31/12/19X7)		£4,550

Profit for the year is derived from workings $(4)+(3)-(1)$

that is, opening capital + net profit – drawings = closing capital.

Therefore net profit = closing capital + drawings – opening capital = $4,550 + 7,430 - 3,720 = £8,260$

Notes

		£
The cost of the tools:	Opening balance	1,200
	Additions	300
		1,500
	Disposals	200
		£1,300

		£
Depreciation of the tools:	Opening balance	500
	Disposal (£200 × 60%)	120
		380
	19X7 charge (£1,300 × 20%)	260
		£640

1.7   Sufficient records

If the business keeps records of all cash spent and received, both through the bank and in note and coin, and the management is capable of giving information about other assets and liabilities at the year end, it is possible to produce a complete and detailed profit and loss account and balance sheet for the business. Indeed, strictly it may not be necessary for there to be *full* records of cash provided that there is only one unknown figure.

Example

Alf keeps a corner shop. All of his sales are for cash. From his records, including his bank statement, Alf is able to tell you that the following payments were made from cash in the till during the year to 31 December 19X7.

	£
Lodgements in (that is, payments into) bank	53,286
Cash payments to suppliers	3,853
Wages	2,680
Motor expenses	523
Alf's drawings	5,780

The till float at the start of the year (1/1/19X7) was £87 (deduced from last year's balance sheet) and the float at the year end (31/12/19X7) was £153.

It is possible, from this information, to prepare the cash (till) account for the year to 31 December 19X7. This will appear as follows:

Cash account (summary)

	£		£
Opening balance	87	Lodgements	53,286
		Payments to suppliers	3,853
		Wages	2,680
		Motor expenses	523
Sales (balancing figure)	66,188	Alf's drawings	5,780
		Closing balance	153
	£66,275		£66,275

Clearly unless there are any items which Alf has not mentioned (for example pilferage), the balancing figure on this account must be the sales figure. In reality deducing one of the figures by this means is a common occurrence.

Note that the above credit item for lodgements will need an equivalent debit entry in the summary bank account.

Since Alf has a business bank account, which presumably gives rise to periodic bank statements setting out all the transactions which have been carried out through the bank account, it will be a simple matter to analyse his statements for the year and to produce a summary 'cash at bank' account. Alf's summary bank account (for the year to 31 December 19X7) was as follows.

Cash at bank account (summary)

	£		£
Opening balance	516	Electricity	462
Lodgements	53,286	Payments to suppliers	41,016
		Shop rent	5,000
		Motor expenses	253
		Telephone	203
		Sundry items	117
		Drawings	2,512
		Closing balance	4,239
	£53,802		£53,802

The balance sheet (in summary) at the start of the year (1/1/19X7) was as follows:

		£	£	£
Fixed assets				
Motor van:	cost		4,000	
	depreciation		800	
				3,200
Current assets				
Stock		2,386		
Cash at bank		516		
Cash in hand		87		
			2,989	
Current liabilities				
Trade creditors		4,342		
Accrued expenses		50		
			4,392	
Working capital				(1,403)

Net assets £1,797

Capital £1,797

Further investigation reveals the following:

1   The stock in trade at 31/12/19X7 was valued at cost as £2,755
2   Alf's file of unpaid invoices for purchases of stock contained invoices totalling £3,763 at 31/12/19X7
3   The rent payments during the year were for the 15 months to 31 March 19X8
4   The accrued expense of £50 in the opening balance sheet relates to the telephone bill for the last quarter of 19X6. At the end of 19X7 a similar situation existed, except that the bill is expected to be £60
5   Alf has decided to depreciate his van at the rate of 20% pa (straight line).

There is now sufficient information to build up Alf's profit and loss account and balance sheet. This could be done in one of two ways:

1   Normal rules could be followed and a full set of double-entry accounts could be written up. This would amount mainly to completing the double entry in respect of each of the items in the cash and bank accounts. Following that the final accounts could be prepared in the conventional way.
2   The double-entry accounts could be bypassed and the final accounts could be prepared directly, with the double entry being effectively completed on the face of the final accounts, rather than in ledger accounts. This is generally the more practical approach, and is undoubtedly the method to use in examinations, since it takes less time.

For example, consider Alf's sales figure, which was deduced from the cash account. If the normal rules are followed an account for sales should be opened and credited with £66,188, thus completing the double entry. The sales account should then be debited with this amount and the trading account credited. However, using the sales account as a half-way stage to debiting the trading account does seem something of a waste of time, and achieves nothing in answering the typical examination question on incomplete records.

Of course in the situation where the sales are not all for cash, but are wholly or partly on credit, the position is likely to be more complex. In the first instance the figure of £66,188, which was the balancing figure on the cash account, may not be the sales figure. It should be treated as cash received from debtors. Either a summary (or total) debtors account or equivalent workings needs to be prepared to deduce the sales figure. The trade debtors account would appear as follows:

Trade debtors account

	£		£
Opening balance	x	Cash received (from balancing figure in the cash account)	x
Sales (the balancing figure)	x	Cheques received (from bank account)	x
		Bad debts written off	x
		Discounts allowed	x
		Closing balance	x
	£x		£x

As before there seems little point in opening a sales account, since this remains a half-way stage to the crediting of sales in the trading account. However where credit sales occur, the use of a debtors account along the lines shown above provides a logical and systematic approach to the derivation of the total sales figure.

In practice, some combination of the above approaches tends to be used. The straightforward entries like sales in Alf's case can be transferred straight to the final accounts. Where there are potential complications (in this case telephone and purchases), ledger accounts can be opened and the double entry followed through the normal route. The level of complication of ledger accounts is clearly a matter of judgment. Many practising accountants would feel that Alf's case is so simple that no ledger accounts are necessary.

1.8 Sequence of steps to follow

Whatever compromise is adopted, the steps which must be followed in preparing a set of accounts from incomplete (single entry) records are always as follows:

Step 1 Establish opening (last year's) balance sheet

Step 2 Prepare a cash summary

Step 3 Prepare a bank summary

Step 4 Open necessary ledger accounts

Step 5 Draft a pro-forma profit and loss account and balance sheet (that is, without figures)

Step 6 Enter the balances from the opening balance sheet into the appropriate ledger accounts or the appropriate place in the final accounts

Step 7 Post the cash and bank account entries *either* to the appropriate ledger accounts or to the draft final accounts. In practice some of the items in the final accounts will be made up of several postings and adjustments. These can be dealt with *either* by opening accounts for these items *or* by showing the detailed figures as notes in the final accounts, and including their totals in the final columns.

Step 8 Enter the closing adjustments (stock, accruals, depreciation, bad debts and so on) *either* in the appropriate ledger account *or* the draft final accounts, making sure that the double entry is observed. (For example closing stock must be shown both as credit in the trading account and as a current asset (debit) in the balance sheet)

Step 9 Post the balancing figure in the ledger account to the final accounts.

Step 10 Tidy up the final accounts, making the necessary calculations to establish the profit figure.

At first sight these steps seem rather complicated, and perhaps difficult to remember. Actually they should not cause too many problems, partly because with a little practice they become second nature and partly because in the typical examination question some of the steps are already completed. For example, the cash and/or bank summaries are quite often given.

1.9 Sequence of steps illustrated

We will now apply the steps to Alf's accounts. We will explain each step in detail and you should follow them through to arrive at a full set of final accounts. You can then compare your version with the one which is shown at the end of this section.

The opening balance sheet, the cash summary and the bank summary have already been prepared, so step 4 can now be considered. Ledger accounts are opened for telephone expense and trade creditors, in the latter case to assist in the calculation of the figure for purchases. However, since it could be argued that this is not strictly necessary in such a simple case, an approach to these areas without opening ledger accounts will be covered, as an alternative.

Next, draft the profit and loss account and balance sheet. This should be fairly simple as these look much the same from one business to the next and, more particularly, from one year to the next in the same business, except for the figures. It is probably sensible to leave a line between each item to accommodate any omissions or adjustments. In Alf's case the year-end balance sheet is going to look much the same as the opening one and his trading and profit and loss account can be easily visualised.

The balances from the opening balance sheet can now be put into an appropriate ledger account, or entered directly into the final accounts.

1   The opening capital (£1,797). It is best to have an expanded capital section of the balance sheet which shows opening balance, additions for capital injections and profits, and deductions for drawings. This means that the £1,797 can be written in as the opening balance.

2   Trade creditors (£4,342). This can be included as the opening credit balance in the trade creditors account, *or* if it was decided not to open such an account it can be written in (as a note) as a negative figure beside the purchases' space in the trading account.

3   Accrued expense (£50). This can be included as the opening credit balance in the telephone account, *or* as a negative figure beside the 'telephone' expense entry in the profit and loss account. It should be shown as a negative because it is a credit balance being shown on the debit side of the profit and loss account. It reflects the fact that it was last year's expense (or part of it) paid this year and should be set against the cash paid this year.

4   Fixed asset (£4,000). Since there have apparently been no acquisitions or disposals, the £4,000 can be written straight into the 'cost' space. As the depreciation will be increased, for the time being, the £800 brought forward should be written in, as a note, beside the 'depreciation provision' entry.

5   Stock (£2,386). This can be written straight into the 'opening stock' position in the trading account.

6   The cash at bank and in-hand balances have already been included in the two summary accounts as opening balances.

The next step is to post the cash and bank summaries. Postings from the cash summary will be as follows:

1   Sales (£66,188). This should be posted direct to the sales space on the credit side of the trading account.

2   Lodgements (£53,286). This item does not need to be posted because it has, in effect, already been posted to the bank summary.

3   Payments to suppliers (trade creditors) (£3,853). This should be posted to the debit of trade creditors account *or* added to the opening balance which has already been written in beside the 'purchases' item in the trading account.

4   Wages (£2,680). This should be put straight into the 'wages' slot on the debit side of the profit and loss account.

5   Motor expenses (£523). This should be posted to 'motor expenses' on the debit side of the profit and loss account.

6   Alf's drawings (£5,780). This should be written in beside the 'drawings' slot in the capital section of the balance sheet.

The bank summary can then be posted as follows:

1   Lodgements (£53,286). No action is necessary since the other side of the double entry is in the cash summary.

2   Electricity (£462). This should be put straight into the 'electricity' slot on the debit side of the profit and loss account.

3   Payments to suppliers (£41,016). Either debit this to the trade creditors account or write it in as a positive item beside 'purchases' in the trading account.

4   Shop rent (£5,000). Post this to 'rent' on the debit side of the profit and loss account.

5   Motor expenses (£253). Post this to 'motor expenses' (beside the £523 already posted) in the profit and loss account.

6   Telephone (£203). Either debit the telephone account *or* post to 'telephone' in the profit and loss account.

7   Sundry items (£117). Post this straight into the 'sundries' slot on the debit side of the profit and loss account.

8   Drawings (£2,512). This should be written in (beside the £5,780 already posted) by the 'drawings' slot in the capital section of the balance sheet.

The closing adjustments can now be made.

1   Stock in trade at year end (£2,755). This should be entered in the 'closing stock' space in the trading account and under current assets in the balance sheet.

2   The unpaid trade creditors (£3,763). This should either be put in as the closing balance on the trade creditors account, that is, as a debit and entered as 'trade creditors' in the current liabilities in the balance sheet, or it should be written, as a positive figure, by the 'purchases' slot in the trading account, and shown as a current liability in the balance sheet.

3   The rent prepayment (£1,000 (3/15 × £5,000)). This should be deducted from the figure of rent in the profit and loss account and shown as a prepaid expense in the current assets in the balance sheet.

4   The accrued expense for telephone (£60). This should be debited to the telephone account and included as accrued expenses in the current liabilities *or* the item should be added to the 'telephone' expense figure in the profit and loss account and included in the balance sheet as a current liability.

5   Depreciation (£800 (£4,000 × 20%)). This should be debited to the profit and loss account and added to the £800 under 'depreciation provision' in the fixed asset section of the balance sheet.

The ledger accounts can now be closed off:

1   Trade creditors. This should be closed by entering the balancing figure (a credit) and debiting the same figure to the purchases slot in the trading account.

2   Telephone. This should also be closed off by entering the balancing figure (a credit) and debiting the same figure to the 'telephone' expense slot in the profit and loss account. Obviously these accounts need not be closed off if the more direct approach was used.

Finally, it is necessary to total the noted figures in the final accounts and insert the resultant figures. The gross profit and net profit figures need to be deduced and the net profit entered in the capital section of the balance sheet. The sections of the balance sheet need to be sub-totalled and the totals inserted. Once this has been done Alf's final accounts should appear as follows:

Trading and profit and loss account for the year to 31 December 19X7

	£	£
Sales		66,188
Opening stock	2,386	
Purchases (− 4,342 + 3,853 + 41,016 + 3,763)	44,290	
	46,676	
Less: Closing stock	2,755	43,921
Gross profit		22,267
Less: Expenses		
Rent (5,000 − 1,000)	4,000	
Electricity	462	
Motor expenses (523 + 253)	776	
Telephone (− 50 + 203 + 60)	213	
Wages	2,680	
Sundries	117	
Depreciation	800	

		9,048
Net profit		£13,219

Balance sheet as at 31 December 19X7

£	£	£
Fixed assets		
Van: cost	4,000	
depreciation provision (800 + 800)	1,600	2,400
Current assets		
Stock	2,755	
Prepaid expenses	1,000	
Cash at bank	4,239	
Cash in hand	153	
	8,147	
Current liabilities		
Trade creditors	3,763	
Accrued expenses	60	
	3,823	4,324
Net assets		£6,724
Capital		
Opening balance		1,797
Profit for year		13,219
		15,016
Less: Drawings (5,780 + 2,512)		8,292
		£6,724

If ledger accounts had been used for creditors and telephone (the more complicated adjustments) the figures for purchases and the telephone expense could have been derived as follows:

Trade creditors account

	£		£
Cash	3,853	Opening balance b/d	4,342
Bank	41,016	Trading account purchases	44,290
Closing balance c/d	3,763		
	£48,632		£48,632
		Balance b/d	3,763

Telephone account

	£		£
Bank	203	Opening balance b/d	50
Closing balance c/d	60	Profit and loss - telephone	213
	£263		£263
		Balance b/d	60

No workings for purchases or telephones would appear in the final accounts if the above accounts were used.

1.10 Note to the solution

The bracketed figures in the above accounts are workings which most users of the accounts will not understand or be interested in. Although in real life these would be omitted from the final typed version of the accounts, for exam purposes they should be left intact.

You should be clear that preparation of the two accounts shown above is an *alternative* to deducing the purchases and telephone expense figures on the face of the final accounts.

In practice, for all but fairly simple situations, the use of accounts for both debtors and creditors is likely to prove to be the easiest way of calculating sales and purchases figures. The use of other accounts is largely a matter of preference, since the workings and end-product are the same. The use of accounts to deal with adjustments results in a neater set of final accounts, since no workings appear on them; but it is time consuming. In examinations this latter fact must be considered.

1.11 Activity

Pedro, a retailer who does not keep proper books of account, started trading on 1 January 19X2. An analysis of the bank statements of the business for the first year gives the following information:

	Receipts £	Payments £
Initial capital contribution	75,000	
Loan from Juan	15,000	
Cash banked	138,180	
Premium on lease		31,500
Fixtures and fittings		30,450
Purchase of van		10,500
Payments to suppliers of stock		128,115
Rent paid		9,000
General rates and water rates		3,300
Electricity		1,425
Insurance		675
Telephone		300
Repayment of loan to Juan		7,500
Bank charges and interest		900
Repairs to van		510

The following cash payments have been made out of takings:

	£
Drawings	11,700
Wages	8,400
Petrol	1,110
Sundry expenses	915

At 31 December 19X2:

1   Stock in trade was valued at £18,000

2   There was unbanked cash in the till of £600

3   Trade debtors totalled £6,150.

The annual rent is £12,000. The premium on the lease is to be depreciated in equal instalments over its 21-year life. Annual depreciation is to be provided at 10% for fixtures and fittings and at 20% on the van, in both cases based on the cost at the year end. A provision against doubtful debts of 20% of the year-end trade debtors is to be established.

Prepare Pedro's trading and profit and loss account for the year ended 31 December 19X2 and a balance sheet at that date.

1.12 Activity solution

Pedro
Trading and profit and loss account
for the year ended 31 December 19X2

	£	£
Sales (160,905 + 6,150)		167,055
Purchases	128,115	
Less: Closing stock	18,000	
Cost of sales		110,115

	£	£
Gross profit		
56,940		
Less: Expenses		
Rent (9,000 + 3,000)	12,000	
Depreciation of lease	1,500	
Rates	3,300	
Electricity	1,425	
Insurance	675	
Telephone	300	
Interest	900	
Van repairs	510	
Depreciation of van	2,100	
Petrol	1,110	
Wages	8,400	
Depreciation of fixtures	3,045	
Provision for doubtful debts	1,230	
Sundry expenses	915	
		37,410
Net profit		£19,530

Balance sheet as at 31 December 19X2

Fixed assets	**Cost**	**Depreciation**	
	£	£	£
Lease	31,500	1,500	30,000
Fixtures and fittings	30,450	3,045	27,405
Van	10,500	2,100	8,400
	£72,450	£6,645	65,805

Current assets			
Stock	18,000		
Trade debtors (6,150 – 1,230)	4,920		
Cash at bank	4,005		
Cash in till	600		
		27,525	
Current liabilities			
Rent accrual (12,000 – 9,000)		3,000	
			24,525
			90,330

Long-term liability
Loan from Juan (15,000 – 7,500)   7,500

     £82,830

Capital

Capital introduced	75,000
Profit for the year	19,530
	94,530
Less: Drawings	11,700
	£82,830

Workings

Cash (till) account

	£		£
Trade debtors	160,905	Bank	138,180
		Drawings	11,700
		Wages	8,400
		Petrol	1,110
		Sundry expenses	915
		Balance c/d	600
	£160,905		£160,905

1.13 Activity

Julia runs a small clothes shop. She does not keep double-entry records, but she has asked you to prepare accounts for the year to 31 March 19X8.

On investigation you discover the following:

1   Julia purchases all of her stock on credit from a number of different suppliers.

2   Sales are mainly for cash, but Julia does have some credit customers.

3   Julia takes £150 each week from the cash takings as drawings and she pays an assistant £75 each week before banking the remainder.

4   All payments other than the above are made by cheque.

5   The following is a summary of the bank statements for Julia's business account for the year to 31 March 19X8:

		£
Receipts:	Opening balance	1,230
	Cheques from customers	11,280
	Takings paid in	47,310
	Additional capital	10,000
Payments:	Suppliers (net of 5% discount)	39,900
	General expenses	2,150
	Heat and light	1,560
	Rates and insurance	2,070
	New cash tills	1,200

6   The balance sheet at 31 March 19X7 showed the following assets and liabilities:

	£
Buildings	50,000
Cash in the tills	450
Stock	15,500
Shop fittings and equipment:	
Cost	15,000
Depreciation	6,000
Cash at bank	1,230
Accrued heat and light	260
Prepaid rates	900
Trade debtors	3,100
Trade creditors	4,750

7   At 31 March 19X8 the trade creditors' balance was £6,200, trade debtors owed £4,550, the stock in trade was valued at £12,600 and there was £530 in the till.

8   Depreciation is charged on all fittings and equipment at 10% per annum straight line. The buildings are not depreciated.

9   The payment for rates and insurance includes £1,000 which covers the period to 30 September 19X8.

10   No electricity bill has been received for the quarter to 31 March 19X8, but it is expected to be about £300.

Prepare Julia's trading and profit and loss account for the year ended 31 March 19X8 and a Balance Sheet as at that date.

1.14   Activity solution

Julia
Trading and profit and loss account for the year ended 31 March 19X8

	£	£
Sales	71,820	
Opening stock	15,500	
Purchases	43,450	
	58,950	
Less: Closing stock	12,600	
Cost of sales		46,350
Gross profit		25,470
Add: Other revenues		
Discounts received		2,100
		27,570
Less: Expenses		
Wages	3,900	
Rates and insurance		
(900 + 2,070 − 1,000)	1,970	
Heat and light		
(−260 + 1,560 + 300)	1,600	
General expenses	2,150	
Depreciation	1,620	
	11,240	
Net profit		£16,330

Balance sheet at 31 March 19X8

Fixed assets	£	£	£
Buildings			50,000
Shop fittings etc Cost (15,000 + 1,200)		16,200	
Less: Accumulated depreciation			
(6,000 + 1,620)		7,620	8,580
			58,580
Current assets			
Stock in trade	12,600		
Prepayments	1,000		
Trade debtors	4,550		
Cash at bank	22,940		
Cash in tills	530	41,620	
Current liabilities			
Accruals	300		
Trade Creditors	6,200	6,500	35,120
			£93,700
Capital			
As at 1 April 19X7			75,170
Capital introduced			10,000
Net profit for the year			16,330
			101,500
Drawings			7,800
			£93,700

Workings

1   *Calculation of opening capital*

Assets	£	£
Buildings		50,000
Stock		15,500
Trade debtors		3,100
Cash at bank		1,230
Cash in the tills		450
Prepaid rates		900
Shop fittings (net)		9,000
		80,180
Liabilities		
Trade creditors	4,750	
Accrued heat and light	260	5,010
		£75,170

2   **Cash at bank summary**

	£		£
Opening balance	1,230	Suppliers	39,900
Cheques from customers	11,280	General expenses	2,150
Takings	47,310	Heat and light	1,560
Capital	10,000	Rates and insurance	2,070
		Tills	1,200
		Closing balance	22,940
	£69,820		£69,820

3   **Cash in till summary**

	£		£
Opening balance	450	Drawings	7,800
Receipts from customers	59,090	Wages	3,900
		Bank lodgements	47,310
		Closing balance	530
	£59,540		£59,540

4   **Trade debtors account**

	£		£
Opening balance	3,100	Cash receipts	59,090
Sales	71,820	Cheque receipts	11,280
		Closing balance	4,550
	£74,920		£74,920

5   **Trade creditors account**

	£		£
Bank	39,900	Opening balance	4,750
Discount (5/X5)	2,100	Purchases	43,450
Closing balance	6,200		
	£48,200		£48,200

Note You may feel that it is not totally necessary to open accounts for trade debtors and trade creditors. It has been done this way above because there are complications both in the derivation of the sales figure (credit customers and both cash and cheque receipts) and of the purchases figure (credit purchases and the existence of discounts for prompt payment).

2   DEDUCING THE VALUE OF ASSETS LOST

2.1   Introduction

Sometimes it is necessary to deduce the value of assets stolen or damaged for the purposes of making an insurance claim. This would arise, for example, where stock has been stolen from a business which does not maintain detailed and up-to-date stock records. Under such circumstances the stock figure will not be available directly and would need to be deduced. Similarly, cash stolen from a firm which does not keep a detailed record of cash transactions will require some kind of estimate to be made.

Typically deducing a missing stock figure relies on knowledge of the gross profit margin (the ratio of gross profit to sales). Any missing or stolen cash can usually be estimated by putting cash as the balancing figure on a balance sheet as at the day of the mishap. Questions on this topic vary considerably so some flexibility of approach is usually required.

Example

The Carnaby Wholesale Clothing Company was burgled on the night of 14 December 19X2. The raiders stole all that day's cash takings together with the petty cash and a selection of the most expensive clothing.

On 30 November 19X2, the owner had taken a physical stock count for which the cost was evaluated as £32,540. The stock of clothing left after the burglary amounted to £11,300 at cost.

Deliveries from suppliers, of further stock items, between 1 and 14 December 19X2, were invoiced at £5,784 after deduction of trade discounts of £732.

Sales to retail customers (at selling prices) had been:

	Cash	Credit
	£	£
1 to 6 December	1,429.71	6,250.29
7 to 13 December	1,644.50	8,079.50
14 December	259.32	1,200.68

The cash and bank accounts showed that during the period 1 to 14 December 19X2:

1   The cash takings for 1 to 13 December, inclusive, had been banked intact

2   Cheques for £168.92 and £192.67 had been drawn to pay staff wages

3   Credit customers had paid cheques amounting to £15,867.11 (all of which had been banked) in full settlement of accounts totalling £16,102.83

4   The company had paid credit suppliers a total of £17,118.36 by cheque after deducting cash discounts of £940.45

5   The petty cash imprest account had been restored to its established level of £25.00 on 1 December by a withdrawal from the bank of £9.74. Subsequent disbursements to 14 December had amounted to £13.69.

Account balances in the firm's books on 30 November 19X2 had been:

	£	
Bank	6,625.08	(debit)
Cash	129.60	
Petty cash	15.26	

Gross profit on sales had been at the rate of 30% throughout 19X2 but on 7 December, as part of a sales campaign, this was reduced to 25% for the remainder of the month.

Calculate, using such of the above information as is relevant.

1   the amount of cash and the value of stock at cost, which had been stolen;

2   the balance on the bank account at close of business on 14 December 19X2.

Solution

The question can be approached as follows:

1   The amount of cash stolen can be derived from a cash summary, or cash account, as follows:

The Carnaby Wholesale Clothing Company

	£	£
Balance in hand – 30 November 19X2		129.60
Receipts		
Cash sales		
1 to 6 December		1,429.71
7 to 13 December		1,644.50
14 December		259.32
		3,463.13
Payments into bank		
6 December	1,429.71	
13 December	1,644.50	
		3,074.21
Balance 14 December		£388.92

The petty cash balance as at 14 December would be £25 – £13.69 = £11.31

The total amount of cash stolen would thus be £388.92 + £11.31 = £400.23

The amount of stock stolen can be calculated by estimating the likely stock in hand on 14 December, and comparing it with the amount actually in hand. This can be done as follows:

	1 to 6 December	**7 to 14 December**
Sales	(1,429.71 + 6,250.29)	(1,644.50 + 8,079.50 + 259.32 + 1,200.68)
	= £7,680	= £11,184
Cost of sales	70% of sales	75% of sales
	= £5,376	= £8,388 Total £13,764

Closing stock is derived from:

	£
Opening stock	32,540
Purchases	5,784
	38,324
less: Closing stock	x
= Cost of sales	£13,764

Therefore closing stock (x) should have been £24,560

Since the actual stock in hand amounted to £11,300 the amount of stock stolen can be estimated at £13,260.

2   The balance on the bank account as at 14 December 19X2 may be derived as follows:

	£	£
Balance at bank at 30/11/19X2		6,625.08
Takings banked (1,429.71 + 1,644.50)	3,074.21	
Receipts from credit customers	15,867.11	18,941.32
		25,566.40
Payments to suppliers	17,118.36	
Staff wages (168.92 + 192.67)	361.59	
Petty cash	9.74	17,489.69
Balance at bank 14/12/19X2		£8,076.71

2.2 **Activity**

The balance sheet at 30 September 19X9 of John East, a long-established trader, is as follows:

	£	£		£	£
Capital account			**Fixed assets**, at cost		140,000
At 30 September 19X8		62,000	*Less:* Depreciation to date		96,000
					44,000
Add: Net profit for the year ended 30 September 19X9		16,000			
			Current assets		
		78,000	Stock in trade	17,000	
Less: Drawings		9,000	Trade in debtors	6,000	
		69,000	Amounts prepaid	400	
			Balance at bank	8,500	31,900
Current liabilities					
Trade creditors	6,200				
Accrued charges	700	6,900			
		£75,900			£75,900

Owing to a long illness, John East has been obliged to leave the day-to-day operation of his business since early 19X0 in the hands of Peter Pink, a trusted employee.

Although his illness has prevented him keeping his accounting records up to date, John was able to make plans for the year ended 30 September 19X0, which showed that during the year the business bank account would never be in overdraft.

A letter from the bank drawing John East's attention to the fact that his business bank account was £5,000 overdrawn on 30 September 19X0 coincided with the sudden disappearance of Peter Pink. Subsequent investigations implicate Peter Pink who it appears has not paid into the business bank account all the monies received from trade debtors; however, all necessary payments have been paid correctly through the business bank account.

It has always been the practice of John East to bank all business receipts intact and to make all payments from the business bank account.

It can be assumed that there were no unpresented cheques at 30 September 19X0 and all amounts paid into the bank account on or before 30 September 19X0 were credited by that date.

John East is now endeavouring to determine the amount of cash misappropriated and also to prepare the annual accounts for the year ended 30 September 19X0. John East is not insured against loss owing to the misappropriation of cash.

Accordingly, the following information has now been obtained concerning the year ended 30 September 19X0:

1   Stock in trade, at cost, at 30 September 19X0 was valued at £11,000

2   Throughout the year, a uniform rate of gross profit was earned of one-third of the cost of goods sold

3   Payments for purchases totalled £110,700 whilst trade creditors at 30 September 19X0 were £3,300 more than a year previously

4   Administrative expenses payments made during the year totalled £11,200 whilst the amount to be charged to the profit and loss account is £11,000

5   Establishment expenses payments were £9,400 and establishment expenses prepaid at 30 September 19X0 amounted to £800

6   Fixed assets bought and paid for amounted to £20,000

7   Depreciation is provided annually at the rate of 5% of the cost of fixed assets held at the end of each financial year

8   John East's cash drawings totalled £10,000

9   Trade debtors at 30 September 19X0 amounted to £6,500 and cash sales during the year under review amounted to £82,000

10   Amounts prepaid at 30 September 19X9 of £400 related to establishment expenses

11   Accrued charges at 30 September 19X9 of £700 related to administrative expenses.

(a)   Calculate the amount of cash misappropriated during the year ended 30 September 19X0.

(b)   Draw up John East's trading and profit and loss account for the year ended 30 September 19X0 and a balance sheet at that date.

Note: The profit and loss account should include an item 'cash misappropriated'.

(c)   Explain the importance of determining gross profit as well as net profit wherever possible.

2.3   Activity solution

(a)

John East
Loss of cash

	£	£
Cash at 30/9/19X9		8,500
Cash sales	82,000	
Credit sales receipts (6,000 + 78,000 − 6,500)	77,500	159,500
		168,000
Less: Payments to trade creditors	110,700	
Administration expenses	11,200	
Establishment expenses	9,400	
Fixed assets	20,000	
Drawings	10,000	161,300
Theoretical cash at 30/9/19X0		6,700
Actual cash at 30/9/19X0		(5,000)
Cash stolen		£11,700

Note The calculation of credit sales is shown below.

(b)

Trading and profit and loss account
for the year ended 30 September 19X0

	£	£
Sales		160,000
Opening stock	17,000	
Purchases (110,700 + 3,300)	114,000	
	131,000	
Less: Closing stock	11,000	
Cost of sales		120,000
Gross profit (1/3 cost of sales)		40,000

Less: expenses

Admin expenses (– 700 + 11,200 + 500)	11,000	
Establishment expenses (400 + 9,400 – 800)	9,000	
Depreciation	8,000	
Cash misappropriated	11,700	
		39,700
Net profit		£300

Note The sales figure is arrived at after the calculation of cost of sales and gross profit has been made. Cost of sales is calculated at £120,000. Gross profit is equal to one-third of this, £40,000. Sales must therefore total £160,000. If cash sales amount to £82,000 credit sales must total £78,000.

Balance sheet at 30 September 19X0

	£	£	£
Fixed assets			
Cost			160,000
Less: Depreciation to date			104,000
			56,000
Current assets			
Stock in trade	11,000		
Trade debtors	6,500		
Amounts prepaid	800	18,300	
Current liabilities			
Trade creditors	9,500		
Accrued charges	500		
Bank overdraft	5,000	15,000	3,300
			£59,300
Capital			
At 30 September 19X9			69,000
Add: Net profit for the year			300
			69,300
Less: Drawings			10,000
			£59,300

If required, accounts could be opened to deal with the more complicated adjustments, namely debtors, creditors, administration expenses, and establishment expenses, as follows:

Debtors

19X9		£	19X0		£
October 1	Balance b/d	6,000		Cash (received)	77,500
19X0 6,500	Sales (credit)	78,000	September 30	Balance c/d	
		£84,000			£84,000
October 1	Balance b/d	6,500			

The credit sales figure is arrived at as shown above. The cash received is deduced since it must be the balancing figure.

Creditors

19X0		£	19X9		£
	Cash (paid)	110,700	October 1	Balance b/d	6,200
Sept 30	Balance c/d	9,500	19X0	Purchases	114,000
		£120,200			£120,200
			October 1	Balance b/d	9,500

The purchases figure must be the balancing figure.

Establishment expenses

19X9		£	19X0		£
October 1	Balance b/d	400	Sept 30	Profit and loss	9,000
19X0	Cash	9,400	Sept 30	Balance c/d	800
		£9,800			£9,800
October 1	Balance b/d	800			

The opening and closing balances and the cash payment come from notes 5 and 10. The transfer to profit and loss represents the balancing figure.

Administrative expenses

19X0		£	19X9		£
	Cash	11,200	October 1	Balance b/d	700
			19X0		
Sept 30	Balance c/d	500	Sept 30	Profit and loss	11,000
		£11,700			£11,700
			October 1	Balance b/d	500

The opening balance, the cash payment, and the profit and loss transfer come from notes 4 and 11. The closing balance is the balancing figure.

(c)   Gross profit is the difference between the sales revenue and how much it cost to buy or to make the goods sold, from which the selling and administrative overheads are deducted to arrive at the net profit. As such it provides a useful item of information about the firm; for example, it could given an insight into the likely effect on net profit of a particular alteration in the level of sales.

Perhaps more importantly, the relationship between gross profit and sales, the gross profit ratio, can give some idea of the reliability of the four inputs of the trading account. A significant error in any one of the opening stock, closing stock, sales and purchases figures will give an unexpected gross profit ratio which should put the compiler of the accounts on guard.

3   CHAPTER SUMMARY

- Not all businesses keep full double-entry ledger accounts. Provided that they keep reasonable records of the transactions which have occurred, even in summary form, it is possible to prepare a complete set of final accounts. In fact it is possible, even where virtually no records are kept, to deduce a profit or loss figure.

- In the typical incomplete records situation, there is usually full information available (or it is able to be reliably deduced) but it is not in the form of a full set of double-entry books. The task facing the person who is to prepare the annual accounts is to establish total figures for such items as various cash and bank payments and receipts, total sales figure and total purchases figure. This can usually be done through the use of summary statements such as a cash at bank summary account, a petty cash (cash in hand) summary account, a total debtors account and a total creditors account. The figures deduced from these summaries can then be used, following strict double-entry principles, to prepare a trading and profit and loss account and a balance sheet.

- Where there has been loss or theft of goods or cash, it may be necessary to deduce the missing figure to support an insurance claim or just to know how much was involved; this can be reliably achieved by applying incomplete records principles.

4 SELF TEST QUESTIONS

4.1 Which one of the following is the most likely reason for some small businesses finding that a full set of accounting records is not particularly useful for management information purposes?

    (a)   because management information is not usually needed in small businesses

    (b)   because there can be other ways of acquiring useful management information

    (c)   because in small businesses the manager is typically the owner

    (d)   because small businesses rarely trade as companies. (1.1)

4.2 In preparing final accounts from incomplete records, on which of the following occasions is it necessary to open an account for trade debtors?

    (a)   when the final accounts will be presented to the Inspector of Taxes

    (b)   when the level of complexity makes it easier to do so

    (c)   when the credit sales figure is a large one

    (d)   when there are discounts allowed to debtors for prompt payment. (1.10)

4.3 Which one of the following is the 'gross profit margin' ratio?

    (a)   Gross profit/cost of sales

    (b)   Cost of sales/sales

    (c)   Gross profit/sales

    (d)   Net profit/gross profit. (2.1)

5 EXAMINATION TYPE QUESTIONS

5.1 George Gittings

George Gittings is a retailer who makes all of his sales for cash. During the night of 11 February 19X8 a fire destroyed all of his stock in trade and his shop fittings. The fire also destroyed all of his records except the unpaid invoices which he kept at his home.

George was insured against destruction by fire of his stock, up to its full amount and for his shop fittings, up to £5,000. On 31 December 19X7, his most recent accounting year end, his balance sheet was as follows:

George Gittings
Balance sheet as at 31 December 19X7

Fixed assets	£	£
Shop fittings (at net book value)		7,500
Current assets		
Stock in trade	24,500	
Cash at bank	2,300	
Cash in hand	100	
	26,900	

Current liabilities

Trade creditors	8,200	
Accrued expenses	1,400	
	9,600	
		17,300
		£24,800

Capital £24,800

During the period 1 January 19X8 to 11 February 19X8 (6 weeks), all takings were banked except for £150 each week for wages to an assistant and £160 for his own living expenses which were taken from the till. On 11 February 19X8 there was £100 in the till (not destroyed by the fire). George paid all shop expenses, apart from wages, by cheque. An analysis of his bank statement for the period 1 January 19X8 to 11 February 19X8 showed the following:

Receipts	£	Payments	£
Balance at 1/1/19X8	2,300	Trade creditors	17,940
Lodgements of cash	21,170	Shop expenses	2,450
		Balance at 11/2/19X8	3,080
	£23,470		£23,470

Selling prices are always based on cost plus 25%.

All of George's suppliers allowed him to deduct a 2.5% discount for prompt payment from the invoice price of his purchases of stock.

At 11 February 19X8, there were accrued expenses of £950 outstanding and unpaid invoices for stock purchases totalled £6,180.

Draw up the following:

(a) A statement of the amount of stock lost in the fire.

(b) A trading and profit and loss account for the period 1 January 19X8 to 11 February 19X8.

(c) A balance sheet, immediately following the fire, assuming that the insurance claims will be met.

(20 marks)

5.2 Snodgrass

The trial balance of Snodgrass, a sole trader, at 1 January 19X8 is as follows:

		Dr £000	Cr £000
Capital			600
Fixed assets (net)		350	
Trade debtors		200	
Prepayments	– rent	8	
	– insurance	12	
Trade creditors			180
Accruals	– electricity		9
	– telephone		1
Stock		200	
Bank		20	
		790	790

The following information is given for the year:

	£000
Receipts from customers	1,000
Payments to suppliers	700
Payments for: rent	30
insurance	20
electricity	25
telephone	10
wages	100
Proprietor's personal expenses	50
Discounts allowed	8
Bad debts written off	3
Depreciation	50

At 31 December 19X8 the following balances are given:

	£000
Trade debtors	250
Prepayments – rent	10
– telephone	2
Trade creditors	160
Accruals – electricity	7
Insurance	6
Stock	230

Prepare a trading and profit and loss account for the year, and a balance sheet as at 31 December 19X8.

(20 marks)

(ACCA, December 1988)

5.3   Tom Smith

Since commencing business several years ago as a cloth dealer, Tom Smith has relied on annual receipts and payments accounts for assessing progress. These accounts have been prepared from his business bank account through which all business receipts and payments are passed.

Tom Smith's receipts and payments account for the year ended 31 March 19X0 is as follows:

	£		£
Opening balance	1,680	Drawings	6,300
Sales receipts	42,310	Purchases payments	37,700
Proceeds of sale of			
grandfather clock	870	Motor van expenses	2,900
		Workshop – rent	700
Loan from John Scott	5,000	– rates	570
Closing balance	1,510	Wages – John Jones	3,200
	£51,370		£51,370

Additional information:

1   The grandfather clock sold during the year ended 31 March 19X0 was a legacy received by Tom Smith from the estate of his late father.

2   The loan from John Scott was received on 1 January 19X0; interest is payable on the loan at the rate of 10% per annum.

3   In May 19X0 Tom Smith received from his suppliers a special commission of 5% of the cost of purchases during the year ended 31 March 19X0.

4   On 1 October 19X9, Tom Smith engaged John Jones as a salesman. In addition to his wages, Jones receives a bonus of 2% of the business's sales during the period of his employment; the bonus is payable on 1 April and 1 October in respect of the immediately preceding six-month period.

Note: It can be assumed that sales have been at a uniform level throughout the year ended 31 March 19X0.

5   In addition to the items mentioned above, the assets and liabilities of Tom Smith were as follows:

At 31 March	19X9	19X0
	£	£
Motor van, at cost	4,000	4,000
Stock in trade, at cost	5,000	8,000
Trade debtors	4,600	12,290
Motor vehicle expenses prepaid	–	100
Workshop rent accrued due	–	200
Trade creditors	2,900	2,200

6   It can be assumed that the opening and closing balances in the above receipts and payments account require no adjustment for the purposes of Tom Smith's accounts.

7   As from 1 April 19X9, it has been decided to provide for depreciation on the motor van annually at the rate of 20% of the cost.

Draw up the trading and profit and loss account for the year ended 31 March 19X0 and a balance sheet at that date of Tom Smith.

(20 marks)

5.4   Mr Bends

On 1 January Mr Bends starts a business buying and selling motor cars. He gives you a summary of the business receipts and payments account as follows, for the year to 31 December (all figures are in £000).

Receipts	£000
Capital introduced (1 January)	100
From customers (after deducting worthless cheque, see note iii below)	400
10% loan from his mother (1 January)	50
	550

Payments	
To suppliers of new cars	320
To suppliers of second-hand cars	93
Wages	36
Rent	15
Purchase of furniture	5
Purchase of showroom display equipment	5
Insurance, electricity and stationery	7
Bank charges	1
Transfers to private bank account	26
	508

You are informed that:

(i) Rent payable is £3,000 for each 3-month period.

(ii) Mr Bends has bought a total of 37 new cars at a cost of £10,000 each. One of these was destroyed by fire the day before Mr Bends signed his insurance policy, two were taken into use by Mr Bends and his senior salesman, and 27 have been sold at a markup of 20% on cost (one of which has not yet been paid for).

(iii) Mr Bends had a problem with the very first second-hand car which he sold. He accepted a cheque for £5,000 which proved worthless, and he has been unable to trace the customer. Since then all sales of second-hand cars have been for cash. All purchases of second-hand cars have also been for cash.

(iv) Four second-hand cars remain in stock at 31 December. The cost of these to Mr Bends was £6,000, £6,000, £7,000 and £8,000 respectively.

(v) All fixed assets are to be depreciated at the rate of 20% for the year.

Prepare in good order:

• Trading accounts for new cars.

• Trading accounts for second-hand cars.

• Profit and loss account for the business for the year.

• Balance sheet as at 31 December.

Indicate clearly the calculation of all figures in your solution.

(20 marks)

(ACCA, June 1989)

5.5   Albert Zweistein

Albert Zweistein began business on 1 January 19X2 as a manufacturer of clocks. He believes his business is relatively successful but he has failed to keep proper records and is unsure of the real financial position. Unfortunately he seems to have been rather absent-minded, and is only able to give you limited information, as shown below. He wants you to prepare a single profit and loss account for the 18 months to 30 June 19X3, and a balance sheet as at 30 June 19X3.

Mr Zweistein gives you a summarised cash book as shown together with the following additional information which he thinks could be relevant.

(i) The stock of clocks at 30 June 19X3 has a cost of £20,000. This figure is obtained from the following table.

	Model A	Model B	Total
Cost	£15,000	£5,000	£20,000
Expected selling price	£28,000	£3,000	£31,000

(ii) All machines and vehicles were bought and put into use on the first day of the relevant six-month period. Depreciation should be calculated pro rata, assuming a five-year life, equal usage in each six-month period, and zero scrap value.

(iii) Items appearing on the bank statement for the business for the month of June 19X3 include the following, none of which are included in the cash book summary given.

Standing order receipt from customer	£3,000
Bank charges	£500
Standing order payment to supplier	£1,000

Albert Zweistein, summarised cash book
January 19X2 to June 19X3

Cash	Bank	Cash	Bank	
				January – June 19X2
	100,000			Capital (1 January)
	120,000			Loan from Russell (1 January)
			10,000	Rent for 12 months
		5,000	25,000	Purchase of material and parts
			5,000	Transfer
5,000		8,000		Factory wages
			3,000	Office wages
			2,000	Business formation costs
			125,000	Purchase of machines and vehicles
		1,000	4,000	Sundry expenses
		1,000	5,000	Personal spending
10,000	30,000			Sales
				July – December 19X2
		6,000	26,000	Purchase of material and parts
		10,000		Factory wages
			4,000	Office wages
			9,000	Purchase of vehicles
		1,500	5,000	Sundry expenses
		1,200	7,000	Personal spending
			12,000	12-month interest to 31 December on loan from Russell
12,000	50,000			Sales
10,000			10,000	Transfers
				January – June 19X3
		7,000	30,000	Purchase of materials and parts
		12,000		Factory wages
			6,000	Office wages
			8,000	Purchase of machines
	20,000			Additional capital
9,000	60,000			Sales
		800	6,000	Sundry expenses
			8,000	Personal spending
11,000			11,000	Transfer
57,000	380,000	53,500	321,000	

(iv)   Items properly included in the cash book summary, but not recorded on the bank statements up to 30 June 19X3, include the following:

Cash deposit	£700
Unpresented cheque	£2,000

(v)   Clocks which had cost £200 and had been sold for a total of £300 had been returned under guarantee and replaced. The returned clocks had been thrown away. The replacements had cost the same as the original ones.

(vi)   Mr Zweistein has produced a pile of papers which suggest that at 30 June 19X3 customers owe him £2,000 for clocks already dispatched. You notice, however, that the pile making up this £2,000 appears to include two identical photocopies of a document confirming a sale of £300. One of the other sales took place on 14 February 19X2, for £200.

(vii) Mr Zweistein had given a clock, cost £100, normal selling price £200, to a supplier in exchange for clock parts for which he would normally have had to pay £150.

(viii) Mr Zweistein produced invoices from suppliers, unpaid at 30 June 19X3, totalling £6,000.

Required

Prepare profit and loss account for the single period 1 January 19X2 to 30 June 19X3 and summarised balance sheet as at 30 June 19X3. Written workings may be in any form and to any volume you find convenient, but should be clear and legible.

(20 marks)

(ACCA, June 1993)

6 ANSWERS TO EXAMINATION TYPE QUESTIONS

6.1 George Gittings

(a)

George Gittings
Statement of loss of stock

	£
Sales: Bankings	21,170
Wages (£150 × 6)	900
Drawings (£160 × 6)	960
	£23,030
Cost of sales (100/125 × £23,030)	£18,424

Closing stock = opening stock + purchases − cost of sales
= 24,500 + 16,380 (see workings) − 18,424
= £22,456

(b)

Trading and profit and loss account
for the period 1 January 19X8 to 11 February 19X8

	£	£
Sales		23,030
Less: Cost of sales (see above)		18,424
		4,606
Add: Discounts received		460
		5,066
Less: Wages	900	
Shop expenses (− 1,400 + 2,450 + 950)	2,000	
Loss on destruction of fittings (7,500 − 5,000)	2,500	
		5,400
Loss for the period		£334

(c)

Balance sheet as at 11 February 19X8

	£	£
Current assets		
Insurance claim (22,456 + 5,000)	27,456	
Cash at bank	3,080	
Cash in hand	100	
		30,636

Current liabilities

Trade creditors	6,180	
Accrued expenses	950	
		7,130
		£23,506

Capital

Balance at 1 January 19X8		24,800
Less: Loss for the period	334	
Drawings	960	
		1,294
		£23,506

Note: The trading and profit and loss account makes no mention of the loss of stock by fire since the loss is totally covered by an insurance claim which is expected to be met in full.

Workings

Trade creditors account

	£		£
Cash	17,940	Opening balance	8,200
Discount received			
(2.5/97.5 x 17,940)	460	Purchases	16,380
Closing balance	6,180		
	£24,580		£24,580

6.2   Snodgrass

Snodgrass
Trading and profit and loss account
for the year ended 31 December 19X8

		£000	£000
Sales (see workings W1)			1,061
Less:	Cost of sales		
	Opening stock	200	
	Purchases (W2)	680	
		880	
	Closing stock	230	650
	Gross profit		411
Less:	Rent (8 + 30 – 10)	28	
	Insurance (12 + 20 + 6)	38	
	Electricity (– 9 + 25 + 7)	23	
	Telephone (– 1 + 10 – 2)	7	
	Wages	100	
	Discounts allowed	8	
	Bad debts written off	3	
	Depreciation	50	
			257
Net profit for the year			154

Balance sheet as at 31 December 19X8

	£000	£000	£000
Fixed assets (net)			300
Current assets			
Stock		230	
Prepayments		12	
Trade debtors		250	
Bank (W3)		85	
		577	
Less: Current liabilities			
Trade creditors	160		
Accruals	13	173	404
Net assets			704
Capital			
Capital as at 1 January 19X8			600
Add: Profit for the year			154
			754
Less: Drawings			50
			704

Workings

W1

Debtors account

	£000		£000
Balance b/d	200	Receipts	1,000
Sales *	1,061	Bad debts	3
		Disc allowed	8
		Balance c/d	250
	1,261		1,261
Balance b/d	250		

W2

Creditors account

	£000		£000
Payments	700	Balance b/d	180
Balance c/d	160	Purchases*	680
	860		860
		Balance b/d	160

* missing figure

W3

Cash (bank) account

	£000		£000
Balance b/d	20	Payments	
Receipts from customers	1,000	– creditors	700
		– rent	30
		– insurance	20
		– electricity	25
		– telephone	10
		– wages	100
		– personal expenses	50
		Balance c/d*	85
	1,020		1,020
Balance b/d	85		

* Missing figure

6.3   Tom Smith

Tom Smith
Trading and profit and loss account for the year ended 31 March 19X0

		£	£
Sales (– 4,600 + 42,310 + 12,290)			50,000
Less:	Opening stock	5,000	
Add:	Purchases (– 2,900 + 37,700+ 2,200)	37,000	
		42,000	
Less:	Closing stock	8,000	
	Cost of sales		34,000
Gross profit			16,000
Add: Special commission (Note 2)			1,850
			17,850
Less:	Wages	3,200	
	Bonus (50,000 x 6/12 × 2%)	500	
	Motor expenses (2,900 – 100)	2,800	
	Depreciation (4,000 × 20%)	800	
	Rent and rates (700 + 570 + 200)	1,470	
	Loan interest (5000 × 3/12 × 10%)	125	
			8,895
Net profit for the year			£8,955

Tom Smith
Balance sheet as at 31 March 19X0

		£	£
Fixed assets			
Motor van –	cost		4,000
	depreciation		800
			3,200
Current assets			
	Stock	8,000	
	Trade debtors	12,290	
	Special commission	1,850	
	Prepaid expenses	100	
		22,240	

Less:	Current liabilities		
	Trade creditors	2,200	
	Accrued expenses (200 + 500 + 125)	825	
	Bank overdraft	1,510	
		4,535	
Working capital			17,705
			20,905
Less:	Long-term loan – John Scott		5,000
			£15,905

Financed by:			
Capital			
Opening balance (note 1)			12,380
Add:	Net profit for the year	8,955	
	Capital introduced	870	9,825
			22,205
Less:	Drawings		6,300
			£15,905

Notes

1

Statement of affairs at 1 April 19X9

		£
Assets:	Cash	1,680
	Motor van	4,000
	Stock	5,000
	Trade debtors	4,600
		15,280
Less:	Liabilities: Trade creditors	2,900
	Capital at 1/4/19X9	£12,380

2   There is doubt about how the 'special commission' should be treated. It could certainly be argued that it is, in effect, a trade discount and as such the normal treatment would be to deduct it from the purchases figure. The treatment does not affect the net profit, but it does affect the gross profit.

6.4   Mr Bends

Mr Bends
Trading account for new cars for the year ended 31 December

	£000
Sales of new cars (27 × £10,000 × 120%)	324
Less: Cost of sales (27 × £10,000)	270
Gross profit on new cars for the year	54

Trading account for second-hand cars for the year ended 31 December

	£000	**£000**
Sales of second-hand cars (see workings)		93
Less: Purchases of second-hand cars	93	
Less: Stock at 31 December (6 + 6 + 7 + 8)	27	
		66
Gross profit on second-hand cars for the year		27

Profit and loss account for new cars for year ended 31 December

		£000	£000
Gross profit:	New cars	54	
	Second-hand cars	27	
			81
Wages		36	
Rent		12	
Insurance, electricity and stationery		7	
Cars destroyed by fire		10	
Depreciation: Showroom display equipment		1	
Furniture		1	
Motor cars		4	
Bad debts written off		5	
Bank charges		1	
Loan interest		5	
			82
Net loss for the year			1

Balance sheet as at 31 December

	Cost £000	Depr'n £000	£000
Fixed assets			
Showroom display equipment	5	1	4
Furniture	5	1	4
Motor cars	20	4	16
	30	6	24
Current assets			
Stock (27,000 + (7 × 10,000))		97	
Trade debtors		12	
Prepaid rent		3	
Cash		42	
		154	
Less: **Current liabilities**			
Trade creditors		50	
Accrued loan interest		5	
		55	
			99
			123
Less: **Long-term loan**			50
			73
Capital			
Cash introduced			100
Less: Net loss for the year		1	
Drawings		26	
			27
			73

Workings

	£000
Cash received from all customers	400
Add: New car not paid for	12
Worthless cheque	5
Total sales revenue (new and second-hand cars)	417
Less: Sales of new cars	324
Sales of second-hand cars	93

6.5   Albert Zweistein

Profit and loss account for the 18-month period to 30 June 19X3

	£	£	£
Sales			175,700
Less Cost of sales			
Purchases		106,150	
Less cost of clocks returned	200		
Cost of exchange for clock parts	100	300	
		105,850	
Factory wages		30,000	
		135,850	
Closing stock		18,000	117,850
Gross profit			57,850
Gain on clock exchange			50
			57,900
Office wages		13,000	
Rent		15,000	
Sundry expenses		18,300	
Cost of guarantee returns		200	
Bank charges		500	
Bad debt written off		200	
Depreciation		40,100	87,300
Operating loss			29,400
Loan interest payable			18,000
			47,400
Formation costs written off			2,000
Net loss for the period			49,400

Balance sheet as at 30 June 19X3

	£	£	£
Fixed assets			
Machines and vehicles at cost		142,000	
Less accumulated depreciation		40,100	101,900
Current assets			
Stock (lower of cost and NRV)		18,000	
Debtors		1,500	
Cash at bank		60,500	
Cash in hand		3,500	
		83,500	
Creditors: amounts due within one year			
Trade creditors	6,000		
Interest payable	6,000		
Rent owing	5,000	17,000	66,500
			168,400

Creditors: amounts owing beyond one year

Loan – Russell   120,000
                                                                                                          48,400

Opening capital   120,000
Net loss for period   49,400
Drawings   22,200   71,600
                                                                                                          48,400

Workings

Sales ledger control account

	£		£
Sales (less returns)	175,700	Receipts from debtors (10,000+30,000+12,000 +50,000+9,000+60,000)	171,000
		Standing order	3,000
		Bad debt	200
		Balance c/d	1,500
	175,700		175,700

Purchase ledger control account

	£		£
Payments to suppliers (25,000+5,000+26,000 +6,000+30,000+7,000)	99,000	Purchases	106,150
Standing order	1,000		
Exchange	150		
Balance c/d	6,000		
	106,150		106,150

Bank account

	£		£
Balance b/d	59,000	Bank charges	500
Standing order	3,000	Standing order	1,000
		Balance c/d	60,500
	62,000		62,000

Clock exchange

	£		£
Purchases	100	Purchase ledger control account	150
Profit	50		
	150		150

Depreciation charges
20% 3 1/2 year 3 £125,000   = £12,500
20% 3 1/2 year 3 £134,000   = £13,400
20% 3 1/2 year 3 £142,000   = £14,200
                                                                          £40,100

16 ACCOUNTING FOR CLUBS, SOCIETIES AND ASSOCIATIONS

INTRODUCTION AND LEARNING OBJECTIVES

So far this book has been concerned with issues relating to the accounts of profit-seeking organisations. However, it was mentioned in Chapter 1 that not-for-profit organisations also need to record their financial transactions and prepare financial reports. Certain not-for-profit organisations operate within the public sector, such as public utilities, nationalised industries and local government. These organisations can be extremely large and complex and can exert an important influence on the economy. Although an understanding of such organisations and the nature of their financial reports in general is outside the scope of the Foundation Accounting syllabus, there are certain not-for-profit organisations which do fall within the syllabus and whose financial reports must be considered. These organisations are clubs, societies and associations which exist for the primary purpose of providing some benefit or facility to members and/or others.

Many such organisations are small and are managed by a committee of unpaid elected officials. One member of the committee usually acts as treasurer and has responsibility for the accounting function. It is not unusual for the treasurer of a small club to have a limited understanding of accounting and to maintain only rudimentary financial records. However, this does not apply to all clubs, societies and associations. Some of these organisations are very large and employ professionally qualified accountants to operate their accounting system. An example is the Automobile Association (AA), a large and complex organisation which provides advice and technical support to its motorist members on a not-for-profit basis.

In this chapter, however, the principal focus will be on the preparation of accounts for smaller clubs, societies and associations. It is common for examination questions concerning this topic to require the preparation of final accounts for a small club from rudimentary financial records. The questions, therefore, represent a form of incomplete records problem and are similar in many respects to the incomplete records problems considered in the previous chapter.

When you have studied this chapter you should be able to do the following:

- Understand the items commonly seen in a receipts and payments account

- Explain why more complicated societies produce an income and expenditure account rather than a receipts and payments account

- Appreciate the form of final accounts presented by a typical club or society.

---

1 RECEIPTS AND PAYMENTS ACCOUNTS

1.1 Introduction

In the case of small clubs, societies and associations it is common for the treasurer to maintain only a cash book in which the cash and bank transactions for the period are recorded. At the end of the financial period the treasurer may summarise the bank and cash transactions and submit this summary as the final accounts. This summary of bank and cash transactions is referred to as a **receipts and payments account**. It should be noted that most clubs, societies and associations do not have a statutory duty to produce accounts. Nevertheless, the members may wish to know the state of the club's finances periodically and the treasurer will normally want the opportunity to account to the members.

A receipts and payments account may be a satisfactory financial report to the members where the organisation has few assets and liabilities and the activities are simple and straightforward. For example, a club which organises occasional social events for its members and has few assets and liabilities may find receipts and payments accounts sufficient. A receipts and payments account will list the cash and bank receipts and payments during the period and will also indicate the opening and closing cash and bank balances. Some receipts and payments accounts may group receipts and payments relating to a particular event together in order to reveal the net result of the event.

Example

The following is the receipts and payments account of the Merrivale Student Accountants Social Club, an organisation which runs a couple of coach trips each year for student accountants in the Merrivale area.

Receipts		£	Payments	£
Opening balance:				
Current account		24	Donation to children's home	100
Deposit account		113		
		137		
Easter trip to Sandup Park Racecourse:				
Ticket sales	218			
Coach hire	(150)			
Refreshment	(46)			
Tip to driver	(10)			
Surplus		12		
August Bank holiday trip to Brightpool-on-sea:				
Ticket sales	237			
Coach hire	(162)			
Group entry to				
Waterland Park	(40)			
Tip to driver	(10)			
Surplus		25		
			Closing balance:	
			Current account	21
Deposit account interest		12	Deposit account	65
		£186		£186

Notes

(a)   Some receipts and payments have been grouped together to show the net position for a particular event, namely each outing.

(b)   Except in the opening and closing balances no distinction is made between the current and deposit account.

These two points are matters of judgement, but producing the account in this way does seem to make it more informative to the typical reader, who is likely to be interested in the net outcome of each trip and who probably is not really interested in whether a particular payment was made from the current or the deposit account.

1.2   Activity

What are the main features of the Merrivale Student Accountants Social Club which make a simple receipts and payments account an adequate form of financial reporting to its members and other interested parties?

1.3 Activity solution

The club appears to have no other asset apart from cash (and bank). The few activities undertaken are simple and straightforward and there are unlikely to be accruals and prepayments arising from these activities. As a result, a receipts and payments account is an adequate form of financial reporting.

2 INCOME AND EXPENDITURE ACCOUNTS

2.1 Introduction

In many clubs and societies, particularly smaller ones, the receipts and payments account is a perfectly adequate form of reporting, because cash is the only economic asset that the club ever owns. In more complicated cases it may be important for members to be able to see how the wealth of the organisation was affected by activities during the year and what the assets and liabilities of the organisation are at the year end. Such information may help members make judgements about such things as the appropriate level of subscriptions for the forthcoming year and the ability of the organisation to increase or maintain its range of facilities and services. It is clear that many clubs, societies and associations need to produce financial statements which are very similar to those produced by profit-seeking organisations.

In fact, many clubs produce an **income and expenditure account** which is similar to the profit and loss account of a profit-seeking business in that it sets out revenues and expenses for the financial period. The title 'income and expenditure account' is not strictly correct as the financial report actually records *expenses* rather than expenditure for the period. Nevertheless this title is in general usage and will be employed in this chapter. Many clubs will also produce a balance sheet which is based on the same principles as the balance sheet of a profit-seeking business.

2.2 Activity

Distinguish between expenses and expenditure. Suggest at least two other titles for the income and expenditure account.

2.3 Activity solution

An expense is an amount of benefit that has been used up during an accounting period. Expenditure usually means an outlay of money. (The benefits of the outlay may or may not be used up during the accounting period in which the outlay occurred.) Other titles could include 'Revenue Account', 'Revenue and Expenses Account' and 'Income and Expenses Account'.

2.4 Terminology of a club's accounts

When preparing the income and expenditure account and balance sheet of a club, society or association the accounting procedures are very similar to those for preparing the final accounts of a profit seeking business. However, there are certain differences in terminology which must be noted. The major differences are:

- the financial statement showing revenues and expenses is referred to as the 'income and expenditure account' for not-for-profit organisations rather than the 'profit and loss account'

- when revenues exceed expenses the difference is referred to as 'surplus of income over expenditure' rather than profit. Similarly, where expenses exceed revenues the difference is referred to as 'excess of expenditure over income' rather than loss

- the capital of a not-for-profit organisation is often referred to as the **accumulated fund** or **general fund**. However, it is also occasionally referred to as 'capital'.

The format of an income and expenditure account of a club will differ from the format of a profit and loss account for a profit-seeking business. The club may generate income from various activities such as subscriptions, functions, outings and donations; each source of income, if material, should be shown separately. Once again it is appropriate to offset expenses against revenues in order to show the net result of a particular activity or event. This can be done on the income and expenditure account or shown in a supporting statement. It is a matter of judgement as to which treatment should be adopted. Where the activity or event is complex it is often useful to relegate the detailed information to a supporting statement and simply show the net result in the income and expenditure account. This will make the report easier to read. It is important to bear in mind that members of clubs, societies and associations may have only a limited understanding of accounting and excessive detail on the face of the accounts could confuse readers and obscure the underlying messages.

An example of a simple income and expenditure account set out in the vertical form is shown below.

Example

The Drake Badminton and Squash Club

Income and expenditure account for the year ended 31 March 19X2

	£	£
Income		
Subscriptions		12,420
Court fees		8,400
Annual dinner	3,100	
Less: Catering expenses	2,860	240
Investment income		1,560
Donations		400
		23,020
Less: Expenditure		
Receptionist's wages	7,000	
Rates	4,200	
Light and heat	2,950	
Repairs and renewals	1,860	
Insurance	230	
Printing and stationery	190	
Loan interest	870	
Depreciation – building	5,340	
		22,640
Surplus of income over expenditure		£380

2.5 Miscellaneous points

In order to prepare an income and expenditure account and balance sheet for a club, society or association it is necessary to be aware of the appropriate accounting treatment for certain items and activities which arise. The following items and activities are of particular importance.

(a) Profit-making activities

Because the club exists for the primary purpose of providing some benefit to members and, perhaps, others it is described as a not-for-profit organisation. It may, nevertheless, engage in certain activities with the intention of making a profit. This will usually be done to help provide additional services and benefits to members. When some profit-making activity is undertaken it is necessary to calculate the net profit (loss) arising from the activity. In some cases the activity may involve some form of trading (operating a bar, restaurant or shop for instance). Where this occurs it is useful to prepare a trading and profit and loss account for each trading activity in order to arrive at the net profit (loss) made. This will usually then be shown as a supporting statement to the income and expenditure account and the net profit (loss) on trading will be transferred to the income and expenditure account.

(b) **Subscriptions in arrears**

Members of a club are often required to pay an annual subscription. Where a member has failed to pay this subscription by the due date some clubs will include the amount owing as part of the total subscriptions for the year and show the amount outstanding as a debtor in the balance sheet. This accounting treatment is in accordance with the accruals convention. However, when a subscription is in arrears it may not be clear whether payment has simply been delayed or whether the member has allowed his membership to lapse without informing the club. Where ultimate receipt of the subscription is uncertain many clubs prefer to apply the convention of prudence and only take credit for those subscriptions actually received. Thus, subscriptions in arrears are generally ignored.

In an examination question it is important to read the question carefully to find out which accounting treatment for subscriptions in arrears is required. In the absence of any specific statement it is recommended that subscriptions in arrears be taken into account in arriving at total subscriptions for the year and amounts due at the year end.

Subscriptions paid in advance should always be adjusted for in arriving at total subscriptions for the year and liabilities outstanding at the balance sheet date. Subscriptions paid in advance should be deducted from subscriptions paid during the year in deducing the subscriptions revenue for the year in which the advance subscriptions were paid.

(c) **Entry fees and life membership**

In some clubs, a fee has to be paid on initial entry in addition to the first annual subscription. Similarly, in some clubs it is necessary, or possible, to pay a fee in order to obtain life membership of the club. In this case no annual subscriptions would be paid. When such fees are received there are three ways in which the amounts could be treated. These are:

1   Include the fee as revenue in the year in which it is received

2   Transfer the fee to a suspense account and then credit an equal portion of the fee received to each year of the member's anticipated period with the club

3   Transfer the fee to the accumulated or general fund.

Method 2 is consistent with the accruals convention. However, the anticipated period of membership is usually difficult to estimate and some arbitrary period is usually selected. In an examination, the question should provide specific instructions if this method is required to be adopted. In the absence of any instructions it is recommended that method 1 or 3 be adopted.

(d) **Special funds**

Not-for-profit organisations may set up a fund for a special purpose. For example, a hockey club may wish to acquire a synthetic all-weather playing surface for their pitch and may set up a special fund for this purpose. Where a special fund has been established any amounts received through donations or fund-raising activities for the particular purpose should be transferred directly to the fund rather than to the income and expenditure account. Similarly, any expenses relating to the special purpose should be charged to the fund rather than the income and expenditure account.

In some cases the club may wish to make a transfer from the accumulated or general fund to a special fund. This is simply a matter of debiting the accumulated fund and crediting the special fund with the amount of the transfer. It is important to appreciate that the setting up of a special fund will not automatically ensure that there will be liquid assets held by the club which are equivalent to the amount of the fund. The special fund, like any form of capital, represents a claim on assets and these assets can take many different forms. If the club wishes to maintain the assets represented by the fund in a liquid form it will be necessary to make special arrangements, such as opening a separate bank account.

(e) **Donations**

The accounting treatment of donations will depend on the nature of the particular donation. Donations which are intended to provide financial support for the day-to-day running of the club should be treated as revenue and credited to the income and expenditure account. However, donations which are extraordinary and non-recurring in nature and which are intended, or earmarked, for a particular project should be transferred directly to the accumulated fund or a special fund assigned for that project.

2.6 Activity

The following is the balance sheet of the Hartley Sea Anglers Club at 30 September 19X6.

	£	£
Fixed assets at cost less accumulated depreciation		52,000
Current assets (excluding cash at bank)	6,000	
Cash at bank	24,000	
	30,000	
Less: Current liabilities	4,000	
		26,000
		£78,000
Accumulated fund		56,000
Special fund – new fishing boat		22,000
		£78,000

On 1 October 19X6 the club purchased and paid for a new fishing boat which cost £22,000.

1   State the accounting entries which are required in order to record the purchase of the new boat.

2   What should happen to the special fund after the acquisition of the new fishing boat?

3   Does the setting up of a special fund ensure that cash is available to acquire the new fishing boat?

4   What is the practical value of setting up a special fund?

2.7 Activity solution

1   To record the purchase of a new boat the accounting entries would be:

    Debit   Fishing boat
    Credit   Bank (or Creditor)
                 with £22,000

2   The balance on the special fund will be transferred to the accumulated fund.

3   No. The special fund represents a claim on assets. In order to ensure those assets are in liquid form special arrangements must be made.

4   The special fund will indicate to members and others that a certain proportion of the assets of the club is earmarked for a specific purpose. As a result they should not be used for other purposes.

3   PREPARING THE FINAL ACCOUNTS

3.1   Steps to follow

Examination questions about the accounts of clubs, societies and associations often require candidates to prepare an income and expenditure account and balance sheet from incomplete records. Typically, a summary of bank and cash transactions (that is, a receipts and payments account) is provided along with information relating to opening and closing assets and liabilities. When this type of question is posed it should be approached in essentially the same way as an incomplete records question concerning a profit-seeking organisation.

In Chapter 15 the steps to be followed in preparing a set of final accounts from incomplete (single entry) records were given. These rules can be applied in the case of clubs, societies and associations with only slight modifications. The steps are as follows:

Step 1   Establish opening (last year's) balance sheet

Step 2   Prepare a cash summary

Step 3   Prepare a bank summary

Step 4   Open such ledger accounts as are deemed necessary (for example, a subscriptions account)

Step 5   Draft a pro-forma income and expenditure account and balance sheet (and if necessary, a pro-forma trading and profit and loss account for each trading activity)

Step 6   Enter the balances from the opening balance sheet into an appropriate ledger account, or in the appropriate place in the final accounts

Step 7   Post the cash and bank account entries to the appropriate ledger accounts or the draft final accounts (or draft trading and profit and loss account for each trading activity)

Step 8   Enter the closing adjustments (accruals, depreciation) either in the appropriate ledger account or the draft final accounts (or draft trading and profit and loss account for each trading activity), making sure that the double entry is observed

Step 9   Post the balancing figure in the ledger accounts to the final accounts (and post any profit (loss) on each trading activity to the income and expenditure account)

Step 10   Tidy up the final accounts, making the necessary calculations to establish the surplus of income over expenditure or the excess of expenditure over income.

In order to illustrate the above rules consider the following example.

Example

The following receipts and payments account for the year ended 31 October 19Y0 has been prepared from the current account bank statements of the Country Cousins Sports Club:

19X9			**£**	**19Y0**			**£**
Nov	1	Balance b/fwd	1,700	Oct	31	Clubhouse rates and insurance	380
19Y0							
Oct	31	Subscriptions	8,600			Decorations and repairs	910
		Bar takings	13,800				
		Donations	1,168			Annual dinner – catering	650

Annual dinner			Bar purchases	9,200
– sale of tickets	470		Stationery and printing	248
			New sports equipment	2,463
			Hire of films	89
			Warden's salary	4,700
			Petty cash	94
			Balance c/fwd	7,004
	£25,738			£25,738

The following additional information has been given:

At 31 October	19X9	19Y0
	£	£
Clubhouse at cost	15,000	15,000
Bar stocks, at cost	1,840	2,360
Petty cash float	30	10
Bank deposit account	600	730
Subscriptions received in advance	210	360
Creditors for bar supplies	2,400	1,900

It has been decided to provide for depreciation annually on the clubhouse at the rate of 10% of cost and on the new sports equipment at the rate of 33.3% of cost. The petty cash float is used exclusively for postages.

The only entry in the bank deposit account during the year ended 31 October 19Y0 concerns interest.

One quarter of the Warden's salary and one half of the clubhouse costs, including depreciation, are to be apportioned to the bar.

The donations received during the year ended 31 October 19Y0 are for the new coaching bursary fund which will be utilised for the provision of training facilities for promising young sportsmen and sportswomen. It is expected to make the first award during 19Y1.

We shall work through the following tasks below:

(a)   An account showing the profit or loss for the year ended 31 October 19Y0 on the operation of the bar.

(b)   An income and expenditure account for the year ended 31 October 19Y0 and a balance sheet at that date for the Country Cousins Sports Club.

Each step will be explained in detail and you should follow them through to the completed income and expenditure account and balance sheet at the end. The workings required in the various steps are shown after the final accounts.

The opening balance sheet must first be prepared. This involves using the information about assets and liabilities at 31 October 19X9 listed in the question to produce the balance sheet. However, it is important not to forget to include the opening balance on the bank account in the opening balance sheet. This is not included in the list of items provided but is shown in the summary of the bank account which is provided. The accumulated fund balance at 1 November 19X9 can then be established as £16,560.

A summary of petty cash can be prepared next. This involves transferring the opening and closing balances of petty cash (that is, the petty cash floats included in the lists of assets and liabilities) to a summary petty cash account. The amount paid from the bank account to the petty cash account must also be credited to the summary petty cash account. The balancing figure on this account (£114) will represent payments from petty cash which, you are informed, is for postage.

The club has a bank deposit account and the opening and closing balances can be transferred to a deposit account. The difference between the opening and closing balance, you are informed, represents interest received during the year. A summary of the bank current account has already been prepared and, therefore, this step can be missed.

The next step is to open the relevant ledger accounts. In this question, ledger accounts may be opened for subscriptions and bar creditors as each have opening and closing balances. However, it is not essential to open these accounts and, instead, adjustments can be made on the face of the final accounts.

The next step is to draft a pro-forma income and expenditure account and balance sheet and a pro-forma bar trading and profit and loss account. As mentioned in Chapter 15, it is probably sensible to leave a line between each item in order to accommodate any omissions or adjustments. In this question the type of revenue and expense items to be shown on the income and expenditure account and bar trading and profit and loss account can be found from an inspection of the cash and bank summaries. The closing balance sheet will look much the same as the opening balance sheet, however; it will be noted from the bank summary there has been the purchase of sports equipment. In addition, a coaching bursary fund must also be included in the closing balance sheet.

The balances from the opening balance sheet can now be put into the appropriate ledger account or entered directly into the final accounts.

1   The accumulated fund (£16,560) will represent the balance before adjustments relating to the current year.

2   Subscriptions received in advance can be put in as the opening credit balance in the subscriptions account *or* if it were decided not to open such an account it can be written in as a positive figure beside the subscriptions item in the income and expenditure account.

3   Bar creditors (£2,400) can be put in as the opening credit balance in the bar creditors account *or* as a negative figure beside the bar purchases entry in the bar trading and profit and loss account.

4   Clubhouse (£15,000). Since there have been no additions to the clubhouse this amount can be written straight into the balance sheet as 'clubhouse – cost'.

5   Bar stocks (£1,840). This can be written onto the opening stock position in the bar trading and profit and loss account.

6   The cash and bank balances have already been placed in the summary cash and bank accounts.

The next step is to post the bank and cash summaries. Postings from the current bank account will be as follows:

1   Subscriptions (£8,600). This should be posted to the subscriptions account *or* if it were decided not to open such an account, it can be written in as a positive figure next to the subscriptions item in the income and expenditure account.

2   Bar takings (£13,800). This should be posted to the bar trading account.

3   Donations (£1,168). This should be posted to the coaching bursary fund.

4   Annual dinner (£470). This should be posted to the income and expenditure account.

5   Clubhouse rates and insurance (£380) and decorations and repairs (£910). Half of these expenses should be posted to the income and expenditure account and half to the bar profit and loss account. This apportionment is in accordance with the information set out in the question.

6   Bar purchases (£9,200). This should be posted to the bar creditors account *or* as a positive item beside the bar purchases item in the bar trading account.

7   Stationery and printing (£248). This should be posted direct to the income and expenditure account.

8   New sports equipment (£2,463). This should be shown as a new asset at cost in the closing balance sheet.

9   Hire of films (£89). This should be posted to the income and expenditure account.

10   Warden's salary (£4,700). Three-quarters of this figure (£3,525) should be posted to the income and expenditure account and one quarter (£1,175) to the bar profit and loss account.

11   Petty cash (£94). This has already been posted to the summary petty cash account.

12   The closing balance on this account should be shown under current assets in the balance sheet.

The bank deposit account has only one entry which is interest received £130. This amount should be posted to the income and expenditure account. The closing balance should be shown under current assets in the balance sheet.

The summary petty cash account can be posted as follows:

1   Transfer from bank account (£94). No action is required since the other side of the double entry is in the bank summary.

2   Postage (£114) should be posted to the income and expenditure account.

3   The closing balance will appear as a current asset in the balance sheet.

The closing adjustments can now be made:

1   Bar stocks at the year end (£2,360) should be entered in the closing stock space in the bar trading account and as a current asset in the balance sheet.

2   The bar creditors (£1,900) should be shown as the closing balance in the bar creditors account *or* as a positive figure beside the bar purchases entry in the bar trading account. The figure must also be shown as a current liability in the balance sheet.

3   Clubhouse depreciation (£1,500). Half of this expense should be posted to the income and expenditure account and half to the bar profit and loss account in accordance with the requirements of the question. The total depreciation charge should be shown as a deduction from the cost of the clubhouse on the closing balance sheet.

4   Sports equipment depreciation (£821) should be posted to the income and expenditure account and deducted from the cost of the asset in the balance sheet.

The ledger accounts can now be closed off.

1   **Subscriptions**

     This should be closed by entering the balancing figure (a debit) and then crediting this figure to the income and expenditure account.

2   **Bar creditors**

     This should be closed by entering the balancing figure (a credit) which represents bar purchases. The double entry can be completed by debiting this figure to the bar trading account.

Where separate ledger accounts have not been used it is necessary to total the noted figures in the final accounts and insert the resultant figures.

The next step is to calculate the bar profit for the year and transfer this amount to the income and expenditure account. Once this has been done it is possible to calculate the surplus of income over expenditure for the year. This amount will be added to the accumulated fund on the balance sheet. The sections on the balance sheet need to be subtotalled and the grand totals inserted. The final accounts of the Country Cousins Sports Club will appear as follows:

Income and expenditure account for the year ended 31 October 19Y0

Income		£	£
Subscriptions (210 + 8,600 – 360)			8,450
Profit from bar			3,050
Annual dinner – sale of tickets		470	
Less: Catering costs		650	(180)
Interest on deposit account			130
			11,450
Less: **Expenditure**			
Clubhouse	– rates and insurance	190	
	– decoration and repairs	455	
Warden's salary 3,525			
Stationery and printing		248	
Postage		114	
Hire of films		89	
Depreciation	– sports equipment	821	
	– clubhouse	750	6,192
Surplus of income over expenditure			£5,258

Bar trading and profit and loss account for the year ended
31 October 19Y0

		£	£
Bar takings			13,800
Opening stock		1,840	
Bar purchases (–2,400 + 9,200 + 1,900)		8,700	
		10,540	
Less: Closing stock		2,360	8,180
Gross profit			5,620
Warden's salary		1,175	
Clubhouse	– rates and insurance	190	
	– decorations and repairs	455	
	– depreciation	750	2,570
Net profit (transfer to income and expenditure account)			£3,050

Note: The workings shown above for subscriptions and bar purchases will only appear if ledger accounts are not opened for subscriptions and bar creditors. If accounts are opened the final figures will be derived in the accounts.

Balance sheet as at 31 October 19Y0

	Cost	**Depreciation**	**WDV**
	£	£	£
Fixed assets			
Clubhouse	15,000	1,500	13,500
Sports equipment	2,463	821	1,642
	£17,463	£2,321	15,142
Current assets			
Bar stocks	2,360		
Cash at bank – deposit account		730	
– current account		7,004	
Cash in hand		10	
		10,104	

Less: **Current liabilities**			
Bar creditors	1,900		
Subscriptions in advance	360	2,260	7,844
			£22,986

Accumulated fund		
Balance at 1 November 19X9	16,560	
Add surplus of income over expenditure	5,258	21,818

Coaching bursary fund	1,168
	£22,986

Workings
Balance sheet as at 31 October 19X9

	£	£	£
Fixed assets			
Clubhouse at cost			15,000
Current assets			
Bar stocks		1,840	
Cash at bank – deposit account		600	
– current account		1,700	
Cash in hand		30	
		4,170	
Less: **Current liabilities**			
Bar creditors	2,400		
Subscriptions in advance	210	2,610	1,560
			£16,560
Accumulated fund			£16,560

Petty cash

	£		£
Balance b/d	30	Postage	114
Bank	94	Balance c/d	10
	£124		£124
Balance b/d	10		

Bank deposit

	£		£
Balance b/d	600		
Interest	130	Balance c/d	730
	£730		£730
Balance b/d	730		

Subscriptions

	£		£
Income and expenditure a/c	8,450	Balance b/d	210
Balance c/d	360	Bank	8,600
	£8,810		£8,810
		Balance b/d	360

Bar creditors

	£		£
Bank	9,200	Balance b/d	2,400
Balance c/d	1,900	Bar trading a/c	8,700
	£11,100		£11,100
		Balance b/d	1,900

3.2 Activity

The treasurer of the Bamford Country Dancing and Rambling Society has prepared the following receipts and payments account for the year ended 31 December 19X8:

Receipts	£	Payments	£
Opening balance	1,760	Purchase of amplifier (bought 1 July 19X8)	700
Subscriptions [see note (i)]:		Country dancing:	
Country dancing	2,410	Musicians' fees	900
Rambling	1,690	Coaching fees	820
Annual dinner – ticket sales	340	Hall – rent	330
Sale of hut	670	– rates for year to 31 December 19X8	800
Country dancing festival – admissions	940	– decorating	110
Sales – clothes	2,100	– cleaning	160
		Annual rambling expedition	1,320
		Annual dinner – hotel and catering	410
		Country dancing festival: Prizes 170	
		Adjudicator's fee	90
		Purchases – clothes	1,800
– refreshments	8,300	– refreshments	7,000
		Closing balance	3,600
	£18,210		£18,210

Additional information:

(i) (a) Subscriptions

	Country dancing £	Rambling £
Received in 19X7 for 19X8	130	60
Received in 19X8 for 19X7	10	140
Received in 19X8 for 19X8	2,300	1,520
Received in 19X8 for 19X9	100	30
	£2,410	£1,690

(b)   It is not the policy of the Society to take into account subscriptions in arrears until they are paid.

(ii)   The hut which was sold during 19X8 had been valued at £800 on 31 December 19X7, and was used for the Society's activities until sold on 30 June 19X8.

(iii)   Immediately after the sale of the hut, the Society rented a new hall at £330 per annum.

(iv)   The above receipts and payments account is a summary of the Society's bank account for the year ended 31 December 19X8; the opening and closing balances shown above were the balances shown in the bank statement on 31 December 19X7 and 19X8 respectively.

(v)   All cash is banked immediately and all payments are made by cheque.

(vi)   A cheque for £200 drawn by the Society on 28 December 19X8, for stationery was not paid by the bank until 4 January 19X9.

(vii)   The Society's assets and liabilities at 31 December 19X7 and 19X8, in addition to those mentioned earlier, were as follows:

31 December		19X7	19X8
		£	£
Stocks of goods for resale, at cost:			
Clothes		1,300	1,100
Refreshments		310	600
Sundry creditors	– Annual dinner (catering)	–	70
Purchases	– Clothes	600	400
	– Refreshments	300	500

The Society has now instructed its treasurer to prepare an income and expenditure account for the year ended 31 December 19X8, and a balance sheet at that date.

It is proposed to provide for depreciation on the amplifier at the rate of 20% per annum on cost, pro rata to time.

1   Draw up he Society's income and expenditure account for the year ended 31 December 19X8, and balance sheet as at that date. Comparative figures are not required.

2   Outline the advantages of income and expenditure accounts as compared with receipts and payments accounts.

3.3   Activity solution

Bamford Country Dancing and Rambling Society
Income and expenditure account for the year ended 31 December 19X8

Income		£	£
Subscriptions	– Country dancing (see workings)		2,440
	– Rambling (see workings)		1,720
Annual dinner	– ticket sales	340	
	– hotel and catering expenses (410 + 70)	(480)	
			(140)
Country dancing festival	– admissions	940	
	– prizes	(170)	
	– adjudicator's fees	(90)	
			680
Profit on sale of clothes (see workings)			300
Profit on sale of refreshments (see workings)			1,390
			6,390

Expenditure

Country dancing	– musicians' fees	900	
	– coaching fees	820	
Annual rambling expedition		1,320	
Hall	– rent (330 – 165)	165	
	– rates	800	
	– decorating	110	
	– cleaning	160	
Stationery		200	
Loss on sale of hut		130	
Depreciation – amplifier		70	
			4,675
Surplus of income over expenditure			£1,715

Balance sheet as at 31 December 19X8

Fixed assets		£	£	£
Amplifier at cost				700
Less: Accumulated depreciation				70
				630
Current assets				
Stocks	– goods for resale		1,100	
	– refreshments		600	
Prepayment			165	
Cash at bank			3,400	
			5,265	
Current liabilities				
Subscriptions in advance	– dancing	100		
	– rambling	30		
Sundry creditors		970		
			1,100	
				4,165
				£4,795
Accumulated fund				
Balance at 1 January 19X8				3,080
Add: Surplus of income over expenditure for year				1,715
				£4,795

Workings

Balance sheet as at 31 December 19X7

Fixed assets		£	£	£
Hut				800
Current assets				
Stocks	– goods for resale		1,300	
	– refreshments		310	
Cash at bank			1,760	
			3,370	

Less: Current liabilities

Subscriptions in advance	– Dancing	130	
	– Rambling	60	
Sundry creditors		900	
			1,090
			2,280
Accumulated fund at 31 December 19X7			£3,080

Subscriptions – country dancing

	£		£
Income and expenditure a/c	2,440	Balance b/d	130
Balance c/d	100	Bank	2,410
	£2,540		£2,540

Subscriptions – rambling

	£		£
Income and expenditure a/c	1,720	Balance b/d	60
Balance c/d	30	Bank	1,690
	£1,750		£1,750

Trading account – clothes

	£	£
Sales		2,100
Opening stock	1,300	
Purchases (– 600 + 1,800 + 400)	1,600	
	2,900	
Closing stock	1,100	
		1,800
Profit		£300

Trading account – refreshments

	£	£
Sales		8,300
Opening stock	310	
Purchases (– 300 + 7,000 + 500)	7,200	
	7,510	
Closing stock	600	
		6,910
Profit		£1,390

4   CHAPTER SUMMARY

- Not-for-profit organisations such as clubs, societies and associations exist, primarily, to provide some service or facility to members and/or others. Many such organisations are small in size and maintain only rudimentary financial records. It is common for the final accounts of a club to take the form of a receipts and payments account which is simply a summary of the bank and cash transactions for the financial period. This form of reporting may be acceptable where there are few assets and liabilities and the activities are simple and straightforward. However, for many clubs it is appropriate to prepare accounts which reveal more fully their performance and financial position.

- The income and expenditure account and balance sheet prepared by many clubs are based on the same principles as those governing the final accounts of profit-seeking organisations. There are, in essence, two differences between the accounts of clubs and societies, on the one hand, and sole trading businesses, on the other. These are:

  - terminology used
  - style of the income statement.

- In the context of clubs and societies we tend to use the word surplus and deficit instead of profit and loss. The financial stake of the members in their club is usually known as accumulated fund rather than capital. The equivalent of the profit and loss account is the income and expenditure account.

- In the final accounts of not-for-profit organisations there is a tendency to look at income analysed activity by activity and to match the expenses activity by activity, so that the surplus or deficit for each activity is separately identified. For example where a tennis club has a clubroom where members can buy refreshments, the revenues from selling the refreshments are matched with the relevant expenses on the face of the income and expenditure account to show what the facility contributed to the club, or cost the club, during the accounting period.

5   SELF TEST QUESTIONS

5.1   For which type of club is a receipts and payments account completely adequate? (1.1)

5.2   Which one of the following will an income and expenditure account of a club, society or association contain?

    (a)   receipts and payments

    (b)   receipts and expenditure

    (c)   income and expenditure

    (d)   income and expenses. (2.1)

5.3   Which one of the following is an alternative name for the accumulated fund of a club, society or association?

    (a)   owner's interest

    (b)   special fund

    (c)   general fund

    (d)   surplus income over expenditure. (2.4)

5.4   Why does the income and expenditure account of many clubs show the results of activities, like running a bar, separately from other of its activities? (2.5)

5.5   What are the three possible methods of dealing with life membership fees in the accounts of a club? (2.5)

6 EXAMINATION TYPE QUESTIONS

6.1 Ilkton Social Club

The following is a summary of the Ilkton Social Club's cash book for the year ended 30 June 19X7:

Payments	£	Receipts	£
Rent	625	Bar sales	583
Rates	200	Entrance fees	60
Lighting	182	Members' subscriptions	2,220
Wages	760	Donations	350
Printing, stationery	126		
General expenses	79		
Creditors for bar purchases	430		
Improvements to club house	388		
Repairs	310		

Additional information available from the records is as follows:

		30 June 19X6	30 June 19X7
		£	£
Creditors for	– wines and spirits	190	130
	– printing	12	16
	– wages	27	38
	– lighting	21	37
Arrears of subscriptions		89	97
Subscriptions paid in advance		45	38
Bar stock		148	123
Cash in hand		60	72
Cash at bank		210	
Premises		7,500	
Fittings (net of depreciation)		1,740	

Depreciation on fittings is to be provided at 10% on the reducing balance.

(a) Draw up a combined cash/bank account for the year ended 30 June 19X7, and

(b) Create an income and expenditure account for the year ended 30 June 19X7, and a balance sheet as at that date. **(22 marks)**

6.2 Scout Troup

A scout troop collects subscriptions from its members, and also has to pay 60% of them to central scouting funds. In the year to 31 December 19X8 the troop receives;

For 19X7	£20
For 19X8	£60
For 19X9	£10

It pays to central funds in that year:

For 19X7	£12
For 19X8	£30
For 19X9	nil

(a) Produce a summary of the subscription position for the troop for the year 19X8, on

(i) a receipts and payments basis

(ii) a revenue and expenses basis.

(b)   Outline the advantages and disadvantages of each basis with reference to appropriate accounting conventions. Give the scout troop leader your recommended method, with reasons. Discuss also any difficult decisions you have to make in deciding your answer to (a) above.   **(20 marks)**

(ACCA, June 1989)

6.3   Greenfinger Gardeners Club

The Greenfinger Gardeners' Club is a member of the Countryside Gardeners' Federation. The annual subscription payable by member clubs to the Federation is 5% of the total subscription income plus 5% of any profit (or less any loss) arising from the sale of seeds and fertilisers for the preceding year.

The receipts and payments account for the year ended 31 December 19X8 of the Greenfinger Gardeners' Club is as follows:

	£		£
Balance at 1 January 19X8	196	Purchase of seeds and fertilisers	1,640
Subscriptions received	1,647	Cost of visit to research centre	247
Sale of tickets for visit to research centre	232	Purchase of garden equipment	738
Sale of seeds and fertilisers	1,928	Repairs to garden equipment	302
Annual garden show:		Annual garden show:	
Sale of tickets	829	Hire of marquee	364
Competition fees	410	Prizes	650
		Balance at 31 December 19X8	1,301
	£5,242		£5,242

The following additional information is given:

At 31 December	19X7	19X8
	£	£
Subscriptions due and unpaid	164	83
Subscriptions prepaid	324	248
Sale of seeds and fertilisers – debtors	220	424
Purchase of seeds and fertilisers – creditors	804	547
Stocks of seeds and fertilisers – at cost	261	390

Provide a computation of the membership subscription for 19X9 payable by the Greenfinger Gardeners' Club to the Countryside Gardeners' Federation.   **(15 marks)**

6.4   Happy Tickers

The accounting records of the Happy Tickers Sports and Social Club are in a mess. You manage to find the following information to help you prepare the accounts for the year to 31 December 19X0.

Summarised balance sheet 31 December 19X9

	£		£
Half-share in motorised roller	600	Insurance (3 months)	150
New sports equipment unsold	1,000	Subscriptions 19X0	120
Used sports equipment at		Life subscriptions	1,400
valuation	700		1,670

Rent (2 months)	200	Accumulated fund	2,900
Subscriptions 19X9	60		
Cafe stocks	800		
Cash and bank	1,210		
	4,570		4,570

Receipts in the year to 31 December 19X0:	£
Subscriptions – 19X9	40
– 19X0	1,100
– 19X1	80
– life	200
From sales of new sports equipment	900
From sales of used sports equipment	14
Cafe takings	4,660
	6,994

Payments in the year to 31 December 19X0	£
Rent (for 12 months)	1,200
Insurance (for 18 months)	900
To suppliers of sports equipment	1,000
To cafe suppliers	1,900
Wages of cafe manager	2,000
Total cost of repairing motorised roller	450
	7,450

Notes:

(i)   Ownership and all expenses of the motorised roller are agreed to be shared equally with the Carefree Conveyancers Sports Club which occupies a nearby site. The roller cost a total of £2,000 on 1 January 19X6 and had an estimated life of 10 years.

(ii)   Life subscriptions are brought into income equally over 10 years, in a scheme begun in 19X5. Since the scheme began the cost of £200 per person has been constant. Prior to 31 December 19X9 10 life subscriptions had been received.

(iii)   Four more annual subscriptions of £20 each had been promised relating to 19X0, but not yet received. Annual subscriptions promised but unpaid are carried forward for a maximum of 12 months.

(iv)   New sports equipment is sold to members at cost plus 50%. Used equipment is sold off to members at book valuation. Half the sports equipment bought in the year (all from a cash and carry supplier) has been used within the club, and half made available for sale, new, to members. The 'used equipment at valuation' figure in the 31 December 19X0 balance sheet is to remain at £700.

(v)   Closing cafe stocks are £850, and £80 is owed to suppliers at 31 December 19X0.

(a)   Calculate profit on cafe operations and profit on sale of sports equipment.

(b)   Prepare a statement of subscriptions income for 19X0.

(c)   Prepare an income and expenditure statement for the year to 31 December 19X0, and balance sheet as at 31 December 19X0.

(d)   Why do life subscriptions appear as a liability?

(22 marks)

(ACCA December 1990)

7   ANSWERS TO EXAMINATION TYPE QUESTIONS

7.1   Ilkton Social Club

Ilkton Social Club
Combined cash/bank account for the year ended 30 June 19X7

		£			£
Balance b/d	– cash	60	Rent		625
	– bank	210	Rates		200
Bar sales		583	Lighting		182
Entrance fees		60	Wages		760
Members' subscriptions		2,220	Printing stationery		126
Donations		350	General expenses		79
			Creditors – bar purchases		430
			Improvements – club house		388
			Repairs		310
			Balance c/d	– cash	72
				– bank	*311
		£3,483			£3,483

* balancing figure

Income and expenditure account for the year ended 30 June 19X7

Income		£
Subscriptions (see workings)		2,235
Bar profit (see workings)		188
Entrance fees		60
Donations		350
		2,833
Less: **Expenditure**		
Rent	625	
Rates	200	
Wages (760 – 27 + 38)	771	
Lighting (182 – 21 + 37)	198	
Printing and stationery (126 – 12 + 16)	130	
General expenses	79	
Repairs	310	
Depreciation – fittings	174	2,487
Surplus of income over expenditure		£346

Balance sheet as at 30 June 19X7

	£	£	£
Fixed assets			
Premises		7,500	
Add: Improvements to clubhouse		388	7,888
Fittings at written-down value			
(1,740 – 174)			1,566
			9,454
Current assets			
Bar stock		123	
Subscriptions arrears		97	
Cash at bank		311	
Cash in hand		72	
		603	

Less: **Current liabilities**

	£	£	£
Subscriptions in advance	38		
Sundry creditors	221	259	344
			£9,798

	£
Accumulated fund (see workings)	9,452
Add surplus income and expenditure	346
	£9,798

Workings

Ilkton Social Club
Balance sheet as at 30 June 19X6

	£	£	£
Fixed assets			
Premises			7,500
Fittings			1,740
			9,240
Current assets			
Bar stock		148	
Subscription arrears		89	
Cash at bank		210	
Cash in hand		60	
		507	
Less: **Current liabilities**			
Subscriptions in advance	45		
Sundry creditors	250	295	212
Accumulated fund			£9,452

Bar trading and profit and loss account for the year ended 30 June 19X7

	£	£
Bar sales		583
Opening stock	148	
Purchases	370	
	518	
Closing stock	123	395
Bar profit to income and expenditure account		£188

Bar creditors account

	£		£
Bank/cash	430	Balance b/d	190
Balance c/d	130	Bar trading account	370
	£560		£560

Subscriptions account

	£		£
Balance b/d	89	Balance b/d	45
Income and expenditure account	2,235	Bank/cash	2,220
Balance c/d	38	Balance c/d	97
	£2,362		£2,362

7.2   Scout Troop

(a)   If the subscriptions were dealt with on a receipts and payments basis the position for the year to 31 December 19X8 would be as follows:

Subscriptions for the year

		£
Cash received	– for 19X7	20
	– for 19X8	60
	– for 19X9	10
Total subscriptions		£90

Payment to central funds

Payments for the year (60% of £90)	54
Less Payments made (12 + 30)	42
Payments due	£12

If the subscriptions were dealt with on a revenue and expenses basis the position for the year to 31 December 19X8 would be as follows:

Subscriptions for the year

	£
Total cash received as above	90
Less: Subscriptions in advance for 19X9	10
Total subscriptions	£80

Payment to central funds

	£
Payment for the year (60% of £80)	48
Less: Payments made (12 + 30)	42
Payments due	£6

(b)   In preparing these calculations it has been assumed that the scout troop adopts the convention of prudence in respect of subscriptions in arrears. This means that the subscriptions received during 19X8 in respect of 19X7 have not been accrued during 19X7. Hence, the subscriptions received late will be credited in the year in which they are received. This approach is often preferred where ultimate receipt of the subscription is uncertain. As credit will only be taken for subscriptions received during 19X8, this means that any amounts arising in respect of this year and received in 19X8 will be credited in that year.

However, under the revenue/expenses basis, subscriptions in advance should always be adjusted before arriving at total subscriptions for the year. This treatment is consistent with the accruals convention.

The advantage of the receipts and payments approach is that it is simple to operate. Subscriptions and payments to central funds are determined by reference to the actual cash received during the year. However, it has the disadvantage that the troop will be taking credit for subscriptions paid in advance. These subscriptions may have to be repaid at some future date due to unforeseen circumstances and this could mean that central funds will receive more than is due to them or that some adjustment will be required in respect of future payments to central funds in order to retrieve the earlier overpayments.

The advantage of the revenue and expenses basis is that it recognises that cash receipts and payments may not provide a good indication of the wealth generated by the scout troop during the period. This approach is based on the accruals convention which states the profit (wealth) is the difference between revenue and expenses during a period and not the excess of cash receipts over payments. The accruals convention would show the net wealth generated for 19X8 as being:

	£
Total subscriptions for the year	80
Less: Payable to central funds	48
Net wealth for the year	£32

The cash position, on the other hand, would be:

	£
Total cash receipts	90
Less: Total cash payments	42
Net cash flow	£48

7.3   Greenfinger Gardeners Club

Greenfinger Gardeners Club
Membership subscription to Countryside Gardeners Federation for 19X9

	£
5% of the total subscription income (5% × £1,642) for 19X8	82
5% of profit on sales of seeds and fertilisers (5% × £878) for 19X8	44
	£126

Workings

Subscriptions account

	£		£
Balance b/d	164	Balance b/d	324
Subscriptions for the year	1,642	Bank/cash	1,647
Balance c/d	248	Balance c/d	83
	£2,054		£2,054
Balance b/d	83	Balance b/d	248

Seeds and fertilisers
Profit and loss account for the year ended 31 December 19X8

	£	£
Sales (see workings below)		2,132
Opening stock	261	
Purchases (see workings below)	1,383	
	1,644	
Less: Closing stock	390	1,254
Profit to income and expenditure account		£878

Debtors account – seeds and fertilisers

	£		£
Balance b/d	220	Bank/cash	1,928
Profit and loss account	2,132	Balance c/d	424
	£2,352		£2,352

Creditors account – seeds and fertilisers

	£		£
Bank/cash	1,640	Balance b/d	804
Balance b/d	547	Profit and loss account	1,383
	£2,187		£2,187

7.4   Happy Tickers

(a)

Happy Tickers Sports and Social Club
Profit on cafe operations

	£	£
Sales		4,660
Less: Opening stock	800	
Add: Purchases (1,900 + 80)	1,980	
	2,780	
Less: Closing stock	850	
Cost of sales		1,930
		2,730
Less: Wages of manager		2,000
Profit		730

Profit on sports equipment

	£	£
Sales		900
Less: Opening stock	1,000	
Add: Purchases of stock for sale	500	
	1,500	
Less: Closing stock (balancing figure)	900	
Cost of sales		600
Profit		300

Note that since the used equipment is sold at book value and therefore yields no profit it has been omitted from this statement.

(b)

Subscription income

	£
19X0 subscriptions paid in 19X9	120
19X0 subscriptions paid in 19X0	1,100
19X0 subscriptions paid in 19X1	80
Portion of life membership subscriptions relating to 19X0 (11 @ £20)	220
	£1,520

(c)

Income and expenditure account for the year ended 31 December 19X0

	£	£
Income		
Subscription income		1,520
Profit on cafe operations		730
Profit on sale of sports equipment		300
		2,550
Expenses		
Rent	1,200	
Insurance	600	
Repairs to roller	225	
Depreciation of roller	100	
Depreciation of sports equipment		
(700 + 500 − 14 − 700)	486	
19X9 subscription income written off	20	
		2,631
Deficit for the year		£81

Happy Tickers Sports and Social Club
Balance sheet as at 31 December 19X0

	£	£
Fixed assets		
Roller net of depreciation		500
Sports equipment, net of depreciation		700
		1,200
Current assets		
Stock of new sports equipment	900	
Stock of cafe supplies	850	
Subscription in arrears	80	
Prepaid insurance and rent	350	
Amount owed by CCSC re roller	225	
Cash at bank (1,210 + 6,994 − 7,450)	754	
	3,159	
Less: **Current liabilities**		
Creditors of cafe supplies	80	
Subscription in advance	80	
	160	
		2,999
		4,199
Accumulated fund at 1 January 19X0		2,900
Less: Deficit for the year		81
		2,819
Life memberships, unexpired (1,400 + 200 − 220)		1,380
		£4,199

(d)   The life subscriptions are in the nature of deferred revenues because they will eventually become revenues. They can be seen as membership which the club 'owes' to the life members and to that extent they are liabilities.

17 PARTNERSHIP ACCOUNTS

INTRODUCTION AND LEARNING OBJECTIVES

This chapter introduces accounting for partnerships. In doing this certain legal aspects of partnership will be introduced, although the emphasis will be on the law as it affects the accounts, rather than on the law itself. A partnership is a business which has more than one owner, when two or more people agree to act together to try to earn profits. Typical partnerships might involve a husband and wife jointly owning and running a small shop, three friends going into business as builders or eight Certified Accountants setting up in practice.

In essence the accounts of partnerships are identical in form and content as the accounts of sole traders (people in business by themselves). But there are some differences. The real differences lie in the fact that all of the owner's capital of the sole trading business, including all of the profit, belongs to just one person. In a partnership it is shared between them. This is complicated slightly by the fact that partners would not necessarily have contributed equal amounts of capital, nor be entitled, under the agreement between the partners, to equal shares of the profits (or losses). In practice the presence of more than one owner means that there is an appendix to the profit and loss account in which the net profit or loss is divided between the partners.

When you have studied this chapter you should be able to do the following::

*   Understand the nature of a partnership

*   Appreciate the contents of a typical partnership agreement

*   Prepare accounts for partnerships involving both capital accounts and current accounts

*   Deal with partnership loans in the accounts.

---

1   DEFINITION AND LEGAL POSITION OF A PARTNERSHIP

1.1   Nature of a partnership

A partnership may be defined as

> the relation which subsists between persons carrying on a business in common with a view of profit. (Partnership Act 1890, Section 1)

Most legal matters relating to partnerships are covered by the Partnership Act, 1890. In addition, under the Limited Partnership Act, 1907, **limited partnerships** may be formed. These are partnerships where at least one partner has liability limited to a certain amount. In any limited partnership there must be at least one unlimited or general partner.

Partnership should be distinguished from joint ownership. Perhaps the two most important differences between these are:

1   A partnership must be the result of agreement (which may be express or implied – in other words the various parties to a partnership may have specifically agreed to act together, or they must have clearly implied that they wish to act together)

2   A partnership involves working for a profit.

A partnership should also be distinguished from a limited company. As will be made clear in later chapters a limited company may be formed by a number of people. However, a limited company has a legal identity quite separate from the individual owners. This is not true of a partnership, which has no separate legal identity.

The maximum size of a partnership is normally 20 persons, although for certain professional practices, such as solicitors and accountants, the number can exceed 20, as long as such partnerships are registered under the Companies Act.

An alternative name given to a partnership is a **firm**. (In passing it is worth noting that the word firm is frequently used in a more general sense to mean a commercial enterprise. In this chapter the word firm is used to describe a partnership.) The firm can be given a suitable name under which to trade, though restrictions on the choice of name may be imposed. Legal action can be taken in the firm's name, but the effect is the same as if the action were taken in the partner's individual names, because the partnership has no separate legal identity. This means that the personal property of a partner is not safeguarded against legal claims in connection with the partnership business. Indeed, if all but one partner became insolvent, the remaining solvent partner could be sued for all the partnership debts. Under most circumstances each partner is an agent of the firm for the purpose of carrying on the normal business of the firm. This means that individual partners can bind the other partners to contracts they negotiate on behalf of the firm. They may also recover from the partnership any funds they spend for the benefit of the partnership.

1.2   The partnership agreement

A **partnership agreement** may be made in writing or orally. The terms of the agreement are entirely at the discretion of the partners, provided of course that such terms are themselves legal. It is common to draw up a partnership deed, a legal document, covering all the details of the partnership. Such an agreement would normally cover such things as:

1   the amount of capital required from each partner

2   whether any interest on capital is to be allowed (to compensate partners for different amounts invested)

3   how profits or losses are to be shared

4   whether any remuneration is to be paid to partners (to compensate for different amounts of work carried out by the partners in the partnership business, or for different levels of expertise used within the business)

5   the arrangements for drawings, including the possibility of interest being charged on drawings (to act as some kind of charge on partners who take out drawings earlier than the other partners)

6   the extent to which each partner can bind the other partners

7   the arrangements necessary to change any of the conditions of the partnership, in particular to change the profit-sharing ratio, or to provide for one or more partners leaving the partnership.

This list is intended to provide an indication of the more usual items included in an agreement. Other elements can be included at the partners' discretion.

Precisely what kind of agreement is reached is likely to depend upon the relative strengths or weaknesses of the bargaining position of each partner. In the final analysis a partnership will normally only be set up if the would-be partners can agree. However, the items identified above provide an indication of the typical areas likely to be covered in discussions.

1.3   Activity

You are considering entering a partnership with two other people, Jane and John. John is to provide most financial support, and will contribute £20,000, while you and Jane will provide only £5,000 each. However, the original ideas for the partnership business came from you, and you are considered to be the 'brains' of the business. Jane will work full-time in the business, while you and John will contribute approximately 10 hours a week. Your work is high-level and technical, while John will deal with some routine lower-level jobs.

Indicate the areas on which the three partners should try to reach agreement with regard to sharing profits, giving reasons why these areas are important, and identifying possible differences in profit shares.

1.4   Activity solution

Rewards should be based on the following:

1   contribution in terms of ideas and expertise

2   the amount of work put into the business, and the degree of expertise associated with such work

3   the amount of capital provided.

Rewards for the first of these are likely to be in the form of profit shares. For the second a salary is likely to be paid, which reflects the amount and level of work undertaken for the business. For the third an appropriate amount of interest on capital would be allowed.

In the example included in the activity it would seem appropriate for you to seek to obtain a greater share of profits than Jane and John, given that the ideas are yours. Jane will expect to be paid an annual salary which is fairly close to what she could reasonably expect to receive in equivalent employment. John will probably want an agreement which gives him an appropriate amount of interest on his capital. The equivalent of the current rate of interest obtainable from securities such as government bonds might be expected.

In the final analysis a partnership will only be set up if the would-be partners can agree. The relative strengths and weaknesses of the bargaining position of each partner will influence the finally agreed profit shares. For example, if John is the only source of funds for the project he will be able to argue for a greater share of the profits than if alternative sources of finance were available. Jane's bargaining position will depend upon her alternative employment prospects. Your position will depend upon just how good your ideas are.

1.5   Provisions in the absence of a partnership agreement

It is important to know the situation if no partnership agreement has been reached. In the absence of agreement the provisions of the Partnership Act 1890 apply. The provisions of the Act in the event of no agreement are as follows:

1   Profits are to be shared equally

2   No interest on capital is to be paid

3   No remuneration is to be paid to any partner

4   Any general partner (that is, not a limited partner) may take part in the management of the business

5   No change in the partnership structure can take place without the agreement of all the partners

6   Differences of opinion in normal trading matters will be settled by a majority decision

7   A partner is entitled to claim on the firm for all payments made in respect of normal trading activities of the firm, or payments necessarily paid to preserve the firm

8   A partner who makes an advance in excess of the agreed capital (say, a loan) is entitled to interest on the advance at 5% per annum.

2   PARTNERSHIP ACCOUNTS – NORMAL TRADING

2.1   The profit and loss account and the appropriation account

There are no special requirements in the preparation of the trading and profit and loss account of a partnership. The calculation of the net profit of a partnership is the same as for a sole trading business. The principles and methods used so far are thus equally appropriate for a partnership.

The main difference between the accounts of a sole trader and those of a partnership result from the fact that, instead of there being one capital account, as in a sole trading business, there will be *one capital account for each partner*. Having arrived at a partnership net profit this profit must be transferred to the various partners' capital accounts. As was pointed out above, the amount transferred will depend upon the agreement about profit sharing which has been made by the partners, or in the absence of agreement, upon the provisions of the Partnership Act 1890. Whatever the agreement, some form of accounting procedure is needed for sharing out the net profit of a partnership. This is provided by the **profit and loss appropriation account**. It should be clear that agreement on such things as interest on capital, profit shares, or partners remuneration does not affect the net profit of the partnership. None of these items are expenses of the partnership. They are merely the agreed method of sharing out the net profit in a way that the partners consider fair.

The function of the appropriation account is to show clearly how the net profit has been shared (or appropriated) between the partners. The appropriation account is opened, and the net profit will be brought down from the profit and loss account to the credit side of the appropriation account. The shares of the partners, for such things as interest on capital, remuneration and profits, are then debited to the appropriation account and credited to the capital accounts.

Example

A firm makes a profit of £40,000 in a particular year. The firm has two partners, Sam and Sally, and they agree to share profits in the ratio 2:1 (two thirds to Sam, one third to Sally), to allow interest on capital at 10% per annum, and to allow Sally a salary of £8,000 a year. At the beginning of the year Sam has capital of £32,000, while Sally has a capital of £48,000.

The appropriation account would appear as follows:

Appropriation account

	£		£
Sam – interest on capital	3,200	Net profit (from profit and loss)	40,000
Sally – interest on capital	4,800		
Sally – salary	8,000		
Sam – profits	16,000		
Sally – profits	8,000		
	£40,000		£40,000

Note that the profit sharing ratio of 2:1 is only applied after the other elements of profit share have been deducted from the net profit. The share of residual profits or losses is thus the last figure to be calculated.

Example

Suppose that the profit in the above example had been only £12,400, but the same agreement on profit sharing existed. The appropriation account would appear as follows:

Appropriation account

	£		£
Sam – interest on capital	3,200	Net profit	12,400
Sally – interest on capital	4,800	Sam – loss	2,400
Sally – salary	8,000	Sally – loss	1,200
	£16,000		£16,000

In both examples shown above the double entries equivalent to the entries in the appropriation account relating to profit sharing will go to the capital accounts of the partners, a credit for an increase in capital, and a debit for a decrease. Hence the capital accounts for Sam and Sally for the above example would appear as follows:

Capital – Sam

	£		£
Appropriation – loss	2,400	Balance b/d	32,000
Balance c/d	32,800	Appropriation – interest on capital	3,200
	£35,200		£35,200
		Balance b/d	32,800

Capital – Sally

	£		£
Appropriation – loss	1,200	Balance b/d	48,000
Balance c/d	59,600	Appropriation – interest on capital	4,800
		Appropriation – salary	8,000
	£60,800		£60,800
		Balance b/d	59,600

Drawings will be debited to partners' capital in the same way as they would be for a sole trading business. If *interest on drawings* is charged the capital accounts will be debited with the appropriate amount, and the appropriation account will be credited. This will, of course, result in a larger figure to be shared out between the partners.

In earlier chapters it was suggested that the trading and profit and loss account should be *presented* in **narrative form**. Where this is done the appropriation account format will need to be modified accordingly. A suggested format is given below, assuming three partners, A, B, and C:

	£	£	£
Net profit			x
Add: Interest on drawings			
– Partner A		x	
– Partner B		x	
– Partner C		x	
			x
			x
Less: Interest on capital			
– Partner A	x		
– Partner B	x		
– Partner C	x		
		x	
Salaries			
– Partner A	x		
– Partner B	x		
– Partner C	x		
		x	
Share of balance (profit/loss)			
– Partner A	x		
– Partner B	x		
– Partner C	x		
		x	x
			£–

2.2   Current accounts

It is clear that using the approach of the last example will result in the capital account balances of the partners fluctuating from one period to the next. However, in many partnerships the capital accounts are kept fixed, and the partners' entitlements to profit are credited to a separate account, usually called a current account. No new principles are involved. The current account is merely the part of the partners' capital which represents his entitlement to profit, as opposed to original capital. Interest on capital is usually paid only on the fixed capital, although partners may agree otherwise if they wish.

Example

Margaret and James are in partnership. During the first year of trading the business makes a profit of £24,000, after the deduction of normal trading expenses. They have fixed capital accounts. At the beginning of the year Margaret introduced capital of £18,000 and James £12,000. The partnership agreement provides for partnership salaries of Margaret £6,000 and James £3,000, interest on capital at 10% and equal division of any remaining profits. During the year Margaret made drawings of £12,000, while James withdrew £9,000.

The appropriation account and current accounts would appear as follows:

Appropriation account

		£		£
Salaries	– Margaret	6,000	Net profit	24,000
	– James	3,000		
Interest on capital	– Margaret	1,800		
	– James	1,200		
Profits	– Margaret	6,000		
	– James	6,000		
		£24,000		£24,000

Current – Margaret

	£		£
Drawings	12,000	Salary	6,000
Balance c/d	1,800	Interest on capital	1,800
		Profit	6,000
	£13,800		£13,800
		Balance b/d	1,800

Current – James

	£		£
Drawings	9,000	Salary	3,000
Balance c/d	1,200	Interest on capital	1,200
		Profit	6,000
	£10,200		£10,200
		Balance b/d	1,200

The closing credit balances on the partners' current accounts represent their share of retained profits in a business. A debit balance represents withdrawals in excess of profit entitlement. Closing balances for one period will clearly be opening balances for the next period.

Note: In examination questions columnar capital and current accounts provide a useful way of saving time. The current accounts shown above could thus be presented as follows:

Current accounts

	Margaret £	James £		Margaret £	James £
Drawings	12,000	9,000	Salary	6,000	3,000
Balance c/d	1,800	1,200	Interest on capital	1,800	1,200
			Profit	6,000	6,000
	£13,800	£10,200		£13,800	£10,200
			Balance b/d	1,800	1,200

2.3 Activity

Paula and Jane are in partnership. Their partnership agreement contains the following provisions. Interest on capital is to be allowed at 10% on fixed capital accounts; salaries are to be £8,000 for Paula and £12,000 for Jane ; the remaining profits are to be shared in the ratio 3:2. Profits for the current year were £22,000. The capital account balances, held throughout the year, were Paula £28,000, Jane £12,000. Drawings amounted to £12,000 for Paula and £8,000 for Jane. There were no balances on the current accounts at the beginning of the year.

Prepare the appropriation account for the year, as well as columnar current accounts.

2.4 Activity solution

Appropriation account

	£		£
Interest on capital – Paula	2,800	Net profit	22,000
Interest on capital – Jane	1,200	Loss – Paula	1,200
Salary – Paula	8,000	Loss – Jane	800
Salary – Jane	12,000		
	£24,000		£24,000

Current accounts

	Paula £	Jane £		Paula £	Jane £
Drawings	12,000	8,000	Salaries	8,000	12,000
Loss	1,200	800	Interest on capital	2,800	1,200
Balance c/d		4,400	Balance c/d	2,400	
	£13,200	£13,200		£13,200	£13,200
Balance b/d	2,400		Balance b/d		4,400

2.5 Activity

Alpha and Beta are in partnership sharing profits and losses in the ratio 3:2. Alpha is to be allowed an annual salary of £6,000, while Beta is to be allowed £10,000. Interest on fixed capital accounts is to be allowed at 5% per annum. Interest is to be charged on drawings at 5% per annum. Both fixed capital accounts and current accounts are to be kept for each partner. The capital balances held throughout the current year are Alpha £25,000, Beta £50,000. Drawings, made in equal instalments halfway through the year and at the end of the year, totalled £10,000 for Alpha and £20,000 for Beta. Profit for the year amounted to £44,375.

Prepare the appropriation account for the year and the partners' current accounts.

2.6   Activity solution

Appropriation account

	£		£
Alpha – Salary	6,000	Net profit	44,375
Beta – Salary	10,000	Alpha – Interest on drawings	125
Alpha – Interest on capital	1,250	Beta – Interest on drawings	250
Beta – Interest on capital	2,500		
Alpha – Profit	15,000		
Beta – Profit	10,000		
	£44,750		£44,750

Current accounts

	Alpha £	**Beta** £		**Alpha** £	**Beta** £
Drawings	10,000	20,000	Salary	6,000	10,000
Interest on drawings	125	250	Interest on capital	1,250	2,500
Balance c/d	12,125	2,250	Profits	15,000	10,000
	£22,250	£22,500		£22,250	£22,500
			Balance b/d	12,125	2,250

Workings

Drawings	**Alpha** £	**Beta** £
mid-year	5,000	10,000
end of year	5,000	10,000

Interest is therefore on the mid-year drawings as follows:

Alpha   £5,000 × 6/12 (months) × 5/100 = £125

Beta   £10,000 × 6/12 × 5/100 = £250

There will be no interest on year-end drawings because they have not taken place before the appropriation of profits.

Profit shares

Profit after preferential claims

£44,750 – £16,000 (salaries) – £3,750 (interest on capital) = £25,000

Profit shared 3:2

Alpha	£15,000
Beta	£10,000

2.7   Changes in capital account balances

The use of the term 'fixed capital accounts' should not be taken to mean that the capital accounts cannot be changed. It is perfectly acceptable for changes in capital to take place, provided that they are within the terms of the partnership agreement, or are agreed to subsequently by the partners. Such changes are often confined to specific additional injections of capital, along with other adjustments, some of which are dealt with later in this chapter. However, increases and decreases in capital associated with profit shares, and decreases associated with drawings, are typically dealt with through the current accounts.

2.8 Guaranteed minimum profit shares

In certain partnership agreements one (or more) partner(s) is guaranteed a certain minimum share of profits. In the event of a share being less than this guaranteed amount a partner will be credited with the guaranteed minimum amount, and the profit remaining will then be shared out between the *other partners* in accordance with the partnership agreement.

Example

Jan, Jeff and David share profits and losses 3:2:1 respectively. David is guaranteed a minimum of £5,000 under the partnership agreement. If profit for the year is £24,000 David's share would be £4,000, a figure which is below his guaranteed minimum. He would thus be credited (in his current account) with the guaranteed minimum, and the remaining profit (£19,000) would be split between Jan and Jeff in the proportions 3:2. The appropriation account would thus appear as follows:

Appropriation

	£		£
David	5,000	Net profit	24,000
Jan	11,400		
Jeff	7,600		
	£24,000		£24,000

In some partnership agreements one partner may guarantee that another partner will have a certain minimum share of profits. In such circumstances any deficiency must be borne by the partner making the guarantee. Hence, if in the above example Jan guaranteed that David would have a minimum of £5,000 share of profits (as opposed to the guarantee being given by all the remaining partners) the shares of profit would be as follows:

Jan – entitlement £12,000 (3/6 of £24,000) less £1,000 to make up David's guaranteed share – £11,000.

Jeff – entitlement (2/6 of £24,000 = £8,000)

David – entitlement (1/6 of £24,000) plus £1,000 from Jan to make up the guaranteed minimum of £5,000.

2.9 Activity

M, J and P are in partnership sharing profits and losses in the ratio 4:2:1. P is guaranteed a minimum share of profits of £10,000 per annum. The profits in the current year total £58,000.

1   Show the appropriation account for the current year.

2   Show the revised appropriation account if M had guaranteed P's minimum profit share.

2.10 Activity solution

(1)

Appropriation account

	£		£
Profit shares		Net profit	58,000
M	32,000		
J	16,000		
P	10,000		
	£58,000		£58,000

Workings

Profit share based upon normal ratio of 4:2:1 (and rounded)

M – £33,142   J – £16,572   P – £8,286

But P is guaranteed £10,000, therefore minimum share given. This leaves £48,000 to be split in the ratio 4:2.

Therefore: M £32,000, J £16,000.

(2)   If M had guaranteed P's minimum share J would have remained entitled to £16,572.

P would be given his minimum of £10,000

M would have the remainder (£33,142 less the amount needed to bring P's share up to £10,000; that is £1,714) – which equals £31,428.

Appropriation account

	£		£
Profit shares		Net profit	58,000
M	31,428		
J	16,572		
P	10,000		
	£58,000		£58,000

2.11   Balance sheet presentation

In a partnership balance sheet the capital section will be somewhat more complicated than that in the balance sheet of a sole trader. The capital section will need to show both fixed capital account balances and current account figures. The detail provided should also be as informative as possible. In practice it is therefore usual to show the capital account and the current account transactions in some detail, to show their major components and any movements in them.

Example

Given below is an indication of the type of approach adopted, using an earlier activity as the base.

Balance sheet – owners' equity only

	Alpha	**Beta**	**Total**
	£	**£**	**£**
Capital	25,000	50,000	75,000
Current			
Opening balance	–	–	
Salary	6,000	10,000	
Interest on capital	1,250	2,500	
Profit	15,000	10,000	
	22,250	22,500	
Less			
Drawings	(10,000)	(20,000)	
Interest on drawings	(125)	(250)	
Closing balance	£12,125	2,250	14,375
Total owners' equity			£89,375

It is clear from the above example that the balance sheet presentation for partnership equity is effectively a duplication of what is in the partners' capital and current accounts. For this reason it is unusual for examiners to require both capital and current accounts and the balance sheet. Clearly both are needed in practice and care should always be taken to ensure that the requirements of a particular question are being met. In fact the balance sheet is rather more intelligible if the final capital and current account balances only are shown on the face of the balance sheet, with supplementary notes showing the breakdown of the figures.

2.12 Partnership loans

Sometimes partners bring funds into the business in the form of a loan, rather than as capital. Such loans have a higher priority than capital as regards repayment on the dissolution (that is, termination) of a partnership. Interest on partnership loans is debited to an 'interest on loan' account and credited to either 'cash' or the appropriate current account. There seem to be some disagreements about whether the 'interest on loan' account should then be transferred to the profit and loss account proper, or to the appropriation account. It can be argued that interest is an expense of the partnership business, and should thus be transferred to the profit and loss account as a business expense.

However, given that the firm has no separate legal identity, both partnership loans and partnership equity may be seen as capital at risk. While a partner's loan may be given priority as regards repayment in the event of a dissolution of the partnership, any shortfall in partnership funds must be made up by the partners, from any other assets they may have. Under such circumstances the idea of a partner lending money to himself (at least in part), and then being charged interest on it, seems inconsistent. It could thus be argued that interest on a partner's loan represents a preferential share of profits, and should therefore be transferred to the appropriation account.

The balance of opinion appears to favour the first treatment, and most suggested solutions adopt this treatment. The relative insecurity of a partnership loan should nevertheless be recognised.

2.13 Activity

Dawn, Edith and Mandy are in partnership as Recreational Suppliers, sharing residual profits and losses in the ratio of 5:2:3 respectively. At 1 November 19X2 their capital and current account balances were:

	Capital account	Current account	
	£	£	
Dawn	8,000	580	(credit)
Edith	10,000	350	(debit)
Mandy	12,000	210	(credit)

By agreement, partners are entitled to interest on capital at the rate of 5% per annum.

On 1 May 19X3, by mutual agreement, Dawn increased her capital by paying a further £2,000 into the partnership bank account, whilst Edith reduced her capital to £6,000 but left her withdrawn capital in the partnership as a loan bearing interest at 5% per annum.

Partners are allowed to withdraw from current accounts at any time during the financial year but are charged interest on the amounts involved. Details of the drawings made and interest chargeable in respect of each partner for the financial year ended 31 October 19X3 are:

	Drawings	Interest on drawings
	£	£
Dawn	2,400	90
Edith	1,800	30
Mandy	3,000	25

Edith is remunerated for her participation in the running of the partnership with an annual salary of £2,500. The trading profit (before interest) of Recreational Suppliers for the year ended 31 October 19X3 was £19,905.

For the year ended 31 October 19X3:

1   Prepare the profit and loss appropriation account for the partnership.

2   Post to and balance the capital and current accounts of the individual partners.

2.14   Activity solution

(1)

Appropriation account

	£		£
Interest on loan*	100	Net profit	19,905
Interest on capital		Interest on drawings	
– Dawn	450	– Dawn	90
– Edith	400	– Edith	30
– Mandy	600	– Mandy	25
Salary – Edith	2,500		
Profits – Dawn	8,000		
– Edith	3,200		
– Mandy	4,800		
	£20,050		£20,050

*   Alternatively interest on loan may be deducted from the net profit figure.

Workings – Interest on loan

Edith: £4,000 left on loan – covers 6 months – 5% interest

Therefore interest = £4,000 × 6/12 × 5/100 = £100

Workings – Interest on capital

Capital: Dawn – £8,000 for 6 months – £10,000 for 6 months

Edith – £10,000 for 6 months – £6,000 for 6 months

Mandy – £12,000 for 1 year

Workings – Profit shares

Profit after other appropriations but before profit shares calculated.

£20,050 – £100 (interest on loan) – £1,450 (interest on capital) – £2,500 (salary) = £16,000, which is to be shared in the ratios 5:2:3.

Therefore	Dawn is entitled to	£16,000 × 5/10 = £8,000
	Edith is entitled to	£16,000 × 2/10 = £3,200
	Mandy is entitled to	£16,000 × 3/10 = £4,800

(2)

Capital

	Dawn £	Edith £	Mandy £		Dawn £	Edith £	Mandy £
19X3				**19X2**			
May 1 Loan		4,000		Nov 1			
				Balance b/d	8,000	10,000	12,000
Oct 31				**19X3**			
Balance c/d	10,000	6,000	12,000	May 1 Cash	2,000		
	£10,000	£10,000	£12,000		£10,000	£10,000	£12,000
				Nov 1			
				Balance b/d	10,000	6,000	12,000

Current

	Dawn £	Edith £	Mandy £		Dawn £	Edith £	Mandy £
19X2				**19X2**			
Nov 1							
Balance b/d		350		Nov 1			
				Balance b/d	580		210
19X3				**19X3**			
Drawings	2,400	1,800	3,000	Oct 31			
				Interest			
				on loan		100	
				Interest			
Oct 31 Interest				on capital	450	400	600
on drawings	90	30	25	Salary		2,500	
Balance c/d	6,540	4,020	2,585	Profits	8,000	3,200	4,800
	£9,030	£6,200	£5,610		£9,030	£6,200	£5,610
				Nov 1			
				Balance b/d	6,540	4,020	2,585

2.15 Activity

Middleton and Teesdale are trading as general merchants and the following trial balance is extracted from the partnership books as 31 December 19X7:

	£	£
Capital – Middleton		40,000
Capital – Teesdale		40,000
Loan – Middleton		30,000
Purchases	180,000	
Debtors	45,000	
Sales		260,000
Creditors		42,000
Salesperson's salaries	13,500	
Discount received		3,800
General expenses	3,500	
Wages	8,000	
Vans – cost	15,000	
– depreciation provision		3,000
Bad debts provision		2,000
Carriage out	3,300	
Carriage in	2,200	
Rent, rates and insurance	13,500	
Bad debts	2,450	
Fixtures and fittings – cost	10,000	
– depreciation provision		1,000
Stock	40,000	
Drawings – Middleton	30,000	
– Teesdale	25,000	
Cash	30,350	
	£421,800	£421,800

Notes:

1   Middleton is to have an annual salary of £10,000. Profits are to be divided according to the provisions of the Partnership Act 1890. Interest on capital, on drawings and the partnership loan are also to be as laid down in the Act.

2   Accrued expenses at the year end were: rent £500; wages £600.

3   Amounts paid in advance at the year end were: rates £1,500; insurance £500.

4   Depreciation is to be written off the vans at 20% per annum and off fixtures and fittings at 10% per annum. The straight-line method of depreciation is to be used.

5   Closing stock is valued at £40,000.

6   The bad debts provision is to be maintained at 5% of debtors.

7   Separate capital and current accounts are to be kept for the partners.

Prepare a trading and profit and loss account for the year ended 31 December 19X7 (including an appropriation account), and a balance sheet as at that date.

2.16   Activity solution

Middleton and Teesdale
Trading and profit and loss account
for the year ended 31 December 19X7

	£	£
Sales		260,000
Opening stock	40,000	
Purchases	180,000	
Carriage in	2,200	
	222,200	
Less: Closing stock	40,000	
Cost of sales		182,200
Gross Profit		77,800
Add: **Other revenues**		
Discount received		3,800
		81,600
Less: **Other expenses**		
General expenses	3,500	
Wages (8,000 + 600)	8,600	
Rent, rates, insurance *	12,000	
Depreciation – fixtures	1,000	
Carriage out	3,300	
Salesperson's salaries	13,500	
Depreciation – van	3,000	
Bad debts	2,450	
Increase in BDP	250	
		47,600
Net profit		£34,000
Interest on loan**	1,500	
Salary – Middleton	10,000	
Profit – Middleton	11,250	
– Teesdale	11,250	
		£34,000

* £13,500 + £500 – £2,000

**or in Profit and Loss account as an expense.

Balance sheet as at 31 December 19X7

Fixed assets	Cost £	Depreciation £	Net £
Vans	15,000	6,000	9,000
Fixtures and fittings	10,000	2,000	8,000
	£25,000	£8,000	17,000

Current assets			
Stock		40,000	
Debtors	45,000		
Less: BDP	2,250		
		42,750	
Prepayments		2,000	
Cash		30,350	
		115,100	
Less: **Current liabilities**			
Creditors	42,000		
Accruals	1,100		
		43,100	
Net current assets			72,000
			£89,000

	Middleton £	Teesdale £	Total £
Capital	40,000	40,000	80,000
Current			
Interest on loan	1,500		
Salary	10,000		
Profits	11,250	11,250	
	22,750	11,250	
Less: Drawings	30,000	25,000	
	£(7,250)	£(13,750)	(21,000)
Loans – Middleton			30,000
Total ownership interest			£89,000

3 CHAPTER SUMMARY

- This chapter has set out the nature and legal position of a partnership. The typical items which are found in a partnership agreement have been identified, as has the position when no agreement has been made on particular issues. The need to share out profits means that the profit and loss account has an additional section, referred to as the appropriation account. The entitlement to profits, and the withdrawal of profits, are typically dealt with through current accounts. This results in the equity or capital section of a partnership balance sheet being rather more complex than that of a sole trading business. Nevertheless you should not forget that the sum of the capital and current account of each partner is simply that partner's stake or investment in the business.

- Sometimes there is a junior partner who is entitled, under the partnership agreement, to a minimum share of profits. In these circumstances, where the partner's percentage share would work out at less than the guaranteed minimum, this partner's share must be taken first, and the other partners, in effect, take less than their normal percentage share.

- The Partnership Act 1890 lays down a number of points about the relationships between partners and between the partnership and the outside world. Particularly important to us are the rules on how profits are to be shared in the event of there being no partnership agreement, or one which is incomplete.

4   SELF TEST QUESTIONS

4.1   What is the maximum number of partners in a partnership which is allowed by law? (1.1)

4.2   Which one of the following applies in the absence of a partnership agreement?

(a)   Interest on capital at 5% is to be paid, and profits are to be shared equally

(b)   No interest on capital is to be paid, and profits are to be shared equally

(c)   Interest on capital at 10% is to be paid

(d)   No interest on capital is to be paid, and profits are to be shared in the proportions of fixed capital. (1.5)

4.3   What does the Partnership Act 1890 say about interest on loans in the absence of a partnership agreement? (1.5)

4.4   Which one of the following is the correct double entry to record interest on drawings?

(a)   Debit interest on drawings, credit the partners' capital accounts

(b)   Debit appropriation account, credit the partners' capital accounts

(c)   Debit the partners' current accounts, credit the appropriation account

(d)   Debit the appropriation account, credit the partners' current accounts. (2.1)

5   EXAMINATION TYPE QUESTIONS

5.1   Bee, Cee and Dee

Bee, Cee and Dee have been holding preliminary discussions with a view to forming a partnership to buy and sell antiques.

The position has now been reached where the prospective partners have agreed the basic arrangements under which the partnership will operate.

Bee will contribute £40,000 as capital and up to £10,000 as a long-term loan to the partnership, if needed. He has other extensive business interests and will not therefore be taking an active part in the running of the business.

Cee is unable to bring in more than £2,000 as capital initially, but, because he has an expert knowledge of the antique trade, he will act as the full-time manager of the business.

Dee is willing to contribute £10,000 as capital. He will also assist in running the business as the need arises. In particular, he is prepared to attend auctions anywhere within the United Kingdom in order to acquire trading stock which he will transport back to the firm's premises in his van. On occasions he may also help Cee to restore the articles prior to sale to the public.

At the next meeting, the three prospective partners intend to decide upon the financial arrangements for sharing out the profits (or losses) made by the firm and have approached you for advice.

Prepare a set of explanatory notes, under suitable headings, of the considerations which the prospective partners should take into account when arriving at their decisions at their next meeting.

(18 marks)

5.2 **Brushe and Partners**

Brushe, Payperr and Paynte are in process of drawing up an agreement for the painting and decorating partnership which they are proposing to form.

They have estimated that after the partnership has become properly established, annual net profit should not be less than £28,200 but is unlikely to exceed £36,400.

Various arrangements for appropriating the net profit have been suggested but the prospective partners have now narrowed down the choice to two:

Arrangement A

1   Drawings are to be permitted throughout the year but no interest is to be charged on them

2   Interest is to be credited at 5% per annum on partners' capital

3   Partnership salary of £2,000 per annum goes to Brushe

4   Residual profits and losses to be shared 3:5:2 between Brushe, Payperr and Paynte respectively.

Arrangement B

1   Drawings are to be permitted only after the profit for the year has been ascertained

2   Interest is to be credited at 10% per annum on partners' capital

3   No partnership salaries are to be paid

4   Residual profits and losses to be shared 4:3:3 between Brushe, Payperr and Paynte respectively.

Capital introduced by the partners will be Brushe, £10,000, Payperr, £14,000 and Paynte £20,000.

One of the prospective partners, Brushe, has asked you which alternative arrangement would be the more beneficial to him.

(a)   Prepare, in tabular format, your calculations of the amounts which individual prospective partners would receive at each of the two stated profit levels.

(b)   State what advice you would give to Brushe, as the result of your calculations in a).

(15 marks)

5.3 **Able and Partners**

(a)   The current accounts of three partners, Able, Baker and Delta at 31 December 19X0 were as follows:

Current accounts

	A	B	D		A	B	D
	£	£	£		£	£	£
Balance at 1 Jan	–	500	–	Balance at 1 Jan	350		800
Drawings	2,100	2,300	2,400	Salary	800	–	–
Goods	210	–	–	Interest on capital	600	400	300
Balance at 1 Dec	1,940	100	1,200	Share of profits	2,500	2,500	2,500
	£4,250	£2,900	£3,600		£4,250	£2,900	£3,600

Give a brief explanation of each type of entry, and suggest reasons why the partnership agreement has allowed for salary, interest on capital and a share of profits, and not just for a share of profits.

(b)   Further investigation of the accounts of Able, Baker and Delta reveals that:

- Interest on capital was credited at 5% but the partnership agreement had allowed for 8%

- A provision for doubtful debts had been increased by £100 but should have been decreased by the same amount

- Goods taken by Able were at sales value (£210) and not at cost (£110)

- The business's cars were shown at a net book value at 31 December 19X0 of £4,500 (original cost £10,000, accumulated depreciation £5,500) but the current year's depreciation had been charged in error at 10% on the written-down value at 1 January 19X0 instead of on a straight-line basis. No cars had been bought or sold during the year, and there was no expected residual value

- The closing stock included some goods (cost £800) which had been invoiced to a customer for £1,000 on 31 December 19X0, but which had not been despatched until 2 January 19X1.

Draw up an extract from the balance sheet as at 31 December 19X0 showing the partners' capital accounts and revised balances on their current accounts.   **(15 marks)**

5.4   Checke and Tikk

(a)   For a number of years you have been employed in a senior position by a firm of certified accountants.

The two partners, Checke and Tikk, have now offered to take you into the firm as a junior partner with effect from 1 April 19X5. Hitherto the partners have contributed capital thus:

Checke	50,000
Tikk	30,000

They receive interest at 5% per annum. They have shared profits (and losses) at the ratio of 3:2 respectively.

After admission to the partnership you will be expected to continue managing the practice for which you will receive exactly half your present annual salary of £14,000 as a partnership salary. You will also be expected to contribute £20,000 as capital (on which you will receive interest at 5% per annum).

The profit-sharing ratio will then be altered to give you a one-sixth share of the profits and losses, without disturbing the relative shares of the other two partners.

For the year ended 31 March 19X5, the total amount appropriated by the two partners was £34,000.

Prepare a statement showing the details of the amounts appropriated by Checke and Tikk during year ended 31 March 19X5 together with details of the amounts which would have been appropriated if you had been taken into partnership on 1 April 19X4.

(b)   The financial arrangements between the members of the partnership are usually contained in an agreement. State:

(i)   the position where a partnership agreement contains financial arrangements which conflict with the requirements of the Partnership Act 1890, and

(ii)   the requirements of the Partnership Act 1890 regarding

- interest on capital
- interest on loans made by partners
- remuneration of partners
- sharing of profits and losses.

(15 marks)

6   ANSWERS TO EXAMINATION TYPE QUESTIONS

6.1   Bee, Cee and Dee

Profit sharing in a partnership will normally reflect a number of factors, relating to the relative contributions of the partners in terms of:

- the amount invested, whether as capital or a loan
- the amount of work to be carried out by the partners
- the relative expertise of the partners.

In addition, some kind of charge may be made to penalise partners who make drawings earlier than other partners. In fact, if no agreement is reached on profit sharing, the provisions of the Partnership Act 1890 apply. However, the partners may, and typically do, come to an agreement which is different to that of the Act, which reflects the particular circumstances of the partnership. Typically a partnership agreement will deal with these by including some or all of the following components in the profit-sharing agreement.

1   **Partnership salaries**

Where a partner puts in a substantial amount of time or expertise into a business it is common to find that a partnership salary is allowed. The Partnership Act does not provide for a salary. In this particular partnership however it would seem appropriate for Cee to be given a full-time salary and for Dee to be given a part-time salary. Such salaries are appropriations of profit.

2   **Interest on capital**

Where the amount of the capital contributed by each partner is different it is common to find an appropriation of profit being allowed to provide interest at an agreed rate on the capital invested. The Partnership Act does not require any such appropriation. In this partnership it is probably appropriate for Bee, the largest provider of capital funds, to receive substantially more than Dee, who in turn should receive substantially more than Cee.

3   **Interest on drawings**

If one partner draws a share of profits earlier than another it may be appropriate to pay interest on these drawings. Since such interest is credited to the appropriation account the total charged will be shared out by the partners in their profit-sharing ratio. This nevertheless results in an additional charge being incurred by any partner who makes drawings at an earlier stage, or in greater amounts, than his partners.

4   **Residual profits**

Once the appropriations referred to above have been carried out the question needs to be asked about how the residual profits should be shared out. Some agreement on the method of sharing out this residual needs to be agreed. In fact, decisions about this element are difficult, since they will reflect a variety of factors such as enterprise, risk, business expertise and acumen and contacts.

Overall the profit-sharing agreement should reflect these kind of elements. In the final analysis, however, some sort of compromise must be reached which the partners can all agree to.

It should be noted that in the absence of agreement to the contrary the Partnership Act 1890 would grant Bee interest on his loan at a rate of 5% per annum which would have the effect of reducing the profit available to be divided between the partners, including Bee.

6.2   Brushe and Partners

(a)

Arrangement A

Lower level of profits	Total	Brushe	Payperr	Paynte
	£	£	£	£
Interest on capital	2,200	500	700	1,000
Salaries	2,000	2,000	–	–
Profit (3:5:2)	24,000	7,200	12,000	4,800
	£28,200	£9,700	£12,700	£5,800

Upper level of profit	£	£	£	£
Interest on capital	2,200	500	700	1,000
Salaries	2,000	2,000	–	–
Residual profit (3:5:2)	32,200	9,660	16,100	6,440
	£36,400	£12,160	£16,800	£7,440

Arrangement B

Lower level of profits	£	£	£	£
Interest on capital	4,400	1,000	1,400	2,000
Profits (4:3:3)	23,800	9,520	7,140	7,140
	£28,200	£10,520	£8,540	£9,140

Upper level of profit	£	£	£	£
Interest on capital	4,400	1,000	1,400	2,000
Profits (4:3:3)	32,000	12,800	9,600	9,600
	£36,400	£13,800	£11,000	£11,600

(b)   Arrangement B gives Brushe a higher share of profits overall, irrespective of the profit level. The same is true of Paynte. Clearly therefore Arrangement A will be most beneficial to Payperr at either level of profit.

6.3   Able and Partners

(a)   (i)   Opening balances – the amount of retained profits to which a partner is entitled. A debit balance means that a partner has withdrawn more than his salary, interest on capital and share of profits entitles him to.

(ii)   Salary – a share of profit specifically identified as salary, usually being related to work done, particular expertise and so on.

(iii)   Interest on capital – a fixed amount of interest in respect of the fixed capital of each partner.

(iv)   Share of profits – a share of the residual profits after all other appropriations have been taken out.

(v)   Drawings – money taken from the business during the year by the partners, in anticipation of their share of profits.

(vi)   Goods – stock drawings by the partner.

The partnership agreement actually decided on will reflect the relative amounts of capital, work done, and expertise.

(b)

Balance sheet as at 31 December 19X0

	A	B	D	Total
	£	£	£	£
Capital	12,000	8,000	6,000	26,000

	A	B	D	
Current	£	£	£	
Opening balance	350	(500)	800	
Salary	800			
Interest on capital	960	640	480	
Profits	1,840	1,840	1,840	
	3,950	1,980	3,120	
Less: Drawings	2,210	2,300	2,400	£2,140
	£1,740	£(320)	£720	£28,140

Workings

	£
Profit before adjustments	
(800 + 600 + 400 + 300 + 2,500 + 2,500 + 2,500)	9,600
Plus doubtful debt provision adjustment	200
Less: Stock drawings adjustment	(100)
(difference between sales value and cost)	
Less: Additional depreciation	(500)
Less: Reduction in closing stock	(800)
	£8,400

6.4   Checke and Tikk

(a)

Appropriations for year ended 31 March 19X5

			£
Total available for appropriation			34,000

Appropriated as follows:	Checke	Tikk	
	£	£	
Interest on capital	2,500	1,500	4,000
Profits (residual)	18,000	12,000	30,000
	£20,500	£13,500	–

If you had entered the partnership on 1 April 19X4 the appropriations would have been as follows:

			£
Total available for appropriation (profits + salary of £14,000)			48,000

Appropriated as follows:	Checke	Tikk	You	
	£	£	£	
Interest on capital	2,500	1,500	1,000	5,000
Salary			7,000	7,000
Profits (3:2:1)	18,000	12,000	6,000	36,000
	£20,500	£13,500	£14,000	–

(b)   (i)   The arrangements contained in the agreement override the requirements of the Partnership Act.

          (ii)

- no interest on capital is to be paid
- interest on loans is payable at 5% per annum
- no partnership remuneration
- profits and losses to be shared equally.

18 PARTNERSHIP ACCOUNTS – PARTNERSHIP CHANGES

INTRODUCTION AND LEARNING OBJECTIVES

When changes occur in a partnership, either with the partners themselves or in the profit-sharing ratios, some adjustment is often necessary to ensure that no partner is disadvantaged as a result. A possible reason for the disadvantage is the fact that the balance sheet value, or book value, of most assets is not the same as their market value. Certain assets, for example goodwill, may have a market value yet not appear in the balance sheet at all. To some extent a similar point can arise with a firm's liabilities, but in practice this is usually not significant. Broadly speaking, the historic cost and prudence conventions tend to cause the balance sheet to understate the value of assets relative to their market values.

Suppose that there is a partnership of two partners who share profits equally. The only partnership asset is a building which is let to tenants. The building is shown in the balance sheet at £100,000. Imagine that a third partner joins the partnership and that the new partnership is to share profits equally (one third to each partner). Suppose now that the partners decide to sell the building for £160,000. This means that each partner will be credited with a profit share of £20,000 ((£160,000 – 100,000)/3). Thus a partner who has only just joined the partnership will gain an immediate profit of £20,000. It also means that instead of the old partners getting half each of the profit, they only get one third. Thus there is a shift of wealth from the old partners to the new one. Fortunately it is simple to make a adjustment which will compensate for this unfairness. This example is obviously oversimplified, but it should illustrate the nature of the problem.

When you have studied this chapter you should be able to do the following:

*   Appreciate the need to introduce goodwill into the partnership assets on a change in partnership

*   Calculate the value of goodwill according to formulas provided

*   Account for the situation when two or more sole traders combine their businesses to form a partnership.

---

1 THE LEGAL AND ACCOUNTING POSITIONS COMPARED

1.1 Introduction

Legally a change in partners means that a new partnership comes into existence. However, in practice the accounting records of the partnership business usually continue, with various adjustments being made to these accounts. The introduction of a new partner will result in an increase in one or more assets (and possibly liabilities, if a new partner is bringing in an existing business), together with an associated capital account. Such entries should pose few problems. Problems are far more likely to arise where the book value of a business and its worth are different. Where this situation exists some adjustments are likely to be needed to the accounts, when new partners are introduced, when existing partners leave, or when profit-sharing ratios change.

1.2 Reasons for adjustment

It should be clear from earlier chapters that the balance sheet of a business, being based upon historic cost, does not necessarily, or even usually, give the worth of that business. The whole question as to what constitutes 'worth' is a somewhat tricky one, since the parties to a transaction must agree on what they think worth is, and this will depend upon perceptions and needs at the particular time of the transaction.

If a new partner is introduced into a firm he only becomes entitled to his share of profits or losses made *after* his introduction. He is obviously not entitled to any profits (or losses) made prior to his introduction, unless a special agreement is made. Such an agreement would overrule the general points made in this section. If no such agreement is made it will generally be necessary to adjust the accounts on the admission of a new partner, to ensure that all of the existing partners' shares of the agreed worth are preserved.

Example

This example will show why adjustments of the type described above are necessary, and the impact on the existing partners of the absence of adjustments.

Charlie and George are in partnership sharing profits and losses in the ratio 2:1. The partnership balance sheet at 31 December 19X7 is as given below:

	£	£
Fixed assets		
Property		40,000
Equipment		10,000
		50,000
Current assets		
Stock	10,000	
Debtors	10,000	
Cash	5,000	
	25,000	
Current liabilities		
Creditors	10,000	
Net current assets		15,000
		£65,000
Capital		
Charlie		40,000
George		25,000
		£65,000

Both partners and the local estate agent agree that the business could be sold as a going concern, for about £95,000. This means that the current worth of the business, £95,000, is £30,000 more than the book value of the owners' equity. This increase in value is not yet a realised profit, so has not yet been recorded in the accounts. Nevertheless, it can be argued that at this particular time the two partners' share of the worth of the business is £30,000 more than the book value. Their respective shares of this are £20,000 and £10,000, since profits are shared in the ratio 2:1; in other words, Charlie's share of the business (when valued at £95,000) is £60,000 (the capital balance of £40,000 plus the £20,000 referred to above), while George's is £35,000 (the capital balance of £25,000 plus the £10,000 referred to above). If the business were to be sold at this time for £95,000, the two partners would take out £60,000 and £35,000 respectively.

If Best were now to be introduced into the partnership with a capital of £25,000, with a new profit-sharing ratio between Charlie, George and Best of 2:1:1, and no adjustment were made, the balance sheet would appear as follows.

Balance sheet as at 31 December 19X7

	£	£
Fixed assets		
Property		40,000
Equipment		10,000
		50,000
Current assets		
Stock	10,000	
Debtors	10,000	
Cash	30,000	
	50,000	
Current liabilities		
Creditors	10,000	
Net current assets		40,000
		£90,000
Capital		
Charlie		40,000
George		25,000
Best		25,000
		£90,000

If the business were to be put on the market immediately, as a going concern, total proceeds from the sale are likely to be about £120,000 (the original worth of £95,000 plus the £25,000 additional cash brought in by Best). If the business were sold for this amount the day after Best joined the partnership, there would be a profit of £30,000, which would be split in the profit-sharing ratio in existence at the time of the sale, namely 2:1:1. Charlie would thus be entitled to £15,000, with George and Best being entitled to £7,500 each. Since in this case the entry of Best into the partnership has not caused any increase in profits or worth there is little justification for him to be entitled to this £7,500. If he were to obtain any such entitlement it would be at the expense of Charlie and George, who stand to lose £5,000 and £2,500 respectively (the difference between their shares of the additional £30,000 before and after the entry of Best). The increase in worth of £30,000 had accumulated before the entry of Best, and should therefore accrue to Charlie and George. Some sort of adjustment is necessary to ensure that after a partnership relationship has changed the old partners retain their proper shares of the worth of the business prior to the change. Without adjustment the kind of problem identified above is almost certain to arise.

1.3   The introduction of goodwill

In practice the differences between book value and current worth may be attributable to certain assets (or liabilities) being missing from the balance sheet or the current value of certain of the individual assets (or liabilities) included in the balance sheet being rather different from their book value.

In practice and, more particularly, in examination questions the asset of **goodwill** is typically omitted from the balance sheet. This can be an important omission since goodwill can be very valuable. The nature of goodwill is discussed in the next section after which the accounting treatment of the necessary adjustments to correct for differences between the book and current value of net assets (including goodwill) will be considered.

1.4   The nature of goodwill

Goodwill in an accounting sense should be distinguished from goodwill in an everyday sense. Non-accountants tend to describe goodwill by reference to such things as a good reputation, high-quality workmanship and pleasantness. When accountants refer to goodwill they are using the term much more precisely. Goodwill, in an accounting sense, arises from the fact that a business can be worth more as a going concern than the sum of the values of the individual assets, net of all debts. For example, suppose that a business finds that by selling the assets individually, and paying off outstanding debts, it could raise a total of £120,000. Suppose further, that it could sell the business as a going concern for £140,000. In such circumstances the goodwill (the excess of the value of the business as a whole over the value of the component parts) would be £20,000.

Someone wishing to buy a business as a **going concern** may be prepared to pay more than the sum of the value of the individual assets because it is perceived that the business would be capable of generating a higher level of profit than might be expected from a similar business being started from scratch. Typical influential factors include: a good reputation with customers and suppliers; the quality of the products or workforce; the location of the business or its outlets; the clientele which is associated with the business; the ability to ensure supply of raw materials; and the technical expertise or research prowess. By their nature these kinds of factors may change fairly quickly over time, with the result that goodwill can change in value (or even be eliminated altogether) over quite short time spans. Typically, goodwill is only formally valued when it is to be the subject of a purchase or sale. A change of partnership membership or profit-sharing ratio is, of course, an event which is, in effect, a purchase or sale of part of the business of the partnership.

1.5   Valuation of goodwill

It is clear from the earlier example that if goodwill exists at the time of a partnership change and it is not already fully reflected in the balance sheet, some kind of adjustment needs to be made to reflect the amount of goodwill at the time of the change. This is no more the case with goodwill than with any other asset or liability whose book value differs from its current value. However, goodwill is often a particularly important example of such a difference, because goodwill can be of significant value and because, typically, it does not appear on the balance sheets of partnerships. Where partners need to make some kind of adjustment for goodwill it is necessary to arrive at a value for goodwill. This can be quite difficult, since each business has its own strengths and weaknesses at any particular point in time, and only limited guidance can be obtained from looking at other businesses, all of which are slightly different. Theoretically the value of a business should be arrived at by estimating future profits and trying to place some value on them. However, in practice a number of traditional rules are typically found to be used. These are often used as the basis of goodwill valuations in examination questions. The more common methods found are:

The average profits method

In this method goodwill is valued at a certain number of times the average profit for the last few years. The number of times and the number of years are factors which need to be identified and agreed.

The average revenue method

Goodwill is arrived at by multiplying the average revenue for a number of years by an agreed factor. This method is often used by professional firms with well-established clientele.

The super-profits method

Under this method a deduction from profits is made for an element of salaries (reflecting work done by owners) and interest (reflecting the amount of capital invested in the business). The remaining profits are known as super-profits. The goodwill is usually arrived at by multiplying the super-profits by an agreed factor.

Each of these methods emphasises **past performance**, which may or may not be a good indicator of future performance. Goodwill should clearly be based upon **expected future performance**. In the final analysis goodwill will reflect agreement between two (or more) parties, and their relative bargaining positions. In a partnership any goodwill estimated on the change of that partnership must be agreed by both existing and new partners. Some partnership agreements include a section which defines how goodwill is to be valued, should it prove necessary to do so.

Before completing this discussion it might be useful to make the point that goodwill is by no means confined to partnerships. From what we have seen, any business whose market value exceeds the break-up value of its individual tangible net assets has goodwill, be it a sole trader, a partnership or a limited company. In fact it is in the context of limited companies that the topic of goodwill tends to be most frequently referred. It tends to arise in the context of one company buying the entire business of another company (a 'takeover'). Where the net tangible assets of the company taken over are exceeded by the amount paid by the company taking over, the asset of goodwill will, initially at least, occur on the taking-over company's balance sheet. The fact that goodwill, even when purchased, does not unarguably meet the definition of an asset for accounting purposes (see Chapter 2), tends to mean that its continued appearance on the balance sheet is seen by many people as inappropriate. There has been much controversy surrounding the treatment of goodwill in the case of companies. This is a topic which you will meet in some detail at a later stage in your studies.

It is not usual for goodwill to be an issue, except where it is purchased, as with a partnership change or a company takeover. It is unusual, and in contravention of the historic cost convention, for non-purchased goodwill to appear on a balance sheet.

2 METHODS OF ADJUSTMENT

2.1 Introduction

Where the current values of individual assets and liabilities are different from their book value, or where particular assets and liabilities are not included in the accounts, the revaluation of these assets and liabilities provides a means of protecting the interests of existing partners. All the assets and liabilities of the partnership are revalued prior to the admission of a new partner, and the existing partners' capital accounts are adjusted by their share of any increase or decrease in value. Such revaluations are bound to have an element of subjectivity, but the use of professional advice should remove some bias.

Although the partners affected by possible differences between the balance sheet value and the current value of the net assets will have agreed with the extent and the reason for the difference, they may not wish to alter the individual asset and claims are not usually meant to reflect realisable values. It is quite simple however to make the necessary adjustments to the partners' capital accounts without touching the individual asset and liability accounts. Thus there are two approaches to the adjustments which may be necessary on a change of partnership. The first involves adjusting individual asset and liability accounts to reflect the revaluation. The second avoids adjusting the individual asset and liability accounts and makes the necessary adjustments only through the capital accounts.

2.2 Adjusting individual asset and liability accounts

The usual procedure is to:

1   Debit any increases in assets to the appropriate asset account, and to credit a **revaluation account**; this may involve opening an account for any asset or liability not previously shown in the accounts

2   Credit any decreases in assets to the asset account, and debit the revaluation account

3   Credit any increases in liabilities to the appropriate liability account, and debit the revaluation account

4   Debit any decrease in liabilities to the liability account, and credit the revaluation account.

After these entries have been made all the asset and liability accounts will now have up-to-date balances, and the revaluation account will contain a summary of all the changes in value. These increases or decreases in value are obviously the entitlement of the existing partners, so the revaluation account is closed off by transferring the total increase or decrease in value to the capital accounts of the existing partners to the profit-sharing ratios.

At this stage the balance sheet of the business shows the existing partners' estimate of the worth of the business, and their individual shares therein. A new partner can now be introduced, as the existing partners' shares are safeguarded. The purpose of the revaluation account is simply to bring together the differences between the book and current values of the various individual assets and liabilities. If there is only one such asset or liability then there is no need to open a revaluation account, since the double entry can be made in the individual asset or liability account and the capital accounts. In examination questions it is quite common for goodwill to be the only item for which adjustment is necessary.

Example

Suppose that, given the basic information contained in the earlier example, Charlie and George agree that the partnership property is worth £65,000, that the equipment is worth only £5,000 and that a bad debts provision of £1,000 should be established. This gives an increase in value of £19,000. It is known that the estimated realisable value of the business as a going concern is £95,000, which represents an increase of £30,000 on book value. The revaluations shown above account for £19,000 of this, which means that the remaining £11,000 must represent the value of the partnership goodwill. If an asset account is opened for this amount, a corresponding credit must be made to the revaluation account. The revaluation account can then be closed to the partner's capital accounts in the profit-sharing ratio. The accounts necessary to record the above adjustments are shown below.

Revaluation

	£		£
Equipment	5,000	Property	25,000
Bad debts provision	1,000	Goodwill	11,000
Capital – Charlie	20,000		
Capital – George	10,000		
	£36,000		£36,000

Equipment

	£		£
Balance b/d	10,000	Revaluation	5,000
		Balance c/d	5,000
	£10,000		£10,000
Balance b/d	5,000		

Bad debts provision

	£		£
		Revaluation	1,000

Property

	£		£
Balance b/d	40,000	Balance c/d	65,000
Revaluation	25,000		
	£65,000		£65,000
Balance b/d	65,000		

Goodwill

	£		£
Revaluation	11,000		

Capital – Charlie

	£		£
Balance c/d	60,000	Balance b/d	40,000
		Revaluation	20,000
	£60,000		£60,000
		Balance b/d	60,000

Capital – George

	£		£
Balance c/d	35,000	Balance b/d	25,000
		Revaluation	10,000
	£35,000		£35,000
		Balance b/d	35,000

If Best now brings in £25,000 and the business is subsequently sold for £120,000, he will recover only his £25,000 capital. The remaining £95,000 will be shared between Charlie and George in line with their capital balances (£60,000 and £35,000 respectively). Their rights to profits made prior to the entry of Best (even though not realised) have been preserved by the above procedure.

2.3 Problems with the above approach

Note that in order to preserve the old partners' rights a departure from certain accounting conventions is necessary. There are departures, at least to some extent, from objectivity and the historic cost conventions. The values placed on assets and liabilities, even on the business as a whole, are likely to be subjective, although they should be based upon such things as professional valuations where possible. Another problem with the above treatment is that profits are in effect recognised before they have been realised, which is also contrary to usual accounting practice. However, without some kind of adjustments the accounts would be very misleading, and could result in unfair treatment of certain partners. The alternative approach dealt with below avoids this problem.

It was pointed out earlier that the factors which give rise to goodwill can change fairly quickly over time. It can arise that goodwill recorded at one point, perhaps on a partnership change, is subsequently regarded as being overstated in the accounts, leading to a desire to reduce or eliminate its book value. Where it has been decided to reduce the book value of the goodwill it is necessary to credit the goodwill account with the amount of the reduction, which might be the entire book value of the goodwill. The corresponding debit will be go to the capital accounts of the partners according to their profit-sharing ratio. The ratio to be used is that applying at the time of the decision to reduce or eliminate the book value. This treatment is not peculiar to goodwill and should be applied to any asset under similar circumstances. However, the nature of goodwill means that there is a greater likelihood of there being a desire to reduce or write off its book value than would be the case with most other types of asset.

2.4 Activity

Lee and Anthea are partners sharing profits and losses in the ratio 3:2. The business balance sheet as at 31 December 19X7 was as follows:

		£	£
Fixed assets			
Property			20,000
Equipment			5,000
			25,000
Current assets			
Stock		5,000	
Debtors		2,500	
Cash		4,000	
		11,500	
Current liabilities			
Creditors		11,500	
Net current assets			–
			£25,000
Capital			
Lee			15,000
Anthea			10,000
			£25,000

The partners agree to admit Bill, subject to the following revaluations being incorporated into the books:

1   Property to be revalued to £35,000

2   Equipment to be revalued to £6,000

3   Stock to be revalued to £4,000

4   A bad debts provision of £250 is to be created

5   Goodwill is estimated to be worth £10,000.

Bill is to bring in capital of £15,000, being represented by vehicles of £5,000, stock of £2,500, debtors of £1,500, cash of £2,000 and goodwill of £4,000.

The new profit sharing ratio is to be in the ratio of 3:2:2 for Lee, Anthea and Bill respectively.

Prepare the accounts necessary to record the above.

2.5   Activity solution

Revaluation account

		£		£
Stock		1,000	Property	15,000
BDP		250	Equipment	1,000
Capital	– share of revaluation		Goodwill	10,000
	– Lee	14,850		
	– Anthea	9,900		
		£26,000		£26,000

Capital

	Lee £	Anthea £	Bill £		Lee £	Anthea £	Bill £
				Balance b/d	15,000	10,000	
Balance c/d	29,850	19,900	15,000	Revaluation	14,850	9,900	
				Various (refer to journal entry)			15,000
	£29,850	£19,900	£15,000		£29,850	£19,900	£15,000
				Balance b/d	29,850	19,900	15,000

Goodwill

	£		£
Revaluation	10,000	Balance c/d	14,000
Bill	4,000		
	£14,000		£14,000
Balance b/d	14,000		

2.6 Not adjusting individual asset and liability accounts but adjusting only through the capital accounts

Even where the amount of the revaluation is not to be reflected in the individual asset and liability accounts, the same process of revaluation will be necessary to discover the net difference between the book and current values of the net assets. Once the amount has been agreed it is necessary to calculate the adjustment needed to the capital accounts. This is done by ascertaining the respective shares in the difference in values (not recorded in the accounts) before and after the change in the partnership membership or profit-sharing ratio. There will be some partners who will have a greater share of this difference under the new agreement than under the old; for other partners the opposite will be true. There needs to be an adjustment to compensate partners who would otherwise suffer as a result of the partnership change.

Example

Continuing the Charlie, George and Best example above, it might be agreed that the £30,000 undervaluation of the net assets should not be adjusted in the individual asset and liability accounts, but, so as not to give Best (the new partner) an undeserved potential benefit, an adjustment should be made only in the capital accounts of the partners.

The shares in (entitlement to) the £30,000 excess of current value over book value are as follows:

	Old agreement (2:1) £	New agreement (2:1:1) £	Difference £
Charlie	20,000	15,000	−5,000
George	10,000	7,500	−2,500
Best	–	7,500	+7,500

The necessary adjustment to the capital accounts can thus be made as follows:

		£	£
Debit	Best capital account	7,500	
Credit	Charlie capital account		5,000
Credit	George capital account		2,500

After making these adjustments and accounting for the cash introduced by Best the balance sheet of the partnership would look identical to that shown earlier, except that the capital section would include the following:

	£	
Charlie	45,000	(40,000 + 5,000)
George	27,500	(25,000 + 2,500)
Best	17,500	(25,000 – 7,500)

At first sight this looks very unfair to Best in that he has immediately 'lost' £7,500 of his capital account balance. It should be remembered, however, that he has gained a 1/4 share of the unrealised difference between the book and realisable value of the net assets, a share which is worth £7,500. What has happened, in effect, is that Best has 'bought' his share in this difference from each of his new partners, £5,000 worth from Charlie and £2,500 worth from George. Note that he has taken profit share from them as follows:

	Old profit share	**New profit share**	**Difference**
Charlie	2/3	1/2	1/6 (decrease)
George	1/3	1/4	1/12 (decrease)
Best		1/4	1/4 (increase)

Thus Best has bought 1/6 of the unrealised difference from Charlie and 1/12 of it from George. Charlie and George have been 'paid' for the shares in the unrealised difference by the net increase in their capital accounts balances, that is, their claims against the business have increased by the appropriate amount.

Note that there is no reason of principle why some revaluations may be reflected in individual asset and liability accounts while others may not be.

2.7   Activity

Using the basic information from the earlier activity, show the balance sheet immediately after the admission of Bill, assuming that full adjustment is to be made for unrealised gains and losses, but only the stock revaluation and the creation of the bad debts provision are to be reflected in the individual asset or claims accounts. Also assume that Bill brings his £15,000 entirely in cash.

2.8   Activity solution

Balance sheet as at 31 December 19X7
(after admission of Bill)

	£	£
Fixed assets		
Property		20,000
Equipment		5,000
		25,000
Current assets		
Stock	4,000	
Debtors (net of provision)	2,250	
Cash	19,000	
	25,250	
Current liabilities		
Creditors	11,500	
Net current assets		13,750
		£38,750

Capital

Lee	18,708
Anthea	12,471
Bill	7,571
	£38,750

Workings

Revaluation account

	£		£
Stock	1,000	Capital – share of revaluation	
Bad debt provision	250	Lee 3/5	750
		Anthea 2/5	500
	£1,250		£1,250

Capital

	Lee £	Anthea £	Bill £		Lee £	Anthea £	Bill £
Reval acc.	750	500	–	Balance b/d	15,000	10,000	–
Adjustment (see note)			7,429	Adjustment (see note)	4,458	2,971	–
Balance c/d	18,708	12,471	7,571	Cash			15,000
	£19,458	£12,971	£15,000		£19,458	£12,971	£15,000
				Balance b/d	18,708	12,471	7,571

Note: The assets whose revaluations are not to be reflected in the individual asset accounts have a total excess or current value over book value of £26,000.

(Property £15,000, Equipment £1,000 and Goodwill £10,000)

Adjustment through the capital accounts

	Old (3:2) £	New (3:2:2) £	Difference £
Lee	15,600	11,142	–4,458
Anthea	10,400	7,429	–2,971
Bill	–	7,429	+7,429

		£	£
Therefore:			
Debit Lee capital account		7,429	
Credit Anthea capital account			4,458
Credit Bill capital account			2,971

2.9   Activity

X and Y are in partnership sharing profit 3:1. They agree to admit Z on condition that he brings in £15,000 capital, and that adjustment is to be made for the goodwill, valued at £6,000. The new profit-sharing ratio is to be 2:1:1 for X, Y and Z respectively.

1   Journalise the entries necessary to record the above, opening a goodwill account.

2   Journalise the entries necessary to then write off the goodwill account.

3   Journalise the entries to record the above if you had been told that no goodwill account was to be opened.

2.10   Activity solution

		£	£
1	Debit Goodwill	6,000	
	Credit Capital – X		4,500
	Credit Capital – Y		1,500

Being adjustment on introduction of goodwill

	£	£
Debit Cash	15,000	
Credit Capital – Z		15,000

Being cash introduced by Z

		£	£
2	Debit Capital – X	3,000	
	Debit Capital – Y	1,500	
	Debit Capital – Z	1,500	
	Credit Goodwill		6,000

Being writing off of goodwill

3   **Shares of goodwill**

	Old	New	Differences
	£	£	£
X	4,500	3,000	–1,500
Y	1,500	1,500	–
Z	–	1,500	+1,500
	£6,000	£6,000	–

Therefore journal entry	£	£
Debit Capital – Z	1,500	
Credit Capital – X		1,500

Being adjustment for share of goodwill on admission of Z

2.11   Activity

N and O are in partnership sharing profits in the ratio 3:2. They agree to admit P into the partnership on condition that he brings in £15,000, £5,000 of which is to be regarded as payment for his share of the goodwill. He is to be entitled to one sixth of the profits, the remainder being shared between N and O in the ratio 3:2. No goodwill account is to be opened.

Journalise the entries necessary to record the above transactions.

2.12 Activity solution

Share of goodwill
(which must be valued at £30,000, since £5,000 buys one-sixth)

	Old £	New £	Differences £
N	18,000	15,000	–3,000
O	12,000	10,000	–2,000
P	–	5,000	+5,000
	£30,000	£30,000	–

Therefore: journal entry	£	£
Debit Cash	15,000	
Credit Capital – P		10,000
Credit Capital – N		3,000
Credit Capital – O		2,000

Being cash received from P on entry
to partnership, and adjustment for goodwill

2.13 Activity

X and Y are in partnership sharing profits in the ratio 3:2. They agree to admit Z into the partnership on condition that he brings in £15,000, £5,000 of which is to be regarded as payment for his share of the goodwill. The new profit sharing ratio is to be 3:1:1 for X, Y and Z respectively.

Journalise the entries necessary to record the above transactions on the assumption that no goodwill account is to be opened.

2.14 Activity solution

Share of goodwill (£25,000)

	Old £	New £	Difference £
X	15,000	15,000	–
Y	10,000	5,000	–5,000
Z	–	5,000	+5,000
	£25,000	£25,000	–

Therefore: journal entry:	£	£
Debit cash	15,000	
Credit capital – Z		10,000
Credit capital – Y		5,000

Being cash brought in by Z and
adjustment for goodwill

2.15 Adjustment outside the partnership books

It may be the case that the necessary adjustments are dealt with by the partners as a completely private matter, in which case the accounts of the business are not affected. Nevertheless, the principles outlined above are likely to be useful in arriving at an appropriate figure for the adjustment.

2.16 Changes in the profit-sharing ratio and departures of existing partners

The same kind of adjustment is also necessary when the profit-sharing ratio of a partnership changes. This is to ensure that a partner gets his fair share of all increases or decreases in equity (whether realised or not) made during the period covered by a particular agreement. Similarly, these adjustments also need to be made prior to the departure of a partner. This should ensure that the balance on the departing partner's capital account reflects that person's entitlement.

2.17 Activity

Danger and Zone are in partnership sharing profits and losses in the ratio 2:1. They agree to share profits and losses equally in future. At the time of the change in the agreement goodwill is estimated at £7,500.

1   Journalise the above assuming that a goodwill account is to be opened.

2   Journalise the above assuming that a goodwill account is not to be opened.

2.18 Activity solution

		£	£
1	Debit Goodwill	7,500	
	Credit Capital – Danger		5,000
	Credit Capital – Zone		2,500
	Being introduction of goodwill		

2

Share of goodwill

	Old £	New £	Difference £
Danger	5,000	3,750	–1,250
Zone	2,500	3,750	+1,250
	£7,500	£7,500	–

	£	£
Therefore journal entry		
Debit Capital – Zone	1,250	
Credit Capital – Danger		1,250
Being adjustment for goodwill		
on change in profit-sharing ratio		

3   THE PROFIT AND LOSS ACCOUNT WHEN A PARTNERSHIP CHANGES

3.1   Introduction

The adjustments described so far relate to under- and over-valuations of assets and claims and are reflected in the capital accounts. A change in the partnership, or in the profit-sharing ratios, which occurs during a financial year, will also require the splitting of the financial results of the period into different time periods, relating to the periods before and after any change. This will require an apportionment of the revenues and expenses in an agreed and appropriate way, from which the profit or loss for each part of the year can be ascertained, and appropriated between the partners in the agreed way. Columnar trading, profit and loss and appropriation accounts are a particularly useful way of approaching this problem.

Example

Sun and Sand organise package holidays. They share profits and losses in the ratio 3:2. Sun is also entitled to an annual salary of £10,000. Interest on capital is payable at 10% per annum. Capital at the beginning of the year amounted to £20,000 for Sun and £25,000 for Sand. On 1 July, Lake joins the partnership, bringing in cash of £15,000. The new profit-sharing ratio is 2:1:1 for Sun, Sand and Lake respectively. Under the new agreement Sun is entitled to an annual salary of £10,000 and Lake £6,000. Interest on capital is to be allowed at 10% per annum. At the time of the change in the partnership, goodwill was estimated at £10,000, and an adjustment is to be made in the partners' capital accounts, without opening a goodwill account. Holidays sold during the year ended 31 December amounted to £250,000, and a fixed gross profit margin of 20% (of sales) is earned. 40% of the value of holidays were sold in the first half of the year. Rent, rates and expenses relating to the property used by the business were £5,000 for the year. Other expenses, which may be assumed to relate directly to the value of holidays sold, amounted to £3,000 for the year.

Prepare the trading, profit and loss and appropriation accounts for the year ended 31 December.

Solution

In dealing with this example it is necessary to deal with two aspects:

1   The adjustment for goodwill
2   The apportionment of profits over the two halves of the year, and between partners.

The **adjustment for goodwill** requires estimates to be made of the relative entitlements to goodwill before and after the change in the partnership.

Partner	Before	After	Difference
	£	£	£
Sun	6,000	5,000	−1,000
Sand	4,000	2,500	−1,500
Lake		2,500	+2,500
	£10,000	£10,000	£0

This means that Sun must be compensated by £1,000, and Sand by £1,500. The entry of Lake may thus be recorded in the books of the partnership as follows:

debit cash	£15,000
credit Lake	£15,000
debit Lake	£2,500
credit Sun	£1,000
credit Sand	£1,500

The apportionment of profit may best be handled by the use of a columnar trading and profit and loss account and appropriation account, as follows:

Trading, profit and loss and appropriation accounts for the year ended 31 December

	Jan–June	July–Dec		Jan–June	July–Dec
	£	£		£	£
Cost of sales (2)	80,000	120,000	Sales (1)	100,000	150,000
Gross profit (3)	20,000	30,000			
	£100,000	£150,000		£100,000	£150,000
Rent etc (4)	2,500	2,500	Gross profit	20,000	30,000
Other expenses (5)	1,200	1,800			
Net profit	16,300	25,700			
	£20,000	£30,000		£20,000	£30,000

Salary – Sun	5,000	5,000	Net profit	16,300	25,700
Salary – Lake	–	3,000			
Interest on capital (6)					
– Sun	1,000	1,050			
– Sand	1,250	1,325			
– Lake	–	625			
Profit shares (7)					
– Sun	5,430	7,350			
– Sand	3,620	3,675			
– Lake	–	3,675			
	£16,300	£25,700		£16,300	£25,700

The numbers in brackets relate to the notes given below, showing the basis of the split between the two periods.

1   Volume of holidays

2   80% of sales

3   20% of sales

4   Split on time basis

5   Split on basis of holidays sold in the period

6   Interest in period January–June calculated on capitals of Sun £20,000, Sand £25,000. Interest in period July–December calculated on capitals after goodwill adjustment, namely Sun £21,000, Sand £26,500, Lake £12,500

7   Profit shares calculated as follows:
     January–June

     Profit after other appropriations £9,050 (£16,300 – £5,000 – £1,000 – £1,250) split in the ratio 3:2.

     July–December

     Profit after other appropriations £14,700 (£25,700 – £5,000 – £3,000 – £1,050 – £1,325 – £625) split in the ratio 2:1:1.

In many examination questions it is not always possible, or necessary, to split the trading account between two periods in the conventional way. The situation often arises in which opening stock, purchases for the year and closing stock figures are available, enabling a cost of sales figure to be calculated for the year. A comparison of this cost of sales figure and the sales figures for the year should enable the gross profit for the year to be calculated. This gross profit is then usually split between the periods in proportion to sales. The resulting figures can then be entered into the columnar profit and loss account.

3.2   Activity

On 1 January Pam and Dick are in partnership, with the following agreement:

1   Profits and losses to be shared equally

2   Salaries to be paid at the rate of £10,000 per annum for Pam and £8,000 per annum for Dick

3   Interest on capital to be 10% per annum.

On 30 June they agree to admit Ellen into the partnership, provided that the premises are revalued to £82,000, and that goodwill (estimated to be worth £28,000) is incorporated into the books, both prior to the admission of Ellen. Ellen is to bring in £25,000 cash.

The new partnership agreement is as follows:

1	Profits and losses are to be shared in the ratio 3:2:2 for Pam, Dick and Ellen respectively
2	Salaries are to be paid at the rate of £8,000 per annum for each partner
3	Interest on capital is to be paid at 10% per annum.

On 31 December the trial balance of the firm is as follows:

	£	£
Property	50,000	
Equipment	12,000	
Depreciation provision – equipment		2,000
Stock (1 January)	15,000	
Purchases	220,000	
Wages	14,500	
Debtors	19,000	
Capital – Pam		30,000
Capital – Dick		30,000
Capital – Ellen		25,000
Current – Pam	8,000	
Current – Dick	10,000	
Current – Ellen	5,000	
Rates	1,000	
Heating and lighting	1,200	
Administration	6,000	
Creditors		15,800
Sales		280,000
Cash	21,100	
	£382,800	£382,800

Other information available at the year end is as follows:

1	Equipment is to be depreciated at the rate of 25% on cost
2	Prepaid wages amount to £500
3	Administration expenses of £1,000 are owing
4	The sales for the period 1 January to 30 June amounted to £120,000
5	Gross profit is always 25% on sales
6	All expenses other than wages accrue evenly over the year
7	Wages are incurred in the same proportions as sales over the two halves of the year
8	The entries relating to the property revaluation and the inclusion of goodwill have not been made
9	The partners decide to write off goodwill on 31 December.

Required

1	Draw up trading, profit and loss and appropriation accounts for the year, in columnar form, clearly distinguishing between the results of the two halves of the year, and a balance sheet as at the year end.
2	Draw up partners' capital and current accounts, incorporating the adjustments for the new partner, and the writing off of goodwill.
3	Create journal entries to show how you would have dealt with the admission of Eddie if the partners had agreed that the revaluation of property and the goodwill were not to appear in the books, even though they represented estimated current value.

3.3 Activity solution

Trading and profit and loss account for the year ended 31 December

	Jan–June £	July–Dec £		Jan–June £	July–Dec £
Cost of sales	90,000	120,000	Sales	120,000	160,000
Gross profit	30,000	40,000			
	£120,000	£160,000		£120,000	£160,000
Wages	6,000	8,000	Gross profit	30,000	40,000
Rates	500	500			
Heating and lighting	600	600			
Administration	3,500	3,500			
Depreciation equipment	1,500	1,500			
	12,100	14,100			
Net profit c/d	17,900	25,900			
	£30,000	£40,000		£30,000	£40,000
Salaries – Pam	5,000	4,000	Net profit b/d	17,900	25,900
– Dick	4,000	4,000			
– Ellen	—	4,000			
Interest on capital					
– Pam	1,500	3,000			
– Dick	1,500	3,000			
– Ellen	—	1,250			
Profits – Pam	2,950	2,850			
– Dick	2,950	1,900			
– Ellen	—	1,900			
	£17,900	£25,900		£17,900	£25,900

Notes

1   Cost of sales for the year arrived at as follows:

	£	
Opening stock	15,000	
Purchases	220,000	
	235,000	
Less: Closing stock	25,000	
= Cost of sales	£210,000	(75% of sales)

split £90,000/£120,000 over the two half years.

2   Interest on capital for the second half year is based on the capitals of Pam £60,000, Dick £60,000, and Ellen, £25,000.

3   Profits remaining after other appropriations – for the second half year (£25,900 – £19,250) shared in the ratio 3:2:2.

Capital

	Pam £	Dick £	Ellen £		Pam £	Dick £	Ellen £
Dec 31 Goodwill	12,000	8,000	8,000	Jan 1 Balance b/d	30,000	30,000	
				June 30 Cash			25,000
Dec 31 Balance c/d	48,000	52,000	17,000	Dec 31 Property (revaluation)	16,000	16,000	
				Dec 31 Goodwill	14,000	14,000	
	£60,000	£60,000	£25,000		£60,000	£60,000	£25,000
				Jan 1 Balance b/d	48,000	52,000	17,000

Current

	Pam £	Dick £	Ellen £		Pam £	Dick £	Ellen £
Dec 31 Balance b/d	8,000	10,000	5,000	Dec 31 Salaries	9,000	8,000	4,000
				Dec 31 Interest on capital	4,500	4,500	1,250
Dec 31 Balance c/d	11,300	7,350	2,150	Dec 31 Profits	5,800	4,850	1,900
	£19,300	£17,350	£7,150		£19,300	£17,350	£7,150
				Jan 1 Balance b/d	11,300	7,350	2,150

Balance sheet as at 31 December

Fixed assets	£	£	£
Property			82,000
Equipment – cost		12,000	
Less: Depreciation provision		5,000	
			7,000
			89,000
Current assets			
Stock		25,000	
Prepayments		500	
Debtors		19,000	
Cash		21,100	
		65,600	

Less:
Creditors due within a year

Creditors	15,800	
Accruals	1,000	
		16,800

Net current assets		48,800
		£137,800

Capital

Pam	48,000
Dick	52,000
Ellen	17,000
	117,000

Current accounts

Pam	11,300	
Dick	7,350	
Ellen	2,150	
		20,800
		£137,800

The journal entries for the third requirement are given below, as are the supporting workings.

Revaluation	£32,000
Goodwill	£28,000
Therefore total 'extra' value not shown on balance sheet	£60,000

The entitlement to this, and the necessary adjustment, can be seen, as follows:

	Before £	**After** £	**Difference** £
Pam	30,000	25,714	–4,286
Dick	30,000	17,143	–12,857
Ellen	–	17,143	+17,143
	60,000	60,000	–

The journal entry is thus:

Dr Pam	17,143	
Cr Dick		4,286
Cr Ellen		12,857

4 TWO OR MORE SOLE TRADERS FORMING A PARTNERSHIP

4.1 Introduction

So far we have looked at the formation of partnerships where all of the new partners bring in cash to start the partnership and where any additional partners bring in cash when they join the partnership. In practice it is not uncommon for new partnerships to be formed by the amalgamation of existing businesses.

Example

A and B intend to start a completely new partnership. It is agreed that they will each bring in cash, £25,000 by A and £40,000 by B. Immediately after the partnership has been formed and the cash paid in the balance sheet of the partnership will appear as follows:

Balance sheet of A and B as at the date of formation of the partnership.

		£
Current assets		
Cash at bank	(£25,000 + 40,000)	65,000
Capital accounts		
A		25,000
B		40,000
		65,000

Obviously this balance sheet was created by adding together the assets (cash only) introduced by each partner.

Example

Suppose that C and D are to go into partnership. C and D are both sole traders. They agree to take all of their existing assets and claims into the new partnership at the current balance sheet values.

The balance sheets of the existing sole trading businesses, at the date of the formation of the partnership, were as follows:

Balance sheet of C

	£000	£000
Fixed assets		
Land and buildings (at cost *less* depreciation)		53
Plant and machinery (at cost *less* depreciation)		21
Motor vehicles (at cost *less* depreciation)		34
		108
Current assets		
Stock	37	
Debtors	16	
Cash	23	
	76	
Less: **Current liabilities**		
Creditors	21	
		55
		163
Capital		163

Balance sheet of D

	£000	£000	
Fixed assets			
Plant and machinery (at cost *less* depreciation)			10
Motor vehicles (at cost *less* depreciation)			12
			22
Current assets			
Stock		11	
Debtors		9	
		20	
Less: **Current liabilities**			
Creditors	8		
Bank overdraft	7	15	5
			27
Capital			27

The balance sheet immediately following the formation of the partnership would be:

Balance sheet of C and D

	£000	£000
Fixed assets		
Land and buildings (at cost *less* depreciation)		53
Plant and machinery (at cost *less* depreciation) (21 + 10)		31
Motor vehicles (at cost *less* depreciation) (34 + 12)		46
		130
Current assets		
Stock (37 + 11)	48	
Debtors (16 + 9)	25	
Cash (23 – 7)	16	
	89	
Less: **Current liabilities**		
Creditors (21 + 8)	29	
		60
		190
Capital		
C		163
D		27
		190

As with partnership changes, where the balance sheet does not represent the value of the assets and claims an adjustment needs to be made, otherwise one of the new partners is likely to gain at the expense of the other one. The revised values can either be left on the face of the balance sheet or written off immediately.

Example

Assume exactly the same circumstances as for the C and D example above, except that C and D agree that the land and buildings of C are worth £74,000, not £53,000. The new partners do not want to increase the balance sheet value of this asset, however. C and D have agreed to share profits and losses in the ratio 2:1. Now the balance sheet immediately following the formation of the partnership will be:

Balance sheet of C and D

	£000	£000
Fixed assets		
Land and buildings (at cost *less* depreciation)		53
Plant and machinery (at cost *less* depreciation) (21 + 10)		31
Motor vehicles (at cost *less* depreciation) (34 + 12)		46
		130
Current assets		
Stock (37 + 11)	48	
Debtors (16 + 9)	25	
Cash (23 - 7)	16	
	89	
Less: **Current liabilities**		
Creditors (21 + 8)	29	
		60
		190

Capital

C (163 + 21 – (21 x 2/3))	170
D (27 – (21 x 1/3))	20
	190

4.2 Partnership accounts linked with other accounting problems

This chapter has so far been concerned with the accounts of partnership for relatively straightforward trading businesses. All the necessary principles of partnership accounts which are included in this syllabus have been covered. However, it is not uncommon for examiners to devise questions which include principles drawn from a number of aspects of accounting.

5 CHAPTER SUMMARY

- It is usually necessary to make certain adjustments on any change of personnel or of the profit-sharing ratio of the partnership. This is usually because the book value of certain assets is likely to be understated relative to their market values. Failure to make the adjustment will tend to advantage new partners at the expense of existing ones.

- Basically there are two approaches which can be taken to making the necessary adjustments.

  - The individual asset and liability accounts can be adjusted, the difference being shared between the existing partners, through their capital accounts. The new balances then remain on the asset and liability accounts concerned.

  - The individual asset and liability accounts can be adjusted, the difference being shared between the existing partners, through their capital accounts. The original values are then reinstated, this time the difference being shared between the new partners. A slight variation on this is that the individual asset and liability accounts are not altered; only the capital account entries are made.

- Where there is a change of partnership part way through an accounting period, it may be felt helpful to draw up a set of final accounts for each part of the period. Alternatively the books can be kept open until the end of the period at which point it will be necessary to divide the period's profit or loss into two elements, each of which will be allocated between partners in a different manner. This can become quite complicated in practice where particular revenues and expenses need to be apportioned, to different parts of the accounting period, in different ways.

6 SELF TEST QUESTIONS

6.1 What is the legal position when a there is a change of partnership personnel? (1.1)

6.2 Suggest three popular methods for valuing the goodwill of a partnership. (1.5)

6.3 Why is there a reluctance by accountants to maintain goodwill on the balance sheet? (1.5)

6.4 Which one of the following is the correct double entry to record the upward revaluation of certain fixed assets?

(a) Debit revaluation account with the increase in value, credit the partners' capital accounts in the profit-sharing ratio

(b) Debit fixed assets with the increase in value, credit the revaluation account

(c) Debit fixed assets with the new value of the assets, credit profit and loss

(d) Debit fixed assets with the new value of the fixed assets, credit capital accounts in the profit-sharing ratio. (2.2)

7   EXAMINATION TYPE QUESTIONS

7.1   Al and Bert

Al and Bert are in partnership, sharing profits equally. At 30 June they have balances on their capital accounts of £12,000 (Al) and £15,000 (Bert). On that day they agree to bring in their friend Hall as a third partner. All three partners are to share profits equally from now on. Hall is to introduce £20,000 as capital into the business. Goodwill on 30 June is agreed at £18,000.

(a)   Show the partners' capital accounts for 30 June and 1 July on the assumption that the goodwill, previously unrecorded, is to be included in the accounts.

(b)   Show the additional entries necessary to eliminate goodwill again from the accounts.

(c)   Explain briefly what goodwill is. Why are adjustments necessary when a new partner joins a partnership?   **(15 marks)**

(ACCA, June 1989)

7.2   Perks and Harvey

On 1 January Perks and Harvey are in partnership. Their partnership agreement is as follows:

(a)   Profits and losses to be shared equally

(b)   Salaries   – Perks £16,000 per annum

                            – Harvey £24,000 per annum

(c)   Interest on capital – 10% per annum

On 31 March they agree to admit Webb into the partnership, subject to the property being revalued to £150,000, and goodwill valued at £30,000 being incorporated into the books, both prior to the admission of Webb. Webb is to bring in £40,000 cash.

The new partnership agreement is as follows:

(a)   Profits and losses to be shared Perks 3/8, Harvey 1/2, Webb 1/8.

(b)   Salaries   – Perks £10,000 per annum

                            – Harvey £20,000 per annum

                            – Webb £10,000 per annum

(c)   Interest on capital – 10% per annum.

On 31 December the trial balance of the firm is as follows:

	Dr £	Cr £
Sales		500,000
Property	100,000	
Equipment	20,000	
Stock – 1 January	30,000	
Purchases	400,000	
Wages	30,000	
Debtors	40,000	
Payment from Webb		40,000
Capital – Perks		60,000
Capital – Harvey		60,000
Depreciation – Equipment	4,000	
Depreciation – provision – equipment		8,000
Creditors		32,000
Drawings – Perks	20,000	
Drawings – Harvey	20,000	
Drawings – Webb	15,000	

Rates	1,000	
Heat and light	2,000	
Administration	3,000	
Cash	15,000	
	700,000	700,000

The trading information covers the period 1 January to 31 December.

Other information available at the year end is as follows:

- Depreciation of equipment is to be 20% per annum straight line

- Prepaid wages amount to £2,000

- Rates of £600 were owing

- Administration expenses of £1,000 remain unpaid

- Sales for the period 1 January to 31 March amounted to £100,000. Gross profit is 25% on sales. All expenses other than cost of goods sold and rates accrue evenly over the year. The rates for the first quarter amounted to £500

- The partners now realise that the entries necessary to record the revaluation of the property, and the goodwill, have not been made

- The partners decide to write off goodwill at the year end.

You are required to provide the following:

(a)   Trading, profit and loss and appropriation account for the year, in columnar form, clearly distinguishing between the results of the first three months and the last nine months.

(b)   Partners' capital and current accounts, including the adjustment for the admission of Webb.

(c)   A balance sheet to show how you would have dealt with the admission of Webb if the partners had agreed that the revaluation of the property and the goodwill were not to appear in the books, even though they represented estimated current market value.

(20 marks)

7.3   ABC Partnership

(a)   The bookkeeper of the ABC partnership needs your help with the following problems. You may assume that the trial balance already includes a suspense account.

    (i)   Partner A has taken from the partnership for his own use a motor car at an agreed value of £600. The car had originally cost £5,000 and had been depreciated down to a net book value of £1,000. The bookkeeper had made no entries relating to this transfer.

    (ii)   Purchase ledger control balance had been understated by £2,000.

    (iii)   Sales day book had been understated by £300.

    (iv)   Purchase returns day book had been understated by £50.

    (v)   The balance on customer P in the sales ledger had been understated by £100.

    (vi)   An invoice for motor repairs of £123 had been paid twice by mistake. The first time it was posted correctly but the second time it was accidentally credited to the motor vans account as an amount of £231 (as well as being quite correctly entered in the cash book a second time).

    (vii)   Carriage inwards of £200 and carriage outwards of £225 have both been put on the wrong side of the trial balance.

Prepare journal entries necessary to correct the above. You may omit narratives provided that each entry clearly states the name of the account to be entered, and is referenced to the note numbers above.

(b)   A new partner has joined the business during the year and has paid in £10,000 'for goodwill'. This £10,000 has been credited by the bookkeeper to the account of the new partner. The senior partner had objected to this, but the bookkeeper had replied 'why not credit the £10,000 to the account of the new partner? It is his money after all'.

Give your advice as to the proper treatment of this £10,000. Explain your reasons fully.

(15 marks)

7.4   Timmy and Lucy

Timmy and Lucy have been in partnership for some years, sharing profits equally.

After the preparation of accounts for the year ended 31 December 19X2 their trial balance is as shown below (all figures £s).

		Dr	**Cr**
Timmy	– capital account		30,000
	– current account		3,000
Lucy	– capital account		40,000
	– current account	4,000	
Land		12,000	
Buildings	– cost	25,000	
	– depreciation		2,000
Machinery	– cost	30,000	
	– depreciation		16,000
Goodwill		10,000	
Net current assets		10,000	
		91,000	91,000

With effect from 1 January 19X3, Charlie is admitted into the partnership, and on that day he pays in £20,000 which is entered in his capital account. From that date the partners are to share profits, Timmy 40%, Lucy 40%, Charlie 20%.

It is agreed that at 1 January 19X3 the land is worth £20,000, the buildings are worth £30,000 and the goodwill is worth £16,000. The necessary adjustments are not to be recorded in the asset accounts, but should be made in the capital accounts.

The operating profit for the year 19X3 is £40,000, after charging depreciation of 1% on cost of the buildings and of 10% on cost of the machinery. There have been no sales or purchases of fixed assets in the year.

The partners are allowed 10% per annum interest on capital account balances on a *pro rata* basis. No interest is allowed or charged on current account balances. On 31 December 19X3 the partners are advised that the buildings are now worth only £20,000 (though the value of the land is not affected). It is agreed that this revised valuation should be incorporated in the accounts as at 31 December 19X3.

Each partner has taken drawings of £4,000 in the year to 31 December 19X3.

Required

(a)   Partners capital accounts in columnar form for the year 19X3.

(b)   Appropriation account for the year 19X3.

(c)   Partners current accounts in columnar form for the year 19X3.

(d)   Summary balance sheet as at 31 December 19X3, taking net current assets as the balancing figure.

(e)   A reconciliation of net current assets at 1 January 19X3 with net current assets at 31 December 19X3.
(22 marks)

(ACCA, December 1993)

8 ANSWERS TO EXAMINATION TYPE QUESTIONS

8.1 Al and Bert

(a)

Capital accounts

	Al £	Bert £	Hall £			Al £	Bert £	Hall £
30 June Balances c/d	21,000	24,000	20,000	20 June Balances b/d		12,000	15,000	
				Goodwill (divided 1:1)		9,000	9,000	
				Cash				20,000
	£21,000	£24,000	£20,000			£21,000	£24,000	£20,000
				1 July Balances b/d		21,000	24,000	20,000
(b)								
Goodwill (divided 1:1:1)	6,000	6,000	6,000					
Balances c/d	15,000	18,000	14,000					
	£21,000	£24,000	£20,000			£21,000	£24,000	£20,000
				Balances b/d		15,000	18,000	14,000

(c) Goodwill is an asset which arises from the fact that an existing profitable business may be worth more than the sum of its tangible assets net of liabilities. It may exist because the business has such attributes as a good reputation, a loyal clientele, a loyal workforce, or a skilled workforce. Goodwill has a value because a business with goodwill will be able to generate greater profits, all things being equal, than a business having no goodwill. The greater the goodwill, the greater the profit potential and the greater the value placed on goodwill.

A new partner joining a partnership is entitled to a share of future profits. This includes surpluses on disposals of fixed assets. Any assets which are undervalued in the books at the time of a new partner joining the firm represent a potential future profit in which the new partner will be entitled to participate. Such undervalued assets amount to a potential gain to the new partner at the expense of the existing partners. An adjustment needs to be made to correct for this unfairness.

Note that there would be no need to make any adjustment where there are no undervalued assets at the time of the new partner's admission to the partnership.

8.2 Perks and Harvey

(a)

Perks, Harvey and Webb

Trading and profit and loss account for the year ended 31 December

	January to March £	April to December £
Sales	100,000	400,000
Gross profit (25% of sales)	25,000	100,000

Wages	7,000	21,000
Depreciation	1,000	3,000
Rates	500	1,100
Heat and light	500	1,500
Administration	1,000	3,000
	10,000	29,600
Net profit	15,000	70,400

Salaries:	Perks	4,000	7,500
	Harvey	6,000	15,000
	Webb	–	7,500
Interest	Perks	1,500	7,500
	Harvey	1,500	7,500
	Webb	–	3,000
Profit	Perks	1,000	8,400
	Harvey	1,000	11,200
	Webb	–	2,800
		£15,000	£70,400

(b)

Capital

	Perks £	Harvey £	Webb £		Perks £	Harvey £	Webb £
Goodwill	11,250	15,000	3,750	Balance b/d	60,000	60,000	–
Balance c/d	88,750	85,000	36,250	Property	25,000	25,000	–
				Goodwill	15,000	15,000	–
				Cash			40,000
	100,000	100,000	40,000		100,000	100,000	40,000
				Balance b/d	88,750	85,000	36,250

Current

	Perks £	Harvey £	Webb £		Perks £	Harvey £	Webb £
Balance b/d	20,000	20,000	15,000	Salaries	11,500	21,000	7,500
Balance c/d	9,900	22,200	–	Interest	9,000	9,000	3,000
				Profit	9,400	12,200	2,800
				Balance c/d			1,700
	29,900	42,200	15,000		29,900	42,200	15,000
Balance b/d			1,700	Balance b/d	9,900	22,200	

(c)

Perks, Harvey and Webb
Balance sheet as at 31 December

Fixed assets	£	£	£
Property			150,000
Equipment			12,000
			162,000
Current assets			
Stock (see below)		55,000	
Prepayments		2,000	
Debtors		40,000	
Cash		15,000	
		112,000	
Current liabilities			
Creditors	32,000		
Accrued expenses	1,600		
		33,600	
Working capital			78,400
			£240,400
Capital accounts			
Perks		88,750	
Harvey		85,000	
Webb		36,250	
			210,000
Current accounts			
Perks		9,900	
Harvey		22,200	
Webb		(1,700)	
			30,400
			£240,400

The stock figure is derived as follows:

Cost of sales   =   Sales less gross profit

            =   £500,000 – 125,000 = £375,000

	£
Opening stock	30,000
Purchases	400,000
	430,000
Less: Closing stock	?
	£375,000

Thus closing stock is £55,000

8.3   ABC Partnership

			Dr £	Cr £
(a)	(i)	Disposal account	5,000	
		Motor car account		5,000
		Motor car depreciation account	4,000	
		Disposal account		4,000
		Partner A - current account	600	
		Disposal account		600
		Profit and loss account	400	
		Disposal account		400
	(ii)	Suspense account	2,000	
		Purchase ledger control account		2,000
	(iii)	Sales ledger control account	300	
		Suspense account		300
	(iv)	Purchase ledger control account	50	
		Purchase returns account		50

(v)   Items (ii)-(iv) assume that the control accounts form part of the double-entry system. Hence, the sales and purchase ledger accounts are simply memoranda accounts and no journal entries are therefore required.

			Dr	Cr
	(vi)	Motor vans account	231	
		Cash account	123	
		Suspense account		354
	(vii)	Carriage inwards	400	
		Carriage outwards	450	
		Suspense account		850

(b)   The goodwill of the partnership, up to the point when a new partner is introduced, has been created by the old partners. These partners should, in the event of any partnership sale, benefit from the goodwill they have created according to their profit-sharing ratio. It is, therefore, essential that on the eve of any partnership change, the goodwill (and other assets) of the partnership be revalued and the profit on revaluation be allocated to existing partners in their existing profit-sharing ratio. The new partner may be required to buy a share of the goodwill created by the old partners as a requirement of entering the partnership. The amount paid in by the new partner should be credited to the accounts of the old partners and should not be credited to the capital account of the new partner.

8.4   **Timmy and Lucy**

(a)

Capital accounts

	Timmy £	Lucy £	Charlie £		Timmy £	Lucy £	Charlie £
Revaluation	8,400	8,400	4,200	Balances b/d (1.1.X3)	30,000	40,000	
Balances c/d (1.1.X3)	32,100	42,100	15,800	Cash			20,000
				Revaluation	10,500	10,500	
	40,500	50,500	20,000		40,500	50,500	20,000
Revaluation	1,100	1,100	550	Balances b/d (1.1.X3)	32,100	42,100	15,800
Balances c/d (31.12.X3)	31,000	41,000	15,250				
	32,100	42,100	15,800		32,100	42,100	15,800
				Balances b/d (1.1.X4)	31,000	41,000	15,250

(b)

Appropriation account for the year ended 31 December 19X3

		£	£
Operating profit			40,000
Less: Interest on capital			
	Timmy	3,210	
	Lucy	4,210	
	Charlie	1,580	
			9,000
			31,000
Profit share			
	Timmy	12,400	
	Lucy	12,400	
	Charlie	6,200	
			31,000

(c)

Current accounts

	Timmy £	Lucy £	Charlie £		Timmy £	Lucy £	Charlie £
Balances b/d (1.1.X3)		4,000		Balances b/d (1.1.X3)	3,000		
Drawings	4,000	4,000	4,000	Interest	3,210	4,210	1,580
				Profit share	12,400	12,400	6,200
Balances c/d (31.12.X3)	14,610	8,610	3,780				
	18,610	16,610	7,780		18,610	16,610	7,780
				Balances b/d (1.1.X4)	14,610	8,610	3,780

(d)

Balance sheet as at 31 December 19X3

		£	£
Fixed assets			
Goodwill			10,000
Land			12,000
Buildings			20,000
Machinery			11,000
			53,000
Net current assets (see (e), below)			61,250
			£114,250
Capital accounts:	Timmy	31,000	
	Lucy	41,000	
	Charlie	15,250	87,250
Current accounts:	Timmy	14,610	
	Lucy	8,610	
	Charlie	3,780	27,000
			£114,250

(e)

Summary of net current asset movements during the year
ended 31 December 19X3

		£
Net current assets at 1 January 19X3		10,000
Add:	Cash introduced by Charlie	20,000
	Net profit	40,000
	Expenses not affecting net current assets (depreciation)	3,250
		73,250
Less:	Partners' drawings	12,000
Net current assets at 31 December 19X3		£61,250

19 ACCOUNTING FOR LIMITED COMPANIES

INTRODUCTION AND LEARNING OBJECTIVES

This chapter provides an introduction to limited liability companies and the accounting procedures associated with this form of business organisation. A limited company is a separate legal person which in many ways has the same sort of legal rights and obligations as a human being. This is probably the most important feature of a company, and most other features of companies arise from it. The owners of the company are the shareholders, each of whom owns a number of equally sized slices of the company's capital. These slices are known as shares. The shareholders of limited companies have limited liability. This means that shareholders cannot normally be required to contribute more capital than they have already done or have promised to do. This limited liability is an important distinction between a company on the one hand, and sole traders and partners on the other.

Forming a company is a fairly straightforward and cheap affair. There are two types of company, which have slightly different legal rules surrounding them. A public limited company (plc) tends to be one of the larger companies with shares fairly widely spread between different shareholders. A private limited company (Ltd) is likely to be a small, perhaps family company, with relatively few shareholders. All companies have an obligation to prepare and make public a set of annual accounts. These accounts must, both in form and content, provide information prescribed by law.

When you have studied this chapter you should be able to do the following:

*   Describe the nature of a limited company

*   Explain the rights and responsibilities of shareholders

*   Distinguish between public limited companies and private limited companies

*   Distinguish between ordinary shares and preference shares

*   Explain the different types of reserves

*   Discuss liabilities, provisions and reserves

*   List the statutory books which a company must keep.

1   THE NATURE OF A LIMITED COMPANY

1.1   Introduction

Limited companies play an important role within the private sector of the UK economy. Indeed, for most industries within the private sector, limited companies represent the dominant form of business organisation. Those businesses which are not limited liability companies tend to be small in size or provide highly specialised professional services, such as firms of accountants or solicitors.

A limited company is, in essence, an artificial person which has been created by law. The fact that a limited company has a separate legal personality means that it can sue (or be sued) in its own name and can enter into legally enforceable contracts in its own name. This contrasts with the position of sole proprietorships and partnerships which do not have separate legal identities from that of their owners and, therefore, cannot take legal action in their own names.

The nature of limited companies makes the **business entity convention** in accounting easy to apply. Because of its separate legal status the boundaries of this form of business organisation can often be drawn more clearly than for sole proprietorships and partnerships. However, it should be emphasised that the business entity convention applies to all forms of business organisation, whether a limited company or not. Separate legal status means that a company may have a perpetual life. It will not be affected by changes in its membership through death, retirement or any other reason.

1.2   Share capital and shareholders

The capital of a limited company may be contributed by a number of people or organisations. The capital is divided into units of equal size which are referred to as **shares**. The purchase of a share entitles the holder to receive distributions from profits and distributions of a share of capital under certain circumstances, for example if the company is eventually wound up.

Under UK law, shares must be assigned a nominal or par value. This can be of any denomination. The nominal value will not necessarily, or even normally, reflect the market value of the share, which is determined by the earnings and growth prospects of the company. Changes in the market value of shares are likely to be of direct concern to investors who hold the shares but not necessarily to the company, which may have received funds from the issue of the shares some time earlier. The company will not record changes in the value of its shares. However, the current market value of shares is important to a company when it is considering issuing further shares to raise funds.

1.3   Activity

It has been stated that limited companies must assign a nominal or par value to their shares and this can be of any denomination.

What factors may influence a company in its choice of a suitable nominal value for its shares?

1.4   Activity solution

The company may issue shares with the aim of attracting the interest of a particular investor group. For example, the company may identify small shareholders as the most likely investor group. It may therefore decide to issue shares of a small denomination.

Widespread share ownership The company may wish to encourage widespread ownership of its shares. This may be to prevent a small group of investors from gaining effective control over the company. It may, however, be for commercial reasons. A retail chain, for example, may wish to sell its shares to existing and potential customers in order to strengthen customer loyalty. In certain cases widespread share ownership may be encouraged for political reasons. In the 'privatisation' of many government-owned businesses it has been an objective to appeal to a wide range of investors. Where widespread share ownership is an objective the company may decide to issue shares of a small denomination in order to appeal to small investors.

Administrative convenience Where shares of a company will be held by a few investors, such as large financial institutions, and the amount of each shareholding is large, it may be administratively convenient to issue shares of a large denomination.

Custom and practice The issue of shares of certain denominations such as £1, appears to be a very common occurrence. A new company, when selecting an appropriate denomination for its shares, may be influenced by the denomination of shares which other companies have issued.

1.5   Delegation of day-to-day running of a company

For practical reasons, shareholders do not usually participate in the day-to-day management of the company. The shareholders who, in effect, own the company and exercise ultimate control over it, will delegate the day-to-day running of the company to a board of directors. Members of the board of directors are elected by the shareholders and will run the business on behalf of the shareholders. The directors may themselves be shareholders in the company. If the performance of the directors is considered to be inadequate shareholders can elect to remove them from office.

1.6 Limited liability

It was mentioned above that a limited company is a separate legal person and like a human person it is fully liable for all debts incurred. Where a company becomes insolvent, that is the assets owned are worth less than the financial obligations, the liability of the company, like that of a human person, is restricted to the assets owned. This means that shareholders are not obliged to introduce funds to pay off the debts of the company beyond the amount of share capital they have purchased or pledged. The term **limited liability**, therefore, refers to the position of the shareholder rather than the company, which is fully liable for debts incurred.

1.7 Formation of a limited company

To form a limited company a minimum of two persons must make an application to the Registrar of Companies (Department of Trade and Industry). The application must be accompanied by certain documents, the most important of which are the Memorandum and Articles of Association. The **Memorandum of Association** defines the company's relationship with the outside world. The Memorandum consists of five main clauses. These are:

- The *name* of the company. The name chosen by a public company must, unless there are exceptional circumstances, end with the words 'public limited company' (plc) and the name chosen by a private limited company must end with the word 'limited' (Ltd). (The distinction between each type of company is discussed below.)

- *Location* of the registered office.

- *Objects* for which the company was formed. Companies are only permitted to engage in activities which are set out under this clause. In practice, this means the clause will be drafted in order to maintain flexibility of operations.

- The *declaration* that the liability of the members is limited.

- *Share capital.* This clause sets out the maximum amount of share capital the company is authorised to issue and the way in which the share capital is divided. A company need not issue all of the share capital it is authorised to issue.

The **Articles of Association** set out the internal rules by which the company is governed. The articles, which are subordinate to the Memorandum, set out how the company will be administered and deal with such matters as directors' duties, voting rights of shareholders, payment of dividends and the raising of capital.

When a company is registered, the Memorandum and Articles of Association become public documents. The documents are kept by the Registrar of Companies and are available for inspection by any member of the public for a small fee.

2 PUBLIC AND PRIVATE LIMITED COMPANIES

2.1 Introduction

UK limited companies may be divided into two types – public companies and private companies. A **public limited company** must state in its Memorandum of Association that it is such and must end its name with the words public limited company (or plc). It must have a share capital of at least £50,000 and must have a minimum of two directors and two members (who can be the same people).

A **private limited company** is a company which does not qualify as a public limited company and it must end its name with the word limited (Ltd). An important distinction between the two types of company is that a public company can make an offer to the general public of its shares and debentures (loans) whereas a private company cannot. In addition, private companies may impose restrictions on their shareholders about the transfer of shares to third parties. They also have less onerous reporting requirements.

In the UK, private limited companies far outnumber public limited companies. However, private limited companies tend to be much smaller, largely due to their inability to offer shares to the general public. It is quite common for private limited companies to be family controlled. Many public limited companies obtain a listing on a recognised stock exchange. This enables shares in the company to be traded through the exchange. By bringing together buyers and sellers in this way, the marketability of the company's shares is enhanced. From the company's viewpoint this can facilitate the raising of finance. Private limited companies cannot obtain a stock exchange listing.

2.2 Activity

Three major forms of business organisation have so far been discussed in this book, namely the sole proprietorship, the partnership and the limited company.

Compare each form of business organisation under the following headings:

1   Legal status

2   Duration of life

3   Ownership risk

4   Transferability of interest

5   Number of owners

6   Management.

2.3 Activity solution

Legal status A limited company is a separate legal entity which is independent of its members. Sole proprietorships and partnerships are not separate legal entities.

Duration of life As a limited company is independent of its members it can have a perpetual existence. This does not occur with sole proprietorships and partnerships.

Ownership risk In the case of a limited company a member's liability is restricted to the fully paid value of the shares subscribed. In the case of a partnership, all partners (except limited partners) are fully liable for the debts of a partnership. Similarly the owner of a sole proprietorship business is fully liable for the debts of the business.

Transferability of interest A shareholder of a limited liability company can sell his/her interest to another person subject to any conditions set out in the Articles of Association. A partner may only sell his/her partnership interest by agreement with the other partners. A sole proprietor can sell his/her interest without having to seek agreement from others.

Number of owners A limited company must have a minimum of two members and there is no maximum. A partnership has a minimum of two and a maximum of twenty members. However, partnerships made up of members of certain professional bodies such as solicitors and accountants have no maximum membership. A sole proprietorship, by definition, has one owner.

Management Members of a limited company will usually delegate responsibility for running the company to a Board of Directors. The members of the board may or may not be shareholders in the company. It is less usual for partners (except limited partners) or sole proprietors to delegate responsibility for running the business to others.

2.4 Issuing share capital

A company must state in its Memorandum of Association its **authorised share capital**, that is the maximum amount of share capital the company is permitted to issue. The authorised share capital may be increased with the agreement of shareholders and subject to certain procedures being completed. The **issued share capital** represents that proportion of the authorised share capital which has been taken up by shareholders.

Shares may be paid for on the date of issue or by instalments. Where shares are purchased by instalments they are referred to as **partly paid** until payment of the final instalment. A company may decide to issue shares by instalments where it does not require all of the funds from the issue at the outset or where it wishes to enhance the marketability of the shares. An investor purchasing a share by instalments must pay each instalment at the due date. Failure to do so will make the shares liable to forfeiture. Once the final payment is made the shareholder has no further financial obligation to the company. **Called-up share capital** is the amount which the company has called to be paid and is an expression used in the context of shares paid by instalments. **Paid-up share capital** refers to the amount of share capital for which the called cash has actually been received.

Although shares are assigned a nominal or par value it is common for companies to issue shares at a price in excess of their nominal value. The difference between the value at which shares are issued and the nominal value is referred to as the **share premium**.

The bookkeeping for a share issue is very straightforward and it closely resembles the introduction of new capital by a sole trader. This is not surprising because, in essence, it is the same thing. The only real difference occurs where shares are issued at a value above their par value, because share premium will be involved; this concept is unknown in the accounts of sole traders (and partnerships).

Example

A limited company issues 100,000 ordinary shares of £1 each at an issue price of £1.35 per share. All of the cash is payable immediately.

The relevant entries will be (in journal form):

	Dr £000	Cr £000
Cash at bank account	135	
Share capital account		100
Share premium account		35

2.5 Types of share capital

There are two major classes of share capital which a limited company may issue:

- ordinary shares (also known as equity shares)
- preference shares.

The basic difference between each class of share is related to prospective risks and returns.

(a) Ordinary shares

These are designed for the investor who is prepared to take a relatively high level of risk in order to obtain high returns. Ordinary shareholders are entitled to receive returns only after all other claims have been satisfied. Thus expenses (including loan interest) and returns to preference shareholders must be met out of profits first. Only if there is residual profit after these prior claims will ordinary shareholders receive a return. This can mean that in poor years ordinary shareholders will not receive a return, while in good years they may benefit from very high returns.

Where a residue of profits occurs, ordinary shareholders may receive a cash return out of these profits which is referred to as a **dividend**. The amount of any dividend is proposed by the directors of the company. The ordinary shareholders cannot demand that the dividend be increased above the level recommended by the directors but can request that the dividend be reduced. The dividend proposed by the directors is sometimes expressed as a percentage of the nominal value of the shares. Thus, if a dividend of 20% were declared on ordinary shares with a nominal value of £1, it would mean the ordinary shareholders would receive 20p for each share held. It is however, becoming increasingly common to express dividends in terms of pence per share.

It may be prudent for directors to decide on the amount of any dividend at the end of the year when profits for the period are known. However, the directors have the power to make interim dividends at some point during the year, if they believe the profits are sufficient to justify this. The payment of interim dividends is often in addition to any final dividend proposed at the year end.

Not all of the residual profits available to ordinary shareholders need be distributed to them in the form of dividends. The directors may decide to plough back profits in order to finance future ventures. However, any profits reinvested remain the property of the ordinary shareholders. If profits are reinvested in profitable ventures this will increase the earning potential of the company and this, in turn, should increase the market value of the ordinary shares held. In assessing returns to shareholders it is therefore necessary to consider both cash returns from dividends and any appreciation in share values arising from expectations concerning earnings and growth prospects.

Ordinary shares will normally be given the **voting rights** within the company and therefore have effective control over the company's activities. Ordinary shares are each given equal rights in relation to dividend payments and capital distributions in the event of the company being wound up. Ordinary shares are also normally given equal voting rights and, therefore, voting power will be determined by the number of ordinary shares held.

(b)   Preference shares

These are designed for the investor who does not wish to take the degree of risk associated with ordinary shares and is prepared to accept the prospect of lower, more secure, returns. Preference shares entitle the holder to a fixed rate of dividend payable before any ordinary dividend is paid. The fixed rate of dividend is expressed as a percentage of the nominal value of the share. Dividends can only be paid to preference shareholders if there are sufficient profits to cover the proposed dividends.

Preference shares are not usually given voting rights within the company. In the event of the company being wound up, preference shares may or may not rank before the ordinary shareholders for capital repayment. The Articles of Association will specify voting rights (if any) and the rankings of shareholders on winding up.

Preference shares may be cumulative or non-cumulative. **Cumulative preference shares** confer on the holders the right to any arrears of dividends out of future profits before any dividend is payable to ordinary shareholders. **Non-cumulative shares** do not confer such rights and, therefore, if profits are insufficient to pay a dividend there is no responsibility to carry forward the arrears.

Preference shares have fallen from popularity in recent years and no longer represent a major source of finance to UK companies. This is probably because preference shares have tax disadvantages compared with borrowing, which is an obvious alternative for most companies.

3   RESERVES

3.1   Introduction

Reserves are gains or profits which accrue to the ordinary shareholders and have been retained within the company. They represent the ordinary shareholders' interests in the company over and above the nominal value of the ordinary share capital. Reserves may be divided into two main categories:

*   revenue reserves
*   capital reserves.

3.2   Revenue reserves

These represent undistributed trading profits. They can be applied by the directors to pay dividends, or in any other way considered appropriate. Revenue reserves are often shown under various headings, the most common being the profit and loss account (or unappropriated profit) and **general reserve**. There is no legal distinction between the different types of revenue reserves found in practice. The allocation of trading profits to a particular revenue reserve is entirely at the discretion of the directors of the company.

3.3 Capital reserves

These represent profits which are not associated with the normal course of trading. The three most common forms of capital reserve are:

(a) **Share premium account**

This arises as a result of the sale of shares in the company. Where shares are issued at a price in excess of their nominal value, a premium will occur. Thus, if 100,000 ordinary shares of £1 nominal value were issued at a price of £2.50 each, the premium per share would be £2.50 less £1 = £1.50 per share. When recording the share issue the nominal value of the shares (£100,000) would be transferred to the share capital account and the total share premium (£150,000) would be transferred to the share premium account. The share premium account is regarded as part of the permanent capital of the company. There are restrictions on how this reserve may be used and it cannot be regarded as available for distribution.

(b) **Revaluation reserve**

This arises as a result of asset revaluation. Any increase in the value assigned to an asset will result in a corresponding increase in capital. The increase in capital will be shown in a revaluation reserve. The balance on the revaluation reserve account represents unrealised profit and cannot be used for dividend distribution.

(c) **Capital redemption reserve**

This arises as a result of a company redeeming or purchasing its shares. Redeemable shares (which may be ordinary or preference shares) are those where the company has the power to repay shareholders and to cancel the shares. Only those shares described on issue as being redeemable may be redeemed. The price at which the shares are to be redeemed will be specified at the time of issue. In addition to this a company may purchase its own shares from shareholders willing to sell them.

In order to protect creditors, there are strict rules concerning the redemption and purchase of shares. A public limited company may only redeem or purchase its shares if it does not reduce its total effective share capital. This means that any shares redeemed or purchased must be replaced by:

- a further issue of shares equal to the nominal value of the shares redeemed or purchased
- a transfer from reserves available for distribution (see below), to a capital redemption reserve, of an amount equal to the nominal value of the shares redeemed or purchased. The capital redemption reserve cannot be used to distribute dividends.

Either one of these two methods, or a combination of the two, can be used to replace share capital lost as a result of a redemption or purchase.

Similar rules apply to private limited companies. However, in certain circumstances private companies may redeem shares out of capital.

3.4 Activity

Why might a limited company wish to issue redeemable shares?

3.5 Activity solution

A new or expanding company may require finance in order to purchase assets. To raise the cash required the company may decide to issue redeemable shares. The issue of this type of share enables the company to replace share capital by retained profits at some future date. The company is not therefore encumbered by a commitment to redeemable shareholders for an indefinite period.

3.6 Legal requirements

The law does not require that companies distinguish between capital and revenue reserves in their accounts. However, separate disclosure of the share premium account and capital redemption reserve is required. Other reserves can be classified in a manner appropriate to the company's activities. It is useful to distinguish between those reserves which are available for distribution and those which are not. Generally speaking, revenue reserves are available for distribution and capital reserves are not.

It is important to appreciate that reserves, like annual profit, need not be represented by an equivalent amount of cash. Thus the fact that a company has accumulated considerable amounts of reserves does not necessarily imply that the company has similar amounts of liquid funds available. Reserves, like other forms of capital, simply reflect the owners' claim on assets owned by the company. The type of assets owned will be determined by management policy.

4 DIVIDENDS

4.1 Introduction

Dividends represent the means by which profits are distributed to shareholders. It is important to be aware, however, which profits are regarded as being available for dividend. The law has established the general principle that dividends can only be distributed out of accumulated realised profits. This will include trading profits plus any profits resulting from the sale of fixed assets. Any accumulated realised losses over the years will be deducted from accumulated profits in order to derive the amount available for distribution. Surpluses arising on share issue (share premiums), the revaluation of fixed assets and the capital redemption reserve are not available for dividend distribution.

4.2 Activity

Simat Engineering Ltd commenced operations on 1 January 19X6. For the first four years the following results were achieved.

Year ended 31 December	Trading profit (loss) £	Profit (loss) on sale of fixed asset £	Profit on revaluation of land £
19X6	(100,000)		
19X7	80,000		
19X8	90,000	30,000	
19X9	60,000	(10,000)	40,000

State, for each year, the maximum dividend the company could pay (assuming a maximum dividend is paid whenever possible)

4.3 Activity solution

Maximum ordinary share dividend for each year:

Year ended 31 December	
19X6	Nil (accumulated loss £100,000)
19X7	Nil (accumulated loss £20,000)
19X8	£100,000 (£90,000 + £30,000 − £20,000)
19X9	£50,000 (£60,000 − £10,000)

4.4 **Practical constants**

It is common for companies to make dividend distributions which fall well below the maximum permitted by law. This may be due to a variety of influences, the most important of which are:

Liquidity

The fact that a company has made profits does not necessarily mean the company has sufficient liquid funds available to pay a dividend. Although a company may be able to borrow in order to finance a dividend payment this may not be regarded as financially prudent.

Retained profits

Ploughing back profits into the business represents an important source of funds to many companies. This may be a particularly important source of finance to new, or high-risk, ventures which may not have ready access to alternative sources of finance.

Taxation

It was mentioned above that returns to shareholders may take the form of cash dividends or an appreciation in share values. Some companies may attract investors who may prefer returns in the form of capital gains rather than cash dividends. This is because there may be certain tax advantages in receiving returns in this form.

5 **LOANS AND DEBENTURES**

5.1 **Introduction**

It is common for companies to borrow funds on a long-term or even perpetual basis. Any amounts borrowed must fall within the limits of the company's borrowing powers which are set out in the Articles of Association. The amounts raised in the form of long-term loans are sometimes referred to as loan capital. The amounts borrowed can be raised by approaching a bank, or other financial institution, by an arrangement with individuals or organisations, or by an offer to the public in the case of public limited companies.

One important form of long-term loan normally associated with limited companies is the **debenture**. These are loans which are usually divided into units (rather like shares) in order to attract a wider range of investors. The debenture issue is usually governed by a trust deed which appoints trustees to act in the interests of the debenture holders and which sets out the rate of interest payable, the date of redemption (if applicable) and the security given by the borrowing company for the loan.

Debenture holders, or other forms of lenders, are often offered **security** for the amount owed in the form of a fixed charge on specific assets owned by the company. From the lenders' point of view, an attractive form of security is freehold land. If a company defaults on interest or capital repayments, the trustees appointed under the debenture deed would be entitled to sell the assets on which the debentures have been secured and use the money to repay any amounts owing to the debenture holders. If there is a surplus after repayment this could be given to the company.

Sometimes debenture holders or other lenders are offered **security** in the form of a floating charge on a group of assets, for example, stock in trade owned by the company. From the borrowing company's viewpoint, this has the advantage that the company retains the right to trade in the assets over which the floating charge 'hovers'. The floating charge will 'crystallise' on the group of assets in existence at the time of default of interest or capital repayments, should the event arise.

Some debentures or loans may be **unsecured**. However, this is not a common occurrence. Investors may only be prepared to offer unsecured loans to very financially sound companies. It is imperative that companies with loan capital meet interest and capital payments at the due dates, as the consequences of not doing so could be very serious indeed. Whereas failure to make dividend payments to shareholders may lead to some embarrassment, failure to meet interest payments to lenders could jeopardise the future of the company.

Debenture interest is usually a fixed amount which is expressed as a percentage of nominal value. It represents a business expense which is deducted, along with other business expenses, in arriving at the net profit of the company. The issue of debentures and other forms of loan capital may be attractive to companies because interest payments are allowable against profits for taxation purposes, whereas dividend payments to shareholders are not.

5.2   Activity

Compare and contrast each of the following forms of long-term finance under the headings set out below:

Debentures   Preference shares   Ordinary shares

Voting rights

Type of cash return to holder

Security on investment

Member/creditor

Tax relief on interest/dividend payment

5.3   Activity solution

Voting rights Debentures do not have voting rights in the company. Preference shareholders do not usually have voting rights but may be given such rights if preference dividends are in arrears. Ordinary shareholders usually have voting rights although some companies issue two classes of ordinary share – non-voting and voting shares.

Types of return to holder Debenture holders receive interest on their investment in the company. This must be paid whether or not the company is earning profits. Preference shareholders and ordinary shareholders may receive a dividend on their investment provided that there are sufficient profits available for distribution and that both directors and shareholders consider it prudent.

Security on investment It is usual for debenture holders to be offered some form of security on their investment. This may take the form of a fixed or floating charge. Preference shareholders and ordinary shareholders do not receive security on their investment.

Member/creditor Debenture holders are creditors of the company whereas preference shareholders and ordinary shareholders are members of the company. In the event of the company being wound up, creditors have priority claims over the assets of the company over shareholders.

Tax relief on interest/dividend payment Interest payable on debentures represents a charge against profits and is an allowable business expense in arriving at taxable profits. Dividends (both preference and ordinary) represent an appropriation of profit and are not allowable against tax.

5.4   Capital gearing (leverage)

Capital gearing (or leverage) refers to the extent to which fixed return capital (that is, preference shares and loan capitals) is employed to provide long-term finance for the company. Gearing can be measured by relating the fixed return capital to the total long-term capital of the business. A ratio which expresses this relationship is:

$$\text{Gearing ratio} = \frac{\text{Fixed return capital}}{\text{Total long-term capital}} \times 100\%$$

(that is, ordinary share capital plus reserves plus fixed return capital)

The higher the ratio (that is, the higher the percentage of fixed return capital to total long-term capital) the higher the gearing of a company.

Gearing is important because it is possible to employ fixed interest capital as a means of magnifying returns to ordinary shareholders. This is possible provided the returns generated from the used of fixed return capital exceed the fixed payments incurred.

To illustrate the effect of capital gearing it may be useful to consider a simple example.

Example

Helena Products plc has the following long-term capital structure:

	£m
£1 ordinary shares	4
10% debentures	6
	10

For the three-year period ended 31 December 19X8 net profits (before debenture interest) were as follows:

Year ended 31 December	Net profit (before debenture interest)
	£m
19X6	1.2
19X7	2.4
19X8	0.8

In this case, the gearing ratio of the company is 60% (6/10 × 100%). This would normally be regarded as high. To show the gearing effect it is necessary to calculate the returns to ordinary shareholders. The returns (ignoring taxation) would be as follows:

Year to 31 December

	19X6	19X7	19X8
	£m	£m	£m
Net profit (before debenture interest)	1.2	2.4	0.8
less: Debenture interest	0.6	0.6	0.6
Available to ordinary shareholders	0.6	1.8	0.2
Earnings per share	£0.15	£0.45	£0.05

$$\text{Earnings per share} = \frac{\text{Amounts available to ordinary shareholders}}{\text{No of ordinary shares}}$$

The calculations above show that although profits doubled in the second year, the returns to ordinary shareholders trebled. The gearing effect, however, can work in both directions. Thus, in the third year, when profits fall to one-third of the second-year level the returns to ordinary shareholders fall to one-ninth of the second-year returns.

If the company had no capital gearing (no fixed return capital) and the company had 10 million £1 ordinary shares as its long-term finance, the returns to shareholders would follow a different pattern from that above.

Year to 31 December

	19X6	19X7	19X8
	£m	£m	£m
Net profit (no interest payable)	1.2	2.4	0.8
Earnings per share	0.12	0.24	0.08

It can be seen that the returns to shareholders are not subject to such wide fluctuations. Fluctuations in returns are in line with fluctuations in profits.

While capital gearing increases the prospective returns to ordinary shareholders it also increases the prospective risks. Profits must be sufficiently high to cover interest payments and therefore dividends before the ordinary shareholders receive a return. From the company's viewpoint it is important to remember that by taking on loans it is committed to paying interest whatever the fortunes of the business.

5.5   Activity

Silo plc has been formed to trade as a food retailer. It is currently considering three possible long-term capital structures. These are as follows:

	Capital structure		
	1	**2**	**3**
	£m	**£m**	**£m**
£1 ordinary shares	4	10	20
10% £1 preference shares	6	4	–
12% debentures	10	6	–
	20	20	20

Profits (before interest) for the next three years are estimated as follows:

Year 1	£3m
2	£5m
3	£1.8m

Taxation on profits is to be ignored.

(a)   Calculate the gearing ratio for each financing option

(b)   Calculate the earnings per share for each of the three years assuming

   (a)   option 1
   (b)   option 2, and
   (c)   option 3 is chosen.

(c)   Which of the three financing options would you choose and why?

5.6   Activity solution

Silo plc

(a)   **Gearing ratio**

	Option		
	1	**2**	**3**
	80%	50%	0%

Gearing ratio
(Gearing ratio = fixed return capital/total long term capital × 100%)

(b)   **Earnings per share**

	Option		
	1	**2**	**3**
	£m	**£m**	**£m**
Year 1 – Profit before debenture interest	3.00	3.00	3.00
Less: Debenture interest	1.20	0.72	–
	1.80	2.28	3.00
Less: Preference dividend	0.60	0.40	–
Available to ordinary shareholders	1.20	1.88	3.00
Earnings per ordinary share	£0.30	£0.19	£0.15

	£m	£m	£m
Year 2 – Profit before debenture interest	5.00	5.00	5.00
Less: Debenture interest	1.20	0.72	–
	3.80	4.28	5.00
Less: Preference dividend	0.60	0.40	–
Available to ordinary shareholders	3.20	3.88	5.00
Earnings per ordinary share	£0.80	£0.39	£0.25
Year 3 – Profit before debenture interest	1.80	1.80	1.80
Less: Debenture interest	1.20	0.72	–
	0.60	1.08	1.80
Less: Preference dividend	0.60	0.40	–
Available to ordinary shareholders	0.00	0.68	1.80
Earnings per ordinary share	£0.00	£0.07	£0.09

(c) **Option 1** represents a high level of gearing. The table in part 2 above indicates that this option produces the highest return in the first two years but the lowest in the third year. The effect of such high gearing is to magnify considerably profit fluctuations on amounts available to equity shareholders.

Option 3 represents a nil level of gearing. The table in part 2 above indicates that this option produces the lowest return in the first two years but the highest return in the third year when profits are at their lowest. In this case, fluctuations in earnings per share follow the same pattern as fluctuations in profit.

Option 2 represents a compromise between the two extremes discussed above. The table above indicates that this option produces the second highest return to ordinary shareholders in each of the three years. (In year 3 the returns are only slightly lower than those achieved under Option 3.)

The choice of option will be determined by investors' attitudes towards risk and judgements about the level and stability of profits over the longer term. On the basis of the information available, Option 2 has the advantage of reaping the benefits of gearing without undue risk to ordinary shareholders.

5.7 Liabilities, provisions and reserves

It is only too easy to confuse these three types of credit balance. The distinction is an important one.

A **liability** is an amount owed by the business which can be determined with substantial accuracy. This would include accrued expenses, as well as borrowings or an amount owed as a result of buying goods and services on credit.

A **provision** is an amount set aside or retained for the purpose of providing for any liability or loss, which is either likely or certain to be incurred, but where the amount is unclear. Thus provisions relate to uncertainties. Examples include depreciation provisions and doubtful debt provisions.

As we have already seen, a **reserve** is a gain or profit which accrues to the ordinary shareholders and has been retained within the company. Reserves represent the ordinary shareholders' interests in the company over and above the nominal value of the ordinary share capital.

6 THE ACCOUNTS OF LIMITED COMPANIES

6.1 Introduction

The basic principles employed in the preparation of accounts of sole traders and partnerships are also employed in the preparation of accounts of limited companies. However, some important differences exist which are considered below. It should be emphasised that it is the preparation of accounts for internal purposes which is the main concern of this section. The preparation of final accounts for publication is considered in Chapter 20.

6.2 Profit and loss account

This financial report will have the same format for limited companies as for sole proprietorships and partnerships. The content, in terms of revenue and expense items, will also be broadly the same. However, there are certain additional items of expense that may be found in the profit and loss account of limited companies. These are:

(a) **Directors' remuneration**

The directors are employees of the company and any remuneration paid to the directors for acting in that capacity is a business expense.

(b) **Debenture interest**

It has already been seen that debentures are a form of loan normally associated with limited companies. The interest payable is a business expense.

(c) **Audit fees**

The law requires that large limited companies have to appoint an independent firm of accountants to report whether the accounts show a true and fair view of the company's position and performance. Audit fees represent the professional charge made by the reporting accountants for performing this task.

6.3 Profit and loss appropriation account

This account shows how the profit, once calculated, is allocated. The first allocation of profit is usually to the payment of corporation tax. This is a tax levied on companies for profits made. The net profit after tax represents the amount available to shareholders in respect of that year. Some of this profit may be transferred to a revenue reserve (for instance, general reserve) and some may be distributed in the form of dividends. Any amounts not allocated in some way will remain on the profit and loss account and will be carried forward to the following year. Thus the balance on the profit and loss account is a revenue reserve.

If a vertical or narrative format for the financial statements is adopted the following would be fairly typical of the profit and loss appropriation account:

	£	£
Net profit for the year		x
Less: Corporation tax		x
Net profit after tax		x
Add: Unappropriated profit brought forward		x
		x
Transfer to general reserve	x	
Preference dividend	x	
Ordinary dividend	x	x
Unappropriated profit carried forward		x

It is worth mentioning again that dividends for the year may be paid in two stages. An interim dividend can be proposed (and will usually be paid) at some time during the year. A final dividend may be proposed at the year end and paid some time after the year end. The distinction between dividends paid and dividends only proposed is sometimes made in the appropriation account.

The profit and loss appropriation account forms an integral part of the double-entry system. Hence allocations shown in the appropriation account must also be shown in another part of the accounts.

Corporation tax will also be shown in a corporation tax payable account. At the year end the amount payable will appear as a creditor in the balance sheet.

Dividends will be shown in a dividends account. Separate dividend accounts will be opened for each class of share. Dividends proposed and not paid at the year end will be carried forward and will appear as a current liability in the balance sheet. Transfer to reserves will appear as an increase in the relevant reserve account.

Unappropriated profit carried forward will be the balance brought forward on the appropriation account at the beginning of the next year. The unappropriated profit carried forward is a revenue reserve and will appear with other reserves on the balance sheet at the year end.

An example of the ledger accounts for corporation tax and dividends is given a little later in this chapter.

6.4   Activity

Pavlo plc reports a net profit for the year ended 31 March 19X3 of £185,000. Corporation tax on these profits is estimated at £68,000. It has been decided to transfer £18,000 to a general reserve and £21,000 to a fixed asset replacement reserve. Unappropriated profits brought forward were £142,000.

Pavlo plc has 300,000 10% £1 preference shares and 400,000 £1 ordinary shares in issue. An interim dividend of 5% was paid to both preference and ordinary shareholders. It is proposed to pay a final dividend to both classes of shareholders totalling £21,000 between them.

Show the profit and loss appropriation account for the year ended 31 March 19X3.

6.5   Activity solution

Pavlo plc
Profit and loss appropriation account for the year ended 31 March 19X3

	£	£
Net profit for the year		185,000
Less: Corporation tax		68,000
Net profit after tax		117,000
Add: Unappropriated profit brought forward		142,000
		259,000
Transfer to general reserve	18,000	
Transfer to fixed asset replacement reserve	21,000	
Interim dividends paid:		
Preference	15,000	
Ordinary	20,000	
Final dividends proposed:		
Preference	15,000	
Ordinary	6,000	95,000
Unappropriated profit carried forward		£164,000

6.6   Balance sheet

The assets and liabilities of a limited company can be grouped in the same way as assets and liabilities in other forms of business organisation. However, current liabilities, that is amounts falling due within one year, can include amounts owing in respect of dividends and corporation tax which will not be found in sole trader and partnership accounts. Similarly, long-term liabilities (amounts falling due beyond one year) can include debentures which will not normally be found in sole proprietorship and partnership accounts.

The more complex capital structure of limited companies leads to the greatest area of difference between the accounts of this form of business organisation and others.

Capital will show the different types of share capital which have been issued at their nominal value.

Reserves will comprise a separate section. There will usually be separate disclosure of the share premium account, capital redemption reserve, and revaluation reserve, and the distributable revenue reserves. The revenue reserves may be further subdivided into such things as general reserve and unappropriated profit.

As an illustration, the final accounts of a limited company for internal reporting purposes are shown below.

Example

Helsim Ltd

Trading, profit and loss account and appropriation account
for the year ended 30 June 19X4

	£	£
Sales		840,000
Less: Cost of sales		
Opening stock	125,000	
Purchases	480,000	
	605,000	
Less: **Closing stock**	85,000	
Cost of sales		520,000
Gross profit		320,000
Less:		
Wages and salaries	78,000	
Directors remuneration	30,000	
Heat and light	18,000	
Rates	6,000	
Repairs and renewals	8,000	
Motor running expenses	20,000	
Insurance	4,000	
Printing and stationery	12,000	
Debenture interest	10,000	
Audit fees	4,000	
Depreciation	45,000	
		235,000
Net profit for the year		85,000
Less: Corporation tax		32,000
Net profit after tax		53,000
Add: Unappropriated profit brought forward		186,000
		239,000

Transfer to general reserve	12,000	
Preference dividend proposed	20,000	
Ordinary dividend proposed	15,000	47,000
Unappropriated profit carried forward		192,000

Helsim Ltd
Balance sheet at 30 June 19X4

Fixed assets	Cost £	Depreciation £	Net £
Freehold property	480,000	48,000	432,000
Motor vehicles	160,000	85,000	75,000
	640,000	133,000	507,000
Current assets			
Stocks		85,000	
Debtors		242,000	
Cash		186,000	
		513,000	
Current liabilities			
Trade creditors	124,000		
Corporation tax	32,000		
Proposed dividends	35,000		
Accrued expenses	4,000	195,000	
Net current assets			318,000
Total asset less current liabilities			825,000
Less: **Long-term liabilities**			
10% Debentures (secured)			100,000
			725,000
Issued share capital			
10% Preference shares of £1 per share			200,000
Ordinary shares of £0.50 per share			150,000
			350,000
Reserves			
Share premium account		100,000	
General reserve		83,000	
Profit and loss		192,000	
			375,000
Shareholders' funds			725,000

6.7 Ledger accounts for limited companies

It should be clear that essentially the same ledger accounts will be maintained for companies as are used by sole traders and partnerships. There are some which are peculiar to companies, however. Several of these are, in effect, created by entries which first appear in the appropriation account. Like the rest of the trading and profit and loss account, the appropriation account is an integral part of the double-entry system. This means that if we charge things to it (debit) we must also credit some account somewhere else in the system.

By way of illustration let us consider the corporation tax and ordinary dividend of Helsim Ltd for 19X4. When we debit the appropriation account with £32,000 and £15,000 for these two items respectively we must credit accounts with those names.

Corporation tax account

		£			£
			30/6/X4	P and L appropriation	32,000

Ordinary dividend account

		£			£
			30/6/X4	P and L appropriation	15,000

These two balances appear on the 30 June 19X4 balance sheet as current liabilities (see previous page).

Nine months following the end of the financial year, the corporation tax will be due for payment. Following this the corporation tax account will look like:

Corporation tax account

		£			£
31/3/X5	Cash at bank	32,000	30/6/X4	P and L appropriation	32,000

Sometimes the amount actually paid, which will be the result of discussion and negotiation with the Inland Revenue, will differ from the amount in the accounts. In these circumstances the balance on the corporation tax account, following the cash payment, will be taken into the following year's appropriation account. It is likely to be a relatively small amount.

A few months into the new financial year, the company will normally hold its annual general meeting of shareholders, at which they will usually agree to the directors' dividend proposal. Shortly following this (say on 30 September 19X4) the dividend will be paid (normally in cash). This will clear the balance on the account.

Ordinary dividend account

		£			£
30/9/X4	Cash at bank	15,000	30/6/X4	P and L appropriation	15,000

6.8   Activity

The Cirrus Company Ltd has the following balances on its books at 31 December 19X0.

	£	£
50p ordinary shares		20,000
6% preference shares of £1 each		14,000
Purchases	240,000	
Sales		310,000
Stock at 1 January 19X0	20,000	
Directors' fees	6,000	
Undistributed profit at 1 January 19X0		35,700
10% Debentures (19X4)		20,000
Debenture interest paid	1,000	
Discounts allowed	500	

Administrative expenses	18,400	
Sales staff salaries	18,500	
Selling and distribution expenses	4,000	
Heating and lighting	2,500	
Rent and rates	1,700	
Debtors	14,000	
Provision for doubtful debts at 1 January		300
Creditors		9,700
Land and buildings at cost	65,000	
Vans at cost less depreciation	19,800	
Cash in hand	400	
Bank balance		2,100
	411,800	411,800

The following information is also given:

1   The stock at 31 December 19X0 has been valued at £32,000. Further investigation reveals that this includes some items originally purchased for £3,000 which have been in stock for a long time. They need modifications, probably costing about £600, after which it is hoped they will be saleable for between £3,200 and £3,500. Other items, included in the total at their cost price of £5,000, have been sent to an agent and are still at his premises awaiting sale. It cost £200 for transport and insurance to get them to the agent's premises and this amount is included in the selling and distribution expenses.

2   The balance on the vans account (£19,800) is made up as follows:

	£
Vans at cost (as at 1 January 19X0)	30,000
Less: Provision for depreciation to 1 January 19X0	13,800
	16,200
Addition during the year	3,600
	19,800

Depreciation is provided at 25% per annum on the diminishing balance method. The addition during the year was invoiced as follows:

	£
Recommended retail price	3,000
Signwriting on van	450
Undersealing	62
Petrol	16
Number plates	12
Licence (to 31 December 19X0)	60
Addition during the year	3,600

3   The directors, having sought the advice of an independent valuer, wish to revalue the land and buildings at £80,000.

4   The directors wish to make a provision for doubtful debts of $2\frac{1}{2}$% of the balance of debtors at 31 December 19X0.

5   Rates prepaid at 31 December 19X0 amounted to £400, and sales staff salaries owing at that date were £443.

6   The directors have proposed an ordinary dividend of 5p per share, and the 6% preference dividend.

7   Ignore VAT.

(a) Explain carefully the reasons for the adjustments you have made in respect of items 1, 2 and 3 above.

(b) Prepare a trading and profit and loss account for the year ended 31 December 19X0, and a balance sheet as at that date.

(c) Briefly distinguish between your treatment of debenture interest and proposed dividends.

6.9 Activity solution

(a) (i) *Stock valuation.* Stocks are valued at the lower of cost and net realisable value. The most prudent assumption gives a net realisable value of £2,600 for the first items. 'Cost' includes the expense of bringing the product to its present location – so for the other items the cost is £5,200. The stock valuation is now £31,800 (£24,000 + £2,600 + £5,200). £200 is transferred to the trading account because it is now treated as part of the cost of the goods.

(ii) The company should capitalise (treat as an asset) only those costs which are of long-term benefit. Hence the petrol and licence costs (£76) will be expenses, leaving the asset value of the new van as £3,524.

	£
WDV at 1/1/19X0	16,200
Addition	3,524
	19,724
Depreciation at 25%	4,931
Balance at 31/12/19X0	£14,793

(iii) The revaluation of land and buildings does not amount to 'revenue (and thus profit) realisation', which requires both independent objective measurement and reasonable certainty of asset value. The increase will be treated as an unrealised profit, and become a **capital reserve**, a reserve not available for distribution by way of dividend.

(b)

Cirrus Company Ltd

Trading and profit and loss account
for the year ended 31 December 19X0

	£	£
Sales		310,000
Stock on 1 January	20,000	
Purchases	240,000	
Transport cost	200	
	260,200	
Less: Stock at 31 December	31,800	
		228,400
Gross profit		81,600
Less: Other expenses		
Directors' fees	6,000	
Administration expenses	18,400	
Rent and rates	1,300	
Heating and lighting	2,500	
Salesperson's salaries	18,943	
Selling and distribution expenses	3,876	
Depreciation on vans	4,931	

Discounts allowed	500	
Provision for doubtful debts	50	
Debenture interest	2,000	
		58,500
Net profit		23,100
Balance brought forward		35,700
Available for appropriation		58,800
Dividends proposed:		
Ordinary: 5p per share	2,000	
Preference: 6%	840	2,840
Balance of retained profits 31 December 19X0		£55,960

Balance sheet as at 31 December 19X0

	£	£	£
Fixed assets			
Land and buildings at valuation			80,000
Vans at cost less depreciation			14,793
			94,793
Current assets			
Stock		31,800	
Debtors less provision		13,650	
Prepayments		400	
Cash in hand		400	
		46,250	
Less: **Current liabilities**			
Creditors	9,700		
Accruals	1,443		
Bank overdraft	2,100		
Dividends proposed	2,840		
		16,083	
Net current assets			30,167
			124,960
Long-term liabilities			
10% Debentures			20,000
			£104,960
Issued share capital			
50p ordinary shares			20,000
6% £1 Preference shares			14,000
			34,000
Reserves			
Revaluation reserves		15,000	
Undistributed profit		55,960	
			70,960
			£104,960

Notes

		£
1	Provision for doubtful debts – at 2.5%	350
	Already provided	300
	Additional provision	£50
2	Selling Expenses	4,000
	Less: Transfer to Trading account	200
		3,800
	Add: Petrol and licence	76
		£3,876

(c) Debenture holders are creditors – therefore the interest is an expense charged against profit (£1,000 + £1,000 accrued). Shareholders – ordinary and preference – are members of the company, so dividends are an appropriation of profit.

6.10 Bonus shares

The directors of a company may decide to make a **bonus issue** of shares (sometimes referred to as a **capitalisation** or **scrip issue** of shares). This involves issuing new shares to shareholders in proportion to their existing shareholdings. The issue of shares is made possible by transferring from reserves an amount equivalent to the nominal value of the shares issued.

Example

Stidwell Enterprises plc has the following capital structure:

	£m
£1 ordinary shares	10
Revenue reserves	20
	30

The directors decide to make a 1 for 2 bonus issue of shares. A 1 for 2 issue means that one new share will be issued to a shareholder for every two shares held. Thus, an issue of five million new ordinary shares will be made.

In order to increase the share capital a transfer from revenue reserves will be made. The double entry is:

Debit	Revenue reserve account
Credit	Share capital account
	with the amount of the bonus issue

After the bonus issue the capital structure will be:

	£m
£1 ordinary shares	15
Revenue reserves	15
	30

It is important to recognise that a bonus issue does not involve a receipt of cash by the company from shareholders. The shares are distributed to existing shareholders without any financial consideration on their part.

A bonus issue can be effected by a transfer from either capital or revenue reserves. The transfer of revenue reserves to share capital account has the effect of making a larger proportion of the capital base of the company permanent, and, therefore, provides greater protection to creditors. The receipt of bonus shares does not imply a 'windfall' gain by shareholders. The issue of bonus shares does not increase the assets or earning potential of the company. As a result, the total value of the company and, therefore, the total value of shares held by an investor in that company should remain the same after the issue.

Example

Pluto plc has 12 million £1 ordinary shares with a market value of £5 each. The directors have decided to make a 1 for 4 bonus issue. We shall show the effect of the bonus issue for an investor holding 100 shares in the company.

In this case the total market value of the shares before the bonus issue is £60 million (12 million at £5 each). After the bonus issue, the total market value should remain unchanged. However, a 1 for 4 bonus issue will result in a total of 15 million ordinary shares in issue. This means that the market value of each share will be £4 (£60m/15m).

An investor holding 100 ordinary shares prior to the issue would experience the following change:

Shareholding prior to bond issue 100 at £5 each	£500
Shareholding after bonus issue 125 at £4 each	£500

The investor would therefore be no better off as a result of the issue.

In practice, the value of a share following a bonus issue may settle at a figure above the value which, in theory, it should settle at. This would mean that the total value of shares held in the company would increase following the bonus issue. There are a number of reasons why this situation may arise.

A bonus issue of shares is sometimes offered to shareholders as an alternative to a dividend. The shareholder is, therefore, given a choice between increasing the holding in the company or receiving a cash return. Those shareholders who elect to receive shares rather than cash will increase the value of their holdings at the expense of those who elected to receive a cash dividend.

6.11 Rights issues

A rights issue is a form of share issue which offers existing shareholders the right to purchase new shares in the company in proportion to their existing shareholdings. It is different from a bonus issue as it results in a receipt of cash from shareholders for the new shares issued. The price of the new shares is often set at a figure below the current market value. Existing shareholders who do not wish to take advantage of the rights offer may decide to sell their rights to other investors wishing to take advantage of the discounted price of the new issue. Rights issues represent a relatively cheap method of issuing new shares. No costs of advertising are incurred and administrative costs are relatively low. As rights are issued in proportion to existing shareholdings the existing shareholders have the opportunity to retain control of the business.

6.12 Activity

The balance sheet of Canvat Ltd is as follows:

Assets	£
Sundry net assets	1,200,000
Share capital	
£1 ordinary shares fully paid	400,000
Reserves	
General reserve	500,000
Profit and loss account (unappropriated profit)	300,000
	1,200,000

The directors decide to make a 1 for 5 bonus issue. This will be followed by a 1 for 3 rights issue. Rights shares will be offered at a price of £1.60 per share.

Show the revised balance sheet of Canvat Ltd after both share issues have taken place.

6.13 Activity solution

Canvat Ltd
Revised balance sheet

	£
Assets	
Sundry net assets	1,456,000
Share capital	
£1 ordinary shares fully paid	640,000
Reserves	
Share premium	96,000
General reserve	420,000
Profit and loss account	300,000
	£1,456,000

The bonus issue of ordinary shares has been carried out by a transfer from the general reserve. However, a transfer from the profit and loss account would also have been appropriate.

7 STATUTORY BOOKS

7.1 Introduction

The law places an obligation on limited companies to keep certain books and registers which are collectively known as **statutory books**. Many of these books are available for inspection by company shareholders and the public. The statutory books are:

(a) **Register of Members**

This sets out the name and address of each shareholder and the number of shares held. The purpose of the register is to allow those interested to identify those who have membership of the company.

(b) **Register of Debenture Holders**

This includes the name and address of each debenture holder and the amount of debentures held. This register fulfils a similar purpose to the Register of Members mentioned above.

(c) **Register of Directors and Secretary**

This sets out personal details of each director and secretary to enable interested parties to discover the identities of each officer of the company.

(d) **Register of Charges**

This gives details of assets owned by the company on which there is a charge, and those who are entitled to the charge. This register enables those interested to know details of security offered in respect of loans. This may be of particular interest to prospective lenders.

(e) **Register of Directors' Interests**

This sets out details of shares and debentures held by directors and their close relatives. This enables those interested to discover the financial interest the directors have in the company and any changes in their financial interest which may occur.

(f) **Register of Substantial Shareholdings**

This sets out details of shareholders in a public company who own more than 3% of the voting shares. This allows those interested to see who may be in a position to exercise influence over the company's affairs.

(g) **Minute Books**

A minute book must be kept for directors' meetings which provides details of items discussed and decisions made. A minute book must also be kept for general meetings of shareholders including details of items discussed and resolutions passed. These books provide a record of matters of business dealt with by directors and shareholders.

(h) **Books of Account**

These set out details of daily financial transactions; amounts received and paid and details of assets and liabilities. This provides a record of the financial transactions and position of the company.

Shareholders have a right to inspect all the statutory books with the exception of the Minute Book of Directors Meetings and the Books of Account. Members of the general public have virtually the same rights of inspection as shareholders but cannot view the Minute Book of General Meetings of Shareholders.

8 CHAPTER SUMMARY

- Limited companies represent the dominant form of business organisation in the UK. They have a separate legal status and are, therefore, independent of the shareholders who are the effective owners. The concept of limited liability has led to a need to protect creditors. Similarly, the fact that day-to-day control of limited companies is vested in directors rather than the owners has led to a need to protect shareholders. In order to protect creditors and shareholders, a legal framework surrounds limited companies. The part of this legal framework relating to the redemption of shares, the keeping of statutory books and the publication of annual reports has been discussed in this chapter.

- The law is particularly strict on the rights of shareholders to pay themselves from company funds. This is because under normal circumstances the shareholders cannot be forced to contribute capital in addition to that which they have already contributed or undertaken to contribute. Dividends may normally only be paid out of reserves which arise from realised profits and gains. It is possible for a company to redeem part of its shares or to buy its own shares. This however can only occur where the legal right of the company to pay dividends is restricted by the amount of the share capital which is redeemed or purchased. This last rule can be relaxed for private limited companies.

- The accounts of limited companies are prepared according to the same basic principles employed for sole proprietorship and partnership businesses. However, some adaptation and extension of the final accounts is required to accommodate the more complex capital structure of limited companies and the different forms of profit appropriation which may occur.

9 SELF TEST QUESTIONS

9.1 Which one of the following is **not** a capital reserve?

(a) share premium account

(b) capital redemption reserve

(c) general reserve

(d) revaluation reserve. (3.3)

9.2 As a general principle, dividends can only be paid out of 'accumulated, realised profits'. Which one of the following best describes this term?

(a) trading profits

(b) trading profits plus profits on sale of fixed assets plus profits on revaluation

(c) trading profits plus profits on sale of fixed assets less realised losses

(d) trading profits plus profits on revaluation less realised losses

(e)   trading profits plus profits on sale of fixed assets plus profits on revaluation less realised losses. (4.1)

9.3   Which one of the following would **not** appear in the profit and loss appropriation account of a limited company?

    (a)   dividends proposed

    (b)   corporation tax

    (c)   transfer to reserves

    (d)   debenture interest

    (e)   net profit for the year. (6.3)

9.4   Which one of the following is a major purpose of a bonus issue of shares?

    (a)   to raise new capital for the company

    (b)   to increase the number of shareholders in the company

    (c)   to provide a 'windfall' gain to shareholders

    (d)   to increase the permanent capital of the company. (6.10)

10   EXAMINATION TYPE QUESTIONS

10.1   Share Capital

The assets employed by limited companies are financed by loans of various sorts and/or by shares. All limited companies, apart from those limited by guarantee, must have a share capital. The two most common types of share are preference and ordinary (equity).

(a)   In what respects are the rights of preference shareholders preferential over the rights of ordinary shareholders?

(b)   For what main reason may a company issue preference shares rather than ordinary shares?

(c)   For what main reason may a company issue redeemable shares rather than those which are irredeemable?

(d)   What form of remuneration do shareholders receive on their holdings?

(e)   How is the remuneration in d) accounted for in a company's profit and loss account?

(f)   Under what main circumstance may a company's share capital be only partly called up?

(g)   What is the main effect of a preference share issue on the capital structure of a company?

(15 marks)

10.2   Helen

The summarised trial balance of Helen Ltd at 31 December after the calculations of the net operating profit, was as follows:

	Dr £	Cr £
Ordinary shares of 50p each		10,000
10% Preference shares of £1 each		9,000
10% Debentures		8,000
Fixed assets at net book value	35,000	
Current assets	30,100	
Creditors		20,000
Capital redemption reserve		5,000
Share premium		4,000
Profit and loss balance 1 January		3,000
Debenture interest	400	

Preference dividend	450	
Preference dividend	450	
Net operating profit for year		8,450
Interim ordinary dividend	2,000	
Corporation tax		500
	67,950	67,950

The following should be taken into account:

(i) A building, net book value currently £5,000, is to be revalued to £9,000.

(ii) Preference dividends of £450 and a final ordinary dividend of 10p per share are to be proposed.

(iii) The balance on the corporation tax account represents an overprovision of tax for the previous year. Corporation tax for the current year is estimated at £3,000.

(a) Prepare completed final accounts for internal use, within the limits of the information available. Ignore taxation except as specifically stated in the question.

(b) What are reserves in the context of limited companies, and what essential features distinguish reserves from debentures and share capital? Explain briefly the differences between capital and revenue reserves, using the reserves in the balance sheet of Helen Ltd as illustrations.

(20 marks)

(ACCA, June 1988)

10.3 Trouble

A friend has bought some shares in a quoted United Kingdom company and has received the latest accounts. There is one page she is having difficulty in understanding. Briefly but clearly answer her questions:

(a) What is a balance sheet?

(b) What is an asset?

(c) What is a liability?

(d) What is a share capital?

(e) What are reserves?

(f) Why does the balance sheet balance?

(g) To what extent does the balance sheet value my investment?

(15 marks)

(ACCA, December 1988)

10.4 Chairperson

The chairperson of a public limited company has written an annual report to the shareholders, extracts of which are quoted below:

Extract 1

In May 19X6 in order to provide a basis for more effective operations, we acquired PAG Warehousing and Transport Ltd. The agreed valuation of the net tangible assets acquired was £1.4 million. The purchase consideration, £1.7 million, was satisfied by an issue of 6.4 million equity shares, of £0.25 per share, to PAG's shareholders. These shares do not rank for dividend until 19X7.

Extract 2

As a measure of confidence in our ability to expand operations in 19X7 and 19X8 and to provide the necessary financial base, we issued £0.50 million 8% Redeemable Debenture Stock 2000/2007, 20 million 6% £1 Redeemable Preference Shares and 4 million £1 equity shares. The opportunity was also taken to redeem the whole of the 5 million 11% £1 Redeemable Preference Shares.

Answer the following questions on the above extracts.

Extract 1

(a)   What does the difference of £0.30 million between the purchase consideration (£1.7m) and the net tangible assets value (£1.4m) represent?

(b)   What does the difference of £0.1 million between the purchase consideration (£1.7m) and the nominal value of the equity shares (£1.6m) represent?

(c)   What is the meaning of the term 'equity shares'?

(d)   What is the meaning of the phrase 'do not rank for dividend'?

Extract 2

(e)   In the description of the debenture stock issue, what is the significance of:

(i)   8%?

(ii)   2000/2007?

(f)   In the description of the preference share issue, what is the significance of:

(i)   6%?

(ii)   Redeemable?

(g)   What is the most likely explanation for the company to have redeemed existing preference shares but at the same time to have issued others?

(h)   What effect will these structural changes have had on the gearing of the company?

(i)   Contrast the accounting treatment, in the company's profit and loss accounts, of the interest due on the debentures with dividends proposed on the equity shares.

(j)   Explain the reasons for the different treatments you have outlined in your answers to (i) above.

(12 marks)

10.5   Percival

The opening balances in the accounts of Percival plc at 1 January 19X1 are given below.

	£000
Share capital	400
Share premium	100
Revaluation reserves	100
Retained profits	200
Debentures (15%)	200
Land at valuation	350
Property – cost	200
– depreciation	24
Plant – cost	450
– depreciation	180
Stock	225
Trade debtors	200
Provision for doubtful debts	20
Trade creditors	220

Expense accruals	11	
Expense prepayments	10	
Bank (positive balance)	20	

You are given the following information in relation to the year 19X1.

	£000	
Cash sales	100	
Credit sales	1,500	
Purchases on credit	900	
Discounts allowed	20	
Discounts received	30	
Purchases of plant	120	
Proceeds of disposal of plant	30	
Original cost of plant disposed of	90	
Profit on disposal of plant	20	
Cost of stock damaged by fire	40	
Scrap proceeds of fire-damaged stock	10	
Contras between debtors and creditors	15	
Bad debts written off	25	
Debenture interest paid	30	
Interim dividend paid	20	
Final dividend proposed	20	
Bank charges	8	
Cheques outstanding at 31/12/X1 per bank reconciliation	35	
Banking of receipts from credit sales	1,450	
Trade creditors at 31/12/X1	280	
Depreciation rate on closing cost balances:		
property	2%	
plant	10%	
Wages and salaries paid	250	
Operating expenses paid	240	
Expense accruals 31/12/X1	12	
Expense prepayments 31/12/X1	14	
Provision for doubtful debts required	10%	of debtors
Closing stock	170	

Prepare trading, profit and loss account and closing balance sheet, for the year 19X1 not for public use. Workings may be in any form, and to any level of detail, you find convenient, but should be logically and clearly presented.

(22 marks)

10.6   Lincoln

You are presented with the following trial balance of Lincoln plc as at 31 December 19X2. All figures are in £000.

Share capital, 50p ordinary shares		1,000
Share premium		500
15% Debentures		800
Profit and loss balance 1 January		200
Purchases and sales	2,400	5,000
Purchase returns and sales returns	100	150
Sales and purchase ledger control balances	1,000	400
Property – cost	800	
– depreciation to 1.1.X2		200
Land – at valuation on 1.1.X3 (12 years earlier)	900	

Machinery – cost	1,600	
– depreciation to 1.1.X2		500
Discounts for prompt payment	20	10
Operating expenses	1,300	
Interim dividends paid	100	
Debenture interest paid to 1.7.X2	60	
Bank		30
Suspense account	210	
Stock at 1.1.X2	300	
	8,790	8,790

The bookkeeper has not recorded certain items, and seems to have only partially recorded others. Details are given below.

(i)   Half of the debentures had been redeemed on 1 July 19X2 at a cost of £380,000. Only one entry, in the bank account, had been made.

(ii)   During the year 19X2 a further 200,000 ordinary shares, identical to those already in issue, had been issued at 110 pence per share. Again only one entry, in the bank account, had been made.

(iii) The managing director has taken £10,000 of the purchases for his own use and no entries have been made for this.

(iv)   The land is to be revalued, as at 31 December 19X2, at £1,500,000.

(v)   Depreciation of 2% p.a. on cost needs to be provided on the property.

(vi)   One tenth of the cost of machinery figure represents items which were fully depreciated down to their estimated scrap value of £10,000 prior to 1 January 19X2. There have been no purchases or disposals of machinery during 19X2. Depreciation of 10% p.a. on the reducing balance basis needs to be provided on the machinery, as appropriate.

(vii) An amount of £50,000 had been paid during the year 19X2 to a customer because of personal injury he had suffered as a result of a fault in the goods delivered to him. Only one entry, in the cash book, had been made.

(viii) A final dividend of 5 pence per share, on all the shares in issue on 31 December 19X2, is to be proposed.

(ix)   Closing stock at 31 December 19X2 is £400,000. Half of this figure represents purchases still included in the purchase ledger control account balance at 31 December 19X2.

(x)   Any balance on the suspense account should be shown in the profit and loss account as a separate item.

Required

Prepare profit and loss account, and balance sheet of Lincoln plc, in good order, as at 31 December 19X2. Your layout and use of headings and sub-totals should be designed to give the maximum of helpful information to the reader. All necessary workings should be clearly shown.

(22 marks)

(ACCA, December 1992)

11   ANSWERS TO EXAMINATION TYPE QUESTIONS

11.1   Share capital

(a)   Preference shareholders have the right to receive dividends out of profit before any dividends are paid to ordinary shareholders. Preference shareholders may or may not have the right to repayment of capital in the event the company is wound up. The rights of each class of shareholder concerning repayment of capital will be set out in the company's documents of incorporation.

(b) Preference shares are designed for investors who do not wish to take the degree of risk associated with investment in ordinary shares. Preference dividends are more certain than ordinary dividends as preference dividends have a prior claim on profits and the amount of the preference dividends is fixed. However, there is no guarantee of dividend. There must be sufficient profits available for distribution.

(c) A new or expanding company may issue redeemable shares to finance the purchase of assets. Once these assets start generating profits the company will be in a position to redeem the shares and will therefore not be committed to the payment of dividends for an indefinite period.

(d) Shareholders receive remuneration in the form of dividends.

(e) Dividends are shown as an appropriation of profits.

(f) A company may issue shares by instalments where the total amount of the share issue is not required at the outset. The company will receive each instalment when the finance is required.

(g) Preference shares represent a form of fixed return capital. The effect of issuing preferences shares will be to raise the gearing of the company.

11.2 Helen

(a)
Helen Ltd
Profit and loss account for the year ended 31 December

	£	£	£
Net operating profit before interest and tax			8,450
Less: Debenture interest			800
Net profit before tax			7,650
Unappropriated profit brought forward			3,000
			10,650
Less: Appropriations			
Corporation tax for the year		3,000	
Less: Overprovision from previous year		500	
		2,500	
Dividends:			
Preference: paid		450	
proposed		450	
		900	
Ordinary: paid		2,000	
proposed		2,000	
		4,000	
			7,400
Unappropriated balance carried forward			£3,250

Balance sheet as at 31 December

	£	£
Fixed assets		39,000
Current assets	30,100	
Current liabilities		
Creditors	20,000	
Corporation tax	3,000	
Accrued interest	400	
Dividends proposed	2,450	
	25,850	
Working capital		4,250
Less: Long-term loan		43,250
10% Debentures		8,000
		£35,250
Share capital and reserves		
10% Preference shares of £1 each		9,000
Ordinary shares of 50p each		10,000
Capital redemption reserve	5,000	
Share premium	4,000	
Revaluation reserve	4,000	
Profit and loss account	3,250	
		16,250
		£35,250

(b)   **Reserves** are part of the owner's claim arising from undistributed profits or gains either realised or unrealised. The other part of the owner's claim is share capital.

Debentures are loans evidenced by deeds. Debenture holders are creditors of the company to whom the company normally has a contractual obligation to pay interest and to repay the principal of the loan at specific dates.

Capital reserves are those which cannot legally be distributed to shareholders by way of dividend. They can arise as a result of the issue shares (share premium account), the redemption of shares (capital redemption reserve) or as a result of the revaluation of fixed assets (revaluation reserve).

Revenue reserves arise from realised profits or gains and can legally be used to pay a dividend. The profit and loss account balance is Helen Ltd's only example of a revenue reserve. This means that the maximum legal dividend which the company could pay (after taking account of the dividends proposed in the final accounts) is £3,250.

11.3   Trouble

(a)   A **balance sheet** is a list of the assets of a business and the various claims against it. Typically it is presented in a way which separates the claims into those which are external to the business and those of the owners. A balance sheet thus typically lists assets and deducts from them the short-term and long-term external claims. The residual represents the claims of the owners.

(b)   An **asset** is a resource of the company which is capable of providing probable future benefits, and which was acquired as a result of a past transaction or event and the right of access of others to it can be restricted.

(c)   A **liability** is a financial obligation of a business to outsiders (non-owners of a business). Liabilities are thus claims on a business by other than the owners.

(d)   **Share capital** is part of the owner's claim on a business. The claim is typically built up from amounts specifically invested in the business by the owners, and amounts which reflect profits made and retained in the business (reserves). That part of the claim which is specifically invested by owners of a company, which cannot normally be repaid, is known as share capital.

(e)   **Reserves** represent the part of the owners' claim which reflect profits made and retained by the business. These reserves may be distributable or not, depending upon their nature. Only realised profits can be distributed, and then only if they are from trading or the sale of fixed assets. Certain reserves, such as share premium and capital redemption reserves, have severe limitations regarding their use. Reserves are *not* cash.

(f)   The balance sheet balances because of the conventions of business entity and duality. The convention of business entity means that any profits or losses will effectively change the claim of the owners. Once this is achieved every transaction must have a twofold effect, following the convention of duality.

(g)   The balance sheet does not value an investment. The owners' claim is based upon assets less external liabilities, where the assets are valued at their cost (less depreciation for fixed assets) at the time of their acquisition. Historic cost does not provide much of a basis for estimating current value. In fact the value of an investment in a business will depend upon its potential future earnings and the risk associated with it. This may be extremely difficult to estimate, and the balance sheet gives a very imperfect guide to it. The value of an investment will be arrived at by the financial markets in a way which reflects supply and demand for the shares in a particular business. High demand will presumably reflect confidence about the level of expected future earnings. The value will also reflect the general confidence of the financial markets about the future state of economy. Clearly the relationship between the balance sheet and market value is tenuous.

11.4   Chairperson

(a)   Goodwill

(b)   Share premium

(c)   Ordinary shares

(d)   The shares are not eligible for dividends

(e)   (i)   8% is the interest rate payable

          (ii)   2000/2007 represents the dates between which the debentures will be redeemed.

(f)   (i)   6% is the maximum rate of dividend payable if a dividend is paid.

          (ii)   'Redeemable' means that the preference shares can be repaid by the company.

(g)   The preference shares redeemed paid a dividend of 11% whereas the new preference shares issued pay a 6% dividend. The replacement of the 11% preference shares, therefore, results in a savings in dividends payable.

(h)   The gearing of the company will be increased.

(i)   Interest due on debentures is a business expense which is chargeable to the profit and loss account. Dividends proposed represent an appropriation of profits.

(j)   Dividends represent a cash return to the owners. The amount of the dividend will be decided upon once the profit for the period has been determined. Interest due represents the charge for borrowing money from outsiders and is an expense incurred in running the business.

11.5 Percival

Percival plc

Trading and profit and loss account for the year ended 31 December 19X1

		£000	£000
Sales		1,600	
Less:	Opening stock	225	
	Purchases	900	
		1,125	
Less:	Stock damaged	40	
		1,085	
Less:	Closing stock	170	
			915
Gross profit			685
Add:	Surplus on disposal of plant		20
	Discounts received		30
			735
Less:	Fire losses	30	
	Discounts allowed	20	
	Depreciation: Property	4	
	Plant	48	
	Bad and doubtful debts	24	
	Wages	250	
	Operating expenses	237	
	Bank charges	8	
	Debenture interest	30	
			651
Net profit			84
Less:	Dividends		40
Net profit retained			44

Balance sheet as at 31 December 19X1

Fixed assets

	Cost £000	Depreciation £000	£000
Land	350	–	350
Property	200	28	172
Plant	480	148	332
	1,030	176	854

Current assets

Stock	170	
Debtors	171	
Prepayments	14	
Cash at bank	147	
	502	

Less:	Current liabilities		
	Creditors	280	
	Accruals	32	312
			190
			1,044
Less:	Long-term liability		200
			844

Share capital	400
Share premium	100
Revaluation reserve	100
Retained profit	244
	844

Percival plc - Workings (in £000s)

Plant account

Cost	450	Cost of disposals	90
Additions	120	Balance c/d	480
	570		570
Balance b/d	480		

Plant depreciation account

Plant disposals a/c	80	Accumulated depreciation	180
Balance c/d	148	Depreciation for year (P+L)	48
	228		228
		Balance b/d	148

Plant disposals account

Cost of disposals	90	Proceeds of disposal	30
Profit on disposal (P+L)	20	Depreciation a/c	80
	110		110

Sales ledger control account

Balance b/d	200	Discounts allowed	20
Credit sales	1,500	Contras to purchases ledger	15
		Bad debts written off	25
		Cash receipts	1,450
		Balance c/d	190
	1,700		1,700
Balance b/d	190		

Purchase ledger control account

Discounts received	30	Balance b/d	220
Contras to sales ledger	15	Credit purchases	900
Cash payments	795		
Balance c/d	280		
	1,120		1,120
		Balance b/d	280

Operating expenses

Prepayments b/d	10	Creditors b/d	11
Cash payments	240	Profit and loss account	237
Creditors c/d	12	Prepayments c/d	14
	262		262
Prepayments b/d	14	Creditors b/d	12

Bank account

Balance b/d	20	Plant additions	120
Cash sales	100	Debenture interest	30
Disposal of plant	30	Interim dividend	20
Scrapped stock sale	10	Bank charges	8
Sales ledger control	1,450	Purchase ledger control	795
		Wages and salaries	250
		Operating expenses	240
		Balance c/d	147
	1,610		1,610
Balance b/d	147		

11.6 Lincoln

Lincoln plc

Profit and loss account for the year ended 31 December 19X2

		£000	£000
Sales (net of returns)			4,900
Less: Opening stock		300	
Purchases (net of returns and private use)		2,240	
		2,540	
Less: Closing stock		400	2,140
Gross profit			2,760
Discounts received			10
			2,770
Less: Operating expenses (general)		1,300	
Depreciation: Property		16	
Machinery		109	(Note 2)
Discounts allowed		20	1,445
Operating profit			1,325
Less: Injury payment		50	
Debenture interest (60 + 30)		90	140
			1,185

Add:	Gain on redemption of debentures		20
Net profit			1,205
Add:	Balance brought forward		200
			1,405
Less: Dividends: paid		100	
	proposed	110	210
			1,195

Lincoln plc

Balance sheet as at 31 December 19X2

	£000 Cost/valuation	**£000** Depreciation	**£000**
Fixed assets			
Land	1,500	-	1,500
Property		800	216
584			
Machinery	1,600	609	991
	3,900	825	3,075
Current assets			
Stock		400	
Debtors		1,000	
Amount owed by director		10	
		1,410	
Creditors: amounts falling due in less than 12 months			
Creditors	400		
Dividends	110		
Accrued interest	30		
Bank	30	570	
Working capital			840
			3,915
Less: Creditors: amounts falling due in more than 12 months			
Debentures			400
			3,515
Share capital and reserves			
Ordinary shares of £0.50 each			1,100
Share premium			620
Revaluation reserve			600
Profit and loss account balance			1,195
			3,515

Notes

1   The suspense account will be cleared by the following journal entry.

	Dr £000	**Cr** £000
Share capital (200,000 @ £0.50)		100
Share premium (200,000 @ £0.60)		120
Debentures	380	

Debentures	380	
Injury payment	50	
Suspense account		210
	430	430

2

	Cost £000	Depreciation £000
Machinery per trial balance	1,600	500
10% depreciated to scrap value	160	150
	1,440	350
	350	
	1,090	
Depreciation @ 10%	109	

20 INTRODUCTION TO PUBLISHED COMPANY ACCOUNTS

INTRODUCTION AND LEARNING OBJECTIVES

This chapter considers the framework of laws and other rules which govern the way in which directors of limited companies must account for the activities of those companies. This chapter naturally follows on from Chapter 19, which introduced and discussed the nature of limited companies.

There are basically three sources of corporate accounting rules. These are:

- statute law, encompassed in the Companies Acts
- accounting standards, established by the accounting profession
- requirements of the Stock Exchange.

Not all of the accounting rules apply to all companies. Smaller companies are exempt from many of the provisions of all three sources. Not surprisingly companies whose shares are not traded on the Stock Exchange will not be bound by its set of rules.

The overriding principle of the law surrounding corporate accounting is that each company's directors should produce and publish (make public) final accounts which show 'a true and fair view' of the company's performance and position. In pursuit of this objective, the Companies Acts lay down a set of items of information, which must be disclosed as a minimum. This information must be disclosed in a prescribed format.

It is probably fair to say that the accounting standards and the Stock Exchange requirements complement the law, rather than pursue their own separate objectives. An obvious question is: Why does the law not encompass all of the regulatory framework? Furthermore, why are there three sources of it? The answer to these questions probably lies in the flexibility which the accounting standard setters and the Stock Exchange have and, therefore, in their ability to respond fairly quickly to new circumstances. Parliament is not noted for its ability to respond quickly.

In Chapter 21 the topic of accounting standards and the Stock Exchange requirements for published accounts will be discussed and a couple of the more important accounting standards will be considered.

When you have studied this chapter you should be able to do the following:

- Explain the statutory framework for accounting for limited companies
- Be familiar with the statutory formats for the balance sheet and the profit and loss account
- Be familiar with the contents of a directors' report
- Appreciate the consequences of satisfying the conditions to be a small or medium-sized company.

1 THE BACKGROUND TO REGULATION

1.1 Introduction

It has long been accepted, in all parts of the world, that limited companies should be required to account, in the sense of publishing information about themselves. Most countries with a developed commercial infrastructure have limited companies and most of these have a framework of regulations surrounding them. These frameworks are a combination of **statutory** and **non-statutory rules**. In 'Anglo-Saxon' countries, like the United Kingdom and the United States of America, the role of non-statutory rules is extensive. This is also true of countries whose law and customs are, or were, heavily influenced by the UK or the USA, such as many Commonwealth countries. However, most continental European countries, and countries with links or former links with them, tend to favour a system of regulation where the law is more far-reaching. These differences of emphasis are purely cultural and historical.

Historically, in the UK, statute law was the only source of accounting regulation. Gradually the Stock Exchange and the accounting profession added their own rules, which extended and complemented those deriving from statute. Originally the law was mainly, if not totally, concerned with protecting those who had financial claims against the company (creditors and shareholders) from unscrupulous directors. As attitudes altered, such that other groups were recognised as having a stake in the company, the role and scope of regulation has been expanded.

1.2　Need for regulation

Currently, in the UK and probably elsewhere as well, regulation is seen as necessary for three main reasons:

1　**Separation of ownership from control.** Except for very small companies, most companies are managed by directors who do not own all of the shares. This means that those who own shares, but are not directors, have a moral right to receive a periodic account of the stewardship of the directors. This right is also enshrined in law.

2　**Limited liability status.** Shareholders cannot normally be required to contribute additional funds to meet unsatisfied creditors' claims against an insolvent company. Potential creditors need certain assurances about a company's future, before they will be prepared to lend money or to provide goods or services on credit. To some extent they can obtain these assurances from accounting information provided by the company.

3　**Economic power.** Certain large companies wield extensive economic power and influence, which affects society generally, as well as affecting those normally seen as having a direct stake in the those companies. For example, a large manufacturing company could employ a significant proportion of the 'breadwinners' in a particular locality. If the company were to go out of business the effect on those living in the locality, even though not employed by the company, could be greatly affected by the closedown. House prices might fall, retailers might be forced to close down and a general economic malaise could pervade the area. Many people would argue that the general economic power of certain companies requires that there is a relatively high degree of accountability by companies to society generally.

Clearly not all of these points apply to companies of all sizes. In particular they do not all tend to apply to smaller companies and the regulations reflect this.

Though regulation may be seen by companies as irksome, in fact a vigorous private sector cannot really exist without it. Unless companies provide accounting information they will find it very difficult to attract investors, lenders and suppliers who will provide goods and services on credit. They may also find it more difficult to attract employees and, in some cases, customers. They may also find resistance by society to accept certain companies operating at all. It is interesting to note that the USA, which is widely seen as a bastion of private enterprise, has one of the strictest and most far-reaching accounting regulatory frameworks. Regulation should not be seen as the enemy of the private sector, rather the opposite.

2　THE LEGAL FRAMEWORK

2.1　Introduction

The current law is set out in the Companies Acts of 1985 and 1989. These pieces of legislation lay down the legal position of a company in every detail, from formation to liquidation and extinction.

The Acts also state the legal rules on company accounting. These require the directors to:

- keep accounting records which are sufficient to show and to explain the company's transactions. The accounting records should also be sufficient to enable the directors to be able to prepare final accounts

- prepare and publish a **profit and loss account** on an annual basis, a **balance sheet** as at the last day of the company's accounting year (the 'final accounts') and a **directors' report** which provides additional financial and other information. The accounts are required to show a true and fair view of the company's trading results and position.

The legislation does not specify what is meant by 'accounting records'. There is no suggestion that these need to be sophisticated, provided that they meet the objectives of being sufficient to show and explain the company's transactions and form a reliable basis for the preparation of the final accounts. In practice, the size and complexity of the company will dictate the necessary level of sophistication. For very small companies, and there are many such companies, very basic, handwritten records, perhaps not even written in double-entry form, will be all that is necessary. For other, larger, companies a computerised system might be absolutely essential to meet the objectives of the accounting records.

2.2 The profit and loss account and balance sheet

A question which any accountant, called on by the directors to prepare the final published accounts, is bound to ask is, what is meant by a 'true and fair view'? The answer to this question is not contained in the legislation. It cannot mean a totally correct view. You have already seen that in areas like stock valuation and depreciation, there is no such thing as complete correctness. All accounting statements contain judgements. While preparers can use their judgement honestly and logically, this does not make the judgements correct. It is probably reasonable to say, however, that accounts which show 'a true and fair view' will not mislead readers into a false view of the company's trading and position.

The published final accounts must be set out in one of the formats which is stipulated in the legislation. These are shown in Appendix 1 of this chapter. There is a choice of four profit and loss account formats and two balance sheet ones. As you can see, each of these sets out the information in slightly different ways. It is up to the company's directors to select a format for each statement. Format 1 for both the profit and loss account and the balance sheet is probably the most popular in practice. Note that Format 1 for the balance sheet is the one which this book tends to follow, whenever the vertical form is used. Companies may select whichever format they prefer to use, but having selected a particular format they must continue to use it from year to year. If there are valid reasons for changing the format it is possible to change, but the reasons for the change must be clearly disclosed in the accounts.

The objective of having legally prescribed formats is to make it easier for users of the final accounts to find the items in which they are particularly interested. They also facilitate making comparisons between different companies and between different time periods for the same company.

Format 1 for the profit and loss account contains some items which perhaps need some explanation. Unfortunately the Companies Acts do not provide any explanation of them, but the popular interpretation is as follows:

Cost of sales

This includes all production expenses, including materials used, productive labour, production overheads and so on.

Distribution costs

These are all of the costs concerned with selling and delivering the products or services which the company provides.

Administrative expenses

This 'mops up' all expenses which are not included in cost of sales, distribution costs or in any other specified expense items (such as interest charges).

Other operating income

This is all income of the company which is not included under any other specific heading.

Where a company has nothing to put into one of the categories in the final account formats, it would normally ignore the item in the accounts. It would not show a nil figure. Companies do not need to show the letters and numbers which appear in the formats in Appendix 1.

2.3 Examples of the formats

The formats in Appendix 1 do not look too much like balance sheets and profit and loss accounts. This is because there are no figures and there are no rulings for sub-totals and totals. The following is an example of a profit and loss account and balance sheet for a company, using Format 1 in each case.

Example

Ducat plc

Profit and loss account for the year ended 31 December 19X3

	£m	£m	£m
Turnover			623
Cost of sales			414
Gross profit			209
Distribution costs		73	
Administrative expenses		32	105
			104
Other operating income			8
			112
Income from other fixed asset investments		2	
Other interest receivable and similar income		16	18
			130
Interest payable and similar charges			15
			115
Tax on profit on ordinary activities			35
Profit on ordinary activities after taxation			80
Retained profit brought forward from last year			46
			126
Transfer to general reserve		40	
Proposed dividend on ordinary shares		50	90
Retained profit carried forward			36

Note: 'Comparative figures' showing the equivalent figures for the previous year must also be included in practice. Note that not all of the items in Format 1 in Appendix 1 appear in this profit and loss account. This is simply because they do not apply to this company for this year or for the previous one. The several lines after 'Profit on ordinary activities after taxation' are not included in Format 1, but they are required to be included under the Companies Acts.

Ducat plc

Balance sheet as at 31 December 19X3

	£m	£m	£m
Fixed assets			
Intangible assets:			
Development costs		35	
Tangible assets:			
Land and buildings	220		
Plant and machinery	103		
Fixtures, fittings, tools and equipment	149	472	507
Current assets			
Stocks:			
Raw materials and consumables	11		
Work in progress	6		
Finished goods and goods for resale	34	51	
Debtors:			
Trade debtors	106		
Prepayments and accrued income	12	118	
Cash at bank and in hand		23	
		192	
Creditors: amounts falling due within one year			
Trade creditors	20		
Other creditors including taxation and			
social security	43		
Accruals and deferred income	13	76	
Net current assets			116
Total assets less current liabilities			623
Creditors: amounts falling due after more than one year			
Debenture loans		110	
Provisions for liabilities and charges			
Pensions		47	157
			466
Capital and reserves:			
Called up share capital			200
Share premium account			40
Revaluation reserve			70
Capital redemption reserve			120
Profit and loss account			36
			466

Note: Again 'comparative figures' have been omitted, but they should be there in practice. Where there is no asset or claim under any of the Format 1 items, that item has been omitted. Where there is a choice of where to place particular items (see Appendix 1), that choice was exercised in preparing this balance sheet.

2.4 Activity

The following is an extract from the trial balance of Unity plc at 31 March 19X4, after the necessary year end adjustments had been made:

	Dr £000	Cr £000
Cost of sales	1,823	
Distribution costs	547	
Sales		4,050
Rents receivable		437
Loan stock interest	647	
Administrative expenses	974	

Show the first part of the published profit and loss account of the company using Format 1.

2.5 Activity solution

The profit and loss account of Unity plc for the year ended 31 March 19X4, using Format 1 is as follows:

Unity plc

Profit and loss account for the year ended 31 March 19X4

	£000	£000
Turnover		4,050
Cost of sales		1,823
Gross profit		2,227
Distribution costs	547	
Administrative expenses	974	1,521
Profit from trading activities		706
Income from other fixed asset investments		437
		1,143
Interest payable on loans		647
Profit on ordinary activities before tax		496

2.6 Activity

The directors of Unity plc (see previous activity) are interested to see how the company's profit and loss account would look if it were prepared following Format 2. You discover that the sum of cost of sales, distribution and administrative expenses which appears in the original profit and loss account as 3,344 (1,823 + 547 + 974) can be alternatively analysed as:

	£000
Decrease in stocks of finished goods and work in progress	52
Raw materials and consumables	875
Depreciation	943
Staff costs	1,065
Other operating charges	409
	3,344

Show the profit and loss account for Unity plc as it would appear if it were to be produced following Format 2.

2.7 Activity solution

The profit and loss account of Unity plc for the year ended 31 March 19X4, using Format 2 would be as follows:

Unity plc

Profit and loss account for the year ended 31 March 19X4

	£000	£000
Turnover		4,050
Decrease in stocks of finished goods and work in progress		52
		3,998
Raw materials and consumables		875
		3,123
Staff costs	1,065	
Depreciation	943	
Other operating charges	409	
		2,417
Profit from trading activities		706
Income from other fixed asset investments		437
		1,143
Interest payable on loans		647
Profit on ordinary activities before tax		496

2.8 Notes to the accounts

In addition to those items which are specified in the formats, the final published accounts must disclose other information by way of notes. This is shown in Appendix 2 of this chapter. Though the formats and the additional requirements add up to quite a lot of information, there is other information which could be given, or given in more detail. Many companies give more information than that which the law demands. To simplify the basic accounting statements, many companies give only the information in outline on the face of the statements, using supporting notes to fill in the detail.

Not only does the law state the objectives of the final published accounts and their form and content; it also specifies certain accounting conventions which must be followed in preparing the accounts. These are:

- **Going concern;** unless the contrary is known to be true, it is assumed that the business of the company will continue indefinitely

- **Consistency;** where different accounting treatments could be made of a particular type of transaction, the one selected should be applied consistently

- **Prudence;** where the outcome of a transaction is not known, a cautious or pessimistic view is taken of it

- **Accruals;** profit (or loss) is the difference between revenues and expenses (properly matched) not the difference between cash receipts and payments.

In addition, published company final accounts must comply with the following:

- Each component of an asset or liability must be looked at separately in deducing the aggregate figure which must be used in the published final accounts. The valuation of stock in trade provides an example of this point. Where there is more than one category of stock, each one must be separately valued (that is, at lower of cost and net realisable value) before being added together to give the total stock figure

- Assets and liabilities must not be netted against one another to arrive at a net figure to be shown in the published balance sheet. It was not unknown, before this point became law, for companies to set a liability arising from a loan to acquire an asset against the value of that asset, showing just the net figure in the balance sheet. This could have the effect of masking the extent of the company's borrowing, an effect which the directors might see as desirable.

Such is the importance which the legislators attach to the true and fair view that one or more of these conventions, or other points, can be ignored if, in the opinion of the directors, they get in the way of a true and fair view being provided. In such a case the directors will need to give a note of details of the departure with the reason for it. This is also true of any of the disclosure requirements.

Preparing company published final accounts and, therefore, following one of the formats does not pose any particular problems, provided that the information is available from the company's accounting system. It is simply a matter of arranging it in the manner required by law, rather than in the manner which the directors may feel is more useful for their own purposes. Most companies, certainly the larger ones, will produce a set of final accounts in a form which they prefer, for internal management use. These accounts will then be amended to put them into a form suitable for publication.

2.9   The directors' report

As well as the final accounts, the directors must also publish a directors' report which contains further information of both a financial and a non-financial nature. This report is a narrative review of the development of the company's business for the year under review. The items which must be included in the directors' report are listed in Appendix 3 to this chapter. The legislation does not require that the directors' report is set out in any particular format.

Many companies, including most Stock Exchange quoted companies, also produce a **Chairman's statement**. Though this can be a valuable source of information to readers, since it tends to make some comment about the future, it is not a legal requirement. In fact many companies give out information about themselves, including press releases, which goes well beyond that which the law requires.

2.10   Small and medium-sized companies

The need to publish full final accounts and a directors' report is reduced for small and medium-sized companies. The objective of relaxing the requirements for smaller companies is partly an attempt to limit the cost burden of complying with legislation. It is also a recognition by the legislators that there is certain information which companies may prefer not to disclose and which, in the case of smaller companies, it is reasonable not to make them disclose.

The criteria which are applied to deduce the size of a company, in this context, come under three separate headings: balance sheet total, turnover and number of employees, as follows:

Size category		
Criterion	**Small**	**Medium**
Balance sheet total (total assets)	£1,400,000	£5,600,000
Annual turnover	£2,800,000	£11,200,000
Average number of employees	50	250

Companies will be able to be treated as small or medium-sized if they can meet two of the above three criteria for both the current and for the preceding year.

The consequences of being deemed a small company are:

* No profit and loss account need be filed with the Registrar of Companies. Also a shorter format may be used for the statement to be placed before the members, if the company chooses

- No directors' report need be filed with the Registrar of Companies
- The balance sheet need only show the total figure for each item against which there is a roman numeral or a capital letter (see Appendix 1).

The consequences of being deemed to be a medium-sized company are:

- The profit and loss account need not show the two items, 'turnover' and 'cost of sales'
- An analysis of 'turnover' and 'profit', normally required in the notes to the accounts, need not be shown
- Certain items in the profit and loss account can be summarised as one figure. Specifically these are:
  - Format 1:   Items 1, 2, 3 and 6
  - Format 2:   Items 1 to 5, inclusive
  - Format 3:   Items A1, B1 and B2
  - Format 4:   Items A1, A2 and B1 to B4, inclusive.

Apart from the items specified, companies of all sizes must comply with all aspects of the Companies Acts' accounting requirements. The exemptions which medium-sized companies are allowed are relatively insignificant compared with those available to small companies.

The published final accounts (including the directors' report, except for small companies) must normally be produced with respect to the same accounting year-end each year. The financial year for which the profit and loss account is prepared must begin on the day following the date to which the last accounts were prepared and must end on the last day of the company's normal financial year. The financial year-end must coincide with, or fall not more than seven days before or after the accounting reference date of the company notified to the Registrar of Companies.

Each shareholder and debenture-holder is entitled to receive a copy of the accounts and a copy must be laid before the annual general meeting of the company. The company must also send a copy of the accounts to the Registrar of Companies (Department of Trade and Industry) which must then be readily available to anyone who wishes to inspect it.

2.11 Audit

The Companies Acts require that the shareholders of large companies must appoint qualified **auditors**, failing which auditors will be appointed by the Registrar of Companies. The role of the auditors is to carry out an independent review of the company's published final accounts and accounting records. The auditors' report expresses the auditors' opinion (either explicitly or implicitly) as to whether:

- the published profit and loss account and balance sheet show a true and fair view of the company's trading and position
- the published final accounts comply with the form and content for them prescribed by the Companies Acts
- the company has maintained accounting records sufficient to show and explain the company's transactions and to enable the published final accounts to be prepared
- accounting standards have been complied with, where appropriate
- the contents of the directors' report is consistent with the published final accounts.

Where the auditors are of the opinion that the company is deficient in any of these respects, they must make this clear in their report. The auditors play a very important role in the regulation of accounting in the UK.

Clearly the nature of the role of the auditors requires that they are completely independent of the company and its directors. The auditors are, in effect, acting as a watchdog for the shareholders, and possibly for society generally, over financial statements produced by the directors.

Many companies employ internal auditors (which is not a statutory requirement) as well as external auditors (which is). The role of internal auditors is rather different from that of the externals. The work of the internal auditor might well include going beyond that which is necessary to form an opinion about the truth and fairness of the final accounts. The internal auditors are usually concerned with the quality of the information which the company's accounting information system provides to management. They are ultimately responsible to the directors and will undertake tasks dictated by the company's senior management. The external auditors, on the other hand, are responsible to the shareholders and their task is defined by law. The directors cannot limit the definition of the task undertaken by the external auditors.

3   APPENDIX 1 COMPANY PUBLISHED FINAL ACCOUNTS FORMATS

3.1   The profit and loss account

Format 1

1	Turnover
2	Cost of sales
3	Gross profit or loss
4	Distribution costs
5	Administrative expenses
6	Other operating income
7	Income from shares in group undertakings
8	Income from shares in participating interests
9	Income from other fixed asset investments
10	Other interest receivable and similar income
11	Amounts written off investments
12	Interest payable and similar charges
13	Tax on profit or loss on ordinary activities
14	Profit or loss on ordinary activities after taxation
15	Extraordinary income
16	Extraordinary charges
17	Extraordinary profit or loss
18	Tax on extraordinary profit or loss
19	Other taxes not shown under the above items
20	Profit or loss for the financial year

Format 2

Format 2 classifies expenses slightly differently and in a little more detail. For example, staff costs are shown separately rather than included in cost of sales, distribution costs or administrative costs, as appropriate.

1	Turnover	
2	Change in stocks of finished goods and work in progress	
3	Own work capitalised	
4	Other operating income	
5	(a)	Raw materials and consumables
	(b)	Other external charges
6	Staff costs:	
	(a)	wages and salaries
	(b)	social security costs
	(c)	other pension costs

7   (a)   Depreciation and other amounts written off tangible and intangible fixed assets

         (b)   Exceptional amounts written off current assets

8   Other operating charges

9   Income from shares in group undertakings

10   Income from shares in participating interests

11   Income from other fixed asset investments

12   Other interest receivable and similar income

13   Amounts written off investments

14   Interest payable and similar charges

15   Tax on profit or loss on ordinary activities

16   Profit or loss on ordinary activities after taxation

17   Extraordinary income

18   Extraordinary charges

19   Extraordinary profit or loss

20   Tax on extraordinary profit or loss

21   Other taxes not shown under the above items

22   Profit or loss for the financial year

Note that in format 2, from item 9 onwards the format is identical to Format 1.

Format 3

	A	Charges		B	Income
	1	Cost of sales		1	Turnover
	2	Distribution costs		2	Other operating income
	3	Administrative expenses		3	Income from shares in group undertakings
	4	Amounts written off investments		4	Income from shares in participating interests
	5	Interest payable and similar charges		5	Income from other fixed asset investments
	6	Tax on profit or loss on ordinary activities		6	Other interest receivable and similar income
	7	Profit or loss on ordinary activities after taxation		7	Profit or loss on ordinary activities after taxation
	8	Extraordinary charges		8	Extraordinary income
	9	Tax on extraordinary profit or loss		9	Profit or loss for the financial year
	10	Other taxes not shown under the above items			
	11	Profit or loss for the financial year			

Format 4

	A	Charges		B	Income
	1	Reduction in stocks of finished goods and work in progress		1	Turnover
	2	(a) Raw materials and consumables		2	Increase in stocks of finished goods and work in progress
		(b) Other external charges			
	3	Staff costs		3	Own work capitalised
		(a) wages and salaries			
		(b) social security costs			
		(c) other pension costs			
	4	a) Depreciation and other amounts written off tangible and intangible fixed assets		4	Other operating income
		(b) Exceptional amounts written off current assets			
	5	Other operating charges		5	Income from shares in group undertakings
	6	Amounts written off investments		6	Income from shares in participating interests
	7	Interest payable and similar charges		7	Income from other fixed asset investments
	8	Tax on profit or loss on ordinary activities		8	Other interest receivable and similar income
	9	Profit or loss on ordinary activities after taxation		9	Profit or loss on ordinary activities after taxation
	10	Extraordinary charges		10	Extraordinary income
	11	Tax on extraordinary profit or loss		11	Profit or loss for the financial year
	12	Other taxes not shown under the above items			
	13	Profit or loss for the financial year			

Note that profit and loss formats 3 and 4 are simply horizontal versions of formats 1 and 2, respectively.

3.2   Balance sheet formats

Format 1

A   **Called up share capital not paid**

B   **Fixed assets**

I   Intangible assets

    1   Development costs

    2   Concessions, patents, licences, trade marks and similar rights and assets

    3   Goodwill

    4   Payments on account

II   Tangible assets

    1   Land and buildings

    2   Plant and machinery

    3   Fixtures, fittings, tools and equipment

    4   Payments on account and assets in course of construction

III   Investments

    1   Shares in group undertakings

    2   Loans to group undertakings

    3   Shares in participating interests

    4   Loans to participating interests

    5   Other investments other than loans

    6   Other loans

    7   Own shares

C   **Current assets**

I   Stocks

    1   Raw materials and consumables

    2   Work in progress

    3   Finished goods and goods for resale

    4   Payments on account

II   Debtors

    1   Trade debtors

    2   Amounts owed by group undertakings

    3   Amounts owed by participating interests

    4   Other debtors

    5   Called up share capital not paid

    6   Prepayments and accrued income

III   Investments

    1   Shares in group undertakings

    2   Own shares

    3   Other investments

IV   Cash at bank and in hand

D   **Prepayments and accrued income**

E   **Creditors: amounts falling due within one year**

    1   Debenture loans

    2   Bank loans and overdrafts

    3   Payments received on account

    4   Trade creditors

    5   Bills of exchange payable

    6   Amounts owed to group undertakings

    7   Amounts owed to participating interests

    8   Other creditors including taxation and social security

    9   Accruals and deferred income

F   **Net current assets (liabilities)**

G   **Total assets less current liabilities**

H   **Creditors: amounts falling due after more than one year**

1   Debenture loans

2   Bank loans and overdrafts

3   Payments received on account

4   Trade creditors

5   Bills of exchange payable

6   Amounts owed to group undertakings

7   Amounts owed to participating interests

8   Other creditors including taxation and social security

9   Accruals and deferred income

I   **Provisions for liabilities and charges**

1   Pensions and similar obligations

2   Taxation, including deferred taxation

3   Other provisions

J   **Accruals and deferred income**

K   **Capital and reserves**

I   Called up share capital

II   Share premium account

III   Revaluation reserve

IV   Other reserves

1   Capital redemption reserve

2   Reserve for own shares

3   Reserves provided for by the articles of association

4   Other reserves

V   Profit and loss account

Notes:

- 'Called up share capital not paid' can appear either at A or as a debtor at C
- 'Prepayments and accrued income' can appear either as a debtor at C or at D
- 'Accruals and deferred income' can appear either as a creditor at E or at J.

Format 2

Assets

A   **Called up share capital not paid**

B   **Fixed assets**

I   Intangible assets

1   Development costs

2   Concessions, patents, licences, trade marks and similar rights and assets

3   Goodwill

4   Payments on account

II   Tangible assets

    1   Land and buildings

    2   Plant and machinery

    3   Fixtures, fittings, tools and equipment

    4   Payments on account and assets in course of construction

III   Investments

    1   Shares in group undertakings

    2   Loans to group undertakings

    3   Shares in participating interests

    4   Loans to participating interests

    5   Other investments other than loans

    6   Other loans

    7   Own shares

C   Current assets

I   Stocks

    1   Raw materials and consumables

    2   Work in progress

    3   Finished goods and goods for resale

    4   Payments on account

II   Debtors

    1   Trade debtors

    2   Amounts owed by group undertakings

    3   Amounts owed by participating interests

    4   Other debtors

    5   Called up share capital not paid

    6   Prepayments and accrued income

III   Investments

    1   Shares in group undertakings

    2   Own shares

    3   Other investments

IV   Cash at bank and in hand

D   Prepayments and accrued income

Liabilities

A   Capital and reserves

I   Called up share capital

II   Share premium account

III   Revaluation reserve

IV   Other reserves

    1   Capital redemption reserve

    2   Reserve for own shares

        3   Reserves provided for by the articles of association

        4   Other reserves

   V   Profit and loss account

   B   **Provisions for liabilities and charges**

        1   Pensions and similar obligations

        2   Taxation, including deferred taxation

        3   Other provisions

   C   **Creditors**

        1   Debenture loans

        2   Bank loans and overdrafts

        3   Payments received on account

        4   Trade creditors

        5   Bills of exchange payable

        6   Amounts owed to group undertakings

        7   Amounts owed to participating interests

        8   Other creditors including taxation and social security

        9   Accruals and deferred income

   D   **Accruals and deferred income**

Format 2 is basically a horizontal version of Format 1, but in Format 2 there is no distinction between creditors falling due within 12 months and those falling due after 12 months.

Notes

- 'Called up share capital not paid' can appear (under assets) either at A or as a debtor at C
- 'Prepayments and accrued income' can appear (under assets) either as a debtor at C or at D
- 'Accruals and deferred income' can appear (under liabilities) either as a creditor at C or at D.

4   APPENDIX 2   NOTES TO THE FINAL PUBLISHED ACCOUNTS

Companies must disclose the following information in the accounts:

1   Directors' emoluments (directors' fees, salaries)

    (a)   The aggregate amount of:

         (i)   the directors' emoluments, including pension contributions and benefits-in-kind

         (ii)   pensions to past directors

         (iii) compensation paid to directors or former directors as compensation for loss of office

    (b)   The emoluments of the chairman and those of the highest-paid director if more than those of the chairman

    (c)   The number of directors who have waived emoluments and the aggregate amount involved

    (d)   The number of directors whose total emoluments (excluding pension contributions) fall into 'bands' of £5,000. Thus the note must disclose the number of directors who were paid between nothing and £5,000, between £5,001 and £10,000, between £10,001 and £15,000 and so on.

Note: (b), (c) and (d) need not be disclosed where total emoluments do not exceed £60,000

2   Directors' loans and other arrangements (for instance, guarantees made by the company in respect of a loan from a third party to a director)

These must include information that such loans or other arrangements exist, the names of the directors concerned and the terms of the arrangement, including its value, if it is not a loan.

Where a loan from the company is involved, there must also be information showing:

(a)   the amount outstanding at the beginning and at the end of the accounting period

(b)   the maximum amount outstanding at any point during the accounting period

(c)   the amount of any arrears of interest

(d)   the amount of any provision which has been made against failure of a director to repay either principal or interest.

3   Employees

(a)   Average number of employees, analysed according to categories of work.

(b)   Staff costs analysed according to:

(i)   wages and salaries

(ii)   social security costs

(iii)   other pension costs

4   Analysis of turnover and profit. This includes:

(a)   an analysis, by major class of business, of both turnover and profit before tax

(b)   a geographical analysis of turnover.

5   Charges

(a)   auditors' remuneration, including expenses

(b)   hire charges for plant and machinery

(c)   interest payable analysed between short-term loans (repayable within five years) and long-term loans (repayable after five years).

6   Fixed assets

Cost

(a)   aggregate purchase price or production cost of each item as at the date of the beginning of the financial year and as at the financial year-end

(b)   the effect on the amount shown in the balance sheet of any alterations in the basis of valuation of the asset, any acquisitions, disposals or transfers.

Depreciation

(a)   the amount of the provision in respect of the financial year and the cumulative amount of the provision as at the financial year-end

(b)   the amount of any adjustment relating to any disposals or transfers or other adjustments.

5   APPENDIX 3   CONTENTS OF THE DIRECTORS' REPORT

Content	Explanation
Principal activities	What these are and how they have changed over the period
Review	A review of the development of the business of the company over the period
Future developments	Some indication of the company's plans for the future

Future developments	Some indication of the company's plans for the future
Dividends	Amount proposed
Reserves	Amounts proposed to be transferred to and from reserves
Post balance sheet events	Any significant events which have occurred since the end of the accounting period
Research and development	Some indication of the activities of the company in this regard
Fixed assets	Significant changes and the difference between book and market value of land and buildings, if significant
Charitable and political	If in excess of £200, separate totals for each donations category. If political donations exceed £200, the names of recipients and amounts must be given
Own shares acquired	Details of any shares in itself which the company has acquired
Employees	Information on health, safety, training and welfare. where employees number 250 or more, also information on company policy towards disabled people

Directors	(a)	Names of those who held office at any time during the period
	(b)	Directors' interests in contracts of third parties and the company
	(c)	Each director's shares and debenture holdings (including a 'nil' return where relevant):
		(i) at the start of the accounting period
		(ii) at the end of the accounting period
		(iii) at the date of appointment for directors appointed during the accounting period

6   SELF TEST QUESTIONS

6.1   What are the three sources of rules which make up the 'regulatory framework' of accounting in the UK? (Introduction)

6.2   What are the three major reasons for it being regarded as necessary that a regulatory framework exists? (1.2)

6.3   What two broad requirements are imposed on directors of UK limited companies in the context of accounting? (2.1)

6.4   Which one of the following is the precise wording of the Companies Act 1985 in its requirement of what the published accounts of UK companies should show?

    (a)   'a fair and reasonable view'

    (b)   'a true and reasonable view'

    (c)   'a true and fair view'

    (d)   'a correct and fair view' (2.1)

6.5   How many formats are there for the profit and loss account and for the balance sheet for UK limited companies, according to the Companies Act 1985? (2.2)

6.6   What are the consequences of being a 'small company' under the Companies Act 1985 in relation to published accounts requirements? (2.10)

6.7   Which one of the following is not required to be included in the directors' report?

(a)   a review of the development of the business of the company over the period

(b)   amount of dividend proposed

(c)   total amount of the company's tax liability for the year

(d)   details of own shares acquired. (5)

7   EXAMINATION TYPE QUESTIONS

7.1   General Warehouses

The trial balance of General Warehouses plc shows the following balances at 31 December 19X3.

	Dr £m	Cr £m
Ordinary share capital		150
Share premium		10
General reserve		10
Profit and loss		25
Stock at 1 January 19X3	30	
Sales		500
Purchases	270	
Purchase returns		13
Sales returns	14	
Carriage outwards	14	
Warehouse wages	40	
Salespersons' salaries	30	
Administrative wages	20	
Warehouse plant and machinery	63	
Delivery vehicle hire	10	
Provision for depreciation – plant and machinery		25
Goodwill	50	
Distribution expenses	5	
Administrative expenses	15	
Directors' salaries	15	
Rents receivable		8
Trade debtors	165	
Cash at bank	30	
Trade creditors (payable by 28/2/19X4)		30
	771	771

Notes: The following final adjustments need to be made:

1   Stock of goods for resale at 31 December 19X3, £50m

2   Provide annual depreciation of £16m on Warehouse plant and machinery

3   Provide for corporation tax, due 30 September 19X4, £25m

4   Proposed dividend, £30m

Prepare the published profit and loss account and balance sheet for the 19X3 financial year. The directors consider that Format 2 should be used.

(20 marks)

7.2 Board of Directors

After the directors of General Warehouses plc had seen the draft profit and loss account and balance sheet for the 19X3 financial year they concluded that the profit and loss showed too much analysis of their expenses and the balance sheet gave no direct impression of the company's net current asset strength.

Prepare a further set of accounts, for publication purposes, for comparison by the Board of Directors of General Warehouses plc. **(20 marks)**

7.3 Small Company

Refer again to the data given in the trial balance of General Warehouses plc. Assume instead of £ million the headings read £000: therefore ordinary share capital would be £150,000 not £150m.

(a) How would this affect the information which the company must provide and publish in respect of its financial statements?

(b) Prepare the appropriate financial statements for the financial year 19X3.

(20 marks)

8 ANSWERS TO EXAMINATION TYPE QUESTIONS

8.1 General Warehouses

General Warehouses plc

Balance sheet as at 31 December 19X3

	£m	£m
Fixed assets		
Intangible assets		
Goodwill		50
Tangible assets		
Plant and machinery		22
		72
Current assets		
Stocks	50	
Debtors	165	
Cash at bank and in hand	30	245
		317
Capital and reserves		
Called up share capital		150
Share premium account		10
Other reserves – general reserve		10
Profit and loss account		62
		232
Creditors		
Trade creditors	30	
Other creditors including taxation	55	85
		317

General Warehouses plc
Profit and loss account for the year ended 31 December 19X3

	£m	£m
Turnover		486
Increase in stock of goods for resale		20
		506
Purchases of goods for resale		257
		249
Staff costs	90	
Depreciation	16	
Other operating charges	59	165
Profit from trading activities		84
Income from other fixed asset investments		8
Profit on ordinary activities before taxation		92
Tax on profit on ordinary activities		25
Profit on ordinary activities after taxation		67
Retained profit brought forward from 19X2		25
		92
Proposed dividend on ordinary shares		30
Retained profit carried forward		62

Note: The figure for other operating charges is as follows:

	£m
Carriage outwards	14
General distribution expenses	5
Vehicle hire	10
General administrative expenses	15
Directors' salaries	15
	59 (Working only)

8.2 Board of Directors

General Warehouses plc
Balance sheet as at 31 December 19X3

Fixed assets	£m	£m	£m
Intangible assets			
Goodwill			50
Tangible assets			
Plant and machinery			22
			72
Current assets			
Stocks		50	
Debtors		165	
Cash at bank and in hand		30	
		245	

Creditors: amounts falling		
due within one year		
Trade creditors	30	
Other creditors including taxation	55	85

Net current assets	160
Total assets less current liabilities	232

Capital and reserves	
Called up share capital	150
Share premium account	10
Other reserves – general reserve	10
Profit and loss account	62
	232

General Warehouses plc

Profit and loss account for the year ended 31 December 19X3

	£m	£m
Turnover		486
Cost of sales		237
Gross profit		249
Distribution costs	115	
Administrative expenses	50	165
Profit from trading activities		84
Income from other fixed asset investments		8
Profit on ordinary activities before taxation		92
Tax on profit on ordinary activities		25
Profit on ordinary activities after taxation		67
Retained profit brought forward from 19X2		25
		92
Proposed dividend		30
Retained profit carried forward		62

8.3   Small Company

(a)   The following test regarding size should be carried out:

	£	Small company limits £
Total assets	317,000	1,400,000
Annual turnover	486,000	2,800,000
Average number of employees	?	50

Although the number of employees for General Warehouses plc is not given, a company need only satisfy two of the three criteria which are applied to deduce the size of a company. Therefore, General Warehouses plc may be classified as a small company for publication of annual accounts.

The consequences of being deemed to be a small company are:

(i)   No profit and loss account need be filed with the Registrar of Companies. A shorter format may be   used for the statement to be placed before the members, if the company chooses.

(ii)   No directors' report need be filed with the Registrar of Companies.

(iii)   The balance sheet need only show the total figure for each item against which there is a letter or roman numeral.

(b)   The published balance sheet would look like this

General Warehouses plc

Balance sheet as at 31 December 19X3

	£000	£000
Fixed assets		
Intangible assets		50
Tangible assets		22
		72
Current assets		
Stocks	50	
Debtors	165	
Cash at bank and in hand	30	
	245	
Creditors: amounts falling due within one year	85	
Net current assets		160
Total assets less current liabilities		232
Capital and reserves		
Called up share capital		150
Share premium account		10
Other reserves		10
Profit and loss account		62
		232

No profit and loss account need be published and filed with the Registrar of Companies. Clearly, the directors would wish to present a form of profit and loss account to the members at the Annual General Meeting.

21 NON-STATUTORY ASPECTS OF PUBLISHED COMPANY ACCOUNTS

INTRODUCTION AND LEARNING OBJECTIVES

In the previous chapter we considered the financial reporting requirements as laid down by the Companies Acts. These requirements have increased over the years to the point where they are now quite onerous. The complexity of modern businesses and the increasing sophistication of the investment community and other major users have required changes in the methods of presentation and an increase in the level of disclosure within corporate reports. However, these statutory requirements are not all that limited companies have to contend with. In addition to the Companies Acts requirements, they must also conform to certain accounting standards which have been laid down by the accounting profession. These standards are designed to support and to supplement the statutory requirements which exist.

In this chapter we consider the role of accounting standards and the nature of the accounting standard process. We also examine, in detail, some of the accounting standards which are included within the syllabus. As we shall see, these standards are aimed at increasing uniformity amongst companies in the way in which they report key accounting issues.

Finally we shall consider the role of the Stock Exchange in financial reporting. For listed companies, the Stock Exchange represents another important source of regulation concerning financial reporting matters.

When you have studied this chapter you should be able to do the following:

*   Understand the need for mandatory accounting standards

*   Explain the current standard setting process

*   Describe the requirements of SSAP 2, SSAP 13, SSAP 17 and SSAP 18

*   Explain the additional rules imposed on listed companies by the Stock Exchange.

---

1 WHY HAVE ACCOUNTING STANDARDS?

1.1 Introduction

The preparation of the final accounts depends upon the exercise of judgement. An example is the method of depreciation chosen; should it be straight line or reducing balance or some other method? Should stock be valued on a first-in, first-out basis (FIFO) or on a last-in, first-out (LIFO) basis? The Companies Acts do not answer these questions.

To see how the exercise of judgement in these areas can affect the accounts, consider this example.

Example

Hardy Ltd and Nelson Ltd are two companies which operate in the same industry. By a remarkable coincidence, they both started trading on 1 January last year. By an even more remarkable coincidence their trading transactions for last year were identical. They were as follows:

	£000
Share capital contributed on 1 January	100
Fixed assets (at cost) bought on 1 January	60
Debtors at 31 December	70
Cash at 31 December	20
Creditors at 31 December	40

Sales for the year	170
Purchases made during the year	130
Overhead expenses (excluding depreciation)	30

Both companies' directors believe that the various fixed assets will have an economic life of four years and then have a residual value of 20% of their original cost.

The directors of Hardy Ltd decide to use the straight-line method of depreciation. This means an annual expense of £12,000 ((60,000 − 12,000)/4). The directors of Nelson prefer to use the reducing-balance method of depreciation. Using the formula to deduce the appropriate rate gives an annual rate quite close to 33.33%, which means a depreciation charge for last year of £20,000.

The physical stock at 31 December was identical for both companies. Hardy's directors preferred to value the stock on a FIFO basis, which gave a closing stock value of £30,000. Nelson's directors favoured using a LIFO basis, which led to a valuation of £20,000.

When the two companies prepared their accounts, they showed the following:

Profit and loss account for the year ended 31 December

	Hardy £000	Hardy £000	Nelson £000	Nelson £000
Sales		170		170
Less: Cost of sales (purchases less stock)		100		110
Gross profit		70		60
Overhead expenses	(30)		(30)	
Depreciation	(12)	(42)	(20)	(50)
Net profit		28		10

Balance sheet as at 31 December

	Hardy £000	£000	£000	£000	Nelson
Fixed assets (at cost)			60,000		60,000
Less: Depreciation			12,000		20,000
			48,000		40,000
Current assets					
Stock		30,000		20,000	
Debtors		70,000		70,000	
Cash		20,000		20,000	
		120,000		110,000	
Less: **Current liabilities**					
Creditors		40,000	80,000	40,000	70,000
			128,000		110,000
Share capital			100,000		100,000
Retained profit			28,000		10,000
			128,000		110,000

The accounts show an apparently quite different picture from one company to the other. Hardy's profit, expressed as a percentage of the end-of-year capital invested, is about 22% ((28/128) x 100). Nelson, on the other hand, looks much less successful at about 9% ((10/110) x 100). Obviously, the example was constructed to make a point and is, therefore, rather an exaggeration. Nevertheless, the point remains that different preparers of accounts, each taking a perfectly honest and reasonable approach to the same set of facts, can produce final accounts which give entirely different views.

1.2   The exercise of judgement

Unfortunate though it may be from the point of view of objectivity and consistency from one company to another, the exercise of judgement is unavoidable in the preparation of final accounts. It is not reasonable to ignore depreciation on the grounds that accounting for it involves a subjective judgement. Ignoring depreciation would lead to an even more distorted view being given by the accounts.

Depreciation and stock valuation are by no means the only areas where judgement has to be exercised by preparers of accounts, though these two tend to be areas of particular importance, because of the highly significant amounts of money involved. Other areas where judgement needs to be exercised are:

- bad and doubtful debts
- the timing of the recognition of revenues (applying the realisation convention)
- the matching of expenses to revenues (applying the matching convention)
- the exercise of prudence (applying the prudence convention)
- deciding when some item is material or not (applying the materiality convention).

This is not a new problem. What perhaps is a fairly recent development is a wide recognition, by users of accounts, that the problem exists. This has, in turn, forced the accountancy profession to take steps to try to limit the effects of the problem. Things particularly came to a head in the late 1960s, when a large number of takeovers and company mergers brought to light the number of different areas in which the exercise of judgement by preparers of accounts was necessary. It also became obvious that the exercise of judgement could have profound effects on the resulting final accounts.

A notable example of this occurred when the General Electric Company Ltd (GEC) took over Associated Electric Industries Ltd (AEI) during 1967. As part of its strategy to defend the company from the takeover, the directors of AEI made a profit forecast for 1967 of £10 million. This was based on actual results for the first ten months of the year (which had already elapsed by the time of the forecast) plus two months budgeted profit. In the end GEC successfully took over AEI. But, when GEC's accountants assessed AEI's actual 1967 financial results, following the end of the financial year, they came to the conclusion that AEI had made a loss of £4.5 million, a figure £14.5 million below their earlier forecast.

When GEC's auditors came to analyse the difference between the forecast profit and the 'actual' loss, they concluded that £9.5 million of it was the result of the difference in judgements made by two sets of accountants.

As a result of the GEC/AEI 'scandal' and of a number of other disturbing, though less spectacular, cases around that time, the UK accountancy profession decided to take some action.

1.3   The standard-setting process

The Accounting Standards Committee (ASC) was established during the 1970s. It was funded by, and its membership drawn from, the six major UK professional accounting bodies:

The Chartered Association of Certified Accountants

The Chartered Institute of Management Accountants

The Chartered Institute of Public Finance and Accountancy

The Institute of Chartered Accountants in England and Wales

The Institute of Chartered Accountants in Ireland

The Institute of Chartered Accountants of Scotland

The membership also included representatives of users of accounts. The objective of this committee was to 'narrow the difference and variety of accounting practice by publishing authoritative statements on best accounting practice which will, wherever possible, be definitive'.

The ASC created a number of Statements of Standard Accounting Practice (SSAPs), each one addressing itself to a particular accounting issue. For example SSAP 12 deals with accounting for depreciation, as was mentioned earlier in this book. The accounting standards are substantially concerned with promoting the preparation of final accounts which show a true and fair view. In creating the accounting standards the ASC went through the following 'exposure draft' process:

- identification of an accounting issue which needed attention
- commission of a research study on the issue identified
- preparation and wide distribution of an 'exposure draft' of a proposed accounting standard
- a period during which any interested party was invited to make comments on the exposure draft
- review by ASC of the comments and issue of the final accounting standard.

Once an accounting standard has been formally issued, it becomes mandatory for all companies for which it is intended. Sometimes an accounting issue may be only of interest to a particular industry or business sector. In such a situation, the lack of general applicability would prevent a SSAP being issued. Instead a Statement of Recommended Practice (SORP) may be issued. As the name suggests, a SORP is not mandatory.

In the late 1980s, the UK accountancy profession sought a review of standard setting and proposals for the future of standard setting. The general conclusion of the committee established for this purpose was that, although the ASC had played a valuable role and the standard-setting process described above had proved successful, a new regulatory structure was required to develop further, and ensure greater compliance with, accounting standards. The committee's main recommendation was that the work of the ASC should be divided into two distinct roles, each to be undertaken by a separate committee. The proposal was accepted. There is now a Financial Reporting Council (FRC), which takes overall, but generalised, responsibility for the direction, funding and public relations of standard setting. The FRC consists of 26 members drawn from the accounting profession and private- and public-sector managers.

A separate body, the Accounting Standards Board (ASB), is a committee of 10 qualified accountants, charged with the more technical role, formerly undertaken by the ASC, of developing the actual standards, now known as Financial Reporting Standards (FRSs). Apart from its narrower role, the ASB differs from the ASC in three important respects:

- The ASB only requires a two-thirds majority to obtain approval for a particular standard whereas the ASC required unanimous approval amongst its members.
- The ASB has two full-time members (a chairman and technical director) whereas the ASC had only part-time members.
- The ASB issues standards in its own right whereas standards produced by the ASC required the approval of the major professional accountancy bodies identified earlier. The process of issuing draft standards for public comment is similar to the ASC process: preliminary ideas are issued as Discussion Drafts (DDs), which following public consultation are issued as Exposure Drafts, which following further consultation are issued as standards. For example a DD may first become a FRED and finally an FRS.

These differences are seen as important in helping to prevent the dilution of accounting standards and in ensuring that the standard-setting process does not take too long.

In addition to the two-tier structure described above, there is also an Urgent Issues Task Force (UITF). A criticism of the ASC was that it was, at times, slow to respond to emerging issues. The UITF is an offshoot of the ASB and aims to provide timely action to deal with issues as they arise. This should help prevent them from growing in scale. The UITF produces 'abstracts' which are designed to come into effect very quickly (usually about one month after the publication of the abstract). The UITF is also available to provide advice and guidance on problems requiring a rapid solution.

In order to ensure that companies comply with the accounting standards laid down, there is now a Financial Reporting Review Panel which monitors financial reporting practices amongst large companies. Any failure to adhere to a standard, which in turn leads to a failure to show a true and fair view of the company's performance and position, can result in the Review Panel (or the Secretary of State for Trade and Industry) taking the delinquent company to court to ensure that its directors fulfil their statutory duties in this respect. The auditors of the company may also face disciplinary action if they did not qualify their report concerning their departure from accounting standards.

1.4 The scope of accounting standards

Accounting standards vary in their scope:

- Some apply to all undertakings whose final accounts are required to show a true and fair view, that is all companies and some other bodies as well
- Some apply only to larger companies
- Some apply only to those companies which are listed on the Stock Exchange.

1.5 Activity

For the sake of uniformity should not accounting standards be imposed on all companies and other bodies, including not-for-profit organisations? What are the arguments for variation in the scope of accounting standards?

1.6 Activity solution

Accounting is not an exact science and the exercise of judgement in the preparation of final accounts is unavoidable. Clearly, uniformity is desirable in these judgmental areas but the cost of effecting an accounting standard may far outweigh the benefits. Thus, with this in mind, the ASC produced accounting standards which vary in scope as follows:

- Some do apply to all undertakings
- Some apply only to relatively large companies
- Some apply only to those companies which are listed on the UK Stock Exchange.

Arguments for such variation might include:

- The cost/benefit argument is relevant; for instance it would not make sense to apply a standard requiring an independent valuation of certain assets to all companies. The relative cost to a company with asset values of a few thousand pounds would be far greater than to a company with multi-million pound assets.

  The relative size of companies is also important as are the different needs of users of accounts – artificial uniformity may be imposed by standards on all companies, however diverse.

1.7 Failure to follow a standard

The standards are mandatory on all companies within their scope. Failure to comply with a particular standard will lead to the auditors commenting on that failure in their report on the company's accounts, unless the auditors concur with the directors of the company that following the particular standard will lead to the true and fair view being obscured. The professional accounting bodies have the power to discipline their members who, as preparers or as auditors, do not comply with standards. The courts look to the accounting standards, where they are relevant, in deciding whether a company's final accounts comply with the Companies Acts' requirement to show a true and fair view. Thus accounting standards are not the law as such, but they have the force of law behind them to some extent.

1.8   Activity

Should accounting standards be incorporated into legislation? What are the arguments for and against such a move?

1.9   Activity solution

Given that standards are mandatory on all companies within their scope and:

- Preparers or auditors who do not comply with standards may be disciplined by the ASB and,

- The courts will look to the standards when deciding whether a company's accounts comply with statutory requirements to show a true and fair view, it would seem a reasonable step to incorporate standards into an Act of Parliament.

However, the following points could be made against such a move:

- For the accounting profession to continue to be a major force in the development of financial reporting, independence is vital.

- Adequate self-regulation of its members appears to be present through the standards system.

- It is difficult to see how auditors could concur with the directors of a company where following a standard embodied in law would lead to a true and fair view being obscured. They would merely be breaking the law.

- There could be a conflict of law between what the standards legislation says and existing Companies Acts requirements.

- Flexibility to changing circumstances. The law may be very slow to change. Parliament may give a low priority to proposed accounting standards which will result in undue delay in their implementation.

1.10   Standards currently in issue

A list of accounting standards which are currently in force is given in Appendix 1 to this chapter. If you look at this list you will see that you have met two of these, SSAP 9 (Stocks and long-term contracts) and SSAP 12 (Accounting for depreciation), and they have been covered in some detail in earlier chapters.

1.11   Types of accounting standards

According to Professor Edey, accounting standards can be seen to fall into four types. These are concerned with:

- **Description**. These are concerned with the manner in which an item is dealt with in the published final accounts. SSAP 12 (Accounting for depreciation), which you have already met, is a good example of this type of standard. SSAP 12 does not seek to prescribe in detail how fixed assets depreciation should be dealt with in the accounts; the standard does require that the way in which the company does deal with it is adequately described.

- **Presentation**. These standards are concerned with the manner in which certain items are actually shown in the accounts. FRS 3 is an example of this type of standard, requiring a profit and loss account to be drawn up to present the amount of turnover and profit relating separately to continuing operations and those operations that have been discontinued in the year.

- **Disclosure**. These standards extend the amount of information which must be disclosed in the published final accounts. For example, FRS 1, the first standard to emerge from the new standard setting board (ASB), requires virtually all companies, except the smallest, to publish a cash flow statement to augment the published final accounts. You will cover FRS 1 in detail in Chapter 22 of this book.

- **Valuation and profit measurement**. These standards deal with how to value certain assets and how to calculate certain items of profit. An example with which you are familiar is SSAP 9 (Stocks and long-term contracts). This standard sets out how stocks should be valued and it gives clear guidelines as to how the profit on long-term projects should be calculated.

1.12   International accounting standards

The growth of multinational companies and the development of international capital markets has created a need for accounting standards to transcend national boundaries. It can be very difficult both for preparers and for users of financial reports to deal with variations in accounting practices between countries. In addition, the growth of accounting standard-setting bodies in different countries has led to a need to harmonise accounting rules. The International Accounting Standards Committee (IASC) was established in 1973 to address these issues. International Accounting Standards (IASs) have now been produced on a variety of topics. However, the problem of reconciling national differences in accounting practice has inevitably meant that the rate of development of standards has been somewhat slower than the process at national level. The IASC is, in essence, a voluntary organisation and so it is important for it to obtain cooperation and agreement amongst member countries on the contents of proposed standards. This has sometimes led to the criticism that in order to obtain support for its standards, the IASC permits too much choice in acceptable accounting practices for a given area. International accounting standards are developed using the 'exposure draft' approach employed in the UK (which is a founder member of the IASC).

1.13   The case for accounting choice

There are some who believe that accounting standards have an adverse effect on the quality of financial reports. They believe that it is better for companies to have some choice about the way in which they report financial matters. The main arguments in favour of accounting choice rather than accounting standards are as follows:

- By permitting a company to choose its own methods of financial reporting, an insight will be provided into its 'corporate personality'. Thus a company which is risk-averse is likely to adopt very conservative accounting policies: for instance, immediate write-off of goodwill or research and development expenditure. A risk-seeking company, on the other hand, would favour less conservative methods of accounting. Whilst this is an interesting point it can be argued that there are other (more direct) ways in which 'corporate personality' may be assessed. Making inferences about attitudes to risk for example, based on the choice of accounting policies, may prove unreliable

- No two companies are exactly the same. Each company is unique and should be allowed to adopt accounting methods which are most suitable for its particular needs. By imposing rigid standards there is a danger that an artificial uniformity will be created which will prevent users from recognising the unique aspects of a particular company. This point is similar to the one above in that it stresses the importance of reflecting individual differences between companies. This again is an interesting argument although there is a danger of overstating the differences which exist between companies and understating those aspects which they have in common. It should be pointed out that many of the standards produced so far permit choice in the methods adopted by a company and cannot be described as being rigid. In addition, a company can depart from a standard if it can be shown that the standard inhibits the reflection of a true and fair view of company performance and position

- Accounting standards are not based on any underlying conceptual framework. Thus, there is no clear rationale for insisting that particular methods of measurement or presentation be adopted by companies. It is true that accounting does not rest on any clear body of knowledge which explains and provides guidelines for accounting practice. In recent years, however, there have been some attempts to develop such a framework. (This issue will be dealt with in more detail in Chapter 23.) The accounting profession has taken a rather pragmatic view in dealing with this point. Although there has been an increasing recognition of the need to develop a conceptual framework, it has been argued that there are accounting problems which are in pressing need of attention and that we cannot wait until a conceptual framework has been developed before addressing these problems. Thus, the search for a conceptual framework and the development of accounting standards must take place simultaneously

- Standards may ossify accounting procedures. By laying down particular procedures to be followed, future development in this area may be inhibited. There is a danger that this may happen, although past experience suggests that there is a willingness by standard setters to review accounting standards and to make changes where necessary. The requirement for companies to produce cash flow statements in preference to funds flow statements to augment their financial reports is a case in point.

The case for accounting choice cannot be dismissed lightly. There is always a danger that rigid rules can be imposed without regard to particular circumstances and that the importance of the accountant's judgement in dealing with technical issues can be undervalued. However, most believe that accounting standards have enhanced the quality of accounting reports in the UK. They have improved levels of disclosure and presentation and have eliminated many confusing differences in reporting methods. They have also helped to stimulate debate concerning important accounting issues. It should be remembered that accounting choice existed during the 1960s. The accounting 'scandals' of this period created the impetus for the development of standards.

2 SELECTED ACCOUNTING STANDARDS

2.1 Introduction

In the remainder of this chapter we will consider the detail of certain accounting standards. These standards form part of the syllabus and so it is important that you understand the nature and purpose of each standard.

2.2 SSAP 2 – Disclosure of accounting policies

This accounting standard was designed to help users of accounts obtain a clearer picture of the accounting policies which companies adopted when preparing their financial statements. Unless users know the way in which certain key accounting figures are derived, the accounts will be difficult to analyse and evaluate. Hence, this standard was seen as being an important contribution towards improving the quality of financial reporting by companies.

The statement begins by distinguishing between three terms: fundamental accounting concepts, accounting bases and accounting policies.

2.3 Fundamental accounting concepts

These are broad basic assumptions employed in preparing the final accounts of a business for a period. The standard identifies four such concepts which are considered to have general acceptance. These fundamental concepts have been covered in earlier chapters and will not, therefore be discussed in detail here. The four concepts are as follows:

- going concern
- accruals
- consistency
- prudence.

The statement recognises that the relative importance of each concept will vary according to the circumstances of a particular situation. However, where there is a conflict between the prudence concept and the accruals concept it is the former which should prevail. The Companies Act 1985 has also recognised these four fundamental concepts although they are referred to in the Act as 'accounting principles'.

2.4 Activity

Can you think of two areas where a conflict between the prudence concept and the accruals concept might occur?

2.5 Activity solution

The accruals concept asserts, in essence, that profit is the excess of revenues over expenses for the period, properly matched, and not between cash receipts and payments.

The prudence concept asserts that accounting should err on the side of caution in the recognition of expenses and claims. Examples of where a conflict between these two concepts could exist are:

(a)   Valuation of trading stock. This item should be valued at the lower of cost or net realisable value in the balance sheet. Clearly, where trading stock is subsequently realised at a figure materially lower than its cost the prudence concept would require the lower figure to be included in the accounts.

Otherwise, profits would be overstated. However, the effect of bringing into the accounts a net realisable value is in conflict with the accruals concept.

(b)   Writing off goodwill. Application of the accruals concept will mean that goodwill is written off over the expected useful life of any goodwill purchased. Application of the prudence concept is likely to result in immediate write-off as the useful life of this asset may be difficult to establish.

2.6 Accounting bases

These are the methods developed for applying the fundamental concepts to financial transactions and items. These bases help preparers in deciding the period in which revenues and expenses are to be recognised and the amounts to be shown in the balance sheet at the end of the period. Some examples of areas where accounting bases are important (and the bases available) are:

•   depreciation of fixed assets (straight-line method, reducing-balance method)

•   stock in trade and work-in-progress (FIFO, LIFO, AVCO)

•   research and development expenditure (immediate write-off or carry-forward of expenditure).

2.7 Accounting policies

These are the bases which have been selected and employed consistently by a business. Thus, for example, a business may decide to use the reducing-balance method for depreciation and this will then become its accounting policy for depreciation. The accounting bases selected by management should be most appropriate to the particular circumstances of the business and should also be best suited to a fair reflection of the performance and financial position of the business.

2.8 Requirements of SSAP 2

SSAP 2 requires companies to explain clearly any departure in the accounts from the four fundamental concepts identified above. In the absence of any such statement, it is presumed that these concepts were adhered to in preparing the accounts. The accounting policies followed when determining material amounts to be shown in the profit and loss account and balance sheet should be disclosed by way of a note to the accounts. Explanations provided should be clear, fair and as brief as possible.

3 SSAP 9 STOCKS AND LONG-TERM CONTRACTS

3.1 Introduction

The following are the essential points of SSAP 9:

- In determining profit, costs should be matched with related revenues. Since the cost of unsold stocks and work-in-progress at the end of an accounting period has been incurred in the expectation of future revenue, it is appropriate to carry these costs forward in the balance sheet, and charge them against profits of the period in which the future sales revenue is earned.

- If there is no reasonable expectation of sufficient future revenue to cover cost incurred, the irrecoverable cost should be charged to revenue in the year under review. Thus stocks and work-in-progress normally need to be stated at cost, or, if lower, at net realisable value.

- The comparison of cost and net realisable value should be made separately for each item of stock, but if this is impractical, categories of similar stock items can be grouped together.

- Net realisable value is defined as the amount for which it is expected that items of stock and work-in-progress can be disposed of without creating either profit or loss at the time of sale, that is, the estimated selling price (net of trade discounts but not settlement discounts) less all further costs to completion and all costs to be incurred in marketing, selling and distributing.

- Cost is that expenditure which has been incurred in the normal course of business in bringing the product to its present location and condition. This expenditure should include, in addition to the cost of purchase, such costs of conversion which are appropriate. Cost of purchase typically includes import duties, transport and handling costs and any other attributable costs, less trade discounts, rebates and subsidies. Costs of conversion comprise costs specifically attributable to units of production (labour, direct expenses and subcontracted work), production overheads and any other overheads which are attributable to bringing the product or service to its present location and condition. *Abnormal* costs of production should be treated as an expense of the accounting period in which they arise.

- SSAP 9 identifies a number of methods which can satisfy the general principles laid down. Interestingly, the standard states that LIFO does *not* do so. This is in spite of the fact that use of LIFO is permitted by the Companies Act. However LIFO is not accepted by the Inland Revenue for taxation purposes.

3.2 SSAP 9 - Stocks and long-term contracts

In Chapter 9 we considered the accounting treatment of stock in trade. We shall now consider the main provisions of the accounting standard which deals with this topic. It will probably be helpful for you to look again at Chapter 9 just to remind yourself of the issues involved.

3.3 Stocks

(a) Disclosure

The amount at which stocks are stated in periodic financial statements should be the total of the lower of cost and nest realisable value of the separate items of stock or of groups of similar items. Stocks should be sub-classified in the balance sheet or in notes to the financial statements so as to indicate the amounts held in each of the main categories in the standard balance sheet formats (as adapted where appropriate) of Schedule 4 of the Companies Act, 1985.

(b) Long-term contracts

The accounting treatment of long-term contracts is also included in SSAP 9. At this stage it is not necessary for you to know the detailed provisions of SSAP 9 in this context, because it is not in the syllabus. The broad principles of dealing with long-term contracts were discussed in Chapter 9 and you are expected to be familiar with these.

4   SSAP 12 - ACCOUNTING FOR DEPRECIATION

4.1   Introduction

In Chapter 8, we considered the subject of accounting for depreciation in a fair amount of detail. At that stage it was made clear that the contents of Chapter 8 are entirely in agreement with SSAP 12. We shall now take a formal look at SSAP 12. Before you read this section, you may find it helpful to reread Chapter 8.

4.2   Activity

Without looking back at Chapter 8, try to define depreciation in the accounting sense.

4.3   Activity solution

Depreciation is defined in SSAP 12 as 'the measure of the wearing out, consumption or other reduction in the useful economic life of a fixed asset whether arising from use, effluxion of time or obsolescence through technological or market changes.'

4.4   Accounting treatment

SSAP 12 starts by making it clear that provision should be made for fixed assets having a finite economic life by allocating the cost (or revalued amount) less the estimated residual value of the assets as fairly as possible to the periods expected to benefit from their use. The depreciation methods used should be appropriate having regard to the types of asset and their use in the business. Thus SSAP 12 does not require the use of any particular method of depreciation (straight line, reducing balance, etc).

4.5   Activity

With which one of the accounting conventions is providing for depreciation most concerned?

4.6   Activity solution

Depreciation is most concerned with matching the expenses of generating revenues to those revenues in the same accounting period.

4.7   Consistency of accounting treatment

The accounting treatment in the profit and loss account must be consistent, so that the charge in the profit and loss account is based on the figure appearing in the balance sheet. The whole of the depreciation charge should be reflected in the profit and loss account. That is to say that no part of the depreciation charge should be taken directly to a reserve.

4.8   Reviewing estimates

The useful economic lives of assets must be estimated on a realistic basis and these estimates need to be reviewed frequently and, where necessary, revised. Normally, where it is felt necessary to revise the estimate of the asset life, future depreciation charges should seek to write off the net book amount over the revised estimation of the remaining life. Where, however, future results would be materially distorted, the adjustment to accumulated depreciation should be recognised in the accounts in accordance with FRS 3 *Reporting financial performance*. This means that the adjustment must be shown as an exceptional item under the same statutory format heading (that is 'cost of sales', 'distribution costs', etc.) as the ongoing depreciation charge.

The allocation of depreciation to accounting periods (the depreciation method) requires judgement by management in the light of technical, commercial and accounting considerations. In view of this, it is also necessary to review this allocation in the light of any changes in circumstances. A change from one method to another is permissible only on the ground that the new method gives a fairer presentation of the results and financial position.

If, at any time, the value of a fixed asset to the business has permanently diminished as a result of lower expectations of residual value and/or future economic benefit from using, the asset, the net book amount should be written down to a more realistic amount. The revised book amount should be depreciated over the remaining useful economic life of the asset.

4.9 Assets within the scope of SSAP 12

SSAP 12 applies to tall fixed assets except:

- Investment properties, which are the subject of a separate accounting standard (SSAP 19 - *Accounting for investment properties*);

- Goodwill, which is the subject of a separate accounting standard (SSAP 22 - *Accounting for goodwill*);

- Development costs, which are dealt with in a separate accounting standard (SSAP 13 - *Accounting for research and development*);

- Investments (outside the business).

4.10 Activity

Would SSAP 12 apply to land and buildings?

4.11 Activity solution

Buildings are normally included within the scope of SSAP 12, but land (because it normally has an infinite economic life and/or its residual value is likely to be no less than it cost) is usually excluded.

4.12 Disclosure requirements

The following should be disclosed in the financial statements for each major class of depreciable asset:

- the depreciation methods used;
- the useful economic lives or the depreciation rates used;
- total depreciation charged for the period; and
- the gross amount of depreciable assets and the related accumulated depreciation.

Where there has been a change in the depreciation method used, the effect, if material, should be disclosed in the year of the change. The reason for the change should also be disclosed.

Where assets have been revalued, the effect of the revaluation on the depreciation charge should, if material, be disclosed in the year of revaluation.

5 SSAP 13 – ACCOUNTING FOR RESEARCH AND DEVELOPMENT

5.1 Introduction

The treatment of research and development (R&D) costs poses a problem for the accountant. On the one hand, it can be argued that such costs are incurred in order to secure future profits and so, in accordance with the matching convention, should be carried forward in the balance sheet and written off in the period in which the revenues generated by the R&D arise. On the other hand, it can be argued that future revenues arising from R&D are often uncertain and so should not be anticipated. The convention of prudence would therefore require the accountant to write off the R&D costs in the year in which they were incurred rather than allow them to be carried forward. In many businesses, R&D costs are incurred on a continuous basis and it may not always be practical to attempt matching such costs against revenues. It can often be difficult, if not impossible, to match R&D costs with related revenues.

5.2   Identifying R&D costs

SSAP 13 states that research and development activity is distinctive from other forms of business activity because a significant amount of innovation is involved and new ground is broken rather than existing patterns followed.

Some examples of R&D costs given in SSAP 13 include:

- experimental, theoretical or other work aimed at discovering new knowledge or advancing existing knowledge
- searching for ways to apply that knowledge
- testing to find or evaluate alternative products, services or processes
- work carried out on pre-production prototypes
- design of products, processes or services involving new technology or substantial improvements
- construction and operation of pilot plants.

Activities which would *not* normally be included as R&D include:

- testing and analysis for either quality or quantity control
- periodic changes to existing products, services or processes even though some improvement may be involved
- operational research not directly related to a particular R&D activity
- costs incurred in taking corrective action for breakdowns during commercial operations
- legal and administrative work relating to applications for, or the sale and licensing of, patents
- design and construction of facilities unless related to a particular R&D project
- market research.

5.3   Accounting for R&D costs

SSAP 13 approaches the problem of accounting for R&D costs by dividing R&D into three separate categories. These categories are as follows:

Pure (basic) research

This kind of research is undertaken to advance scientific or technical knowledge without there being any specific objective or clear understanding of the likely outcome.

Applied research

This involves using knowledge acquired from pure research in order to meet a specific objective of the business.

Development

This is work undertaken with a view to either developing new or improving existing products, services, systems and processes. Development work is undertaken before commercial operations begin.

5.4   Activity

What problems may arise for a company when attempting to apply these categories to its R&D costs?

5.5   Activity solution

SSAP 13 identifies examples of R & D costs. It also provides three categories under which R & D costs are analysed.

- The most difficult problem a company may face in this analysis is where there are shared facilities, such as a building and equipment, which may be used to carry on any one or more of the categories at the same time. How are overheads administration and so on to be allocated; any method must be purely arbitrary?

- There is also, clearly, a problem of definition in that the boundary between each category in practice may be very fine.

- What happens in a situation where applied research suddenly generates another line of thought or investigation, such as pure research? How much of the costs should be transferred from category to category?

5.6   Requirements of SSAP 13

SSAP 13 requires that both pure and applied research costs be written off in the period incurred rather than carried forward to future years. For these types of costs, the arguments put forward above concerning the uncertainty of future returns and the difficulties of matching are seen as more compelling.

SSAP 13 also requires development expenditure to be written off when incurred. However, it recognises that, in some cases, there is a reasonable expectation that profits will arise directly from development expenditure being incurred and such expenditure may be matched against future revenues. As a result, it would be acceptable to carry this expenditure forward. The amounts carried forward would be shown as an intangible fixed asset on the balance sheet.

The standard sets out certain conditions which must be met if development expenditure is to be carried forward. These conditions are that:

- the project must be capable of being clearly defined
- development expenditure relating to the project must be separately identified
- the outcome of the project must be reasonably certain concerning its technical feasibility and its commercial viability. In the latter case factors to consider include market conditions, competition, and environmental and consumer legislation
- further costs, including development, production, selling and administration costs, relating to the project are expected to be covered by future revenues relating to the project
- there are adequate resources, or there is a reasonable expectation that they will be available, to complete the project and provide any additional working capital arising from the project.

These are stringent conditions; all of them must be satisfied for development expenditure to be carried forward. Moreover, at the end of each accounting period, any development expenditure carried forward on the balance sheet must be reviewed to ensure the conditions relating to each project are still being met. Where the conditions are no longer being met the development expenditure must be immediately written off.

It should be emphasised that development expenditure does not have to be carried forward if the above conditions are met. The company is given a choice of either immediate write-off or deferral. Where the company chooses the latter, the period over which the development expenditure is written off will be the period in which the product is expected to be sold and begins when commercial production commences. Moreover, the policy selected concerning the treatment of development expenditure must be applied consistently by the company.

5.7   Activity

How might it be possible, in practice, to get around the requirement to treat development expenditure relating to different projects in a consistent manner?

5.8   Activity solution

- SSAP 13 only allows R & D costs on development expenditure to be carried forward providing a stringent set of conditions is met.

- All of these conditions must be met.

- In certain cases the company could argue that all the conditions can no longer be met in the annual review.

- Clearly, the expenditure on different projects is being treated inconsistently – there is now a mixture of write-off *and* deferral.

5.9   Fixed assets acquired for R & D purposes

Sometimes fixed assets are employed in research and development activities. These assets should be capitalised, like other fixed assets, and written off over their useful lives. The depreciation charge will form part of the total depreciation charge disclosed under the requirements of the Companies Acts and will also be included in the profit and loss account as part of any research and development costs written off.

5.10   Disclosure in the accounts

Where development costs have been deferred and therefore appear on the balance sheet of the company, SSAP 13 states that there must be disclosure of movements on the deferred development expenditure account, including balances brought forward and carried forward at the beginning and end of the period. There should also be a clear explanation of the accounting policies used in relation to R&D.

SSAP 13 also requires that public companies and certain other large companies disclose the total R&D expenditure charged to the profit and loss account. R&D expenditure for the current period and any development expenditure amortised (depreciated) during the period must be separately disclosed.

6   SSAP 17 – ACCOUNTING FOR POST BALANCE SHEET EVENTS

6.1   Definition of post balance sheet events

Post balance sheet events are defined in this standard as being:

> ...those events, both favourable and unfavourable, which occur between the balance sheet date and the date on which the financial statements are approved by the board of directors.

We have seen in earlier chapters that the balance sheet is designed to reflect the financial position of the business at the point in time when the balance sheet is drawn up. However, it is possible that certain events may occur between the date of the balance sheet and the date the accounts are approved by the board of directors which shed new light on conditions existing at the balance sheet date. If the balance sheet is to provide a true and fair view of the financial position of a business then some form of disclosure of these conditions is really required.

6.2   Adjusting and non-adjusting events

SSAP 17 draws a distinction between an 'adjusting' event ' and a 'non-adjusting event'. An adjusting event is one which provides new or additional information about conditions at the balance sheet date. A non-adjusting event, on the other hand, relates to conditions which did not exist at the balance sheet date but, nevertheless, provides information which can be useful in understanding fully the financial position of the company.

An adjusting event, as the name suggests, must be incorporated in the final balance sheet to be approved by the board of directors (and for subsequent publication). The appendix to SSAP 17 provides several examples of items which would normally be considered as being an adjusting event. These include the following:

- assets purchased or sold during the financial year whose price was determined after the year-end

- the permanent diminution in value of property arising during the financial year where the valuation took place after the year-end

- information received (such as a copy of the accounts) relating to an unlisted company which provides evidence that there has been a permanent diminution in the value of the investment in that company

- evidence after the year-end which sheds new light on the profit taken on long-term contracts or the net realisable value of stocks and work-in-progress

- information concerning the insolvency of a debtor or the renegotiation of the amount of debt outstanding

- the subsequent announcement of tax rates relating to the financial period

- the discovery of errors or fraud which result in inaccuracies in the final accounts

- insurance claims received or agreed which were still being negotiated at the balance sheet date.

Sometimes events occurring after the balance sheet date may lead to a situation where it is no longer appropriate to apply the going-concern convention when preparing the accounts. Hence some adjustment will also be required in these circumstances.

A non-adjusting event will not be taken into consideration when preparing the final accounts. However, it may be necessary to disclose such an event as a note to the accounts. Disclosure is required where the amount is material and, therefore, its non-disclosure would have a significant effect on the ability of users to assess properly the financial position of the company.

Disclosure of a non-adjusting event is also required where the event is simply to reverse or complete a transaction arising before the year-end and which was designed to alter the appearance of the balance sheet. This type of transaction is referred to as 'window dressing' and is usually carried out to provide a much healthier view of the financial position of the company than is really the case. Such transactions are normally regarded as being misleading and unacceptable.

Disclosure of a non-adjusting event requires details about the nature of the event and either an estimate of the financial effect of the event or a statement that the financial effects cannot be quantified. The financial effects should be stated on a pre-tax basis, although the tax effects should be explained where it is necessary for a proper understanding of the accounts.

The appendix to SSAP 17 also provides examples of non-adjusting events. These include the following:

- acquisitions and mergers
- exchange rate fluctuations
- industrial disputes
- share or debenture issues
- increases in pension benefits
- government action (such as nationalisation or privatisation)
- changes in trading activities
- sale or purchase of fixed assets
- loss of assets through a catastrophe such as fire or flooding.

6.3 Activity

Place each of the following events in the relevant column below.

		Adjusting event	Non-adjusting event	Neither
1	Government nationalisation of fixed assets on the balance sheet date			
2	The sale of a fixed asset after the balance sheet date at a much lower price than it was stated on the draft balance sheet			
3	The sale of stock after the balance sheet date at a much lower price than it was stated on the draft balance sheet			
4	The takeover of a rival company after the balance sheet date			

6.4 Activity solution

		Adjusting event	Non-adjusting event	Neither
1	Government nationalisation of fixed assets on the balance sheet date			✓
2	The sale of a fixed asset after the balance sheet date at a much lower price than it was stated on the draft balance sheet		✓	
3	The sale of stock after the balance sheet date at a much lower price than it was stated on the draft balance sheet	✓		
4	The takeover of a rival company after the balance sheet date		✓	

7 SSAP 18 – ACCOUNTING FOR CONTINGENCIES

7.1 Definition of a contingency

SSAP 18 defines a contingency as:

a condition which exists at the balance sheet date, where the outcome will be confirmed only on the occurrence or non-occurrence of one or more uncertain future events.

A contingency differs from a post balance sheet event in that the former exists at the balance sheet date whereas the latter arises between the balance sheet date and the date of approval of the accounts by the board of directors. Some examples of contingencies may be:

- legal action where the outcome has yet to be decided
- guarantees undertaken on behalf of other entities
- options available to acquire assets.

However, uncertainties arising as a result of estimates that have to be made in preparing the accounts such as the residual value of fixed assets, the net realisable value of stocks held, and the amount of bad debts, are not regarded as contingent items and, therefore, do not fall within the scope of the statement.

7.2 Requirements of SSAP 18

A contingency may result in either a gain or loss arising at some future date. Where a contingent gain is probable then it should be disclosed in the notes to the accounts. However, where a contingent gain is anything less than probable no disclosure is required in the accounts.

In the case of a contingent loss, a provision should be made where the loss is probable and can also be estimated with reasonable accuracy at the date at which the accounts are approved by the board of directors. If there is only a reasonable *possibility* that the contingent loss will arise then disclosure in the notes to the accounts only is required. If a contingent loss is considered to be remote then no disclosure in the accounts is required at all. It is clear from the above that SSAP 18 does require the use of subjective judgement when determining the appropriate accounting treatment for contingencies.

We can see from the above that contingent gains and losses may be treated quite differently in the accounts. Whereas a contingent gain is never adjusted in the accounts, a contingent loss may be taken into account when measuring profit and financial position. This difference in treatment is, of course, consistent with the convention of prudence discussed earlier in this book.

When either a contingent gain or contingent loss is required to be disclosed as a note to the accounts the following information should be supplied:

- the nature of the contingency
- the uncertainties which will affect the final outcome
- a prudent estimate of the financial effect of the contingency (on a pre-tax basis) or a statement that it is not possible to quantify the financial effect.

7.3 Activity

Herex Ltd produces a range of pharmaceutical products. At the balance sheet date the following information is available:

- Ms Entwhistle took one of the company's products and then felt drowsy when driving home from work. She crashed her car and suffered serious injury which she claims was due to the medication she took. There were no warnings on the product packaging concerning possible side-effects and the company's legal advisors believe that Ms Entwhistle has a good chance of winning the forthcoming court case and that the court will agree to the damages claim of £80,000.

- Another company Derex Ltd has launched a new product which Herex Ltd believes infringes its patent rights. The company's legal advisors are confident the current court case will find in favour of Herex Ltd and that the damages requested of £200,000 will be agreed.

- A Ms Sidebotham drank one of the company's cleaning products by mistake and became violently ill. The packaging on the product stated clearly that it was not for internal consumption. The company's legal advisors do not think there is much chance that the claim before the courts for damages of £30,000 will be accepted.

What accounting treatment and disclosure would you recommend for of each of the above?

7.4   Activity solution

(1)   The legal advisers state that 'Ms Entwhistle has a good chance of winning the forthcoming court case'.

- This is an example of a contingent loss,
- The loss has a high degree of probability of arising
- The loss can be quantified with reasonable accuracy

'. . . the Court will agree to the damages claim of £80,000'.

Recommended: disclosure is by way of a provision of £80,000 to reduce pre-tax profits.

(2)   The legal advisors 'are confident the current court case will find in favour of Herex Ltd.'; 'damages requested of £200,000 will be agreed':

- This is an example of a contingent gain
- The gain has high probability of arising.

Recommended: disclosure by way of a note which makes it clear pre-tax profits are likely to be increased by £200,000 in a future year.

(3)   The legal advisors, probably quite rightly, given the facts of the case, 'do not think there is much chance that the claim of £30,000 will be accepted'.

- This is an example of a contingent loss
- The outcome of a decision against Herex Ltd is remote.

Recommended: that no disclosure be made in the accounts.

8   FRS 3 REPORTING FINANCIAL PERFORMANCE

8.1   Introduction

This is an important accounting standard which sets out radical changes to the way in which financial performance must be reported. The standard represents an attempt to shift the emphasis of the profit and loss account away from the final profit figure, by ensuring that users are provided with a more complete picture of the various gains and losses arising during the year.

There are two major changes arising from the standard. The first is that the **format of the profit and loss account** has undergone significant alteration. The second is that a number of new **statements and notes to the accounts** must now be prepared in order to provide a more complete picture of the movements in wealth during the period. Below we consider in detail both of these major changes.

8.2   Profit and loss account format

Various elements of financial performance must now be shown separately in the profit and loss account. These elements are:

1   *Results of continuing operations* (including any operations acquired during the period).

2   *Results of discontinued operations.* The analysis between continuing (including acquisitions) and discontinued operations should be disclosed to the level of operating profit. The minimum disclosure requirements are to show separate analysis of turnover and operating profit for continuing operations (including acquisitions) and discontinued operations.

3   *Certain exceptional items,* which are as follows:

- Gains or losses on the sale or termination of an operation.
- Gains or losses on the disposal of fixed assets.
- Any costs occurred in relation to fundamental reorganisation and restructuring.

Exceptional items are material items which fall within the ordinary activities of the business but which need to be disclosed because of their size or incidence. Although as already indicated the three exceptional items listed above must be shown separately in the profit and loss account, other forms of exceptional item should be included under the statutory headings to which they relate. This requirement is designed to ensure that users do not place too much emphasis on the profit figure *excluding* exceptional items. The exceptional items that do not fall within the three categories listed above should be disclosed separately as a note to the accounts, or, if the amount is of sufficient importance, it can be given more prominence by placing it on the face of the profit and loss account.

4   *Extraordinary items.* These are abnormal items which are not part of the normal operations of the reporting entity and are not likely to recur. They do not include exceptional items such as those listed in 3 above. FRS 3 points out that extraordinary items would be very unusual and offers no examples of items which may fall within this category. This item is now expected to appear in financial reports very rarely, if at all. Before FRS 3 was published, extraordinary items regularly appeared in the accounts of companies and became, according to one member of the ASB, '...a convenient repository for all unwanted costs'. As a result, comparisons of performance between years and between companies became difficult.

The layout required for the profit and loss account can be illustrated diagrammatically as follows:

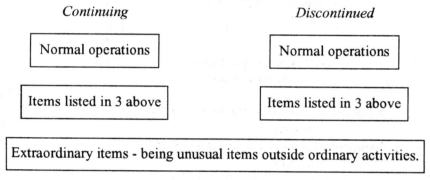

8.3   Activity

Why do you think it is necessary to show separately the different elements of financial performance? How might this be of value to users?

8.4   Activity solution

FRS 3 points out that different elements of the company's activities may differ in respect to stability, risk and predictability. By disclosing each element separately, users should gain a better understanding of the results for the period and should help them in deciding the extent to which past results are a guide to the future.

8.5   Earnings per share

The earning per share (EPS) of a Stock Exchange listed company must be shown on the face of the profit and loss account. EPS is an important investor ratio which is considered later in this text in Chapter 24. The ratio divides the profit attributable to ordinary shareholders by the number of ordinary shares issued in order to derive a measure of share return. FRS 3 states that the profit attributable to ordinary shareholders must be derived after taking into account extraordinary items and preference dividends. If an additional measure of EPS, based on another measure of profit, is shown, this must be calculated on a consistent basis and must be reconciled with the figure calculated in accordance with FRS 3. The EPS figure as required by FRS 3 must be at least as prominent in the accounts as any additional EPS measure and the reasons for calculating the additional measure must be explained.

8.6   Acceptable formats

FRS 3 provides illustrative examples of acceptable profit and loss account formats which include the presentation of earnings per share. One such example is reproduced below, along with a note expanding on the information contained in the profit and loss account.

Profit and loss account example

	19X3	19X3	19X2 as restated
	£m	£m	£m
Turnover			
Continuing operations	550		500
Acquisitions	50		
	600		
Discontinued operations	175		190
		775	690
Cost of sales		(620)	(555)
Gross profit		155	135
Net operating expenses		(104)	(83)
Operating profit			
Continuing operations	50		40
Acquisitions	6		
	56		
Discontinued operations	(15)		12
Less 19X2 provision	10		
		51	52
Profit on sale of properties in continuing operations		9	6
Provisions for loss on operations to be discontinued			(30)
Loss on disposal of discontinued operations	(17)		
Less 19X2 provision	20		
		3	
Profit on ordinary activities before interest		63	28
Interest payable		(18)	(15)
Profit on ordinary activities before taxation		45	13
Tax on profit on ordinary activities		(16)	(6)
Profit for the financial year		29	7
Dividends		(8)	(1)
Retained profit for the financial year		21	6
Earnings per share		**39p**	**10p**
Adjustments		xp	xp
(to be itemised and an adequate description to be given)			
Adjusted earnings per share		yp	yp

(Reasons for calculating the adjusted earnings per share to be given)

8.7 Additional financial statements and notes

These additional financial statements and notes provide a number of benefits to users. In particular, they:

- bring together related and relevant information which appears in different parts of the financial statements;
- provide additional information for evaluation and comparison purposes;
- show the effect of movements in wealth on shareholders funds.

Each of the additional statements is considered below.

8.8 Statement of total recognised gains and losses

This statement brings together the recognised gains (both realised and unrealised) which have arisen during the period from whatever source. It is regarded as an important financial statement as it enables users to see the total gains and losses which have been recorded since the last accounts. This statement is valuable because not all gains and losses may pass through the profit and loss account.

8.9 Activity

Can you think of any gains or losses which are recognised during a period but which may not pass through the profit and loss account?

(Hint: Think about gains and losses arising from holding certain fixed assets)

8.10 Activity solution

This is quite a difficult activity as you have not yet come across some of the items shown below. However, the following items would be relevant in answering this activity:

- Unrealised gains or losses on the revaluation of freehold land and buildings
- Unrealised gains and losses on (long-term) trade investments held
- Gains or losses arising from currency translation differences on overseas investments.

8.11 Illustration

An illustration of the required statement of total recognised gains and losses is set out in FRS 3 and is reproduced below.

Statement of Total Recognised Gains and Losses

	19X3	19X2 as restated
	£m	£m
Profit for the financial year	29	7
Unrealised surplus on revaluation of properties	4	6
Unrealised (loss)/gain on trade investments	(3)	7
	30	20
Currency translation differences on foreign currency net investments	(2)	5
Total recognised gains and losses relating to the year	28	25
Prior year adjustment	(10)	
Total gains and losses recognised since last annual report	18	

8.12 Note of historical cost profits and losses

Companies which revalue their fixed assets will depreciate those assets on the revalued amount rather than on the original cost of the assets. This can create problems when making comparisons between companies. FRS 3 aims to make comparisons easier by requiring a note, or memorandum, to the accounts. This memorandum restates the accounts, in abbreviated form, on the basis of depreciation being charged according to the historic cost of assets rather than their revalued amounts.

The note is required where there is a material difference between the results shown on the profit and loss account and the results on an unmodified historic cost basis. This note, or memorandum, must be presented immediately after the profit and loss account or the statement of total recognised gains and losses.

An illustration of the required note of historical cost profits and losses is set out in FRS 3 and is shown below.

Note of historical cost profits and losses

	19X3	19X2 as restated
	£m	£m
Reported profit on ordinary activities before taxation	45	13
Realisation of property revaluation gains of previous years	9	10
Difference between a historical cost depreciation charge and the actual depreciation charge of the year calculated on the revalued amount	5	4
Historical cost profit on ordinary activities before taxation	59	27
Historical cost profit for the year retained after taxation and dividends	35	20

8.13   Reconciliation of movements in shareholders' funds

FRS 3 points out that the profit and loss account and the statement of total recognised gains and losses reflect the performance of the company, or other reporting entry, for the period. However, other changes may occur to the shareholders' funds which can be important in understanding the financial position of the company. The reconciliation of movements in shareholders' funds sets out the effect on shareholders' funds of the various changes that occurred during the period which, in addition to recognised gains and losses, may include dividends announced and the issue and redemption of shares. Any amounts written off to shareholders' funds, such as goodwill, will also be shown.

An illustration of this statement is set out in FRS 3 and is reproduced below.

Reconciliation of movements in shareholders' funds

	19X3	19X2 as restated
	£m	£m
Profit for the financial year	29	7
Dividends	(8)	(1)
	21	6
Other recognised gains and losses relating to the year (net)	(1)	18
New share capital subscribed	20	1
Goodwill written-off	(25)	
Net addition to shareholders' funds	15	25
Opening shareholders' funds (originally £375m, before deducting prior year adjustment of £10m)	365	340
Closing shareholders' funds	380	365

8.14   Prior period adjustments

Often, adjustments which relate to prior periods are shown in the accounts for the current period. In most cases, these adjustments arise because, in practice, it is necessary to make estimates when preparing accounts. When these estimates turn out to be incorrect, an adjustment is required. These adjustments are dealt with in the profit and loss account of the period in which the need for adjustment is identified and do not represent exceptional or extraordinary items.

8.15 Activity

Can you think of *three* expense items where estimates have to be made when preparing accounts and where some adjustment may be necessary in future periods?

8.16 Activity solution

Three examples of such expense items are:

* provision for doubtful debts
* bad debts written-off
* provision for depreciation.

8.17 Adjustments made against reserves

However, in some cases, prior period adjustments should not be passed through the profit and loss account, but instead should be adjusted against the opening balance on retained profits or reserves. This would be appropriate where the adjustment arose from a change in accounting policy or from a fundamental error.

These types of adjustments are normally regarded as rare occurrences. Changes in accounting policy, for example, should not be made lightly as this contravenes the convention of consistency. Change is only justified if the new policy provides a fairer presentation of the results of the company than the old policy. Similarly, fundamental errors which may destroy the validity of the published financial statements of prior periods are not expected to be a common event.

An illustrative example of movements on the reserves, including prior year adjustments is given in FRS 3 and is reproduced below.

Reserves

	Share premium account	*Revaluation reserve*	*Profit and loss account*	*Total*
	£m	*£m*	*£m*	*£m*
At beginning of year as previously stated	44	200	120	364
Prior year adjustment			(10)	(10)
At beginning of year as restated	44	200	110	354
Premium on issue of shares (nominal value £7m)	13			13
Goodwill written-off			(25)	(25)
Transfer from profit and loss account of the year			21	21
Transfer of realised profits		(14)	14	0
Decrease in value of trade investment		(3)		(3)
Currency translation differences on foreign currency net investments			(2)	(2)
Surplus on property revaluations		4		4
At end of year	57	187	118	362

Note: Nominal share capital at end of year £18m (19X2 £11m)

9   STOCK EXCHANGE REQUIREMENTS

9.1   Introduction

The Stock Exchange of the UK and the Republic of Ireland has added its own rules to those imposed by the law and accounting standards in respect of the published final accounts of those companies which are traded by Stock Exchange members.

The Stock Exchange requirements mainly extend the requirements of the Companies Acts and of accounting standards. The requirements include the following:

- final published accounts must be sent to the normal recipients within six months of the end of the relevant accounting period
- details or analysis must be provided, including:
- geographical analysis of turnover
- the principal countries in which the company operates
- details of holdings of more that 20% of the equity shares of other companies
- the amount of any interest which has been capitalised, that is, treated as an asset.
- explanations resulting from any significant departures from any accounting standards and of any significant differences between published forecasts of trading results and the actual results
- interim (six-monthly) accounts must be prepared and published. These must give an outline of the company's trading for the half-year, but not its position.

9.2   Sanctions for non-compliance

The sanction which the Stock Exchange can invoke against companies which do not comply with these requirements is to deny the Stock Exchange members the right to trade in the shares of the company. This is a powerful sanction. Existing shareholders are denied the opportunity to sell their shares in an orderly market and this would have a very adverse effect on the company's share price. This would put a lot of pressure on the directors.

10   CHAPTER SUMMARY

- In this chapter we have considered the role of accounting standards and the nature of the accounting standard-setting body. We have seen that accounting standards aim to narrow the differences which exist in the accounting practices of companies. By ensuring greater uniformity of measurement and presentation of accounting areas the quality of financial reporting should be improved.

- We have examined a number of important SSAPs in some detail in this chapter. SSAP 2 – Disclosure of accounting policies - was designed to help users gain a better understanding of how key figures appearing in the accounts were derived. The basic requirement is that there should be disclosure of accounting policies adopted by the company which are important for determining the profit for the period or stating the financial position at the end of the period. The SSAP makes a clear distinction between fundamental concepts, accounting bases and accounting policies and identifies four fundamental concepts which are regarded as generally accepted.

- SSAP 13 – Accounting for research and development – deals with the accounting problems relating to this area by making a distinction between pure research, applied research and development. Pure and applied research must be written off in the period incurred whereas development costs may be carried forward and written off in subsequent years. The rationale for this difference in treatment is that, in some cases, there is a reasonable expectation that profits will arise directly from development expenditure being incurred and such expenditure may be matched against future revenues. As a result, it would be acceptable to carry this expenditure forward. However, the SSAP lays down stringent conditions to be met before development expenditure can be carried forward in the accounts.

- SSAP 17 – Accounting for post balance sheet events – makes a distinction between two types of post balance sheet events – adjusting events and non-adjusting events. Adjusting events provide new information about conditions existing at the balance sheet date and therefore must be taken into account when preparing the final balance sheet for approval by the board of directors. Non-adjusting events concern conditions which arise after the balance sheet date and will not affect the figures shown in the accounts. However, if material, a non-adjusting event will require disclosure as a note to the accounts.

- SSAP 18 – Accounting for contingencies – requires that contingent losses be provided for in the accounts if it is probable that a future event will confirm the loss and that the amount of the loss can be estimated with reasonable accuracy. Where no provision is made there should be full disclosure as a note to the accounts unless the possibility of a future loss is unlikely. A contingent gain is never accrued but should be shown as a note to the accounts if it is probable the gain will eventually be realised.

- FRS 3 provides guidance for the detail that must be disclosed on the face of the profit and loss account, and the notes that must accompany the profit and loss account in order that a true and fair view can be given of a company's financial performance for a period.

- Finally we considered the role of the Stock Exchange in financial reporting. We have seen that, for listed companies, there are further financial reporting requirements which must be taken into account. These are laid down by the Stock Exchange and are designed to extend the requirements as set out in the Companies Acts and relevant accounting standards.

11 APPENDIX   UK ACCOUNTING STANDARDS

		Year of issue/revision
SSAP 1	Accounting for associated companies	1982
SSAP 2	Disclosure of accounting policies	1971
SSAP 3	Earnings per share	1974
SSAP 4	Accounting for government grants	1990
SSAP 5	Accounting for value added tax	1974
SSAP 8	The treatment of taxation under the imputation system in the accounts of companies	1977
SSAP 9	Stocks and long-term contracts	1988
SSAP 12	Accounting for depreciation	1987
SSAP 13	Accounting for research and development	1989
SSAP 15	Accounting for deferred tax	1985
SSAP 17	Accounting for post balance sheet events	1980
SSAP 18	Accounting for contingencies	1980
SSAP 19	Accounting for investment properties	1981
SSAP 20	Foreign currency translation	1983
SSAP 21	Accounting for leases and hire purchase contracts	1984
SSAP 22	Accounting for goodwill	1989
SSAP 24	Accounting for pension costs	1988
SSAP 25	Segmental reporting	1990
FRS 1	Cash flow statements	1991
FRS 2	Accounting for subsidiary undertakings	1992
FRS 3	Reporting financial performance	1992
FRS 4	Capital instruments	1993
FRS 5	Reporting the substance of transactions	1994
FRS 6	Acquisitions and mergers	1994
FRS 7	Fair values in acquisition accounting	1994

Several standards have been issued and subsequently withdrawn, which explains the gaps in the numerical sequence.

Many of the standards have been revised and reissued. The issue dates given are the reissue dates, where relevant. This explains the fact that the standards are not listed in chronological order.

12   SELF TEST QUESTIONS

12.1   Identify the four types of accounting standard mentioned in the chapter. (1.11)

12.2   Distinguish between 'accounting bases' and accounting policies' as defined in SSAP 2 – Disclosure of accounting policies. (2.6, 2.7)

12.3   Which one of the following items would not be regarded as research and development expenditure for the purpose of SSAP 13 – Accounting for research and development?

    (a)   construction and operation of pilot plants

    (b)   work on pre-production prototypes

    (c)   market research

    (d)   searching for applications of new knowledge. (3.2)

12.4   Distinguish between an 'adjusting event' and a 'non-adjusting event' for the purpose of SSAP 17 – Accounting for post balance sheet events. (4.2)

12.5   What is a 'contingency' as defined by SSAP 18 – Accounting for contingencies'? How does a contingency differ from a post balance sheet event? (5.1)

13   EXAMINATION TYPE QUESTIONS

13.1   Demand for Rules

'The demand for rule making...comes largely from an insatiable appetite for rules.'

What are the arguments against accounting standards and for greater choice in financial reporting?

(20 marks)

13.2   Accounting Concepts

SSAP 2 (Disclosure of accounting policies) states that there are four fundamental accounting concepts which have general acceptability.

(a)   State and briefly explain each of the these four fundamental concepts.

(b)   State and briefly explain three other accounting concepts.

(c)   In what circumstances might you abandon one of the concepts in either part a) or part b) when preparing a financial statement?

(20 marks)

13.3   Development Expenditure

(a)   Discuss the criteria which SSAP 13 (Accounting for research and development) states should be used when considering whether development expenditure should be written off in an accounting period or carried forward.

(b)   Discuss to what extent these are consistent with fundamental accounting concepts as defined in SSAP 2 – Disclosure of accounting policies.

(20 marks)

13.4 Financial Statements

'Financial statements should be prepared on the basis of conditions existing at the balance sheet date' (SSAP 17 – Accounting for post balance sheet events).

(a) Recognising the possibility of time lags in establishing what conditions actually exist at the balance sheet date, how does SSAP 17 seek to ensure that financial accounts are prepared in accordance with this rule?

(b) How does SSAP 17 seek to ensure that financial accounts prepared in accordance with this rule are not misleading?

Your answer should include three examples relating to (a) and a further three examples relating to (b).

(20 marks)

13.5 Disagreement

Your managing director is having a polite disagreement with the auditors on the subject of accounting for contingencies. Since the finance director is absent on sick leave he has come to you for advice. The auditor has given him the text of Part 3 of SSAP 18, and this is attached as Appendix A.

It appears that your firm is involved in four unrelated legal cases, P, Q, R and S. In case P the firm is suing for £10,000, in case Q the firm is suing for £20,000, in case R the firm is being sued for £30,000 and in case S the firm is being sued for £40,000. The firm has been advised by its expert and expensive lawyers that the chances of the firm winning each case are as follows:

Case	Percentage likelihood of winning
P	8
Q	92
R	8
S	92

Required

Write a memorandum to the managing director which

(i) explains why SSAP 18 is relevant to these situations,

(ii) states the required accounting treatment for each of the four cases in the published accounts,

(iii) gives journal entries for any necessary adjustments in the double-entry records,

(iv) suggests the contents of any Notes to the Accounts that are required by the SSAP,

(v) briefly discusses whether SSAP 18 leads to a satisfactory representation of the position.

Appendix A Part 3 – Standard accounting practice

15 In addition to amounts accrued under the fundamental concept of prudence in SSAP 2 *Disclosure of accounting policies*, a material contingent loss should be accrued in financial statements where it is probable that a future event will confirm a loss which can be estimated with reasonable accuracy at the date on which the financial statements are approved by the board of directors.

16 A material contingent loss not accrued under paragraph 15 above should be disclosed except where the possibility of loss is remote.

17 Contingent gains should not be accrued in financial statements. A material contingent gain should be disclosed in financial statements only if it is probable that the gain will be realised.

18   In respect of each contingency which is required to be disclosed under paragraphs 16 and 17 above, the following information should be stated by way of notes in financial statements:

(a)   the nature of the contingency;

(b)   the uncertainties which are expected to affect the ultimate outcome; and

(c)   a prudent estimate of the financial effect, made at the date on which the financial statements are approved by the board of directors; or a statement that it is not practicable to make such an estimate.

19   Where there is disclosure of an estimate of the financial effect of a contingency, the amount disclosed should be the potential financial effect. In the case of a contingent loss, this should be reduced by:

(a)   any amounts accrued; and

(b)   the amounts of any components where the possibility of loss is remote.

The net amount only need be disclosed.

20   The estimate of the financial effect should be disclosed before taking account of taxation, and the taxation implications of a contingency crystallising should be explained where necessary for a proper understanding of the financial position.

21   Where both the nature of, and the uncertainties which affect, a contingency in respect of an individual transaction are common to a large number of similar transactions, the financial effect of the contingency need not be individually estimated but may be based on a group of similar transactions. In these circumstances the separate contingencies need not be individually disclosed.

Date from which effective

22   The accounting practices set out in this statement should be adopted as soon as possible and regarded as standard in respect of financial statements relating to accounting periods beginning on or after 1 September 1980.

(20 marks)

(ACCA, Pilot paper)

14   ANSWERS TO EXAMINATION TYPE QUESTIONS

14.1   Demand for Rules

There are some who believe that accounting standards have an adverse effect on the quality of financial reports. They believe that it is better for companies to have some choice in the way in which they report financial matters. The main arguments in favour of accounting choice rather than accounting standards are as follows:

•   By permitting a company to choose its own methods of financial reporting, an insight will be provided into its 'corporate personality'. Thus a company which is risk averse is likely to adopt very conservative accounting policies, such as immediate write off of goodwill and research and development expenditure. A risk-seeking company, on the other hand, would favour less conservative methods of accounting. Whilst this is an interesting point it can be argued that there are other (more direct) ways in which 'corporate personality' may be assessed. Making inferences about attitudes to risk for example, based on the choice of accounting policies may prove unreliable.

•   No two companies are exactly the same. Each company is unique and should be allowed to adopt accounting methods which are most suitable for its particular needs. By imposing rigid standards there is a danger that an artificial uniformity will be created which prevent users from recognising the unique aspects of a particular company. This point is similar to the one discussed above insofar that it stresses the importance of reflecting individual differences amongst companies. This again is an interesting argument although there is a danger of overstating the differences which exist between companies and understating those aspects which they have in common. It should be pointed out that many of the standards produced to date permit choice in the methods to be adopted by a company and could not be described as being rigid. In addition, a company can depart from a standard if it can be shown that the standard inhibits the reflection of a true and fair view of company performance and position.

- Accounting standards have not been based on any underlying conceptual framework. Thus, there is no clear rationale for insisting that particular methods of measurements or presentation be adopted by companies. It is true that accounting does not rest on any clear body of knowledge which explains and provides guidelines for accounting practice. In recent years, however, there have been some attempts to develop such a framework. The accounting profession has taken a rather pragmatic view in dealing with this point. Although there has been an increasing recognition of the need to develop a conceptual framework, it has been argued that there are accounting problems which are in pressing need of attention and that we cannot wait until a conceptual framework has been developed before addressing these problems. Thus, the search for a conceptual framework and the development of accounting standards must go on simultaneously.

- Standards may ossify accounting procedures. By laying down particular procedures to be followed, future development in this area may be inhibited. There is a danger that this may happen, although past experience suggests that there is a willingness by standard setters to review accounting standards and to make changes where necessary. The requirement for companies to produce cash flow statements in preference to funds flow statements to augment their financial reports is a case in point.

The case for accounting choice cannot be dismissed lightly. There is always a danger that rigid rules can become imposed without regard to particular circumstances and that the importance of the accountant's judgement in dealing with technical issues will become undervalued.

14.2   Accounting Concepts

(a)   Fundamental accounting concepts are:

- The going concern concept asserts that a business will continue indefinitely, unless contrary evidence is available.

- The accruals concept asserts that profit (loss) is the difference between matched revenues and expenses for the period rather than the difference between cash receipts and payments.

- The consistency concept asserts that the application of a policy should be consistent over time.

- The prudence concept asserts that accounting should err on the side of caution in recognition of expenses and claims.

(b)   Three additional accounting concepts are:

- The realisation concept asserts that revenues should normally be recognised when the goods or service pass to, and are accepted by, the customer.

- The historical costs concept asserts that assets should be shown in the accounts at their original cost.

- The matching concept asserts that in calculating profits, expenses should be matched against the revenues to which they relate.

(c)   The accounting concepts may be abandoned in the following circumstances.

- Where clearly to apply it would result in a true and fair view not being shown by the company accounts.

- In times of rapid price inflation, the historic cost concept can lead to the incorrect measurement of profit and asset values.

14.3   Development Expenditure

(a)   **SSAP 13** set out certain conditions which must be met if development expenditure is to be carried forward. These conditions are:

- The project must be capable of being clearly defined

- Development expenditure relating to the project must be separately identified.

- The outcome of the project must be reasonably certain concerning its technical feasibility and its commercial viability. In the latter case factors to consider include market conditions, competition, and environmental and consumer legislation.

- Further costs, including development, production, selling and administration costs relating to the project should be covered by future revenues relating to the project.

- There must be adequate resources, or a reasonable expectation that they will be available, to complete the project and provide any additional working capital arising from the project.

These are stringent conditions to be applied and all of these conditions must be satisfied for development expenditure to be carried forward. Moreover, at the end of each accounting period, any development expenditure carried forward on the balance sheet must be reviewed to ensure the conditions relating to each project are still being met. Where the conditions are no longer being met the development expenditure must be immediately written off.

It should be emphasised that development expenditure does not have to be carried forward if the above conditions are met. The company is given a choice of either immediate write-off or deferral. Where the company chooses the latter, the period over which the development expenditure is written off will be the period in which the product is expected to be sold and begins when commercial production commences. The policy selected for the treatment of development expenditure must be applied consistently by the company.

(b)   Where the company makes a choice to carry forward R & D expenditure, the going concern concept is being acknowledged. It also permits the accruals concept to be applied in that R & D will be set against future earnings from the product. Clearly, it is vital to apply the concept of consistency. Finally, it could be argued that the concept of prudence is being abandoned.

An immediate write off of all R & D expenditure (the alternative) could result in:

- no real transgression of the going concern concept

- the accruals concept being abandoned as future income will not be properly matched with all relevant expenditure

- the concept of consistency being acknowledged.

- the prudence concept being interpreted rather too harshly.

14.4   Financial Statements

(a)   The balance sheet is designed to reflect the financial position of the business at the point in time when the balance sheet is drawn up. However, it is possible that certain events may occur between the date of the balance sheet and the date the accounts are approved by the board of directors which shed new light on conditions existing at the balance sheet date. If the balance sheet is to provide a true and fair view of the financial position of a business then some form of disclosure of these conditions is really required.

SSAP 17 draws a distinction between an 'adjusting event' and a 'non-adjusting event'. An adjusting event is one which provides new or additional information concerning conditions at the balance sheet date. A non-adjusting event, on the other hand, relates to conditions which did not exist at the balance sheet date but, nevertheless, provides information which can be useful in fully understanding the financial position of the company.

(b)   An **adjusting event**, as the name suggests, must be incorporated in the final balance sheet to be approved by the board of directors (and for subsequent publication).

A **non-adjusting event** will not be taken into consideration when preparing the final accounts; however, it may be necessary to disclose such an event as a note to the accounts. Disclosure is required where the amount is material and, therefore, its non-disclosure would have a significant effect on the ability of users to assess properly the financial position of the company.

Examples of adjusting events are:

*   Assets purchased or sold during the financial year whose price was determined after the year end.

*   The permanent diminution in value of property arising during the financial year where the valuation took place after the year end.

*   Information received (such as a copy of the accounts) relating to an unlisted company which provides evidence that there has been a permanent diminution in the value of the investment in that company.

Examples of non-adjusting events are:

*   Exchange rate fluctuations

*   Changes in trading activities

*   Sale or purchase of fixed assets.

14.5   Disagreement

(i)   Each of the four legal cases are examples of contingencies. SSAP 18 is relevant because it deals with accounting for contingencies in the financial statements. This standard defines contingencies as follows:

'A condition which exists at the balance sheet date, where the outcome will be confirmed only on the occurrence or non-occurrence of one or more uncertain future events.'

The uncertain future event referred to in the standard would be the outcome of the court case in each of the legal cases mentioned.

(ii)   P and Q can be classified as contingent gains for the purposes of SSAP 18. As there is only a small likelihood of winning in the case of P it should not be mentioned in the accounts. However, there is a strong probability that, in the case of Q, the gain will be realised. This means that there should be some mention of the case in the notes to the accounts only.

R and S can be classified as contingent losses for the purposes of SSAP 18. In the case of S, there is a reasonable possibility that a loss will be incurred and this should be disclosed by way of a note to the accounts only. However, in the case of R there is a strong probability that the loss will occur and so a provision should be made in the accounts for the amount of the loss.

(iii)   Only R needs to be entered in the accounts. The double entry is simply to debit the P&L account and credit a provision for legal damages account.

(iv)   In the case of Q the note should point out that there is a court case being fought where the company is suing for £20,000 and that the company believes it has a strong case. However, the outcome is contingent on the decision of the court. In the case of S, the note should again point out that there is a court case being fought where the company is being sued for £40,000. Although the company believes it has a strong defence the outcome is contingent upon the decision of the court.

(v)   SSAP 18 is a further illustration of the bias shown by accountants towards prudence in financial reporting. We can see that contingent gains and contingent losses with the same likelihood of occurrence are treated quite differently. Thus, a strong probability of occurrence of a contingent gain will merit a note to the accounts whereas a similarly strong probability of a loss will merit a provision being made in the accounts. A possibility of a contingent gain will be ignored whereas a similar possibility of a contingent loss will be shown as a note to the accounts. There is an argument which states that it would be better for investors to be given all the contingent gains and losses and the likelihood of occurrence by way of a note to the accounts and to allow investors to adjust the accounts themselves to take account of these uncertainties.

22 THE CASH FLOW STATEMENT

INTRODUCTION AND LEARNING OBJECTIVES

In this chapter we examine the cash flow statement in some detail. The chapter begins by pointing out the importance of cash to a business and emphasising the point that profitability alone is not enough. The purpose of the cash flow statement is explained and the main features of FRS 1 (Cash flow statements) are considered. The cash flow statement is viewed as being potentially very informative to users. It is likely to become a popular examination topic.

FRS 1 superseded an earlier standard (SSAP 10) which required all but the smallest companies to prepare a funds flow statement as part of their published accounts. The nature and purpose of the funds flow statement is examined in this chapter. In addition, we discuss the reasons why it was considered appropriate to withdraw the earlier standard on funds flow statements and replace it with a new standard requiring companies to prepare a cash flow statement.

When you have studied this chapter you should be able to do the following:

- Explain the importance of cash generation in a business

- Draft a cash flow statement in a format acceptable to FRS 1

- Distinguish between a cash flow statement and a funds flow statement.

1 THE IMPORTANCE OF CASH

1.1 Introduction

In order for a business to survive, the ability to make profits may not be enough. It is also important for the business to generate sufficient cash in order to meet maturing obligations. In the final analysis, an inability to meet current financial obligations will often force businesses to cease trading. Even in less extreme circumstances, careful management of cash is needed to pursue all the opportunities desired by management. It is not at all unusual for quite profitable businesses to be severely restricted as a result of inadequate management of cash. It is clear, therefore, that businesses must pay great attention to liquidity as well as profitability if they are to succeed. It should also be clear that profitability and liquidity do not necessarily go hand in hand. The different effects, in terms of profitability and liquidity, need to be recognised.

1.2 Activity

In respect of each of the following transactions, state the effect on both profit and on cash (increase/decrease/no effect).

Transaction		Effect on profit	Effect on cash
1	Purchase of new plant for cash		
2	Sale of stock for cash		
3	Issue of loan stock		
4	Purchase of stock on credit		
5	Writing off a bad debt		
6	Payment of a dividend		
7	Transferring profit to reserves		

1.3   Activity solution

Transaction	Effect on profit	Effect on cash
1	no effect	decrease
2	increase*	increase
3	no effect	increase
4	no effect	no effect
5	decrease	no effect
6	no effect	decrease
7	no effect	no effect

* assuming that it is sold for more than it cost.

2   THE PURPOSE OF A CASH FLOW STATEMENT

2.1   Introduction

FRS1 (Cash flow statements) requires certain companies to publish a cash flow statement as part of the final accounts. The purpose of this statement is to reveal to users how cash was generated and then used by the company during the period under review. The cash flow statement should be useful to users in a number of ways. For example, it should help in assessing:

- the ability of the business to generate future cash flows
- the effect of major events such as a share issue or acquiring another business on the liquidity of the business
- the ability of the business to meet future commitments such as loan repayments, interest payments, taxation due and onerous contracts
- likely future financing needs.

The cash flow statement should therefore be a valuable addition to the information supplied in the annual reports of companies.

2.2   Defining the term 'cash'

In order to prepare a cash flow statement in accordance with FRS1, it is necessary to understand how the term 'cash' is defined for the purpose of this standard. The term will include cash in hand and cash on deposit with a bank or other financial institution. However, it will also include 'cash equivalents' which are short-term liquid investments, 'Cash equivalents' are investments which can be converted into cash without notice and which are within three months of maturity when acquired. Short-term advances from banks which are repayable within three months of the date of the advance must be deducted from the total of cash and cash equivalents in order to derive the net cash balance.

This rather broad definition of cash has been used because it was felt that it would provide a clearer picture of how cash is managed during the period. If a narrow definition of cash is used, the true liquidity position of the business could be obscured. For example, a business may have a relatively small amount of cash in hand or in the bank at any given time. However, this may be due to the fact that any spare cash available is channelled into short-term investments in order to generate additional revenues for the business.

It should be mentioned that this definition of cash has not met with universal agreement. Since the standard was issued, there has been some criticism of employing such a broad definition.

2.3   Activity

Can you think of any reasons why this definition of cash may be unacceptable to some preparers or users?

2.4 Activity solution

Short-term investments are often made to generate income for the business. Spare cash used could perhaps be invested in stock-market securities. Government securities may guarantee some income, ordinary shares would not. However, both could suffer from a major reversal in the stock market – loss of capital could result. Thus, in general there is a possibility that any 'cash equivalent' investment could pay back less than invested, which in turn overstates the liquidity position. The three-month definition used here is an arbitrary one.

3 PREPARING THE CASH FLOW STATEMENT

3.1 The FRS 1 format

FRS1 lays down a format for the cash flow statement which identifies separately the main activities resulting in cash inflows or outflows. The standard requires that five separate categories of cash flow should normally be shown on the face of the cash flow statement. These are:

- **Operating activities**, that is the net cash flows which have been generated from trading operations during the period

- **Returns on investments and servicing of finance**, that is interest received and paid and dividends received and paid during the period. Also included in this category is the interest element of finance lease payments

- **Taxation**, that is corporation tax payments and any tax rebates or returns of overpayments

- **Investing activities**, that is proceeds from the sale of fixed assets, and investments in other entities. Payments to acquire fixed assets and investments in other entities will also be included

- **Financing**, that is receipts from the issue of shares, loans and debentures. Payments to reacquire or redeem shares of the company and repayments of amounts borrowed will be shown. Also included is the capital element of finance lease payments, rental payments and any expenses incurred in the issue of shares, loans or debentures.

Not only does the standard require that each of these categories be separately identified (unless there are no material cash flows to be reported under them) but also the categories must be shown on the cash flow statement in the above order.

3.2 The cash flow statement format in detail

Having explained the various types of cash flow that need to be reported, we can now examine a cash flow statement which has been prepared in accordance with the standard. Note that the headings shown in bold are necessary to comply with the standard.

C. Simon Ltd

Cash flow statement for the year ended 30 June 19X3

	£	£
Net cash inflow from operating activities		10,000
Returns on investments and servicing of finance		
Interest received	2,000	
Interest paid	(3,000)	
Dividends paid	(4,000)	
Net cash inflow/(outflow) from returns on investments and servicing of finance		(5,000)
Taxation		
Corporation tax paid	(3,200)	
Tax paid		(3,200)

Investing activities

Payments to acquire intangible fixed assets	(200)	
Payments to acquire tangible fixed assets	(1,200)	
Receipts from sales of tangible fixed assets	300	
Net cash inflow/(outflow) from investing activities		(1,100)
Net cash inflow before financing		700
Financing		
Issue of ordinary capital	2,000	
Repurchase of debenture loan	(1,000)	
Expenses paid in connection with share issue	(100)	
Net cash inflow/(outflow) from financing		900
Increase/(decrease) in cash and cash equivalents		1,600

3.3   Calculating cash flows

In order to prepare a cash flow statement we must be clear about how to calculate or derive the figures to be shown on the statement. In this section we will consider each of the categories of cash flow in turn to see how the amounts to be shown are determined. In order to reinforce the basic principles of calculation, the profit and loss account and balance sheets of a particular business are given in the example below. The information contained in these statements will be used to show how a cash flow statement can be prepared from the other two statements and their related supporting notes.

Example

The balance sheets of Priority plc as at 31 December 19X8 and 19X9 and the summary profit and loss account for the year ended 31 December 19X9 were as follows:

Balance sheet as at 31 December

	19X8		19X9	
	£m	£m	£m	£m
Fixed assets				
Land and buildings at cost	130		130	
Less accumulated depreciation	30	100	32	98
Plant and machinery at cost	70		80	
Less accumulated depreciation	17	53	23	57
		153		155
Current assets				
Stock	25		24	
Debtors	16		26	
Short-term investments	5		20	
Cash at bank and in hand	3		7	
	49		77	
Creditors: Amounts due in less than one year				
Trade creditors	19		22	
Taxation	15		17	
Proposed dividends	12		14	
	46		53	
Net current assets		3		24
		156		179

Creditors: Amounts due beyond one year

10% Debentures	20	40
	136	139

Financed by:

Share capital	100	100
Revenue reserves	36	39
	136	139

Profit and loss account for the year ended 31 December 19X9

	£m	**£m**
Sales		173
Less: Cost of sales		96
Gross profit		77
Interest receivable		2
		79
Less		
Sundry expenses	24	
Interest payable	2	
Loss on sale of fixed asset	1	
Depreciation – buildings	2	
– plant	16	45
Net profit before tax		34
Corporation tax		17
Net profit after tax		17
Proposed dividend		14
Unappropriated profit added to revenue reserves		3

During the year plant costing £15 million and with accumulated depreciation of £10 million was sold for £4 million.

3.4   Net cash flows from operating activities

There are two approaches which can be used to determine this figure – the **direct method** and the **indirect method**. FRS 1 allows companies to calculate the net cash flows from operating activities using either method. The choice of method is not of critical importance as the same figure for net cash flows should be derived whichever method is adopted.

The direct method arrives at the required figure by employing information contained within the accounting records of the company. These records can be used to identify cash movements relating to operating activities. The relevant cash movements will include cash sales, cash received from trade debtors, cash purchases, cash paid to trade creditors and suppliers as well as other cash expenses. To calculate the net cash flows from operating activities the following calculation must be performed:

	£	**£**
Cash sales		x
Cash received from debtors		x
		x
Less		
Cash purchases	x	
Cash paid to trade creditors and suppliers	x	
Cash expenses	x	x
Net cash flow from operating activities		x

The indirect method does not rely on the underlying accounting records to derive the net cash flows from operating activities. Instead, the information contained in the profit and loss account and balance sheet is used. The 'net profit before taxation' figure in the accounts provides the starting point for calculations. By making certain adjustments to the net profit before taxation figure, it is possible to derive the net cash flows from operating activities.

Depreciation and profits and losses on the disposal of fixed assets may be included in the profit and loss account of a business but will not involve movements of cash. These items are simply book entries and so it will be necessary to adjust for them in order to derive the net cash flow from operations. (The cash proceeds on disposal of a fixed asset will, of course, result in a cash inflow; however, this inflow is dealt with in another part of the cash flow statement.)

Movements in the level of stocks, debtors and creditors must also be taken into account. A decrease in stocks or debtors will increase the cash generated from operating activities, whereas a decrease in creditors will reduce cash. Similarly, an increase in stocks and debtors will reduce the cash generated whereas an increase in creditors will effectively increase the cash available to the business.

Interest payable and receivable may also appear in the profit and loss account of a business. Although these items may well result in cash movements during the period (depending on the timing of interest payments and receipts), they must nevertheless be adjusted for in deriving the net cash flow from operating activities. This is because these items will be dealt with elsewhere in the cash flow statement.

The above items would be taken into account in order to deduce the net cash flows from operating activities as follows:

	£m	£m
Net profit before taxation		x
Add back:		
Depreciation of fixed assets	x	
Loss on sale of fixed assets	x	
Interest payable	x	x
		x
Deduct:		
Profit on sale of fixed assets	x	
Interest receivable	x	x
		x
(Increase)/decrease in stock	x	
(Increase)/decrease in debtors	x	
Increase/(decrease) in creditors	(x)	x
Net cash flow from operating activities		x

It is important that you understand both of the methods described above. The examiner may require you to calculate net cash flows from operating activities using either of the methods.

Using the information contained in the example above we can calculate the net cash flows from operating activities as follows:

	£m	£m
Net profit before taxation		34
Add back:		
Loss on sale of fixed assets	1	
Depreciation of fixed assets	18	
Interest payable	2	21
		55

Deduct:

Interest receivable		2
		53
(Increase)/decrease in stock	1	
(Increase)/decrease in debtors	(10)	
Increase/(decrease) in creditors	3	(6)
Net cash flow from operating activities		47

3.5 Returns on investments and servicing of finance

We have seen earlier that this includes interest received and paid during the period and dividends paid. The dividends shown in the cash flow statement should be the dividends actually paid during the period. There is a lag between the proposal of dividends and their payment. Dividends paid in one year usually relate to dividends proposed in another year. The only exception to this arises where interim dividends are paid. These are both an appropriation of profits and an outflow of cash.

In the example above, the dividend to be shown on the cash flow statement for the year ended 31 December 19X9 will be £12 million. This is the amount shown as a creditor due within one year in the balance sheet as at 31 December 19X8. The dividend will be paid in the following year.

3.6 Taxation

The cash flow statement should reflect the corporation tax actually paid. Since corporation tax in the UK is typically paid some nine months after the financial year end, it is reasonable to assume that the tax provided in the profit and loss account will not be paid until the next year. This provision will appear in the balance sheet as a creditor due within one year.

In the example above the corporation tax paid by Priority plc will be £15 million, the provision at 31 December 19X8. The liability for tax at 31 December 19X9 represents the provision for the year ended 31 December 19X9, and is effectively the double entry for tax in the appropriation account.

3.7 Investing activities

Changes in fixed assets over a period can arise in a number of ways, namely:

*   depreciation of assets – a decrease
*   purchase of new assets – an increase
*   sale of existing assets – a decrease.

We have seen earlier that depreciation of fixed assets will appear as an adjustment in arriving at 'net cash flows from operating activities' together with any profit or loss on disposal. The purchase of fixed assets and the proceeds from the sale of fixed assets are shown under the heading of 'investing activities'.

In many examination questions the problem is often one of calculating one of the components of fixed asset changes. The best way to deduce the figures needed for the cash flow statement under this heading is to set out a pro-forma statement of movements in the value of fixed assets. This can be set out as follows:

	Cost	Depreciation provision	Net
Opening balance	x	x	x
Less: Disposals	(x)	(x)	(x)
	x	x	x
Add: New acquisitions	x	x	x
	x	x	x
Depreciation	–	x	(x)
	x	x	x

The figure available can be inserted and any missing figures deduced.

In the case of Priority plc, there have been changes in the plant and machinery account and the pro-forma can be applied as follows:

	Cost	Depreciation provision	Net
	£m	£m	£m
Opening balance	70	17	53
Less: Disposals	15	10	5
	55	7	48
Add: New acquisitions	25*	–	25
	80	7	73
Depreciation	–	16	16
	80	23	57

        * Missing figure

The figures relating to the plant and machinery account for Priority Ltd will appear in the cash flow statement as follows:

- depreciation for the year (£16 million) – added back to net profit to deduce net cash flows from operating activities

- loss on disposal (£1 million) – added back to net profit to deduce net cash flows from operating activities

- plant acquired (£25 million) – shown under investing activities

- proceeds on the disposal of plant (£4 million) – shown under investing activities.

Sometimes only the written-down values of assets held and disposed of are provided in a question. In this case only the last column of the pro-forma shown above need be used to deduce the missing figure for fixed assets acquired.

Where there are no disposals of fixed assets during the year, the new acquisitions may be calculated simply by deducting the cost of fixed assets held at the beginning of the period from fixed assets held at the end of the period. This information will usually be given in the opening and closing balance sheets.

3.8   Activity

A company has plant and machinery whose written-down value at 1 January 19X8 was £36,280 and at 31 December 19X8 was £43,050. Depreciation for the year was £9,400 which did not include the deficit on a piece of plant which had a written-down value of £2,800 when it was sold for £2,500.

Calculate the value of plant and machinery acquired during the year.

3.9   Activity solution

The best way to deduce the figures needed for the cash flow statement for the year ended 31 December 19X8 is to set out a 'pro forma' statement of movements in the written down value of the plant and machinery. If all known values are inserted any missing figures can be deduced, thus:

	£
WDV at 1 January 19X8	36,280
Less: Disposal (at WDV)	2,800
	33,480
Add: Acquisition (balancing figure)	18,970
	52,450
Depreciation for the year	9,400
WDV at 31 December 19X8	£43,050

From this it can be deduced that the cost of the acquisitions must have been £18,970.

3.10 Financing

We have seen earlier that this section will include the receipts from the issue of shares, loans and debentures, as well as payments to reacquire or redeem shares of the company and repayments of any amounts borrowed. Also included is the capital element of finance lease rental payments and any expenses incurred in the issue of shares, loans or debentures.

In the case of Priority plc, we can see by comparing the opening and closing balance sheets that there has been an increase of £20 million in the amount of debentures outstanding (£40 million – £20 million) and this increase will appear as a financing activity for the year. There has been no change in the number of shares issued by Priority plc during the year.

It is worth mentioning that an increase in shares attributable to a bonus issue will not be shown on the cash flow statement, since it is only a transfer from reserves to capital, and not an issue of shares for cash. In some cases, shares will be issued at a premium. A comparison of the opening and closing balances on the share premium account will ascertain whether this is so. When shares are issued at a premium the cash flow statement will reflect the total cash generated by the issue (that is, the par value of shares issued plus any premium).

Now that we have considered the way in which the various figures that appear on the cash flow statement are derived it is possible to prepare a cash flow statement for Priority plc. The statement will be as follows:

Priority plc
Cash flow statement for the year ended 31 December 19X9

	£m	£m
Net cash inflow from operating activities		47
Returns on investments and servicing of finance		
Interest received	2	
Interest paid	(2)	
Dividends paid	(12)	
Net cash inflow/(outflow) from returns on investments and servicing of finance		(12)
Taxation		
Corporation tax paid	(15)	
Tax paid		(15)
Investing activities		
Payments to acquire tangible fixed assets	(25)	
Receipts from sales of tangible fixed assets	4	
Net cash inflow/(outflow) from investing activities		(21)
Net cash outflow before financing		(1)
Financing		
Issue of debenture loan	20	
Net cash inflow/(outflow) from financing		20
Increase/(decrease) in cash and cash equivalents		19

3.11   Notes to the cash flow statement

FRS 1 requires the following notes to be shown to the cash flow statement:

*   Reconciliation of operating profit to net cash flow from operating activities
*   Analysis of changes in cash and cash equivalents during the year
*   Analysis of the balances of cash and cash equivalents as shown in the balance sheet
*   Analysis of changes in financing during the year.

These notes are designed to provide the user with additional information to help reconcile the figures shown in the accounts and to analyse the changes which have occurred during the year. They are considered to be an integral part of the cash flow statement. These notes are considered in detail below.

3.12   Reconciliation of operating profit to net cash flow from operating activities

This note starts with the operating profit (the profit before interest paid or received) and then adjusts for items, as described earlier, in order to derive the net cash flow from operating activities.

The operating profit for Priority plc can be calculated as follows:

	£m
Net profit before tax	34
Add: Interest payable	2
	36
Less: Interest receivable	2
Operating profit	34

The note to the cash flow statement will appear as follows:

*Reconciliation of operating profit to
net cash inflow from operating activities*

	£m	£m
Operating profit		34
Add:		
Loss on sale of fixed assets	1	
Depreciation of fixed assets	18	19
		53
Deduct:		
(Increase)/decrease in stock	1	
(Increase)/decrease in debtors	(10)	
Increase/(decrease) in creditors	3	(6)
Net cash inflow from operating activities		47

As you can see, this note is very similar to the calculations undertaken earlier except that the adjustments for interest payable and receivable are taken into account in arriving at operating profit and, therefore, need not be shown in the note.

3.13   Analysis of changes in cash and cash equivalents during the year

The increase in cash and cash equivalents over the year can be reconciled with the final figure shown above as follows:

Analysis of changes in cash and cash equivalents during the year

	£m
Balance as at 1 January 19X9	8
Net cash inflow during the year	19
Balance as at 31 December 19X9	27

3.14   Analysis of the balances of cash and cash equivalents as shown in the balance sheet

This note simply shows the movements in the balances of cash and cash equivalents. The note will appear as follows:

Analysis of the balances of cash and cash equivalents
as shown in the balance sheet

	Jan 1 £m	19X9 Dec 31 £m	Change in year £m
Cash at bank and in hand	3	7	4
Short-term investments	5	20	15
	8	27	19

3.15   Analysis of changes in finance during the year

This note will reflect movements in the shares and debentures outstanding. The note for Priority plc will be as follows:

Analysis of changes in finance during the year

	10% Debentures £m
Balance at 1 January 19X9	20
Cash inflow from financing	20
Balance as at 31 December 19X9	40

Another column would be used if there were also changes in shares issued during the year. Where shares are issued at a premium, a third column would be required to show movements in the share premium account.

3.16   Interpretation of the cash flow statement

The cash flow statement gives useful insights into the financing and investing activities of the business over the period. Looking back at the solution to Priority plc, we can see that this shows that the business generated most of its cash (nearly two thirds) from operating activities. The remaining cash generated was largely from the issue of debentures. Much of the cash generated was used to purchase new fixed assets, to meet the corporation tax liability and to pay the dividend. However, as there was more cash generated during the year than was used, there was also a significant rise in the amount of cash and cash equivalents held by the company.

By examining cash flow statements for a number of years it is possible to detect the trends in financing and investing activities of the business over time. This may be very useful in predicting likely future trends.

3.17   Preparing the statement without a profit and loss account

In certain examination questions, the profit and loss account is not given. If such a situation arises, it is necessary to make a supplementary calculation to arrive at the net profit before tax. As with fixed asset movements, a pro-forma approach is suggested, with known figures being inserted, and the resulting profit figure being deduced. A suggested pro-forma is given below.

	£	£	
Net profit before tax		x	deduced as balancing figure after all other figures inserted
Profit and loss account balance brought forward		x	from opening balance sheet
Total available for distribution		x	

Less: Appropriations			
Corporation tax	x		from closing balance sheet
Dividend proposed	x		from closing balance sheet
Transfers to reserves	x		deduced by comparing reserves in
		x	opening and closing balance sheets
Equals:　Profit and loss			
account balance carried forward		x	from closing balance sheet

4　THE SOURCE AND APPLICATION OF FUNDS (FUNDS FLOW) STATEMENT

4.1　Introduction

In the past, companies were not obliged to prepare a cash flow statement. Instead, all but the smallest companies were required to prepare a **source and application of funds statement** (also known as a **funds flow statement**) for the year. This requirement was set out in SSAP 10 (Statements of source and application of funds). This statement was seen as providing a link between the balance sheet at the beginning of the period, the profit and loss account and the balance sheet at the end of the period. SSAP 10 recognised that the funds flow statement did provide information already contained in the profit and loss account and balance sheet. However, as will be seen below, the statement sets this information out in a way which makes the statement both complementary and supplementary to the profit and loss account and balance sheet.

The objective of the funds flow statement is to show how a business obtained funds and how those funds were used during the year. It is therefore similar in purpose to the cash flow statement discussed above. Indeed, the cash flow statement discussed earlier can really be viewed as a form of funds flow statement. The major difference between the cash flow statement and the funds flow statement that was normally prepared lies in the way in which the term 'funds' is defined. In the case of the cash flow statement, the term 'funds' is defined as being cash and cash equivalents. However, the funds flow statement, as prepared by companies to comply with SSAP 10, usually defines the term 'funds' as being working capital, that is, current assets less current liabilities (where current liabilities excludes tax and dividend payments due). Thus, a broader definition of the term 'funds' is being used.

Based on this definition, the principal sources of funds are as follows:

- trading profit
- injections of capital (such as share issues)
- borrowings (such as debenture and loan stock issues)
- proceeds of sales of fixed assets.

The principal applications of funds are as follows:

- purchase of fixed assets
- repayment of borrowings
- withdrawals of capital (for example dividends)
- tax payments
- trading losses.

4.2　The format of the funds flow statement

Although there is no uniquely 'correct' way to set out a funds flow statement, many companies appeared to have adopted the following format:

Statement of source and application of funds for the year ended..........

	£	£
Sources		
Funds from operations		
Net profit	x	
Adjusted for items not involving a movement of funds	x	x
Other sources		
Capital injected	x	
Loans raised	x	
Sale of fixed assets	x	x
Total sources		x
Applications		
Purchase of fixed assets	x	
Loan repayments	x	
Tax paid	x	
Dividends/drawings	x	
Total applications		x
Net change in funds		x
Working capital changes		
Increase/(decrease) in stock	x	
Increase/(decrease) in debtors	x	
(Increase)/decrease in creditors	x	
Increase/(decrease) in liquid funds	x	x

The difference between the the total sources of funds and the total applications represents the the change in funds over the period.

Since funds have been defined as working capital, it should be clear that the net change in funds should reconcile with the sum of the differences in the individual components of working capital, namely, stock, debtors, creditors and liquid funds (cash and similar balances). The 'working capital changes' section of the above statement provides this reconciliation. Note that an *increase* in current assets will result in an *increase* in working capital and an *increase* in creditors will result in a *decrease* in working capital (and vice versa).

4.3 Calculating the figures for the funds flow statement

The figure 'funds from operations' is generally arrived at by taking the net profit before tax and adjusting it for any items in the profit and loss account which do not involve the movement in funds. Typically, such items include depreciation and profits and losses on the disposal of fixed assets. You may recall that these adjustments are also necessary to derive the net cash flow from operating activities under the indirect method described earlier. However, unlike the cash flow statement, no adjustment is required for interest payable or receivable. These items are not separately identified for purposes of preparing the funds flow statement. Similarly, no adjustment is required to the net profit before tax for movements in stock, debtors and creditors. These are working capital items whose movement will be reflected only in the lower part of the funds flow statement.

Using the information contained in Priority plc above the figure 'funds from operations' will be derived as follows:

	£m
Net profit before tax	34
Add back:	
Loss on sale of fixed assets	1
Depreciation of fixed assets	18
Funds from operations	53

The calculation of movements in capital, borrowings and the proceeds of such things as the sale of fixed assets can be derived in the same ways as described earlier when discussing the preparation of the cash flow statement.

4.4   Preparing the funds flow statement

In order to illustrate the way in which a funds flow statement is prepared we can prepare a funds flow statement using the information given for Priority plc above. This statement will be as follows:

Statement of source and application of funds for the year ended 31 December 19X9

	£m	£m
Sources		
Funds from operations		
Net profit	34	
Adjusted for items not involving a movement of funds		
Loss on sale of fixed asset	1	
Depreciation	18	53
Other sources		
Debentures issued	20	
Sale of fixed assets	4	24
Total sources		77
Applications		
Purchase of fixed assets	25	
Tax paid	15	
Dividend paid	12	
Total applications		52
Net increase in funds		25
Working capital changes		
Increase/(decrease) in stock	(1)	
Increase/(decrease) in debtors	10	
(Increase)/decrease in creditors	(3)	
Movement in liquid funds		
Increase/(decrease) in cash	4	
Increase/(decrease) in short-term investments	15	25

4.5   Criticisms of the funds flow statement

The funds flow statement prepared by companies to comply with SSAP 10 was subject to much criticism. A major criticism was that there was no clear definition of the term 'funds' set out in SSAP 10. Whilst most companies chose to define the term as being working capital, other ways of defining this term were also possible. In particular, some companies chose to take a narrower definition of the term 'funds', based on cash rather than working capital. This ambiguity of the term 'funds' helped to create variety in accounting practices and confusion amongst users.

A further problem with the funds flow statement was that the standard did not lay down a particular format to be followed. Although there was an illustrative format in the appendix to SSAP 10, companies did not have to adopt this format. Furthermore, the format in the appendix to SSAP 10 has, itself, been criticised for being based on balance sheet headings rather than activities undertaken by a business.

Soon after being created, the ASB undertook a fundamental review of SSAP 10. It was felt that the cash flow statement was preferable to the funds flow statement, as set out in SSAP 10, for a number of reasons. In particular, it was felt that the cash flow statement was more clearly related to a fundamental objective of users, that is, to identify future cash flows of the business. The funds flow statement can be criticised for obscuring the cash position by including this item with other elements of working capital such as stock, debtors and creditors. By adjusting these other elements of working capital in arriving at the net cash flow from operations, the changes in net cash flow arising from increase or decreases in stock, debtors and so on become clearer.

This preference for a statement of cash flows rather than funds flows led to the withdrawal of SSAP 10 and the publication of FRS 1 to replace it.

5   CHAPTER SUMMARY

- In this chapter we have seen that most companies are required to produce a cash flow statement as part of their published accounts in order to comply with FRS 1. The purpose of this statement is to show users how cash was generated and then applied by a company during a particular period. FRS 1 defines the term 'cash' in order to include both cash in hand or at bank and 'cash equivalents' that is, short-term liquid investments held, less any short-term advances. This broader definition of the term 'cash' is designed to provide users with a clearer picture of how cash was managed during the period.

- FRS 1 sets out the main headings under which cash flows must be shown. These are:
  - operating activities
  - returns on investments and servicing of finance
  - taxation
  - investing activities
  - financing.

  The format of the cash flow statement has been discussed in some detail and the ways of calculating or deriving figures for this statement have also been explained.

- FRS1 supersedes SSAP 10 which obliged all but the smallest companies to produce a source and application of funds statement (commonly known as a funds flow statement) as part of their published accounts. The funds flow statement was designed to provide users with an insight into the financing and investing activities of a business and so is similar in purpose to the cash flow statement. Indeed, the cash flow statement can be viewed as a form of funds flow statement. The major difference lies in the way in which the term 'funds' is defined. In the case of the cash flow statement, it is defined as being cash and 'cash equivalents' whereas the funds flow statement usually defines 'funds' as being working capital.

- SSAP 10 was criticised because of its lack of a clear definition for the term 'funds' and its lack of an agreed format for the funds flow statement. It was also felt that a funds flow statement did not meet the needs of users as well as a cash flow statement would. SSAP 10 has now been withdrawn, and replaced by FRS1.

6 SELF TEST QUESTIONS

6.1 What are the five categories of cash flows identified in FRS 1 – Cash flow statements? (3.1)

6.2 The depreciation charge for the year is added to profit in arriving at net cash flow from operating activities because:

  (a) Depreciation is a source of cash

  (b) Depreciation is a use of cash

  (c) Profit before depreciation is a source of cash

  (d) It is necessary to do so to deduce the cost of any fixed assets acquired. (3.4)

6.3 Which of the following results in a cash inflow?

  (a) An issue of bonus shares

  (b) A rights issue

  (c) A depreciation charge

  (d) Revaluing a fixed asset. (3.10)

6.4 Identify and explain each of the notes which should accompany a cash flow statement drawn up in accordance with FRS1. (3.11)

6.5 Following the usual form of the source and application of funds statement (the one used in this chapter), which profit figure is used in the sources?

  (a) Net profit before interest and tax

  (b) Net profit before tax

  (c) Net profit after tax and preference dividend

  (d) Net profit after tax, dividends and transfers to reserves. (4.2, 4.3)

7 EXAMINATION TYPE QUESTIONS

7.1 Helouise

The balance sheets of Helouise Ltd for the years ended 30 June 19X3 and 19X4 and the profit and loss account for the year ended 30 June 19X4 are shown below.

Balance sheet as at 30 June 19X4

	19X3 £	19X3 £	19X4 £	19X4 £
Fixed assets				
Land and buildings at cost	130,000		140,000	
Less: Accumulated depreciation	30,000	100,000	34,000	106,000
Plant and machinery at cost	82,000		100,000	
Less: Accumulated depreciation	27,000	55,000	43,000	57,000
		155,000		163,000
Current assets				
Stock	28,000		36,000	
Debtors	26,000		24,000	
Short-term investments	8,000		10,000	
Cash at bank and in hand	7,000		15,000	
	69,000		85,000	

Creditors: Amounts due in less
than one year

Trade creditors	18,000	26,000
Taxation	18,000	10,000
Proposed dividends	10,000	11,000
	46,000	47,000

Net current assets	23,000	38,000
	178,000	201,000

Creditors: Amounts due beyond one year

10% Debentures	30,000	10,000
	£148,000	£191,000

Financed by:

Share capital	100,000	130,000
Share premium	22,000	28,000
Revenue reserves	26,000	33,000
	£148,000	£191,000

Profit and loss account for the year ended 30 June 19X4

	£	£
Sales		185,000
Less: Cost of sales		103,000
Gross profit		82,000
Interest receivable		10,000
		92,000
Less:		
Sundry expenses	32,000	
Interest payable	5,000	
Loss on sale of fixed asset	3,000	
Depreciation – buildings	4,000	
– plant	20,000	64,000
Net profit before tax		28,000
Corporation tax		10,000
Net profit after tax		18,000
Proposed dividend		11,000
Unappropriated profit added to revenue reserves		£7,000

During the year plant costing £19,000 and with accumulated depreciation of £4,000 was sold during the year for £12,000.

(a)   Prepare a cash flow statement for Helouise Ltd for the year ended 30 June 19X4 in accordance with FRS1.

(b)   Comment on the significant features revealed by this statement.   **(24 marks)**

7.2   Funds Flow

(a)   Using the information contained in 1 above prepare a source and application of funds statement for the year ended 30 June 19X4.

(b)   Compare and contrast the cash flow statement and source and application of funds statement prepared for Helouise Ltd for the year ended 30 June 19X4. Which do you consider to be more useful for an investor and why?   **(18 marks)**

7.3   Genesis

The balance sheets of Genesis Engineering Ltd for the years ended 30 April 19X3 and 19X4 and the profit and loss account for the year ended 30 April 19X4 are shown below.

Balance sheet as at 30 April

	19X3 £	19X3 £	19X4 £	19X4 £
Fixed assets				
Land and buildings at cost	160,000		160,000	
Less: Accumulated depreciation	40,000	120,000	44,000	116,000
Plant and machinery at cost	95,000		110,000	
Less: Accumulated depreciation	35,000	60,000	55,000	55,000
Motor vans at cost	42,000		50,000	
Less: Accumulated depreciation	16,000	26,000	26,000	24,000
		206,000		195,000
Current assets				
Stock	22,000		19,000	
Debtors	36,000		44,000	
Short-term investments	18,000		32,000	
Cash at bank and in hand	5,000		12,000	
	81,000		107,000	
Creditors: Amounts due in less than one year				
Trade creditors	28,000		36,000	
Taxation	15,000		8,000	
Proposed dividends	15,000		21,000	
Short-term loan	10,000		15,000	
	68,000		80,000	
Net current assets		13,000		27,000
		219,000		222,000
Creditors: Amounts due beyond one year				
10% Debentures		60,000		50,000
		£159,000		£172,000
Financed by:				
Share capital		120,000		150,000
Share premium		30,000		–
Revenue reserves		9,000		22,000
		£159,000		£172,000

Profit and loss account for the year ended 30 June 19X4

	£	£
Sales		280,000
Less: cost of sales		120,000
Gross profit		160,000
Interest receivable		12,000
		172,000

Less:		
Sundry expenses	76,000	
Interest payable	6,000	
Loss on sale of fixed asset	8,000	
Depreciation – buildings	4,000	
– plant	20,000	
– motor vans	16,000	130,000
Net profit before tax		42,000
Corporation tax		8,000
Net profit after tax		34,000
Proposed dividend		21,000
Unappropriated profit added to revenue reserves		£13,000

Notes:

(a) During the year motor vans costing £18,000 and with accumulated depreciation of £6,000 was sold during the year.

(b) There was a 1 for 4 bonus issue of shares during the year.

Prepare a cash flow statement for the year ended 30 April 19X4 in accordance with FRS1.

(24 marks)

7.4 Cash Flow

SAF (1979) Ltd
Balance sheets as at 31 March

19X5				19X6	
£	£	**Fixed assets**	£	£
		Tangible assets		
		(at written down values)		
200,000		Land and buildings	196,000	
830,700		Plant and machinery	925,800	
		Fixtures, fittings,		
182,400	1,213,100	tools and equipment	204,600	1,326,400
	10,800	Investments		72,000
		Current assets		
421,500		Stock	381,000	
134,600		Debtors	110,200	
89,200		Bank and cash	92,400	
645,300			583,600	
		Creditors: amounts due in		
		less than one year		
–		Bank loans and overdrafts	77,300	
120,900		Trade creditors	9,400	
16,000		Bills of exchange payable	51,900	
157,300		Taxation	163,200	
175,000		Proposed dividends	190,500	
469,200			492,300	
	176,100	Net current assets		91,300
	1,400,000	Total assets less current		
		liabilities		1,489,700

	Creditors: amounts due in more than one year	
400,000	Debenture loans	150,000
	Provisions for liabilities and charges	
56,000	Provision for legal damages and costs	–
	Capital and reserves	
700,000	Called up share capital	700,000
5,000	Share premium	5,000
239,000	Profit and loss	634,700
1,400,000		1,489,700

Notes:

1   The amounts shown in 19X5 for taxation, proposed dividend and legal damages and costs were paid in year ended 31 March 19X6 at the amounts stated.

2   Debenture interest expense (and payment) for the year ended 31 March 19X6 were £40,000.

3   Interest received on investments totalled £6,000 for the year ended 31 March 19X4.

4   During the year ended 31 March 19X6, £231,100 was spent on additional plant and £50,300 on additional fixtures. Old plant, with a book value of £25,800, was sold for £22,400.

(a)   Prepare a cash flow statement for SAF (1979) Ltd for the year ended 31 March 19X6.

(b)   Comment briefly on the financial position of the company disclosed by your answer to a).

(24 marks)

8   ANSWERS TO EXAMINATION TYPE QUESTIONS

8.1   Helouise

(a)

Helouise Ltd

Notes to the cash flow statement

1   Reconciliation of operating profit to net cash inflow from operating activities

	£'000	£'000
Operating profit		23
Depreciation charges	24	
Loss on sale of fixed asset	3	27
		50
Increase in stock	(8)	
Decrease in debtors	2	
Increase in trade creditors	8	2
Net cash inflow from operating activities		52

2   Analysis of changes in cash and cash equivalents during the year

	£'000
Balance at 1 July 19X3	15
Net cash inflow	10
Balance at 30 June 19X4	25

3   Analysis of the balances of cash and cash equivalents as shown in the balance sheet

	19X4 £'000	19X3 £'000	Change in year £'000
Cash at bank and in hand	15	7	8
Short-term investments	10	8	2
	25	15	10

4   Analysis of changes in financing during year

	Share capital £'000	Share premium £'000	Debentures £'000
Balance at 1 July 19X3	100	22	30
Cash inflow (outflow)	30	6	(20)
Balance at 30 June 19X4	130	28	10

Helouise Ltd
Cash flow statement for the year ended 30 June 19X4

	£'000	£'000
Net cash inflow from operating activities		
Returns on investments and servicing of finance		52
Interest received	10	
Interest paid	(5)	
Dividends paid	(10)	
Net cash outflow from returns on investments and servicing of finance		(5)
Taxation		
Corporation tax paid	(18)	
Tax paid		(18)
Investing activities		
Payments to acquire tangible fixed assets	(47)	
Receipts from sales of tangible fixed assets	12	
Net cash outflow from investing activities		(35)
Net cash outflow before financing		(6)
Financing		
Issue of share capital	30	
Premium received on issue of shares	6	
Redemption of debentures	(20)	
Net cash inflow from financing		16
Increase in cash and cash equivalents		10

Helouise Ltd

Changes in plant and machinery

	Cost £'000	Depreciation £'000	Net £'000
Opening balance	82	27	55
Less: Disposals	19	4	15
	63	23	40
New acquisitions	37*	–	37
	100	23	77
Depreciation	–	20	20
Closing balance	100	43	57

* This is the missing figure of cash additions	37
to which must be added additions to land and buildings	10
	47

Calculation of operating profit

	£'000
Net profit before tax	28
Interest payable	5
	33
Interest receivable	10
Operating profit	23

(b)   The solution will probably include comments on the following:

- Less than 50% of all cash inflows came from operating activities
- About 20% of all cash inflows came from interest on investments and sales of tangible assets
- The remaining one third comes from the issue of new shares at a premium.
- About 40% of the cash raised was used to purchase fixed assets
- Tax, dividends and redemption of debentures accounted for another 40% – 50%
- The remaining 10% has not yet been spent and is held in cash or cash equivalents.

A tentative conclusion might be drawn that the company is retrenching after a period of poor trading. Capital assets are acquired and paid for. A buildup of cash or cash equivalents is held ready to finance a projected increase in working capital requirements.

8.2   Funds Flow

(a)

Helouise Ltd

Statement of sources and applications of funds for the year ended 30th June 19X4

Sources	£m	£m
Funds from operations		
Net profit before tax		28
Adjustments for items not involving a movement of funds:		
Depreciation	24	
Loss on sale of fixed asset	3	27
		55

Other sources

Issue of share capital	36	
Sale of fixed assets	12	48
		103

Applications

Purchase of fixed assets	47	
Repayment of debentures	20	
Tax payments	18	
Dividends	10	95
Net change in funds		8

Working capital changes

Increase in stock	8	
Decrease in debtors	(2)	
Increase in trade creditors	(8)	
Movement in liquid funds		
Increase in cash	8	
Increase in short-term investments	2	8

(b) Solutions would include the following points:

- The different formats
- Net funds from operations obscure certain servicing of finance costs, for instance interest payable
- The cash flow statement clearly identifies the movement in cash and cash equivalents
- The wider definition of funds, that is including working capital items, tends to obscure the movement in liquid funds
- The cash flow statement has a mandatory format
- A long-term investor would probably find the cash flow statement easier to interpret.

8.3   Genesis

Genesis Engineering Ltd

Cash flow statement for the year ended 30 April 19X4

	£'000	£'000
Net cash inflow from operating activities		87
Returns on investments and servicing of finance		
Interest received	12	
Interest paid	(6)	
Dividends paid	(15)	
Net cash outflow from returns on investments and servicing of finance		(9)
Taxation		
Corporation tax paid	(15)	
Tax paid		(15)
Investing activities		
Payments to acquire tangible fixed assets	(41)	
Receipts from sales of tangible fixed assets	4	
Net cash outflow from investing activities		(37)
Net cash flow before financing		26

Financing

Redemption of debentures	(10)	
Net cash outflow from financing		(10)
Increase in cash and cash equivalents		16

Note: the 1 for 4 bonus issue has no effect on cash balances.

Genesis Engineering Ltd

Notes to the cash flow statement

1   Reconciliation of operating profit to net cash inflow from operating activities

	£'000	£'000
Operating profit		36
Depreciation charges	40	
Loss on sale of fixed assets	8	48
		84
Decrease in stock	3	
Increase in debtors	(8)	
Increase in trade creditors	8	3
Net cash inflow from operating activities		87

2   Analysis of changes in cash and cash equivalents during the year

	£'000
Balance at 1 May 19X3	13
Net cash inflow	16
Balance at 30 April 19X4	29

3   Analysis of the balances of cash and cash equivalents as shown in the balance sheet

	19X4 £'000	19X3 £'000	Change in year £'000
Cash at bank and in hand	12	5	7
Short-term investments	32	18	14
Bank overdrafts	(15)	(10)	(5)
	29	13	16

4   Analysis of changes in financing during year

	Debentures £'000
Balance at 1 May 19X3	60
Cash outflow	10
Balance at 30 April 19X4	50

Genesis Engineering Ltd

Calculation of operating profit

Net profit before tax	42
Interest payable	6
	48
Interest receivable	12
	36

Changes in plant and machinery

	Cost £'000	Depreciation £'000	Net £'000
Opening balances	95	35	60
New acquisitions	15*	–	15
	110	35	75
Depreciation	–	20	20
Closing balance	110	55	55

Changes in motor vans

	Cost £'000	Depreciation £'000	Net £'000
Opening balance	42	16	26
Less: Disposals	18	6	12
	24	10	14
New acquisitions	26*	–	26
	50	10	40
Depreciation	–	16	16
Closing balance	50	26	24

* = cash acquisitions in year

cash received on sale of vehicles, cost (net) £12m – loss on sale £8m gives £4m.

8.4 Cash Flow

(a)

SAF (1979) Ltd

Cash flow statement for the year ended 31 March 19X6

	£	£
Net cash inflow from operating activities		862,400
Returns on investments and servicing of finance		
Interest received	6,000	
Interest paid	(40,000)	
Dividends paid	(175,000)	
Net cash outflow from returns on investments and servicing of finance		(209,000)
Taxation		
Corporation tax paid	(157,300)	
Tax paid		(157,300)
Investing activities		
Payments to acquire plant	(231,100)	
Payments to acquire fixtures	(50,300)	
Payments to acquire investments	(61,200)	
Receipts from sales of plant	22,400	
Net cash outflow from investing activities		(320,200)
Net cash flow before financing		175,900

Financing

Debentures redeemed	(250,000)

Net cash outflow from financing	(250,000)
Decrease in cash and cash equivalents	(74,100)

Notes:

1   *Derivation of net cash inflows from operating activities*

	£
Increase in profit and loss account balance (634,700 – 239,000)	395,700
Dividends	190,500
Taxation	163,200
Net profit before tax	749,400
Interest paid	40,000
Interest received	(6,000)
Operating profit	783,400
Depreciation	142,300
Deficit on disposal of plant	3,400
Reduction in stock (421,500 – 381,000)	40,500
Reduction in debtors (134,600 – 110,200)	24,400
Reduction in creditors (120,900 – 9,400)	(111,500)
Increase in bills (51,900 – 16,000)	35,900
Legal charges paid	(56,000)
Net cash inflows from operating activities	£862,400

2   Fixed assets

	Buildings £	P & M £	F & E £
Balance at 1/4/19X5	200,000	830,700	182,400
Less: Disposals (WDV)	–	25,800	–
	200,000	804,900	182,400
Less: Depreciation for the year (balancing figures)	4,000	110,200	28,100
	196,000	694,700	154,300
Acquisitions	–	231,100	50,300
Balance at 31/3/19X6	£196,000	£925,800	£204,600

(b)   The liquidity of the company deteriorated significantly over the year. This arose particularly as a result of major investment in new fixed assets and other investments and as a result of major expenditure in redeeming part of the debentures. The weakening of liquidity manifested itself in reductions in stocks and debtors and in increases in bank loans and bills payable. These were partially offset by decreases in creditors and a small increase in cash.

23 PROFIT MEASUREMENT AND VALUATION

INTRODUCTION AND LEARNING OBJECTIVES

In this chapter the conventional approach to profit measurement and valuation is reviewed. The major measurement conventions which underpin the conventional approach, which we discussed in earlier chapters, are restated and the problems associated with each of them are examined. In recent years, there has been increasing recognition of the fact that accounting conventions alone provide an inadequate foundation for the development of accounting. There have been calls for the development of a conceptual framework for accounting which will both help provide a rationale for accounting practices and also help guide accounting standard setters in their work. In this chapter, we consider the need for a conceptual framework and examine the contribution of the ASB towards the development of such a framework.

This chapter also considers the way in which inflation can create distortions in financial statements prepared using conventional measurement rules. The chapter concludes with a brief discussion of other approaches to profit measurement and valuation which might be adopted during a period of changing prices. The problem with the conventional approach is that decision makers, who rely on accounting information to help them to make decisions, may be misled. The distortions caused by inflation are particularly important in this context since there is a tendency for profits derived following the conventional approach to accounting to be overstated. This can influence managers to make decisions which could seriously damage the business and its ability to survive in the future. It must be remembered that the provision of information to aid decision making is the primary purpose of accounting.

When you have studied this chapter you should be able to do the following:

- Discuss the limitations of the conventional approach to profit measurement and valuation

- Argue the case for and against constructing a conceptual framework of accounting

- Discuss the progress of the ASB's Statement of Principles in this area

- Discuss the problems faced by conventional accounts in times of changing prices.

---

1 CRITICISMS OF THE CONVENTIONAL APPROACH

1.1 Introduction

The conventional approach to profit measurement and valuation has already been explained. This approach has undergone little real change for many years and it seems unlikely that there will be any radical change to the conventional rules in the foreseeable future. However, the conventional approach to profit measurement and valuation is not without its critics. Some believe that the fact that this approach is widely used does not necessarily mean it is always useful to those who read financial reports. It has been suggested that some users (and preparers) may support the conventional approach simply because it is familiar to them. Having understood the conventional approach, some users may be reluctant to learn other possible approaches. In addition, some users may simply be unaware that there are other possible approaches.

The conventional approach to profit measurement and valuation rests on four major conventions. Each of these has been subject to serious criticism. These conventions have already been outlined in earlier chapters. However, it is useful to restate each convention and to examine the criticisms levelled against them.

1.2   Historic cost

This convention holds that assets should be shown in the accounts at their outlay cost to the business. This convention is usually supported on the grounds that it provides an objective, reliable base for financial statements. Outlay (historic) cost can be determined by reference to fact rather than opinion; hence the figures produced are free from bias and capable of independent verification.

Critics of the historic cost convention take the view that, whilst the provision of objective, reliable information is important, this is not in itself enough. It was stated in Chapter 1 that the primary quality of accounting information is relevance, that is, accounting information must be capable of influencing the decisions of users. Rigid adherence to the historic cost convention can mean that information which has potential relevance to user decisions is not provided. A simple example can be used to illustrate this point.

Example

Simon Developments Limited acquired a piece of freehold farming land for £100,000 on 30 September 19X6. During the following year the company applied for planning permission to build eight 'executive' detached houses on the site. On 30 September 19X7 planning permission was granted by the local council. As a result the market value of the land increased to £180,000. During the months which followed the company decided against using the land for building detached houses. Instead, the company applied for new planning permission to build 40 'starter' houses on the land. On 30 September 19X8 planning permission for the 'starter' houses was granted by the local council. As a result the market value of the land increased to £300,000. A few days after planning permission for the 'starter' houses was granted a local builder offered the company £300,000 for the land, which was accepted. The company's year-end is on 30 September. Adherence to the historic cost convention will mean that any change in the value of the freehold land will be ignored until the land is finally sold. Hence, the freehold property will be shown on the balance sheets as at 30 September 19X7 and 19X8 at the original cost of £100,000, despite the increases in value which have occurred. Users may, however, feel that this outdated value appearing on the balance sheets does not provide an appropriate basis for assessing performance and position and may prefer information about the property's current market value.

The fact that increases in value are only recognised when the land is eventually sold means that profits recorded within a particular period may represent increases in value arising in previous periods. In the above example the profit on the sale of the land of £200,000 (£300,000 – £100,000) will be recognised during the accounting year ended 30 September 19X9. However, it can be argued that £80,000 (£180,000 – £100,000) of the profit can be attributed to the year ended 30 September 19X7 and £120,000 of the profit (£300,000 – £180,000) can be attributed to the year ended 30 September 19X8. Thus, all of the profit earned can be attributed to previous periods. Some believe that it would be more useful to recognise the profits when the change in value occurs rather than when a sale is finally achieved.

1.3   Realisation

This convention is closely linked to the historic cost convention and holds that profit should only be recognised when realisation has occurred. The point at which realisation is deemed to occur is not clear-cut. The general criteria applied to identify realisation are that:

- a point must be reached where the amount of revenue can be determined with substantial accuracy
- the activities required to generate the revenue have been substantially completed
- there is reasonable certainty that the cash can eventually be collected.

For most businesses these criteria are considered to be met when the goods are passed to the customer (or when the service is rendered to the customer) and are accepted by the customer. However, it is possible to interpret these general criteria in different ways. For example, a civil engineering business will usually have a long time span of production and will probably be unwilling to wait to recognise profit until a contract is finally completed. Instead it is usual practice to recognise a proportion of the expected final profit at particular stages of the contract based on a percentage of work completed.

The fact that the realisation convention is closely linked to the historic cost convention means that it provides support for delaying any recognition of profit in the accounts. Such delays may seriously hinder comparisons of performance and position between businesses. A simple example may be used to illustrate this point.

Example

Three separate commodity dealers, A, B and C, started business on 1 January 19X6 with £20,000 capital and £20,000 cash at bank. On their first day of trading each purchased £20,000 worth of cocoa in the expectation that prices would rise. By 31 January 19X6 the price of cocoa had doubled. On that day A decided to sell all of his stock of cocoa and B decided to sell half of his stock of cocoa for cash. C decided, however, to retain all of his stock of cocoa in the hope that there would be future price rises.

We need to prepare for each business a profit and loss account for the period to 31 January 19X6 and a balance sheet at that date.

Applying the conventional rules of measurement the profit and loss account for each business would be as follows:

Profit and loss accounts for the period to 31 January

	A	B	C
	£	£	£
Sale of cocoa	40,000	20,000	–
Cost of sales of cocoa	20,000	10,000	–
Profit on sale	£20,000	£10,000	–

The balance sheet for each business prepared using conventional rules would be as follows:

Balance sheets as at 31 January

	A	B	C
Assets	£	£	£
Stock of cocoa at cost	–	10,000	20,000
Cash at bank	40,000	20,000	–
	£40,000	£30,000	£20,000
Opening capital	20,000	20,000	20,000
Add: Profit	20,000	10,000	–
Closing capital	£40,000	£30,000	£20,000

From the above statements a reader may deduce that A has been the most successful, B the next most successful and C the least successful trader during the period. The profit and loss account and balance sheet for each business certainly convey quite different views of financial performance and position. However, in reality, each business has experienced the same increase in wealth over the period and each business has the same amount of wealth at the end of the period. The differences in recorded profits and asset values between each business arise because unrealised profits are not recognised. B's decision to sell only half his stock of cocoa means that only half of the increase in value of £20,000 (£40,000 – £20,000) is recognised. Similarly, C's decision to retain all of his stock of cocoa means that none of the increase in value will be recognised during the period.

1.4   Activity

State, with reasons, whether you agree with each of the following arguments in defence of the realisation convention:

1   The value of an asset may increase in one period but may fall again in a subsequent period. It is therefore better not to recognise changes in value until the asset is finally sold.

2   It is often difficult to establish the current value of an asset until a market transaction takes place. Thus changes in value can often only be determined with substantial accuracy when a sale finally takes place.

1.5   Activity solution

It is difficult to argue that increases in the value of an asset arising in one period should not be recognised simply because there may be a fall in its value in a subsequent period. If an increase in value arises during a period it may be useful to recognise that fact in order to portray a more realistic view of the financial performance and position of the business. If a fall in value occurs in a subsequent period then this too may be recognised in the period in which it occurs for similar reasons.

In many cases it is difficult to measure precisely the change in any asset's value which arises during a period where there has been no sale of the asset. As a result, attempts to measure any such change in value are likely to be subject to a margin of error. The key issue is, however, whether information provided concerning changes in value is relevant to user needs. Not providing information concerning changes in value may mean that users are deprived of something which has potential relevance to their decisions. Users may, therefore, be prepared to accept information which is not precisely accurate if the information is relevant to their needs.

1.6   The special case of land and buildings

In the late 1980s, before the onset of the recession of the early 1990s, there was a significant rise in the general value of freehold land and buildings. In such a situation the original cost of land and buildings acquired by a business may bear little resemblance to the current market value of these assets. This fact has led some businesses to abandon the realisation convention for these assets. This means that freehold land and buildings are periodically revalued and any increases in value recognised as a revaluation gain which is transferred to a revaluation reserve. However, for other assets the realisation convention is still applied.

The revaluation of freehold land and buildings contravenes a number of the major measurement conventions in accounting and therefore represents a radical departure from the conventional approach. It can be seen as contravening both the realisation convention and the cost convention referred to above. It also contravenes the convention of prudence in accounting which is discussed below.

1.7   Matching

This convention states that expenses should be matched with the revenues to which they relate, such that revenues and associated expenses should be recognised in the same accounting period. In order to apply the matching convention it is necessary to examine costs incurred and to make a judgement concerning:

•   the amount which has been consumed in the process of generating revenues during the period under review

•   the amount which has not been consumed at the end of the period and which can be used to help generate revenues in future periods.

The costs consumed to generate revenues during a period are regarded as expired costs or expenses of that period. The unexpired costs are carried forward and shown as assets on the balance sheet.

The matching convention has been subject to considerable criticism because of the often arbitrary nature of the matching process. For example, when a fixed asset is purchased it is usually necessary to allocate the cost (less residual value) of the asset over its useful life using a depreciation method. The depreciation charges in the first period will represent an expense of that period and this amount is then deducted from the original cost in order to arrive at the unexpired cost element which should be carried forward and shown on the balance sheet at the period end. However, there is no underlying theory to guide preparers of accounting reports when deciding how much the depreciation charge should be in a particular period and, therefore, how much should be carried forward to future periods. Although various methods of calculating depreciation are available, there is no conclusive means of deriving the most appropriate method. Thus, determining the expired element of a cost can be highly subjective and this can create problems for both preparers and users. The problem of matching is, of course, further compounded by the practical difficulties often associated with establishing the useful life and residual value of an asset.

One effect of the matching convention is that the assets side of the balance sheet simply provides details of unexpired costs to be allocated to future accounting periods. The balance sheet, therefore, reveals what remains after matching for the period has taken place.

1.8 Prudence

This convention holds that those who prepare financial statements should err on the side of caution. This convention requires that losses, whether actual or anticipated, be recognised whereas profit should only be recognised when realised. This can be seen as generally supporting the historic cost convention and realisation convention discussed above. However, the requirement to recognise anticipated losses can result in a conflict between the historic cost and prudence convention.

1.9 Activity

Can you provide an example of a conflict between the conventions of prudence and historic cost? Which convention dominates in your example?

1.10 Activity solution

A good example of a conflict between the conventions of prudence and historic cost arises in the case of stock valuation. The historic cost convention requires that assets be recorded at their cost of acquisition. The convention of prudence requires that all losses whether actual or anticipated be recognised and, therefore, where the net realisable value of stock is below its cost of acquisition the stock must be shown at its net realisable value. In this case, as in other cases, the convention of prudence dominates.

1.11 Criticisms of the prudence convention

Although the convention of prudence supports the realisation convention, it does create inconsistencies in the rules of profit measurement and valuation. Whereas profits are not recognised until realised it is permissible to recognise losses before they are realised. The origins of this convention can be traced to an earlier period when lenders were the dominant user group and when those granting credit preferred to adopt a cautious approach in any lending decision.

Critics of this convention believe that the convention of prudence introduces an unnecessary bias towards understatement into financial reports. The effect of this may work to the advantage of some users and the disadvantage of others. For example, the recording of all losses, whether realised or unrealised, and the refusal to recognise profits until realised may work to the advantage of an investor wishing to purchase shares in a particular company but may work to the disadvantage of an investor wishing to sell shares in that company.

Prudence can be viewed as a philosophy of financial reporting as much as a specific measurement rule. However, the problem which arises is that some preparers of accounts may adopt this philosophy more enthusiastically than others. As a result the degree of bias towards understatement in the accounts may vary between businesses. The effect of this will be to hinder comparisons between businesses.

The convention of prudence is, in essence, a means of dealing with uncertainty regarding the future. However, some would argue that it is a poor method of dealing with uncertainty. It has been suggested that, rather than providing a single (cautious) view of the future, it would be more useful to provide a range of values regarding a likely future outcome (for instance, a pessimistic, a realistic and an optimistic value) along with some assessment of the likelihood of each possible outcome. Users can then decide for themselves which value they wish to adopt.

1.12   The defence of the conventional approach

Although it is clear that the conventional approach to profit measurement and valuation has its weaknesses and limitations, arguments can be provided in support of this approach. One such argument is that the conventional approach is well suited to the **stewardship function** of accounting. Managers are appointed by the owners of the business to run the business on their behalf. In order to help assess the managers' stewardship of the business, the managers are required to account to the owners of the business periodically for the resources with which they have been entrusted. The conventional approach can be said to reveal more clearly than other methods the cause and effect of past transactions and their relationship with the current financial condition of the business. The conventional balance sheet, for example, is a list of sources and deployments of funds which is historically based. Also, the fact that the conventional approach provides more objective measures than other approaches means that managers, when accounting to the owners, have less scope to manipulate the figures to their advantage.

As the conventional approach is generally considered to be more objective than other approaches, there is less likelihood of disagreement arising over the values shown on the financial statements. This fact enhances the credibility of the conventional approach.

2   THE DEVELOPMENT OF A CONCEPTUAL FRAMEWORK

2.1   Introduction

The conventions described in this text have been developed over many years in response to problems encountered by accountants when preparing financial statements. These conventions represent practical solutions to practical problems and offer the accountant guidelines concerning *which* items should be recorded and *how* they should be recorded. The conventions have been criticised from time to time because they offer only broad guidelines to the accountant which may, at times be in conflict with each other. Nevertheless, they have, for many years, provided the only framework for accountancy practice.

Although many of the conventions have proved to be extremely robust when tested over time, there has been a growing recognition that accounting conventions do not provide an adequate basis for the development of accounting. Conventions offer guidelines concerning *how* and *what* to record without offering any clear explanation as to *why* we should record in a particular way. This has posed a major problem for standard setters in particular. Accounting standards are usually designed to reflect 'best practice'; however, it is difficult to say what 'best practice' really is unless there is a clear justification for doing things in a particular way.

It has been argued that if we are to advance the subject of accounting in order to deal with the complexity and problems of modern businesses, we need to supply a sound foundation to the subject. This means we need to develop a framework which provides a rationale for accounting and for the ways in which we prepare and present financial information. This conceptual framework, as it is often called, should provide us with answers to fundamental questions such as: What is the nature and purpose of accounting? Who are the users of accounting reports? What kind of accounting reports should be prepared and what should they contain?

If answers to these questions can be formulated, we shall then have the foundations necessary to develop accounting practices in a more logical and consistent manner. Accounting standard setters can justify more clearly why a particular accounting method is preferred over another and why particular accounting reports should be prepared.

During the 1970s and early 1980s the Financial Accounting Standards Board (FASB) in the USA devoted a considerable amount of time and money to the development of a conceptual framework for accounting. This pioneering work has been followed by further statements about a conceptual framework which have been produced by other standard-setting and professional bodies, including the International Accounting Standards Committee (IASC), the Canadian Institute of Chartered Accountants and the Australian Accounting Standards Review Board. More recently, the Accounting Standards Board (ASB) in the UK has produced a draft version of a Statement of Principles. This statement draws heavily on earlier work produced by the FASB and IASC concerning the development of a conceptual framework.

2.2 Statement of Principles

The Statement of Principles attempts to set out the concepts which underpin the preparation of financial statements. It is designed to help the ASB in both the formulation of new standards and the review of existing standards. However, it should also be of value to preparers, auditors and users of financial reports.

2.3 Activity

Explain how a conceptual framework may be of value to:

1   preparers
2   auditors
3   users.

2.4 Activity solution

A conceptual framework should help preparers apply accounting standards and to help them deal with issues which are not the subject of an accounting standard.

A conceptual framework should help auditors in assessing whether financial statements have been drawn up in accordance with accounting standards.

A conceptual framework should help users in analysing and interpreting the information contained in a financial standard.

2.5 Topics to be considered

In September 1991, the ASB produced the first part of its Statement of Principles as an exposure draft. In the first part of the statement, the topics which should be considered in developing accounting principles are identified. These are:

1   the objective of financial statements
2   the attributes of financial information that enable financial statements to fulfil their purpose
3   the elements that make up financial statements (the nature of assets, capital, liabilities, revenue and expenses)
4   when items are to be recognised in financial statements (when an item is recognised as an asset, revenue, expense and so on)
5   how net resources and performance are measured
6   how items can best be presented in the financial statements
7   the principles underlying accounting for groups of companies.

These topics are similar to those identified by the FASB in its earlier work on the development of a conceptual framework. The ASB propose to issue a separate chapter of its Statement of Principles to deal with each topic. Draft chapters for each topic have now been issued; we consider below the main points contained within each of the first six chapters. The content of chapter 7 is outside the scope of your syllabus.

2.6 Users and their information needs

The draft introduction to the Statement of Principles identifies the major users of financial statements prepared for external use. These users are:

- investors
- employees
- lenders
- suppliers and other trade creditors
- customers
- government and their agencies
- the public.

This list of users is very similar to other lists which have been prepared by academics and professional bodies over the past two decades. As a result the list is not likely to be contentious.

The information needs of each of these user groups are examined in the exposure draft.

2.7 Chapter 1 - The objective of financial statements

This chapter begins by stating:

> The objective of financial statements is to provide information about the financial position, performance and financial adaptability of an enterprise that is useful to a wide range of users in making economic decisions

This objective is broad in nature and is rather bland in tone. However, it is interesting to note that 'financial adaptability' is mentioned as part of this objective. A useful indicator of financial adaptability is the cash flows generated by the business. Hence, the cash flow statement now required of companies should be of particular value in this respect.

The ASB points out that financial statements may not provide all the information required by users. Financial statements are historic documents and do not include non-financial information which may be important to a user in assessing the future prospects of the business.

2.8 Activity

What other sources of information, apart from financial statements, may be used to assess the future prospects of a business?

2.9 Activity solution

Other sources of information include:

- Information relating to the industry as a whole (market size, level of competition). This may be found in industry reports by government bodies, newspapers, trade magazines, journals, financial analysts' reports and reports from information-gathering agencies (such as Dun and Bradstreet).

- Information relating to the economy as a whole (interest rates, levels of inflation, GNP forecasts). This may be found in government reports, newspapers, magazines, journals and reports by forecasting bodies.

- Information relating to the particular business. This may come from the business itself, from a competitor business, from newspaper or magazine reports, from a government report, from financial analysts' reports or the reports of a forecasting body.

2.10 Chapter 2 - Qualitative characteristics of financial statements

We saw in Chapter 1 of this text that qualitative characteristics are those characteristics which make accounting information useful. The ASB exposure draft has identified *relevance* and *reliability* as being the primary qualitative characteristics. The secondary characteristics are seen as being *comparability* and *understandability*. It is pointed out that accounting information which lacks these secondary characteristics would only be of limited usefulness despite being both relevant and reliable.

These characteristics have been considered earlier in the text and so will not be discussed in detail here.

In addition to the four characteristics above, there is the threshold quality of *materiality* to be considered. This characteristic needs to be considered before considering the other characteristics. Unless an item is material (that is, its omission or mis-statement could influence decisions), there is no need to consider it further.

2.11 Trade-offs in relation to relevance and reliability

In practice, a trade-off between qualitative characteristics may be necessary. Thus an increase in the level of one quality may only be achieved by a decrease in the level of another. Where a conflict arises between two or more characteristics the relative importance of each characteristic in a particular situation is likely to be a matter of judgement. Thus, differences between preparers on such matters are likely to arise.

2.12 Activity

Can you think of any situations where there may be a conflict between two or more qualitative characteristics?

2.13 Activity solution

There is a potential conflict between prudence and neutrality. Both of these are attributes of reliability. However, neutrality implies freedom from bias whereas prudence implies a bias towards reducing profit and asset values.

There may also be a conflict between relevance and reliability. Information which is relevant to users may not always be reliable (such as current values of assets).

2.14 The inter-relationship between characteristics

In addition to the possible trade-offs between characteristics there are other trade-offs to consider. Sometimes, the need for *timely reporting* of information will lead to a sacrifice in the level of a quality (for instance, reliability). Thus, preparers may at times also have to balance the need for timeliness against the need for reliability. Preparers must also weigh the *benefits* of providing information to users against the *costs* involved.

The ASB exposure draft includes a diagram which attempts to illustrate the inter-relationship between the various characteristics. This diagram is reproduced below.

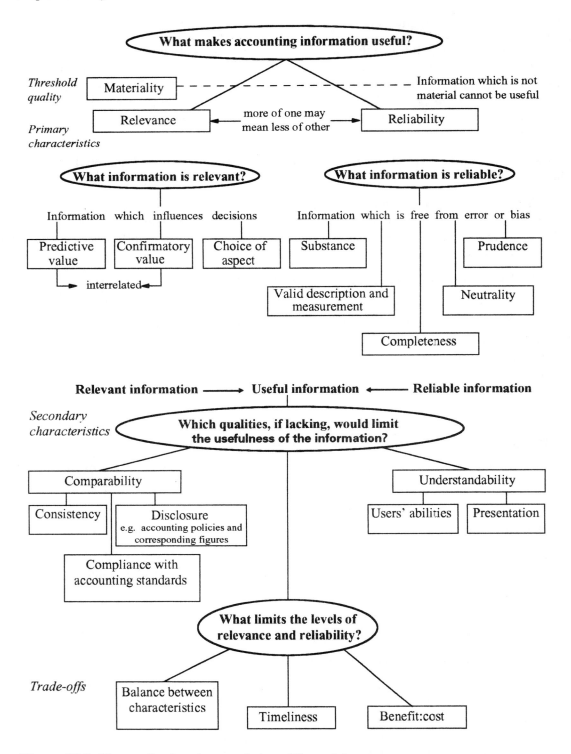

Figure 23.1 The qualitative characteristics of financial statements

2.15   Chapter 3 - The elements of financial statements

This chapter is concerned with defining certain key items which appear in the financial statements. Definition is important because, unless we have a clear view of what these items represent, differences can arise over which items are to be included in the financial statements and how those items are to be measured. Although items which do not fall within the definitions given should not be included in the financial statements, items which fall within these definitions will not be automatically included. The issue of recognition of key elements is dealt with in the following chapter of Statements of Principles.

The individual elements defined are:

- Assets
- Liabilities
- Equity
- Gains and losses
- Contributions from and distributions to owners.

2.16 Assets

The chapter defines **asset** as:

> rights or other access to future economic benefits controlled by an entity as a result of past transactions or events.

This definition stresses the right to control access to economic benefits rather than legal ownership. Thus leasing, rather than owning, a property or piece of plant can give rise to an asset. Future economic benefits are seen in terms of prospective cash receipts (or the avoidance of future cash payments).

2.17 Activity

Febrraro Fish Food plc has invested heavily in advertising its 'Captain Cod Fish Pie' (One bite and you're hooked!) over the years. Now it has a strong customer loyalty towards the pie.

Can the 'Captain Cod Fish Pie' brand be regarded as an asset to the company?

2.18 Activity solution

A business can create an asset by advertising a product and developing customer loyalty towards it. The advertising and customer loyalty should lead to an expectation of future benefits which will be controlled by the company. However, the valuation of this type of asset can be a problem, so it does not automatically follow that a brand will appear on the balance sheet of the company.

2.19 Liabilities

This chapter defines a **liability** as:

> an entity's obligations to transfer economic benefits as a result of past transactions or events.

The obligations referred to in the definition need not constitute a legal duty. Taxation arising on the profits for a period, for example, may not arise until several months after the end of the reporting period but would, nevertheless, appear as a liability on the balance sheet at the end of the period. The key issue is whether or not the transfer of economic benefits can be avoided.

Items which meet the definitions of assets and liabilities are not automatically included on the balance sheet of an enterprise. To be recognised for such inclusion, the item must also meet the recognition criteria set out in Chapter 4 of the Statement, which is discussed below.

2.20 Activity

When you buy certain goods (e.g. a motor car), a warranty may be provided. Do you think a liability would arise for the business when providing a warranty agreement or only if a claim is made under the warranty?

2.21   Activity solution

When a warranty is provided with goods, the liability is recognised when the warranty is issued, which is usually on the date of sale, rather than when a claim is made under the warranty. By entering into a warranty agreement the business takes on an obligation.

2.22   Other definitions

Equity is defined as:

> the ownership interest in the entity: it is the residual amount found by deducting all liabilities of the entity from all the entity's assets.

In the case of a limited company, the equity will be represented by the share capital plus any reserves. The residual nature of equity will mean that the market value of the equity is likely to differ from the figure recorded in the balance sheet. (This point is considered in Chapter 5 of the Statement.)

Gains are defined as:

> increases in equity, other than those relating to contributions from investments made by owners in their capacity as owners.

Losses are defined as:

> decreases in equity other than those relating to distributions to owners.

These may be regarded as balance sheet definitions of gains and losses as they are defined in terms of movements in the equity of the entity.

Contributions from, and distributions to, owners are defined in terms of movements in ownership equity. Hence, **contributions from owners** are defined as:

> increases in equity resulting from investments made by owners in their capacity as owners.

Distributions to owners are defined as:

> decreases in equity resulting from transfers made to owners in their capacity as owners.

2.23   Activity

As a result of a boardroom dispute at Rochester Rovers Football Club Ltd, the chairman resigned and his shares were bought by another one of the directors.

Has there been a contribution from owners or a distribution to owners as a result of this transaction?

2.24   Activity solution

No. There has been no increase or decrease in the equity of the company as a result of the transaction. There has simply been a transfer between owners.

2.25   Chapter 4 - The recognition of items in financial statements

This chapter deals with the criteria for recognising items in the financial statements. Recognition is, perhaps, one of the most difficult areas of accounting. It involves:

> depiction of the item in words and by a monetary amount and the inclusion of that amount in the statement totals.

The chapter states that an item should be recognised when:

- the item conforms to the definition of an element appearing in the financial statements (see above), and

- there is sufficient evidence that the changes an assets or liabilities, which is inherent in the item, has occurred (including, where appropriate, evidence that a future inflow or outflow of benefit will occur), and

- the item can be measured in monetary terms with sufficient reliability.

These criteria represent general guidelines. To develop specific rules from these general statements may be extremely difficult in practice.

The chapter goes on to state that the event which triggers recognition must have occurred before the balance sheet date and must have resulted in a **measurable change** in assets or liabilities. This measurable change, we are told, can be caused by three types of past events:

- *Transactions.* These involve the transfer of assets or liabilities to, or from, an external party.

- *Contract for future performance.* This refers to an enforceable contract where both parties have yet to complete their obligations. (Where at least one party has carried out his/her part of the contract a transaction will have occurred.)

- *Other events.* Other events may arise through decisions taken by third parties or governments, which can result in changes in assets and liabilities e.g. changes in the market value of assets, or taxation by government.

2.26 Activity

Which type of measurable change, if any, would each of the following be described as?
- A sale on credit where delivery has not taken place.
- A sale on credit where delivery has taken place but no payment has yet been received.
- Placing an order with an advance payment being made in full.
- Expropriation of overseas assets by a government.

2.27 Activity solution

- A credit sale where no delivery has taken place is a contract for future performance as both parties have yet to complete.

- A credit sale where delivery has taken place is a *transaction* as one party has completed his/her part of the contract.

- An order where payment is made in full is a transaction, as one party has completed his/her part of the contract.

- Expropriation of assets is an 'other event' as there has been a change in assets due to a decision taken by a third party.

2.28 Gains in the profit and loss account

This chapter also states that gains shown in the profit and loss account should be both *earned* and *realised.* These two criteria will ensure both the existence and the amount of the gains possess a high degree of certainty. If there is less certainty surrounding the gain (e.g. the revaluation of freehold land) the gain should be shown in the statement of total recognised gains and losses for the period.

2.29 Chapter 5 - Measurement in financial statements

Chapter 5 starts by reminding us of the fundamental balance sheet equation:

$$\text{Assets} - \text{Liabilities} = \text{Equity (or capital)}$$

This equation makes it clear that equity (or capital) is a residual which will be affected by the way in which we value assets and liabilities. In practice, the recorded equity or capital does not equate with economic wealth because goodwill is not usually included in the balance sheet and assets are not shown at their current economic value.

The chapter examines the various bases which can be used in the valuation of assets. We consider the bases next.

2.30   Historic cost

This is the conventional approach to the measurement of assets. It is defined in the chapter as the cost of acquiring an asset, and the measurement of the value will therefore occur as the result of a transaction.

The advantages of historic cost are that it can produce dependable and verifiable figures, it is familiar and understandable to most users and is relatively cheap to use. However, the main disadvantage is that asset values are recorded at their date of acquisition and this is typically earlier than the balance sheet date. As we shall see later in the text, this can be a real problem during a period of rapidly changing prices.

2.31   Activity

To what extent is it true to say that historic cost is the conventional system of measuring asset values? In the UK, do we depart from the use of historical cost when accounting for assets?

2.32   Activity solution

We depart from historic cost when we revalue fixed assets (usually freehold property) and when we employ the 'lower of cost and net realisable value' rule in relation to stocks. The conventional system is, in reality, 'a hybrid mixture of historical cost and unsystematic and illogical modifications of it' (ASB Discussion Paper).

2.33   Current value accounting

Instead of using historic cost, it is possible to employ a measure based on the current value of the assets acquired. The chapter examines three approaches to measuring current value:

- *Entry value.* This is based on the cost of acquiring an asset in current market conditions.
- *Exit value.* This is based on the net realisable value (i.e. selling price less any selling costs) of the asset.
- *Values in use.* This is based on the present value of future net cash flows from using the asset in the business.

These three methods may provide more relevant information than historic cost but are likely to be less reliable since there are measurement problems associated with each one. Although it would be possible to provide information based on all the current value methods, the Statement believes this option is likely to be both confusing to users and expensive to operate.

A more feasible solution may be to employ the 'value to the business' approach which employs whichever basis appears most relevant to each particular asset. The 'value to the business' of an asset is the lower of the replacement cost of the asset and its recoverable amount. The recoverable amount, in turn, is the higher of the net realisable value of the asset and its value in use.

Identification of 'value to the business'

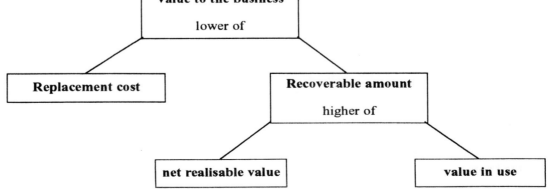

Although this method overcomes some of the problems identified with current value accounting, it also inherits the measurement problems of each valuation basis.

A 'value to the business' approach can also be used to value the liabilities of an enterprise.

2.34 Chapter 6 - Presentation of financial information

This chapter considers the way in which information should be arranged in financial reports. The chapter states that accounting information should be presented in the form of a structured set of financial statements. Proper structuring will ensure that items are given due prominence in the financial statements. The chapter points out that the volume of financial information available creates a need to structure the information and also to condense by aggregating certain information. The degree of aggregation to be used involves a weighing of likely benefits and costs.

The chapter notes that classifying items according to their nature or function can help in the analysis of performance and position It also points out that the financial statements should articulate, or interrelate, with each other so that different aspects of a transaction can be shown in the different financial statements. For example, the effect of the annual depreciation charge will reduce the reported profit in the profit and loss account and the written down value of assets in the balance sheet. This need for articulation means that the financial statements must be built on the same foundations.

2.35 The primary financial statements

The chapter identifies and discusses the major (or primary) financial statements, which are:

- the profit and loss account (including the note of historical profits and losses)
- the statement of total recognised gains and losses
- the balance sheet
- the cash flow statement.

The first two statements are concerned with financial performance, and the chapter discusses the features of good presentation including such matters as reporting unusual items separately, reporting the performance of different operating segments separately, distinguishing between different categories of gains and losses, and giving sufficient detail to users for understanding the composition of gains and losses. It is interesting to note that the statement of total recognised gains and losses and the note of historical profits and losses are recent additions to the financial reports, yet they are seen as being of primary importance.

The limitations of the financial statements are also addressed. The chapter recognises that the balance sheet is not a statement of value, although the information contained within it may help users in arriving at their own view of the value of the enterprise. It also recognises that the cash flow statement does not offer a comprehensive guide for assessing future cash flows.

The chapter refers to the need for notes to the financial statements to amplify or explain items in the financial statements. Notes may also provide additional information relating to items not included in the financial statements. Where supplementary information is provided, such as a directors' report or chairman's report, the contents should be consistent with the picture portrayed in the financial statements.

The chapter stresses the importance of financial adaptability, defined as:

> the ability of an organisation to take effective action to alter the amounts or timing of cash flows so that it can respond to unexpected needs or opportunities.

Financial adaptability will be reflected in the ability of the enterprise to raise finance quickly, to sell assets without dislocating trading operations and to improve cash flows from operations. In order to asses financial adaptability, each of the financial statements mentioned above may provide useful information.

2.36   Criticisms of the Statement of Principles

The Statement is seen by many as an important contribution to the development of accounting in the UK. At the very least, it should make standards more consistent with each other and should be of assistance when considering an accounting issue for which there is no accounting standard. However, a number of specific criticisms have been made of the Statement which include:

- *Definitions.* Some think it is strange that items that meet the definitions for assets and liabilities are not automatically included in the balance sheet. It has been suggested by one eminent academic that definitions which fail to do this are no more helpful than defining those who can vote in elections as adult humans. Whilst all voters are adult humans, not all adult humans can vote. (For example, prisoners and aliens are excluded from voting.) Thus, the definitions for assets and liabilities are inadequate.

- *Limitations of accounting information.* It has been argued that there should be a prominent statement setting out the limits of accounting information, particularly as a basis for investment decisions. It is argued that such a statement would provide a clearer perspective on the value and role of accounting information in making decisions. As we have seen, the Statement of Principles mentions the limitations of particular financial statements and so this criticism appears to be concerned with the degree of emphasis given.

- *The role of prediction.* Not all accountants are happy with the idea that accounting information should have a predictive role. Some would prefer to limit its scope to assessing the financial stewardship of directors and confirming the accuracy of predictions made by users themselves. They believe that prediction should not be a function of financial reporting and this is best left to users who will make gains and losses according to their ability to predict. However, the fact that accounting information *has* predictive value (as mentioned in Chapter 2 of the Statement) is not quite the same as saying that it should predict the future. Facts relating to past events can have predictive value. For example, accounting information showing the trend of sales over past years may help users in predicting future sales.

- *Accounting standards.* It can be argued that the Statement of Principles should be developed *before* accounting standards are developed rather than produced in tandem with the development of new standards. After all, the Statement is meant to guide the development of accounting standards. This argument has already been considered in Chapter 21. Although in an ideal world this argument may be correct, the ASB cannot ignore the pressing need to reform accounting practices. In order to maintain and improve the credibility of accounting reports and to avoid government intervention, the ASB must continue to produce standards whilst it develops the Statement of Principles.

The Statement of Principles is not yet complete. Before the Statement is finalised the whole of the document will be exposed to further comment and consultation.

2.37   Problems in developing a framework for accounting

The Statement of Principles should be seen as an important first step towards the development of a conceptual framework in the UK. However, developing a conceptual framework is not an easy task. According to Professor Robert Anthony, part of the problem is the lack of skilled theorists in accounting. Most accountants are practitioners and only a few are interested in analysing theoretical issues. Moreover, Professor Anthony argues that:

> accounting requires a special kind of theorist, a person who has a thorough knowledge of both real world accounting and concepts

This suggests that progress on developing a sound framework will be slow.

Some people appear to believe that the development of a conceptual framework will be a panacea for the problems which beset accounting. However, this is unlikely to be the case. Even if we can develop such a framework, and if it is adopted by the ASB, it is unlikely that everyone will accept it. There will still probably be fundamental differences among preparers, users and commentators concerning the nature and purpose of accounting.

Nor will the development of a conceptual framework resolve issues where judgement is called for. We have seen earlier that, when preparing financial statements, judgement is required in trading off qualitative characteristics. In addition, judgement will continue to be required when dealing with uncertainty (such as with the provision of doubtful debts) or when making allocations over time (such as with depreciation).

A conceptual framework cannot remain static. It must continue to evolve over time in response to changes in society and business. The pace and direction of changes in the established framework are likely to provide another fertile area for debate.

Although problems exist in developing a conceptual framework, this does not imply that effort should not be spent on this issue. At the very least it should help us identify and address the key issues in accounting. It should also go some way towards putting the discipline of accounting on a sounder footing and in helping standard setters make more rational policy decisions.

3 THE PROBLEM OF INFLATION

3.1 Inflation and the monetary unit

The conventional approach to accounting employs money as the unit of measurement and assumes that the particular currency (pounds sterling in the UK) will remain stable over time. However, history has shown that money is not always a stable measurement scale and that changes in the value of money can occur due to inflation (and very occasionally deflation). Inflation can be described as a reduction in the general purchasing power of a particular monetary unit which results from a rise in prices.

The effect of inflation is to create further distortions in the process of profit measurement and valuation which help to undermine the usefulness of the conventional approach. Overall, profit can be overstated, and the problem of outdated values on the balance sheet is worsened during a period of inflation.

3.2 Overstatement of profit

It can be argued that profit is overstated during a period of inflation. This problem arises because of the **time lag** which occurs between acquiring a particular resource and utilising or selling that resource. An example of the time lag problem arises in the case of stocks for resale.

Example

Helen Louise (Fashions) Limited purchased an evening gown as part of its stock for resale in one of its stores. The gown was acquired on 1 January 19X3 at a cost of £2,500. On 30 June 19X3 the gown was sold to a customer for £3,250. On that day the company purchased an identical gown to replace the gown sold. The purchase cost of the gown had risen during the period by 10% in line with the general rate of inflation.

In order to calculate profit, the conventional approach would match the original purchase cost of the gown with the sale price. Hence, the profit on sale would be:

	£
Sale of evening gown	3,250
Less original purchase cost of evening gown	2,500
Profit on sale	750

However, during the period in which the gown was in stock prices rose and the current purchase cost of the gown at the date of sale was £2,750 (£2,500 plus 10% of £2,500). Thus, it can be argued that a more realistic measure of profit would be achieved by matching the current purchase cost of the gown with the selling price. Hence, the profit on sale would be:

	£
Sale of evening gown	3,250
Less current purchase cost of evening gown	2,750
Profit on sale	500

The problem with the conventional approach is that current revenues are being matched with past outlays. During the period the gown was held there was a general rise in the buying-in price of the gown of 10%. This means that the original outlay is no longer a realistic measure of either the general purchasing power or the specific purchasing power sacrificed. As a result the cost of sales figure represents an understatement of resources consumed and this in turn leads to an overstatement of profit. By matching the purchase cost of the item expressed in current terms with the final selling price we can overcome the time lag problem and provide a more realistic measure of profit.

3.3   Activity

Conventional accounting rules offer a choice of three main approaches to determining the cost of stock held at the end of a period and the cost of sales during the period. These approaches are:

1   first in, first out (FIFO)

2   last in, first out (LIFO)

3   weighted average cost (AVCO)

In practice there will be a time lag between acquiring stock and utilising that stock. Each approach mentioned above will make different assumptions about this time lag.

Which of these approaches assumes:

(a)   The longest time lag?

(b)   The shortest time lag?

What are the implications for the calculation of profit of these different assumptions during a period of inflation?

3.4   Activity solution

The FIFO method assumes the longest time-lag between acquiring and utilising stock and the LIFO method assumes the shortest time-lag. During a period of inflation the FIFO method can match current revenues with an outdated figure for the value of stock consumed during the period. As a result profits will be overstated. The LIFO method, on the other hand, will match current revenues with a more up-to-date figure for stock consumed and will therefore derive a more realistic measure of profit. The FIFO method, however, will provide a more up-to-date stock figure for the balance sheet than the LIFO method.

3.5   The time lag problem as it affects fixed assets

The time lag problem also arises with fixed assets which must be depreciated. Under the conventional approach, the annual depreciation charge will represent a proportion of the original cost of the asset. However, during a period of rising prices, the depreciation charge in each successive period will become increasingly out of date in terms of purchasing power sacrificed. The effect, once again, will be to understate the expenses for the period and thereby overstate profits.

3.6   Activity

Can you suggest a way in which a more realistic annual depreciation charge could be calculated during a period of rising prices?

3.7   Activity solution

One way in which a more realistic annual depreciation charge could be calculated during a period of inflation would be to calculate the charge on the basis of the replacement cost of the asset rather than its original cost. During a period of inflation the replacement cost will rise and, therefore, the periodic depreciation charge will also rise.

3.8 Profit overstatement and capital depletion

Profit can be seen as the increase in wealth (capital) which arises during a period after adjusting for new capital injected and capital withdrawn. Viewed from this perspective, profit will only arise if the existing capital base of a business is maintained intact. The maintenance of the capital base, that is, the fixed assets and working capital, is important if a business wishes to operate at the same level of activity. However, during a period of inflation, maintenance of the capital base may be threatened. It has been seen that under the conventional approach, which matches current revenues with past outlays, there is a danger that profits will be overstated. If these profits were to be distributed as a dividend (or drawings) a business might well find itself in a position where it is unable to replace assets and thereby maintain its productive capacity. By distributing conventionally determined profits, during a period of inflation the business will suffer a reduction in the purchasing power of its capital base. The result is likely to be that the business will have to reduce the scale of operations unless there are fresh injections of capital or increased borrowings to compensate. Any system of measurement which permits depletion in the purchasing power of the capital base must be regarded as suspect.

A simple example can be used to illustrate the above problem.

Example

A business has the following balance sheet at the beginning of a period

	£		£
Stock of widgets (100 units)	1,000	Capital	1,000

During the period the business sold all of the widgets for cash at a price of £15 each. At the end of the period the owner decided to withdraw the profit made and to replenish the stock of widgets for sale in the next period. During the period there was a rise in the price of widgets of 20% which was in line with the general rise in prices.

The profit made using the conventional approach would be:

	£
Sales (100 × £15)	1,500
Less cost of sales (100 × £10)	1,000
Profit	500

If we draw up a balance sheet after the owner has withdrawn the profit as calculated above but before the stock is replenished we have:

	£		£
Cash (1,500–500)	1,000	Capital	1,000
		Profit	500
			1,500
		Less: Drawings	500
	1,000		1,000

The balance sheet reveals that the business has £1,000 available to replenish the stock of widgets. This represents the same amount in monetary terms that was invested in widgets as at the beginning of the period. However, the price of the widgets is 20% higher at the end of the period than it was at the beginning. Thus, in order to acquire a stock of 100 widgets and therefore have the same physical quantity as at the beginning, the business will need £1,200 (100 × £12). Unless the owner introduces more capital or borrows, the business will be unable to maintain the same level of operations.

3.9   Valuation of assets

It has been seen earlier that the historic cost convention and realisation convention require that changes in the value of an asset will not be recognised until realisation has taken place. Even during a period of general price stability specific price changes may occur which can result in the balance sheet reflecting out-of-date values. However, the problem of outdated values becomes much more acute during a period of inflation. As a result the balance sheet is further undermined in attempting to portray the financial position of a business. Moreover, a problem of **additivity** also arises. In order to explain this problem it may be useful to consider a simple example.

Example

The balance sheet of Asgard Limited showed freehold land at a cost on 31 December 19X9 of £500,000. Further enquiry revealed that the freehold land was purchased on the following dates:

	£
July 19X1	100,000
March 19X6	150,000
May 19X9	250,000
	500,000

During the period 19X1 to 19X9 the annual rate of inflation varied between 6 and 10%.

In this example, there has been a price level change each year and, hence, a change in the purchasing power of the pound. As the measurement scale has changed each year it is not really valid to add together pounds of different years. A 19X1 pound could acquire more goods and services, and a 19X6 pound in turn had greater purchasing power than a 19X9 pound. The pound at these different points in time could be regarded as quite different units of currency. Thus, it is no more valid to add together these pounds than adding together, say, US dollars, French francs and Dutch guilders. The final result is meaningless.

3.10   Assessment of performance

The impact of inflation on financial reports can hinder attempts to assess performance. An important ratio used to assess the performance of a business relates the profits earned during a period to the amount of assets in use. This ratio provides a measure of the return on capital employed. However, the problems of profit overstatement and outdated balance sheet values can combine to produce return figures which are misleadingly high.

For example, suppose that a business held assets which cost £100,000 ten years ago and made profits in the current year of £30,000. The return on assets would be 30%. However, suppose the assets could be sold for £300,000 and it was estimated that profits were overestimated by £5,000 as a result of the time lag distortions arising from increases in stock prices and depreciation. It can be argued that a more realistic measure of assets would be £300,000. This represents the current realisable value which could be put to other uses. In effect there is an 'opportunity' to use the assets differently and it can therefore be argued that in calculating returns the 'opportunity cost' of £300,000 should be used. Similarly, a more realistic measure of profit would be £25,000 (£30,000 – £5,000) as this would take account of the time lag distortions. Using the revised figures, the return on assets would now be £25,000/£300,000 which, expressed as a percentage, is 8.3%. Whereas a return on assets of 30% would typically be regarded as very good, a return of 8.3% is unlikely to be regarded in the same light since this kind of return can frequently be obtained from very low-risk investments such as government securities.

3.11   Monetary items

Another criticism which has been made of the conventional approach is that, during a period of inflation, it fails to recognise gains and losses which arise from holding **monetary items**. In order to understand this point it is first necessary to be clear what is meant by the term. A monetary item can be either an asset or a claim which is fixed (by contract or statute) in terms of a certain number of pounds, irrespective of changes in the price level. Examples of monetary assets are debtors, prepayments, fixed interest investments and cash. Examples of monetary claims are debentures, loans, preference shares, taxation owing, dividends proposed and accrued expenses. Non-monetary items are items which are not fixed in money terms. Examples of non-monetary items are freehold land, plant, motor vans and stock.

During a period of inflation the effect of holding monetary liabilities is to make a gain in purchasing power. A loan of £100 taken out in 19X5 and which is due for repayment in 19X8 will be paid back in the same number of pounds as the original amount received, irrespective of the rate of inflation. If the rate of inflation during the three-year period of the loan was 25% it is clear that the purchasing power of the £100 repaid in 19X8 will be less than the purchasing power of the £100 received in 19X5. In order to preserve the purchasing power of the £100 borrowed, £125 would have to be repaid. Since the loan is a monetary item only repayment of the £100 borrowed (plus interest) is required. As a result there is a purchasing power gain on borrowing of £25 (£125 – £100). In periods of high inflation there have been occasions when the inflation gain on borrowing has compensated for the interest payable.

Whereas the holding of monetary liabilities during a period of inflation leads to a purchasing power gain, the holding of monetary assets will result in a purchasing power loss. It can be argued that measurement of such gains and losses is important for a proper assessment of business performance.

3.12 Problems of purchasing power maintenance

The above problems indicate the need for a system which enables some measure of changes in purchasing power to be made. However, such a system requires a clear definition of the purchasing power which is to be maintained. In fact two major schools of thought exist in this area.

(a) General purchasing power maintenance

One possible definition of purchasing power is that of the general purchasing power of the owner. The aim of a system based upon this definition is to provide a measure of profit after the owners' purchasing power (in terms of goods and services generally in the economy) has been maintained. The measure of purchasing power most commonly used in the UK is the **Retail Price Index**, an index prepared on the basis of changes in the price of a selected range of goods and services used by the majority of the population.

(b) Specific purchasing power maintenance

The second definition of purchasing power is concerned with maintaining the specific purchasing power of the organisation for which accounts are being prepared. A business organisation does not buy goods and services generally. It trades in certain specific items. It is thus concerned with ensuring that its purchasing power in terms of these specific items is maintained. Thus, specific purchasing power maintenance is concerned with ensuring that the business can maintain its specific assets and thereby maintain the quantity of goods and services provided. It reflects a concern for the business entity rather than the owners, a concern which is the focus of the general price maintenance approach.

In a system of adjusting accounts for changing prices, revenues are set against expenses which have been adjusted to ensure that they reflect the purchasing power sacrifice. In the evening gown example above it was assumed, for the sake of simplicity, that a specific increase in price (an increase in the purchase cost of the evening gown) was in line with the general increase in prices. However, in many cases this situation does not occur. If different definitions of purchasing power are used different adjustments can result. The differences between the two approaches identified above can be demonstrated by considering the following example.

Example

A company purchases stock for £1,000 when the retail price index is 100. It sells the stock for £1,100 some time later, when the retail price index is 103. At the time of the sale the stock will cost £1,050 to replace.

Using the general purchasing power basis, the profit would be measured as follows:

	£
Sales	1,100
Cost of sales (£1,000 × (103/100))	1,030
Profit	£70

Using the specific purchasing power basis profit would be measured as follows:

	£
Sales	1,100
Current cost of sales	1,050
Profit	£50

Both are correct figures. The two concepts of profit are different. The £70 profit represents the increase in purchasing power of the owners, as measured by their claim on the business. If this £70 were to be taken out of the business as a distribution to the owner the remaining claim on the business would still have the same purchasing power over goods and services generally as the owner's claim at the beginning of the year. Such a distribution would, however, result in the specific purchasing power of the business being diminished. No more than £50 (the profit based upon specific purchasing power maintenance) can be distributed without the purchasing power of the business being reduced.

It is worth noting that the historic cost profit related to the above transaction (£100) overstates real profits, whichever definition of purchasing power maintenance is adopted. Clearly, historic cost profits cannot all be distributed without reducing the scale of operations of the business and reducing the purchasing power of the owner's equity, in a period of rising prices.

3.13   Practical proposals for dealing with accounting for changing price levels

A very considerable debate has taken place in the UK over the last 20 years about accounting practice in a period of changing prices. Proposals have been made based upon the concept of general purchasing power maintenance, and the concept of specific purchasing power. Some attempts have also been made to obtain the maximum benefit by combining various aspects of the two systems of adjustment. At present the situation may be said to remain unresolved.

The proposal based upon general purchasing power maintenance is referred to as current (or constant) purchasing power accounting (**CPP accounting**). The proposal based upon specific purchasing power maintenance is generally known as current cost accounting (**CCA accounting**).

3.14   Notes on examination questions

Examination questions relating to accounting for changing price levels will be limited to basic principles. It is important to recognise, however, that the ideas and problems identified above may well be useful in answering questions which appear to be concerned with more basic concepts.

Example

This is an example of a typical exam question.

1   Explain clearly, in terms which a non-accountant would understand, the following accounting terms:

    (a)   historic cost

    (b)   historic cost accounting

>   (c)   objectivity

>   (d)   prudence.

2   To what extent is historic cost accounting objective and prudent?

Solution

Clearly this question can be answered fairly fully on the basis of the information contained in earlier chapters. However, it may be useful to contain at least some passing reference to alternative systems of accounting, in discussing historic cost accounting. In referring to objectivity, it is possible to criticise the narrow definition of objectivity used in accounting. The use by accountants of a centrally prepared index number for purposes of adjusting accounts for inflation (such as the Retail Price Index in the UK) could be said to be objective, in that there is no scope for any personal bias in the choice of the index. Objectivity could easily be maintained in a system of CPP accounting. In the case of the prudence convention, the implications of the purchasing power maintenance concepts identified above may be included. The so-called prudent system of historic cost accounting has been shown to lead to the overstating of profits at a time of changing price levels. If this is not recognised it is possible that unduly large distributions of profit may be made, which will reduce the scale of operations. Such an accounting system would not appear to be prudent.

4   CHAPTER SUMMARY

*   The primary purpose of accounting is the provision of information which will enable decision makers to make more informed and, therefore, better decisions. It has been seen that the conventional approach to profit measurement and valuation has been subject to serious criticism. Each of the major measurement conventions has been examined and has been found wanting. This means that decision makers are often likely to be making judgements based on flawed information. Despite this problem the conventional approach still appears to enjoy considerable support amongst preparers and users of accounting information. Those who support the conventional approach can point to the relatively objective nature of the information provided and its potential usefulness in assessing stewardship. There is also a typical human resistance to accept changes in attitudes and approaches.

*   However, in recent years there has been a growing demand for the discipline of accounting to be placed on a sounder footing. There has been increasing recognition of the need for a conceptual framework which will help explain accounting practice and which will help guide decisions concerning accounting alternatives. In this chapter we have considered the benefits and problems of developing such a framework and have considered the contribution of the ASB towards this debate.

*   The problem of inflation in modern economics has created further problems for the conventional approach. The principal problems concern the overstatement of profit and the understatement of asset values. Several ways have been suggested to overcome these problems. One method based on general purchasing power maintenance and one method based on specific purchasing power maintenance have been discussed in this chapter. However, to date no method of dealing with the problem of inflation has managed to gain widespread acceptance.

5   SELF TEST QUESTIONS

5.1   Between which of the following does the convention of matching provide a link?

>   (a)   the recognition of revenues and expenses

>   (b)   the realisation and historic cost conventions

>   (c)   the recognition of costs and objectivity

>   (d)   the recognition of revenues and realisation. (1.7)

5.2 Which one of the following does the convention of prudence underpin?

    (a)   historic cost and matching

    (b)   historic cost and realisation

    (c)   realisation and matching

    (d)   matching and objectivity. (1.8)

5.3 What are the four qualitative characteristics identified in the ASB Exposure Draft Statement of Principles? (2.10)

5.4 During a period of inflation, which one of the following does the conventional approach lead to?

    (a)   an understatement of profit and asset values

    (b)   an overstatement of profit and asset values

    (c)   an overstatement of profit and understatement of asset values

    (d)   an understatement of profit and overstatement of asset values. (3.2, 3.9)

5.5 Which one of the following does CPP accounting aim to maintain?

    (a)   the general purchasing power of the business

    (b)   the general purchasing power of the owners

    (c)   the specific purchasing power of the business

    (d)   the specific purchasing power of the owners. (3.12)

5.6 Which one of the following does CCA accounting aim to maintain?

    (a)   the general purchasing power of the business

    (b)   the general purchasing power of the owners

    (c)   the specific purchasing power of the business

    (d)   the specific purchasing power of the owners. (3.12)

6 EXAMINATION TYPE QUESTIONS

6.1 Terms

Explain clearly four of the following terms as an accountant would understand them:

1   financial accounting

2   realisation

3   matching

4   materiality

5   inflation.   **(20 marks)**

6.2 Going Concern

The annual final accounts of businesses are normally prepared on the assumption that the business is a going concern.

Explain and give a simple illustration of:

    (a)   the effect of this convention on the figures which appear in those final accounts

    (b)   the implications for the final accounts figures if this convention were deemed to be inoperative.   **(15 marks)**

6.3   Users

Company financial statements, including profit and loss accounts, balance sheets and cash flow statements, are used by a variety of individuals and institutions for a wide variety of purposes.

Specify six different types of users of financial statements and explain in each case the aspect of performance or position in which they are interested.   **(18 marks)**

6.4   Margan

The accounts of a small business have recently come into your possession and are reproduced below.

M. and A. Margan
Trading and profit and loss account for year ended 30 April 19X5

	£	£
Sales – cash	72,010	
– credit	83,206	
		155,216
Less:		
Opening stock	18,352	
Purchases	123,693	
	142,045	
Closing stock	(21,824)	
Goods used by owner	(640)	
Cost of sales		119,581
Gross profit		35,635
Add:		
Trade discounts received on purchases	16,530	
Value added tax included in purchases	14,500	
		31,030
		66,665
Less:		
Wages and salaries	28,726	
Value added tax included in sales	16,000	
Goods used by owner	640	
Heating and lighting	6,127	
Depreciation	5,760	
Other expenses	4,036	
		61,289
Net profit for year		£5,376

M. and A. Margan
Balance sheet as at 30 April 19X5

	£	£
Fixed assets		
Premises	44,000	
Vehicles	10,240	
		54,240
Current assets		
Stock 21,824		
Debtors 6,017		
Bank and cash	511	
	28,352	

Current liabilities		
Creditors	27,809	
		543
		£54,783

Capital: opening	53,000	
Net profit for year	5,376	
	58,376	
Drawings	(6,000)	
		52,376
Unidentified difference in books		2,407
		£54,783

Explanatory notes:

Sales

The figure shown comprises amounts actually received (including value added tax) for both cash and credit sales after deducting cash discounts for prompt settlement of accounts. The value added tax element is then charged as an expense.

Cost of sales

Opening stock has been valued at FIFO (first in, first out) purchase cost but during the year it has been thought appropriate to take account of storage and handling charges; consequently closing stock includes a surcharge of 5% to cover this item.

Purchases are included at gross catalogue price (including value added tax). Both reclaimable value added tax and trade discounts on purchases are then shown as additional items of revenue.

Wages and salaries

This item comprises the amounts actually paid within the year, irrespective of the period in which they were earned.

Depreciation

Premises have been depreciated on a straight-line basis on cost, assuming a 50-year life.

Vehicles have been depreciated at the rate of 20% per annum on a reducing-balance basis.

Identify and comment upon the specific instances in which the accounts of this business have been prepared in apparent conflict with generally accepted accounting principles, practices and conventions. **(18 marks)**

6.5   More Terms

(a)   Explain the following terms used in financial accounting.

   Matching convention

   Prudence convention

   Inflation

   Price changes

   Going concern

   Objectivity

(b)   Should price changes be taken into account during the matching process? Give reasons for your answer. **(18 marks)**

6.6   Statements

'The shareholder needs a statement of financial prospects, i.e. an indication of future progress. However, the supplier of goods on credit needs a statement of financial position, i.e. an indication of the current state of affairs.'

Required

(a)   Explain the extent to which you think this statement is true.

(b)   It is general practice in most countries to prepare published accounting reports either based on historical costs, or based on historical costs but with the occasional revaluation of some fixed assets. To what extent do you think that accounting reports prepared in such ways do actually meet the needs of shareholders and suppliers of goods on credit?   **(15 marks)**

(ACCA, December 1992)

6.7   Information

It is frequently suggested that accounting information and accounting reports should attempt to be relevant and reliable. These terms could be explained as follows.

'Information has the quality of relevance when it influences the economic decisions of users by helping them evaluate past, present or future events or by confirming, or correcting, their past evaluations.

'Information has the quality of reliability when it is free from material error and bias and can be depended on by users to represent faithfully in terms of valid description that which it either purports to represent or could reasonably be expected to represent.'

Required

(a)   Explain what accountants mean by the convention of objectivity.

(b)   Why do shareholders need to read published accounts of companies in which they own shares?

(c)   'From the viewpoint of shareholders, objectivity will tend to lead to accounts being more reliable, but less relevant.' Do you agree?   **(15 marks)**

(ACCA, June 1993)

7   ANSWERS TO EXAMINATION TYPE QUESTIONS

7.1   Terms

(a)   **Financial accounting**

Financial accounting is concerned with providing economic information to 'outsiders' (user groups other than managers). The information provides a general overview of the financial position and performance of the business and is not as specific or detailed as the information produced for managers. The major financial accounting statements are the balance sheet, the profit and loss account and the cash flow statement.

Financial accounting information is usually backward looking. Forecast information is rarely disclosed for fear that the forecasts may be misunderstood by investors or that it may help competitors. Financial accounting information relating to a business may be used for comparison with other businesses. To facilitate comparisons it is useful if each business prepares and presents the financial accounting statements in a similar way. The law and accounting profession have intervened to ensure that the financial accounting statements published by limited companies are produced in a fairly uniform fashion.

(b)   **Realisation**

It is important that consideration is given to the question of at which point a revenue should be treated as having occurred. For example, should a credit sale be recorded in the accounts of a business:

- when the order is received from the customer
- when the goods pass to the customer
- when the customer pays for the goods?

There is no precise, objective answer to this question. However, in accounting we usually apply the realisation convention to resolve this issue. This convention states that the sale should normally be recognised when the goods physically pass to the customer and they are accepted by him or her. It is based on the idea that at this point there is some measure of achievement that can be made, that there is acceptance by the customer of some kind of obligation to pay, and that there is a good chance that such payment will be made by the customer. It is important to recognise that application of the realisation convention can mean that revenue is recognised before the cash is received from the customer. Indeed, a revenue may be recognised in one accounting period and the cash may be received in a later period.

(c)   **Matching**

Having established in which accounting period revenues should be recognised, typically by following the realisation convention, it is necessary to ensure that the expenses relating to them are allocated to the same accounting period. Failure to match revenues with expenses which arise in relation to them can cause very considerable distortions and therefore misleading information. The matching convention asserts that expenses should be matched to the revenues to which they relate such that both the revenues and the expenses are recognised in the same accounting period.

Where a good is produced over two accounting periods it will be necessary to carry forward costs of production to the period in which the good is sold, so that these costs can be matched against revenues arising from the actual sale. Costs carried forward in this way must be shown as a current asset on the balance sheet usually as stock or work-in-progress. With certain types of expenses it is not possible to match expenses with revenues in the way that cost of sales can be matched with sales. For example, rates cannot be related to any particular sales in the direct way that cost of sales can. The only logical approach here is to match on a time basis. This means that the revenues recognised in the accounting period are matched with the expenses relating to that period.

(d)   **Materiality**

Costs may be divided into two elements – an expense element and an asset element. The expense element represents that portion of the costs which has been used up in the process of generating revenues. The asset element represents that portion of the costs which has not yet been used up and is carried forward to future accounting periods. Where the amounts involved are trivial it is not necessary to identify precisely the point at which costs become expenses. For example, in order to follow strictly the accruals convention it would be necessary to assess the physical quantities and then to value every item of stock, not just stock in trade but also stocks of things such as stationery, so that they could be treated as assets rather than expenses in the final accounts. According to the materiality convention this should be ignored except where the value of these stocks is material. What is material is a matter of judgement for those preparing the accounts. It will also vary from business to business. What is a material amount for a small business may be immaterial to a large business.

(e) **Inflation**

Inflation has been defined in various ways over the years. A popular definition of inflation is a rise in the general level of prices or a fall in the value of money. This definition suggests a change in the relationship between the amount of money in the economy and the amount of goods. Strictly, inflation refers to a general rise in the price of goods and services within the economy and should be distinguished from rises in the price of individual goods or services. It is possible for prices of individual goods and services to rise and yet for the general level of prices to stay constant. Price rises of certain goods and services will be cancelled out by price falls among other goods and services. Rises in the general level of prices result from macroeconomic factors such as an increase in the supply of money, whereas individual price rises may result from particular market conditions or microeconomic factors. Inflation can be measured by the use of an index. In the UK the Retail Price Index is a widely used measure of the rate of inflation.

Inflation accounting is concerned with the accounting implications of changing price levels. Although it can be argued that inflation accounting should be concerned only with the general rise in prices within the economy many commentators believe it is more important to consider the implications of specific price changes on the business.

7.2 Going Concern

(a) The going concern convention is normally applied when preparing the annual accounts of a business. This means that the business is assumed to continue in operation into the forseeable future. The practical implication of this convention is that fixed assets are recorded at their historic cost in the accounts and depreciation is calculated by allocating the cost (less residual value) of the asset over its estimated useful life rather than measuring changes in the market value of the asset.

In order to provide an illustration of this convention consider a business which commenced trading for the first time on 1 January 19X1. On that date a machine was purchased for £10,000. The machine is expected to have a useful life of four years and a residual value of £2,000. The business adopts the straight-line method of depreciation. At the year-end the realisable value of the machine was £6,000.

Where the business is a going concern the relevant balance sheet and profit and loss account extracts after the first year of operations would be as follows:

Balance sheet as at 31 December 19X1

	Cost	Depreciation	WDV
	£	£	£
Machine	10,000	2,000	8,000

Profit and loss account
for the year ended 31 December 19X1

	£
Depreciation – machine	2,000

In this case information concerning realisable value is irrelevant when preparing the accounts.

It is sometimes queried whether the going concern convention should provide support for the historic cost convention. The fact that a business is deemed to continue into the indefinite future need not imply a commitment to pursuing certain activities or holding certain fixed assets. Knowledge of current market values of fixed assets may help in the formulation of future strategies.

(b)   If the going concern convention is considered to be inoperative for a particular business the practical implication would be that assets should be shown at their realisable values rather than their historic cost. These hypothetical market values may be difficult to establish with reasonable accuracy. Given the information concerning a business in a) above the relevant balance sheet and profit and loss account extracts for such a business would be as follows:

Balance sheet as at 31 December 19X1

	£
Machine at valuation	6,000

Profit and loss account
for the year ended 31 December 19X1

	£
Loss in value of machine	4,000

7.3   Users

(a)   **Owners**

Owners invest in a company to increase their wealth, in order for prospective and existing owners to make decisions concerning whether to invest in, remain in, or disinvest from a company, they require information about potential risks and rewards. To assess risk, information about liquidity, financial structure and the variability of earnings would be useful. To assess rewards, information about levels of profits, dividends and capital appreciation would be useful. Where the owners leave the day-to-day running of the company to professional managers, information about financial position and performance is required in order to assess whether the managers have been honest and efficient and have acted in the best interests of the owners.

(b)   **Employees**

Employees often have a substantial and longstanding relationship with a company. The principal concerns of employees are those of job security and remuneration. These matters are related to the survival and economic success of the company. Hence, information about the growth and stability of sales and profits, liquidity and the amount of net assets held would be useful.

(c)   **Lenders**

Where lenders provide finance to a company on a short-term basis their principal concern will be with the liquidity of the company. However, providers of long-term finance have a more general concern for the financial health of the company. In order to assess the ability of the company to pay interest and repay capital over the longer term, lenders would require information concerning growth and stability of profits, the company's financial structure and the market value of assets held.

(d)   **Competitors**

Competitors will have an interest in the financial performance of the company so they can make comparisons of efficiency and effectiveness. Thus, information about trends in sales, expenses and profits will be of value. Competitors will also have an interest in the resources of the company so that they can assess its ability to compete and survive in the future.

(e)   **Government**

Government may have a number of reasons for requiring economic information from a business. Information relating to performance, such as profits, will be of interest for taxation purposes. In addition, information relating to sales, profits and resources may be helpful in deciding upon the level of financial assistance to be given to a company or industry. Government may be interested in sales and profits for regulatory purposes, for instance to encourage competition and prevent the growth of monopoly.

(f) Customers

Customers may require information to assess whether the company is capable of supplying goods or services when needed. This will be important where large contracts are involved and binding commitments have been made. Thus, information concerning the growth and stability of profits and the resources of the company will be useful.

7.4 Margan

Sales

The calculation of sales contravenes generally accepted principles concerning revenue recognition. Credit sales should reflect the amounts receivable rather than amounts actually received. The realisation convention requires that sales should normally be recognised when the goods have been passed to the customer and are accepted, and not when the cash is finally received.

Cash discounts should not be deducted when arriving at the sales figure. Sales should be shown at the gross amount and any cash discounts should be regarded as a selling expense which should be shown separately in the profit and loss account.

VAT should not be included in the sales figure and should not be included as an expense. The business is simply a collector of this form of taxation and the accounts should reflect this fact. This means that VAT should not normally be regarded as either revenue or an expense and should normally only appear in the accounts to the extent it is owed to, or reclaimable from, the taxation authorities.

Cost of sales

The change in the valuation of stocks contravenes the convention of consistency. A business should be consistent in its valuation method from period to period unless there are compelling reasons not to be so. Where a change in valuation method occurs this should be clearly stated and its impact on profit also stated.

Trade discounts are regarded as a lowering of the initial purchase price and should not therefore be included in the accounts. The purchases figure should be shown after trade discounts have been taken. VAT should normally be excluded from the purchases figure for the same reasons as those stated above.

Wages and salaries

The wages and salaries figure has not been prepared in accordance with the accruals convention. The amounts should reflect the amounts earned rather than the amounts actually paid.

Depreciation

It is permissible to employ different methods of depreciating fixed assets for different classes of asset.

Further points

Goods used by the owner represent drawings which should be deducted from capital. Goods used by the owner should also be deducted from purchases in arriving at the cost of goods sold.

An explanation of the basis on which fixed assets have been valued in the balance sheet should be given.

It is not acceptable for an unexplained difference to appear in the final accounts. The reason(s) for any difference should be established and appropriate corrections made.

7.5   More Terms

(a)   The matching convention is an accounting rule which asserts that in computing profits, expenses should be matched against the revenues to which they relate.

The prudence convention asserts that accountants should err on the side of caution in recognition of expenses and claims.

Inflation is the average rise in the general level of prices measured by some standard 'basket of goods'. A common measure used is the Retail Price Index which is a weighted average of a number of common household items. The result is the same amount of money will buy less goods; it can be said therefore that there is an average fall in the value of money.

Price changes are, on the other hand, relative to a specific good or service. The change in the price may be either in costs or sales, or indeed both, during an accounting period. There may be an index available by which specific price changes are measured – an example is the Capital Goods Index.

The going concern convention is an accounting assumption that a business will continue indefinitely or at least into the foreseeable future. Thus, in arriving at the value of fixed assets and the depreciation thereof a consistent basis may be used.

The objectivity convention asserts that the figures which appear in accounts should be free from bias and capable of independent verification.

(b)   During a period of rapid general price rises or specific price changes, profits may become overstated. This situation arises because of the time lag between the acquisition of an item and its sale. The result of applying the matching rule is that historic cost items are compared with inflated current selling prices at a later date. However, if the historic cost price is increased to a current cost price then like is being compared to like and a lower profit calculated. This is the prudence convention in operation. Nevertheless, although a more realistic number has been calculated there may be an argument that objectivity has been lost. Despite this objection, if no adjustment is made, profits will be overstated and perhaps commensurate distributions will be made. This could result in a permanent reduction in the size of operations which could be carried on in the future. In this case the prudence convention has or perhaps should override the objectivity convention.

7.6   Statements

(a)   The following points should be included:

- The statement is probably generally true. The short-term creditors are most interested in the ability of the company to meet its short-term commitments, whereas shareholders have a longer-term stake in the company.

- The company will have no long term if it cannot meet its short-term commitments, so shareholders have more than a passing interest in financial position.

- Short-term creditors will be interested in the financial prospects of the company since these will relate to the company's ability to generate cash.

(b)

- Historic figures are relatively objective, other figures tend to be less so.

- There is often a conflict between objectivity and relevance/usefulness.

- Historic figures tend to lead to imprudently large profit figures and, potentially therefore, dividend payments.

- 'Occasional revaluation' probably does help in the usefulness of the accounts. Many people, however, would argue that this is too limited and haphazard an approach to dealing with the deficiencies of historic cost information.

7.7 Information

(a) Objectivity implies that accounting statements should be, in so far as possible, based on facts rather than opinion. They should be free from bias and should be capable of independent verification. The presence of objectivity is seen as giving greater credibility to the accounting statements.

(b) Shareholders invest in a company with a view to increasing their wealth. They will, therefore, be interested in the financial statements in order to help assess the financial performance and position of the company. This assessment will, in turn, help them decide whether to hold, buy or sell shares in the company. The directors of the company act for and on behalf of the shareholders. The shareholders will also be interested in the financial statements in order to help assess whether the directors have acted honestly, efficiently and in the best interests of the shareholders.

(c) Basing accounts on objective verifiable evidence should have a positive influence on the reliability of the information presented in so far as it reduces bias. However, the relevance of the information for decision-making may be undermined as a result. Objectivity supports the continuing adherence to the use of historic cost which may not be relevant to a wide range of management decisions. There is support for other valuation methods which rely more on the use of subjective judgement in order to increase the relevance of financial reports. Some, however, would argue that for certain types of decisions (for example, stewardship decisions) the continued use of historic cost (and by implication the use of objectivity) is important.

24 ANALYSIS AND INTERPRETATION OF FINAL ACCOUNTS

INTRODUCTION AND LEARNING OBJECTIVES

The point has been made at various points in this book that the principal objective of accounting is to provide decision makers with useful information which will enable them to make better decisions as a result of having that information. In the main, the earlier chapters of this book have tended to be concerned with the collection and analysis of accounting information, rather than with its interpretation and use. This chapter, however, is concerned with the analysis and evaluation of final accounts as a basis for decision making. Here the main emphasis will be on the use of accounting ratios as a means of drawing logical conclusions from accounting statements, which should enable more informed decisions to be made. We start with a consideration of why ratios can be useful and how they can provide insights which the basic accounting statements cannot provide. The chapter then goes on to consider the classes of accounting ratios which users are likely to find most useful. The different classes are:

- profitability ratios – those concerned with levels of earning
- activity ratios – those concerned with the effective use of the assets of the business
- liquidity ratios – those concerned with the ability of the business to meet its short-term obligations
- gearing ratios – those concerned with the long-term financing of the business
- investors' ratios – those used by shareholders, potential shareholders and others to try to assess the performance of the business specifically from that perspective.

Examples are discussed which use a variety of ratios to build up a picture of the business over past periods. The chapter concludes with a discussion and examples of how accounting ratios can be useful in formulating financial plans and budgets.

The subject of analysis and interpretation of accounts through accounting ratios is a particularly important one. It will come up again throughout your studies and questions which require a sound knowledge of it are likely to be met in several of the later papers, particularly Papers 5, 10 and 13.

When you have studied this chapter you should be able to do the following:

- Calculate and interpret all the key accounting ratios for a set of financial statements
- Appreciate the limitations of such ratio analysis.

---

1 FINANCIAL RATIOS

1.1 Introduction

Accounting statements can be analysed and evaluated in a number of ways. One of the most important of these in practice is through the use of **ratio analysis**. It is also particularly important from an examination point of view, since questions involving ratio analysis frequently arise.

Financial ratios are simply measures, often expressed in percentage terms, which relate one financial figure to another. Typically, the two financial figures come from the same set of final accounts. The objective of calculating such ratios is to enable useful comparisons to be made in order that insights into past performance and present positions may be gained.

Assume, for example, last year's net profit of a particular business was £50,000. Those who are, for one reason or another, interested in that business are likely to want to know how effective a performance by the company's management this represents. The obvious course of action for interested parties is to compare this profit with that of another company engaged in the same type of activity during the same period, or perhaps to compare it with the previous year's profit of the same business. A major problem of seeking to make such a comparison is that the other company may be much smaller or larger in scale, so that direct comparison of the two companies' profits could be misleading. The same problem could also arise if comparison is sought between the business's profit this year and last year, since it would be unusual for a company to have exactly the same level of assets tied up in the business from one year to the next.

The obvious solution to this problem of lack of comparability is to express profits in terms of some measure of the size of the company, for example the net assets (fixed assets and working capital).

If the net assets of the business during this year averaged £300,000 this would imply a return on net investment of 17% (50,000/300,000 × 100%). This is a measure that could now usefully be used as a basis of comparison with similarly derived ratios for other businesses or earlier years.

Thus financial ratios may be regarded as key indicators which can be a practical and valuable basis of comparison.

1.2 Basis of comparison

There are broadly three bases of comparison for ratios derived from final accounts.

(a) Past periods

A comparison can be made between the most recent period and previous periods in the life of the same business. It may then be possible from this to detect trends which may be useful in planning for the future. A problem with such comparisons is that merely because a particular ratio may seem better than it has been in the past does not necessarily mean that it is really acceptable. In other words, restricting the basis of comparison to the same business may be too narrow. Another problem with this basis of comparison is that the economic environment in which the particular business operates could easily alter dramatically from one period to the next.

(b) Planned performance

Businesses often formulate their financial plans in terms of financial ratios, in order to compare the actual ratios which occur with planned ratios. This is a valid and useful activity provided the planned ratios are based on realistic assumptions about the future. Later in the chapter, consideration will be given to using financial ratios as financial planning tools.

(c) Other businesses in the same industry

This is a very useful basis of comparison, particularly if several businesses can be identified as being valid for comparison. A problem here is that differences in accounting policies on issues such as depreciation and stock valuation can hinder valid comparison. Statements of Standard Accounting Practice (SSAPs) tend to reduce the impact of such hindrances but they do not eliminate them. The difficulty is also reduced where there is some sort of 'inter-firm comparison' scheme in existence. Such schemes are sometimes organised by various trade associations. Here the accounting figures of individual businesses are often adjusted to try to eliminate the differences caused by the fact that businesses do not all use the same accounting policies.

1.3 Ratio classification and users

Ratios are usually classified according to the particular aspect of the business which they seek to address. The major classifications include the following:

(a) Profitability

These ratios relate profit to other aspects to try to assess the effectiveness of the business in achieving its central objective; that is, generating profit.

(b)   **Activity**

These try to assess the effectiveness of the business in using its assets. They can give insights into managerial policy.

(c)   **Liquidity**

These seek to assess the ability of the business to meet its short-term financial obligations.

(d)   **Gearing**

These ratios look at the long-term financing structure of the business and provide some indications of the level of risk inherent in that structure. Liquidity and gearing ratios are sometimes useful in giving an indication of the financial stability of a business.

(e)   **Investors' ratios**

These look at the business from the particular perspective of a shareholder or a potential shareholder. More particularly they tend to used for companies which are traded in an established Stock Exchange.

One of the reasons for classifying ratios in this way is to gather together those ratios which might be of particular interest to particular users of the final accounts. It might be useful at this point to recall the users identified in Chapter 1 and to identify which group of ratios will most likely interest each of them.

User	Class of ratio	Reason
Owner (shareholders)	Profitability Activity Gearing Investors'	Shareholders will be particularly interested in what profits have been made and what prior calls there may be on these profits before shareholders can participate. They will also be interested in how effectively management have used the resources at their command.
Government Revenue)	Profitability	The Inland Revenue will be interested in (Inland profits and how they are earned
Management	Profitability Activity Liquidity Gearing	Management should be interested in every facet of the business. They have a responsibility for the overall financial position and performance of the business.
Customers	Liquidity	Customers will tend to be interested in the ability of the business to survive in the short-term and to continue to supply.
Suppliers	Liquidity	Suppliers will also often be most interested in the ability of the business to survive in the short-term and to meet its trade credit obligations.
Lenders	Liquidity Gearing	Short-term lenders will be particularly concerned with the ability of the business to meet its short-term financial commitments.Long-term borrowers will be interested in the extent to which the business is financed by long-term lenders.
Employees	Profitability Activity Liquidity	Employees are suppliers of labour and have similar interests to those of other suppliers. Their more close involvement with the business tends to make them interested in profit as well.

None of the foregoing should be taken to imply that the specified users will be uninterested in aspects other than those mentioned. All that is being said is that particular users will have a particular interest in some ratios more than others.

The ratios will now be introduced class by class in relation to the following example.

Example

Riosta plc's final accounts for the two most recent years are as follows:

Riosta plc
Trading and profit and loss account for the year ended 31 December

	19X8	19X9
	£000	£000
Sales	10,874	11,450
Less: Cost of sales	6,351	6,907
Gross profit	4,523	4,543
Less: Trading expenses	3,452	3,098
Net profit before interest and taxation	1,071	1,445
Less: Long-term loan interest	350	280
Net profit before tax	721	1,165
Less: Taxation	203	327
Net profit after tax	518	838
Less: Dividend	200	200
Retained profit	318	638

Balance sheet as at 31 December

	19X8		19X9	
	£000	£000	£000	£000
Fixed assets				
(cost less depreciation)				
Freehold premises	4,025		5,025	
Plant and equipment	2,167		2,750	
		6,192		7,775
Current assets				
Stock	2,625		1,863	
Trade debtors	2,277		1,980	
Cash	198		193	
	5,100		4,036	
Less: **Creditors** Amounts falling due in under 1 year				
Trade creditors	1,175		1,432	
Taxation	203		327	
Dividend due	200		200	
	1,578		1,959	
Net current assets		3,522		2,077
Total assets less current liabilities		9,714		9,852
Less: **Creditors** Amounts falling due in more than 1 year				
Loan		2,500		2,000
		7,214		7,852

Capital and reserves

Share capital (4,000 shares of £1 each)	4,000	4,000
Reserves	3,214	3,852
	7,214	7,852

2 PROFITABILITY RATIOS

2.1 Introduction

Three ratios are commonly used to assess the effectiveness of the business in generating profit.

2.2 Return on capital employed

This ratio relates the net profit to the level of investment used to earn it. There are several definitions for this ratio. The differences involve such considerations as whether to take profit before or after tax, whether to consider the assets net of current liabilities or net of both current and long-term liabilities. To some extent the definition should depend on the use to which the ratio is to be put. Two definitions will be considered here.

(a) **Return on net assets**

$$\text{Return on net assets} = \frac{\textbf{Net profit before long-term loan interest and tax}}{\textbf{Fixed assets plus working capital}} \times 100\%$$

For Riosta plc this would give:

	19X8	**19X9**
Return on net assets	$= \dfrac{1,071}{9,714} \times 100 = 11.0\%$	$\dfrac{1,445}{9,852} \times 100 = 14.7\%$

Theoretically, the higher the ratio the better, since a high ratio suggests effective trading. On this basis 19X9 is an improvement on the previous year. Whether 14.7%, as a pre-tax return, is really satisfactory when compared with the safe returns available from bank deposit accounts is an important question. Returns must be weighed against the risks involved. The higher the level of risk associated with a business the higher the expected returns should be.

(a) **Return on equity**

$$\text{Return on equity} = \frac{\textbf{Net profit after long-term loan interest and tax}}{\textbf{Share capital and reserves}} \times 100\%$$

For Riosta plc this would give:

	19X8	**19X9**
Return on equity	$= \dfrac{518}{7,214} \times 100 = 7.2\%$	$\dfrac{838}{7,852} \times 100 = 10.7\%$

This also suggests a distinct improvement. There is a distinction between these two definitions of return on capital employed. *Return on net assets* seeks to assess the effectiveness of management in generating profit from the assets (net of current liabilities) at its disposal. Note that the ratio is calculated before long-term interest. This is because the assets concerned are those provided from funds supplied both by shareholders and by long-term lenders. It is calculated *before* tax because the control which management has over its tax charge is limited and the object of the ratio is to assess management's effectiveness in terms of use of net assets. *Return on equity* looks at the position from the shareholder's point of view. It is more concerned with how much the shareholders get by way of a return on their investment, after accounting for all prior claims, including interest and tax.

The return on capital employed ratios measured by each of these definitions are likely to be highly correlated. Where this is not the case it probably indicates a high level of gearing (see below).

2.3 Gross profit margin

This relates gross profit to sales and is therefore:

$$\text{Gross profit margin} = \frac{\text{Gross profit}}{\text{Sales}} \times 100\%$$

For Riosta plc this would give:

	19X8	**19X9**
Gross profit margin $=$	$\dfrac{4,523}{10,874} \times 100 = 41.6\%$	$\dfrac{4,543}{11,450} \times 100 = 39.7\%$

Put another way, in 19X8, for each £ of sales, 41.6 pence remained after meeting the cost of goods sold. During 19X9 this had fallen to 39.7 pence.

The ratio gives some idea of pricing policy. It cannot be said that one of these figures is better than the other. The lower ratio for 19X9 means that, relative to cost, stock is being sold at a lower price than it was in 19X8. If it assumed that stock buying prices were more or less the same in both years, it must mean that selling prices were lower in 19X9 than in 19X8. This may have been part of a deliberate policy to generate more sales. If this were so it was not very successful in profitability terms, since the extra sales brought only a marginal increase in gross profit.

2.4 Net profit margin

This expresses the net profit as a percentage of sales. For this ratio net profit is usually taken before tax.

It is defined as:

$$\text{Net profit margin} = \frac{\text{Net profit before tax}}{\text{Sales}} \times 100\%$$

For Riosta plc this would give:

	19X8	**19X9**
Net profit margin $=$	$\dfrac{721}{10,874} \times 100 = 6.6\%$	$\dfrac{1,165}{11,450} \times 100 = 10.2\%$

Thus, in 19X8, 6.6 pence of profit was left out of each £ of sales after meeting trading expenses. This had increased to 10.2 pence in the pound by 19X9. On the face of it 19X9 was a more successful year than 19X8. Inspection of the profit and loss account shows this to be attributable to the lower expenses.

3 ACTIVITY RATIOS

3.1 Introduction

There are four ratios which are commonly used to assess the effectiveness of the business in using its assets.

3.2 Net asset turnover

This attempts to assess how effective the business is at generating sales compared to the amount invested in net assets (fixed assets plus working capital). This is calculated as:

$$\text{Net asset turnover} = \frac{\text{Sales}}{\text{Net assets}}$$

For Riosta plc this would give:

	19X8		**19X9**	
Net asset turnover	$= \dfrac{10{,}874}{9{,}714}$	$= 1.1$ times	$\dfrac{11{,}450}{9{,}852}$	$= 1.2$ times

The company was rather more effective at generating sales in 19X9 than it was in 19X8. A low figure for this ratio indicates ineffectiveness on the part of management in using the assets of the business. Too high a figure could mean that the business is overtrading, that is, overstretching its financial resources.

3.3   Stock-holding period

This ratio identifies the average length of time that stock spends in the business before it is sold (or used in production). It can be calculated for the stock as a whole or for sections of the stock. It is calculated by relating the stock level to the annual usage of stock (cost of sales in a merchant business) and converted into a time period by conversion into days, weeks or months. It is calculated as:

$$\text{Stock-holding period (in days)} = \frac{\text{Stock}}{\text{Cost of sales}} \times 365$$

For Riosta plc this would give:

	19X8		**19X9**	
Stock-holding period $=$	$\dfrac{2{,}625}{6{,}351}$	$\times 365 = 151$ days	$\dfrac{1{,}863}{6{,}907}$	$\times 365 = 98$ days

In the above calculations the closing stock figure for each year has been used. It is probably better to use the figure for average stock held during each year. However, in this case, this information is not available for both years and therefore, for reasons of consistency, year-end stocks have been used.

This represents a fairly dramatic drop in the stock-holding period from 19X8 to 19X9. Even at the lower level it still means that stock is on the premises for about 14 weeks before it is sold. It may be in the nature of the trade in which the company operates that it needs to maintain high stock levels, for example in order to be able to offer its customers sufficient choice. This is something which should be assessed and if the high levels of stock are not really necessary the level should be further dropped.

Stock holding is expensive in terms of storage costs, finance tied up and the dangers of the stock becoming obsolete. Therefore it is important that stock is kept at the lowest level which is practical, bearing in mind the need to be able to supply customers and to have raw material stock available to put into production.

A variation of this ratio is the **stock turnover ratio** which is calculated by dividing cost of sales by stock. Thus it is, in effect, the inverse of the stock-holding period ratio. It indicates how many times a year, on average, the stock is used and replaced.

3.4   Debtors collection period

Here the objective is to identify the average period for which trade debts remain outstanding, that is, the length of time between the credit sale being made and the cash being received. It is calculated as:

$$\text{Debtors collection period (in days)} = \frac{\text{Trade debtors}}{\text{Credit sales}} \times 365$$

For Riosta plc this would give:

19X8 **19X9**

$$\text{Debtors collection period} = \frac{2,277}{10,874} \times 365 = 76 \text{ days} \quad \frac{1,980}{11,450} \times 365 = 63 \text{ days}$$

(assuming that all of Riosta plc's sales are on credit)

This appears to be an improvement, though 63 days still seems a long period. It may be that Riosta has to offer credit periods of this scale in order to attract custom, but it may simply be mismanagement of debtors. This is probably something worthy of investigation. Giving credit is expensive in terms of interest lost and the dangers that customers will not eventually pay. Selling on credit is almost unavoidable in most areas of commerce and industry; in order to compete businesses usually need to offer it. As with stock, an appropriate balance must be sought.

3.5 Creditors payment period

This ratio assesses the average time taken between buying stock on credit and paying for it. It is calculated as:

$$\text{Creditors payment period (in days)} = \frac{\text{Trade creditors}}{\text{Credit purchases}} \times 365$$

Even assuming that all of the purchases of stock are on credit, there is not sufficient information to calculate this ratio for Riosta plc. This is because the purchases figure is not given in the accounts. Where the stock figure is fairly constant from one year to the next, using the cost of sales figure as a substitute would probably be reasonable. In the case of Riosta plc this is clearly not true, as there is a significant drop between 19X8 and 19X9.

If the value of stock in trade at 31 December 19X7 was available, the purchases figure for the two years could be deduced. Assuming that this was £2,487,000, the calculation for this is carried out as follows:

It is well established that:

Cost of sales = opening stock + purchases – closing stock

This can be rearranged to give:

Purchases = Cost of sales + closing stock – opening stock

For 19X8

Purchases = 6,351 + 2,625 – 2,487 – 6,489

For 19X9

Purchases = 6,907 + 1,863 – 2,625 = 6,145

This enables the creditor payment ratio to be calculated:

19X8 **19X9**

$$\text{Creditor payment period} = \frac{1,175}{6,489} \times 365 = 66 \text{ days} \quad \frac{1,432}{6,145} \times 365 = 85 \text{ days}$$

This represents a significant increase in the creditor payment period from one which was already fairly long. On the face of it, this is good for Riosta plc because it was receiving more benefit from free credit in 19X9 than it was in 19X8. However, the increase may, unless it is with the agreement of suppliers, lead to suppliers refusing to accept any more orders from the company.

4   LIQUIDITY RATIOS

4.1   Introduction

There are two ratios commonly used to assess the ability of a business to meet its short-term commitments.

4.2   The current ratio

This ratio tries to assess how well the business could meet its short-term financial commitments from its current assets. It is calculated as:

$$\textbf{Current ratio} \quad = \quad \frac{\textbf{Current assets}}{\textbf{Current liabilities}}$$

For Riosta plc this would give:

	19X8	19X9

$$\text{Current ratio} \quad = \quad \frac{5,100}{1,578} = 3.2{:}1 \qquad\qquad \frac{4,036}{1,959} = 2.1{:}1$$

Without knowing what is typical for the industry it is impossible to say whether or not these ratios look reasonable. Generally the current ratios found in practice fall into the range 1:1 to 2:1. Retailers tend to be at the lower end, because they typically turn their stock over fairly quickly and because they tend to have few or no trade debtors. Manufacturers tend to be at the higher end because they tend to hold quite large stocks, in various stages of completion, and they sell on credit.

Too low a current ratio implies financial weakness and a possible inability to meet short-term (current) liabilities without strain. Too high a current ratio tends to imply excessive and inefficiently managed stocks, debtors and cash and perhaps a failure to utilise sufficiently the free trade credit available. The reduction in the ratio for Riosta plc implies a more effective use of its working capital.

4.3   The quick asset ratio (acid-test ratio)

Here the question is whether the business can meet its short-term financial commitments at short notice, from its own liquid resources, should it be required to do so. Thus it is a more stringent test of liquidity than the current ratio.

The ratio is calculated as:

$$\textbf{Quick asset ratio} = \frac{\textbf{Current assets less stocks}}{\textbf{Current liabilities}}$$

The reason for excluding stock is that in most types of business stock is not very liquid. That is to say that it may take quite a long time to be turned into cash, because first it must be sold, typically on credit, then payment from the customer must be received.

For Riosta plc this would give:

	19X8	19X9

$$\text{Quick asset ratio} = \frac{5,100 - 2,625}{1,578} = 1.6{:}1 \qquad\qquad \frac{4,036 - 1,863}{1,959} = 1.1{:}1$$

This is fairly high for both years. Given the nature and purpose of this ratio a figure of 1:1 is usually seen as satisfactory, though it does vary from one industry to another. As with the current ratio, too high an acid-test ratio implies underutilisation of working capital.

5 GEARING RATIOS

5.1 Introduction

Two ratios are commonly used to assess the long-term financing structure of a business.

5.2 Debt to equity ratio

This relates the long-term funds provided by outsiders and on which interest must be paid to the finance provided by the owners through their capital (shares and reserves in the case of companies). The ratio is calculated as:

$$\text{Debt to equity ratio} = \frac{\textbf{Borrowings (long-term plus bank overdrafts)}}{\textbf{Total equity}} \times \textbf{100}$$

For Riosta plc this would give:

	19X8	19X9

$$\text{Debt to equity ratio} = \frac{2,500}{7,214} \times 100\% = 34.7\% \qquad \frac{2,000}{7,852} \times 100\% = 25.5\%$$

Whether these are seen as large or small figures depends on the average for the industry. Generally, higher levels of gearing are more appropriate where the levels of profit tend not to fluctuate from year to year. High gearing levels are also often associated with the purchase of certain types of expensive fixed assets such as property or ships.

The decline in the ratio for Riosta plc clearly arises from the fall in the long-term loan, arising from repayment of £500,000 during the year.

5.3 Times interest earned (interest cover) ratio

This ratio quantifies the relationship between loan interest obligations and profit before tax and interest. It seeks to assess how well interest payments are covered by the profits available to meet them. It thus provides a measure of the confidence that a lender may have that interest payments will be met.

$$\text{Times interest earned ratio} = \frac{\text{Net profit interest and tax}}{\text{Interest charges}}$$

For Riosta plc this would give:

	19X8	19X9

$$\text{Times interest earned ratio} = \frac{1,071}{350} = 3.1 \text{ times} \qquad \frac{1,445}{280} = 5.2 \text{ times}$$

The level of coverage has increased over the two years, partly because profit has increased and partly because the interest obligation has reduced, with the reduction in the loan.

6 INVESTORS' RATIOS

6.1 Introduction

This set of ratios tends to be used by shareholders or potential shareholders of Stock Exchange quoted companies. Shareholders, though actually part-owners or potential part-owners of the company, can also be seen as external to the company in the sense that they are not likely to be able to exert much influence on the company. Thus they tend to be particularly interested in the company's profitability per share and the company's ability to pay dividends, for obvious reasons, as they affect shareholders' individual wealth.

So that we can use Riosta plc as an example for the calculation of several of the investors' ratios, we need to know the market value per share at each of the relevant year ends. These are:

	19X8	19X9
Market price per £1 ordinary share	£1.75	£2.50

6.2   Earnings per share

This ratio simply takes the net profit after tax (and preference dividends, if any) and divides it by the number of ordinary shares. This is widely regarded as a useful measure of performance. A company may increase its profit, but if it has also increased its share capital, the benefit to a particular shareholder may not necessarily have increased – hence the usefulness of this ratio.

It is calculated as follows:

$$\text{Earnings per share} = \frac{\textbf{Net profit after tax and preference dividends}}{\textbf{Number of ordinary shares at issue}}$$

For Riosta plc this would give:

19X8	19X9
$\text{EPS} = \dfrac{518}{4,000} = 13.0 \text{ pence}$	$\dfrac{838}{4,000} = 21.0 \text{ pence}$

This implies a genuine 'organic' earnings growth, rather than growth through raising additional finance.

6.3   Earnings yield

This relates earnings per share to the current market value per share. Thus it is, from the investor's point of view, a measure of return on investment.

It is calculated as follows:

$$\text{Earnings yield} = \frac{\textbf{Earnings per share}}{\textbf{Market price per share}} \times 100$$

For Riosta plc this would give:

19X8	19X9
$\text{Earnings yield} = \dfrac{13}{175} \times 100 = 7.4\%$	$\dfrac{21}{250} \times 100 = 8.4\%$

This shows that shareholders earn a higher return on their investment in the second year despite the increase in share price.

6.4   Price earnings ratio (PE)

This relates earnings per share to the current market value per share, as does the earnings yield ratio. The PE ratio calculates the number of years that it would take for the earnings from the share to pay back the price of the share.

It is calculated as follows:

$$\text{PE} = \frac{\textbf{Market price per share}}{\textbf{Earnings per share}}$$

For Riosta plc this would give:

	19X8	**19X9**
PE ratio =	$\dfrac{175}{13}$ = 13.5	$\dfrac{250}{21}$ = 11.9

This suggests that investors generally were prepared to pay more for this share compared with its past earnings in 19X8 than in 19X9. Perhaps this is because they saw the prospect in 19X8 of the growth in earnings which occurred in 19X9.

6.5 Dividend per share

This ratio simply takes the ordinary dividend paid and/or proposed for the year and divides it by the number of ordinary shares.

It is calculated as follows:

$$\textbf{Dividend per share} \quad = \quad \frac{\textbf{Total dividend for the year}}{\textbf{Number of ordinary share at issue}}$$

For Riosta plc this would give:

	19X8	**19X9**
Dividend per share =	$\dfrac{200}{4,000}$ = 5.0 pence	$\dfrac{200}{4,000}$ = 5.0 pence

Thus, the dividend per share has remained the same, even though the earnings per share has increased over the period.

6.6 Dividend yield

This relates dividend per share to the current market value per share. Thus it is a measure of cash return on investment.

It is calculated as follows:

$$\textbf{Dividend yield} \quad = \quad \frac{\textbf{Dividend per share}}{\textbf{Market price per share}} \quad \times \textbf{100}$$

For Riosta plc this would give:

	19X8	**19X9**
Dividend yield =	$\dfrac{5}{175}$ × 100 = 2.9%	$\dfrac{5}{250}$ × 100 = 2.0%

Since the dividend per share remained constant while the share price increased, the yield fell over the period. This fact might make the share unattractive to an investor who was keen to receive dividends. Of course the profits not paid out as dividends are no less the property of the shareholders; in theory at least, this part of the profit simply goes to increase the share price.

6.7 Dividend cover

This ratio indicates the extent to which the company pays its profits out as ordinary dividends.

It is calculated as follows:

$$\text{Dividend cover} = \frac{\textbf{Net profit after tax and preference dividends}}{\textbf{Dividends for the year}}$$

For Riosta plc this would give:

	19X8	**19X9**
Dividend cover	$= \dfrac{518}{200} = 2.59$	$\dfrac{838}{200} = 4.19$

This suggests a rather conservative dividend policy in 19X9, compared with 19X8. In 19X9 there was £4.19 of profit for each £1 of dividend paid.

Summary of Riosta plc's recent performance

There is only limited information with which to try to assess the company. It would be particularly useful to also have some typical ratios for the industry in which the company operates. In the absence of further information only tentative conclusions can be drawn.

The return on capital has increased from a level which was probably unacceptably low, in the light of returns from relatively safe investments, to a more reasonable level. This was achieved (despite a lower gross profit margin) through a cut in expenses which more than compensated for the gross profit margin to give a higher net profit margin. In 19X9 the company seemed to use its assets more effectively in generating sales. This was partly due to a much lower stock-holding period, a lower debtor collection period and a longer creditor payment period.

In terms of liquidity, the company seems to be very safe, with an apparently more effective deployment of working capital. The level of gearing has fallen and interest cover increased as a result of the repayment of part of the long-term loan.

From an investor's point of view, there was strong earnings per share growth and good earnings yield growth. The company's dividend policy looks a bit conservative in 19X9 relative to 19X8 and this may cause discontent with some shareholders.

In general the company looks to be in a strong and stable position, with increasing profitability.

7   GENERAL POINTS ABOUT FINANCIAL RATIOS

7.1   Caution in interpretation

Dogmatic conclusions should be avoided. For example, a reduction in the stock- holding period may be a good thing, but if it is likely to cause loss of customer goodwill or production dislocations due to stock shortages, it may not be such an advantage. Ratios rarely answer questions but they can highlight areas where questions might usefully be asked.

7.2   Balance sheet figures

Many of the ratios considered in this chapter involve the use of balance sheet figures. These ratios should be interpreted with caution since the balance sheet shows the position at a specific moment only and this may not be typical of the general position. This point is particularly important where the ratio is derived from a balance sheet figure in conjunction with a figure from the trading or profit and loss account. This is because the first figure relates to a moment in time whereas the second is a total for a period. A sensible way to try to avoid possible distortions here is to use the average figure for the balance sheet figure. So, for example, the debtor collection period would relate credit sales to the average of the trade debtors figures at the beginning and at the end of the year. But in many industries the existence of recurrent seasonal factors may mean that averaging beginning- and end-of-year figures will not solve the problem. It may, for example, be that the date up to which a business draws up its final accounts has been selected because it is a time when stock levels are always low, so that stock is relatively easy to value. In such cases, averaging the stock figures for two consecutive year-end dates would simply be averaging two figures which were totally untypical of stock levels throughout the rest of the year. Averaging monthly figures would usually be the solution to this problem. However, outsiders would not typically have access to such information.

In fact, past examination questions involving ratios have not given sufficient information to enable averages to be used, so candidates will have been forced to use year-end figures. This makes the calculations a little easier even if the resulting ratio is a little less valid.

7.3 Other financial ratios

There are an almost infinite number of ratios which can be calculated from a set of final accounts. The ones shown above are those most commonly used in practice and include those which have been specifically asked about in examination questions. It should be noted, however, that there are many other ratios which could be useful in particular contexts.

7.4 Partial sightedness of ratios

It is usually unwise to limit analysis and interpretation only to information revealed by ratios. For example, sales for a business could double from one year to the next. This would be a dramatic and important development, yet none of the ratios whose use is advocated in most textbooks would reveal this, at least not directly. However, this significant increase in turnover would be fairly obvious from even a superficial glance at the final accounts. There is the danger that excessive reliance on ratios in interpretation and analysis can lead to a 'blinkered' approach.

7.5 Notes on examination questions

Financial ratio questions are popular with the examiners. Questions involving calculation of financial ratios fall into two categories. Some questions ask for specific ratios to be calculated and commented on; others leave it to the candidate to select the ratios, though questions tend to specify the class of ratio required. It seems fairly common for examination questions to require candidates to deduce missing figures from information supplied. An example of this sort of deduction arose in the case of Riosta plc when the creditor payment period could be calculated only after the purchases figure had been deduced. Multiple choice questions on ratios will tend to focus on some specific area, rather than the broader approach which written test questions could take.

7.6 Activity

The outline balance sheets of the Nantred Trading Co. Ltd were as shown below:

Balance sheets at 30 September

19X5 £	19X5 £		19X6 £	19X6 £
		Fixed assets (at written-down value)		
40,000		Premises	98,000	
65,000		Plant and equipment	162,000	
	105,000			260,000
		Current assets		
31,200		Stock	95,300	
19,700		Trade debtors	30,700	
15,600		Bank and cash	26,500	
66,500			152,500	
		Current liabilities		
23,900		Trade creditors	55,800	
11,400		Corporation tax	13,100	
17,000		Proposed dividends	17,000	
52,300			85,900	

14,200	Working capital		66,600
£119,200			£326,600
	Financed by		
100,000	Ordinary share capital	200,000	
19,200	Reserves	26,600	
119,200	Shareholders' funds		226,600
–	7% Debentures		100,000
£119,200			£326,600

The only other information available is that the turnover for the years ended 30 September 19X5 and 19X6 was £202,900 and £490,700 respectively, and that on 30 September 19X4, reserves were £26,100.

1   Calculate, for each of the two years, six suitable ratios to highlight the financial stability, liquidity and profitability of the company.

2   Comment on the situation revealed by the figures you have calculated in your answer to 1 above.

Hint: It is necessary to deduce the profit figure from knowledge of opening and closing balance of reserves for each year.

7.7 Activity solution

Nantred Trading Co Ltd

		19X5	**19X6**
1	Return on net assets (Net profit before interest and tax/fixed assets plus working capital)	$\frac{21,500}{119,200} \times 100 = 18.0\%$	$\frac{44,500}{326,600} \times 100 = 13.6\%$
2	Net profit margin (Net profit before tax/sales)	$\frac{21,500}{202,900} \times 100 = 10.6\%$	$\frac{37,500}{490,700} \times 100 = 7.6\%$
3	Net asset turnover (sales/net assets)	$\frac{202,900}{119,200} = 1.7$ times	$\frac{490,700}{326,600} = 1.5$ times
4	Debtors collection period (Trade debtors/credit sales × 365)	$\frac{19,700}{202,900} \times 365 = 35$ days	$\frac{30,700}{490,700} \times 365 = 23$ days
5	Current ratio (Current assets/current liabilities)	$\frac{66,500}{52,300} = 1.3:1$	$\frac{152,500}{85,900} = 1.8:1$
6	Quick asset ratio (Current assets – stock/current liabilities)	$\frac{66,500 - 31,200}{52,300}$ $= 0.7:1$	$\frac{152,500 - 95,300}{85,900}$ $= 0.7:1$
7	Debt to equity ratio (Borrowings/equity)	$\frac{\text{Zero}}{119,200} \times 100 = 0\%$	$\frac{100,000}{226,600} \times 100 = 44\%$

In terms of stability, the company is much more dependent on outside finance in 19X6 than it was in 19X5 with an obligation to make annual interest payments of £7,000 on the debentures. Liquidity is mixed. The current ratio is stronger, but the company still could not meet its current obligations from quick assets. The change in the debtor's collection period suggests tighter credit control. The company is losing ground in terms of profitability because the return on capital employed has reduced due to lower margins and lower asset turnover. This company has expanded fairly dramatically over the year mainly through new share and debenture finance. It may well be the case that the full fruits of the expansion have yet to show.

Workings

Calculation of profit

Closing reserves = opening reserves + profit before tax − debenture interest − taxation − dividends: therefore profits before tax = closing reserves + debenture interest + taxation + dividend − opening reserves

For 19X5

Profit before tax = 19,200 + 11,400 + 17,000 − 26,100 =   £21,500

For 19X6

Profit before tax = 26,600 + 13,100 + 17,000 − 19,200 =   £37,500

Note: This answer assumes that the corporation tax is payable less than 12 months after the year end.

8   THE USE OF RATIOS IN FINANCIAL PLANNING

8.1   Introduction

Financial ratios define relationships between various financial factors. Much financial planning is concerned with establishing pre-specified relationships between those same factors. It is not surprising therefore that much financial planning by businesses uses ratios. For example, the senior management of a business may decide that they plan to earn a particular return on capital, or that they plan that debtors should, on average, pay within a particular period.

What is typically involved in formulating financial plans in this way is the building up of a set of final accounts for a forthcoming period from several key financial figures and a series of ratios which enable the other figures to be deduced. The activity is not unlike putting the pieces into a jigsaw puzzle. Quite often the cash figure is deduced as the balancing figure in the balance sheet.

Probably the best way to approach this topic is through an example.

Example

Michael Telford plans to start a business selling a device for saving fuel in cars on 1 January 19X9. During his first year he envisages that:

1	Sales will be £240,000 spread more or less evenly over the year
2	The gross profit ratio will be 40% of sales
3	At the year-end the current ratio and the quick asset ratio will be 2:1 and 1:1 respectively
4	The creditors' payment period will be two months. Once the business is under way purchases will replace the stock sold each month
5	The debtors collection period will be one month
6	Various fixed assets will be bought and paid for immediately at a total cost of £200,000. These will be depreciated at 10% per annum straight line
7	All cash transactions will be through the bank. Michael will open an account and put in £220,000 of his own money to start the business
8	Various expenses other than stock and depreciation are expected to total £60,000 for the year. There will be no accruals or prepayments at the year end
9	Michael will make drawings of any cash in excess of the amount necessary to meet the above plans.

Michael needs to prepare a projected trading and profit and loss account for the year ending 31 December 19X9 and a balance sheet as at that date, in as much detail as the information available to him allows.

Probably the best way for him to approach this task is firstly to draft the final accounts without any figures. A glance at the facts makes it fairly easy to see what the various items are likely to be. Then it is a matter of working through the information and inserting figures in the draft final accounts as they emerge.

Michael Telford
Trading and profit and loss account for the year ended 31 December 19X9

	£	£	£	See note
Sales			240,000	
Gross profit			96,000	1
Less: Various expenses		60,000		
depreciation		20,000	80,000	
			16,000	

Balance sheet as at 31 December 19X9

	£	£	£	See note
Fixed assets: cost			200,000	
Less: Depreciation			20,000	
			180,000	
Current assets				
Stock	24,000			5
Trade debtors	20,000			2
Cash	4,000	48,000		4
Less: Current liabilities				
Trade creditors		24,000		3
Net current assets			24,000	
			£204,000	
Capital				
Capital introduced			220,000	
Profit for the year			16,000	
			236,000	
Less: Drawings			32,000	6
			£204,000	

Notes to the solution

1   The gross profit is 40% of the sales figure.

2   Trade debtors represent one month's sales, that is, £240,000/12 = £20,000.

3   Trade creditors represent the stock usage for two months, since the purchases replace stock usage each month, once the business is under way. The gross profit ratio is 40%, therefore the stock used each month is 60% of sales, (£20,000 x 60% = £12,000) which for two months is £24,000.

4   The quick assets ratio is 1:1, therefore trade debtors + cash = trade creditors = £24,000. Therefore cash is £4,000.

5   The current ratio is 2:1, therefore trade debtors + cash + stock = 2 × (trade creditors = £24,000) = £48,000.
Since cash + trade debtors = £24,000
stock = £24,000

6   The net assets (total assets less current liabilities) = £204,000. The closing capital must therefore be £204,000. Thus, capital introduced + profit for the year (£16,000) – drawings = £204,000. Drawings for the year must therefore be £32,000.

8.2   Activity

For a number of years Martin Smith has been employed as the works manager of a company which manufactures cardboard cartons. He has now decided to leave the company and to set up a similar business of his own on 1 January 19X6 but, before taking this step he wants to see what his financial results are likely to be for his first year of operations.

In order to do this, he has obtained certain 'average industry' ratios from his trade association, the Cardboard Carton Manufacturers' Association (CCMA), which he wants to use as his norm for predicting the first year's results. At this stage he consults you, asks for your professional assistance and supplies the following information.

	CCMA statistics 19X4 (based on year-end figures)
Sales/Net assets employed	2.8 times
Gross profit/Sales	28.0%
Net profit/Sales	10.0%
Fixed assets/Working capital	1.5:1
Current assets/Current liabilities	2.25:1
Debtors collection period	36.5 days
Creditors payment period	58.4 days

He informs you that he is able to contribute £40,000 as capital and has been promised a long-term loan of £6,000 from a relative. Initially, he intends to acquire a stock of materials at a cost of £20,000 but his (simple) average stock for the first year will be £18,500. Purchases of materials for the year, excluding the initial purchase of stock, £20,000, will be £97,800. All purchases and sales will be on credit.

Sundry accruals at 31 December 19X6 are estimated at £350 and bank and cash balances at £5,000.

He proposes to withdraw £10,000 during the year for living expenses.

Prepare, in as much detail as can be elicited from the information supplied, a forecast trading and profit and loss account for Martin Smith's proposed business for the year ended 31 December 19X6, and a forecast balance sheet as at that date. All figures should be stated to the nearest £10.

Marks will be awarded for workings, which must be shown.

8.3   Activity solution

Martin Smith

Trading and profit and loss account
for the year ending 31 December 19X6

	£	£	see note
Sales		140,000	2
Less: Purchases			
(including initial stock)	117,800		
Less: closing stock	17,000		1
Cost of sales		100,800	
Gross profit		39,200	
Less: Expenses		25,200	
Net profit		£14,000	3

Balance sheet at 31 December 19X6

	£	£	£	
Fixed assets (net of depreciation)			30,000	6
Current assets				
Stock 17,000				
Trade debtors	14,000			4
Cash	5,000			
		36,000		
Current liabilities				
Trade creditors	15,650			5
Accrued expenses	350			
		16,000		
Working capital			20,000	
Net assets employed			50,000	
Less: Long-term loan			6,000	
			£44,000	
Capital				
Introduced			40,000	
Add: Profit for the year			14,000	
			54,000	
Less: Drawings			10,000	
			£44,000	

Notes to the solution

1   The closing stock is deduced from the fact that the initial stock was £20,000 and the simple average stock is £18,500 ; (20,000 + closing stock)/2 = £18,500. Therefore closing stock = £17,000.

2   Gross profit/sales = 28%. Therefore cost of sales/sales = 72% and sales = 100,800/72% = £140,000.

3   Net profit/sales = 10%. Therefore net profit = £140,000 × 10% = £14,000.

4    $\frac{\text{Trade debtors}}{\text{Sales}}$ × 365 = 36.5 days. Since sales = £140,000, Trade debtors – £14,000.

5    $\frac{\text{Trade creditors}}{\text{Purchases}}$ × 365 = 58.4 days. Since purchases = £97,800, Trade creditors = £15,650.

(excl. initial stock)

Note that the examiner clearly meant the purchase figure to exclude initial stock purchases otherwise the resultant net assets employed figure would not bear the required relationship to sales (sales/NAE = 2.8 times).

6   Fixed assets/working capital = 1.5:1. Since working capital = £20,000, then fixed assets = £30,000.

9   CHAPTER SUMMARY

- Accounting is concerned with providing information which will enhance the quality of business decisions made by those who need to make them. Ratios are one set of the tools of analysis which decision makers can use to help them make judgements. Ratios can help to provide insights which basic accounts cannot directly provide.

- Ratios can be useful because they make it easier to make comparisons between:
    - the performance of different businesses
    - the performance of the same business over different periods
    - the actual and planned performance of the same business over a particular period.

- Ratios most often used are of five basic types:
    - profitability ratios, including return on capital employed, gross profit and net profit margin ratios
    - activity ratios, including net asset turnover, stock-holding period, debtors collection and creditors payment period
    - liquidity ratios, including the current ratio and the quick assets ratio
    - gearing ratios, including debt to equity and times interest earned
    - investors' ratios, including dividend yield and earnings yield

- Users tend to vary with the extent to which each of these classes particularly interest them.

- Ratios must be interpreted with caution. They are drawn directly from the accounting statements and, therefore, are likely to be flawed in the same way as are the accounts themselves, by such factors as a failure to take account of the distortions caused by inflation. Ratios also may have their own inherent weaknesses, such as the fact that some ratios tend to mask scale. Ratios also tend to pose questions rather than to provide answers.

- Ratios are nevertheless very often used in the formulation of the financial plans of a business.

10   SELF TEST QUESTIONS

10.1   Of which one of the following types of ratio is return on capital employed an example?

    (a)   profitability

    (b)   activity

    (c)   liquidity

    (d)   gearing. (2.2)

10.2   When calculating the stock-holding period ratio, which one of the following is the reason why is it best not to use the stock figure at the end of the accounting period?

    (a)   because not all businesses hold stock

    (b)   because this is the stock which has not been turned over yet

    (c)   because the year-end figure is not easily available

    (d)   because it may not be typical of the level of stock held during the period. (3.3)

10.3   If the creditor payment period ratio is calculated using the cost of sales figure as the denominator, which one of the following does this imply?

    (a)   that no stock was purchased during the year

    (b)   that the level of stock increased during the year

    (c)   that the level of trade creditors increased during the year

    (d)   that the level of stock was constant over the year. (3.5)

10.4   Of which one of the following types of ratio is the current ratio an example?

     (a)   profitability

     (b)   activity

     (c)   liquidity

     (d)   gearing. (4.2)

10.5   Relatively low levels of current ratio tend to be associated with which of the following types of business?

     (a)   retailers

     (b)   manufacturers

     (c)   housebuilders

     (d)   shipbuilders. (4.2)

10.6   Ratios tend to be most useful in which one of the following ways?

     (a)   to tell you what's wrong with the business

     (b)   to tell you what's right with the business

     (c)   to highlight areas where questions might usefully be asked

     (d)   to tell you whether to sell your shares in the business or not. (7.1)

11   EXAMINATION TYPE QUESTIONS

11.1 Optimistic

Optimistic Traders plc is planning its activities for next year. In outline its plans are as follows:

1   **Sales** These are planned to be £3.6m spread fairly evenly over the year

2   **Expenses** The gross profit ratio is planned to be 40% of sales. Other expenses are planned to be 75% of the gross profit

3   **Taxation** Corporation tax will be charged at 30% of net profit. This will be the only outstanding tax liability at the year-end

4   **Working capital** Throughout the year the following relationships are planned to exist:
     (a)   Stock – 2 months' usage
     (b)   Trade debtors – 1.5 months' sales
     (c)   Trade creditors – 2.5 months' purchases

     At the year-end other working capital items will be provision for corporation tax (see 3 above), dividend (see 5 below) and cash.

5   **Dividend** The company plans to pay a dividend on its ordinary share capital of 30% of the nominal value (ignore taxation on dividends)

6   **Share capital and reserves** The company is financed by 500,000 ordinary shares of £1 each (fully paid). At the start of the year reserves totalled £230,000

7   **Fixed assets** At the start of the year the only fixed assets will be plant which cost £800,000 and on which accumulated depreciation is £150,000. During the year £100,000 is planned to be spent on new plant. The depreciation for next year (already included in other expenses, see 2 above) will be charged at 20% on the cost of the plant owned at the year end.

Prepare a projected trading and profit and loss account for next year and a balance sheet as at the year-end. These should both be in narrative form.

(18 marks)

11.2   Algernon

You are given below, in summarised form, the accounts of Algernon plc for 19X6 and 19X7.

	19X6			19X7		
	Balance sheet			*Balance sheet*		
	Cost	Depn	Net	Cost	Depn	Net
	£	£	£	£	£	£
Plant	10,000	4,000	6,000	11,000	5,000	6,000
Building	50,000	10,000	40,000	90,000	11,000	79,000
	60,000	14,000	46,000	101,000	16,000	85,000

	19X6	19X7
Investments at cost	50,000	80,000
Land	43,000	63,000
Stock	55,000	65,000
Debtors	40,000	50,000
Bank	3,000	–
	237,000	343,000
Ordinary shares £1 each	40,000	50,000
Share premium	12,000	14,000
Revaluation reserve	–	20,000
Profit and loss account	25,000	25,000
10% Debentures	100,000	150,000
Creditors	40,000	60,000
Proposed dividend	20,000	20,000
Bank	–	4,000
	237,000	343,000

	19X6	19X7
	Profit and loss a/c	*Profit and loss a/c*
	£	£
Sales	200,000	200,000
Cost of sales	100,000	120,000
	100,000	80,000
Expenses	60,000	60,000
	40,000	20,000
Dividends	20,000	20,000
	20,000	–
Balance b/f	5,000	25,000
Balance c/f	25,000	25,000

(a)   Calculate for Algernon plc, for 19X6 and 19X7, the following ratios:

- Return on capital employed
- Return on owners' equity (return on shareholders' funds)
- Debtors turnover
- Creditors turnover
- Current ratio
- Quick assets (acid test) ratio

- Gross profit percentage
- Net profit percentage
- Dividend cover
- Gearing ratio.

(b) Using the summarised accounts given, and the ratios you have just prepared, comment on the position, progress and direction of Algernon plc. **(20 marks)**

11.3 Bert

At the end of its first year of trading Bert plc has the following summarised balance sheet. The fixed assets were bought, and the debentures issued, at the beginning of the year.

	£
Fixed assets at cost	120,000
Current assets	130,000
	250,000
Shares	100,000
Profits	65,000
Debentures (10%)	50,000
Creditors	30,000
Bank overdraft	5,000
	£250,000

This balance sheet contains all adjustments except for depreciation of fixed assets. The bank overdraft is temporary.

(a) Prepare in columnar form five balance sheets, headed (i) to (v), incorporating the assumptions that respectively:

    (i) no depreciation is to be provided

    (ii) depreciation of 10% (straight-line basis) is to be provided

    (iii) depreciation of 20% (reducing-balance basis) is to be provided

    (iv) fixed assets are to be revalued by plus 20% and no depreciation is to be provided

    (v) fixed assets are to be revalued by plus 20% and depreciation of 10% (straight-line basis) is to be provided

(b) For each of the five balance sheets, calculate (showing workings clearly):

    (i) return on closing owner's equity (ROOE)

    (ii) return on closing capital employed (ROCE)

(c) Explain clearly but simply, in your own words, what these two ratios (ROOE and ROCE) are designed to show.

(d) Assuming that the estimated useful life of the fixed assets is correct at 10 years, which of the five balance sheets is likely to be most useful for the calculation of these two ratios if the fixed assets are buildings? Why?

(e) Would your answer to d) above be altered if the fixed assets were machines used in manufacturing? Why?

(20 marks)

11.4   Businesses

Business A and Business B are both engaged in retailing, but seem to take a different approach to this trade according to the information available. This information consists of a table of ratios, shown below:

Ratio	Business A	Business B
Current ratio	2.1	1.5:1
Quick assets (acid test) ratio	1.7:1	0.7:1
Return on capital employed (ROCE)	20%	17%
Return on owner's equity (ROOE)	30%	18%
Debtors turnover	63 days	21 days
Creditors turnover	50 days	45 days
Gross profit percentage	40%	15%
Net profit percentage	10%	10%
Stock turnover	52 days	25 days

(a)   Explain briefly how each ratio is calculated.

(b)   Describe what this information indicates about the differences in approach between the two businesses. If one of them prides itself on personal service and one of them on competitive prices, which do you think is which and why?

(20 marks)

(ACCA June 1991)

11.5   Electrical

You are given summarised results of an electrical engineering business, as follows. All figures are in £000.

Profit and loss account
Year ended

	31.12.X1	31.12.X0
Turnover	60,000	50,000
Cost of sales	42,000	34,000
Gross profit	18,000	16,000
Operating expenses	15,500	13,000
	2,500	3,000
Interest payable	2,200	1,300
Profit before taxation	300	1,700
Taxation	350	600
(Loss) profit after taxation	(50)	1,100
Dividends	(600)	600
Transfer (from) to reserves	(650)	500

Balance sheet

Fixed assets		
Intangible	500	
Tangible	12,000	11,000
	12,500	11,000
Current assets		
Stocks	14,000	13,000
Debtors	16,000	15,000
Bank and cash	500	500
	30,500	28,500

Creditors due within one year	24,000	20,000
Net current assets	6,500	8,500
Total assets less current liabilities	19,000	19,500
Creditors due after one year	6,000	5,500
	13,000	14,000
Capital and reserves		
Share capital	1,300	1,300
Share premium	3,300	3,300
Revaluation reserve	2,000	2,000
Profit and loss	6,400	7,400
	13,000	14,000

(a)   Prepare a table of the following 12 ratios, calculated for both years, clearly showing the figures used in the calculations.

- current ratio
- quick assets
- stock turnover in days
- debtors turnover in days
- creditors turnover in days
- gross profit %
- net profit % (before taxation)
- interest cover
- dividend cover
- ROOE (before taxation)
- ROCE
- gearing.

(b)   Making full use of the information given in the question, of your table of ratios, and your common sense, comment on the apparent position of the business and on the actions of the management.

(20 marks)

(ACCA June 1992)

11.6   Fred

You are given the attached information about Fred plc, comprising summarised profit and loss accounts, summarised balance sheets, and some suggested ratio calculations. You should note that there may be alternative ways of calculating some of these ratios. The holder of a small number of the ordinary shares in the business has come to you for help and advice. There are a number of things he does not properly understand, and a friend of his who is an accountancy student has suggested to him that some of the ratios show a distinctly unsatisfactory position, and that he should sell his shares as quickly as possible.

Required

(a)   Write a report to the shareholder commenting on the apparent position and prospects of Fred plc, as far as the information permits. Your report should include reference to liquidity and profitability aspects, and should advise whether, in your view, the shares should indeed be sold as soon as possible.

(b) Explain the following issues to the shareholder:

(i) What is the loan redemption fund, and how has it been created?

(ii) How on earth can there be £49m of assets on the balance sheet 'not yet in use'? Surely if it is not in use it is not an asset. What are assets anyway? And coming back to that £49m, the depreciation on these items will be artificially reducing the reported profit, won't it?

(iii) What is all this about interest being capitalised? What does it mean, and why are they doing it?

Fred plc
Summarised balance sheets at year end (£m)

		19X2		**19X1**	
Fixed assets					
Tangible	– not yet in use		49		41
	– in use		295		237
			344		278
Investments			1		1
Loan redemption fund			1		1
				346	280
Current assets					
Stocks			42		41
Debtors	– trade	4		4	
	– other	4		4	
			8		8
Bank			2		5
Cash			2		2
			54		56
Creditors – due within one year					
	– trade	60		60	
	– other	87		112	
			147		172
Net current liabilities			93		116
Total assets less current liabilities			253		164
Creditors – due between one and five years			61		1
Provision for liabilities and charges			4		3
Net assets			188		160
Capital and reserves					
Ordinary shares of 10p each			19		19
Preference shares of £1 each			46		46
Share premium			1		1
Profit and loss account			122		94
			188		160

Fred plc
Summarised profit and loss accounts for the year (£m)

	19X2		**19X1**	
Sales		910		775
Raw materials and consumables		730		633
		180		142
Staff costs	77		64	
Depreciation of tangible fixed assets	12		10	
Other operating charges	38		30	
		127		104
		53		38
Other operating income		4		3
		57		41
Net interest payable		5		4
		52		37
Profit sharing – employees		2		1
		50		36
Taxation		17		12
		33		24
Preference dividends		2		2
		31		22
Ordinary dividends		3		2
		28		20

Note
Net interest payable:

	19X2	19X1
interest payable	12	9
interest receivable	(1)	(1)
interest capitalised	(6)	(4)
	5	4

Fred plc
Some possible ratio calculations (which can be taken as
arithmetically correct)

	19X2		**19X1**	
Current ratio	$\frac{54}{147}$	= 36.7%	$\frac{56}{172}$	= 32.6%
Acid test ratio	$\frac{12}{147}$	= 8.2%	$\frac{15}{172}$	= 8.7%
ROCE	$\frac{57}{249}$	= 22.9%	$\frac{41}{161}$	= 25.5%
ROOE	$\frac{33}{188}$	= 17.5%	$\frac{24}{160}$	= 15.0%
EPS	$\frac{31}{190}$	= 16.3 pence	$\frac{22}{190}$	= 11.6 pence
Trade debtors turnover	$\frac{4}{910}$	× 365 = 2 days	$\frac{4}{775}$	× 365 = 2 days

Trade creditors turnover	$\dfrac{60}{730} \times 365 = 30$ days		$\dfrac{60}{633} \times 365 = 35$ days
Gross profit %	$\dfrac{180}{910} = 19.8\%$		$\dfrac{142}{775} = 18.3\%$
Operating profit %	$\dfrac{57}{910} = 6.3\%$		$\dfrac{41}{775} = 5.3\%$
Stock turnover	$\dfrac{42}{730} \times 365 = 21$ days		$\dfrac{41}{633} \times 365 = 24$ days
Gearing	$\dfrac{61}{188} = 32.4\%$		$\dfrac{1}{160} = 0.6\%$

(20 marks)
(ACCA, June 1993)

12 ANSWERS TO EXAMINATION TYPE QUESTIONS

12.1 Optimistic

Optimistic Traders plc
Trading and profit and loss account for next year

	£000
Sales	3,600
Cost of sales	2,160
Gross profit	1,440
Expenses	1,080
Net profit before tax	360
Corporation tax (30%)	108
Net profit after tax	252
Add: Reserves, brought forward	230
	482
Less: Proposed dividend	150
Reserves carried forward	332

Balance sheet as at next year

Fixed assets	£000	£000
Plant: cost		900
Less: Accumulated depreciation		330
		570
Current assets		
Stock	360	
Trade debtors	450	
Cash	160	
	970	
Less: **Current liabilities**		
Trade creditors	450	
Proposed dividend	150	
Corporation tax	108	
	708	

Working capital	262
Net assets employed	832
Financed by:	
Ordinary shares of £1 each	500
Reserves	332
	832

Note that cash is the balancing figure. Also it has been assumed that the opening and closing stocks remained constant. Hence the cost of sales could be used to calculate the year-end trade creditors.

12.2 Algernon

(a)

	19X6	19X7
Return on capital employed		
$\dfrac{\text{Net profit before interest}}{\text{Share capital plus reserves plus long-term liabilities}} \times 100\%$	28.25%	13.51%
Return on owner's equity		
$\dfrac{\textit{Net profit available to ordinary shareholders}}{\text{Ordinary share capital plus reserves}} \times 100\%$	51.95%	18.35%
Debtors turnover (see note 2)		
$\dfrac{\textit{Sales}}{\text{Trade debtors}}$	5.00T	4.00T
Creditors turnover (see note 3)		
$\dfrac{\textit{Cost of goods sold}}{\text{Trade creditors}}$	2.50T	2.00T
Current ratio		
$\dfrac{\textit{Current assets}}{\text{Current liabilities}}$	1.63	1.37
Quick assets (acid test) ratio		
$\dfrac{\textit{Current assets less stock}}{\text{Current liabilities}}$	0.72	0.60
Gross profit percentage		
$\dfrac{\textit{Gross profit} \times 100\%}{\text{Sales}}$	50.00%	40.00%
Net profit percentage		
$\dfrac{\textit{Net profit} \times 100\%}{\text{Sales}}$	20.00%	10.00%
Dividend cover		
$\dfrac{\textit{Profit available for dividend}}{\text{Dividends}}$	2.00T	1.00T
Gearing ratio		
$\dfrac{\textit{Total long-term borrowings (plus bank overdraft)}}{\text{Share capital plus reserves}}$	129.87%	141.28%

Notes

1   In order to calculate ratios which employ balance sheet figures the figures appearing in the balance sheet at the year-end rather than average figures have been employed.

Although it is often appropriate to use average figures in the calculation of certain ratios insufficient information is available to do this for both years.

2   It is assumed all sales are on credit.

3   Strictly speaking, the purchases figure should be used rather than the cost of goods sold figure when calculating this ratio. However, insufficient information is available to calculate the purchases figure for both years.

(b)   Sales have remained constant at £200,000 but the gross profit percentage and net profit percentage have both decreased. The reduction in the gross profit percentage appears to be due to an increase in the cost of sales from (£100,000 to £120,000). Expenses have remained constant over the period. Despite the fall in profits, dividends have remained constant. As a result the dividend cover has fallen from 2.0T to 1.0T.

The liquidity of the company has declined. In 19X7 the acid test ratio has fallen to 0.60 and must give rise to some concern. The wisdom of paying such high dividends should be reconsidered given the liquidity problems of the company.

The debtor turnover ratio has declined from 5.0T to 4.0T. This may be due to either a more liberal credit policy or failure to control debtors. The liquidity problems mentioned above may have resulted in the decline of the creditors turnover ratio (from 2.5T to 2.0T).

The company has increased its net assets over the period. The effect of this and the decline in the net profit percentage has been a substantial fall in the return of capital employed and return on owner equity ratios. However, the benefits of the expansion policy may not filter through until a later accounting period.

There has been a slight increase in the gearing ratio in 19X7. This increase would have been higher had there not been a revaluation of assets during 19X7.

12.3   Bert

(a)

Bert plc
Balance sheet as at year end

	(i)	(ii)	(iii)	(iv)	(v)
	£	£	£	£	£
Fixed assets	120,000	108,000	96,000	144,000	129,600
Current assets	130,000	130,000	130,000	130,000	130,000
	£250,000	£238,000	£226,000	£274,000	£259,600
	£	£	£	£	£
Shares	100,000	100,000	100,000	100,000	100,000
Revaluation reserve	–	–	–	24,000	24,000
Profits	65,000	53,000	41,000	65,000	50,600
Debentures (10%)	50,000	50,000	50,000	50,000	50,000
Creditors	30,000	30,000	30,000	30,000	30,000
Bank overdraft	5,000	5,000	5,000	5,000	5,000
	£250,000	£238,000	£226,000	£274,000	£259,600

(b)

(i)   ROOE $\dfrac{65 \times 100}{165}$ $\dfrac{53 \times 100}{153}$ $\dfrac{41 \times 100}{141}$ $\dfrac{65 \times 100}{189}$ $\dfrac{50.6 \times 100}{174.6}$

$= 39\%$ $=35\%$ $=29\%$ $=34\%$ $=29\%$

(ii)   ROCE* $\dfrac{70 \times 100}{215}$ $\dfrac{58 \times 100}{203}$ $\dfrac{46 \times 100}{191}$ $\dfrac{70 \times 100}{239}$ $\dfrac{55.6 \times 100}{224.6}$

$=33\%$ $=29\%$ $=24\%$ $=29\%$ $=25\%$

* Net profit before debenture interest ÷ (owner's equity + debentures)

(c)   ROOE is designed to show the return on the shareholders' investment in the business. It is an input-output measure which compares the shareholders' capital plus reserves (input) against the profit available to shareholders (output). It represents a useful measure of investment performance.

ROCE is designed to show the return on the long-term capital invested in the business. Once again this is an input-output measure which compares the long-term capital (shareholders' equity plus long-term loans) with the net profit before interest and tax. It is a widely used measure of performance and efficiency.

(d)   Balance sheet (v) is likely to be most useful as a basis for calculating the two ratios. By revaluing the fixed assets, a revaluation reserve is created. This represents an unrealised gain which increases shareholders' equity and provides a more realistic view of the shareholders' stake in the business and of capital employed. However, revaluation of buildings represents a departure from the convention of historic cost accounting.

(e)   No. The arguments set out in (d) above apply whether the fixed assets are buildings or machinery. By showing assets at current values the balance sheet provides a more realistic view of shareholders' equity and capital employed. Hence, the relevant rates of return should be more useful than when they are based on historic costs.

12.4 Businesses

(a)   Current ratio $=$ $\dfrac{\text{Current assets}}{\text{Current liabilities}}$

Quick assets ratio $=$ $\dfrac{\text{Current assets less stocks and other non-liquid assets}}{\text{Current liabilities}}$

ROCE (%) $=$ $\dfrac{\text{Net profit before interest and tax}}{\text{Owners' capital and reserves plus long-term loan}} \times 100$

ROOE (%) $=$ $\dfrac{\text{Net profit after long-term interest and tax}}{\text{Owners' capital and reserves}} \times 100$

Debtors turnover (average days) $=$ $\dfrac{\text{Trade debtors}}{\text{Credit sales}} \times 365$

Creditors turnover (average days) $=$ $\dfrac{\text{Trade creditors}}{\text{Credit purchases}} \times 365$

$$\text{Gross profit percentage} \quad = \quad \frac{\text{Gross profit}}{\text{Sales}}$$

$$\text{Net profit percentage} \quad = \quad \frac{\text{Net profit before tax}}{\text{Sales}} \times 100$$

$$\begin{array}{l}\text{Stock turnover} \\ \text{(average days)}\end{array} \quad = \quad \frac{\text{Stock}}{\text{Cost of sales}}$$

(b)

Differences in approach to trading/management

	Business A	Business B
Current ratio	Clearly, A has a higher working capital requirement than B	–
Quick ratio	–	Indicates by relation to current ratio that high stocks are held relative to current liabilities (0.8=1)
Debtors turnover	A probably has large debtors figure included in current ratio: 63 days average payment period (B only has 21 days)	–
ROCE	A is squeezing about 3% extra out of its long-term capital relative to B	Nearly the same % as for ROOE
ROOE	A is squeezing about 10% extra out of its owners capital relative to ROCE. This would suggest large long-term borrowings or interest rates thereon at considerably less than 20%	Nearly the same % as for ROCE. Either B has low borrowings or paying interest rates at approximately 18%
Stock turnover	Is held for twice as long on average as stocks held for B	–
Gross profit %	25% points higher than B	–
Net profit %	10% These two facts suggest A has considerably higher overheads than B	10%

The above summary indicates that A relative to B has high debtors, low stock levels which sell slowly, but at a larger gross profit margin. There are likely to be higher borrowings by A than B. Finally, A has significantly higher overhead costs than B. As regards B, it would appear that there are high stock levels which sell quickly at much lower gross profit margins than achieved by A: a high-volume, low- price situation.

Given that no indication of absolute size of A or B is provided, a tentative suggestion, from the above analysis, is that A sells on a personal service, whereas B concentrates on competitive pricing. All comparisons in the above analysis are provided on a relative rather than absolute basis.

12.5   Electrical

(a)   **Profitability ratios**

	19X1		**19X0**	
ROCE	$\dfrac{2,500}{19,000}$	= 13%	$\dfrac{3,000}{19,500}$	= 15%
ROOE (before taxation)	$\dfrac{300}{13,000}$	= 2.3%	$\dfrac{1,700}{14,000}$	= 12%
Gross profit %	$\dfrac{18,000}{60,000}$	= 30%	$\dfrac{16,000}{50,000}$	= 32%
Net profit %	$\dfrac{300}{60,000}$	= 0.5%	$\dfrac{1,700}{50,000}$	= 3.4%

Activity ratios

	19X1		**19X0**	
Stock turnover	$\dfrac{14,000}{42,000}$	$\times 365$ = 122 days	$\dfrac{13,000}{34,000}$	$\times 365$ = 140 days
Debtors turnover	$\dfrac{16,000}{60,000}$	$\times 365$ = 97 days	$\dfrac{15,000}{50,000}$	$\times 365$ = 109 days
Creditors turnover	$\dfrac{24,000}{42,000}$	$\times 365$ = 209 days	$\dfrac{20,000}{34,000}$	$\times 365$ = 215 days

Gearing ratios

	19X1		**19X0**	
Debt ratio	$\dfrac{6,000}{19,000}$	= 32%	$\dfrac{5,500}{19,500}$	= 28%
Interest cover	$\dfrac{2,500}{2,200}$	= 1.14 times	$\dfrac{3,000}{1,300}$	= 2.31 times

Liquidity ratios

	19X1		**19X0**	
Current ratio	$\dfrac{30,500}{24,000}$	= 1.27	$\dfrac{28,500}{20,000}$	= 1.43
Quick assets ratio	$\dfrac{16,500}{24,000}$	= 0.69	$\dfrac{15,500}{20,000}$	= 0.78
Dividend cover	$\dfrac{(50)}{600}$	= (0.08)	$\dfrac{1,100}{600}$	= 1.83

(b)   Generally, only tentative conclusions may be drawn since there are no comparative ratios for the electrical engineering industry. However, use of the ratios for 19X0 and 19X1 may enable tentative conclusions about the position of the company and ability of management to be drawn.

19X0

Turnover ratios appear high, although this may be traditional in the electrical engineering industry. The liquidity ratios are probably acceptable given that a normal range for the current ratio is between 1 and 2. Profitability ratios are again not outstanding. Gearing ratios are not considered excessive at about 25% of the long-term capital being borrowed and the interest charges being covered about 2.3 times. The management performance is judged to be no more than average.

19X1

Turnover ratios are still on the high side; for example, 14 weeks are required to collect sums owing to the company! The accounts show that turnover, cost of sales, stocks, debtors and creditors due within one year have all increased in absolute terms but the relative relationships have been allowed to deteriorate, for instance, see the drop in the liquidity ratios. This deterioration is further demonstrated by lower gross profit %, a result of cost of sales increasing disproportionately to an increase in sales.

The 19X1 accounts show substantial increases in the absolute amounts expended on operating expenses and interest payments. These increases are reflected in drastic reductions in the remaining profitability ratios. Management is perhaps not controlling overhead costs properly and may be the victim of external interest rate increases. This latter point is demonstrated by the significant changes in the gearing ratios. Long-term borrowing has risen from over a quarter to nearly a third. The interest rate cover has halved. The consequence of these deteriorations is clearly indicated by the way in which there is now no cover for the dividend payment which has been maintained at the 19X0 figure.

In general, the management performance may be judged to be below average, although this should be tempered by considering general economic conditions for the year 19X1. There has clearly been an attempt to expand – see comments above on turnover and profitability ratios, and the balance sheet showing an increase of £1.5 million in fixed assets. Perhaps management were caught unawares by the external factors or were already irrevocably committed to the expansion programme. Holding the dividend constant is a management ploy which reflects management's confidence in itself for the future. Time will tell as to whether their confidence is justified.

12.6   Fred

(a)   The company has a number of interesting features. The company appears to make most of its sales by cash – there are few debtors and so the debtors turnover ratio is very low indeed. In addition, stocks appear to be turned over rapidly. For both years, the trade creditor period is longer than the stock turnover and debtors turnover period combined. This is a very satisfactory position from the company viewpoint as it indicates that stocks and debtors are being more than financed by creditors. Although the liquidity ratios of the company are low, this need not be a cause for concern, providing the creditors are satisfied with the creditor turnover period. This type of situation can often be found in the case of large supermarket chains.

The profitability ratios, with the exception of ROCE, indicate an improvement over the period. The increase in ROOE and EPS over the period should be of particular interest to shareholders. The decline in ROCE can be attributed to the substantial increase in gearing. However, the gearing ratio is not particularly high in 19X2 and the company appears to still have a considerable amount of unused debt capacity, judging from its strong asset base and profitability.

In absolute terms, there has been a significant increase in both sales and profits over the period. In addition the company appears to be generating strong cash flows from operations. Thus, there does not appear to be any foundation for the recommendation to sell the shares in the company.

(b)   (i)   A loan redemption fund represents an amount which has been set aside out of the company's assets in order to repay the loan outstanding at some future date. The amount set aside may take the form of cash or an investment in securities or, perhaps, some form of policy.

(ii)   The criteria for determining an asset do not include whether or not the asset is currently in use. In order to be defined as an asset, the resource must be owned or controlled by the business as a result of some past transaction and be capable of providing future benefits. It is, perhaps, this last point which is most relevant to this question. Providing the resource provides benefits in the future, it does not have to be currently providing benefits in order to be considered an asset.

(iii)   The notes to the profit and loss account indicate that part of the interest payable during the year has been charged to the current year and part has been capitalised, i.e. treated as an asset and carried forward on the balance sheet to be written off in future years. The argument for adopting this policy is that where a loan is taken out to finance the purchase of a fixed asset, the interest payable on the loan represents a cost of acquiring the fixed asset. This policy, however, fails to adhere to the convention of prudence and requires a clear link to be made between particular investing activities and their financing.

GLOSSARY

Account

A means of recording financial transactions. An account is opened for each particular kind of transaction and each individual or organisation with whom the organisation has credit transactions.

Accounting

The process of identifying, measuring and communicating economic information to users in order to aid economic decision making.

Accounting conventions

The ground rules which underpin financial accounting. They are also referred to as **concepts, principles, assumptions** and **postulates**.

Accounting standards

See Statement of Standard Accounting Practice.

Accruals convention

The accounting rule which asserts that profit (or loss) is the difference between revenues and expenses for the period rather than the difference between cash receipts and payments.

Accrued expenses

Expenses relating to a period which has not been paid by the end of that period.

Accumulated depreciation

The sum of the period-by-period depreciation expenses relating to fixed assets which continue to be held by the business.

Accumulated fund

The members' interest in a not-for-profit organisation such as a club, society or association. Also referred to as the **general fund**.

Analysis books

Books of account (such as the cash analysis journal) which both record and list transactions according to the type of transaction undertaken. These listings can then be used to post entries in the accounts, where possible substituting totals for detailed entries.

Appreciation

An increase in value of an asset.

Appropriation account

A double-entry account which is part of the final account of companies and partnerships. In this account the net profit is allocated or appropriated to various ends: for instance, transfer to the owners, taxation provision.

Articles of Association

Part of the constitution of a company. The Articles set out the internal rules of the company and form part of the documents of incorporation.

Assets

Resources of the company which are capable of providing future benefits and which can be measured in monetary terms.

Assumptions

See *accounting conventions*.

Audit

An independent review of a set of accounts.

Audit trail

The ability to audit a set of accounts is important, and requires a clear set of documentary evidence leading from the original transaction to its inclusion in a set of final accounts. This evidence is frequently described as the audit trail.

Authorised share capital

The total amount of share capital which the directors are authorised to issue without obtaining the sanction of the shareholders.

Average cost (AVCO)

A stock valuation system where the stock withdrawals are valued at the weighted average value of the stock held.

Bad debts

Those debts which are regarded by a business as irrecoverable.

Balance sheet

A list of assets of a business and of the claims against it.

Balancing off

A system within ledger accounts where the two sides of an account are totalled and the net balance carried forward.

Batch processing

Where batches of documents, broadly corresponding to those found in the subsidiary books, are typically punched onto paper tape and fed into a computer for analysis and printing.

Bill

See Invoice.

Board of directors

The most senior management group of a company. Directors are elected by the shareholders to act in this role.

Bonus issue

An issue of shares to existing shareholders, created by transferring owners' capital from reserves to share capital. Also known as a **scrip issue** or **capitalisation issue.**

Bookkeeping

The recording of financial transactions in a systematic and logical manner.

Book value

The value at which assets are shown in the accounting records of a business. The expression is particularly applied to fixed assets.

Books of prime (original) entry

The books in which financial transactions are recorded prior to their posting to the relevant ledger accounts. They are also referred to as **subsidiary books.**

Business entity convention

The accounting rule which asserts that for accounting purposes the business and its owner(s) are separate.

CCA
(current cost accounting)

A system of accounting which shows items in the final accounts at their current cost (rather than their historic cost as occurs in conventional accounting). The system of current cost accounting is based on the idea of determining 'the value to the business' of assets held. In practice, the value to the business of an asset is usually the cost of replacing it.

CPP accounting
(constant purchasing power or current purchasing power accounting)

A system of accounting which adjusts the historic cost accounts of a business to take account of changes in the purchasing power of the currency (or to put it another way,

changes in the price level). The CPP accounts are a restatement of the historic cost accounts to reflect the current purchasing power of the currency. The Retail Price Index is often used to adjust the historic cost accounts for changes in the purchasing power of money.

Called up share capital

That part of a company's authorised share capital for which the shareholders (owners of the share capital) have already been required to pay the company.

Capital

The owner's claim against a business.

Capital account

The account in which the owner's claim (against the business) of a sole trader or a partner is recorded. In the case of partnerships the capital accounts may record only part of the partners' claims against the partnership; the other part of the claim may be recorded in current accounts.

Capital expenditure

The purchase of fixed assets or expenditure which adds to the value of existing fixed assets.

Capital gearing

See *Gearing.*

Capital redemption reserve

The reserve which is created from previously distributable reserves to replace shares, ordinary or preference, which are redeemed.

Capital reserve

Gains arising from events outside the normal course of trading of a company.

Capitalisation issue

See *Bonus issue.*

Carriage in

The expense of transporting stock purchases to a business's premises. Where it is borne by the purchasing business it is treated as part of the cost of purchases and is dealt with in the trading account.

Carriage out

The expense of transporting stock sold to the premises of the customer. It is dealt with in the profit and loss account.

Cash discount

See *Discount allowed* and *Discount received.*

Claims

Financial obligations to others.

Concepts

See *Accounting conventions.*

Conservatism convention

See *Prudence convention.*

Consistency convention

The accounting rule which asserts that the application of a convention should be consistent over time.

Contingent liability

A potential claim, frequently associated with such things as legal cases, which might arise. As such it does not appear as a liability in the balance sheet, but is usually separately disclosed, given its potential significance.

Continuous method of stock valuation

A method of accounting for stock in trade usage where each acquisition and withdrawal of stock is recorded so that the balance should always represent the stock held at any particular moment. Also known as the **perpetual method.**

Contra

This type of entry arises where there are balances on both creditor accounts and debtor accounts for the same individual or business. A person or business may be both customer and supplier, and it is sometimes necessary to set off one balance against the other. In such cases entries will be needed in the personal accounts in both the sales ledger and the purchases ledger, together with corresponding entries in the two control accounts.

Control accounts

Accounts which are prepared using the total balances and transactions relating to a particular ledger with the objective of checking the accuracy of recording to that ledger. Also known as **total accounts.**

Conventions

See *Accounting conventions.*

Conversion costs

Any costs incurred in converting raw materials to final product.

Copyright

An intangible asset. Relates to the exclusive right to produce copies and to control an original piece of work.

Corporation tax

A form of taxation relating to limited companies which is levied on trading profits and capital gains.

Credit

An entry on the right-hand side of a ledger account.

Creditors

Those to whom a business has a financial obligation.

Cumulative preference shares

Preference shares where there is a right not only to receive a dividend in respect of the current year in priority to the ordinary shareholders, but also to receive any arrears of past preference dividends unpaid.

Current assets

Those assets which are intended to be turned over in the normal course of trading. Stock in trade, debtors and cash are typical examples of current assets.

Current liabilities

Financial obligations which must be discharged in the short term, typically within 12 months.

Database

This concept refers to the storage of data in an appropriate way (one which can be accessed and analysed easily), supported by a set of software which effectively 'manages' the data. Software typically permits such things as the selection, updating, analysing, sorting and printing of appropriate information. Some of this will relate to relatively routine parts of the activities of the organisation like sales invoicing, payment of wages and payment of cheques to suppliers.

Day books

See *Books of prime (original) entry.*

Debenture

A loan evidenced by a deed, usually made by a company, and usually broken down into small equally sized units.

Debit

An entry on the left-hand side of a ledger account.

Debtors

Those who have a financial obligation to a business.

Deferred revenue

Cash received for goods or services rendered to customers in advance of the recognition of the revenue concerned.

Depreciation

The wearing out, consumption or other reduction in the useful life of an asset arising from use, the passage of time, or obsolescence.

Director
Someone elected by the members of a company to act as a member of the board of directors, the senior management level of the company.

Directors' report
Part of the published accounts of a limited company. The report acts as a supplement to the financial information contained in the profit and loss account and balance sheet.

Discount allowed
Discount for prompt payment allowed to debtors whereby a percentage of the invoice value of sales is deducted, provided that the debt is settled within a pre-specified period. The amount appears as an expense in the profit and loss account.

Discount for prompt payment
See *Discount allowed* and *Discount received.*

Discount received
Discount allowed by trade creditors to be deducted from the invoice value of purchases provided that the debt is settled within a pre-specified period. The amount appears as a revenue in the profit and loss account.

Dividend
A cash return to the shareholders of a company. The law has established the general rule that dividends can only be paid out of accumulated, realised profits.

Double entry
The process of recording the dual effect of each transaction.

Doubtful debts
Debts which may not be recoverable.

Duality convention
The accounting rule that asserts that each transaction has two effects.

Equity share
See *Ordinary share.*

Expenditure
An outlay of money.

Expense
A trading event which has the effect of decreasing capital (owner's claim).

External liabilities
A claim on the assets of a business other than by the owners.

Final accounts
The expression usually applied to the profit and loss account for a period (typically a year) and the balance sheet as at the end of the period. It usually also includes a cash flow statement.

Financial accounting
The process of providing economic information to users who are external to the organisation (such as shareholders, creditors, employees, customers and government) for decision-making purposes.

Firm
A firm is a business organisation. Historically it meant partnership only, but it is now used to refer to companies as well.

First in, first out (FIFO)
A stock valuation system where the stock withdrawals are valued as if they consisted of the longest-held stock.

Fixed assets
Those assets which are intended to be held to help generate profit rather than to be turned over in the normal course of trading.

Fixed charge
Security offered to lenders covering specific assets of the business which prevents the business from selling the assets.

Floating charge
Security offered to lenders covering the general assets of the business. The business retains the right to sell the assets on which there is a floating charge, in the normal course of trading, unless an event occurs which causes the charge to crystallise (become fixed).

Fully paid share
A share, the whole of the financial obligation for which the shareholder has met.

Funds
Variously defined, but most popularly either as working capital or as cash and short-term investments and deposits.

Funds flow statement
See *Sources and application of funds statement.*

Gearing
The long-term financial structure of the business.

General fund
See *Accumulated fund.*

General purchasing power accounting
A system of inflation accounting where the values used are adjusted for the general rate of inflation as measured by an index such as the Retail Price Index (RPI).

General reserve
An amount set aside out of distributable profit for general use within the company. A form of revenue reserve.

Going-concern convention
The accounting assumption that the business will continue indefinitely, unless the contrary is known to be true.

Goodwill
An asset which arises from the ability of a particular business to generate higher profits than would otherwise be the case by virtue of skilled workforce or a good reputation.

Gross profit
See *Trading account.*

Historical cost accounting
The system of accounting where the historical cost convention is adopted.

Historical cost convention
The accounting rule which asserts that assets should be shown in accounts at their original cost.

Imprest
An agreed maximum amount of petty cash which can be held. This amount is also referred to as a **float**.

Income and expenditure account
A financial statement setting out revenues and expenses for a period of an organisation. It is prepared by not-for-profit organisations such as clubs, societies and associations.

Income statement
See *Profit and loss account.*

Incomplete records
The accounting records of a business which does not maintain a complete set of double-entry ledger accounts.

Inflation accounting
A system of accounting where the historical cost convention is not faithfully followed. Instead, values are applied which reflect the existence of price inflation.

Intangible assets
Non-physical fixed assets which represent certain rights or commercial advantages, such as patent, copyright, goodwill.

Inventory
See *Stock in trade.*

Invoice (bill)
A document issued by a seller to a buyer listing the goods or services supplied and setting the sum of money due.

Issued share capital
That part of the authorised share capital which has been issued by the company.

Journal, the
A diary of financial transactions which do not pass through any other book of prime entry.

Last in, first out (LIFO)
A stock valuation system where the stock withdrawals are valued as if they consisted of the most recent acquisitions.

Ledger
A 'book' of accounts. Usually referred to by this name even where the accounts are maintained on a computer.

Ledger accounts
The basic system of recording transactions in which every transaction is recorded in ledger accounts, typically by the use of two entries, hence the name double-entry bookkeeping.

Liabilities
Financial obligations of a business to 'outsiders', that is, non-owners.

Limited company
An entity where the obligation of shareholders to contribute to its liabilities is limited to the amounts that they have already paid for their shares and any amounts which may be outstanding on partly paid shares.

Limited liability
The situation which exists when shareholders cannot be asked to contribute to meet the debts of the company, except to the extent that the shares may not be fully paid.

Limited partner
A partner who has limited his or her liability in respect of the partnership debts.

Liquidity
The extent of holding assets in cash or in some form which can quickly be converted into cash.

Lodgement
A deposit of cash or cheques into a bank account.

Long-term liabilities
Financial obligations which are not due for payment in the short term; typically they cannot be enforced in less than 12 months.

Loss
The excess of expenses over revenues.

Loss on sale
The excess of the net book value over the sale proceeds of an asset.

Lower of cost and net realisable value rule
The rule which states that stock is valued at the lower of cost or its net realisable value, following the convention of prudence.

Management accounting
The process of providing economic information to internal users (those managing the business) for decision-making purposes.

Management information system

A system which is designed to collect, analyse and distribute throughout the organisation information relevant to the management of the entire organisation. This will typically include information needed for both internal and external users, and information of both an accounting and a non-accounting nature.

Matching convention

The accounting rule which asserts that in computing profit, expenses should be matched against the revenues to which they relate.

Materiality convention

The accounting rule which asserts that, in the interests of expediency, it is possible to write off the cost of an asset in the year in which it is purchased if the amount involved is not material.

Member

See *Shareholder.*

Memorandum of Association

Part of the constitution of a company. The Memorandum defines the company's relationship with the outside world and forms part of the documents of incorporation.

Money measurement convention

The accounting rule which asserts that only aspects of a business which can be expressed in money terms are considered.

Narrative form

A way of presenting financial statements so that the reader can read down the page, rather than in a strict double-entry form where the entries will tend to be made in two columns, one on the left (debit) and one on the right (credit).

Net book value

See *Written-down value.*

Net realisable value

The actual or anticipated selling price of an item less any expenses which must be incurred to sell the item.

Nominal value

The face value of shares. Typically this is the price at which the original shares of the company were first issued. Also known as **par value.**

Objectivity convention

The accounting rule which asserts that what appears in accounts should be free from bias and capable of independent verification.

Ordinary share

A portion of the ownership of the company which is entitled to receive dividends only after all other claims have been fully met. Also known as an **equity share.**

Over-depreciation

The amount by which the fall in value (calculated by comparing costs of acquisition with the disposal value) is less than the total depreciation taken in the profit and loss over the life of the asset.

Par value

See *Nominal value.*

Partnership

The relation which subsists between two or more people carrying on a business in common, with a view to profit.

Partly paid share

A share for which there is a potential financial liability still to be met by the shareholder.

Patent

Grant given to an inventor giving him sole rights to make, use and sell an invention for a limited period.

Periodic method

A method of accounting for stock in trade usage which relies on recording all acquisitions and relying on periodic valuations of the stock to deduce the value of the stock used.

Perpetual method of stock valuation

See *Continuous method of stock valuation.*

Posting

Entering transactions in the ledger accounts.

Postulates

See *Accounting conventions.*

Preference share

A part of the ownership of a company which has a priority right to a fixed slice of any dividend which is paid.

Prepaid expenses

See *Prepayments.*

Prepayments

Payments relating to expenses of a future period. Also known as **prepaid expenses.**

Principles

See *Accounting conventions.*

Private limited company

A private limited company is one which is distinguished from a public limited company in several ways, principally in the fact that it is prohibited from making an appeal to the public to subscribe for its shares.

Profit

The excess of revenues over expenses.

Profit on sale

The excess of the sale proceeds of an asset over its net book value.

Profit and loss account

A statement which compares the revenues and expenses of a business, or part of a business, for a period. The culminating figure is the net profit or net loss for the period. It is also known as the **income statement**.

Profitability

The effectiveness of a business in generating profit.

Provision

An amount set aside out of profits to cover losses or a known liability the amount of which cannot be established with substantial accuracy.

Prudence convention

The accounting rule which asserts that accounting should err on the side of caution in recognition of expenses and claims.

Public limited company

A public limited company is one which is distinguished from a private limited company in several ways, principally in the fact that it has the right to make an appeal to the general public to subscribe for its shares.

Published accounts

The final accounts of a company which the law requires are made public.

Ratio analysis

Direct comparison of one figure with another, usually from a set of accounts. The comparison is facilitated by dividing one of the figures by the other.

Realisation convention

The accounting rule which asserts that revenues should normally be recognised when the goods or service pass to, and are accepted by, the customer.

Receipts and payments account

A summary of the cash book for a period which sets out cash and bank receipts and payments and opening and closing cash and bank balances. Sometimes prepared by small, not-for-profit organisations such as clubs, societies and associations as their final accounts.

Reducing-balance depreciation

A method of apportioning depreciation such that succeeding periods bear a decreasing share of the total.

Reserves

Amount attributable to the shareholders in excess of their nominal share capital.

Residual value

The amount which a business recovers, or is expected to recover, from a fixed asset at the end of its useful life.

Retail Price Index

An index prepared by the government which attempts to measure the change in retail prices over time. The Index is compiled by reference to a 'basket of goods' which is consumed by an 'average family'. The base for the Index is set at 100 and changes in prices are measured by reference to this base.

Returns (of purchases)

Purchases which are sent back to suppliers, with a consequent need for further entries in the accounts.

Revaluation reserve

A capital reserve of a company which arises from revaluing an asset, typically a fixed asset.

Revenue

A trading event which has the effect of increasing capital (owner's claim).

Revenue expenditure

The incurrence of costs, the benefits of which do not extend beyond the period in which the costs were incurred.

Revenue reserve

Undistributed trading profits of a company, which can be used to pay dividends.

Rights issue

An issue of shares to existing shareholders, typically at a discount on the current market price, such that each shareholder has a right to take up a fixed number of shares by virtue of the number of shares already owned by him or her.

Scrip issue

See *Bonus issue*.

Shares

Portions of the ownership of a company. See *ordinary share* and *preference share*. The total is known as **share capital**.

Share capital

See *Shares*.

Shareholder

A person who owns shares in a company. Also referred to as a **member**.

Share premium account
The excess of the proceeds of a share issue over the nominal value of the shares concerned. It is a capital reserve whose use is restricted.

Sole proprietor
See *Sole trader.*

Sole trader
A person in business by him or herself (as compared with a partnership or limited company). Sometimes referred to as a **sole proprietor**.

Sources and application of funds statement
An accounting statement which shows from where a business derived and how it deployed its funds during a period.

Specific purchasing power accounting
A system of inflation accounting where the values used are adjusted for the specific rate of inflation which applies to the individual items of cost concerned.

SSAP
See *Statement of Standard Accounting Practice.*

Stable monetary unit convention
The accounting assumption that the currency units in which accounts are expressed remain at constant value.

Statement of affairs
A balance sheet of a business which has not been prepared from underlying accounting records.

Statement of sources and application of funds
See *Sources and application of funds statement.*

Statement of Standard Accounting Practice (SSAP)
Procedures established by the accounting profession to standardise and improve accounting methods and disclosure.

Statutory books
The books and registers which statute law requires to be kept by limited companies.

Stewardship function
In the case of limited companies (and sometimes other forms of business as well), there can be a separation of ownership from the day-to-day control. The directors of a company will usually have day-to-day control and, thus, may be described as the stewards of the company. They will be accountable to the owners (shareholders) on a regular basis for their stewardship of the company. The financial statements provided to the owners of a company should help them assess the way in which the directors have discharged their stewardship duties. These statements should help the owners decide whether the directors have acted honestly and with integrity. In recent years the stewardship function has been expanded to include the notions of efficiency and effectiveness. Thus, the owners may also scrutinise the financial statements to help assess the directors' performance in these areas.

Stock Exchange
A market for the sale of 'second hand' shares and loan stocks.

Stock in trade
Goods which are owned by a business which are intended to be sold either in their present state or to be processed into a form where they can be sold. Also known as **stock** and **inventory**.

Straight-line depreciation
A method of apportioning depreciation such that each period bears an equal share of the total.

Subsidiary books
See *Books of prime entry.*

Super profits
Levels of profit which are greater than the normal profit which would normally be expected from a business like the one under review. Super profits would arise because the particular business has some trading advantage like a particularly good reputation or a particularly skilled and loyal workforce.

Suspense account
A temporary account which is posted with items requiring clarification or with differences arising from preparation of the trial balance.

Taxable output
Goods and services which are supplied by a trader who is registered for VAT and which are of such a nature that they are charged to VAT at either the standard or the zero rate.

Total accounts
See *Control accounts.*

Trade creditors
Those to whom a business has a financial obligation arising from buying goods or services on credit.

Trade debtors
Those who have a financial obligation to a business arising from buying goods or services on credit.

Trade discount

A discount allowed to customers by virtue of them being in business, rather than private individuals. The sales or purchases figure is shown in the trading account net of trade discount. Typically trade discount does not appear in the accounts.

Trading account

A part of the profit and loss account in which sales for the period are compared with the cost of those sales to deduce the gross profit or loss.

Trial balance

A list of balances extracted from the double-entry accounting system used as a check on the accuracy of the data recording.

Under-depreciation

The amount by which the fall in value (calculated by comparing costs of acquisition with the disposal value) is more than the total depreciation taken in the profit and loss over the life of the asset.

Value added tax (VAT)

A tax on consumers which is chargeable on a wide range of goods and services. It is collected at each transfer point in the chain which leads from producer to final consumer.

Voting rights

The legally enforceable power to vote. It is the expression used to indicate the power of shareholders to exercise power over various aspects of the company.

Voucher

Documentary evidence such as a sales invoice or a purchase invoice which can be used as source data for the recording of financial transactions.

Work-in-progress

Stocks of partly finished goods held by a manufacturer.

Working capital

The excess of current assets over current liabilities.

Written-down value (WDV)

The cost of an asset less any amounts written off. It is particularly applied to fixed assets. Also referred to as net book value.

Zero-rated

VAT outputs by a registered trader where the rate of VAT is zero. Books, newspapers and most items of food are current examples of zero-rated outputs.

Accounting bases	452
Accounting concepts	451
Accounting conventions	60
Accounting for depreciation	131
Accounting information system	5
Accounting policies	451
Accounting records	185
Accounting Standards Board (ASB)	447
Accounting Standards Committee (ASC)	446
Accounting standards	444, 449
Accounts of limited companies	396
Accruals	60
Accruals accounting	40
Accrued expenses	94
Acid-test ratio	544
Activity ratios	541
Adjusting and non-adjusting events	458
Annual subscription	307
Applied research	456
Appropriation account	332
Asset replacement	130
Assets	16, 26
Assets lost	282
Audit	429
Auditing	4
Bad and doubtful debts	165
Balance sheet	16
Balance sheet equation	17, 29, 70
Balance sheet formats	27, 432
Bank reconciliation statements	258
Bonus issue	404
Books of original (or prime) entry	189
Business entity	60
Business entity convention	17
Capital (the owner's claim)	23
Capital expenditure	45
Capital gearing (leverage)	392
Capital redemption reserve	389
Capital reserves	389
Carriage in	101
Cash book	187, 195
Cash discounts	58
Cash flow statement	477
Cash flow statement format	479
Cash journals	198
Characteristics of financial statements	10
Claims	17, 26
Clubs, societies and associations	303
Computerised accounting systems	234, 243
Conceptual framework	508
Consistency	60
Contingency	460
Continuous (perpetual method) of recording stock	146
Control accounts	234
Conventions and principles	21
Accruals	60, 427
Business entity	60
Consistency	60, 427
Duality	17, 60
Going concern	21, 60, 427
Historic cost	21, 60
Matching	40, 60
Materiality	60
Money measurement	21, 60
Objectivity	60
Prudence	60, 427
Realisation	39, 60
Stable monetary unit	60
Cost of sales	54, 99
Cost or net realisable value rule	156
Costs	45
Creditors payment period	543
Current assets	26
Current ratio	544
Database	244
Day books	189
Debentures	391
Debt to equity ratio	545
Debtors collection period	542
Definitions of accounting	1
Depreciation	104, 125, 454
Depreciation expense account	135
Development costs	456
Directors' report	428, 437
Discounts	58
Disposal of fixed assets	135
Dividend cover	547
Dividend per share	547
Dividend yield	547
Dividends	390
Division of the ledger	187
Double-entry bookkeeping	72
Doubtful debts	166
Duality	60
Earnings per share (EPS)	463, 546
Earnings yield	546
Expenses	45
Expenses paid in arrears	41
Final accounts from a trial balance	115
Financial accounting	4
Financial management	4
Financial ratios	536
Financial Reporting Review Panel	448
Financial statements	8
First in - first out (FIFO)	147
Fixed assets	26, 125
Format of the profit and loss account	37
Formation of a limited company	385
FRS 1 (Cash flow statements)	478
FRS 3 Reporting financial performance	462
Fundamental accounting concepts	451
Funds flow statement	488

Gearing ratios — 545
General ledger — 187
Going concern — 60
Going concern/continuity — 21
Goodwill — 353
Gross profit margin — 541

Historic cost — 21, 60

Income and expenditure accounts — 305
Incomplete records — 265
Inflation — 519
Interest earned ratio — 545
Interest cover — 545
International accounting standards — 450
Interpretation of final accounts — 536
Inventory — 145
Investors' ratios — 545
Issued share capital — 386

Journal — 198, 209

Last in - first out (LIFO) — 148
Layout of the profit and loss account — 55
Ledger — 187
Ledger accounts — 70
Legal framework — 422
Liabilities — 17, 395
Life membership — 307
Limited companies — 383
Limited liability — 385
Liquidity ratios — 544
Loans and debentures — 391

Management accounting — 3
Management Information Systems (MIS) — 244
Matching convention — 40, 60
Materiality — 60
Methods of depreciation — 127
Money measurement — 21, 60

Net asset turnover — 541
Net profit margin — 541
Nominal ledger — 187
Not-for-profit organisations — 6, 307
Notes to the final published accounts — 436

Objectivity — 60
Ordinary shares — 387

Partnership accounts — 329
Partnership Act 1890 — 331
Partnership changes — 351
Periodic method of recording stock — 145
Petty cash book — 199
Post balance sheet events — 458

Preference shares — 388
Preparation of final accounts — 48, 82
Prepayment of expenses — 93
Prepayment of revenues (deferred revenues) — 95
Price earnings ratio (PE) — 546
Prior period adjustments — 466
Private ledger — 187
Profit and loss account — 34
Profit and loss account format — 430
Profit and loss appropriation account — 396
Profit measurement and valuation — 503
Profitability ratios — 540
Provisions — 395
Prudence — 60
Public and private limited companies — 385
Published company accounts — 421
Purchases ledger — 187
Purchase ledger control account — 238
Purchasing power maintenance — 523
Pure (basic) research — 456

Quick asset ratio — 544

Ratio analysis — 536
Realisation — 60
Realisation convention — 39
Receipts and payments accounts — 303
Recognition of revenues — 39
Reducing-balance method of depreciation — 128
Register of Charges — 406
   of Debenture holders — 406
   of Directors and Secretary — 406
   of Directors' Interests — 406
   of members — 406
   of Substantial Shareholdings — 406
Research and development (R & D) — 455
Reserves — 388, 395
Return on capital employed — 540
Returns — 101
Revaluation reserve — 389
Revenue expenditure — 45
Revenue reserves — 388
Role of accounting — 1

Sales ledger — 187
Sales ledger control account — 235
Scrip issue — 404
Share capital and shareholders — 384
Share premium — 387
Small and medium-sized companies — 428
Small businesses — 265
Software packages — 245
Sole traders forming a partnership — 370
Source and applications of funds (funds flow) statement — 488
Special funds — 307
SSAP 2 - Disclosure of accounting policies — 451
SSAP 9 - Stocks and long-term contracts — 157, 453
SSAP 12 - Accounting for depreciation — 139, 454

SSAP 13 - Accounting for research and
  development   455
SSAP 17 - Accounting for post balance sheet
  events   458
SSAP 18 - Accounting for contingencies   460
Stable monetary unit   22, 60
Statement of Principles   509
  Chapter 1 - The objective of financial statements 510
  Chapter 2 - Qualitative charateristics of financial
    statements   511
  Chapter 3 - The elements of financial statements 512
  Chapter 4 - The recognition of items in financial
    statements   514
  Chapter 5 - Measurement in financial statements 515
  Chapter 6 - Presentation of financial information 517
Statutory books   406
Statutory framework for accounting for limited
  companies   421
Stock   99, 145
Stock and work-in-progress   157, 453
Stock Exchange requirements   468
Stock in trade   54
Stock valuation methods   147
Stock-holding period   542
Straight-line method of depreciation   127
Subscriptions   307
Subsidiary records   185

Tax consultancy   4
Times interest earned ratio   545
Trade discount   58
Trading and profit and loss account   82
Trial balance   80
True and fair view   423
Types of accounting   3
Types of share capital   387

UK accounting standards   469
Urgent Issues Task Force (UITF)   447
Users of accounting information   2

Valuation of goodwill   354
Valuation of stock   145

Weighted average cost (AVCO)   149

Year-end adjustments   92, 216

PUBLICATIONS AND DISTANCE LEARNING COURSE ORDER FORM

AT FOULKS LYNCH

	ACCA Textbooks	ACCA Revision Series	ACCA Examination Notes	Distance Learning Course (Includes all materials Helpline & Marking)	Open Learning Course (Includes all materials)	Open Learning Optional (Helpline & Marking)
	£17/Subject	£9/Subject	£5/Subject	£79/Subject	£99/Subject	£20/Subject
Foundation Stage						
Module A						
Accounting Framework	☐	☐	☐	☐	☐	☐
Legal Framework	☐	☐	☐	☐	☐	☐
Module B						
Management Information	☐	☐	☐	☐	☐	☐
Organisational Framework	☐	☐	☐	☐	☐	☐
Certificate Stage						
Module C						
Information Analysis	☐	☐	☐	☐	☐	☐
Audit Framework	☐	☐	☐	☐	☐	☐
Module D						
Tax Framework	☐	☐	☐	☐	☐	☐
Managerial Finance	☐	☐	☐	☐	☐	☐
Professional Stage						
Module E						
Info for Control & Dec Making	☐	☐	☐	☐	☐	☐
Accounting & Audit Practice	☐	☐	☐	☐	☐	☐
Tax Planning	☐	☐	☐	☐	☐	☐
Module F						
Management & Strategy	☐	☐	☐	☐	☐	☐
Financial Reporting Environment	☐	☐	☐	☐	☐	☐
Financial Strategy	☐	☐	☐	☐	☐	☐
Postage UK Mainland	£2.00/Text	£1.00/Rev Series	£1.00/Note	£5.00/Subject	£5.00/Subject	
NI, ROI & Overseas	£5.00/Text	£3.00/Rev Series	£3.00/Note	£15.00/Subject	£15.00/Subject	

AT Foulks Lynch Student Number (if applicable) ☐☐☐☐☐☐   ACCA Registration Number ☐☐☐☐☐☐☐   Intended Examination Date ☐ Dec 95   ☐ June 96

1 I enclose my cheque (payable to **AT Foulks Lynch Ltd**) for £_____ *(please include postage)*
Signature _____   Date _____

2 Charge Access/Visa card number ☐☐☐☐☐☐☐☐☐☐☐☐☐☐☐☐   Expires ☐☐ / ☐☐
Signature _____   Date _____

3 Payment by employer. I agree to pay the fees detailed on this form. Please invoice the Company.
Name (*print*) _____   Position _____
Company name _____
Address _____
_____   Postcode _____
☎ _____   Fax number _____
Signature _____   Date _____

Terms and conditions: Employers who sign above are liable for the full fee. Fees include VAT. No refunds for cancelled courses.
  All fees in £ Sterling.
Note: Please tick box if you require a monthly report on this student ☐

STUDENT DETAILS
Name _____   ☎ _____
Home address _____
_____   Postcode _____

Please deliver to: Home ☐   Work ☐

Expected delivery: Up to 5 working days UK mainland business addresses
Up to 10 working days UK mainland home addresses (must be someone available to sign)
Up to 6 weeks Overseas addresses
Should you have special delivery requirements please do not hesitate to contact us

Send your completed order to: AT Foulks Lynch Ltd, Number 4, The Griffin Centre, Staines Road,
Feltham, Middlesex, TW14 OHS
VISA/ACCESS Hotline: 0181 831 9990, Fax: 0181 831 9991